A HISTORY OF MODERN

INDIA
1480–1950

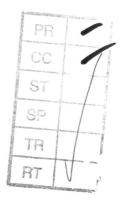

PR	
CC	
ST	
SP	
TR	
RT	

A HISTORY OF MODERN

INDIA
1480–1950

Edited by

Claude Markovits

Translated by
Nisha George and
Maggy Hendry

Anthem Press

Anthem Press is an imprint of
Wimbledon Publishing Company
PO Box 9779
London
SW19 7QA

This paperback edition published by Anthem Press 2004
First published in English translation by Anthem Press 2002

© Librairie Arthème Fayard 1994
First published by Librairie Arthème Fayard as
'Histoire de L'Inde Moderne'

This book is supported by the French Ministry for Foreign Affairs,
as part of the Burgess programme headed for the French Embassy
in London by the Institut Français du Royaume-Uni.

Liberté • Égalité • Fraternité
RÉPUBLIQUE FRANÇAISE

British Library Cataloguing in Publication Data
Data available

Library of Congress Cataloging in Publication Data
A catalog record has been applied for

ISBN 1 84331 152 6

1 3 5 7 9 10 8 6 4 2

Printed by Cromwell Press, Trowbridge, Wiltshire.

CONTENTS

PART SIX
On the margins of the Empire   **493**

LIST OF MAPS

CONTRIBUTORS TO THIS VOLUME

Geneviève Bouchon, Honorary Director of Research at CNRS; Conference Co-ordinator at the New University of Lisbon and Member of the Marine Academy of Lisbon: Chapters 1, 3, 4, 7 and 8.

Marc Gaborieau, Director of Research at CNRS and Director of Studies at EHESS: Chapters 2, 3, 4, 5, 6, 7, 9, 10, 18, 24.

Christophe Jaffrelot, Research Co-ordinator at CNRS (CERI): Chapters 18, 24.

Claude Markovits, Director of Research at CNRS; Director of the Centre of Indian and South Asian Studies (EHESS): Introduction, chapters 14, 15, 17, 18, 19, 20, 23, 24, 25, conclusion.

Eric Meyer, Director of Research at CNRS: Chapter 27.

Jacques Pouchepadass, Director of Research at CNRS: Chapters 16, 21 and 22.

Jacques Weber, Master of Conferences at the University of Nantes, Member of the Centre of Indian and South Asian Studies (EHESS), Member of the Academy of Overseas Sciences: Chapters 11, 12, 13, 14, 26.

INTRODUCTION

From Buddha to Gandhi, India has given the world a message of wisdom and deep spirituality. The cradle of an age-old civilization, her riches have always lured foreigners. Since the mythical Aryans, countless waves of invaders have swept across the land, encroaching on it either through the Khyber Pass or by landing on its hospitable shores. Be it the Greeks, the Huns, the Scythians, the Arabs, the Turks, the Portuguese or the English, India has received them all; their words have added colour to her languages; she has borrowed their techniques, but she has always succeeded in preserving her unique genius. On her soil many empires have risen and fallen.

The Maurya dynasty (324–185 BC) created the first of these empires. It was in this era that Buddhism, under the influence of the great emperor Ashoka (268–231 BC), spread across the country. During this age, Indian civilization experienced a remarkable development both spiritually and technologically. But the Maurya Empire, which extended its dominion over almost the whole of India, declined rapidly and the subcontinent entered a phase of political fragmentation during the following five centuries. Thereafter, the Gupta dynasty reconstructed a vast empire in AD 319–20. During the reign of Chandra Gupta II (375–415), Indian civilization reached a new cultural high, as the works of the poet Kalidasa testify. This splendour was however short-lived: in the fifth century, the invasion of the Ephtalite branch of the Huns put an end to it. Harsha (606–47) succeeded in building another empire, but this unity did not last and North India entered a dark age. The Brahminic renaissance gradually began to root out Buddhism from the country. In 712, the Arabs established themselves in Sind, but India resisted the penetration of Islam for another three centuries. During this period, the subcontinent divided into several kingdoms. One of the most important of these, the Chola kingdom in the South, built a civilization that radiated as far as Southeast Asia.

Towards the year 1000, two new powers come into prominence in North India: the Rajputs, a Hindu warrior caste, and the Turks of Afghanistan who, under the leadership of Mahmud of Ghazni, led a series of devastating raids into Hindustan. The decisive clash took place in 1192: the Rajputs were decimated by a second Turkish wave spearheaded by Muhammad of Ghur. The Turkish cavalrymen conquered the greater part of the Gangetic basin, subjugated Bengal and in 1206 founded a powerful Muslim State, the Sultanate of Delhi. In the beginning of the fourteenth century, they expanded further into the peninsula. Towards 1340, the Hindu kingdom of

Vijayanagar and the Muslim Bahmani Empire asserted their supremacy in the Deccan. At the close of the century, the invasions of Timur (known as Tamerlane in Europe) menaced the Sultanate of Delhi, which had already been considerably weakened. It was due to this that India fragmented into the countless states that the first Portuguese navigators encountered at the close of the fifteenth century, followed thirty years later by a new wave of Turkish invaders, the Moguls.

Hinduism and the caste system

In the course of nearly three thousand years, India was the breeding ground for an original system of thinking and belief, (called 'Hinduism' since the nineteenth century). It is not a revealed religion, but a set of practices and rites transmitted by oral tradition and partly transcribed in texts written in Sanskrit, a language that had not been spoken for a long time when the Moguls established their rule in India.

The earliest seminal texts on which Hinduism is based are the *Vedas* (literally, 'Knowledge'). The oldest of these are collections of hymns and ritualistic formulas – the most widely known, the *Rig Veda* and the *Atharva Veda*, were probably composed between the fifteenth and tenth century BC. The more speculative Upanishads date from BC 800 to 300.

Hinduism then took shape as a devotional religion (*bhakti*), based on the *Smrti* or 'tradition entrusted to memory'. These collections of precepts did not constitute a radical deviation from the Vedic religion, but signalled nevertheless a drift away from it, insofar as they were accessible to all Hindus. With the appearance of a pantheon of divinities in these texts, the dominant figure was no longer an impersonal Absolute. Furthermore, these texts propound the theory of *dharma*, or the socio-cosmic order, which is a central notion in Hinduism. For instance, the *Dharmashastras*, or the 'Treatises on Universal Order,' containing the famous Laws of Manu, lay down 'the rights and duties inherent to the various castes at the various stages of one's life'.[1]

The two great epics, *Ramayana* and *Mahabharata*, which are also related to the *Smrti*, give a concrete illustration of this *dharma*. The *Bhagavad Gita* or 'The Song of the Blessed One', one of the most famous episodes of the *Mahabharata*, explains the quintessence of the *Bhakti* religion. It portrays Krishna, an incarnation of the god Vishnu, teaching the hero Arjuna the paths to salvation. This text, which has become canonical, offers every Hindu, whether a Brahmin or member of the lowest of castes, the hope of participating in the divine work and of receiving grace in return. Finally, the *Smrti* includes other texts, in particular the *Puranas* or 'Antique tales', which narrate the mythology of the important gods.

Bhakti has inspired a remarkably rich literature. The early poems were composed in the Tamil language from the seventh century BC onwards. Then the movement spread to North India where it found expression in several languages (Hindi, Marathi, Bengali, etc.). Devotional worship as defined by *Bhakti* revolves primarily around three deities: Vishnu, Shiva and the Goddess (*Devi*). Vishnu, the 'Preserver' and Shiva, the 'Destroyer', form a trinity with Brahma, the 'Creator'. The latter is however not worshipped (except in Pushkar in Rajasthan, where a temple is dedicated to him).

Vishnu, the pure god, the god par excellence of the high castes, represents the *dharma*. Mythological tales recount his periodic descents (*avatara*) in our universe in order to restore the *dharma*. The most venerated of these incarnations are the Lion Man (Narasimha) and, even more so, Rama and Krishna. Rama, the hero of the Ramayana, is worshipped with particular fervour in North India. The identification of this deity with Ayodhya, where some of his devotees want to build a temple on the site of a mosque (razed to the ground by Hindu fanatics in December 1992) has become a source of communal tension in present-day India. As for Shiva, he embodies the forces of obscurity, the principle of excess. He is worshipped in his numerous forms, often awesome, (but he is also Nataraja, the cosmic dancer, represented in the sublime bronzes of the Chola period), both by those belonging to low castes, especially in South India, and by certain Brahmins in Kashmir. He is also, and above all, the god of the ascetics, of those who have renounced life in society. The third great figure of the Hindu pantheon is the Goddess (Devi). Her aspects and names are numerous, from the countless village deities to the great pan-Indian goddesses, Durga and Kali. The sister of Vishnu, the Goddess is also the consort of Shiva in her form as Parvati. As Lakshmi, she is venerated by merchants, and as Saraswati, she is the patroness of students and scholars.

Though there are innumerable gods in the Hindu pantheon, this multiplicity must not mislead us. If the great majority of Hindus claim to be either Vishnuites or Saivaites, these denominations do not correspond to any theological divisions. Hinduism is a polytheistic system, but it can also be construed as monotheistic, inasmuch as the devotee who worships a god is oblivious of all the others in the moment of grace. Some have therefore described it as 'alternating monotheism'.[2]

Hinduism is a religion of the home. The cult of the gods is primarily a domestic cult. Each family possesses an altar on which they perform their *poojas* (devotions). The priests, mostly Brahmins, are not indispensable for the celebration of everyday worship, but intercede during ceremonies that punctuate the cycle of life (birth, marriage, death). Thus, strictly speaking, there is no Hindu clergy, at least, no secular clergy, nor hierarchy. Everyone born a Hindu remains a Hindu, regardless of his personal philosophical beliefs, provided he performs certain rites. One can thus be a Hindu and an atheist simultaneously.

There are Hindu monastic orders originating from the time of the great reformer Shankara (eighth century AD). These orders are part of the vaster movement of renunciation. Against *dharma*, which ties the Hindu to caste society, stands the figure of the ascetic (*sanyasi*) who distances himself from the social world and practises *ahimsa* or absolute non-violence. The ascetics consider deliverance (*moksa*) the supreme objective of mankind, placing it even above *dharma*.

Hindus believe in the transmigration of souls, manifest in the chain of more or less noble or base rebirths, depending on the acts performed during the previous life/lives. It is this perpetual cycle of reincarnations that the ascetic strives to escape. In a society governed by caste, renunciation appears to be the only path available for the affirmation of the individual. Hence the role played by Gandhi, who owes his prestige largely to the fact that he was perceived as the last of the great ascetics.

Hinduism is not a 'religion' in the meaning that this term has in the West, imply-
ing a distinction between the sacred and the profane. It is a set of beliefs and rites
that pervade life as a whole and determine an individual's place in society.

The caste system has considerably intrigued European observers since the arrival
of the Portuguese in India in the sixteenth century. The word 'caste' is in fact
derived from the Portuguese '*casta*': species, race. To designate 'caste,' Indians use
two distinct terms, *varna* and *jati*. *Varna* refers to the ideal hierarchy of 'orders' which
appears in the Vedic texts and which corresponds to the 'tri-function' defined by
Georges Dumézil: at the top are the priests (the Brahmins), then the warriors (the
Kshatriyas) and the producers (the *Vaishyas*): these orders are 'twice born' (*dvija*), as they
have experienced the 'second birth' brought about by the knowledge of the Vedas.
Added to these is the fourth order, that of servants (the *Shudras*), who are at the service of the other three.

In practice, however, Hindu society is divided into thousands of groups, or *jatis*, a
term sometimes translated as 'caste' and sometimes as 'sub-caste'. Some of these exist
only in certain regions, others all over India. *Jatis* constitute the real, observable
system of castes. The hierarchy established among the castes, based on the opposition
between the pure and the impure, also draws on the model of the *varnas*, as shown by
Louis Dumont.[3] In this context, it is necessary to correct a common error. The
untouchables are not casteless. A certain number of *jatis* are called 'untouchable'
because the members of these are considered particularly impure, to the extent that,
for the 'pure' castes, touching them or even looking at them results in very serious pollution. But the untouchables are a part of the system; they are even indispensable to
it, because if they did not take the impurities upon themselves, the pure castes would
be unable to eschew certain pollutions and would consequently lose their status.

The caste system does not wholly encompass Indian society. Aboriginal populations called 'tribals', scattered all across the subcontinent, are in principle outside the
world of castes, but in the modern age, a number of them have, over the course of
several centuries, come under the umbrella of Hinduization and have been increasingly integrated into the caste system. Besides, several non-Hindu religions exist in
India: most importantly, Islam, but also Christianity, Sikhism, Jainism, Buddhism,
Zoroastrianism and Judaism. The Muslims in the subcontinent follow a caste system
different from that of the Hindus, but which seems to be modelled on it. The distinction between the descendents of the Prophet and those who are not (*ashraf* and
ajlaf), fundamental in Muslim society in India, coincides with the opposition
between the pure and the impure, even though Muslims do not subscribe to the
theory of *varnas*. Among the Syrian Christians in Kerala, who have had ties with
Rome since the sixteenth century, the distinction between 'Roman Syrians' and
'Latin Christians' is akin to an opposition between high and low castes. Jains and
Sikhs, who do not accept the existence of castes, nevertheless have attitudes and
practices not much different in reality from those of the Hindus.

Caste thus defines social status in terms of degrees of purity and impurity. The
principal characteristics of such a system are endogamy, commensality and
hereditary specialization. According to the principle of endogamy, a Hindu is obligated to marry within his own caste and to this day inter-caste marriages are rare.

This principle, however, encompasses considerable regional differences, a South Indian model is in sharp contrast with a North Indian model. Commensality, or sharing one's meals exclusively with the members of one's caste, has become increasingly difficult to observe in urban milieus. Besides, reform movements have focused their attention on this practice, urging the members of high and low castes to share the same table.

The caste system, even though it does not fundamentally imply a division of labour, lays down rules with respect to the exercise of occupations that imply contact with what is impure, particularly, with the defilement that death represents for the Hindus. Only untouchable *jatis* may engage in transporting corpses or in the making of leather (which is an impure material, as it comes from the dead bodies of animals, especially of cows). Other professions are, in practice, open to all. It is thus quite frequent to see Brahmins engaged in trade, a hereditary specialization of the *banias* (a merchant class) and the *shudras* exercising armed professions, in principle reserved for the *kshatriyas*.

Has the caste system been an obstacle to economic progress, as it has often been suggested, since it hampers social mobility and consequently individual initiative? This view is highly questionable. Hindu merchant castes and Jains have produced remarkable businessmen in the course of the centuries. The existence of caste-based networks has for a long time compensated for the absence of an efficient official banking system and has made the mobilization of huge amounts of capital possible. Thus the caste system per se does not explain the economic backwardness of India, which is a recent phenomenon dating only from the nineteenth century.

Is the caste system responsible for the political fragmentation of India, which made it an easy prey for Muslim, and eventually British, conquerors? There is no simple answer to this question. The tendency of the Rajput royal families to split into various branches certainly did not favour the development of vast political entities. In the sixteenth century, even the Vijayanagar Empire did not constitute a state comparable to the European monarchies of the same period. But neither did the Muslim Sultanate of Delhi escape this susceptibility to fragmentation. It is therefore difficult to establish that political disintegration is directly linked to the caste system.

The sources at our disposal are inadequate to enable us to reconstitute with accuracy the evolution of castes prior to the beginning of the nineteenth century. From this time, it appears that caste society successfully adapted itself to the changes, albeit limited, introduced by colonization. Certain castes organized themselves into pressure groups, and the high castes could on the whole maintain their dominant position. The low castes, far from seeking to overthrow the system, strove to find a more advantageous place within it. Caste hierarchy has thus remained by and large intact, undergoing only minor changes.

Modern India

This history of modern India begins at the end of the fifteenth century. The arrival of Vasco de Gama in Calicut in 1498 does not constitute a major watershed in the history of the subcontinent. Though the Portuguese succeeded in creating a maritime empire in Asia, their endeavours to gain territorial expansion in India failed, except in Goa, which remained under their control until 1961. They nevertheless opened the sea route to India, paving the way for Europeans to make commercial inroads into the country, which resulted three centuries later in domination by the British. Almost concurrently with the Portuguese, Turco-Mongol conquerors led by Babur, a descendant of Timur, infiltrated India through the Khyber Pass, the classic gateway for terrestrial invasions. After endless trials and tribluations, they succeeded in creating an empire in India, which endured as the only centralized political structure until the first third of the eighteenth century. It was definitively abolished only in 1858.

The quasi-concomitance of the arrival of the Portuguese and the Moguls is one of history's accidents. But the birth of the Mogul Empire coincides with a trend, prevalent in the Muslim world, of creating political entities that have sometimes been called 'gunpowder empires', as exemplified by the Ottoman Empire and the Safavid Empire in Persia. In the Indian context, the Mogul Empire appeared as a new incarnation of the Sultanate of Delhi. These two waves of invaders – the former arriving by sea, lured by spices and the partially well founded rumour, of the presence of Christians, the latter, conquerors on horseback, fascinated by the riches of the Indian plains, advancing southward from the arid plateaus of Central Asia – remained separated from each other for more than two centuries, until the East India Company built an empire that was both terrestrial and maritime, superior by virtue of its population to the greatest empires in History.

Nevertheless, nothing could have led one to foresee that the conquests spearheaded by Vasco de Gama and Babur would necessarily lead to the conquests by Clive and Wellesley. At the end of the seventeenth century, while the presence of the Portuguese remained confined to certain coastal regions, the Moguls had subjugated almost the entire subcontinent, excepting the far South. But it would be a mistake to see the Mogul Empire as the pre-figuration of the British Indian Empire, as was customary with several nineteenth-century British historians. It would also be misleading to discern in it the embryo of an Indian national State, as did a certain Indian nationalist school of historians. The Mogul Empire was a Muslim political entity, a part of the Islamic world, ruling over a Hindu population on the whole recalcitrant to conversions.

A tableau of India at the end of the fifteenth century shows the diversity of ethnic origins and lifestyles of its population. Besides the sedentary farmers and city dwellers, two other groups occupied the major part of the subcontinent: on the one hand, nomadic or semi-nomadic pastoralists, and on the other, hunter-gatherers scouring the forest regions that covered much vaster areas then than today, and who were also engaged in slash-and-burn cultivation. These groups of people, called 'tribals', were much more numerous at the time than the five to ten per cent attributed to them by contemporary Indian censuses.

The Mogul Empire reinforced the links between India and the Islamic world through the constant influx of Iranian, Turkish and Afghan immigrants, who came to occupy high political positions and to be doctors of the Law and spiritual leaders. Muslims, however, remained a minority. In comparison to those immigrants who settled down and founded families by marrying Indian women, both Muslim and Hindu, the European traders appeared only as visitors, except the Portuguese, some of whom also made India their home. Nevertheless, it was a group of British merchants who, taking advantage of the dissolution of the Mogul Empire, asserted their political supremacy over the entire subcontinent, a feat that the Moguls even at the height of their splendour were unable to accomplish.

From the end of the fifteenth century, these groups of foreign traders and adventurers started to establish relations with Indian society, especially with the Hindus. The dynamics of the Hindu world and the extent to which it went along with the logic of the foreigners still remain unclear. In this respect, Indian historiography, despite the remarkable advances it has made in the last few decades, lags behind that of Europe and China. The picture of an unchanging Hindu society has now been qualified and growing attention given to traders and bankers has enabled historians to enlarge the vision of a sociology that had mostly been interested in the educated and warrior castes and in the rural masses. In fact, in medieval India there existed powerful trade networks through which circulated not only merchandise and credit (by the extensive use of bills of exchange or *hundi*), but also men, techniques and ideas. These networks functioned in symbiosis with the dominant Brahmin and warrior castes, but they were open to contacts with the outside. Though we do not know the role that these networks played in the establishment and expansion of the Mogul supremacy, we do know that they were invaluable allies for the British penetration, as made clear by the role of the great family of Marwari bankers, the Jagat Seths, in the East India Company's conquest of Bengal.

This book largely focuses its attention on states on the one hand, and on economic phenomena, on the other. The various states founded by conquerors, like the Estado do India, the Mogul Empire and the British Indian Empire, were above all preoccupied with the levying of taxes. They had to accept the fact the spiritual and cultural life of their subjects continued largely outside their control. The elite class that made its appearance in the wake of these conquests, though politically and even economically dominant (as in the case of the British), was not in a position where it could claim to exercise cultural hegemony in India. Hindu society continued to consider its Brahmins and its princes as models to emulate, at least until the second half of the nineteenth century. It seems that politico-economic changes had little immediate influence on mentalities. But the socio-cultural history of the Indian people remains a relatively uncharted territory owing to the dearth of written sources. It may only be presented through the eyes of the dominant elite classes of foreign origin, as they alone have left behind abundant written documents.

In a single volume, it is not possible to do justice to the great regional diversity of India. This book has deliberately adopted a pan-Indian point of view and has highlighted those regions that have played the most active role on the political and economic scene. Its main thrust has been the evolution of the relationship between states and society. Empires have a prominent place in it, as modern India experienced two phases of imperial unity: under the Moguls (1580–1739) and the British (1818–1947). However, the years 1480–1580 on the one hand and the interlude of eighty years separating these empires merit our attention, because political fragmentation during these periods was accompanied by dynamism in the economic, social and even intellectual spheres. In the eighteenth century in particular, the subcontinent witnessed a political reorganization, a process that was eventually interrupted by the colonial conquest. This resulted in stagnation, which became particularly acute at the end of the nineteenth century. During this period the backwardness of India in comparison with the most advanced countries only increased. From then onwards, Indian nationalism became the principal driving force. But it came up against the growing difficulties in the relation between the two largest religious communities of the country, a crisis that it failed to overcome. Hence, the partition in 1947, which tragically closed the chapter of what could have been the exemplary victory of a non-violent anti-colonial movement.

PART ONE

AT THE TURN OF THE SIXTEENTH CENTURY

For centuries, India was a meeting point for people, religions, civilizations and trade networks. At the beginning of the sixteenth century, two external forces came into prominence, changing the course of the modern history of Asia: the arrival of the Europeans and the birth of the Islamic Mogul Empire.

India has always been the crossroads of a maritime trade system connecting the Middle East and the Mediterranean on the one side to the Far East on the other, a system parallel to the famous 'Silk Route'. Contrary to a long-held misconception, this system was not in decline in the fifteenth century, and the Portuguese cannot be given credit for reviving it, or blamed for destroying it. In fact, it enjoyed tremendous vitality and evolved considerably during this period. Indian traders, particularly Gujaratis, took control over the network at the expense of Arab merchants who had dominated in the course of the previous century. From Aden to Malacca (in the straits), Gujaratis, most of whom had converted to Islam, exercised their hegemony on the sea routes. Thus it was a powerful and organized trade network that Vasco da Gama and the early Portuguese navigators encountered in the Indian Ocean at the close of the fifteenth century (Chapter I)

Gujarat's control of maritime trade circuits did not however reflect political domination over the entire subcontinent. The sultanate founded in the early years of the fifteenth century was certainly a prosperous and powerful state, but it was only one in a multitude of sultanates that emerged in the wake of the Turko-Afghan conquests. The political situation in India was characterised by the fragmentation of authority among a large number of entities of varying dimensions. Several of them were governed by Muslim rulers, while the subjects, excepting those of Sind and the Kashmir Valley, largely remained faithful to Hinduism. However, Hindu kingdoms did continue to maintain their supremacy in certain regions of the subcontinent, particularly in Rajputana and in the South, where an empire had risen around the city of Vijayanagar in the fourteenth century (Chapters II and III).

The arrival of the newcomers, the Portuguese and the Moguls, did not cause any immediate upheavals. The Portuguese, unable to destroy the Gujarati network, would strive, successfully to a certain extent, to counter or to circumvent it. Meanwhile the Moguls were to fight resolutely against the Afghans for more than half a century following the victory of the emperor Babur at Panipat in 1526, before they were able to consolidate their supremacy under Akbar. (Chapter IV).

I

A CHANGING WORLD

India and its ocean

In India, land is sacred and the sea impure – this was not the least of the paradoxes of this subcontinent, given the fact that it owed the greatest part of its resplendence to the ocean surrounding it, to such an extent that it has lent its name to it: the Indian Ocean, around which the greatest civilizations of the Old World flourished.

Foreigners infiltrated India in two ways. They either came overland by the Central Asian route and the Himalayan passes. This was the route taken by Alexander the Great, the Ephtalite branch of Huns, the Afghans and the Turks who successively invaded India in the course of centuries. Or by sea, by the maritime routes taken by Greco-Roman navigators, the Arabs and the Chinese, and subsequently by the Europeans during the period we are interested in. Those who came overland were warriors, while those who arrived by sea were maritime traders.

The Indian peninsula is at the heart of the ocean, at the crossroads of the paths connecting the three continents of the Old World. The seasonal monsoons brought ships to its shores all the way from Africa, the Middle East and the China Sea. The southwest monsoon breaks out on the Malabar coast during the first days of June, lashing the coast with storms that in times of old forced the ports to be closed at least until August. The northeast monsoon blows from October to January on the Coromandel coast with less violence. For all seafarers, India was the indispensable stopover where they replenished their supplies of water and wood, renewed the rigging and awaited favourable winds for pursuing a cruise that was impossible to accomplish in a single monsoon. From the height of Antiquity, Indian ports had been linked by coastal shipping to the ports of the Persian Gulf, and to South East Asia, and Egypt by deep-sea navigation.

Natural obstacles as well as the lack of roadways and bridges made communication with inland regions difficult. Ports along the Indian Ocean emerged at the mouths of rivers or at the starting points of caravan routes that allowed only limited penetration into the subcontinent. Circulation between coastal cities was easier than between cities and the hinterland. Thus in the course of centuries, Indian merchandise, men and belief systems were carried by sea to the edges of the Mediterranean and the Pacific Ocean.

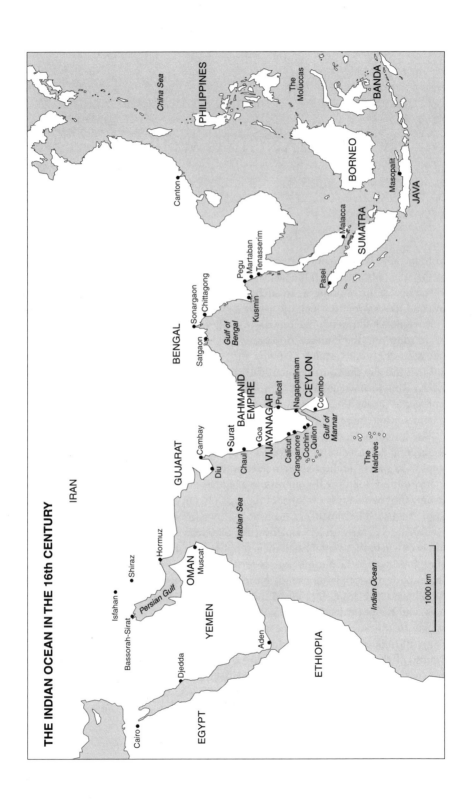

THE INDIAN OCEAN IN THE 16th CENTURY

EGYPT

Cairo

Djedda

YEMEN

Aden

ETHIOPIA

Bassorah-Sirat

Isfahan

Shiraz

IRAN

OMAN

Muscat

Hormuz

Persian Gulf

Indian Ocean

1000 km

Arabian Sea

GUJARAT

Diu

Cambay

Chaul

Surat

Goa

BAHMANID EMPIRE

VIJAYANAGAR

Calicut

Cranganore

Cochin

Quilon

The Maldives

Gulf of Mannar

Colombo

CEYLON

Nagapattinam

Pulicat

BENGAL

Satgaon

Sonargaon

Chittagong

Kusmin

Gulf of Bengal

Pegu

Martaban

Tenasserim

Pasei

SUMATRA

Malacca

BORNEO

The Moluccas

BANDA

JAVA

Masopalit

PHILIPPINES

China Sea

Canton

From the Romans to the Arabs

Archaeological excavations carried out at the mouth of the Indus River have unearthed evidence of a thriving maritime trade since the time of Mohenjo-Daro which had spread to the shores of Gujarat and Kerala. At the dawn of the Christian era, when navigators began to make use of the southwest monsoons to reach the Indian shores in a straight course from the Red Sea, Roman seafarers embarked on regular voyages to buy spices and precious stones. The great Tamil poems evoke the memory of 'the magnificent vessels of the *Yavana*,[4] which arrived laden with gold, splashing the waters of the Periyar with white foam ... and returned replete with pepper.' The ports of Muciri (now Cranganore) in the Malabar, and of Barygaza (now Broach) in Gujarat have been cited among others in the books of Pliny the Ancient. Roman coins and vestiges of trading posts have been discovered as far as the Coramandel coast.

At the same time, coastal cities of the Bay of Bengal were at the height of their commercial activity, spurred both by the proselytizing of the great Buddhist empires and by the intensity of trade with the Southeast Asian islands and with western Indochina. Born in the Gangetic region, Buddhism radiated to Southeast Asia where pilgrims, monks and sea traders were often travelling companions. Open to all horizons, India left its stamp on the art and culture of all coastal countries along the Indian Ocean for several centuries.

Latin authors have maintained that trade with India contributed to the fall of the Roman Empire, thereby highlighting the greed of Indian kings and merchants for gold. Gold from Rome, and subsequently from Byzantium and East Africa would continue to accumulate in the treasuries of coastal kingdoms. While empires disintegrated and others came to power, the Persians and the Chinese made a foray into the markets. In the ninth century when the Abbasid caliphate gave Islam a political dimension, the Arabs infiltrated all the existing trade networks. From Siraf to Canton, they marked out the itinerary of the 'Spice Route', while creating in their ports of call a network of communities converted to the faith of the Prophet.

The islamization of the coastal regions

It is certainly worthwhile bringing to light the circumstances under which the Muslim faith pervaded the Indian Ocean, so tremendous has been the influence of the Islamic expansion on the history of India during medieval and modern times. In the course of their voyages, the Arabs made long halts on Indian coasts. Driven by the monsoon, their vessels reached the shores of Gujarat or the Malabar; the traders stayed there for several months during which time they negotiated cargoes and waited for the sea to become navigable once again so that they could return to their port of registry or sail further to South China. During these sojourns, Muslim seafarers, ostracized by the local society, had relations with women of low caste, who alone were prepared to cook their food. These unions were legalized by a form of marriage peculiar to Islamic institutions (the *muta*), which allowed the sailors to have a family at every port of call. The children belonged to their mothers, who received certain material benefits provided they raised their children in the Islamic faith. This was how Muslim communities sprang up in the course of time on the periphery of the vast Brahminic and Buddhist empires. These communities, flourishing in the obscurity of the poor districts of the ports, laid the groundwork for a network destined to flourish for the next hundred years, the first network of its kind to connect India both to the Mediterranean basin and to the China Sea.

The evolution of maritime trade and the circumstances that determined its exceptional prosperity need to be examined. In the case of India, a conjunction of religious and political movements resulted, among other things, in the setting up of economic and social structures that would prevail until the advent of the colonial age. The revival of Brahminism, the extinction of Buddhism and the expansion of Islam would be decisive factors in the constitution of oceanic networks and markets.

The influence of the Hindu reformers who swept across the peninsula as early as the ninth century had led to the elimination of the Buddhists, breaking the momentum that carried them across the seas. For Indians, firmly bound to their land, sea voyages constituted a serious sin as they exposed the navigator to the inevitable contaminations caused by impure food and encounters. Although their observance varied between regions, these interdictions deterred members of the high castes from embarking on maritime adventures, while hardly inciting the others to do so either. Thus transoceanic trade was to a large extent in the hands of non-Hindu communities, in other words, of those not under the purview of such constraints. In Kerala, guilds of Jewish or Christian traders, settled there at the latest since the fifth century,[5] made the most of this situation, following the example of the Jains of the coastal cities of Gujarat and Karnataka or that of the Buddhist maritime merchants of Nagapattinam whose presence subsisted for a long time in the Coromandel.

At the same time, Islamic expansion, which had remained marginal until then, consolidated itself, thanks to the rise in association of Egyptian maritime traders, the Karimis, who, in the course of the twelfth century, had succeeded in establishing their agents in every port in the Indian Ocean and in coordinating all the mercantile activities of these ports. These foreign Muslim merchants (or Pardeshis) built mosques and Koranic schools in the ports of west India for the benefit of indigenous Muslim communities, like the Navayats in Karnataka, the Mappillas in Kerala and the Illappats in the Coromandel, who had obtained the right of citizenship as early as the twelfth century. These communities that had devoted themselves to overseas commerce found their primary social role by occupying the place left vacant by the merchants of the Buddhist age.

Hindu rulers granted protection to Muslims only under the condition that they respected the established order, did not consume beef, abstained themselves from all acts of iconoclasm and did not interfere with the caste structure. These Islamic settlements were obligated to pay taxes and to contribute to the defence of the territory. They had their own judicial system and participated in the administration of the ports, but they did not exercise any political functions. They had more extensive powers in areas relating to the sea and they had the right to engage in warfare on sea when their interests were jeopardized and to levy taxes from islanders. Organized into guilds or family corporations, these maritime merchant communities had a remarkable sense of solidarity and built networks of correspondents in charge of establishing links between producers and consumers everywhere.

In this context, it must be emphasized that the pacific propagation of the Muslim religion in coastal regions took place totally independently of the Turko-Afghan incursions, which resulted in the subjugation of Delhi and a part of continental India during the same period (twelfth to fourteenth century). Though different in origin and nature, the islamization brought about by conquest was beneficial to the coastal minorities, as it signified Muslims in their respective hinterlands now enjoyed considerable political power. During the fourteenth century, the Muslim invaders, after sweeping through the entire peninsula in successive waves, withdrew to the Gangetic Plain, leaving in the backwash chiefs and governors who would repeatedly reject the supremacy of Delhi, even while remaining faithful to the Islamic religion. Thus were born, among others, the sultanates of Bengal (1336) and of Gujarat (1401), both of which gave a decisive fillip to maritime trade.

The forces that thus came into prominence gave rise to new conflicts and needs. The kingdoms in the Deccan organised themselves in two blocs: the Muslim chiefs joined together under banner of the Bahmani Empire on the one hand, and on the other, Hindu and Jain rulers, spurred by the will for survival, united under the tutelage of the Rajas of Vijayanagar. The parallel expansion of these two powers would significantly change the political map of the peninsula. Their mutual antagonism, which became evident in the middle of the fourteenth century, led to incessant wars. The wars opposing them that lasted for more than two centuries would create considerable domestic demand, to such a degree that they stimulated trade in all the ports along the coast.

After the chaos of the Turk-Afghan invasions, the sultans of Gujarat and Bengal quickly recovered their economic prosperity, which encouraged them to prospect for new export markets. The Islamic settlements on their shores developed increasingly close links with the ports of East Africa and the Southeast Asian islands. The Bengali expansion to the north coast of Sumatra opened the way to the South Seas. Bengali names appear in the necropolises of the island precisely at the time when the ports of Pasei and Pidir started to export pepper from the hinterland towards the China Sea. Even as the power of the Muslims became predominant in Sumatra, the Hinduized kingdom of Majopahit controlled the major part of the archipelago. Java, which remained Hindu at the beginning of the fifteenth century, had already been affected by the proselytizing undertaken by Indian-born Muslims – from Bengal, the Malabar and Gujarat – joined by the Arabs and Persians who had boarded their vessels. These Muslims from various quarters secured their hold by creating breeding grounds for Islamization in every port, without however eliminating the Malay merchants who were engaged in coastal shipping between islands, nor the traders of the Coromandel who had settled there long before.

At the dawn of the fifteenth century, the rise of Malacca on the ruins of a nest of pirates had intensified the coordination of trade. This city, situated where the winds of the two monsoons die down, attracted to its calm waters all ships sailing on the Indian Ocean and the China Sea. When in 1403 the Bengalis persuaded the Raja of Malacca to convert to Islam, the 'Spice Route' had fallen entirely into the hands of Muslims.

The founding of the sultanate of Malacca was the primary factor of change in a century in the course of which the economic structures of the modern age would be laid down. During the thirty years that followed, two movements developed on either side of the Ocean. The first of these emanated from China, where the Ming emperors sent to the South Sea seven expeditions mobilizing hundreds of junks armed for war to raise tribute and to scout for markets as far as the East African coast (1403–33). The second movement was sparked by Barsbay, the sultan of Egypt who arrogated in 1429 the monopoly over the spice trade to the detriment of the Karimi merchants. Some of them took refuge in the ports of west India where they struck partnerships with local traders. At around the same time, driven by internal difficulties, the Ming emperors ceased their incursions.

The withdrawal of the Chinese and the decline of the Arabs gave a golden opportunity to Indian maritime traders. At the dawn of the sixteenth century, they had indeed become the unchallenged masters of the oceanic routes.

The spice route: new networks, new markets

The maritime 'Spice Route' accounted for only a part of an immense network whose bases were established on the Indian shores. Though it has been established that the turn of the sixteenth century marked a high point for the economy of the Indian Ocean, sources dating from this period are inadequate to enable us to understand its infinite complexity. They do, however, help us to discern certain main currents around which secondary mercantile activities were organized.

The countries on the Indian Ocean are rich in archaeological remains, but are disappointing when it comes to manuscripts. The humidity of the tropical climate in South Asia has destroyed historical documents, which have come to our knowledge only through apocryphal copies dealing more with territorial conquests and court intrigues than with maritime trade. Archives have been better preserved in the Middle East, especially in Egypt and Arabia, where legal and fiscal documents, track charts and the genealogies of navigators have survived.

In the absence of comprehensive documents, only travelogues written by voyagers enable us to synthesize the disparate information available to us: Ibn Battuta of Tangiers in the fourteenth century, who has provided us with an overview that is indispensable for any background study; then in the fifteenth century, Chinese scribes aboard the junks of Zheng-He, the admiral of the Ming emperors; Abdurrazzaq, the Persian ambassador to Vijayanagar; the Russian voyager Athanase Nikitine; and Italian traders who succeeded in infiltrating into caravans, often at the price of converting to Islam, like Nicolo de Conti, Girolamo da Santo Stefano and Ludovico di Varthema. From the early years of the sixteenth century, the Portuguese, who had settled on the Malabar Coast, started to keep diaries of their observations. Sources like log books, inventories of cargoes and reports sent to the king constitute the most valuable and the most comprehensive documentation for the study of the Indian seas. Dating from an age still reeling from the upheavals of the preceding period and on the eve of great changes, of which the Portuguese were both witnesses and players, these documents offer a bird's eye view of the economic and social structures of seafaring life.

Products and trade

The Indian seas owed their riches to the exploitation of the natural resources of the tropics, which were traded for manufactured products from the Middle East, China and even from India itself.

Spices were indigenous to the coastal areas of the equatorial ocean. In India, pepper grew in the undergrowth on the slopes of the Western Ghats and ginger in the hinterland of the Malabar Coast. Local merchants bartered them for rice and textiles, and then carried them to the ports on the coasts. Cinnamon grew abundantly in Ceylon, where the same merchants exchanged it for rice, coral and mercury, before distributing it in the emporiums of the Indian coast.

These merchants travelled every year to Malacca to get supplies of the most precious spices from the islands of Southeast Asia: long pepper from Sumatra, greatly appreciated by their Chinese clientele, cloves from the Molucca Islands, nuts and mace from the Banda Islands, where Javanese merchants exchanged them for rice, pots and low quality cotton goods before transporting them to Malacca. Since time immemorial, the spice trade had been closely linked to the trade of foods and textiles, of which India was the largest producer.

Even though Java and Pegu had many rice fields, India remained the primary source of food products for South Asian countries. Two regions practising intensive cultivation were the major suppliers of rice: first, the Vijayanagar Empire which, from its western and eastern ports, guaranteed the subsistence of peninsular India, Ceylon, and countries on the Red Sea and the Persian Gulf; second, Bengal, which from Sonargaon, Satgaon and Chittagong supplied rice to Orissa, Arakan and the Maldives. The cultivation of sugarcane flourished in these two regions, especially in Bengal where it was used for the preparation of preserves, exported as far as Malacca. The islanders of the Maldives produced the greatest share of the dried fish that navigators required for their journeys.

Aromatic and medicinal plants were plentiful among the tropical flora. Betel and areca nuts, used for chewing, grew along the shores and were distributed all across India by coastal fleet. Egyptian opium, exported from Aden to the entire East, began to face competition from Gujarati opium, which was less expensive and had prospects of large-scale distribution in western Indochina. Ships loaded with cargoes of spice sailing all the way to the Mediterranean also carried other plants like, galbanum, Borneo camphor, tamarind and the myrobalan fruit from Malabar.

India, a large consumer of perfumes, imported Arabian incense and rose water from the Middle East, benzoin and musk from Pegu and from Siam. White sandalwood, used for various purposes, came from the island of Timor (Indian red sandalwood was reserved for construction).

The fauna supplied not only aromatic products (like musk from Siam and amber-gris from the Maldives), but the animals themselves were also objects of trade. Elephants, used all over India as domestic animals, were trained in Ceylon especially for warfare and then exported by sea by Malabar traders. The rulers of the Deccan, plagued by incessant conflicts, needed them as much for parade as for military operations. They appreciated horses from Persia and Arabia even more, and they were imported by the hundreds every year because the South Indian climate did not allow their natural renewal. These steeds, bought in exchange for rice in Ormuz, were transported by sea as far as the west coast of India. Then they were sent over-land to the courts of princes who paid for them with gold.

Rajas, sultans and affluent merchants amassed precious stones and metals. 'Amassing treasure is an eminent act of glory and honour for the kings of these lands,' observed the Mogul emperor Babur in 1526.[6] Spending it would be 'infamy' and it had rather be destroyed than fall into the hands of the enemy. The kings of Ceylon, 'where jewels grow',[1] exercised monopoly over sapphires, emeralds and other gems abundant in their lands and which were sold and mounted in the mar-kets of Calicut. The Deccan possessed diamond mines that were worked especially in Vijayanagar and Berar. The quarries in Gujarat produced semi-precious stones like cornelian, agate and amethyst, used in making jewels highly appreciated in the Middle East and in Africa. The southern Coromandel coasts and the Mannar Gulf possessed pearl fisheries. India thus accumulated gold and silver, whether coined or not, in diverse forms: as Venetian ducats, Egyptian *ashrafi*, Persian larins, silver rings from Siam or as gold powder from East Africa.

We can gauge the importance of the slave trade as an economic activity only by the number of foreigners whose liberation or servility is recorded in documents. The majority of them – referred to under the generic term of Abyssinians – were exported from the sultanates of East Africa. The best among them served in the armies, especially in Bengal where they were so numerous that they succeeded in overthrowing the sultan at the end of the fifteenth century and in founding their own dynasty. White slaves, abducted or bought as children in the Balkans and converted to Islam, were extremely popular with Indian rulers. Some of them, after being lib-erated, were promoted by their masters to high positions, like Malik Ayaz, Governor of Diu. Merchants sometimes bought children in India itself, particularly in the Silhet region (Bengal). Castrated and well nourished, these children were raised in the Islamic faith and resold to clients in neighbouring countries. Khaja Ata, the pow-erful governor of Ormuz, was a Bengali eunuch, like the Governor of Chittagong and the *braja*, the highest ranking functionary of the Pegu kingdom.

India did not only supply food and raw materials, it also produced manufactured goods. The majority of these depended on the local craft industry – weaponry, jewels and finely wrought furniture. However important these might have been, they were nothing compared to the textile industry. Whereas China and Persia remained unchallenged for the diversity and quality of their silk, India was the largest cotton producing country in the world. Three regions supplied the bulk of the production: Bengal, whose fabrics were woven with the help of skilful techniques, was especially famous for Sonargaon muslin, in demand as far as Europe; the Coromandel, whose painted cloth was marketed in Ceylon, Java and countries in western Indochina; Gujarat, which specialized more in the manufacture of printed cloth, strove to take the lead over other cotton producing countries by the efficiency of its distribution networks.

The rhythm of the monsoon orchestrated trade movements. Every year in July ships on the quest for spices, driven by the south-westerly winds, departed from ports like Aden, Jedda, Ormuz, situated at the terminuses of land routes, where products from the Middle East and the Mediterranean arrived in caravans – Venetian ducats, Egyptian *ashrafi*, copper, lead, mercury and coral, carpets and gilt leather, opium, weaponry and mirrors. Some of these ships set sail for Calicut where pepper was exchanged for coined gold, ginger for copper, spices from Malacca for other products from the West. These ships returned to their ports of registry in the early months of the following year. Others were bound for the ports of Gujarat where they traded a part of their cargo for textiles, which they loaded onto Gujarati ships in order to trade the whole cargo in Malacca for products from the Far East.

There were also ships that left Gujarat for the ports of north Sumatra – Pasei, Pidir or Atjeh. There they exchanged cotton goods for pepper and raw silk. Some of them sailed up the Bay of Bengal to the ports of Pegu where they bartered this pepper, rose water and opium for rubies, benzoin and lacquer. All these vessels returned to the western side of the Indian Ocean during the northeast monsoon by two different routes. Some of them sailed towards Ceylon, left their merchandise in the Malabar ports and returned to Gujarat, while others took the straight route through the Maldive atolls to reach Aden and the ports of the African Horn. On the shores of the Red Sea and the Persian Gulf caravans awaited, which transported the spices and merchandise from Suez and Ormuz as far as the Mediterranean ports. But the quantity that reached these destinations cannot be compared to what was consumed in East Asia and India itself. Ibn Battuta observed – and the Portuguese Alfonso de Albuquerque would corroborate it at a later period – that what went across to the West was only a small fraction of an immense trade.

The Indian peninsula thus divided the ocean into two zones characterized by two different types of trade. In the western part of the ocean, pepper, ginger and cinnamon were traded for rice at the site of production, then for gold, silver and utility metals in the ports of distribution. In the eastern part of the ocean, pepper, cloves, nuts and mace were bartered in situ principally for rice, then for manufactured products (porcelain, weaponry and especially textiles) on the markets of Malacca. This brief outline of the 'spice route' shows how gold poured into India without ever getting drained out of it. It also points out that beyond the peninsula textiles served as the basis for all trade.

Coastal cities and merchant societies

Seafaring life was concentrated in and around the ports situated most often at the mouths of rivers. The main port, sheltered in an estuary on the west coast or in a delta on the east coast, was linked to satellite ports, each of which was involved in a specialized activity. In the course of the centuries, these ports experienced the vicissitudes of fortune. On the west coast, the ports in Gujarat were grouped around Cambay, which remained the largest of them even though it silted up to such an extent that it was accessible only at high tide. The open city with white houses adorned with finely wrought wood offered foreign merchants all the products of the hinterland: raw cotton, indigo, handicraft objects and, above all, an infinite range of woven and dyed textiles. Each of its satellite ports – Surat, Randa, Gogha and the military town of Diu – had more specific links with one or other of the cities on the Indian Ocean.

As early as the beginning of the sixteenth century, the Portuguese had measured the extent of the expansion of Gujarati trade: 'Cambay spreads out two arms,' wrote Tomé Pires in 1516, 'one touching Aden and the other Malacca'.[2] Cotton goods – grey, bleached or dyed with indigo – were loaded in huge quantities for shipment at all the ports of the country, along with jewels mounted with semi-precious stones, objects of wood, ivory and tortoiseshell, weaponry and perfumes. These manufactured goods, often of mediocre quality, were distributed in all the markets of the Indian Ocean in exchange for the most precious assets: gold, ivory and slaves from Africa, spices and gems.

It appears that the entire Gujarati society participated in mercantile activities. Muslims – generally Bohra or Khoja – were more willing to expatriate themselves than the others. Gujarati merchants and mariners embarked on their own ships or on ships owned by the lords of the kingdom. Their crew boasted the ablest sailors, the most experienced pilots and a corps of archers who defended the fleets. The predominance of Muslims should not, however, eclipse the role played by Hindus in overseas trade. In Cambay, finance was almost entirely in their hands. Though certain Brahmins did not consider it beneath their dignity to commission ships, thereby amassing enormous fortunes, most of the businessmen belonged to the *vaishya* caste of *banias* (Sanskrit: *bania*: 'merchant'), who were experts in all sorts of mercantile transactions. Established in all the ports of the Indian Ocean, principally in Malacca, living as a community in special neighbourhoods with their temples at the centre, these merchants had a network of active and closely-knit correspondents in charge of creating links between ship owners and producers. Voyagers seem to have often mistaken them for Jains, who were also engaged in the same activities and who showed the same sense of honour in their conduct.

Irrespective of the social group they belonged to, Gujarati businessmen filled all those who came in contact with them with admiration. Present in all the ports of call of the spice route, they were the masters of the textile market and the coordinators of almost all trade activities spanning from the China Sea to as far as East Africa. By the end of the fifteenth century, they had succeeded in making Gujarat the largest economic power in the Indian Ocean and perhaps the entire Old World.

The other cities on the west coast served as bases for the coastal fleet, which distributed food, textiles, betel and articles of common use. The only oceanic trade of import was, as we saw earlier, that of horses, transported from Ormuz to Dabhol, Chaul, Goa and Bhattkal by Persian merchants who had settled down in the Deccan. Further to the south, another hub of international trade emerged in the ports of Kerala, which had always been prosperous, thanks to the pepper and ginger that grew abundantly in this region. Whereas certain recent physical modifications had favoured the fortune of some of these ports, they proved to be detrimental to others. In 1341 the swelling of the Periyar River had led to the decline of Cranganore, which tilted the balance towards the port of Cochin. Blocked by an offshore bar, the old port of Eli had been abandoned a few decades prior to the arrival of the Portuguese, which gave the edge to Cannanore. These changes led to the emergence of Calicut as the leading port of Kerala at the expense of the antique Kollam (Quilon).

Three factors were conducive to Calicut's rise to pre-eminence: the safety of its waters, where pirates did not dare to venture; the existence of a stringent organization, which protected foreign traders from fraudulent negotiations; and the official protection granted by the Hindu ruler to Islamic institutions. Thus Muslim merchants of all nations, from Tlemcen all the way to Canton, were drawn to the markets of Calicut, where spices and precious stones were abundant. The city sprawled between the Ghats and the beach, its houses of whitened stone with palm roofs stood amidst gardens in which pepper grew entwined around trees. The city, with its copper-plated temples overlooking it, had not less than twenty mosques.

Travellers have left us only scanty descriptions of coastal cities on the Bay of Bengal, but they give us a glimpse into the nature and extent of their trade activities. Generally situated in deltas covered with rice plantations, these cities provided for the subsistence of neighbouring regions: near the mouths of the Brahmaputra, Sonargoan, the great warehouse of Bengal, exported sugar and precious fabrics; Satgoan, located on the oldest arm of the Ganges, controlled the maritime network of Hindu countries in the Bay of Bengal; and at the edge of Arakan, Chittagong was home to a large Muslim community. On the east coast of Vijayanagar, Pulicat and Nagapattinam distributed the rice and cotton goods of the Coromandel, while Kayal and Kalikarai specialized in the trade of horses and pearls. All these ports were oriented towards the ports of Pegu-Martaban, Dagon and Kusmin, which produced benzoin, lacquer and rubies, and towards Tenasserim, which exported merchandise from Siam. Thanks to these economic activities, the ports of the Bay of Bengal built powerful cultural bonds between the Indian subcontinent and western Indochina.

The growing influence of the Gujaratis on most of the trade in the eastern part of the Indian Ocean was at the expense of merchants of Bengal. The activity of the Bengalis remained nevertheless quite important, thanks to the network of their settlements in coastal regions: in Sumatra, where they formed the ruling class as well as the majority of the inhabitants of Pasei; in Malacca, which they had populated from its origin; in Pegu; in Java and as far as the Maldives, where they came every year to barter rice for cowry shells.

Tamil overseas merchants had settled down in the Hinduized states of Indochina and the islands of Southeast Asia, as far back as the early centuries of the Christian era. They continued to have numerous trading posts and energized the overseas trade of Vijayanagar. The Chettis of the Coromandel had the upper hand in money changing, pearls and precious stones. The Klings of Telangana, who specialized in the export of textiles, were unchallenged masters in Java and Malacca, where the threat of Gujarati competitors began to overshadow them.

Indian businessmen formed companies when they embarked on long distance voyages. In the eastern part of the Indian Ocean, ships from the Coromandel transported the Malabars, while those of Bengal carried merchants from the Bahmani Empire. In the course of the fifteenth century, the Arabs and the Persians increasingly used Gujarati ships to sail beyond the Indian peninsula.

This brief account cannot do justice to the complexity of mercantile networks, entire branches of which remain unknown to this day. We are still searching for answers to several questions but it is risky to look for clues in documents dating from later periods under the erroneous pretext that nothing changes in the East.

At the dawn of the sixteenth century, everything had changed and more changes were in store. In retrospect, we are able to gauge the significance of the transformations that occurred in the preceding century. The most significant of these was the simultaneous rise of the sultanates of Malacca and of Gujarat whose combined interests altered the economic structures of the time by creating new markets and new networks of overseas traders. Around the 1500s, even as the Portuguese began to explore the eastern part of the Indian Ocean, a fundamental mutation was underway in the Indonesian archipelago: the agrarian medieval kingdoms of Hindu culture had completely become Islamized. The supremacy of Muslim overseas merchants extended henceforth beyond the Molucca Islands. What was new was that their companies were no longer controlled by the Arabs or the Persians, but by Muslims of Indian stock. The Gujaratis were all set to consolidate their hold over all other networks, taking up the place left vacant by the decline of the Arabs, who now remained predominant only in the port of Calicut.

Other changes were in the pipeline which would have heavy consequences for seafaring life. In 1511, three key ports – Ormuz, Goa and Malacca – fell into the hands of the Portuguese. The subsequent years would witness the irruption of the Ottaman Turks in the Indian Ocean in the wake of their conquest of Egypt (1517), the rise of the Safavids in Iran and the beginnings of the Mogul expansion in India.

II

THE INDIAN STATES

The Sultanates

The heritage of the Sultanate of Delhi

At the beginning of the sixteenth century, India was under the shadow of an aborted empire, that of the Sultanate of Delhi, founded by Iranized Turks at the turn of the thirteenth century. Pursuing the conquest of the Indus Basin led by the Ghaznavids (977–1186), a new dynasty of Afghan Turks, the Ghurids, undertook the invasion of the Ganges Valley and founded Delhi in 1193. As this wave surged back to Afghanistan, it left in its wake Turkish slaves or Mameluks, who under Qutbuddin Aibak and Iltutmish, established the first dynasty of 'Slave Sultans' (1206–60). The Turkish dynasties that followed, the Khaljis (1290–1320) and the Tughluqs (1320–1414), extended their control beyond the Ganges Valley and imposed their political hegemony on the entire subcontinent, pushing their raids of conquest to Madurai in the far south. This Muslim conquest would eventually give rise to a common literary, religious and political culture, called the Indo-Persian culture, drawn from the models of tenth and eleventh century Iran and Afghanistan.

The Delhi sultanate determined the political geography of the subcontinent: after its disintegration in the course of the fourteenth century and the beginning of the fifteenth, the states that remained under Muslim domination were sultanates, while those that had safeguarded or regained their autonomy were Hindu kingdoms.

How did sultanates emerge? In the northwest, the Ghaznevid Turks had conquered the Indus Basin (approximately present Pakistan) in the beginning of the eleventh century: Lahore became a Muslim capital in 1022. The decisive move that consolidated Muslim hegemony in India was the establishment of a new capital, Delhi, some four hundred kilometres farther south in the Ganges Basin.

With this strategic position as their base, Turkish armies took possession of the subcontinent in less than a century by advancing in three directions. Firstly, Ghurid armies, marching towards the east, descended the Ganges Valley and conquered Bengal as early as 1205. At the turn of the fourteenth century, the Khaljis gained their principal access to the sea by moving southwest, crossing the mountains and the desert of Rajasthan to take control of the ports of Gujarat. Finally, between 1304 and 1311, following a double expedition conducted from Delhi for five years, their armies annexed the Deccan Plateau. For twenty-five years, under the last Khaljis and

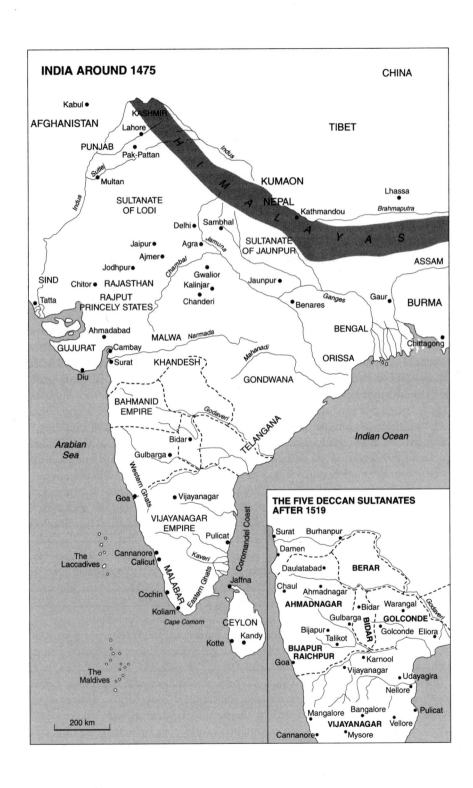

INDIA AROUND 1475

CHINA

Kabul ●
AFGHANISTAN
KASHMIR
Lahore ●
PUNJAB
Pak-Pattan ●
Multan ●
SULTANATE
OF LODI

Sutlej
Indus

Indus

TIBET

KUMAON
Lhassa ●
NEPAL
Brahmaputra
Kathmandou ●

Delhi ● ● Sambhal
Jaipur ● ● Agra
Ajmer ●
Jodhpur ●
Chambal
Jamuna
Gwalior ●
Kalinjar ●
Chanderi ●
SULTANATE
OF JAUNPUR
Jaunpur ●
Benares ●
Ganges
Gaur ●
ASSAM
BURMA

SIND
Chitor ● RAJASTHAN
Tatta ●
RAJPUT
PRINCELY STATES

Ahmadabad ●
GUJURAT
Cambay ●
Surat ●
Diu ●
MALWA *Narmada*
KHANDESH
Mahanadi
GONDWANA
TELANGANA
BENGAL
ORISSA
Chittagong ●

BAHMANID
EMPIRE
Godaveri

Bidar ●
Gulbarga ●

*Arabian
Sea*

Western Ghats

Goa ●
● Vijayanagar
VIJAYANAGAR
EMPIRE
Pulicat ●
Kaveri

The
Laccadives
Cannanore ●
Calicut ●
MALABAR
Eastern Ghats
Cochin ●
Koliam ●
Cape Comorn
CEYLON
Kandy ●
Kotte ●
Jaffna ●

Coromandel Coast

Indian Ocean

The
Maldives

200 km

**THE FIVE DECCAN SULTANATES
AFTER 1519**

Surat ● Burhanpur
Damen ●
Daulatabad ●
BERAR
Chaul ●
Ahmadnagar ●
AHMADNAGAR
● Bidar
Warangal
Gulbarga ●
BIDAR
GOLCONDE
Bijapur ●
Talikot ●
Golconde ● Eliora
BIJAPUR
RAICHPUR
Goa ●
● Karnool
● Vijayanagar
Godaveri
● Udayagira
Nellore ●
Pulicat ●
Mangalore ●
Bangalore ●
VIJAYANAGAR
Vellore ●
Cannanore ●
● Mysore

the early Tughluqs, India formed a single empire: in 1327, the greatest of the sultans, Muhammad ibn Tughluq (1325–51), sovereign of the whole of India, transferred his capital to the Deccan, to the city of Deogir, renamed Daulatabad. The euphoria was, however, short-lived: the provinces seceded one after the other, starting with Bengal around 1338, then the Deccan in 1347. The Mongol invasion led by Timur (1335–1405) that culminated in the sack of Delhi dealt the deathblow.

During the fourteenth and fifteenth centuries, the subcontinent underwent another phase of political fragmentation. Muslim and Hindu states co-existed during this period. The former, conventionally called the 'regional sultanates', emerged in the aftermath of the disintegration of the Delhi sultanate – only Kashmir would remain linked to Central Asia until the end of the sixteenth century. The Hindu states were either situated on the fringes that had remained inaccessible to the Muslim armies or were powerful Hindu confederations, like the Rajput and Vijayanagar kingdoms, that had reorganized themselves in order to fend off the threat posed by the sultanates. All these kingdoms were nevertheless home to Muslim minorities of merchants or mercenaries. Was this period of political fragmentation an age of misery as it has been generally believed, or on the contrary, an age of prosperity and economic expansion, as the period under the Delhi sultanate had undoubtedly been? The clues we have at our disposal are contradictory. The sultanates are often believed to have lived through a dark age. In fact, whereas the Sultanate of Delhi had produced a magnificent and abundant gold and silver currency, the regional sultanates returned to a poorer copper coinage containing a small fraction of silver. Nevertheless, literary and architectural testimonies that have survived as well as accounts of awe-struck voyagers point to a period of prosperity, diversification and innovation.

The sultanate as a political model

The 'nobility'

The sultanate was a state of conquest, dominated by a military oligarchy of foreign origin reigning over a population that was for the most part composed of natives, the majority of whom remained Hindu. Specialists of Muslim India refer to this oligarchy as 'nobility' (Arabic: *umara*, plural of *amir*, head, dignitary). Contrary to what was customary in the West at the close of the Middle Ages, this nobility was not hereditary and did not possess lands. It emerged from the system of slaves (Mameluks), in operation in a large part of the Muslim world, especially in Egypt. In India, slavery had gradually given way to the recruitment of free men, but the ascension of a noble still depended on the reigning sultan: the latter could promote him or reduce him to nothing, if he so desired; the destiny of even his own sons hung on the wishes of the sultan.

The nobility of the sultanates had their roots in diverse ethnic groups that divided a heterogeneous political entity rife with potential conflicts. The most prestigious groups were of foreign origin, with the first generation immigrants enjoying additional esteem. Muslims of pure Indian stock, and even more so Hindus, were pushed to the bottom of the hierarchy.

Reigning families and the high aristocracy came primarily from three ethnic groups: the Turks, the Afghans and the Abyssinians (*Habshi*). The Turks or Turanians (*Turani*), of varied ethnic origins that were more or less Iranized, who had dominated the Islamic world since the eleventh century, rose to eminence in India also. They were indeed its earliest conquerors and it was from them that the slave sultans, the Khaljis, the Tughluqs and most of the regional sultans, descended.

The Afghans, relegated to the lower rungs of the ladder until the middle of the fourteenth century, gradually began to assert their ascendancy to eventually become a politically dominant group in North India, where they came to power under the Lodi dynasty (1451–1526). The Abyssinians, who had come to India as slaves, had a more limited role: they constituted a politically important faction in the Deccan and in Gujarat; they even acquired prominence in the sultanate of Bengal.

The Iranians (*Irani*), often Shiites, formed a faction opposed to the Turks and the Afghans, who were invariably of the Sunni faith. They were, above all, men of letters who propagated Persian cultural models. Influential at the top levels of the administrative machinery, they were also involved in international trade, which at the time was not incompatible with politics.

As for the Arabs, who were mostly religious leaders or traders, they had little representation in the nobility, the Arab dynasties in Khandesh and Bengal being the exception. The so-called 'Indian' Muslims, including local converts or descendants of long established naturalized immigrants, formed a distinct class. Often ostracized by recent immigrants, they had little access to the corridors of power. Finally, a certain number of Indian Hindus were elevated to the ranks of nobility: former ruling families, collectively called *zamindar* (or masters of the land) in Persian, in particular, the famous Rajputs, served the sultans as war chiefs with their own troops; Hindu scholars of the Brahmin caste, or of the caste of scribes, like the Kayasthas or Khatris, indispensable instruments in the Muslim administration, sometimes occupied high offices in the imperial court.

The State apparatus

The State functioned, to use the terminology of Iranian theoreticians who had codified it, as a 'circle of justice': this figure represented the relationships between the four building blocks of society: 1) the peasants; 2) the treasury; 3) the army; and 4) the sultan. The peasants paid taxes to the treasury (the bureaucracy), which supported the army, which in turn protected and extended the power of the sultan; the sultan completed the circle dispensing even-handed justice, that is, by fixing equitable taxes and by protecting the peasants from oppression. The circle of justice was believed to maintain order and peace in the kingdom, while placing it in harmony with the cosmos, thus bringing rain, prosperity and harvests.

Islam, as we shall see in this chapter, had a marginal place in the State machinery. The centre of authority was concentrated in the person of the sultan: a military entrepreneur, he owed his kingdom to a conquest, a coup d'état, or on rare occasions, to heredity, as the same families seldom maintained themselves in power in the Islamic world which did not acknowledge dynastic rights.

The sultan governed with the help of the two branches of his administration, the army and the bureaucracy, the former having precedence over the latter. Indeed, political formations in medieval India were fundamentally military states. The highest dignitaries of the sultanate, both at the centre and in the provinces, were nobles trained in martial arts and the cavalry. The king had his personal guard, while the state dignitaries had to levy taxes and maintain a contingent of soldiers on their salary. The union of these contingents constituted the army of the sultan: a cavalry of archers mounted on imported horses trained for warfare, and whose mobility, power and rapidity of shooting guaranteed total mastery over the terrain. To these techniques borrowed from Central Asia, the sultans added elephants as a buttress for the cavalry.

Bureaucracy was clearly subordinate to the army: at the service of the latter, it was in charge of levying taxes to maintain the armed forces and to enrich the nobles and the sultan, the primary beneficiaries of the system. The idea of a civil administration completely distinct from the military apparatus was unknown at the time. Bureaucrats in high positions were all soldiers. Only at the lower echelons of the hierarchy were found scribes, most often Hindus, devoid of military functions.

The other, more technical, State departments functioned under the supervision of the army and the bureaucracy. The most notable of these were the postal department, primarily focused on espionage, and the department of religious affairs.

The agrarian administration

The State apparatus was organized around the levying of land taxes and was based on a principle also codified by Persian authors. Contrary to the letter of the Islamic law, which laid emphasis on private property, this principle concurred with traditional notions prevalent in India: the sultan was the ultimate master of the land; the peasants were therefore under obligation to pay him a substantial part of the harvest, amounting from a third to even half of the produce. This land tax (*kharaj*) brought in the largest share of revenue to the state exchequer. So great were these incomes that they ultimately proved to be the weakness of the bureaucracy.

It would have been ideal if the sultan's functionaries were to collect these taxes themselves directly from the producers. But this principle was inapplicable, as the functionaries of the king administered only a small part of the lands called the 'reserve' (*khalisa*, or crown-land). Fiscal rights on the rest of the territory were delegated to nobles by way of salary: these revenue rights over a specified area were denoted by the Arabic term *iqta* (which would subsequently be replaced by the Persian *jagir* during the Mogul period). In this institutional set-up, prevalent all across the medieval Muslim world, the central administration gave the beneficiary a statement in writing specifying the territory whose taxes were reserved for him, the amount to be collected and the use to which he may put it. But the beneficiary did not enjoy any right over the people living on the land in question; nor was he the proprietor of the land. In fact, he was often transferred from one region to another to preclude the constitution of fiefs.

The second factor that weakened the power of the sultan's administrators was the fact that the provinces were ruled by powerful governors, eagerly waiting for an opportunity to rebel. The situation was no different even at the level of cantons (denoted by the Hindi term *pargana*), where small rural towns (*qasba*) were the last Islamized pockets in a countryside that had remained overwhelmingly Hindu. Here the administration was in the hands of local Hindus, like the *chaudhari*, the head of a *pargana*, assisted by his accountant (or *patwari*). Besides, the bureaucracy, lacking the resources to deal with the peasants individually, resorted to local intermediaries, who were placed in charge of levying taxes in return for a percentage theoretically fixed at ten per cent. These intermediaries of varying importance – from the modest village chief or the head of a lineage to former kinglets or local kings who retained their private armies – were all potential rebels.

Sultans, merchants and artisans

However preoccupied the sultans were with appropriating the agrarian surplus, they did not overlook the importance of trade. They needed to import warhorses and luxury products, while the export of spices and fabrics, markedly more advantageous in the balance of trade, brought in coinage that accumulated in their treasuries. They also levied customs duties (called *zakat*, or alms), which complemented the land taxes. Just as there was no clear demarcation between a civil administration and the army, there was nothing incompatible about simultaneously playing the role of a warrior and a merchant. Thus the sultan and the nobles could invest in commercial enterprises; the sultans had their own manufactures (*karkhana*), particularly in the weaving sector. The economic development that had marked the second expansion of Islam from the twelfth century onwards continued under the sultanates.

The extent of trade activities, which was relatively circumscribed everywhere, depended on the base of the operations. Whereas traffic was limited in scale in the landlocked principalities of North India, it was extensive in Bengal, Gujarat and in the Deccan, largely open to the Middle East and especially to Iran. Muslims played only a comparatively insignificant role: like the peasantry and the scribes, merchants were more often Hindus or Jains, and the latter included moneychangers who doubled as bankers. Little is known about artisans of this period. More particularly, we do not know when they started to convert en masse to Islam.

The sultans and Islam

How could the sultanates, dominated by a Muslim minority, adapt to a Hindu majority? But first, to what extent were they governed by Islam?

The sultanates were created in the ninth and tenth centuries in the wake of the disintegration of the Abbasid caliphate of Baghdad which had wielded temporal and spiritual authority over the entire Muslim world since AD 750. The sultans were 'warlords' who had acquired autonomy in their regions after obtaining the official recognition of the caliph. It was thus that the Ghaznavids became the first sultans of Delhi. When the Mongols put an end to the Baghdad caliphate in 1258, the sultans, both in India and elsewhere, came to enjoy an autonomous legitimacy recognized by the doctors of the Law; then they began to invest themselves with the title of caliph, which had by then become devalued, to signify that they also commanded spiritual authority. Or else they pledged their allegiance either to the puppet caliph who in the wake of 1258 had taken refuge among the Mameluks of Egypt (1250–1517), as was the case with Muhammad ibn Tughluq (1325–51) and the early sultan of Gujarat, or else to more potent sultans, like Timur and subsequently the Safavids of Iran (1501–1722), whose protection was sought by the Shiite sultans of the Deccan.

The sultans had to declare themselves Muslims and the sultanates were therefore in theory islamic states. The symbol of this adherence to Islam was the inscription of the sultan's name on the coinage that also contained the profession of faith and the mention of his name in the sermon of Friday's main prayer. At the centre of the capital, adjacent to the palace, stood the mosque-cathedral as a testimony to the Islamic conquest. Islamic Law, or the *Shariah*, was in theory the law of the kingdom and the sultan was responsible for appointing *qadis* in order to ensure its application at the level of the canton. The mark of this allegiance to Islam was the discriminatory poll tax, the *jizya*, which was levied on the non-Muslims, that is the Hindus. The latter had always been considered, much like the Christians and Jews in the other Islamic lands, 'protected persons' (*dhimmi*), in other words, inferior subjects.

In order to preserve the islamic character of the state, the sultan was required to maintain, or support by granting aid, a religious staff made up of two, often overlapping, groups. The first were the *ulamas* or Doctors of the Law, who were well versed in exoteric[1] religious sciences in Arabic. They served in the mosques, sat as *qadis* or as experts of the law (*mufti*) and taught in religious schools. The branch of Islam that was predominant in India, as among the Turks in general, was Sunnism of the Hanafi school of law, the fundamental works of which were introduced to India, commented and imitated. With the increasing influence of Iran, especially in the Deccan, a minority belonging to the Twelver Shiah emerged during this time. Finally, perpetuating a movement inaugurated in Sind well before the Delhi sultanate, the merchants of the west coast converted to the Ishmaili sub-sect of the Shiah. These two Shiite sub-sects followed their own laws.[2]

The second category of religious leaders was the Sufi mystics (*mashaikh*, singular: *shaikh*). They were the necessary intermediaries between Allah and men, and benevolence towards them was supposed to guarantee the prosperity of the kingdom: the sultans and his nobles bestowed gifts of cash or land on their hospices (*khanqah*). After the death of the Sufis, these hospices accommodated their tombs, which subsequently became places of pilgrimage called *dargah*, literally 'palace'. While the army was primarily composed of Turks and Afghans, these religious leaders were mostly of Arab stock. The mystics, who were secluded ascetics during the early years of Islam, gradually congregated in hospices around famous founder-leaders, and towards the end of the twelfth century, they began to form orders whose members shared the same spiritual genealogy. The most advanced disciples who frequented these hospices received a mystical education, which, by means of techniques of ecstasy, enabled them to experience immediate contact with the divine. For more common believers, the mystic saints served as intermediaries for obtaining divine favours. The earliest mystical orders established in the subcontinent at this time had come from abroad as far back as the thirteenth century. Thus, the Chishtiyya, which had originated in Afghanistan, reached India along with the conquerors: its four great saints, Muinuddin (died 1233, in Ajmer), Qutbuddin (died 1236, in Delhi), Fariduddin (died 1265, in Pak-Pattan) and Nizamuddin (died 1325 in Delhi) have remained the patrons of Muslim India. Radiating from Delhi under Nizamuddin, and following the trail of the armies of Muhammad ibn Tughluq towards the South, the Chishtiyya spread its roots all across India. Two other brotherhoods were established during this age: the aristocratic Suhrawardiyya and the Qalandariyya, which was a congregation of wandering ascetics, shaven and sometimes nude, resolutely anti-conformists and at times violent. From the fifteenth century onwards, new fraternal orders sprang up. The orthodox Qadiriyya was established everywhere. The Rafaiyya, whose followers went into trances, in which they engaged in violent exercises, pierced their bodies or walked on fire, gained a foothold in Gujarat, and then in the South. Finally, under the sultanates, Indian Islam began to create its own mystical orders: the Shattariyya, extremely successful all over South Asia and the Madariyya, which was confined to the low castes in North India.

To fulfil his religious obligations, the sultan maintained, in tandem with the army and the administration, a third branch of the government: a ministry, so to speak, of religion and justice, under the control of the *sadr as-sudur*. The *sadr as-sudur* supervised the attribution of 'benefits' by way of lands or money to religious dignitaries. He was at the same time in charge of the functioning of the courts of the *qadis* and the appointment of the latter.

On paper, the sultanate seemed to be a perfectly islamized state and it is highly tempting, especially in Pakistan, to consider it as the model of an islamic state so desired by neo-fundamentalists. Nothing could be further from the truth. In fact, the feeling that pervaded the relationship between the religious staff and the Turko-Afghan aristocracy was one of mutual distrust. For the ulamas and the Sufis, the sultanate was, as affirmed by the fourteenth-century historian and moralist Barani, a necessary evil: one ought to accept it as one would accept the consumption of dead bodies at the time of famine, although the Law prohibited such an act. Religious leaders, often of Arab origin, and religion itself were subordinated to the political exigencies of the Turko-Afghans who were in power.

The application of Islamic law was confined to family and penal law; for matters relating to the agrarian administration and for a major part of the penal law, the government and the sultan enjoyed absolute sovereignty, with the *qadis* having no say. The same was true with the *jizya*, the symbol par excellence of the superiority of Muslims over non-Muslims: it is highly doubtful that it was in reality levied as a tax distinct from the land tax; the terms *jizya* and *kharaj* are interchangeable in the texts dating from this time. The extremely theoretical nature of this discrimination must be kept in mind when there is reference to its abolition or its restoration under the Moguls.

The sultanate was thus in principle placed under the aegis of the Muslim faith, but Islam did not govern the conduct of the government, which gave the sultans sufficient leeway for adapting themselves to the local context.

The limits of the power of the sultans

The power of the sultan, absolute in theory, was limited in reality. In his relation with his nobility, the sultan was less the absolute chief than the first among equals in a heteroclite coalition that had allowed him to come to power or to inherit it. The nobles, endowed with incomes from *iqta* lands and backed by armed contingents, could at any time form coalitions to overthrow him; similarly the administrators of the provinces had the military and financial resources to secede. The sultanate was therefore not a centralized state, but rather a fragile edifice, under the shadow of the constant threat of disintegration. What had happened to the Delhi sultanate in the fourteenth century duplicated itself on a smaller scale in the regional sultanates, especially in the Deccan.

The ruling Muslim class was a small minority with little leeway in comparison with the Hindu majority. The intransigence with which the Sultan Muhammad ibn Tughluq (1325–51) treated the Hindu intermediaries had sparked off a long series of revolts, as recounted by the Moroccan traveller Ibn Battuta. Was the political strategy of regional sultans more effective?

The sultanates in the Indian context

Political compromises with the Hindu majority

In order to survive, the regional sultanates had to compromise with the local population to a much greater degree than the vast centralized sultanate, which had at its command an army and considerable resources. As a minority, with only a rudimentary State apparatus, the sultans had to rely on Hindu intermediaries for collecting taxes and for maintaining order. Furthermore, contrary to what has generally been believed, it was not with a passive and unarmed peasantry that they had to contend; recent studies have shown that the Muslim chiefs had to strive not only against former potentates well accustomed to warfare but also against a peasantry trained in martial arts and only too eager to sell their services to the highest bidder, in other words, a real 'armed peasantry'. In the subcontinent, which at the time had probably more than a hundred million inhabitants, supply in this 'military labour market' by far exceeded the demand.[3] Local potentates, especially Rajput chiefs all across North India, or the Polygar and the Marathas in South India, could effortlessly raise armies capable of standing up to the armies of the sultans.

In order to neutralize these sources of threat, sultans resorted to two strategies of differing boldness. The first, classical since the Delhi sultanate and which would be employed extensively in the Mogul Empire under Akbar (1555–1605) and his successors, consisted of admitting a variable proportion of Hindu chiefs into the ranks of nobility. This solution had the advantage of maintaining them in a subaltern position: they could give their daughters in marriage to the sultan or to the Muslim nobility, but the converse was prohibited. This was moreover in keeping with the Law, which stipulated that non-Muslims were inferior to Muslims.

The other form of compromise was even more audacious: sultans and Muslim nobles in Gujarat, Malwa, Rajasthan and eventually all across North India, treated the Rajputs as equals. In particular, they allowed women to circulate in both directions: thus Muslim women were sometimes seen to enter the harems of Hindu chiefs. In this connection, it must be underscored that the Rajputs too had to infringe Hindu orthodoxy. As a matter of fact, they had not yet emerged as the champions of Hinduism, a role that they would subsequently carve out for themselves. This bold compromise could not be generalized owing to the opposition of the ulamas who began during this period to assert their authority as a pressure group.

The religious scene: compromises, convergences, conversions

Compromises like these were not restricted to politics, but were prevalent in the most varied aspects of society, from language to cuisine to mysticism and architecture. Was this a compromise between totally opposed ideologies, as is asserted today in political propaganda and in fundamentalist discourses? This mode of questioning only leads to laborious and inconclusive theories on the influence of Islam on Hinduism and vice versa.

In reality, it was an 'acclimatization' of Islam to the situation in which it found itself: the classical Arabo-Persian culture of the period of the Delhi sultanate adapted itself to the local cultures by borrowing certain features from them. The fifteenth and sixteenth centuries in particular witnessed the development of vernacular literatures: the form of Hindi that is today called Urdu[4] gained the status of the lingua franca of India and appeared in Sufi poetry.

In the wake of the fragmentation of political power, this acclimatization brought about the regional diversification of Muslim cultures. Urdu itself split into two branches: that of the North and that of the Deccan, called Deccani. Muslim literatures in Bengali, Gujarati and Kashmiri began to find expression. Architectural styles took on regional peculiarities. The conquerors adopted regional languages and customs. With their local converts, they constituted Muslim ethnic groups peculiar to each region and often duplicated the regional varieties of the caste system.

Despite all this, are we right to speak about syncretism in this context? We must keep in mind the innocent accommodation to local customs and take into consideration an often forgotten fact, namely convergence, which alone explains the reciprocal adaptation that both the communities underwent. Muslims, like Hindus, possessed a hierarchical vision of society and did not find the caste system shocking. On the other hand, both Hindu and Muslim mystical literatures developed the same themes: disdain for social hierarchies and instituted religions, while giving pre-eminence to the mystical union with a formless divinity, present in everyone's heart.[5] Hindu mystics, poets (sant) from the modest castes of artisans, and ascetics belonging to the order of the Yogis thus had to vie with the Sufis in an over-saturated market for mysticism.

Mystics from all quarters have left behind testimonies of this convergence. The most remarkable of these mystics include: the poet Kabir (around 1440–1518), born in a Muslim family of weavers in Benares, who eventually embraced the Hindu tradition; the Muslim Abdulquddus Gangohi (1456–1537) of the Sufi brotherhood of Chisthiyya, who composed verses in a similar vein and who frequented the Yogis from whom he borrowed the techniques of yoga; and finally the most ecumenical of them all, Guru Nanak, (1469–1539), founder of the Sikh sect that became a distinct religion, which borrowed equally from both Hindu and Muslim poets.

It is from this perspective that we can speak about conversions. Muslims were a minority and were fully aware of this fact: this is just about everything that we know from sources contemporary to this age, as no statistics exist prior to the censuses taken by the British at the end of the nineteenth century. In fact, forced conversions were most certainly the exception. The attraction to a supposed Muslim egalitarianism is a myth, proved wrong by the current distribution of converts: the untouchables have eschewed Islam. No document attests to the peaceful preaching of the Sufis that most defenders of Islam put forward today.

The attraction exercised by the politico-economic benefits that Islam offered seemed to have been the primary motivation for conversions, which particularly affected the middle strata of society. The convergences we have underscored above facilitated the gradual passage from one religion to the other, more often experienced as a group (entire castes or lineage) than as individuals. It is however remarkable that, in contrast with other regions in the Muslim world, after six centuries of Muslim domination, less than twenty per cent of the population had converted to Islam (according to the first census of 1872–4): Muslim converts had only become the majority – in which era still remains unknown – only in certain marginal regions of the Indus Basin (present Pakistan), of East Bengal (present Bangladesh), Kashmir and Kerala. In the great centres of Muslim supremacy, the population of converts had not exceeded fifteen per cent (the Delhi region) or not even reached the ten per cent mark (Gujarat and the Deccan).

A voyage into the sultanates

The Deccan: Bidar, Berar, Ahmednagar, Bijapur and Golconda

The Deccan had in store a destiny very different from that of the sultanates of the North. After seceding from Delhi in 1347, it formed, under the banner of the Bahmani dynasty, a compact empire till the end of the fifteenth century, an empire whose configuration has found no equivalent in India. The Muslim nobility was a small minority lost in an ocean of Hindus, speaking Dravidian languages like Telugu, Tamil, or Indo-Aryan languages like Marathi. It imported from Delhi a ready-made culture including not only Persian but also the lingua franca of the north, Urdu, whose local variety, Deccani, was elevated as early as the fourteenth century (much earlier than in the North) to the status of a literary language. The Bahmanis also brought from Delhi the Sufism of the Chishtiyya brotherhood under Sayyid Muhammad Gesudaraz (died 1492), who settled and died in the first capital of Gulbarga during the reign of Feroz Shah (1397–1422). The latter, who is considered the veritable architect of the kingdom, founded the new capital of Bidar.

The nobility, more complex than that of the north, was divided in to two factions whose relentless conflicts constitute the framework of the history of the Deccan. On one side was the faction of the Deccanis, which regrouped Indian Muslims from the North, or who were purely of local origin, as well as the Abyssinians, who made common cause with them. On the other side were the 'foreigners' called the Pardesis, Afaqis or Gharibs, who were Arab, Iranian, and Turkish immigrants, who believed in their own superiority. An enumeration of these rival groups shows to what extent the region was open to foreign influences through its ports on the west coast, including Goa (which was to be recaptured by the Portuguese): in addition to African slaves, the Deccan welcomed the Arabs who, introduced the Qadiriyya fraternal order to India as early as 1422 (earlier than in North India); and more importantly, immigrants from Iran who arrived by sea and who were to become increasingly powerful in the affairs of the kingdom. The principal sign of this Iranian leverage was the emergence, in the first half of fifth century, of the Nimitullahiyya brotherhood, which owed its particularity to its affiliation to the Twelver Shiahs; this was the beginning of the influence of Shiism, which was to become the preferred religion of the sultans of Turkish stock and of the 'foreign' nobility. This predilection for the Shiahs was also a distinctive feature of the Deccan, whose sultans had to pledge allegiance to the Safavids of Iran in order to resist the Mogols, who were, on the contrary, the champions of Sunnism.

The final characteristic feature of politics in the Deccan was the sultans' early endeavour to improve their relations with Hindus, who could rise to the highest positions in the government; the arts were to a large extent open to the Hindu influence. This eclectic confluence of different cultures gave the Deccan an original and ecumenical inflection as much in politics as in art: the compromises made with the Hindu majority proved to be more long-lasting than in the North.

The most famous statesman was the Iranian scholar and merchant Mahmud Gawan. The unchallenged sovereign of the Bahmani Empire between 1453 and 1481, he was a minister and held the title of *malik at-tujjar*, chief of the merchants. He commissioned Iranian architects to construct in Bidar a monumental school of religious sciences (*madrasa*), on which he bestowed substantial gifts. His multifaceted activities were typical of an age where there was no clear-cut demarcation between politics, trade and religion.

His assassination in 1481, at the instigation of the Deccanis, signalled the beginning of the disintegration of the Bahmani Empire, which was to give rise at the turn of the sixteenth century to five distinct sultanates created by the classic process of secession by the provincial governors. The first few provinces broke away from the empire around the year 1490. Fathulla Imadulmulk (died 1490) founded the dynasty of the Imad Shahis of Berar in 1487 in the north. In 1490, Malik Ahmed Nizalmulmulk Bahri (1490–1509) founded, again in the north, the sultanate of Ahmednagar where his descendants reigned under the name of Nizam Shahi. These two early dynasties, which descended from Brahmin families converted to Islam, were of the Sunni sect and were part of the Deccani faction.

The two following dynasties, of foreign origin, were Shiites. They founded the two most powerful sultanates, which would endure until their annexation by the Moguls in 1668–87. In 1490, the governor of Bijapur founded the first of these sultanates, the dynasty of the Adil Shahis (1490–1686): his vast sultanate covered the entire western Deccan and encompassed the country of the Marathas, formidable warrior peasants who would make India tremble in the eighteenth century. His sultanate enjoyed a long coastal front on Indian Ocean, and he had to contend with the Portuguese, to whom he was forced to give up Goa in 1510. The second sultan of this dynasty, Ismail (1510–35) was the first in the Deccan to acknowledge the suzerainty of the Safavids of Iran.

In the east, Sultan Quli Qutbulmulk (1512–43), an Azerbaijani who had become governor of Telingana, gained autonomy in his capital of Golconda. He officially proclaimed his independence in 1512 and founded the dynasty of the Qutb Shahis (1512–1687). This sultanate ruled over the warriors of the Telugu country; it was also largely open to the sea and to large-scale international business. The riches of Golconda, which have become legendary, were partly derived from diamonds of which it was a large producer and whose market it controlled all over Asia. This sultanate had a relatively calm and prosperous history; it built a new capital in Hyderabad at the beginning of the seventeenth century and it established good relations with Safavid Iran. It had to accept the English and Dutch who set up trading posts on the east coast in the beginning of the seventeenth century. Eventually, after 1528, what had remained of the Bahmani Empire in Bidar formed a fifth sultanate governed by the Barid Shahis. It would ultimately be annexed by Bijapur in 1619.

According to the sarcastic remark of a historian, each of these sultanates of the Deccan 'produced more history than it could consume locally'. Besides the internal disputes between the Sunnite Deccanis and the Shiite newcomers, three important external conflicts punctuated their history. The sultanates fought among themselves with a view to expand their territories at the expense of their neighbour, sometimes striking an alliance with their Muslim neighbours in the north (Gujarat, and later with the Moguls) or even with the Hindu empire of Vijayanagar in the south. Their second great undertaking was to restrict the ambitions of the same Vijayanagar kingdom, which particularly coveted the fertile lands of the *doab* (confluent) of Raichur: the only instance when the sultanates of the Deccan would make common cause would in fact be the ultimate campaign of Talikota, in 1565, which enabled them to destroy Vijayanagar and to share its territory. This episode, contemporaneous with the Mogul expansion in the north, marked the consolidation of Muslim supremacy over the entire subcontinent. The third conflict, which was a fight doomed to failure, arose from the need of the sultanates of the Deccan to defend themselves from the encroachments by the sultanates of the north, firstly by Gujarat and Malwa, and subsequently by the Mogul Empire, which began to appropriate Ahmednagar and Berar as early as the end of sixteenth century. The expansionist policy of the Moguls in this region would culminate in 1686–7 with the conquest of Bijapur and Golconda.

The western block: Gujarat, Sind, Malwa, Khandesh

Gujarat was the first port of call for ships arriving from the Near East. As a large producer of fabrics that were exported to the entire Asian continent and as the normal access to the sea from Delhi, the sultanate owed its prosperity to its role as the hub of maritime commerce and trade with the hinterland. More cosmopolitan than the other sultanates, it welcomed not only the habitual Turks and Iranians, but also the Arabs and the Abyssinians. It tolerated Sufi mystical orders of the Arabic world like the Magribiyya and the Rifaiyya, which could not make inroads into the north. Its sultans in fact received their certificate of investiture from the Caliph of Cairo. Finally, it was mainly in Gujarat that the Ishmaili merchant communities established themselves. Gujarat controlled the entire west coast as far as the confines of the Ahmadnagar territory. In 1411, its prosperous ports were buttressed from the inland by a grandiose capital, destined to become the biggest trading city of India, Ahmadabad, founded by the second king of the dynasty, Ahmad I (1410–42). The architecture of this sultanate is among the finest and the most beautiful of this sub-continent.

Mahmud I Begarha (1459–1511) was considered as the greatest sovereign of the dynasty. He brought his Muslim neighbours under the sway of his domination and extended his possessions towards the northwest at the expense of Rajputs. Faced with the Portuguese who had landed in India in 1498, he suffered a naval defeat in 1509 and had to make peace with them after they settled down in Goa in 1510. His successor Muzaffar II (1511–26) pursued the policies of his father and endeavoured to resist the Portuguese.

His successor Bahadur Shah (1526–37), the last great figure of Gujarat, was much more energetic. He conducted frontal attacks on two of his greatest adversaries, the Portuguese and the Rajputs, which led him to strive against the Moguls. In 1531, armed with the alliance of the Ottomans, he defeated the fleet of the Portuguese, but five years later he could not prevent them from fortifying Diu and eventually died at their hands in 1537. In the meantime, he had embarked on the task of curbing the power of Rajputs. After annexing the sultanate of Malwa, which he controlled during a brief interlude, he subjugated the great Silhadi chief and with the help of the Turkish artilleryman Rumi Khan, he stormed the fortress of Chitor, the telling symbol of the resistance of the Rajputs. Rumi Khan subsequently passed to the side of the Mogul emperor Humayun, who made incursions into Gujarat and seized Ahmadabad, but the rebellion of Sher Shah Sur (1540–5) forced the emperor to return to Delhi. Gujarat was thereafter torn between the Portuguese (who were becoming increasingly powerful and whom the latest attack by the Ottoman fleet in 1538 could not root out), the Abyssinian faction and a Mogul faction, that of the Mirzas; it was to fall into the hands of Moguls in 1572–3. Notwithstanding its economic and strategic importance, Gujarat remained overwhelmingly Hindu, and its merchants were more often Hindus or members of the ascetic sect of the Jains than Muslims.

History unfolded quite differently in Sind, which was governed until the end of the fifteenth century by the obscure local dynasty of the Sammas; and the majority of its population was probably already Muslim. It became the area of contention between Gujarat and the Mogul family of the Arghuns who ruled over Kandahar and Multan. The latter succeeded in taking control of the region in 1527.

Two more sultanates, those of Malwa and Khandesh, were landlocked and served as a buffer between Delhi, the Rajputs, Gujarat and the Deccan. Malwa was famous and prosperous under the Turkish dynasty of the Khaljis, illustrated notably by Mahmud Kalji (*c.* 1436–69), Gujarat eventually put an end to their rule in 1531. Thereafter, the sultanate was annexed by Humayun and Shersha. Restored for a short period by Baz Bahadur (1555–1661), it ultimately surrendered to Akbar. The modest Kandesh, whose sultan claimed to be Arab stock, was especially known for its patronage of Sufis of the city of Burhanpur. Its political history was above all made up of the series of incursions that it suffered at the hands of its powerful neighbours.

Eastern India: Bengal and Jaunpur

The Ganges basin, to the east of Delhi, was the seat of two of the most dazzling sultanates. The enigmatic kingdom of Jaunpur, under the dynasty of the Sharqis (1394–1479) (literally 'Eastern') flourished along the median course of the Ganges. Prosperous, and constantly in rivalry with Bengal, this sultanate experienced an astonishing cultural development under the rule of Ibrahim (1402–40) and of Mahmud (1440–57): at the time Jaunpur was in effect a centre for Persian-style philosophical speculation, to such an extent that it was called the Shiraz of India. Under the influence of Ibn Arabi, it became the breeding ground for diverse forms of Sufism, whose masters, like Abdulquddus Gangohi (1456–1537), practised syncretism and composed poems in Hindi. It witnessed the rise of Sayyid Muhammed Kazimi (1443–1537) who claimed to be the *mahdi* whom the Muslims awaited to re-establish Islam at the end of the world. After receiving the revelation of his vocation during his pilgrimage to Mecca, Kazimi returned to Gujarat in 1497 as a preacher, but was forced to flee to Khorasan where he eventually died. The sect that his disciples formed propounded the doctrine of Mahdawism; it was persecuted, but remained active during the sixteenth and seventeenth centuries. Jaunpur created its own style of architecture. The sultanate had at one time the most powerful army of North India, before the Lodis of Delhi annexed it in 1479, a conquest that would give the Afghans, as we shall see, control over the greatest part of the Ganges basin. The Sharqis, who had took refuge in Bengal, continued to harass the Afghans. But, the cultural heritage of Jaunpur left its stamp on eastern India for a long time.

The only political and economic pole of the eastern region was henceforth Bengal. Like Gujarat, it was open to the sea, and cumulated the profits from trade with agricultural incomes. For a long time, traders from all horizons were present in the Bay of Bengal, which had a double delta, that of the Ganges and the Brahmaputra on the Indian side, and that of the Irrawaddy on the side of Burma. The history of Bengal, a large exporter of cotton fabrics and silk, was very atypical in comparison with the rest of India. By a process that still remains obscure, the majority of the population converted to Islam. While local dynasties elsewhere fawningly imitated Persian models, the sultanate of Bengal encouraged a purely local style of architecture. At the turn of the sixteenth century a vernacular literature of Muslim mysticism in Bengali flourished, a literature that is one of the most original in the whole of India.

Bengal had a turbulent history in course of the fifteenth century during the

Hindu restoration under Rajah Ganesha (1415–8) and, later, at the time when the Abyssinian guard brought the region under its sway (1487–94). At the turn of the sixteenth century, Bengal regained its prosperity under a new dynasty of Arab origin, that of the Husain Shahis, which produced in succession two great sultans Aladdin Husain Shah (1494–1519) and Nusrat Shah (1519–31). During this period, Bengal boasted of its greatest expansion: it advanced northward to Assam in the Brahmaputra Valley and in the east, it strived against the Burmese of the Arakan coast in order to gain control of the port of Chittagong, a necessary port of call for ships sailing upstream in the delta of the Ganges towards Gaur, the Bengali capital. We have knowledge of the splendour of Bengal under the Husain Shahis particularly through the narrative accounts of the first Portuguese diplomatic mission in 1521.[6]

Subsequently Bengal became the object of rivalry between the early Moguls (Babur and Humayun) and the Afghan, Sher Shah, who ruthlessly sacked its treasures. It was subsequently governed by a short-lived Afghan dynasty, before the emperor Akbar annexed it in 1574.

The Lodis: the rise of Afghan power in north of India

In 1414, the last Tughluqs, definitively devastated by the invasion of Timur in 1398, left Delhi and its environs at the hands of the obscure dynasty of the Sayyids,[7] who for some time renounced all imperial ambitions that might be legitimized by the possession of Delhi. From 1451 they were replaced by the Afghan dynasty of the Lodis, who would endure until the Mogul conquest led by Babur in 1526.

The ascendancy of the Lodis represents a watershed in the history of North India for several reasons. First, they restored the currency of imperialistic drive, by reconstituting the Sultanate of Delhi under their control: in the east, they annexed Jaunpur and for a moment extended as far as Bengal; in the south, they undertook the conquest of Malwa. Second, their intrusion marked the definitive ascension to soverignty of the Afghans in the political scenario of North India. Afghan colonies were widespread all across the territory: they were semi-nomadic groups of great mobility, still speaking Pashto, and they readily sold their services to the highest bidding warlords, regardless of whether the latter were Hindus or Muslims. The amazing autobiography of the one of them, Dattu Sarvani, who witnessed the arrival of Babur's army, has survived.[8]

Once in power, the Lodis encouraged further immigration. The newcomers formed pressure groups powerful enough to aspire to royal dignity: they vied with the Rajputs, on the Hindu front; on the Muslim front, they competed with the Turks, who dominated North India before and after them (the Moguls were of Turkish origin). Henceforth, all those who harboured any claims to hegemony had to reckon with them.

The Lodi dynasty witnessed an age of splendour under the first two kings, Bahlul Lodi (1451–1489) and Sikandar Lodi (1489–1517). The former, who already governed the Punjab and Multan on behalf of the Sayyids, seized from the latter the throne of Delhi. The only obstacle to the constitution of an empire was the sultanate of Jaunpur, which at that time had one of the most powerful armies in India, and which threatened to recapture Delhi at the call of Sayyids. Bahlul defeated it in 1479, thereby becoming the sovereign of the Gangetic Valley as far as the confines of Bengal. The territory of the Lodis, however, remained a rather fragile confederation: at the death of Bahlul, it was parcelled out among relatives and influential nobles.

Sikander Lodi, the greatest sultan of this dynasty, ascended to the throne in 1489 and reversed the course of events by instituting a policy of centralization. Firstly, he tightened his grip over the territory: he infringed on Jaunpur to supplant his incompetent brother who governed the region, and in 1494 he defeated the Sharqis who attempted to regain their supremacy with Bengal as their base. During the four ensuing years, he held his court in Sambhal, to the northwest of Delhi. Thereafter, he resolutely embarked on the conquest of the confines of Rajasthan, to the south of Delhi. For this purpose, around 1505 he transferred his capital to the obscure little town of Agra, about a hundred kilometres to the south of Delhi, which was to thrive as the greatest metropolis of North India until the British era. He tried in vain to capture Gwalior from the Rajputs. He brought the sultanate of Malwa under his tutelage and annexed a part of it as far as the city of Chanderi. He died in Agra in 1517.

Sikander's reign carved out a place in history as the example of a successfully implemented centralization, which was to serve as a model for another Afghan dynasty, that of Sher Shah, and later for the Moguls. Instead of considering himself the first among equals, as was customary with the Afghans, he re-established the superiority of Sultan over the nobles. He tightened the reins on the accounting of the administrators and on the maintenance of armed contingents by the nobles.

His son and successor Ibrahim (1517–26) could not match up to his father. At the instigation of the nobility, the sultanate was divided between him and his younger brother Jalal Khan, who established his capital in Jaunpur. In his tentative attempt to reunify the empire, Ibrahim showed tactlessness and brutality, which sparked off a series of revolts. Jalal Khan, aided by the Farmuli and the Lohani clans, declared war against his brother. The Lodis launched a counter-attack from Lahore. As the sultanate was soon torn between rival factions, the close relatives and partisans of Ibrahim called upon the Mogul Babur, who reigned in Kabul at the time, to arbitrate.

The gates of Central Asia: Afghanistan and Kashmir

Kashmir remained very marginal in relation to India until its annexation at the end of sixteenth century by Akbar, who made it a summer residence of the Moguls. Oriented more to Central Asia, it was the centre for the propagation of Buddhism, while remaining a great hub of Hindu culture. Islam infiltrated into this region rather belatedly and it spread by conversion and not by conquest: Rinchana, a Buddhist Tibetan from Ladakh, who had usurped the throne but had not obtained the allegiance of the Hindu nobility, converted to Islam towards 1320. Thus he opened the road for the ascension of a Muslim dynasty native to Swat, the dynasty founded by Shah Mir (1339–42), who officially came to power by marrying the widow of the last Hindu sovereign. The islamization of the population was very progressive: later hagiography attributes a special role to the theologian and mystic Sayyid Ali Hamadani (died 1385) who came from Iran with six hundred Sayyids to preach Islam; he introduced to Kashmir the Kubrawiyya brotherhood, which was widespread in Central Asia but unknown in India.

Medieval Kashmir was the seat of a sophisticated Persian culture and was a great producer of luxury products. Its history is dominated by the contrasting figures of two emblematic Sultans: Sikander (1389–1413) nicknamed 'Butshikan', or the destroyer of idols, who, with the help of a converted Brahmin minister, wanted to undertake an Islamization by force, particularly by demolishing temples; his successor Zainulabidin (1420–70) adopted on the contrary a policy of conciliation. Kashmir witnessed a massive Islamization and only a minority of Brahmins refused to convert. As in the Deccan, an eclectic regional culture, which embraced local influences, flourished in this part of the country. Zainulabidin developed the various cottage industries to which the region owes its reputation even today; he also introduced the manufacturing of paper and gunpowder. His successors, of lesser importance, followed the same politics until external forces began to make incursions into the region, undermining the independence of Kashmir from 1540 onwards.

The anarchy that prevailed after Zainulabidin opened the road to an adventurer from Central Asia, Mirza Haidar Dughlat, cousin of Babur from his mother's lineage, who conquered Kshmir in 1540. He made it his base for his expansionist encroachments to the east, especially towards Tibet, which he attempted to conquer without success. Unable to gain the confidence of the local nobility, he was killed during a rebellion in 1541. The Shah Mir dynasty was then restored, and subsequently replaced in 1561 by the local family of the Chakks, who maintained their rule until the Mogul annexation in 1588.

As for Afghanistan, it had fallen again into the sphere of influence of Central Asia during the three preceding centuries, pledging its allegiance to the Mongols and then to the Timurids. But in 1504, after the conquest of Kabul by the Timurid prince Babur, it started to turn once again towards India. Since the middle of the fifteenth century the Uzbeks had dominated Central Asia; they had chased out of the region a descendant of Timur, Babur, who lost his principality of Ferghana, near Samarkand. Babur advanced towards the east to seek his fortune: he carved out his first kingdom in the north of Afghanistan by conquering Kabul and already set his eyes on India, which he was to bring under his supremacy a quarter century later. From 1516 onwards, he conducted a series of raids on the marches of India, then crossed the Indus River. In 1521, he conquered Kandahar, pushing another Mogul family, that of the Arghuns to the east, towards Sind, and arresting the progression of the Safavids: thus he gained control of the principal land trade route between India and the Middle East. Nothing could now deter him from trying his fortune in India.

III

THE INDIAN STATES

The kingdoms

The ideal kingdom

The principles of the royal office which had been codified as early as the formulation of the laws of Manu were revived and developed in later texts. The king (*rajah*) had to belong to the *kshatriya* caste, the second caste after the priests (Brahmins), in the social hierarchy.

According to tradition, in the early days of the world the *kshatriya* was elected by an assembly of men to preserve social order and property, in exchange for which they would give him a share of their harvests. From the outset the status of the *rajah* was defined as protector of the order of the society which was itself a reflection of the order of the world (*dharma*). He was the defender and administrator of the territory, its population and its riches. From this position it followed that he would be responsible for the police, the exercise of justice, and the initiation and conduct of battles. Together these duties gave him the power of chastisement (*danda*), without which 'the strong would roast the weak' (The Laws of Manu, VII, 13–34). It was a power which must be exercised faultlessly and impartially. In the Brahminical tradition, the king is of divine nature, created 'for the protection of all' from the 'eternal particles' of Indra, Yama, Varuna, and wind, sun and fire. 'Because he has been formed from the fragments of all these gods, the king surpasses all the other beings in splendour' (The Laws of Manu, VII, 5–5).

Along with his sacred mission of maintaining the world in good order came the duty to guarantee peace and prosperity in the kingdom, a duty which belongs in the domain of *artha*, and which could not be performed according to the same moral criteria. *Artha* concerns the 'subsistence of men' and is codified in the *Arthshastra*, a treatise on political strategy, which highlights the pragmatic aspect of the kingly office. It does not conceal in any way the compromises and pitfalls inherent to all politics overtly dissociated from the traditional moral values of which the king was nevertheless the custodian. Such a contradiction was only apparent, since the temporal authority of the king could not be accepted without the support of the spiritual authority of a Brahmin (a *purohita*) closely associated with the exercise of power. This *purohita* was simultaneously chaplain, counsellor and guarantor of the legitimacy of the king. A kingdom without a *purohita* to perform the sacrifice was cursed by the gods, stricken with drought and other disasters. Spiritually superior to the kings, the Brahmins depended on them for their subsistence, which implied for the former the obligation of protecting the latter. Thus, the fundamental alliance of two representatives of the high castes, the priests and the warrior princes, was the cornerstone of the great Hindu empires. The Portuguese reported this *rajah-purohita* partnership several times in the course of the sixteenth century.

The theoretical model of the kingdom certainly never became reality, but it remained as a reference. Before dealing with the history of the Hindu kingdoms, we need to underline some essential traits of the secularization of the royal office. References to these are frequently found among the sources dating from this period, in spite of the diversity of the regions and the peoples.

Any takeover of power, inherited or usurped, required the stamp of legitimacy of a Brahmin, himself the guarantor of the king's relation with the gods. Palace revolutions and regicides, abundant in the history of India, reinforced the power of the Brahmins, without whom no other power could hope to last long. Every reigning sovereign had to mark his accession and justify the permanence of his authority by ensuring the prosperity of temples and the promotion of places of pilgrimage. A wave of legends, which bards propagated from cities to villages, then proclaimed the divine origin of his dynasty.

The observation of the *Arthashastra*, according to which, 'princes are like crabs and eat their relatives' (XVII, I), perfectly illustrates the precariousness of the situation of the rajah whose suzerainty could be called into question by the members of his family under the pretext of his incompetence or military setbacks. The king then would have to renounce the world and retire to a sanctuary. This was the case with the Zamorin[1] of Calicut in 1504, after his defeat by the Portuguese. We come across many an example of the crucial role played by the princes of the royal household, seen by European travellers as the 'vassal' lords of a principal king, who were related to each other. In fact, epigraphic and numismatic sources testify rather to a sharing of the royal office, often practised in the Indian world by the princes of a particular family who all bore the title of rajah and, sometimes, minted coins in their own name. This sharing was subject to diverse rules: sometimes the princes took on a specific role; sometimes they took turns at reigning. The principal king designated a *yuvarajah*, that is a crown prince, who immediately participated in the affairs of the kingdom, promulgating edicts and granting donations independent of the reigning sovereign. A system like this did not always imply a territorial division of power, but was a breeding ground for bloody rivalries.

The responsibility for the prosperity of the kingdom, which was incumbent on the king in the traditional texts, seems to have been shared during the medieval age with the heads of trading communities. The king's domain consisted of his lands – which belonged to him – and his agricultural and mining production, over which he often had the monopoly. On the other hand, commercial activities were in the hands of the merchant classes, usually composed of Jains or Muslims. The princes and traders exercised their respective powers in two different areas which overlapped only at the sharing of profits and payment of taxes to the king. The policies of the State were not always those of the businessmen, particularly in the maritime domain, which meant that rajahs could be at war without compromising commercial prosperity, and merchants could conduct their naval operations without involving the monarch. 'War at sea is the business of merchants,' said Sultan Bahadur of Gujarat, 'it does not concern the prestige of kings.'

In the sixteenth century, the Hindu kings of peninsular India took pride in being the custodians of law and order in society. The correspondence addressed by the kings of Kerala to the Portuguese authorities reveal for instance that they reproached the newcomers primarily for putting cattle to death and consuming their meat, for flouting the caste system by encouraging their servants to convert to Christianity and by promoting them on the social ladder, and for neglecting to respect the Brahmins. These grievances gave rise to more lasting resentments than those created by the damage caused to their economic and political interests. They accepted the military presence of Portugal because she sought to control only the coasts, without ever compromising the integrity of their territory and their rights over the lands.

The islamization of a part of the medieval empires could not always eclipse the traditional character of the royal office. For the overwhelmingly Hindu population, as in Bengal or Gujarat, the sultan had to assume the duties of a rajah, while he enjoyed some of his privileges. A poet contemporary to Alauddin Husain Shah, sultan of Bengal (1484–c.1519), described his master as 'Arjuna in combat,'[2] assimilating him with the hero of the *Baghavad Gita*. The legends of islamization, widespread in Malabar as in Bengal, relate the sultan or the Islamic chief – though he might be the vilest of usurpers – to the lineage of the Prophet, much like the legends of legitimisation of the Brahminic tradition.

The empire of Vijayanagar, 'The city of Victory'

The destiny of what was to be the last great medieval empire began to take shape in the humiliation of defeat. In the early years of the 1330s, two young princes from Warangal, Harihara and Bukha, were brought to Delhi, bound in chains. Soon converted to Islam, they were sent back to their native country to govern it on behalf of the sultan. But it was not long before they exercised power in their own right, renounced Islam, restored Hindu worship and crowned themselves in Hampi (1336). Thus, from its very beginnings, the future kingdom of Vijayanagar was to exemplify the most notable infringement of tradition: two brothers, branded with infamy for having lost their caste after a conversion to Islam, re-conquered their caste status by the grace of a few Brahmins, who saw in them the only solution to the prevalent distress and chaos. This exceptional reintegration was all the more significant as it heralded the birth of an empire that claimed to be the model of a traditional Hindu kingdom. Harihara and Bukha hurried to build their capital, dedicated to Virupaksha, a local Saivaite deity, and which received the name of Vijayanagar ('city of triumph'), later extended to refer to the entire kingdom.

The close alliance between the kings and the Brahmins guaranteed the power of Vijayanagar, because it rested on an uncontested tradition. The influence of the Brahmins was reinvigorated everywhere, the teachings of the disciples of Sankara were widely propagated, and the *bhakti*[3] cult was encouraged in the villages. The monarchs lavished gifts on the temples and new temples sprang up everywhere, attracting crowds of pilgrims. Brahmins, for their part, applied themselves to exalting the glory of the king, the triumphant warrior and the creator of riches, whose divine origin they tirelessly repeated.

Hindus, Jains and Muslims

The unrelenting struggle raging on the frontiers obliged the founders of Vijayanagar to preserve the domestic peace of the kingdom. At the same time as they pursued their policy of expansion, making one conquest after another, they had to deal with a mess of religious rivalries, and at times curb the ambitions of the Brahmins which had been unleashed by the political void in certain areas. When they annexed the provinces of the Canara country to their empire, they also had to come to terms with the large Jain communities that had settled there since Antiquity. The Sravana-Belgola inscription declares that 'the Vaishnavites and the Jains are one and the same, and that as long as the sun and the moon shall endure,' the former should protect the latter. While several Hindu lords, more inclined to claim their independence, were replaced by governors, most of the Jain lords, secluded in their small provincial courts, retained their authority and counted on the monarchs of Vijayanagar to ensure their defence. Epigraphic documents testify that a number of Jain traders were pre-eminent in commercial guilds. As elsewhere, the interdictions that the Brahminical law imposed on maritime trade had dissuaded the Hindus from it, giving the Jains full dominion in this sphere. But the latter must confront the threat of the islamic merchants who were multiplying in the ports.

Extending across the length of the west coast, the conquests of Vijayanagar had respected the civil and religious institutions of Muslim cities, established on the shores. Most of them had as their head a sultan of adventure, invested with power by the communities that controlled economic life, for the most part made up of the Navayats, the Mappillas or the Ilapats. The importance of their economic function soon became evident to the kings of Vijayanagar. Were they not the masters of the horse market, whose monopoly the rajahs wanted to arrogate? The kings of Vijayanagar, while still pursuing their struggle against the Islamic states, were obliged to turn to Muslim merchants for help. These merchants who were paid in gold by the rajahs and the sultans, were careful not to take into account the antagonism of either side towards the other. This seemingly paradoxical situation can be explained by the fact that the ruling castes did not indiscriminately show the same aversion for the invaders from Delhi and the Muslims who had peacefully settled down in the ports on the coast. These last do not seem to have been discredited by the violence of those who shared their faith. It appears that the attitude of the Hindus towards the Muslims was hostile only to those who imposed the Koranic law and destroyed the Brahminic order. This marked the beginning of a long era of compromises, in which waves of persecution broke out only from time to time.

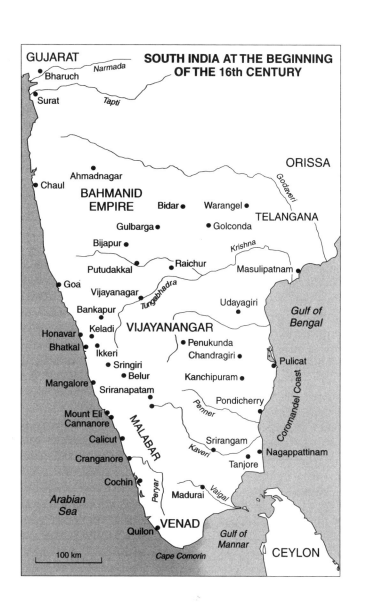

SOUTH INDIA AT THE BEGINNING OF THE 16th CENTURY

GUJARAT

Narmada

• Bharuch

• Surat

Tapti

ORISSA

• Ahmadnagar

• Chaul

BAHMANID
EMPIRE

• Bidar   • Warangel •

Godaveri

TELANGANA

Gulbarga •   • Golconda

Bijapur •

Krishna

Putudakkal •   • Raichur

Masulipatnam •

• Goa

Vijayanagar •

Tungabhadra

Bankapur •

• Udayagiri

Gulf of
Bengal

Keladi •   VIJAYANANGAR

Honavar •

Bhatkal •   • Ikkeri

• Penukunda

Chandragiri •

• Pulicat

• Sringiri

• Belur   Kanchipuram •

Mangalore •

Sriranapatam •

Coromandel Coast

Penner

Pondicherry •

Mount Eli •
Cannanore •

MALABAR

Calicut •

Srirangam •

• Nagappattinam

Kaveri

Cranganore •

Tanjore •

Cochin •

Peryar

Madurai •

Vaigai

Arabian
Sea

VENAD

Gulf of
Mannar

CEYLON

Quilon •

100 km

Cape Comorin

A warring kingdom: treasures and manpower

The incoherence of epigraphic records does not enable us to define the territorial limits of the states in the beginning of the sixteenth century. The bombast of the inscriptions flatters the donating kings by attributing to them control over provinces that they had irrevocably lost or claimed in vain. Furthermore, the inconsistency of the relations of dependence, and the limited but incessant wars in which rival rajahs were engaged make it impossible to put precise dates on the political map of India.

Nevertheless we can establish that the Vijayanagar Empire extended 'from coast to coast,' that is, from the Arabian Sea to the Bay of Bengal. Since 1370, the year in which Madurai was conquered, its dominion spread over the entire South, where only the kings of Malabar had retained a relative independence. To the north there sprawled a frontier with shifting limits that kept varying according to the outcomes of the battles between the armies of Vijayanagar and those of the sultanates that had emerged out of the Bahmanid Empire. Fighting was concentrated around the fortress of Raichur, the key to the food supplies and the mineral riches of the Krishna and the Tungabhadra valley. Further to the east, the diamond mines of Golconda fanned the flames of everyone's covetousness. The possession of Goa, the hub of the trade of horses, was another bone of contention; the Hindu city, under the domination of Vijayanagar, had been captured and burnt by the sultans of Bijapur in 1470, then replaced by a Muslim city which was conquered by the Portuguese in 1510. While the fire that raged in the confines of the Islamic states consumed within two centuries the greatest part of the armies of Vijayanagar, other wars led them to strive relentlessly against other Hindu kingdoms, like Venad and especially Orissa, on both dynastic and economic grounds.

The administration of the empire was designed to deal with such conflicts. Its cohesion hinged on various systems that linked the subjugated rajahs among themselves: traditional alliances inherited from the former Chola, Hoysala or Chera Empires, the obligation that weighed on the lords to pay a tribute in exchange for royal protection, the control of governors belonging to the imperial family who administered entire provinces following the model of the capital. Whatever the nature of the relations of dependence may have been, they all had the common objective of striving for the military expansion of the empire, which was presented as the only guarantee for the maintenance of Hindu values.

Treasure and manpower were the insatiable demands of the central power on its subjects. Whether they were rajahs or lords, the nobles all owed their lands to the king. Land tax was sometimes as high as half the agricultural revenue. Each year, in September, all the nobles were obliged to go to Vijayanagar, where the tax was collected for nine days, and they received a sash of honour as recompense. Furthermore, each of them had to maintain a contingent of soldiers, war elephants and horses (up to 600,000 men and 24,000 horses in 1524, according to the Portuguese Fernao Nunes). Those who could not maintain the forces required of them had their lands confiscated. Thus, some of them, like the rajah of Honavar (Karnataka) in 1510, had to resort to the profits of piracy to be able to pay up the 80,000 *varahas* of gold that the emperor claimed as his due.

To increase land revenues, forests were cleared, large-scale hydraulic works were undertaken – irrigation tanks,[4] dams – giving added value to the lands which were immediately distributed and capitalized. They made profit out of everything. The main gate of the city was leased out for 12,000 *varahas* per year, which was covered by the renting of market places and payments for the right of entry from the men and merchandise arriving in chariots from all the corners of the empire. Countless taxes affected customs, profits from trade, professional activities, as well as judicial acts and marriages. These methods of raising revenues were supplemented by exceptional contributions in cases of military emergency, or a call for funds for the embellishment of temples, for example. A mass of gold, silver and precious stones accumulated from one reign to the next, further increased by coinage and jewels brought as tribute and by the spoils of war.

At the beginning of the sixteenth century, the domestic situation was not exactly trouble free. For the previous two decades, power had been in the hands of palace mayors whose titles passed from father to son. Narasa Nayaka (1490–1503) was the prime minister of a puppet king, Immadi Narasimha, and assumed the office of the 'Protector' of an empire of which he was also the supreme commander of the armies. Upon the death of Narasa, his son Vira Narasimha instigated the assassination of Immadi and arrogated the royal titles. The bloody conflicts that followed his death (1509) propelled his half-brother Krishna Deva Raya to power. This heralded the beginning of a long reign, in which the southern countries experienced an exceptional flourishing in their economic and cultural life.

The king in majesty: Krishna Deva Raya (1509–29)

In the Portuguese reports of the time Krishna Deva Raya appears barefoot, seated on a diamond throne crowned with a sparkling tiara and shaded by parasols. The conquest of Goa and of the horse market had opened the gates of the kingdom and occasionally those of the court to the Portuguese. Their testimonies tally with those of local historiography, which presents Krishna Deva Raya as a magnanimous monarch, possessed of a formidable wrath, a creator of riches but also an amateur poet. The only Europeans to have known Vijayanagar at the hour of its greatest splendour, the Portuguese left detailed accounts of it. They were dazzled by the city and above all by the glorious army, the movement of warhorses and elephants with tusks spiked with javelins. This military apparatus was deployed the length and breadth of the subcontinent and along the northern provinces which were constantly threatened by the pressure of the Muslim forces.

On his accession to the throne, Krishna Deva Raya succeeded in leading his turbulent noblemen in victorious campaigns. In 1510, after repulsing the forces of Bijapur, he laid siege to the fortress of Raichur, which he did not capture until 1520. He reinforced his hold on the far south and created a new province in Mysore with Srirangapatnam as its capital. In the northeast, he defeated the king Prataparudra of Orissa and extended his control over the fertile valleys of both the Krishna and the Godaveri. Incessant wars flared up in the frontiers even as the disintegration of the Bahmani Empire reached its culmination. Far from eliminating danger for the ruler of Vijayanagar, this process gave birth to five sultanates whose dynamism would cause distress to such a degree that it would help the last Bahmani emperor to cling on long enough to make a last vain attemt to impede their development.

With successive conquests, the administration took shape based on the model of the capital, and absolute power returned to the king, advised by the *purohita* and assisted by a prime minister surrounded by high functionaries with hereditary offices. Governed by *nayaks*, generally from the royal family, the provinces were vast but few. Each of them was divided into *vishayas* and into *nadus*, where subjected rajahs reigned in compliance with the local traditions, which, however, increasingly tended to conform to the central power. Krishna Deva Raya held the lords within his sphere of influence by strict constraints: they did not have the right to build fortresses without his authorization, nor the right to reside in cities, though they all had to be present in the capital during the celebration of festivals. Two hundred of them stayed permanently in the court, and some of them wore finely wrought gold ankle bracelets as a mark of their willingness to defend the king with their lives. Treasons, felonies and violations of public order were punished with implacable retributions which included mutilation, impalement and hanging by a hook under the jaw.

A flourishing economy

Land and its resources belonged to the king who employed them as he pleased. This principle, on which all the medieval Hindu empires rested, closely linked the agrarian economy to political power and to its administrative structures.

Vijayanagar threatened war on the countries of the South to which it added the weight of economic constraint. The empire owed its power not only to the strength of its armies, but also to the possession of food-producing lands. Sowed every year on the king's orders and meticulously cultivated, these lands brought him considerable rights, partly paid with gold coins.

Rice was cultivated in the basins of the main rivers, which, from the water source of Mysore, flowed to the countries of Canara, Kerala and the Coramandel. In the mouths of these rivers, the ports of Bhatkal, Mirjan, Barkur and Mangalore opened to the west, while Pulicat, Nagapattinam and the ports of mouths of the Cauveri to the east. Canara rice, of superior quality, ensured the subsistence of Gujarat, Oman, Ormuz and the Persian Gulf; it was exported as far as Aden and the ports of eastern Africa, while rice from the Coramandel, which was four times less expensive, supplied food to Ceylon and southern Malabar. With sugar following the same circuits, it can be said that most of the countries in the western side of the Indian Ocean depended on Vijayanagar for their subsistence. These food products were supplemented by industrial crops, such as cottons and dyes, and by the exploitation of diamond mines, of pearl fisheries in the far south, and of forests of teak, sandal and other precious woods.

Small cities and big urban centres held bustling markets where products from a diversified craft industry poured in, including finely wrought metals and woods, jewels, lacquer, ivory and especially textiles. Spun in villages, cotton was transported to the cities of the Coromandel, where cloth was woven and dyed.

The influence the big traders exercised in the court of Vijayanagar was not exactly negligible, all the more so as Krishna Deva Raya attached great importance to the prosperity of foreign trade. He protected foreign merchants so as to dissuade them from turning to his enemies and thereby enriching them. The favour that the Portuguese enjoyed is a salient example of this policy. It enabled them to settle down on a permanent basis in Goa, because they loyally ensured the renewal of the emperor's cavalry.

Designed along the lines of the medieval ideal of a Hindu city, Vijayanagar was the symbol of royal power. Dedicated to Rama, it was also placed under the protection of Virupaksha, a local Saivaite deity, and of an avatar of Vishnu, Narasimha, the man-lion, whose image was ubiquitous. Gigantic fortifications, wide paved roads, canals and aqueducts celebrated the benevolent king. Punctuated by the monumental gates of its temples, the city sprawled over more than thirty square kilometres. Houses, made of brick and plaster, stood around stone sanctuaries, while crowds lingered at the gates where the marriages of the gods were constantly being celebrated.

To the north, the city of the Brahmins bordered the steep banks of the Tungabhadra. To the southwest, the immense royal citadel housed barracks, army camps and stables for thousands of elephants and horses. The narrow gates of the palace opened to a row of interior gardens, ponds and pavilions with sculpted ivory panelling. The columns of the courtroom rose around a vast esplanade where one could contemplate the king in all his resplendence. Described by travellers, excavated by archaeologists, Vijayanagar still has impressive vestiges, witnesses of the apogee of the last great Hindu Empire on the eve of its collapse.

The fall of Vijayanagar and the disintegration of the subcontinent

Krishna Deva Raya's successors were incapable of continuing his work and, after his death (1529), revived the chain of regicides and usurpations. Thus Ramaraja, son of his minister Saluva Timma, came to power on behalf of the two young princes who had no choice but death or oblivion. Ramaraja believed he could divide and rule, taking advantage of the rivalries among the neighbouring sultans, by allying with one against the other – a dangerous game which resulted only in reconciling the sultans and cementing their coalition. On 23 January 1565, in Talikota, the sultans crushed the charge of the elephants and horses of Vijayanagar. Ramaraja was decapitated by the sultan of Ahmadnagar and the Muslim armies entered the city. Plundering and massacres went on for three whole days. The sultans left plunder for everyone – jewels, slaves, precious clothes – retaining only the elephants loaded with treasures. When in 1568 the Venetian traveller Cesare Federici visited the site of the city, it had already degenerated into a den of brigands, a pile of carbonised ruins invaded by creepers and tigers. A few Hindu princes managed to flee to Penagonda, thereafter to Chandragiri, where they founded minor dynasties. The empire broke up, opening the road for the Mogul conquest and the enterprises of the Europeans.

The Vijayanagar Empire favoured the blossoming of a civilization that inherited the legacy of the traditions and expressed the genius of all the peoples of the South. It is rather surprising that Vijayanagar, so marked by the Hindu culture, failed to inspire the vocation of a great reformer, like Kabir in the Punjab or Chaitanya in Bengal. The only great mystic of Telugu origin, Vallabhacharya (1479–1531) was born in Benares and lived in Mathura, near Agra. More conformist than innovative, Vijayanagar nevertheless gave the southern countries a certain cultural unity. By developing *bhakti* cults everywhere, by encouraging the teachings of Brahmins, the kings of Vijayanagar contributed to the propagation of the great Sanskrit texts all across the subcontinent. The precepts of Shankara and Ramanuja were translated into vernacular languages. Saivaite works were written in the Kannada language, while Telugu literature developed and Tamil culture penetrated erudite circles. This set of traditions, common to the whole of South India, was to preserve its identity in the course of the following centuries.

The Malabar states

The 'chessboard kings'

Malabar is the name that the Arabs gave to Kerala – the former Chera Empire – which extended along the west coast of India, from Mangalore down to Cape Comorin. In the twelfth century, in the wake of the fall of this empire, Kerala disintegrated into several kingdoms. When the Portuguese landed on its shores (1498), four principal royal families assembled around them rajahs of less importance. The Zamorins of Ernad wielded the biggest temporal power, while the princes of Venad outshone everyone else in prestige. The *Kolathiri*[5] of Eli, who were proud of their illustrious lineage, watched over the marches of the North. Though independent, the kings of Perumpadappunad occupied an inferior position, no doubt owing to the more recent prosperity of their domains and to certain constraints imposed on them by their rivalry with the Zamorins. Portuguese authors referred to these kingdoms by the name of their principal city: Calicut, Quilon, Cannanore and Cochin.

The confusion of the inscriptions does not help to define the territorial limits of these states, tiered up from north to south along the seashore. The lands under the control of the *Kolathiri* of Eli spread out between the Nileshvaram and the Tellicherry river; the sphere of influence of the Zamorins of Calicut extended from the left bank of the same river as far as the port of Cranganore, for which the king of Cochin contended. The kingdom of Cochin encompassed the region of lagoons to the south of the Periyar River. The royal families of Venad controlled the provinces covering the southern tip of the subcontinent, up to the delta of the Tambraparni. In each of these kingdoms, dynastic law, which was matrilineal, invested with supreme power the eldest male of all the branches put together, but it did not preclude sovereigns from favouring their own children and giving them entire provinces as gifts. These parallel lines of descent sparked off conflicts caused by never ending disputes. One such quarrel involving the kings of Cochin and Calicut escalated into an endemic war wherein the Portuguese had to play a decisive role. In 1583, the Florentine Filippo Sassetti described the Malabar princes as 'chess-board kings'[6] – such was the extent of the fragmentation of power and local rivalries that played into the hands of foreign powers.

Power was shared within all the royal families. Brothers and cousins of the rajah administered cities and fortresses. Sequestered in the garden of the palace, the dowager princess enjoyed considerable authority. In collusion with the Brahmins and the soothsayers, she could force the rajah to retire from the world in order to push one of her brothers to the throne. Fratricidal rivalries played a vital political role. The Portuguese, and others after them, knew how to take advantage of these pretenders always ready to seek their alliance to supplant the incumbent rajah.

As in Vijayanagar, the royal entourage was marked by the presence of Brahmins and warriors. The turmoil that had followed the fall of the Chera Empire had favoured the fortune of the priestly caste, and prompted the legitimisation of the rajahs of adventure who bestowed on them donations of territories respected by all the Hindu armies, even by enemies. Another caste emerged from the shadow, the Nayars, of *shudra* origin, whose military qualities had covered with privileges. Portuguese narrators have left behind vivid descriptions of these warriors who walked semi nude, armed with a dagger and a sword, which never left their side. Protected by a round shield and at times by a silk coat, they fought on foot and knew how to handle the spear and how to shoot with a bow and a harquebus. Trained from an early age in military academies, they had taken an oath to protect cows and Brahmins. There were several thousand of them in each court. Their families lived outside the city, in vast rural properties, under the authority of mothers and aunts, custodians of the matriarchal traditions which gave them total freedom to choose their way of life.

Kerala did not escape the influence of two external powers – the belligerence of Vijayanagar and the commercial hegemony of Gujarat. Even though the kings of Malabar were independent, the rajah of Vijayanagar intruded very often on their affairs and inspired a respectful fear in them. Only the kings of Venad dared to confront him in a declared war and contended with him for the domination of the Tamil country. Gujarat exerted its influence through its trading communities whose power was to grow in the course of sixteenth century to the point of threatening the authority of the kings.

The role of the Muslims

In their efforts to assert their sovereignty and to preserve the integrity of a territory weakened by civil wars, the rajahs of Malabar not only relied on the Brahmins and the Nayars, but also on the producers of wealth. With the elimination of Buddhist and Jain traders in the wake of the reactions provoked by the preaching of Hindu reformers (from the ninth century onwards), other social groups had taken over the country's economy.

Nature had endowed Kerala with a long sea front and a land that produced pepper and ginger. Growing wild on the forelands of the Ghats, pepper was also cultivated in gardens on the coast. Harvested in lands owned by Nayars or Christians, pepper from the mountains was loaded on to small boats that sailed down the rivers to lagoons where traders from the neighbouring ports took over. As for ginger, it grew abundantly in the countryside of Eli and Calicut.

Only enterprising communities that escaped the prohibition on sea travel could undertake trade in spices, which on its own accounted for substantial profits. We know that guilds dominated by Jewish and Christian leaders took charge of the spice trade in Cranganore (in the ninth century) and in Quilon (in the fourteenth century), even though we cannot affirm that their predominance had been constant throughout. On the other hand, it is certain that the expansion of the Islamic communities continued uninterrupted. As early as 1121, the year of the construction of the mosque of Matayi (Eli), they enjoyed the right of citizenship and the right of religious worship. By the beginning of the sixteenth century, they had attained the zenith of their power, and, according to the Portuguese, they were more numerous in India than from Fez to Tunis.

'All maritime traders are Muslims,' wrote the Portuguese Tomé Pires towards 1515, 'because the Gentiles never sailed.'[7] The ancient mercantile communities were then in decline. A few Jews survived in Matayi (Eli), in Cranganore and above all in Cochin. Undisputed masters of the pepper market just a century earlier, the Christians had gradually lost their supremacy in Calicut, Kayankulam and Quilon. The agents of Islamic merchants infiltrated everywhere and earned the favour of the princes. The legends of Islamization were actively propagated to legitimize the alliance of the Muslims and the royal families. The most popular myth was that of Cheraman Perumal, the last Chera emperor, who had renounced his kingdom to convert to Islam. Before embarking for Mecca, he had attributed a territory to each of his nephews and had especially entrusted the protection of Muslims to the rajah of Calicut. Historically baseless, this tradition testifies to the support granted by the Zamorins to the Islamic communities who had made their fortune. Calicut was the chosen land of resident or seasonal 'pardeshi' – Persians, Turks, North Africans and Arabs from all nations but also from other parts of India – Gujaratis, Deccanis or Bengalis. Their power was so overwhelming that the princes of Calicut, sometimes exasperated by their arrogance, sought other alliances. The Chinese and subsequently the Portuguese enjoyed these short-lived spells of favour which represented no threat to Islamic ascendancy.

Though they were a minority in Calicut, the Mappillas were predominant in most of the other ports and specialised in domestic trade, 'from India to India', rather than in transoceanic commerce. The kingdom of Eli was an example of an old association between the Hindu kings and the Muslim sea traders. The traditions of the Mappilla family of the Arakkal had ties with the royal household. In the beginning of the sixteenth century, its chief held the title *ali rajah* (king of the high sea) and ruled over the world of business. He had the right of submission over the populations of the overseas territories and levied a tribute in his name in certain atolls of the Maldives. In Cochin, the spice trade was in the hands of the Marakkar, a Mappilla family who had the monopoly of pepper and cinnamon, but little influence on the royal family. Excluded by the princes of Quilon in the past, the Muslims began to infiltrate into this kingdom too, taking advantage of the disgrace of Christians whom they soon supplanted.

Cemented by the Gujaratis, who had agents and warehouses in all the ports, the Islamic presence proved to be a factor of cohesion between the different kingdoms of Malabar. Territorial divisions and the rigidity of the Brahminical institutions contrasted with the mobility of the Muslims, whose activities knew no boundaries. The constant evolution of their societies gained impetus from their conflicts with the Portuguese. An important transformation was to take place in the end of the sixteenth century, when the Mappillas, belonging to mercantile circles, would be led to exercise military functions and even to aspire for political power. The ascendancy of the *ali rajahs* of Cannanore was significant inasmuch as they succeeded in founding the only Muslim dynasty that lastingly ruled in Kerala.

Orissa

The land of the gods

'This country is not made for conquests nor for the designs of human ambitions, it belongs to the gods,' wrote Abul-Fazl at the time of the submission of Orissa by the armies of his master the Mogul Akbar, in 1592.

Orissa is still a conservatory of natural species and a repository of traditions. In the beginning of the sixteenth century, it extended the length of the east coast, between Bengal and Telangana. Towards the interior, jungles and woods covered an impenetrable territory as far as the confines of the Bahmani Empire. These highlands were the domain of primitive tribes – the Gond, the Santal and others.

Orissa entered history with the Buddhist kingdom of Kalinga, which reached its apogee at the beginning of the Christian era and whose influence radiated as far as Ceylon and Southeast Asia. After that it had a period of obscurity until the dawn of the seventh century AD, when Saivaite sanctuaries began to rise in the coastal plains. From the twelfth century onwards, the Ganga dynasty encouraged the worship of Vishnu-Jagannath, the 'master of the world.' Medieval life revolved around the great temples of Bhubaneshwar, Konarak and Puri, while Orissa had the reputation of a redemptive and sacred land.

Orissa affirmed its cultural identity under the reign of Kapilendra Deva (1435–69), founder of the Gajapati dynasty (master of elephants), placed under the sign of the sun. Derived from Sanskrit, the Oriya language developed and began to be written at the expense of Tamil, which had earlier been imposed by the Chola emperors. The king led victorious campaigns, confronted the sultan of Bengal and the rajah of Vijayanagar, ravaged the Bahmani city of Bidar and succeeded in extending his boundaries to the Ganges and Krishna valleys. He subdued the turbulent lords of his kingdom, who had to work for justice and prosperity.

Under the dynasty of the sun, Orissa attained the pinnacle of its power. The successors of Kapilendra pursued his conquests until the death of Prataparudra Deva, whose sons were assassinated by the minister Govinda Vidyadha, who seized the throne for himself (1541). This usurpation marked the end of an epoch that is remembered as a golden age. Mukunda Deva (1559–68), the successor of Govinda, was unable to prevent the incursions of the neighbouring sultans and the pillaging provoked by Muslim iconoclasm. After his death, Orissa stagnated until its conquest by the Mogul emperor Akbar (1592).

An economy based on natural resources

Like neighbouring Bengal, Orissa was rich in food crops: rice in the delta of the Mahanadi, sugar cane, spices (pepper and ginger) in the plains, salt in the coastal swamps.

The craft industry flourished thanks to an abundance of natural resources: the enormous tree trunks that drifted down the rivers from the forests of the highlands, blocks of stone, and iron and copper were made into innumerable objects – chariots, arms, tools, chains for elephants and for the casting of 'bell metal'[8], which was exported to the whole of Indochina. The perfumes and therapeutic balms made from the profusion of local medicinal plants became famous all over South Asia.

Specialist villages and small enterprises took up the fabrication of textiles. However, their importance cannot be compared with the textile industries of Gujarat or Bengal, from where the weavers of Orissa borrowed certain techniques. They produced luxury fabrics, in particular, fine white cotton blended with silk threads.

Economic life was irrigated by the numerous pilgrimages and fairs in the region. Puri was the largest commercial city – most of the other cities being only market towns enlivened by a daily bazaar and several markets a week. Buffalo carts and porters thronged the roads leading to the ports. In the north, Balasore and Pipli were the most active towns, associated with the coastal Hindu network on the sea of Bengal, which, since ancient times, connected the countries of the Coromandel coast with the Buddhist kingdoms of Ceylon and western Indochina, Arakan, Pegu and Siam. Pipli was the largest slave market in the region where Arakan pirates sold their captives.

In the course of the sixteenth century, the ports of Orissa escaped domination by the Muslim sea traders, who had succeeded in infiltrating the Hindu network of Southeast Asia. It was the Portuguese who obtained the right to engage in trade in Pipli and who imposed their control on pepper, iron, copper, wood and spices.

The Himalayan Kingdoms

Between the eastern delta of the Ganges and the Brahmaputra (present day Bangladesh) and Kashmir, which were the most Islamized regions in the subcontinent, extended the kingdoms of the Himalayan chain. Though Islam had only a negligible impact on these kingdoms, Muslim influence was never completely absent. There are records of invasions as early as the thirteenth and the fourteenth century in Kumaon (present day central Himalayas, in India), in Nepal and in Assam, but these conquests did not lead to any permanent domination; minor Himalayan kings, since the fourteenth century, had pledged their allegiance to the sultans of the plains and subsequently to the Mogul emperors. There is also evidence of the existence of small colonies of Muslim traders and artisans, linked particularly to trans-Himalayan commerce (three per cent of the current population of Nepal and Bhutan are Muslims).

Dozens of kingdoms, generally Hindu but occasionally Buddhist, as in Bhutan and Sikkim, and many of them very small, shared the Himalayan chain. Two of these kingdoms – Assam and Nepal – are important for their role in history and for being the repository of Indian institutions that have disappeared from the plains.

Assam

The name Assam loosely refers to the entire lower valley of the Brahmaputra which forms an undefined zone of contact between the last advances of Indian civilization and the peoples on the borders of India, Tibet and Burma, some of whom were still largely hunter-gatherers. In the fifteenth century, Assam was divided into two kingdoms.

In the south-west, the kingdom of Kamata, (called Kamrup in the Muslim chronicles), more hinduized, was comprised of the region of Kamrup – feared all over India as a land of magicians – and the city of Gauhati. Often invaded by the Muslims, Kamata was finally ruined between 1498 and 1502, by the sultan of Bengal, Aladdin Husain Shah. Soon after, a new kingdom, Cooch Bihar, emerged, governed by a Hinduized tribal family.

In the northeast, power was in the hands of a dynasty of the tribe of the Shans, of Thai origin, who, under the name of Ahom, exercised their suzerainty from the beginning of the thirteenth century from the capital city of Garghgaon. The most glorious reign was that of Suhungmung (1497–1539). As a sign of the growing Hinduization of the dynasty, Suhungmung took the name of Swarga Narayan (which means 'Divine Vishnu'). He extended his territory considerably at the expense of primitive local tribes and he successfully repulsed an attempted conquest by the sultan of Bengal Nusrat Shah (1519–31).

From the reign of the Mogul emperor Jahangir, Cooch Bihar was progressively absorbed into the Mogul Empire. The kingdom of Ahom resisted till the end: under Aurangzeb, after six years of war (1661–7), it inflicted a humiliating defeat on a Mogul army of conquest led by the famous Mir Jumla (died 1663). It was annexed by India only under British rule, but Assam remained a quasi-virgin land, populated overwhelmingly by tribal peoples.

Nepal

At that time, what was called 'Nepal' covered only the valley of Kathmandu and its immediate vicinity. This historical Nepal forms a special case in North India for two reasons. As the great French Orientalist Sylvain Lévi underlined at the beginning of the twentieth century, Nepal's history is preserved in the form of chronicles and 'newspapers' compiled by scholars, a privilege it shares with the other two marginal regions, Kashmir and Ceylon. The rest of non-Muslim India lacks these archives.[7] It also shares with Ceylon the honour of having kept alive the tradition of Indian Buddhism: it is in Nepal that the canonical books of the Buddhism of the Great Vehicle, written in Sanskrit, were found, and are in use up to today. The stamp of the Buddha is ubiquitous in the most ancient city of the valley, Patan, with its Buddhist monuments called *stupa*, erected in the centre and in the four cardinal points. The descendants of the ancient monks form a caste of Buddhist priests.

The prosperity of Nepal hinged on commerce between India and Tibet and the main route between the Ganges Valley and Lhassa passed through Kathmandu. The indigenous people of the valley, Indianized Tibeto-Burmese called Newar, were skilful traders and artisans; furthermore, the kings of the valley had the privilege of minting money for the Tibetans, in exchange for metal-money produced in Tibet.

Nepal experienced great turmoil in the middle of the fourteenth century. The valley of Kathmandu was sacked by Hindu warriors called Khas, who arrived from the west of present Nepal. Above all, it had to suffer the backlash of the Muslim invasions of India. First, in 1350, when the sultan of Bengal Shamsuddin Ilyas (1342–57) raided the valley and destroyed the temples and palaces. Earlier the Hindu kingdom of Mithila, in the plain on the southern flank of Nepal, had been annexed by the sultan of Delhi Ghiyathuddin Tughluq (1320–5); as a result of which the king of Mithila, Hari Singh Deva, sought refuge in Nepal in 1326. His descendants were to rise to power with Jayasthiti Malla (1382–1395), founder of the last Malla dynasty, which reigned in the valley until its conquest by the present Gorkha dynasty in 1768–9.

Jayasthiti Malla re-built Nepal from its ruins and restored its splendour. The region would attract the admiration of Catholic missionaries who resided there from the seventeenth century. Reaffirming the primacy of Hinduism, the king brought the Bhatta Brahmins from South India to officiate in the temple of Pashupatinath, the great Saivaite sanctuary of Nepal; he abandoned the old capital of Patan for Bhatgaon and reorganised the caste system with the help of Brahmin counsellors. He is also given the credit for creating a code of laws.

Less than a century later, Jaya Yaksha Malla (1428–80), the last great king of the unified valley, briefly embarked on a career of conquering. Taking advantage of the transient weakness of the Lodis in the plain, he conducted raids towards Mithila, Gaya and even Bengal and extended his control over the route to Tibet by conquering the city of Shekar Dzong. The chronicles trace back to his rule the settlement in Nepal of Muslims of Kashmiri origin, specialized in commerce between India and Tibet. They were joined on the trans-Himalayan road by Hindu traders from the plain, ascetics dedicated to commerce and soon even by Armenians. Missionaries (Jesuits, then Capuchins) followed the same routes as early as the first half of the seventeenth century.

Upon his death, towards 1480, Jaya Yaksha Malla divided the valley into three kingdoms, assigned to each of his sons: Bhatgaon; Kathmandu, which became a capital for the first time; and Banepa, which was to be supplanted by Patan in the seventeenth century (Patan recovered at the time its status as capital).

From this epoch the history of Nepal settled into a pattern which became familiar. The three kings vied with each other to invest the money earned from trade in monuments. The capitals, surrounded by ramparts, formed an organized world: in the centre, rose the royal palace, dominated by the temple of the patron deity Taleju; in front of it was a vast square where temples lavishly endowed by the king stood. Everything revolved around this central point: professions and castes had their own quarters – the more noble surrounding the palace, the lower castes relegated to the periphery of the city. All lay and religious architecture was of the same style: in harmony with an Indian model that has survived only in Nepal, it was based on the combination of brick, wood and tiles. Houses and monasteries, both Hindu and Buddhist, which stood around a courtyard, had two to four floors, covered by a single roof. The isolated temples, of square or rectangular plan, had one to five roofs: they are called pagodas.

So, in a high Himalayan valley a model has been perpetuated of the civilization that existed in Bengal before the Muslim invasions, based on an alliance of commerce and agriculture, and on the coexistence of diverse religious traditions, and Buddhism in particular, which has disappeared elsewhere in India.

The regions situated to the west of Kathmandu were progressively colonised by the Khas, Hindus of the central Himalayas, who introduced the Indo-Aryan language today called Nepali. Like their counterparts in the central and western Himalayas (now in India), they claimed to be Rajputs – which is highly doubtful – but they certainly imitated the Rajputs of the plains; they imposed Hinduism at the expense of Buddhism and the tribal religions of the Tibeto-Burmese native populations. They dominated the mountains of present western Nepal, where they founded two confederacies of twenty-two and twenty-four principalities. Gorkha, the closest to Kathmandu, was destined to found the great modern unified Nepal.

The Rajput states

The 'sons of the king'

The Ephtalite branch of the Huns and other hordes from Central Asia who ravaged North India in the fifth century left in their wake wandering warrior tribes. The bravest of them distinguished themselves as early as the ninth century and enjoyed an age of glory at the head of various dynasties, those of the Chalukyas and the Chandellas of Khajurao being the most famous. These new lords took the name of Rajput (Sanskrit: *Rajaputra*, sons of the king) and claimed to be the inheritors of solar or lunar lineages. Their bards wasted no time in propagating the legend of their origin. Emanating from the sacred fire of the Mount Abu, four warriors founded the four Rajput clans -Parihara, Chauhan, Solanki and Pawar – to which flocked captains of adventure, soldiers and pastors.

In fact, the myths of the origin of these clans found a definitive version only in the seventeenth century, which led to a rationalization of the social structures that became traditional. Until then, their legitimacy was established by bards who tirelessly sang the feats of the heroes of the 'family of fire' (Agnikula) and by totally fabricated genealogies. Without a Brahminical past, the Rajputs identified themselves with the *Kshatriyas* in order to integrate into the hierarchy of castes.

Overrun by Islamic invasions, defeated by Mahmud of Ghazni at Tarain (1192), the Rajputs withdrew to the south of the Ganges, without ever giving up enlarging their territory at the expense of the neighbouring Muslim states. By the end of fifteenth century, when the sultan Mahmud of Gujarat had seized Kathiawar from them, the Rajputs had retreated to the arid plateaus, bordered in the west by the Thar Desert and diagonally traversed by the eroded chain of the Aravalli, covered by jungles parched by lack of rain.

According to the bard Chand, Rajput society had thirty-six royal races (some bards suggested even ninety-nine), eighty-four mercantile lineages, apart from a few tribes of aboriginal farmers. Rajahs and vassals called themselves *kshatriyas*. Practising exogamy, they ate meat, drank wine and ate game together in grand feasts. Respect for cows, the prohibition of the marriage of widows, the practise of *sati* were their only concessions to the Brahminical customs. Generously compensated, the Brahmins barely overstepped their traditional functions. When they acceded to the throne, their descendants became *kshatriyas*.

This society of knights was organized according to a system based on non-codified martial laws. In times of war, each lord brought his men and his horses in exchange for gifts of land. When an enemy entered a besieged city, he would not be able to find even single soul: the men would have perished to the last, while a huge fire of *jauhar* consumed the jewels and the women who preferred to be burnt alive than to suffer the defilement of slavery.

Administration and economy

At the beginning of the sixteenth century, the Rajput states had succeeded in constituting a coherent entity, based on family alliances. Internal order was guaranteed by a rigorous distribution of judicial and military powers, the rajah being the only one to exercise both these powers. Each rajah governed with the assistance of a council (*darbar*) of ministers and notables, with the exception of vassal lords and chiefs of war. Like everywhere else in India, the village assemblies (*panchayat*) managed local interests and rendered justice according to the customary law.

A Rajput state comprised several administrative divisions each consisting of about a hundred villages defended by small forts. The citadels on the frontiers, in which transit duties were collected, were each commanded by two chiefs, one military and the other civil, the latter presiding over a small court whose members were elected. The cities were administered by a hereditary magistrate, the *nagarseth*, independent of the citadel, which came under the jurisdiction of the military authorities.

The splendour of the cities of Ajmer, Udaipur, Jodhpur, Bikaner and others testify to the prosperity of urban life. The resources of the country were nevertheless mediocre, as agriculture was difficult in the craggy lands. The mines of silver, iron, tin and the brass, and the marble quarries belonged to the king. The riches of the country depended on the spoils of war, which constituted the fortune of the families, and on commercial activities. Trade was entirely in the hands of *bania* businessmen, often Jains, who were among the most competent in the Indian world. The political independence of these traders and the immunity that they enjoyed ensured that border fights did not hinder the movement of merchandise. Goods transited by caravans from the immense emporium of Gujarat as far as Delhi or Golconda, passing through the Rajput cities whose handicrafts were highly prized everywhere. As physically fit men were destined to the profession of arms, the labour force included a large number of slaves, generally prisoners of war, who were in the service of noble or mercantile families. As the status of slaves was hereditary by maternal afiliation, it was a common practice to fill one's own house with bastards whose destiny was domestic work.

To meet the expenses of a warring state and to ensure that fortresses were properly equipped, taxes compensated for the meagre agricultural revenues. Everything was taxed – lands, horses and cattle, transactions, marriages, ploughs and the very lucrative transit of merchandise.

The Hindu bastion

Tradition presents the Rajput country as the last Hindu bastion resisting the attacks of the Muslim powers that encircled it on all sides. Though it is true that the defence of their sanctuaries and their values strongly motivated their battles, this fact should not eclipse the importance of the political issues at stake. The Rajput citadels were at the heart of a thousand-year-old battle whose goal was the possession of territories that separated the Delhi sultanate from Gujarat and the Islamic states of the Deccan. The game was played out between three powers: the lords of Delhi who strived to extend their conquests towards the south, the sultans of Gujarat and the Rajput chiefs who all craved for the throne of Delhi.

The sixteenth century witnessed the strategies of many different forces, which very often collapsed in the face of the inescapable presence of the Rajputs. Not all had entered the alliance that had taken shape around the rajahs of Marwar (Jodhpur) and Mewar (Udaipur). The descendants of the Chandellas still ruled in Gondwana over the tribes of the jungles. For having helped the Khalji sultan of neighbouring Malwa, the Purbiya Rajput princes retained a preponderant influence in this principality, even reserving for themselves an independent enclave to the east of the country.

The greatest part of the Rajput territory was then dominated by the union of the States of Marwar and of Mewar. The former state was shared among the princes of the Rathore clan, themselves allied to the Sisodyas of Mewar by marriages that did not fail to trigger off conflicts of precedence. The discovery of mines of silver and lead in Mewar had considerably enriched the rajahs whose strong personality eventually helped in asserting their supremacy. Rana Kumbha (1432–69) had been a courageous chief of war, an expert in military architecture and one of the best poets of his times. The prestige of his dynasty escaped the tarnish of the spree of murders and poisonings that marked the reign of his son Rana Malla (1473–1509) and that preceded the accession of Rana Sanga (1509–27), who is traditionally portrayed as the ultimate champion of the Rajputs. Strengthened by an alliance with the Mogul prince Babur, he had resolved to march on Delhi to overthrow Ibrahim Lodi and to take over the throne. But he had not taken into consideration the harassment of the Gujarati armies that had re-launched an offensive on the frontiers of Mewar, obliging him to withdraw towards the south. In the meanwhile, the battle of Panipat (1526) had given Babur both victory and the crown. The alliance was broken and Rana Sanga was in turn defeated by Babur at Kannua in 1527.

The union of the Rajput states collapsed following the simultaneous attacks of the Moguls and of Bahadur Shah of Gujarat (1526–37). The campaigns led against the Rajputs were a pretext to immense territorial conquests. After the annexation of Malwa (1531), the citadels of Ujjain, Ranthambor and Ajmer fell one after another. By besieging the citadel of Chitor, which controlled the route to Delhi, Bahadur provoked a conflict with Humayun, the successor of Babur. Humayun had not forgotten that Bahadur, exiled to Delhi during his youth, had almost become its master by attempting to defeat him. Neither was he unaware of the plans engineered by his rival to arrogate hegemony over the Deccan. In 1535, the Mogul invasion swept through Gujarat, devastating on its way the Rajput fortresses. A few years later, the Afghan Sher Shah (1536–45), who had supplanted Humayun for a while, attempted to conquer them for himself. The frequency of these raids and the annihilation of the Rajput treasures accelerated their decline.

IV

THE NEWCOMERS

The Portuguese

'Christians and spices'

On 20 May 1498, three dilapidated caravels dropped anchor at Kappatt, to the north of Calicut. Those on board were no strangers to the North African traders of the city who understood the Spanish language. The first Portuguese messenger who set foot on terra firma told them they had come in search of 'Christians and spices'.

This famous statement aptly defined the objective of the reconnaissance expeditions that had been relentlessly conducted in the Atlantic for more than half a century at the behest of Prince Henrique of Portugal, known as Henry the Navigator (1394–1460) and Kings Afonso V and Joao II. In 1488, Bartholomew Dias had crossed the Cape of Good Hope, opening the routes of the Indian Ocean to the Portuguese. Ten years later, guided by a Gujarati pilot, Vasco de Gama sailed across the Arabian Sea and finally reached Calicut.

His mission was part of the great messianic project conceived by King Manuel I with a view to establishing an alliance with the Christians of the East and destroying the growing power of the Islamic States. With the liberation of the Holy Land rendered impossible by the presence of the Turkish fleet in the Mediterranean, the Portuguese had schemed to attack the Muslim world from the rear by naval operations in the newly discovered Indian Ocean. They thereby hoped to impose a blockade of the Red Sea and to corner the spice trade for their own advantage, in order to ruin the sultan of Cairo and to finance the construction of a universal Christian Empire.

Unimpressed by their maritime feats, the population of Calicut showed but little curiosity towards the Portuguese navigators. The rustic presents that they brought for the Zamorin soon made them the laughing stock of the city. The natives greatly underestimated the perseverance of these foreigners, who braved the perils of two oceans in order to return to India each year. Vasco de Gama took a few samples of spices back to Lisbon along with the firm conviction that Hindus were Christians with strange rites. Nobody in Malabar could have had the slightest suspicion that this captain had just changed the course of history by opening the sea-lanes of India to the Europeans.

The first impressions cleared up on either side during the expedition of Pedro

Alvares Cabral who, on 13 September 1500, entered the port of Calicut at the head of a squadron armed for war, laden with gold, merchandise, and gifts befitting the Zamorin, who, furthermore, received an offer of alliance. The city authorities accommodated the Portuguese in a stronghold formerly reserved for Chinese merchants. The king, with a view to defying Muslim businessmen, who were exercising a growing influence on Hindu power, bestowed special favours on the newcomers. Incapable of disentangling court intrigues, swayed by the blunders or the ill will of their interpreters, the Portuguese refused to be treated like other foreigners and persistently claimed priority over the Arab traders. It is not possible to gauge the share of misunderstanding, carelessness and sheer perfidy that pushed Cabral to capture a sambuque already loaded with spices and the population of Calicut to resort to violence. The trading post was attacked and about forty Portuguese were massacred even as they fled to their ships. In retaliation, the armada bombed the city. This tragic incident was to leave its imprint long into the future. As early as 1501, the die was cast: the Portuguese presence in Kerala would be characterized by an endemic war with Calicut and by the capricious alliance of the other kingdoms.

In the following years, the Portuguese consolidated their position. When Cabral returned to his country, the illusion of a Christian India was dissipated: the kings were 'pagan' like most of their subjects; Christians were only a respected minority claiming descent from the Mesopotamian patriarch; and the Zamorin favoured the Muslims. However, there remained the promise of abundant riches, spices and gems – sufficient motivation to pursue the adventure.

Each year, in September, a Portuguese squadron of four to twenty vessels landed in Cannanore, where a trading post had been established at the end of a deserted point, under the guard of the Nayars. Then the Portuguese ships sailed to Cochin, where another trading post had been set up near the royal palace. The ships berthed there during the months of November and December, the time needed to constitute the cargo of pepper and the cinnamon supplied by the Mappilla traders of the city, and to make a few captures at sea. In January, they returned to Cannanore where they loaded ginger, navigational equipment, rice and dried fish, to set sail to Lisbon before the headwind rose.

By sparking off hostilities with Calicut, the Portuguese had burst in on the political arena of Malabar. The hospitality that the rajah of Cochin had shown to them gave the Zamorin a pretext for triggering off yet another war and for invading the kingdom of his adversary in the beginning of 1503. Rather than abandoning the handful of Portuguese left under his guard to the hands of his conqueror, the rajah of Cochin sought refuge with his protégés in a sacred island of the lagoon. The arrival of a new armada in September changed the situation to his favour, driving back the troops of Calicut. The Portuguese restored his lands and his rights to the rajah of Cochin, providing him the defence that their meagre means allowed: two caravels and about a hundred men under the command of the famous Duarte Pacheco Pereira. This captain succeeded in repulsing the rush of the armies of Calicut who had re-launched an offensive.

Thus was established the climate of the first years of the Portuguese presence: avowed friendship for the Hindu princes, and war against Calicut and against all those who protected the Islamic trade. Nevertheless, the Portuguese had to temper their attitude towards the Muslims. Their prejudices, nurtured by their own history, by their already distant conflict with their North African invaders, served to create in them the same aversion to the communities of India as they felt for the communities of the Arab world. Meanwhile, they soon learned to distinguish between the Pardeshi and the Mappillai. They attacked the former, whom they wanted to drive out of the Indian Ocean and they conciliated with the latter, who supplied them with spices.

The position of the newcomers remained precarious. Between the departures and arrivals of fleets, the agents of the trading posts were alone, helplessly dependent on the protection of rajahs, who were reluctant to aggravate the hostility of the Muslim merchants. However marginal and seasonal, the Portuguese presence, by its very nature, provoked a negative reaction from the Islamic communities established all along the west coast, from Malabar to Gujarat. The Muslims solicited the assistance of the sultan of Cairo. The victories of Duarte Pacheco Pereira in the lagoon of Cochin, the setting on fire of the merchant fleet of Calicut in Kappatt harbour (1505) had rendered the arrival of spices in the ports of the Red Sea a rare event. Nothing could, however, discourage the tenacity of the Portuguese, which was much more redoubtable than their firepower. On the other hand, the cargoes unloaded in Lisbon were becoming substantial enough to threaten traditional commerce between Egypt and Venice. The political difficulties of the sultan were such that he could not afford to face a financial crisis. He dispatched a Franciscan of Jerusalem to Rome to request the Pope to exert pressure on the Iberian monarchs to make them cease their activities against Islamic interests, thus jeopardizing the access of Christians to the Holy Land. At the same time, the sultan fulfilled the expectations of the Muslims of India by announcing the constitution of a warfare fleet geared to annihilate the Portuguese. This simultaneous attack on two fronts reinforced the determination of both the king of Portugal and the Muslim communities of India, who united in the vain hope of a rapid intervention of the Egyptian forces.

A 'seaborne empire'

In 1505, King Manuel decided to establish a virtual Portuguese state in Malabar, because he did not possess a territorial base other than a small fort in Cochin and a few pavilions at the tip of Cannanore. He entrusted the first viceroy, Dom Francisco de Almeida, with the mission of creating this state, giving him precise instructions to follow: the construction of fortresses in these two cities and on the island of Anjedive, the dispatch of reconnaissance missions to the South Seas, the pursuit of war with Calicut and the capture of all the loaded ships bound for the Red sea. The king of Portugal believed that he had the prerogative to appropriate monopoly over the spice trade. It was with this objective in mind that he instituted a system of safe-conducts (*cartaz*) that the Asian navigators had to buy from the Portuguese authorities, on the penalty of being boarded and often of being sunk with their vessel. The viceroy was requested to send an ambassador to Vijayanagar and to make contact with the leaders of Ormuz, Gujarat, Ceylon and Malacca.

The movements of the fleet ensured a permanent presence in the waters of Kerala, where a squadron served under the command of the viceroy, while another, composed of three or four ships, was stationed in India only during the time of loading of spices and merchandise.

This plan had been engineered in Portugal in the light of the experience of the commanders of previous expeditions. In the beginning, the viceroy complied with the instructions he had received. Built in laterite, with a square dungeon and a compound with four towers, the citadels were raised in a matter of few days. As early as 1506, a reconnaissance mission was sent to the Maldives, and thereafter to Ceylon, from where it returned with its first tribute of cinnamon paid by the rajah of Kotte. In 1509, a squadron reached the ports of the north coast of Sumatra and then Malacca, where around twenty Portuguese had been caught in an ambush laid by Gujarati merchants. In fact, as early as the end of 1506, the viceroy had to face a perilous situation. The armada, scheduled to arrive in September, had missed the monsoon. This delay gave fresh hope to the Muslims, even more because rumour had it that the Egyptian fleet was due to arrive shortly. Skirmishes became more frequent. In 1507, the fortress of Cannanore was besieged; it was only the arrival of the much-awaited armada that saved it.

The necessity to adapt to local realities urged the viceroy to opt to exploit the riches of India rather than to conquer it. He did not, however, give up his war against Calicut and against the traders of the Arab world, because they hampered the consolidation of Portuguese control over the spice trade. He tolerated private commercial transactions between his subjects and the Malabar traders, and offered the latter the protection of his squadrons during their over-seas expeditions. These escort missions enabled the Portuguese to infiltrate into the Asian trade networks and to reconnoitre the routes. It was thus that they discovered the extent of the Gujarati network that had just succeeded in extending its branches to all the oceanic markets.

The commercial hegemony of Gujarat resided in its political power, of which the Portuguese were soon to make an assessment. The territorial conquests of Mahmud I extended as far as the gates of the sultanate of Delhi, and encompassed a vast sea front in the west. A champion of Islam, the sultan had allied himself with the anti-Portuguese league and declared a holy war. In 1508, when the Egyptian fleet finally left its shipbuilding yards in Suez, it headed towards the Gujarati port of Diu, which had been chosen as a naval base.

The sphere of seaborne trade drifted towards the north. At the end of the previous year, Afonso de Albuquerque, the then captain-major of the Arabian Sea, had succeeded in reducing the cities of Oman and Ormuz to submission, forcing them to pay a tribute. Dom Francisco de Almeida, in disapproval of Albuquerque's violence, had sent a message of friendship to the regent of Ormuz. Both of them were anxious to maintain commercial exchanges, much like Malik Ayaz, the governor of Diu. The latter was in fact infuriated at the havoc that the Egyptian crew were wreaking in the port and apprehensive about a possible interference of the sultan of Cairo in the affairs of India. These preoccupations eventually overrode their zeal for a crusade and a holy war. In February 1509, Malik Ayaz ambushed the Egyptian fleet in the port of Diu and left it to be destroyed by the Portuguese artillery.

The Battle of Diu was fraught with consequences. Henceforth, Gujarat, like all the powers of peninsular India, had to reckon with the Portuguese presence, either accepting or rejecting it. The Muslim communities of Malabar learned to rely on themselves rather than on the Mameluk sultan of Egypt, whose prestige had proved to be deceptive. Ruined by the Portuguese enterprises, the Egyptian ruler had indeed lost his naval force and had to depend on the Ottoman Turks to re-constitute it.

The consolidation of the Portuguese Empire gained momentum with the arrival of Alfonso de Albuquerque, who succeeded Dom Francisco de Almeida at the end of 1509 and was invested with the title of 'captain-major and governor of the Indies'. Alfonso's political project signalled a break from that of his predecessor. The line of action was no longer to prefer profit to conquest, but to place one at the service of the other. If he succeeded in imposing his will on his men by sheer intransigence, he also led them on the most audacious expeditions, thanks to his talents as a strategist and to his unwavering faith in the success of his mission. In seven electrifying years, Albuquerque conquered the key areas of the Indian Ocean – Goa (1510), Malacca (1511) Ormuz (1508–11) – and constructed a fortress in Calicut (1513). Only his failure at the hands of Aden stopped him from acquiring absolute mastery over the Indian seas.

Albuquerque led his expeditions of conquest in extremely precarious conditions. He had under his command never more than two thousand Portuguese fighters, often debilitated by fever and by the ordeals of navigation. He did not run the risk of confronting on open terrain the waves of Indian armies, well equipped with horses and war elephants. He always preferred to take position on board his ships, which were hardly in better condition than his men, but which had the advantage of being higher than the Asian vessels and of being mounted with numerous well-maintained cannons, ready to be fired by seasoned artillerymen.

Though the firepower of the Portuguese enabled them to score a few spectacular triumphs in the early years, it cannot be considered the only reason for their victories. In fact, the Indian princes lost no time in upgrading their cannons and in enrolling the services of European deserters to operate them. We should also take into consideration the role of the armies of the allied rajahs, like the Nayars of Cochin, expert in combat in lagoons, and the *nayaks* (commanders) of Honavar, whose men invaded Goa by land. These professional warriors initiated the Portuguese into local strategies, notably into the conduct of battles in rivers. One of the most interesting features of Portuguese accounts is indeed to reveal certain war tactics of medieval India, like that the siege of cities at the time of the monsoon, which prevented help from arriving by sea.

Firstly, the Portuguese attempted to draw mileage from the antagonism between Hindus and Muslims, but they soon discerned more subtle cleavages. Their victories were often thought to be inconsequential successes, and their presence was tolerated inasmuch as their naval power served the interests of Indian princes. The political genius of Albuquerque inspired him to start his round of conquests with that of Goa, a strategic place at the meeting point of the Hindu and Muslim worlds, and for which the sultans of Bijapur and the rajahs of Vijayanagar vied with each other. Consigned to the flames several times by successive armies, it also fell victim to the fire set by the Portuguese (1510), who, after exterminating the Muslims, entrusted the administration of the territory to Brahmins. The conquest of Goa heralded the entrance of the Portuguese on Indian political scene. Its ports received every year ships carrying horses from Persia and Arabia, indispensable for the renewal of the cavalry of rajahs and sultans. Having acquired total control of Ormuz and the city of Oman, which traditionally exported these animals towards the Indian ports, Albuquerque held the powers of the Deccan under his sway, particularly as Portuguese ships patrolled the length of the coasts and diverted to Goa transport ships carrying horses bound for other ports.

Very reluctantly, the rajah of Vijayanagar sent a diplomatic mission to Goa, while Muslim princes, more discreetly, dispatched only emissaries. The sultan Mahmud of Gujarat took the initiative of organizing peace talks. All of them were taken by surprise by the escalation of the conquests of Albuquerque, who brought Malacca under his control in less than a year following the capture of Goa. This conquest dealt the first blow to the commercial hegemony of Gujarat, of which Malacca was the base oriented towards Southeast Asia. Even as the Gujarati traders were on the verge of supplanting their Tamil rivals with whom they vied for the favour of the sultan of the city, the Portuguese reversed the situation by supporting the Tamils because they were not Muslims. It was on board armed junks fitted out by the maritime traders of the Coromandel that they reconnoitred the Molucca Islands, Siam and Pegu. In partnership with them, they started to exploit the markets of these regions. Thus, they cut through the mesh of the network that the Gujaratis had strived to establish in the South Seas.

Portuguese domination of the key points of eastern trade made it no longer necessary to spread out their armies in the ports of Kerala. Albuquerque accepted the peace offers of Calicut. The Zamorin granted him the site of a fortress where the spice trade was to be centralized to the detriment of the kings and traders of Cochin and Cannanore. Thus, Albuquerque's conquests sanctioned the rupture of interests that had hitherto bound the Mappillas of the Malabar with their Portuguese clientele.

Albuquerque created the most ancient European colonial society in Goa. Very different from the others, it modelled itself more on the example of the Greeks and the Romans than on the economic imperatives of the modern world. As the Portuguese navigators never took their wives overseas, they were encouraged to repopulate Goa by marrying Indian women who were baptized beforehand and provided with a dowry. These *casado* (bridegrooms) enjoyed privileged status. They received lands confiscated from the Muslims, while the Hindus retained their properties and their religious liberty. The city of Goa itself was rebuilt in the image of a Portuguese city.

The 'seaborne empire'[1] was not the fruit of ephemeral successes. These conquests would ensure the supremacy of the Portuguese over Ormuz and Malacca for more than a hundred years and over Goa for more than four centuries. At the death of Albuquerque (1515), the newcomers had established their place in the political, economic and social life of the coastal regions of western India.

The Portuguese catalyst

The viceroys and governors who succeeded Albuquerque were caught up, sometimes against their will, in the mutations that transformed the face of the Indian peninsula during the course of the sixteenth century. Throughout this period, they succeeded in maintaining and even expanding the Portuguese domain in spite of their internal disputes and their financial difficulties, because the crown hardly invested in India the profits that it earned there. The scarcity of able-bodied men in the kingdom – which had barely more than one million inhabitants – made it necessary to recruit either outsiders or adolescents who were still too feeble to carry arms and were decimated by disease in no time. Consequently, the Portuguese had to resort to soldiers of Hindu origin, often placed at their service by the allied rajahs, and to the infantry recruited from the territories under their domination. The predominance of Indian elements in the Portuguese army has often been underestimated, due the fact that a large number of them were baptised and carried a Portuguese name.

The presence of the Portuguese served as a catalyst inasmuch as it triggered the reactions that were to occasion durable transformations. The capture of Malacca (1511) and the submission of Calicut (1513) had led to the mobilization of the Gujaratis, who had to chart new maritime routes and create new networks in collusion with all those to whom Portuguese expansion was detrimental. One among them, the *ali rajah* of Cannanore, had in fact succeeded in making the most of the new conditions created by the Albuquerque's policies. Most of the ships coming from the East Indian spice islands were steering clear of an encounter with the armada by diverting their route from the Malabar ports to put in at the ports of the Maldives. Certain ports in this archipelago began to compete with the pepper-exporting ports of Sumatra and opened new channels for spices towards the Red Sea. By acquiring control of the islands and by transporting the products from Malabar and Ceylon to these new destinations, the *ali rajah* found a way to thwart the Portuguese plan and opened markets outside their blockades. He continued to support the Mappillas of Kerala, who, in view of the impending war, secretly fitted out their own fleet in estuaries and lagoons.

The Islamic communities started to take up arms even as uprisings broke out almost everywhere against the Portuguese strongholds. These reactions were encouraged, even orchestrated, by the powerful Gujarati groups that reigned at the time over transoceanic trade. The fortresses of Quilon, Colombo, Pasei (Sumatra) and Ormuz were besieged in succession and the factory of Martaban was destroyed. The Malabar fleets succeeded in taking over the citadel of Calicut, which fell in 1525.

The need to defend Goa and Malacca, under constant threat and occasionally besieged, did not allow the Portuguese to station their armies on all the fronts. At the same time, their governors had to mobilise all their forces in view of conquering the Red Sea. A year after the death of Albuquerque, the Ottoman Turks invaded Egypt and took position on its shores (1516–7). Several armadas were dispatched to the spot in the futile hope of preventing the Turks from gaining access to the maritime routes of India. The threat of an anti-Portuguese coalition re-emerged. The successors of the sultan Mahmud of Gujarat, who were waging a holy war against the

Rajputs, were ready to begin hostilities against the Portuguese with the support of the naval forces of the Turks. The latter, however, conveyed only a few vessels to the ports of Gujarat that Sultan Bahadur (1526–73) had opened for them.

It was the Moguls – who were also newcomers – who gave new impetus to Portuguese expansion. In 1534, Humayun's armies entered Gujarat and burned the fleet that Bahadur had prepared against the armadas. Faced with the inertia of the Turks, the sultan did a volte-face and, when the Mogul invasion confirmed his defeat, sought help from his enemies of the day before, promptly offering them Bassein, then Diu the following year. He died by drowning, during an interview to which the governor Nuno da Cunha had invited him. After repulsing the Moguls, the Portuguese retained possession of Diu, which remained under their authority until 1961.

Portuguese citadels lined thereafter the length of the west coast. The strongholds of the North (Chaul, 1521, Bassein, 1534, Diu, 1535, Daman, 1539) had a status modelled on the customs of Islamic India: each of them was composed of aldees[2] afforded as recompense to Portuguese nobles for three generations.

Despite the harassment that the Turks and the Malabars inflicted on it on sea, notwithstanding the two sieges faced by Diu (1538 and 1546), Portuguese India experienced a revival of its prosperity in the middle of the sixteenth century. It maintained good relations with the rajahs of Vijayanagar thanks to the rigorous organization of the trade in horses that the Portuguese transported each year as far as the capital. The sums of gold that they thereby earned amply compensated for their loss on the spice trade that the Malabar maritime traders continued to carry, concealed under bundles of cloth, towards the ports of the Islamic world.

In the wake of this economic prosperity, countless churches, convents and social service institutions, whose architecture reflected a fusion of cultures, sprang up in the city of Goa. In the countryside, populated by a Hindu majority, life continued peacefully until the 1540s, which were marked by the simultaneous annexation of the territories of Bardes and Salsete, the arrival of Jesuits and the establishment of an inquisition tribunal occasioned by the persistence of Hindu rites and crypto-Judaic beliefs among the Christian population. Temples were demolished following the Brahmins' rejection of conversion, which for the first time became an obligation rather than an invitation. A significant number of them accepted to be baptised, followed suit by all the inhabitants of their villages, who nevertheless maintained their social stratification and avoided mixing with the Portuguese Christians. Two trends marked the hitherto multiracial society: on the one hand, a minority of Portuguese origin who looked for European unions; and on the other, an influx of converted Hindus who retained their castes and rules of endogamy. While these two groups tended to live in closed communities, a large population, formed of bastards of mixed blood and converted of low caste Indians and Muslims, lived in a climate of amalgamated traditions. The city welcomed refugees fleeing the Mogul conquests and was filled with individuals who came from countries affected by the Portuguese expansion, from Africa to Japan.

Neither the compartmentalization of society nor the harshness of the Counter-Reform prevented Goa from being a cultural crossroads. In 1570, the Jesuit college

Saint Paul had nearly two thousand students from all over India, speaking eighteen different languages, even as the first grammars of Indian languages were being published by the Catholic printing press. As early as 1576, the Mogul emperor Akbar received Father Juliao Pereira and requested the authorities of Goa to delegate two Jesuit scholars to participate in the theological discussions held in Fatehpur Sikri.

The intensification of missionary activities that spread out of Goa profoundly modified the character of the Christian population of South India. It gave rise to numerous communities of new converts, generally from the low castes, in Kerala, Ceylon and particularly in the pearl fisheries of the Coromandel coast. The Christians of Saint Thomas, of ancient stock, were hardly inclined to mix with the recently baptized converts. A large number of them nevertheless accepted the establishment of ties with Rome during the Synod of Diamper (1599).

For the mastery of the ocean

In the second half of the sixteenth century, the Indian subcontinent was the stage for upheavals that were not without consequences for the Portuguese state of India. When the Vijayanagar Kingdom disintegrated in 1565, the Mogul Akbar started to expand his conquests towards the Deccan, annexing one after the other the kingdoms that had dominated this region. The fall of Vijayanagar was followed shortly after by the fall of Gujarat (1572) which had been ruined following a bloody resistance. Thus collapsed, in the space of seven years, the powers that had given peninsular India two thousand years of prosperity.

After the annihilation of Vijayanagar, the Portuguese took advantage of the ensuing state of disarray to secure their positions on the coast of Karnataka, in Honavar, Barkur, Mangalore, from where rice and pepper were exported. Mogul domination had not posed a threat to their strongholds in Gujarat. The maritime traders of Gujarat tried to safeguard their overseas markets and accepted the escort of Portuguese squadrons. Diu served overtly as the intermediate port for trade exchanges established between Surat and the countries of the Red Sea. Goa's prosperity received a fillip at the time, but it was primarily thanks to Gujarati trade whose volume was almost as extensive as the Crown's. Thus, the Portuguese compensated for the crash of the horse trade whose profits had dwindled twenty-fold in the wake of the fall of Vijayanagar.

The Portuguese were not the only ones to attempt to draw mileage from the new conjunction of circumstances. The Islamic communities of Kerala now had an opportunity to appropriate the maritime power of Gujarat. The sea was theirs to take and their fleets had proved their efficacy during their clashes with the Portuguese forces. The necessity to eliminate the newcomers was henceforth part of a larger scheme of action and the defence of their interests was exalted to the status of a holy war. From Gujarat down to Ceylon, the navigators of Malabar maintained a constant tension that provoked frequent skirmishes. The violence with which the Portuguese reacted obliged the rajahs to take up arms. Though the rajahs generally accepted the services of corsairs, they also dreaded their influence. By vying with the

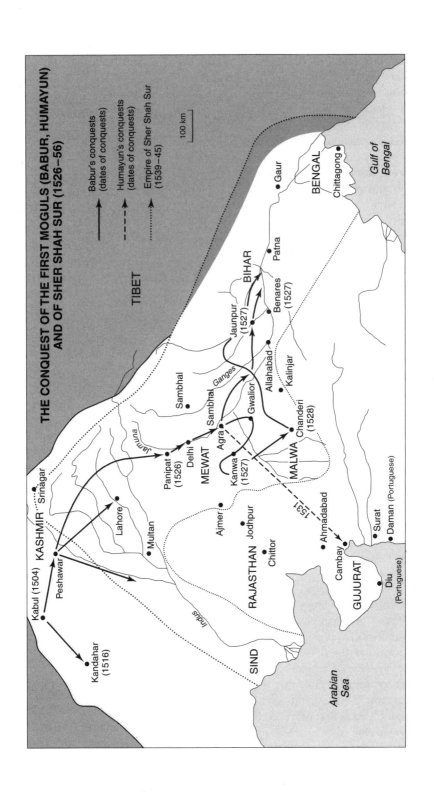

THE CONQUEST OF THE FIRST MOGULS (BABUR, HUMAYUN) AND OF SHER SHAH SUR (1526–56)

Babur's conquests (dates of conquests)
Humayun's conquests (dates of conquests)
Empire of Sher Shah Sur (1539–45)

100 km

TIBET

BENGAL

Gulf of Bengal

Chittagong

Gaur

BIHAR

Patna

Jaunpur (1527)

Benares (1527)

Allahabad

Kalinjar

Sambhal

Ganges

Sambhal

Gwalior

Chanderi (1528)

MALWA

Agra

Kanwa (1527)

Jamuna

Panipat (1526)

Delhi

MEWAT

KASHMIR

Srinagar

Lahore

Multan

Ajmer

Jodhpur

Chittor

RAJASTHAN

Ahmadabad

1531

Cambay

Surat

Daman (Portuguese)

GUJURAT

Diu (Portuguese)

Kabul (1504)

Peshawar

Kandahar (1516)

Indus

SIND

Arabian Sea

Portuguese for the control of the Indian Ocean, the Mappilla chiefs found the opportunity to liberate themselves, as was the case with the *ali rajah* of Cannanore, who had established his own dynasty and had relegated the rajah of Eli to the inland territories.

A precedent like this incited the Zamorin of Calicut to establish close ties with the Portuguese, who had ruined his kingdom but had never contested his suzerainty. A war flared up when the most valiant of his captains, Pate Kunjali Marakkar, flouted his authority and proclaimed himself emperor of Malabar. The coalition of Mappillai navigators, hitherto indomitable, was defeated by the combined forces of the Portuguese fleet and the royal army of Calicut. Thus ended the ultimate attempt to retain control of the oceanic trade in the hands of Indian maritime traders.

The Portuguese, however, did not succeed in asserting their supremacy in the maritime space that had been the undisputed domain of the Gujaratis. Exhausted by the naval war that they had to wage concurrently against the Malabars and the Turks, and by their continuing combat with the pirates of Mascate and of Southeast Asia, they lacked the resources needed to seize this opportunity. The transformations of the Luso-Indian society had dampened their pioneering spirit. The traders preferred to restrict themselves to Indian domestic trade, while captains of adventure were content to found, as in Bengal, independent corsair communities that maintained only sporadic links with Goa. The Portuguese presence thus entrenched itself in Asia to give rise to Christians of mixed race with Portuguese names who often integrated into the economic or military life of the country.

A new order was emerging in the Indian subcontinent. At the behest of Akbar, the development of the road network gave another dimension to trade exchanges. Products from the coastal regions penetrated the subcontinent by wagon. Thanks to the dynamism of its businessmen, the Gujarati trade concentrated its activities around Surat. In Malabar itself, caravans of two to three thousand buffaloes loaded with pepper travelled from Cochin towards Agra and the Central Asian market. The Florentine trader Filippo Sassetti observed in 1588: 'With his court and his military camps, the Great Mogul consumes everything, to a much greater degree than Vijayanagar. His trade is as vast as was Cambay, with the only difference that it is not carried out by sea, but overland.'[3]

Other newcomers were soon to take advantage of this conjunction of circumstances: in the abandoned ocean, the British and the Dutch were already scouting around for the routes of the future.

The Mogul-Afghan contest for supremacy (1526–56)

While the Portuguese were building their overseas empire and while the sultanates of the Deccan were consolidating their power by plotting the ruin of Vijayanagar, the north of India became a bone of contention between the Afghans who were already there and the Moguls, who had recently arrived from Central Asia via Afghanistan. Like the early Sultans of Delhi, both these powers were driven by an imperial ambition: with the Punjab and Delhi as their respective base, they intended to extend their control until the sea, which brought them into conflict with the sultanate of Bengal in the east and in the west with Gujarat and the principalities of Rajasthan, which controlled the approaches to Gujarat.

Babur conquers North India (1526–30)

Babur, born in 1483, a descendant of Genghis Khan (through his mother) and of Timur, belonged to a branch of Turkified Mongols, the Caghatays, henceforth considered as Turks. The term 'Mogul' (Arabo-Persian: *mogul*) which signifies 'Mongol' thus underscores this descent. Like the great men of his age, Babur received a twofold education. He was a warrior and a man of letters. At the age of ten, in 1494, he inherited from his father's side the small principality of Ferghana, in Central Asia. From then on, he led the life of a conqueror in the quest of an empire. He first attempted to build one near his native city around Samarkand and Boukhara, but he was driven from there in 1501 by Shaibani Khan (ruled from 1501 to 1510) who established the supremacy of the Uzbeks for a long time in this region.

Babur then withdrew to Afghanistan. In 1504, he captured Kabul from one of his uncles and established a solid base in the region by obtaining the allegiance of the local emirs. An episode that proved significant for his future was his marriage to an Afghan: Kabul was to remain one of Babur's capitals until his death, and more importantly, Afghanistan would be in the sphere of influence of the Moguls until its emergence as an autonomous political entity in the eighteenth century. It was in Kabul that Babur took the Persian title *padsha* or *badsha*, which we translate as 'emperor' and which supplanted the Arabic synonym *sultan* hitherto in vogue.

For more than ten years, Babur led an indecisive policy swaying between India and Central Asia, while being wary of his powerful neighbours, the Safavids of Iran. Between 1505 and 1507, he launched a few raids into India in the upper valley of the Indus. On the other hand, after the defeat of Shaibani Khan by the Safavid Shah Ismail, he allied himself temporarily with the latter and attempted to stage a comeback in Central Asia. In 1511, he seized Samarkand and reigned for a while as a vassal of the Safavids by professing his adherence to the Shiah creed. He thus gave himself a pretext for resisting the Sunnite Uzbeks; the latter rallied to a nephew of Shaibani Khan, Ubaidullah Khan, who ousted Babur definitively from Samarkand in 1513. Neither Babur nor his successor would get over its loss; they would attempt several times to re-conquer it.

After returning to Kabul, Babur changed his strategy. He broke away from the Safavids to turn definitively towards India. Between 1517 and 1522, he first snatched dominion over Kandahar, in present Afghanistan, from the Arghun Moguls. This advance was important for two reasons: Kandahar controlled the principal terrestrial trade route between India on the one hand, Iran and the Middle East on the other. A strategic position prized by these same countries, it was to become the symbol of the rivalries between the Moguls and the Safavids: the city would change hands not less than seventeen times between the sixteenth and the seventeenth century.

The rest of Babur's reign was devoted to the conquest of India. From 1516 onwards, he conducted raids on his own initiative. Subsequently, he found a providential ally in the internal dissensions of the Afghan Lodis who ruled in North

India: he was invited by Daulat Khan Lodi of Lahore and by Alam Khan to back them in their rebellion against Ibrahim Lodi, the then master of Delhi. Babur complied, but with his own interests at heart. He first conquered Lahore in 1523, then returned to Kabul to mobilize a larger army and came back in 1525 to march towards Delhi.

The decisive battle took place in April 1526 at Panipat, a few dozen kilometres to the north of Delhi. Ibrahim Lodi aligned a hundred thousand cavaliers and a thousand elephants; Babur led ten thousand archers on horseback, but he had the advantage of the artillery that was to play a decisive role for the first time in India. Taking up position behind the gun carriages and his chariots attached to one another forming a barrier, Babur launched his cavalry on the flanks and the rear of his enemy, whom he bombarded with his artillery. The army of the Lodis was hacked to pieces and their elephants captured. Babur secured control of both the capitals, Delhi and Agra, and seized an immense plunder; in Agra, his son Humayun appropriated the famous diamond *Koh-i nur* ('mountain of light'); Babur had virtually become the master of North India, where he resided until his death, constructing mosques and the first Mogul gardens.

During the last four years of his life, Babur established effective control over the country. In a first campaign from Agra, he advanced in 1572 as far as Jaunpur and Ghazipur. The same year, he came up against the Rajputs in the southeast. He defeated a redoubtable coalition led by Rana Sanga of Chitor in Kannua and conquered the city of Chanderi. The following year, he had to face a rebellion by the Afghans in Bihar: he won a decisive victory in 1529, in the confluent of the Gogra and the Ganges, against the army the Afghans had mobilized with the help of the sultan Nusrat Shah of Bengal. After definitively securing his supremacy, he returned to Agra where he died in December 1530; his body was conveyed to Kabul a few years later.

In his Memoirs,[4] Babur has given us a candid day-to-day record of his observations, his thoughts and his feelings. He admits frankly that he did not like India: its luxuriant vegetation and architecture frightened him; he preferred the isolation of the civilized gardens that he had constructed there, with their geometric patterns and their cruciform canals, evocative of the rivers of paradise. Nevertheless, he was drawn to India for its riches and for the power that it afforded him. In fact, as a Turk, he believed himself to be its legitimate owner, perpetuating the Turkish dynasty of old, after driving out the Afghans whom he considered as usurpers. Sincerely pious, he translated in verse a manual of Muslim law and a treatise on Sufi morality written by his spiritual master, Khwaja Ubaidullah Ahrar (died 1490), of the Naqshbandiyya brotherhood. He does not hide his weaknesses, in particular, his fondness for alcohol, which he gave up only in 1527, on the eve of the battle against the Rajputs. Like many devout Muslims in their forties, he began to mend his ways and considered his campaigns a *jihad* (holy war). His memoirs and the abundant poetry he authored place him among the best Turkish writers: his writings have won him acclaim for his sincerity and for the precision and finesse of his expression; the limpidity of his language pleasantly contrasts with the bombastic Persian, which was to become the norm under the Moguls.

The early years of Humayun and the consolidation of the Moguls (1530–40)

Humayun, the first born of Babur, was born in Kabul in 1508. As cultured and scholarly as his father, he wrote poetry, loved painting, and founded the Mogul school of miniatures with the painters that he brought with him from his exile in Iran. He was also interested in mathematics and astronomy, but he had neither the political perceptiveness nor the military genius of Babur. He was often inclined to inactivity and opium abuse.

From the age of ten, Humayun took part in the affairs of his father. When his father died, he was on his way back from a futile campaign for the re-conquest of Samarkand and had taken ill in Sambhal, to the north of Agra. In spite of conspiracies, he was recognized as his successor within three days, but had to immediately face a twofold threat from rival Moguls and from the potentates of India.

The pastoral custom of the Turko-Mongols, which Akbar brought to an end, stipulated a collective sovereignty: besides the first-born, who was the sultan in title, the younger sons had the right to administer parts of the empire granted as fiefs. Therefore, Humayun had to come to terms with his three half brothers, who were endlessly hatching plots to seize the throne from him. In the beginning, the most enterprising among them, Kamran (1509–57), who had obtained Kabul and Badakhshan as his fiefdoms, appropriated the Punjab also, cutting Humayun off from Central Asia; the other two, Askari and Hindal, were content with just assignments of land rights (*jagirs*) in Mewat and in Sambhal.

Humayun's other possessions were also precarious, as they were menaced simultaneously in the east by the Afghans and in the west by Gujarat. His first campaigns enabled him to contain the Afghans beyond Benares. He spent the years 1532 and 1533 in Agra and in Delhi, where he founded a new fortified city (where he was to be buried). He then had to strive with the sultan Bahadur Shah (1526–37) of Gujarat, who, marching through Malwa and the principalities of Rajasthan, besieged Chitor. Humayun overran Gujarat and drove out Bahadur Shah, who had to seek refuge from the Portuguese; in 1536, he conquered Champaner and Ahmadabad, the capital, and amassed enormous spoils.

However, Humayun could not enjoy the fruits of this spectacular victory. He committed the error of granting Gujarat as fief to his second half-brother Askari, who, incapable of consolidating his power, fled, abandoning all the Mogul conquests; thereafter, Askari also strove, in rivalry with his two brothers, to seize Humayun's throne for himself.

For his part, Humayun had to confront an even more serious danger: the Afghans of Bihar. Taking advantage of the respite that Humayun had given him, the great Afghan chief Sher Khan, the future emperor Sher Shah, had consolidated his power around his fief of Sahsaram. Whilst the Moguls besieged his fort of Chunar, he succeeded in conquering Bengal. Humayun pursued him there, but on his way back, in 1539, he suffered a defeat in Chausa. After returning hastily to Delhi to negotiate with his half-brothers, he launched a second campaign against Sher Khan, which culminated the following year with yet another defeat at Kannauj. The Afghans were once again the masters of North India.

Humayun had to flee in humiliation, evading both the Afghans and his half-brothers by the circuitous routes of Rajasthan and of Sind – where the future emperor Akbar was born in October 1542. He reached Afghanistan and eventually Iran, where he found refuge with the Safavid emperor Shah Tahmasp (1524–76): to secure his support, he had to surrender the jewel *Koh-i nur* to him and profess his adherence to the Shiah creed. He was to spend fifteen years of exile wandering between Iran, Afghanistan and Central Asia; and only succeeding in 1553 in wrenching his base in Kabul from Kamran.

The return of the Afghans: Sher Shah Sur (1540–5) and his successors (1545–55)

The victory of Sher Shah over Humayun was not an improvization but a rise to supremacy that had been meticulously prepared well in advance, and of which we know all the details, thanks to the biographies that his nostalgic Afghan admirers, such as Abbas Khan Sarwani,[5] wrote under the reign of Akbar.

Nothing predestined the young Farid to a career of glory – he later took the name Sher Khan and then Sher Shah, upon his accession to the throne. He belonged to the clan of the Surs, deemed inferior among the Afghans. The initiative to revolt against the Moguls had been first taken in 1537 by an aristocrat of the Lodi clan, Sultan Mahmud, who attempted to rally the Afghan nobility, but unsuccessfully. To succeed there where the legitimate aristocracy had failed, Sher Shah had to invent a new method. What did it consist of?

The beginnings of Sher Shah are shrouded in obscurity. His father, Hasan Sur, of mixed blood, partly of Rajput descent, came from the Punjab; he settled down in 1498 in the east of India, in Bihar, at the behest of Sikandar Lodi, who pursued a systematic policy of implanting Afghan colonies in his territory. It was there that the young Farid grew up, acquiring a twofold education as a soldier and as a man of letters. Soldier of fortune, he had relations with the Afghans and with the Rajputs until 1511, the year in which he inherited the administrative office of his father: after this first experience, he travelled around the world to gain knowledge, even serving in the army of Babur between 1527 and 1529. From 1530 onwards, under the reign of Humayun, he returned to establish a powerful base in Bihar by creating his own army.

The secret of his success is twofold. Firstly, he established among his men an egalitarian military discipline, designed to surmount the barriers of origin and rank and to abolish factions: he replaced the model of the segmentary state prevalent among the Afghans by the ideal of a centralized administration. His camp – armies at the time were always mobile – served as a model: a novelty, it was surrounded by earthen fortifications and all the men, irrespective of their rank, had to pitch in to build them. Despite its harshness, this discipline attracted the Afghans as much as the Rajputs, because it gave them the opportunity to rise into prominence by merit and break free from the fetters of their origin; it made them believe in victories with the promise of substantial plunders, the main source of enrichment for soldiers; lastly, and most importantly, it guaranteed them a regular salary.

The second ingredient in Sher Shah's recipe for success was his capacity for the mobilization of resources. During the years 1530–40, he amassed a colossal fortune that propagated his reputation all across North India. He in fact exploited three sources of wealth: an efficient administration of the lands under his jurisdiction; several marriages with rich widows; and spoils of war. With regard to this last point, he had the chance, during the final conflict with Humayun, of reducing the sultanate of Bengal to his mercy and of looting its treasures; his fortune at the time was greater than that of his Mogul adversary.

The first task of Sher Shah was to reunify and even to expand the empire that he had just wrenched from the Moguls. His progress was breathtaking. He seized Agra and Delhi, re-captured Lahore and overran the Punjab, which he protected by a string of forts. As early as 1541 he strengthened his control over Bengal, which he integrated into his empire. On the other side of the subcontinent, in 1543, he conquered Sind and reached the shores of Indian Ocean. However, his most arduous task, from 1541 to 1545, was to bring the Rajputs under his domination. He subdued Gwalior and annexed Malwa, wiped out the family of Silhadi Purbiya in Chanderi, extended his conquests as far as the heartland of Rajasthan, to Marwar, Jodhpur and Ajmer, before subjugating the fortress of Chitor, the symbol of Rajput resistance. He died accidentally in 1545 following the explosion of a mine while he was besieging the marginal fortified city of Kalinjar.

By his audacious conquests, Sher Shah perpetuated the imperial successes of the Khaljis, the Tughluqs and heralded the Mogul Empire. His policy towards the Rajputs, whose submission was indispensable to secure control over North India, also left its stamp in the history of India: Sher Shah was victorious from the military standpoint, but his diplomacy towards the vanquished was indecisive. He vacillated between two lines of conduct. The first favoured dealing with the Hindu Rajputs on equal terms, even with regard to the exchange of women: this practice then had currency among the Muslims, in spite of the edicts of orthodoxy, and Sher Shah wanted to adopt it, because he considered it the best way of reconciling with the Rajput forces. But he came up against the opposition of the ulemas, who with the native Muslim population, claimed the superiority of Islam. Thus, he had to assert his supremacy by force and massacres, instituting a policy that Akbar was to pursue, a policy founded on submission and unequal terms; the Rajputs gave women to the Moguls, while the converse was prohibited. Sher Shah died prematurely, making it impossible for us to speculate whether he would have been successful in this second strategy.

Sher Shah also prefigured the Mogul administration. His short reign was, in effect, marked by measures that were to be largely imitated by subsequent rulers. After more than a century of rather mediocre coinage, he reintroduced a double currency of high quality, in silver (the famous rupee, which will be in use even under the British) and in copper. He reorganized the agrarian administration. He tightened his control over the armed contingents of his nobles, by ensuring the regular payment of soldiers, and by imposing the branding of horses to exclude fraud.

He ordered the relaying of the long route which ran from one end of his empire to the other and equipped caravanserai, favouring the development of the small rural cities, or *qasba*. Thus, he provided the model for the Mogul administration of Akbar and his successors, which is in fact less original than we often believe it to be.

The successors of Sher Shah would prove to be less brilliant. During the long authoritarian reign of his younger son Islam Shah (1545–54), the Afghan Empire survived in spite of internal disputes within the aristocracy, in particular, the rebellion of the Niyazi tribe in the Punjab; the heresy of the Madhawis was definitively repressed with the execution of Shaikh Alai in 1550. Thereafter, under the reign of Muhammad Adil Shah (1554–5), a controversial usurper, the empire disintegrated into three rival kingdoms, leaving the way open for the return of Humayun.

The restoration of Humayun (1555–6)

In the autumn of 1554, Humayun embarked on the re-conquest of India with extraordinary courage and determination. He seized Lahore in 1555, defeated the army of Sikander Shah Sur in Sirhind: the route was open to Delhi, which he entered in the July of the same year. Historians attribute to him a plan for the reorganization of the aristocracy, aimed at confiscating the power of the Mogul princes who had brought about his ruin. However, he could not enjoy his victory. He died in January 1556, after falling from the stairway of his library, on the roof of which, following his lifelong interest in astronomy, he had climbed to contemplate the rising of Venus.

The last days of Humayun had an unexpected witness in person of the Ottoman admiral Sidi Ali Rais,[6] who had come to defend Gujarat against the Portuguese. Defeated at sea, he returned overland to his country passing through Delhi, where, as Humayun's guest, he observed the first days of Akbar. This first and the only direct contact between the Moguls and the Ottomans in the sixteenth century was accidental: nearly a century would elapse before the establishment, under the reign of Shah Jahan (1628–58), of formal exchanges, which would, however, remain sporadic.

Until this date, the imperial power in North India belonged to the Afghans allied to powerful Rajput confederacies, capable of mobilizing the immense resources of the land and of the armed peasantry. The Moguls were still only foreigners who had not yet settled down. The models of administration were also those of the Delhi sultanate that Sher Shah had implemented once again and perfected.

It would be the vocation of Akbar, the son of Humayun, to conceive a new recipe for building a truly Mogul Empire.

PART TWO

THE MOGUL EMPIRE

(1556–1739)

In August 1947, the flag of independent India, hoisted for the very first time, fluttered above the Red Fort in Delhi, the citadel of the last Mogul dynasty. This dynasty was not only the most enduring and the most powerful in the history of modern India; it also epitomized political legitimacy even in the wake of decadence. How did the Moguls as relative newcomers succeed in identifying their destiny with that of India?

When Akbar ascended the throne in 1556, Mogul supremacy was far from consolidated in North India. At the time of his death, in 1605, the former sultanate of Delhi had been reconstituted and other regions, like Kashmir and Assam, which had never formed a part of it, had been incorporated into the empire. However, of greater import than this territorial expansion, impressive without any doubt, is the edification of durable institutions of control, which is the true hallmark of Akbar's reign (Chapter V).

In the eighteenth century, under the three successors of Akbar – Jahangir, Shah Jahan and Aurangzeb – the Mogul Empire reached the zenith of its history. This age of glory elicited the admiration of European voyagers, particularly that of the Frenchman, François Bernier. There then commenced a period of further territorial expansion with Aurangzeb's annexation of the Deccan sultanates, which brought the empire in contact with the formidable armed peasantry of the Marathas that it could never succeed in reducing to submission (Chapter VI).

The dynamism of trade and the consolidation of the urban network testify to the prosperity of India under the Mogul emperors. Nonetheless, the empire remained above all agrarian, and its resources depended on its capacity to appropriate a part of the surplus exacted from the peasantry (Chapter VII).

This prosperity attracted European traders. The Portuguese were soon followed by the English, the Dutch and the French, who arrived with their trading companies. Though they established trading posts in most of the coastal regions of the subcontinent, their presence was only a marginal factor in the political arena. Chapter VIII throws light on their commercial activity and its impact on the Indian economy.

Mogul India witnessed the emergence of a glorious civilization to which splendid architectural wonders bear testimony to this day. A certain symbiosis occurred between Muslim and

Hindu elements, though we cannot go as far as to speak of a trend towards religious syncretism (Chapter IX).

The death of Aurangzeb portended the decline of the Mogul Empire, which nevertheless did not collapse at once. For more than three decades, through crises and short-lived restorations, the empire persevered, remaining at the heart of the political struggles of the subcontinent (Chapter X).

V

AKBAR AND THE CONSTRUCTION OF THE EMPIRE

(1556–1605)

At the death of Humayun, the Mogul Empire had not yet come into existence. The sixteenth century witnessed only a nascent empire – under the Lodis and thereafter under Sher Shah – which the Moguls had appropriated for themselves. It fell upon Akbar to consolidate, to expand, and above all, to remodel the empire: the institutions that were to make the grandeur of the Moguls were those established by Akbar. As early as the eighteenth century, Akbar had become for his Muslim adversaries the symbol of an opening towards non-Muslims and consequently, that of contempt for Islam. His great grandson Aurangzeb (1658–1707), who returned to a more puritanical religious approach, figured on the contrary as the champion of Islam.

This Manichean vision entered political discourse and historiography at the end of nineteenth century, when the competition between Hindus and Muslims for power increased. In history books written in Urdu and Hindi, Akbar and Aurangazeb, became respectively the champions of the Hindus and the Muslims. For the Hindus, Akbar was the benevolent emperor, who favoured the participation of all in the life of the empire, and Aurangzeb the evil emperor, who shattered this harmony, whereas the Muslims evidently saw Aurangzeb as the good emperor.[1]

More generally, the Hindus, the British and the promoters of the Indian union after independence, make Akbar their hero, projecting on him an anachronistic vision of an architect of national unity who rose above religious differences and who was also an apostle of tolerance; Aurangzeb was, for them, the villain of the story. The Muslims, on the contrary, particularly in the ideological vision prevalent in Pakistan, consider Akbar an apostate and Aurangzeb as the restorer and defender of the Islamic community. The poet-philosopher Iqbal (1877–1938), the spiritual father of Pakistan, was the first bard to promulgate this interpretation.[2]

This approach hinges on an anachronistic and narrow vision of religion. It implies that Akbar had a choice only between, on the one hand, a fundamentalist conception of Islam, which implied exclusion of the Hindus, and on the other, apostasy. Recent studies[3] have enabled us to discredit this misleading alternative and have given us an insight into the nature of religious problems at the time of Akbar.

The testimonies of foreign travellers on Akbar are not many, because only the Jesuits were invited to the court from 1578 onwards. On the other hand, there exists a substantial collection of historic texts written in Persian. In fact, reviving the tradition of the Delhi sultanate, Akbar reintroduced the writing of the official chronicles of the dynasty. Two historians are of special importance for those interested in his rule: Abul-Fazl Allami (1551–1602),[4] who, at the behest of Akbar, wrote a monumental chronicle of the dynasty, particularly on the rule of his master, the *Akbar nama*, that is, 'The book of Akbar'[5] and his main rival at the court, the orthodox *mulla* Abdulqadir Badauni (1540–1651). His posthumous book, *Muntakhab al-tawarikh* ('A selection of stories') often took the opposite viewpoint to the *Akbar nama* and filled in the lacunas that had been left intentionally.

Akbar's early years: the Regency of Bairam Khan (1556–61)

Akbar, son of Humayun, was born in 1542 in Sind, in the south of present Pakistan, at the time when his father was on his way to his exile in Iran. During his youth and the early years of his reign, he came under a twofold influence. On the one hand, he was under the sway of the harem where his foster-mother Maham Anaga, possessed of a strong personality, formed along with her sons and her courtiers an influential faction. On the other hand, he was also moulded by his tutor, Bairam Khan (*c.* 1513–61), a Shiite Turk of noble lineage, who had been a faithful companion of Humayun during his exile and the main architect of his reconquest of India.

Unlike his father and his grandfather, both of whom were great scholars, the future emperor showed more interest for play and sports than for studies. Besides, he would retain the reputation of being 'illiterate' (*ummi*). This term has given rise to a hagiographic theme, which could be misleading: the prophet Muhammad and many great Sufi saints are also supposed to have been illiterate: this was not a shortcoming but a virtue, as they could thus receive divine inspiration without distorting it. Hence, Akbar rose above the common mortals, as an elect of God. In reality, even though he had texts read out to him, he was highly cultured, particularly in mystical poetry and, all his life, he showed great interest for music, painting and architecture.

Akbar was only thirteen and a half years old at the time of Humayun's death. The responsibility of the government fell on the shoulders of his tutor, Bairam Khan. He was then in the Punjab with the new emperor, who, initiated early on into the art of administration, had already become the governor of this province. Bairam Khan improvised the coronation on the spot to assert the rights of his master. He also had to confirm his possessions against the Afghans, mobilized by two pretenders to the throne. The most dangerous of his adversaries was a skilful soldier who belonged to a Hindu low caste, Hemu. Warlord and champion of Afghan interests, Hemu proclaimed himself king under the name of Vikramaditya; he was defeated at the second Battle of Panipat, in 1556, taken prisoner and executed. The second pretender to the throne, Sikander Shah Sur, was forced into capitulation the following year. The control of the strategic places of Jaunpur, Gwalior, and Ajmer was now assured. The heritage of Humayun was secure.

Bairam began to play an increasingly important role in the court and married Salima, a daughter of Humayun's sister. His rise into prominence displeased both Akbar, who wanted to stand on his own two feet, and his stepmother, who supported her own faction. He was accused of showing favouritism to his men, to whom he granted important offices, like Shaikh Gadai Kamboh, who was appointed the Chief *Sadr* (*sadr as-sudur*, the Chief Justice and highest religious official combined) and consequently the master of the endowments granted to the religious leaders: this provided a pretext to eliminate him. Bairam sought salvation in an armed rising, and under cover of going to Mecca, he stirred up a rebellion in Bhattinda, in the Punjab. Defeated and demoted, he went on a pilgrimage, for good this time, but was assassinated by an Afghan in 1561 in Patan, in Gujarat. Akbar does not seem to have been implicated in this act of vengeance. In accordance with his wishes, Bairam was buried in Iran, in Meched. His son Abdurrahim Khan-i Khanan (1556–1627), a politician and a fine scholar like his father, as well as a mystic, would be one of Akbar's most important right-hand men, and the tutor of his son Salim, the future emperor Jahangir.

So Akbar embarked on his career as a statesman, conqueror and mystic. As early as 1562, he put an end to the intrigues of his foster-mother's faction. He would undertake the construction of the Mogul Empire simultaneously on several fronts.

The Territorial Expansion of the Empire (1561–76)

No sooner had he broken free from his tutor, Akbar set out on the expansion of his empire. He achieved this expansion mainly between 1561 and 1576: later conquests were to add very little to the already constituted empire. Drawing on the politics of the Kaljis and the Tughluqs, Akbar advanced seawards, concurrently in two directions, towards Bengal in the east and towards Gujarat in the west, neutralizing beforehand the obstacle posed by the Rajputs.

The first phase, the longest and by far the most complex, resulted in the pacification and the lasting submission of North India, in particular of the Rajputs, who controlled the strategic passes of Rajastan and could mobilize the armed peasantry of North India. Akbar also brought under his domination other groups, the Gakkhars of the Punjab for example, whom he defeated in 1563–4, and the Gonds of eastern India, vanquished in 1564. However, he initially deployed a major part of the Mogul forces in the conquest of Rajasthan. The first conquest was of Malwa in 1561. The following year Akbar subjugated the Rajah Bihara Mal Kachwaha, the first Rajput to enter the service of the Moguls and to give his daughter in marriage to Akbar: in 1569 she would give birth to Salim, the future Jahangir, who was to perpetuate the dynasty. From this time onwards, Akbar alternated between compromises and deployment of force. In 1564, Ram Singh Rathor, the king of Marwar, entered the service of the Moguls, who, as the price of his submission, helped him to re-conquer his ancestral throne. In 1568, on the other hand, Akbar had to resort to force against the principality of Mewar, which had once again

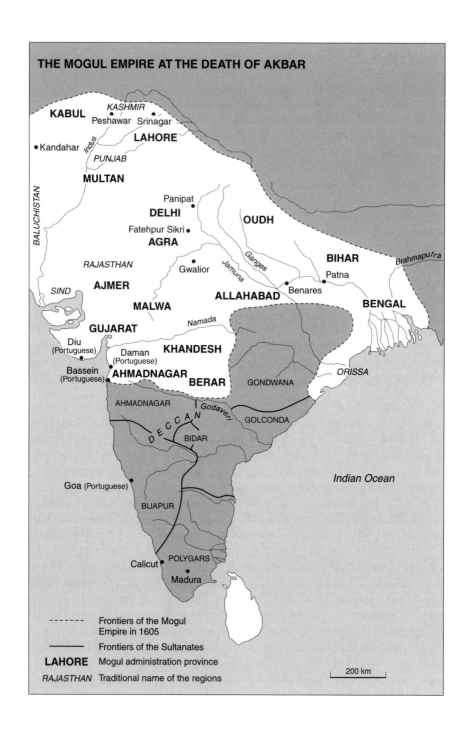

THE MOGUL EMPIRE AT THE DEATH OF AKBAR

KABUL
KASHMIR
Peshawar Srinagar
LAHORE
• Kandahar
Indus
PUNJAB
MULTAN
BALUCHISTAN
Panipat
DELHI
Fatehpur Sikri •
AGRA
OUDH
RAJASTHAN
Gwalior •
Jamuna
Ganges
BIHAR
Patna •
Brahmaputra
AJMER
SIND
MALWA
ALLAHABAD
Benares •
BENGAL
GUJARAT
Namada
KHANDESH
Diu
(Portuguese)
Daman
(Portuguese)
Bassein
(Portuguese)
AHMADNAGAR
BERAR
GONDWANA
ORISSA
AHMADNAGAR
Godaveri
DECCAN
GOLCONDA
BIDAR
Goa (Portuguese) •
BIJAPUR
Indian Ocean
Calicut •
POLYGARS
Madura

- - - - - Frontiers of the Mogul
          Empire in 1605
———— Frontiers of the Sultanates
LAHORE Mogul administration province
RAJASTHAN Traditional name of the regions

200 km

become the spearhead of the Rajput resistance: with King Udai Singh declining all negotiations, Akbar undertook the first great siege of his reign, that of the famous fortress of Chitor, which he captured, ordering the massacre of its garrison. The last great fortress of Rajasthan, Rathambor, succumbed following a brief siege in 1569.

These victories eventually convinced the Rajputs of the military superiority of the Moguls: Rajput principalities outside Rajasthan, like Kalinjar, were reduced to subjection. The last great chiefs, Chandra Sen of Marwar and Rai Kalyan Mal of Bikaner, bowed to the supremacy of the Mughals when Akbar was in Ajmer in 1570; Kalyan Mal gave his daughter in marriage to the emperor; Rawal Har Rai of Bikaner also gave in his turn a daughter, but refused to pay court to him. The Rajput alliance was now sealed: it would prove to be the strength of the Mogul Empire.

After securing his bases North India, Akbar rapidly proceeded with the annexation of the two sultanates that controlled access to the sea, namely Gujarat and Bengal.

Gujarat, already weakened by the decadence of its dynasty and by the first Mogul conquest under Humayun, was plagued by conflicts between the local nobles and the Mogul faction of the Mirzas. The Moguls were eager to resolve the problems caused by the Portuguese presence, which hampered the pilgrimage to Mecca. Akbar succeeded in winning to his cause one of the two political schemers of Gujarat, Itimad Khan, to whom he granted half of the sultanate as fief, while annexing the other half. It was not long before Itimad Khan became less docile: Akbar had to conduct two new campaigns in 1573 to annex the whole of the sultanate. Notwithstanding the sporadic rebellions that continued until the end of sixteenth century, Gujarat had definitively become part of the empire. The emperor placed administrative and financial development of the region in the hands of reliable men, like the famous Hindu finance minister (diwan) Raja Todar Mal.

Bengal had fallen into the hands of an Afghan dynasty in the wake of its invasion by Sher Shah. The sultan who reigned in 1573 was Daud Khan Kararani, who also exercised his supremacy over Bihar and Orissa. For ten months, the Moguls besieged the city of Patna, in Bihar, which fell only after the arrival of Akbar. Pursued in Bengal all the way to Tukaroi, Daud surrendered in 1574. The death of the Mogul governor Munim Khan soon gave him an occasion to rebel, but in 1576, he was once again defeated in the Battle of Raj Mahall, which marked the definitive integration of Bengal, Bihar and a part of Orissa into the Mogul Empire.

It thus took only sixteen years to build the Mogul Empire. This rapidity has raised questions as to the means and methods employed by Akbar. The military edge that he enjoyed no doubt played a role, even though it is not so easy to pinpoint the exact nature of this superiority. Were the political formations of the Ottomans, the Safavids and the Moguls really 'Gunpowder Empires'?[6] In reality, artillery was not always present and was probably less effective than the combination of the archers on horseback (extremely mobile, with remarkable power) and the artillery, which served as leverage. The Mogul armies could thus defeat forces that were far superior in number but less swift, relying on elephants.

Furthermore, under Akbar and his successors, the Moguls resorted to force only when diplomacy had failed. It is by intrigues and interference in internal conflicts that they gained the submission of Ram Singh Rathor of Marwar and that they obtruded on the affairs of Gujarat. However, persuasion prevailed over force, for instance, in Rajasthan with Bihara Mal, their first ally, and with Rawal Har Rai of Bikaner, the last to surrender. This presupposed the effective establishment of a stabilized imperial universe, of which the emperor was the unique centre; a hierarchical conception, according to which all the members of the empire were convinced that they had more to gain by entering the system, even in a subordinate position, than by staying out of it. This system functioned neither by pure force nor by pure persuasion, but by a combination of both.

The Alliance with the Portuguese

The conquest of Gujarat brought Akbar into direct contact with the Portuguese and laid bare the limits of his power. The sultans of Gujarat, with the help of the Ottomans, had unsuccessfully tried to resist Portuguese domination. However, their relations had not been normalized and the route of the pilgrimage to Mecca, which traversed Gujarat, remained impeded by the control that the Portuguese exercised over navigation in the Indian Ocean. Incapable of competing with the newcomers on the seas, Akbar, soon after the definitive annexation of Gujarat, opted for a policy of entente so as to ensure a regular flow of pilgrims, on understanding that, in exchange, the Portuguese retained their control over trade: an accord was negotiated with the envoy of the viceroy of Goa, Antonio Cabral.

From that time onwards, Akbar unceasingly cultivated his relationship with the Portuguese, who remained the only intermediaries with the West until the end of his reign. The emperor would try to make them his allies during his conflict with the Deccan, and subsequently at the time of his strife with his son Salim. The Portuguese supplied imported luxury goods to him. It is through them that the emperor obtained the delegation of missions of Jesuits to participate in religious discussions and, generally, to serve as intermediaries in his relations with the West: the first two missions arrived in 1580–3 and in 1590–2 respectively; the third, which commenced in 1595, would become permanent.

The Organization of the Empire (1572–80)

The subjugation of the factions

Even as he pursued the expansion of his empire, Akbar started concurrently to give shape to its organization. He endeavoured firstly to subjugate the ethnic factions that were vying for scraps of power: Akbar was not content with being the first among equals or an arbitrator, but did his utmost to become the pivot of the political system. After subduing individual rebellions, such as that of Sharafuddin Husain Ahrari, the great grandson of the mystic Ubaidullah Ahrar, in league with Sayyid Abul Maali in 1562, he focused his attention on the submission of two powerful factions.

The Indian Muslims, who had reacted negatively to the change in the dynasty, which was to their detriment, posed the first threat. Their party, as we saw earlier in the wrangles of Sher Shah with the orthodoxy, was powerful because it produced most of the *ulemas*, reputedly of Arab stock, who were essential for the empire. It was from among them that Akbar recruited his two Chief *Sadrs* (*sadr-as-sudur*), Shaik Gadai Kamboh and Shaikh Abdunnabi (died 1584), both of whom were later dismissed. The emperor survived an attempted assassination while he was on a pilgrimage to Nizamuddin. In 1565, to distance himself from the ancient Muslim community with whom he, however, negotiated agreements on an individual basis, he transferred the capital from Delhi first to Agra, where he built a new fort (a fortified palace), and then, in 1571, to Fatehpur Sikri, near Agra, where he built a new city.

Akbar also had to fight off the ambitions of clans of Central Asian origin, who had helped Babur and Humayun conquer India and who believed that they had the prerogative, in accordance with the pastoral tradition of collective royalty, to withhold a part of power and its benefits. Akbar systematically refused this sharing of power either by negotiation or by force. The main threat emanated from the Uzbek clan, whose leaders were Khan-i Zaman Ali Quli Khan and his half-brother Abdullah. Formidable war chiefs spearheading an army of experienced archers on horseback, they were stationed in the east, in the Ganges Valley, to keep the Afghans at bay; between 1565 and 1569, after three rebellions interrupted by spells of submission, Akbar led the campaign in person to defeat them once and for all. He dispersed his foster-mother's clan, the Atga Khails, all across the empire so as to preclude any concerted revolt.

The most difficult to bring into line were the recalcitrant Mirzas. Like the emperor, they belonged to the Timurid family and were authorized, by custom, to lay claim to a part of the sovereignty. These rebels took refuge in Gujarat, where, until its annexation, they formed one of the factions that resisted conquest. After the victory over Gujarat, which was subjugated in 1573, Akbar neutralized them by marriage into the imperial family; the Mirzas, stripped of any share in the sovereignty, were thereafter treated as if they were nothing more than officials of the state.

From then on the Indian Muslims and the Central Asian factions were no longer prominent in the corridors of power. The principle of collective sovereignty that had compromised the reign of Humayun had become outdated. The emperor had risen above the factions: at least in appearance, because Akbar's half brother, Mirza Muhammad Hakim, was fomenting a latent rebellion in Kabul.

The centralization of the administration

Akbar began to implement administrative reforms as early as 1561, placing the eunuch Itimad Khan in charge of increasing the revenues of the centre at the expense of the governors of provinces. In 1564, he appointed Muzaffar Khan Turbati the minister of finance (*wazir* or *diwan*), entrusted with the responsibility of establishing a new land-tax base and of specifying the obligations of the high officials of the empire (*mansabdari*), who were obliged to raise and maintain armed contingents.

The years 1572–80 witnessed the great administrative reforms of his reign. The obligations of the officials of the State were more rigorously defined: they were attributed a numerical hierarchy, two numbers that defined their grade (*mansab*) corresponding to their personal salary index and to the size of their contingent. To rule out any fraud, they were under the obligation to bring their contingents for periodic musters and to brand their horses.

It was at this time that the most daring move towards centralization was made in the whole history of the Moguls, and perhaps of the whole of Muslim India. Even after the arrival of the Moguls, the system of *iqtas* introduced by the sultanate of Delhi had persisted under the Persian name of *jagir*: the beneficiary of these grants of land was obliged to ensure the collection of taxes in the territory that was assigned to him by way of salary. The abolition of this system enabled the imperial administration to levy taxes directly everywhere and to pay all the officials of the empire in cash, so that they became little more than functionaries.

These reforms had other constituents. With a view to tightening the reins of the central power, Akbar reorganized the administrative structure of the provinces. The empire was divided in twelve provinces (*suba*), namely, from west to east, Kabul, Lahore, Multan, Ajmer, Gujarat, Delhi, Agra, Malwa, Oudh, Allahabad, Bihar, Bengal. The functions of the officials who governed them were fixed, and they were urged to control one another. The provinces thus acquired the physiognomy that they would retain up to and even after the British conquest. Concurrently, in order to increase the revenue of the empire, Akbar decreed a systematic revision of privileged tenures or 'advantages' granted to religious leaders so as to check misuses and to diminish, or perhaps even to abolish, these privileged tenures. These revisions were customary in India as in the entire Muslim world, but in the 1570s, when Akbar and his religious and civil staff were at loggerheads, this measure had the overtones of a prosecution for some. However, by the beginning of the 1580s, Akbar had to temper the momentum of the centralized administration, because an important revolt, the causes of which were not religious as generally believed but secular, forced him to back-pedal.

The court ceremony and the new capital of Fatehpur Sikri

The court ceremony, the most visible manifestation of centralization, has often been represented in miniature paintings illustrating the chronicles of the reign: the emperor is portrayed as a sort of a sun king around whom gravitates the whole life of the court as well as that of the empire.

The ceremony took place in several settings because Akbar did not always stay in the capital. Like the Mongols and the Safavids of Iran, the Moguls remained partly nomadic: it has been calculated that they spent forty per cent of their time in sumptuous camps (*urdu*), mobile capitals where hundreds of thousands of people assembled. In the summer months, they settled down in the gardens that had made them famous since Babur's time, or in gardens surrounding certain monumental tombs, like that of Humayun in Delhi.

Irrespective of where the emperor was, the ritual was the same. In Delhi or in Agra, Akbar had to adapt himself to already existing capitals and palaces. In 1571, he engineered the plans for the grandiose capital of Fatehpur Sikri, where, it appears, the ritual would be established. He would dwell until 1585 in this city where life revolved around the person of the emperor. At sunrise, his subjects could contemplate his appearance (*darshan*) at a window especially designed for this purpose (*jharoka*) and make their requests to him. In the morning, the emperor dealt with the routine affairs of the empire (administration, justice, recruitment and promotion of the officials of the State) in the Public Audience Hall (*diwan-i am o khas*): this was the ceremony of the *darbar* that the British would subsequently adopt. In the afternoon and the evening, a few privileged high officials, privy to the secrets of the emperor and select religious leaders and artists were admitted to the Private Audience Hall (*diwan i khas*).

This kind of initiatory ritual served as a means of grading the approach to the person of the emperor: the more the day advanced, the more the official could progress into the interior of the palace and approach the emperor, provided his status allowed it. Thus, in the Public Audience Hall, the emperor sat at the back on his throne, raised to a height of two metres; a cordon of gold touching the throne circumscribed a first zone reserved for the princes of the royal family; a silver barricade delimited a second zone reserved for high officials and ambassadors. The other officials of the State, officers and cavaliers had to stand further away from the throne; the infantrymen and the servants were relegated to the periphery, a barricade of stoneware separating them from the others.

The ceremony also stipulated more or less different forms of salute. When Akbar appeared at the window, it was sufficient to greet him by a *kurnish*, raising one's hand to one's forehead and bowing down. In the Public Audience Hall, one had to execute the *taslim* by bending and touching the ground with the right hand and by placing it on the head while getting up; as for the privileged few admitted into the Private Audience Hall, they were forced to prostrate themselves, the *sijda*. Similarly, the closer an official approached the emperor the more important were the presents that he was expected to bring to the emperor. The princes and the high-ranking officials brought as tokens of their allegiance (*nadhr*) huge sums in gold coins, while the officers of lower rank gave less valuable tributes or *peshkash*. The gift that the emperor gave in return also depended on the status of the receiver: the most salient favour was a robe of honour (in fact a seven-piece suit) that the emperor had worn, or at least, was presumed to have worn.

A new religion or an imperial cult?

From the beginning of his reign, Akbar had had strained relationships with the Sunnite ulemas who were primarily recruited from among the Indian Muslims of the old stock. To improve the situation, he invited them to lead the religious discussions that he organized from 1575 in the Hall of Worship (*ibadat khana*), constructed for this purpose near the mosque of Fatehpur Sikri. The emperor, seated at the centre of the hall, arbitrated in the debates of the protagonists gathered around him. Or rather, he was keeping the score, as it soon became evident that the ulemas could not agree on any question regarding religion or law. Akbar underhandedly encouraged these conflicts to ridicule the ulemas and to get rid of them. The rupture in their relations occurred when the chief *Sadr*, Shaikh Abdunnabi, instigated the execution, against Akbar's will, of a Brahmin who had made derogatory remarks about the Prophet; he would be exiled to Mecca with the Sheikh Makhdumulmulk at the end of the year 1579.

Akbar then undertook a series of measures designed to undermine the religious authority of the ulemas. In the spring of 1579, he took the place of the preacher at the grand mosque of the capital to recite the *Khutba*, or the sermon of the main Friday prayer. A few months later, he goaded the prominent ulemas to promulgate and sign a decree known as a *mahzar* (proclamation), which stipulated that in the event of disagreement among the ulemas on a point in the canonical law, the emperor, as the 'just sultan', had the prerogative to decide on the solution to adopt in accordance with the revealed texts and in the interest of his subjects. Akbar thereby projected himself as a legal expert (*mujtahid*) and identified himself with the caliph of early Islam, who was concurrently the political and religious head, as the 'commander of the faithful' (*amir al muminin*), the shadow of God on earth.

Finally, probably in the same year, Akbar turned his back on orthodoxy by a move that distinguished him from the contemporary Safavids and Ottomans: he abolished the *jizya*, the discriminatory poll-tax imposed on non-Muslims. Muslims thus ceased to be privileged subjects, while the ulemas lost the leverage that they had enjoyed until then. This new religious policy, denoted by the Sufi expression *sulh-i kull* 'perfect reconciliation' had in effect negligible fiscal implications, because it is not certain that the poll-tax had been really collected. It was surely a potent symbol of Akbar's liberalism: a century later Aurangazeb would signal the return to a strict orthodoxy by re-establishing the *jizya*.

From 1579 onwards, Akbar expanded the circle of his religious discussions in the Hall of Worship in Fatehpur Sikri by inviting Shiites, Hindus, Jains, Zoroastrians, and the following year some Christians, the Jesuits. This eclecticism – which had precedents in the Islamic world at the time of the Mongols – illustrates the diversity of religious influences that contributed to the formation of the Mogul ideology.

As early as 1580, Akbar came under the influence of the Shiah creed but also of Madhawism, a sort of millenarianism, which was widespread in the Muslim world of the time, the most influential counsellors at the court from 1574 onwards, Shaikh Mubarak and his two sons (the ideologist Abul-Fazl and the poet Faizi) had been raised in Madhawism. The year 1000 of the hegira calendar was in effect to fall in the year 1591–2: it was believed that this epoch would herald the regeneration of Islam. Some believed – or Akbar himself wanted to project – that he was the expected saviour, a sort of *mahdi*. From 1581–2 the emperor himself commissioned the writing of the first official chronicle the *Tarikh-i alfi*, 'History of the [first] Millennium,' of Shiite and millenarian inspiration, where he is presented as a miracle-worker.

Akbar also performed certain Hindu rites. He recited a prayer to the rising sun by chanting a Sanskrit mantra, then to the noontime sun and to the setting sun. He appeared at the window of his palace like a god in his temple; on solar and lunar anniversaries, he had himself weighed and donated the equivalent of his weight in gold and precious objects. Pursuing the more modest attempts of the Sultanate of Delhi, Akbar ordered the systematic translation of the classics of Sanskrit literature into Persian, which produced illuminated volumes. He prohibited the slaughtering of cows. Like Jains, he encouraged asceticism, vegetarianism and non-violence.

Given the importance that the emperors attached to the sun and light, the influence of Zoroastrianism on the Mogul ideology has been in general inflated. This worship is in reality at the confluence of several traditions, since according to a legend, the Mongols descended from the sun whose rays had fertilized the ancestor queen Alan Qua: Akbar celebrated his Mongol descent in 1580 by a first official chronicle, which would remain uncompleted, the *Tarik-i khandan-i timuriyya* ('History of the lineage of Timur'). We also know that the worship of light holds an important place in Iranian theosophy, in particular in the works of the mystic Shihabuddin Suhrawardi Maqtul (1153–91) from whom the chronicler Abul-Fazl drew inspiration. Lastly, though the Jesuits realized that it was impossible to convert the Mogul court, the religious works and the paintings that they had brought with them played an important role. Abul-Fazl produced a translation of the Bible; and in the seventeenth century, miniature paintings would portray the Mogul emperor dominating the terrestrial globe like Christ the King.

Was Mogul ideology nothing more than a potpourri? The contribution of Hinduism and Jainism, like the Mongol base itself, was marginal. Akbar drew inspiration above all from Sufism and from Iranian theosophy. Until 1585, Sufism exerted an increasingly powerful influence on the emperor. In order to legitimize his regime in the eyes of the Indian Muslims and to reinforce his control over the strategic region of Rajasthan, Akbar became a devotee of the greatest of the Indian saints, Muinuddin, of the Chishtiyya brotherhood: from 1562 onwards, he got into the habit of going on a pilgrimage, at times on foot, to his tomb in Ajmer. In 1568, the saint appeared in a dream to the guards of his tomb to declare that Akbar had attained spiritual maturity and that he no longer needed to come there on a pilgrimage. Thereupon, he became a follower of a living saint this time, Salim Chishti, who interceded to obtain for him the divine favour of having three sons to perpetuate the dynasty – his first son, Salim, born in 1569, was to succeed him under the name of Jahangir. Akbar constructed his new capital, Fatehpur Sikri, around the tomb of Salim Chisti at his death in 1571. It was sanctified by the *baraka* of the saint.

Soon Akbar acquired the reputation of being a saint himself. In 1577, during a hunting trip, he experienced a mystical crisis. From 1582, he became a spiritual guide and started to enrol disciples. The candidate, admitted into the presence of the emperor in the Private Audience Hall, on a Sunday, the day of the sun, prostrated himself at his feet and swore to liberate himself from the customary forms of Islam based on blind imitation and to join the 'divine religion' (*din-i ilahi*) of the emperor. The high-ranking officials who were initiated into the new faith, very few in number after all is said and done – probably about twenty, including the Hindu Birbal –, considered Akbar as a Sufi master. His successors, including Aurangzeb, continued to initiate disciples, with Akbar retaining the reputation of being the perfect man, the greatest saint of his time. Miracles were attributed to him during his lifetime and even after his death.

This 'divine religion' that Akbar preached has given rise to certain misconceptions: the first translator of the *Ain-i Akbari*, H Blochmann, and following him, V Smith, saw it as a new syncretic religion built on apostasy. Fundamentalist Indian, and especially

Pakistani, historians have fallen in behind them and have projected Akbar as a rene-gade who seriously jeopardized Indian Islam. Yet, the initiation text speaks not only about the 'divine religion', but also about 'divine or Islamic uniqueness', about the 'four degrees of sincerity', and about 'submission to a Sufi master'. It does not require the follower to renounce Islam per se, but to eschew certain degenerated and irra-tional aspects of this religion. The 'divine religion' of Akbar thus remained within the sphere of influence of Islam, which was at the time heavily influenced by Sufism.

For all this, was it a humble and sincere faith? After 1585, Akbar never per-formed any act of devotion publicly, neither in a mosque nor in a tomb of a saint. The only tomb that he had ostensibly venerated was that of his father, Humayun, in Delhi. Ultimately, the emperor himself and his dynasty became objects of worship: the 'divine religion' had become an imperial cult.

It is in this perspective that we have to understand the official ideology exposed by Abul-Fazl in the *Akbar-nama* and in the *Ain-i Akbari*, between 1590 and 1595. More than just panegyrics, these works elucidate the imperial cult by reinterpreting the great themes of Sufism and of the Mongol legend in the language of the Iranian theosophy of a Suhrawardi: the emperor emanated from the divine light that had progressively revealed itself through the descendants of Genghis Khan and Timur; he received divine inspiration without any intermediary; he held in his hands both temporal and spiritual power to guide his subjects towards happiness and to spiritual realization. In other words, the emperor had confiscated for his own advantage the religious authority of the ulemas and the Sufis, from whom he demanded the strictest subordination. In religion as in politics, everything had to revolve around him. These claims, which could seem excessive to us, were routinely accepted in the Islamic world of the time, notably among the Safavids who had provided a prece-dent and without doubt a model.

Revolts and Compromises (1580–5)

In 1580–2, the most serious revolts facing Akbar in his long reign broke out in var-ious parts of the empire. The major pockets of rebellion were the eastern provinces of Bihar and Bengal, controlled at the time by officials of Central Asian origin, who had been the spearhead of the conquest. The revolt perhaps had a religious aspect to it, because the qadi of Jaunpur, who was a Shiite, decreed a *fatwa* condemning the religious innovations introduced by Akbar – the reason for which he would ultimately be put to death. Nevertheless, what annoyed the officials more than anything else was the impact of the administrative reforms, which had substantially scaled down their resources. The rebels seized the city of Patna and advanced towards Bengal where they repulsed the imperial armies that had been despatched to subdue them. All the while, discontent was brewing in the other provinces.

The revolt assumed another dimension when the insurgents of Bengal recited the *Khutba* in the name of Akbar's half brother, Muhammad Hakim Mirza, who held Kabul as his fief, thereby designating him the legitimate sovereign of India. Spurred on by this encouragement, the prince started to invade the Punjab. In 1581, Akbar himself had to lead a lightning campaign in Lahore and as far as Kabul where his half brother did not offer any resistance: he pardoned him and left him Kabul, which he would retain until his death in 1584.

In India, the rebels were pacified by a compromise before being forced into submission. Akbar offered them a scapegoat, the principal architect of the administrative centralization, Shah Mansur Shirazi, whose intransigence in the application of reforms had exposed him to public condemnation. Akbar resigned himself to condemning him to death, which he soon regretted because it transpired before long that the documents that had justified his condemnation were false. The death of Mansur Shirazi marked the end of excessive centralization. The *jagirs* were re-established and the rules for controlling the armed forces of the officials were relaxed.

The resulting compromise gave final shape to the organization of the empire, as described by Abul-Fazl twelve years later in the *Ain-i Akbari*. To make eastern India less vulnerable, Akbar constructed a fortress in Allahabad, in the median valley of the Ganges, at the confluence of the Jamuna, at the gates of Bihar and Bengal.

The territorial consolidation of the empire (1585–1601)

Once he had secured the solidity of his power, Akbar devoted himself to the task of expanding and consolidating the boundaries of his empire. He successfully focused his attention for some time on the northwest. Like his great grandfather Babur and his successors Jahangir and Shah Jahan, Akbar nurtured the secret hope of reconquering Central Asia. He was, however, apprehensive over the ascendancy of the Uzbek sultan Abdullah Khan (1556–98) and his designs on Kabul (which had become vulnerable following the death of Mirza Muhammad Hakim). To fend off this threat, Akbar transferred the court, abandoning Fatehpur Sikri for good (he would see it again only once in 1601), and created a new capital in Lahore where he resided for thirteen years. It would be the favourite residence of his son Jahangir.

After securing control of Kabul and after repulsing the Uzbek menace, Akbar pursued the expansion of his possessions. Towards the north, he seized Kashmir in 1586, which entered for the first time within the sphere of influence of Muslim India: it was to become the favourite summer residence of the Moguls. Nevertheless, it was attached – and this was a significant fact – to the province of Kabul. Baltistan and Ladakh, which were Tibetan provinces, also pledged their allegiance to Akbar. In the beginning of the following decade, the emperor concentrated his efforts on his western boundaries and annexed one after another Sind, Baluchistan and finally, the 'lock' of Kandahar, which was recaptured from the Safavids in 1594. The northwest was henceforth under control and pacified: the last indomitable Afghan tribes, stirred up by the Shiite sect of Raushaniyya, surrendered in 1600. At the death of Abdullah Khan in 1598, Akbar returned to Agra with the belief that he had averted all the threats.

The emperor could thereafter devote himself entirely to the Deccan, whose control he had endeavoured to secure since 1591. His son Murad, appointed the viceroy of the province, tried diplomacy first and then resorted to war. The sultanates of Khandesh and Ahmednagar surrendered for a while, but soon rose up in rebellion. Akbar dispatched Abul Fazl to the scene – this was the latter's first ordeal by fire –

arriving in person in 1599. He easily conquered Burhanpur, the capital of Khandesh, but came up against defence of the most formidable fortress of this sultanate, Asirgarh. The siege dragged on for two years; Akbar requested the assistance of the Portuguese artillery in vain; in the end he had to bribe the defenders into betrayal. The revolt of his son interrupted the Deccan campaign. Akbar could eventually take possession of only two and a half provinces: Kandesh, Berar and part of Ahmednagar. The Mogul Empire thus came to number fifteen provinces.

The rebellion of Prince Salim and the death of Akbar (1601–5)

The Moguls did not acknowledge the right of succession, and every change in the reign gave rise to wars between father and son or between brothers. During the four last years of his life, Akbar had to face the problems of his own succession. Salim, placed in charge of safeguarding Agra during his father's absence, seized the opportunity to revolt and took up position in the fort of Allahabad. In 1602, he succeeded in instigating the murder of Abul-Fazl, whom his father had sent to fight him. The conflict resolved on its own: Akbar's two younger sons, Murad and Danyal, having died of alcoholism in 1599 and 1604 respectively, Salim was the only possible successor, unless his own son Khusrau was to bypass him. Faced with this threat, Salim returned to Agra to surrender and after a few days of imprisonment, he was treated as crown prince.

Akbar died in September, 1605, in the fiftieth year of his reign, at the age of almost sixty-three years. He was buried without ceremony in the mausoleum that he had started to construct in Sikandara, near Agra. Salim, who ascended the throne as the emperor Jahangir, would replace it with a new grandiose monument. This tomb would be venerated as that of a saint and miracles would be attributed to it. In the wake of Mogul decadence, it would be pillaged by the Jats in 1791 and the remains of the emperor would be unearthed and burnt.

Myths surrounding Akbar

Beyond the contradictory images that are in vogue today, what portrait of Akbar are we to retain?

Akbar was certainly not an anti-Islamic apostate, as projected by those who have distorted the testimonies of the Portuguese, of disappointed ulemas, like Badauni, and of later Sufi hagiography. He did not cross the limits tolerated at that time and was never perceived as a non-Muslim in the Islamic world.

It is even more anachronistic to present him as the promoter of a secular state because religion was at the time an indispensable ingredient of political power. In reality, he confiscated for himself all forms of religious authority: according to the situation and his interlocutors, he used the most contradictory religious arguments: he preached in turns holy war and 'perfect reconciliation', legalistic Islam and the most liberal Sufism. Rather than syncretism, it would be more appropriate to speak of eclecticism aimed at developing, by any means, an imperial cult.

Neither was Akbar the promoter of a national state. The Mogul Empire remained a medieval Islamic formation, not unlike the Delhi sultanate, or the Safavid Empire and the Ottoman Empire: it was constructed so as to benefit a very small cosmopolitan elite class, most of whom were of foreign stock. Akbar opened the corridors of power to the Hindus, particularly the Rajputs: and yet, among the officials in the top and middle rungs of the hierarchy, Hindus accounted for less than twenty per cent and Muslims of Indian origin were even more under-represented. The Hindus were confined to administrative jobs and to the lower ranks of the army, whereas the honours and the profits of the empire were reserved first for the Turks and the Iranians. Akbar comes across above all as a clever politician who knew how to make the most of the ideas and tools of his time in view of establishing a well-governed empire that would be long-lasting. The exaltation of his dynasty was his great driving force, which, however, did not preclude him from showing a real interest for the most diverse aspects of religion and culture. Like most of the Sufis of the time, he believed that one could find the same God through various religious traditions; pursuing the reticent precedents of the sultanate of Delhi, he commissioned the translation of the great Hindu classics into Persian and was curious to discover all religions. Interested in all the arts, including music, he invited the best Indian singers to his court, including the famous Tansen. Robust and well built, he was keen on sports and hunting. Tradition has kept alive the memory of his vivacity and his kind-heartedness. Supervising every detail in the administration of the imperial household as well as that of the empire, he had the reputation of being attentive to everyone. He was 'great towards the great, small towards the small'.

The Hindu oral tradition, today recorded in the pamphlets found in every bazaar, has conserved the figure of a lackadaisical Akbar grappling with his Hindu disciple Birbal; the latter appears as his finance minister, which is not a historical fact. The emperor, who in the beginning tries to act smart, always ends up eating humble pie. Thus, one day, Akbar promised a huge amount of money to a man capable of spending an entire winter night in a pond of freezing water. A Brahmin passed the test. Akbar asked him how he managed to hold out that long. The man answered, 'All through the night, I contemplated the light that was shining at the window of your Majesty; this warmed my heart and I could hold out until the morning.' Akbar decreed that this was cheating and refused to give the promised sum. Birbal remained silent, but did not appear in the court the next day. Akbar went in search of him and found him in a garden of the palace. The minister had constructed an immense tripod with three bamboos and had hung a pot on the top. On the ground, between the bamboos, he was keeping a small fire going.

'What are you doing?' asked Akbar.

- 'I am cooking some rice for my food,' answered Birbal.
- 'Idiot! How can this fire heat a pot hung so far from it?'
- 'How could the distant light from your window warm the Brahmin immersed in the freezing water?'

Akbar declined to answer but gave the Brahmin the promised recompense.

VI

MOGUL SPLENDOUR

The successors of Akbar
(1605–1707)

After the death of Akbar, the Mogul Empire experienced almost a century of institutional stability while expansion towards the south continued reaching its apogee with Aurangzeb's conquest of the Deccan. There are innumerable testimonies to the splendour of the empire, provided in the first place by the empire itself. The writing of chronicles in Persian, a custom revived by Akbar, continued to be practised; literary works and miniatures richly illustrate life in the empire, just as the monuments and the cities still preserve its memory.

Testimonies borne by foreigners also become more abundant because the Portuguese, the only Europeans present under Akbar, had now been eclipsed by the British, the Dutch and subsequently the French. Traders, travellers and missionaries have left behind books and archives enabling us to reconstitute not only the economic history of the empire but also the ambience of everyday life.[1]

The Mogul Empire, reputed to be stable, came across as paradoxical to Westerners because every change in reign gave rise to wars between father and son or among brothers. In fact, according to the ideal of the caliphate, the most deserving candidate to the throne was 'elected'; dynastic succession was a fact, not a right. The Mogul rule is reminiscent of the one prevalent in the Ottoman empire in the sixteenth century, after the custom of systematically massacring co-heirs had been brought to an end, but before the institution of the practice of imprisoning the sons of the sultan or of choosing the most senior member of the lineage. Therefore in India, struggle to the death among the pretenders to the throne remained the rule: the son revolted against the father and brothers fought among themselves: the most famous example has been provided by Aurangzeb, who, in 1657–8, simultaneously eliminated his ageing father and his three brothers in order to accede to power.

Any candidate for power who wanted to secure his chances of success had to constitute a clientele of high officials (with their armed contingents) for himself. Indian historians call these interest groups 'factions', as they tend to underscore ethnic or religious alignments. In fact, the loyalties of these officials seem to have been motivated more by their own interests, the closeness of the family relation and above all the charisma of the pretenders than by ideological divides.

This struggle, however, had its own rules, which ensured the continuity of the empire. The winner could imprison his rivals and their closest associates; he could also blind them or (more rarely) put them to death. On the other hand, he was forbidden from taking revenge on the clients of his rivals, who were integrated into the service of the new emperor. In the eighteenth century, the systemization of vengeances like these, rare up till then, would be interpreted as a sign of the decadence of the empire.

Once his power had been made secure, the emperor engaged himself in conserving, and if possible, extending his territory. This presupposed constant use of the armed forces, always paraded to instil fear but very rarely employed. Within the empire, rebellion was in effect endemic: local chiefs integrated into the empire, or who were vassals in the marches, showed a ready disposition to lead their peasants in revolt. The success of the empire depended primarily on the maintenance of a precarious order with a view to ensuring good tax revenues.

Another way to enhance power and income consisted of extending the limits of the empire. Towards the west and the north, Akbar seemed to have reached its natural frontiers: even so, until Shah Jahan, the Moguls would attempt to reconquer Central Asia, the land of their ancestors. In the northeast, they would colonize eastern Bengal (Dacca is a Mogul creation) and advance towards the virgin lands of Assam. However, it was in the South that the most enticing treasures existed: the sultanates of Bijapur and Golconda, both of which had been enriched by the conquest of Vijayanagar, and which ruled the entire south of India, had resisted Akbar. The conquest of these two sultanates would remain the overriding obsession of the Moguls throughout the seventeenth century.

These attempts at expansion had repercussions on the relations that the Great Moguls maintained with the neighbouring empires. Safavid Iran blocked the positions in the northwest but in a certain way also encircled the Mogul Empire, because it had ideological and economic interests in the Shiite sultanates of the Deccan, whose resistance it encouraged. These rivalries resulted in the comings and goings of embassies, punctuated by episodes of war, between the Mogul court and the Safavid court and vice versa. Hereafter isolated from the Ottomans by the rise into supremacy of Western fleets in the Indian Ocean, the Moguls had only sporadic relations with them. But for all that, exchanges between India and the rest of the Muslim world were not limited to these affairs. The land routes by way of Iran and Central Asia as far as Istanbul and the Arab world were used up until the disorders of the eighteenth century. Similarly, maritime routes continued to be in use, notably the pilgrimage route to Mecca, with the Portuguese safe-conduct and subsequently – thanks to the obliging favour of the British and the Dutch, because the Moguls never possessed a fleet worthy of the name – on the one hand India was connected to the Persian Gulf, the Red Sea and eastern Africa (from where slaves continued to arrive) and on the other, its networks extended towards the East Indian islands and China. On these terrestrial and maritime routes, traders, pilgrims, Sufis and ulemas in the quest for science travelled, disseminating Mogul culture all across Asia, thanks to Persian being the current lingua franca. They also played an important role in the islamization of the East Indian islands.

Jahangir (1605–27): a reign without great eclat

Of all the Mogul emperors, Jahangir is without doubt the one whose personality we know the best. The Persian chronicles and the accounts of the early ambassadors and traders, notably that of the British ambassador, Thomas Roe, who resided four years in his court, and of his chaplain Terry, as well as Dutch sources, give us abundant information on this very genial and complex figure.

More than all this, Jahangir has himself left us his testimony. Educated by the great scholars of his time, including Abdurrahim Khan-i Khanan (1556–1627) – the son of Akbar's tutor, Bairam Khan – he revived the tradition of autobiography inaugurated by his great grandfather Babur. His memoirs, the *Tuzuk-i Jahangiri*, form an almost complete account of his reign. Like Babur, he makes sincere confessions, without hiding his weaknesses, in particular his fondness for alcohol, which he could never get over. Contemplative rather than active, and generally affable, he was also capable of fits of anger and vengeance, which shocked western observers.

Like his grandfather, the new emperor loved nature, landscapes and gardens, which occupy a predominant place in the paintings of his reign. Unlike his father, he was not a builder of cities, but he constructed tombs – Akbar's and his own – he also supervised the decoration of palaces, notably the one in Lahore, but above all designed gardens, those in Kashmir are still famous today. In this respect, he takes after Babur.

Oral tradition portrays him as a romantic. In his youth, Jahangir is said to have fallen madly in love with a servant, Anarkali. To put an end to this love affair, Akbar is said to have immured the loved one alive in a mausoleum at Lahore, which can be visited today and which houses a tombstone carrying a mysterious inscription; 'mad [with love] [*majnun*], Salim, son of Akbar'. The legend of his marriage with the beautiful Nur Jahan draws inspiration from the story of David and the wife of Uri; he apparently sent the husband of the future empress on an expedition to meet his death in a war so that he could marry her.

No sooner had Jahangir acceded to power in 1605 than his sovereignty was challenged. A faction led by the Rajput Mansingh tried in vain to propel his son Khusrau to the throne. Six months later, Khusrau in turn revolted. He left the court and formed a power base in the provinces of Lahore and Kabul, with the help of his faction of high officials – who were numerous since he was so popular – and with the full blessing of certain Sufis and even of the guru of the Sikhs, Arjun (died 1606).[2]

Often indecisive, Jahangir reacted this time with promptness. He launched himself in the pursuit of Khusrau; in less than three weeks, he defeated his army half way between Lahore and Peshawar. His vengeance – perhaps a sign of his weakness – was uncommonly cruel: he put the guru Arjun to death; on the way back, near Lahore, he ordered from two hundred to eight hundred of Khusrau's partisans to be hanged or impaled and obliged his rebellious son to review the dead bodies. Following a new conspiracy, Khusrau was wounded in the eyes, but his injuries were not serious and he recovered his vision. He would remain a prisoner until 1622 (he was then probably assassinated by his younger brother Khurram, the future Shah Jahan). Another younger brother, Parvez, was proclaimed heir to the throne.

In 1611, Jahangir fell in love with a lady of the court, of Iranian origin, the famous Nur Jahan (light of the world) whose husband had died four years earlier in Bengal under mysterious circumstances after being accused of treason. This marriage marked a turning point in the history of Jahangir. Around the new queen soon formed a new faction under the leadership of her father, Itimaduddaula, and her brother, Asaf Khan, who gave his daughter Mumtaz Mahal in marriage to Khurram, who used Nur Jahan to seize the throne for him. As time went by and Jahangir became increasingly disinterested in the affairs of kingdom and increasingly sunk in alcoholism, Nur Jahan acquired more and more influence and acted as the true head of the state; in what is an exceptional historical fact, even coins were for some time struck in her name.

Jahangir is reputed to have been diligent in observing the etiquette of the court, always punctual in his audiences and zealous to dispense impartial judgements. Even though, like all the Moguls, he nurtured ambitions of territorial expansion, his achievements were limited. In the north, he contented himself with subjugating the pockets of rebellion that had been brewing since the time of Akbar; in Rajasthan, he forced the last recalcitrant Rajputs of Mewar into submission: in Bengal, he built the new provincial capital of Dacca (initially called Jahangirabad). His most illustrious conquest was the capture of the fortress at Kangra, in the Himalayas, to the north of the Punjab. Habitually tolerant, he celebrated this campaign like a holy war; to humiliate the defeated, he committed a deliberate sacrilege: he ordered the defilement of the temple that dominated the fortress by slaughtering cows in the precincts. Less impressive was his accomplishment in the Deccan, where he waged a war of attrition against the Abyssinian chief of war, Malik Anbar, who commanded the troops of Ahmadnagar: the city was soon lost to the Moguls. His reign plunged into even greater gloom with the outbreak of a plague that ravaged the empire from 1616 to 1624.

From the beginning of his reign, relations with the Portuguese and the English had been growing more complicated. Jahangir forged cordial relationships with the Portuguese through the mediation of the Jesuits who resided in the court; he sent an embassy to Goa in 1607–8. During this time, the first British envoy, Captain W Hawkins arrived at the court and gained concessions that broke the monopoly of the Portuguese, who protested and procured the revocation of these benefits. Acts of war ensued: the British defeated a Portuguese fleet; on the other hand, acts of piracy perpetrated by the Portuguese against Mogul ships triggered an imperial retaliation against the trading post of Daman, while the Jesuits and their converts were persecuted for some time. Henceforth, the Moguls would play the British against the Portuguese. From 1615 to 1619, the first embassy sent by King James I was received at the court; it was led by Thomas Roe, who, failing to negotiate a formal treaty, nevertheless obtained substantial commercial concessions; these were the starting point for the establishment of the powerful English East India Company in India.

As for relations with the Safavid Iran, they seemed idyllic for a long time. Shah Abbas I (1587–1629) convinced Jahangir that he sought to maintain peace with him; he even disowned the governor of Herat who had launched an attack on Kandahar in 1606; from 1610 to 1622, the two emperors tried to outdo each other in letters, gifts and sumptuous embassies. Jahangir believed in the sincerity of his interlocutor: in 1602, he represented himself in a miniature embracing the Iranian ruler, while before them a lion and a lamb slept in peace on a globe. When Abbas I attacked Kandahar in 1622, the garrison had only three hundred soldiers and could not offer any resistance. Jahangir tried in vain to make an alliance with the Uzbeks in an effort to recapture the fortress.

With respect to religious affairs, Jahangir seems to have led a conciliatory policy. Several episodes of his reign, however, have given rise to debatable interpretations. The execution of Guru Arjun has been considered a sign of hostility towards the Sikhs, while it was aimed at quelling the revolt of Khusrau and members of all the communities were condemned: a Sufi, Shaikh Nizam Thaneshwari, was in fact exiled and sent to Mecca. It is true that, with the faction of Nur Jahan rising into prominence, Iranians were increasingly represented among the high officials of the empire, but does this necessarily suggest that the emperor showed a predilection for the Shiah sect? Historians have often discerned, erroneously, a sectarian motivation in the alignments of factions, which were in fact determined by sheer expediency.

The rule of Jahangir has also been distorted by a modern myth derived from Sufi hagiography. The emperor is presumed to have triggered an orthodox reaction against the heterodoxy of Akbar under the influence of a Sufi of the Naqshbandiyya brotherhood, Ahmad Sirhindi (1564–1624). In effect, according to Jahangir's memoirs, this Sufi, towards the end of his life, claimed to be superior to the early caliphs: in 1619, Jahangir summoned the imposter to the court demanding an explanation: in the face of his arrogance, the emperor wrote 'I have reached the conclusion that the best thing for him was to imprison him to calm his agitation and his confusion.' The Sufi was consigned to imprisonment for one year in the fortress at Gwalior and released with gifts including a robe of honour and money. The testimony of the emperor was unequivocal: it was Sirhindi who stood accused of heterodoxy (he was to retain this reputation even under Aurangzeb). Jahangir therefore appeared as a defender of the official orthodoxy.

The religious views of Jahangir fell in line with the legacy of Akbar; it remained within the sphere of influence of Islam, but following a liberal and ecumenical approach. He loved the company of Sufis of various orders, whose presence, if we are to give credence to a miniature of his reign, he even preferred to that of kings, which did not prevent him from assiduously frequenting a Hindu yogi called Jadrup.

During the last five years of his life, debilitated by alcohol and illness, having abdicated all power, Jahangir was at the mercy of the two factions that prepared his succession. Khurram, the future Shah Jahan, revolted as early as 1622, refusing to go and combat the Iranians at Kandahar: pushed back towards the Deccan, he awaited the death of his father, having secured the support of his father-in-law, Asaf Khan, the brother of Nur Jahan. In the meantime, the empress was manoeuvring to place on the throne Shahryar, who was both her stepson (born to Jahangir out of a previous marriage) and her son-in-law (husband of a daughter born from her first marriage). The astute Mahabbat Khan, loyal to Jahangir, tried in vain to free the emperor from the influence of Nur Jahan by abducting him; he had to flee and join Khurram in the Deccan.

Jahangir died in November 1627, while he was on his return from Kashmir to spend the winter at Lahore. Shahryar, who was on the scene, was the first proclaimed emperor. But doomed by his incompetence, he was forthwith dismissed by Asaf Khan, who blinded him and proclaimed Shah Jahan emperor. Returning in haste from the Deccan, the new sovereign massacred all his male attendants.

Shah Jahan (1628–58): The builder and the patron of the arts

An ambitious emperor

The history of Shah Jahan has been neglected since the monumental biography by H B P Saksena, published in 1932.[3]

The new emperor came across to western travellers as cold, enigmatic and ruthless. The profuse official documentation concerning the reign of this ambitious emperor indulgently describe the public man and the ritual of his court, which reached its greatest splendour under him. Shah Jahan contrasted with the feeble and hesitant Jahangir. Possessed of decisiveness right from the war of succession, he walked over the corpses of his brothers to reach the throne, and consolidated his authority by immediately repressing the first rebellions sparked off by the Rajputs and Muslim high officials. First, he transferred his capital from Lahore to Agra. Far from being content with preserving his inheritance as his father had been, he launched an ambitious policy of large-scale construction projects and of expansion in the Deccan and even towards Central Asia.

From the beginning of his reign, notwithstanding the terrible famine of 1630–1632, Shah Jahan indulged in costly expenditures in his effort to embellish the empire. From 1628 to 1635, he spent one million rupees for the making of the throne decorated with peacocks, a potent symbol of Mogul splendour.

In 1631, the death of his favourite wife, Mumtaz Mahal, set before him the occasion to inaugurate the new style which gave its identity to Mogul architecture: in 1632, he launched the construction of her mausoleum in Agra, the famous Taj Mahal (corruption of 'Mumtaz Mahal'), which would be completed with its gardens only in 1643.

All the buildings of the Agra fort, which would serve him as his palace until 1648, were reconstructed in the new style: those of the fort of Lahore were also altered. The magnum opus of his reign was certainly the construction of the new capital of Shajahanabad in Delhi from 1638 onwards, on the banks of the river Jamuna. In this grandiose city, the two principal arteries – bazaars watered by canals – are perpendicular to each other and converge on the citadel in the northeast, the Red Fort, which is the palace of the emperor. The ramparts of the fort are made of sandstone, but white marble is predominant in the palatial buildings. The court moved to Shahjahanabad in 1648, reinvesting the historical seat of the sultanate of Delhi, and of Humayun: the Moguls would reside there until the revolt of 1857, which enabled the British to abolish what was then left of the dynasty.

Readily posing as the renovator of Islam, Shah Jahan also commissioned the construction of an impressive series of mosque-cathedrals – most of them in sand-stone – in the capitals of Delhi, Agra and Lahore and in several provincial towns. It was under his reign that Mogul painting reached its zenith: his school is character-ized by portraits, notably that of the emperor and the princes, miniatures being more and more often inserted in albums to the detriment of illustrated books.

Conflicts, conquests and failures

The establishment of western trading posts continued under the reign of Shah Jahan. But the Portuguese, who had settled down and consolidated themselves in Hoogly, in the lower delta of the Ganges, exasperated the emperor for two reasons: they engaged themselves in the raiding and trading of slaves on a large scale: besides the monopoly of salt that had been conceded to them, they levied exorbitant cus-toms duties, notably on the newly introduced tobacco. Shah Jahan despatched an imperial army of one hundred thousand men to sack the fort of Hoogly in 1632. In further retaliation, Christians were persecuted all across the empire until 1635; they would never again receive the preferential treatment that they had thus far enjoyed. Hoogly was later reopened: but it was never to recover its former prosperity. The advance of the British would be marked by the foundation of Madras in 1639.

The first great design of Shah Jahan was certainly the subjugation of the Deccan. It transpires that initially Shah Jahan, like Akbar in his time, had only sought to bring the two remaining big sultanates, Bijapur and Golconde, to surrender as vassals and not to conquer them.

The campaign started from the beginning of his reign. The emperor camped at Burhanpur, in the defunct kingdom of Khandesh, his stay interrupted in 1631 by the death of his wife, Mumtaz Mahal. His officials pursued the war and bribed the chief of the armies of Ahmadnagar, Fath Khan, son of Malik Anbar, who assassinated the ruling sultan to replace him with his son, Husain Nizam Shah, still only a child. Fath Khan's act of treason gave the Moguls a pretext to annex Ahmadnagar.

In the meantime, Shah Jahan had ordered Asaf Khan to lay siege to Bijapur, on the grounds that its sultan, Muhammad Adil Khan (1626–56), was illegitimate; a war of attrition that devastated the country ensued. A second Mogul offensive in 1635 was more successful. Shah Jahan sent the two sultans an ultimatum enjoining them to accept his suzerainty. The ruler of Golconda, deprived of all means of resistance, capitulated immediately; he struck coins in the name of Shah Jahan, ordered that the Friday sermon be recited in his name and paid an annual tribute. The sultan of Bijapur refused to surrender: he saved his capital by flooding its approaches, but his country was ravaged by three Mogul armies. It must be pointed out that in the course of the conflict the Hindu Maratha soldiery made its appearance for the first time in history: it fought for Bijapur under the direction of Shahji Bhonsle, the father of Shivaji, who would neu-tralize Mogul power in the Deccan under the reign of Aurangzeb. Muhamed Adil Khan had to surrender and recognize the suzerainty of the Moguls under terms better that those subscribed by Golconda: he undertook by virtue of a treaty signed in 1636 to pay a peace indemnity (and not a tribute) of two million rupees, to respect the fron-tiers of Golconda and to abstain from helping the Marathas.

It is at this time that the prince Aurangzeb, the future emperor, then eighteen years old, was appointed the viceroy of the Deccan, the administration of which proved to be very tricky. He stayed there for eight years, from 1636 to 1644. After a leave of one year, he became the governor of Gujarat before being sent to Central Asia.

From the beginning of his reign, Shah Jahan had nurtured the desire to re-conquer the land of his ancestors around Samarkand in Central Asia: he was also keen to recover Kandahar. With a view to realizing these ambitions, he lowered the guard of the Safavids by giving them an opulent embassy and, in secret, bought the governor of Kandahar, who delivered him the city in 1638 and then entered his service.

In 1646, he took advantage of the dynastic quarrels among the Uzbeks and launched the most audacious expedition of his reign. His son Murad Bakhsh was sent at the head of an army to conquer Central Asia. He succeeded in gaining control of Balkh and Badakhshan, halfway between Kabul and Samarkand, but hating the country, he requested to be relieved of his command. He was replaced by his brother Aurangzeb, who won another battle against the Uzbeks. The reluctance of his officers to continue the war, then the intervention of the Safavids in the conflict forced him to retreat in 1647 under disastrous circumstances.

This was the end of the dream of reconquering Central Asia. However, the emperor would always have his eyes fixed on this cradle of the dynasty; during his entire reign, he would favour officials of Turanian origin, appointing them to the highest positions. Diplomatic relations with the Ottomans would remain sporadic and formal.

Shah Jahan did not have any more luck with Kandahar. The new Safavid king Shah Abbas II (1642–66) reinvested the city in 1649 and reinforced it in order to resist the Moguls. Aurangzeb was despatched, but twice, in 1649 and 1652, he failed to recapture the city. A third siege in the following year under the direction of Shah Jahan's first son, Dara Shukoh (1615–59), also failed deplorably. The Moguls, incapable of equalling the military techniques of the Iranians, had to renounce Kandahar.

With the interlude of their dreams of annexing Central Asia coming to a close, the Moguls turned their attention again to the Deccan, their land of natural expansion. Disowned for his failures in Balkh and in Kandahar, Aurangzeb was once again appointed viceroy of the Deccan and resided in Aurangabad, which was to become a new capital. First, he had to make good the negligence of the governors who had replaced him during the nine years of his absence and who were incapable of organizing the levy of taxes properly. To do so, he employed the services of a 'finance minister' (diwan) of Iranian origin, Murshid Quli Khan, who extended to the Deccan the practice of registering the population established in North India under Akbar. He restored the confidence of the peasantry and brought prosperity back to the region.

At the same time, under his impetus, the nature of Mogul politics changed. The viceroy was no longer content with just the allegiance of Golconda and Bijapur: he wanted to annex them to appropriate their riches, which were reputedly fabulous. Aurangzeb's ambitions were favoured by the act of treason committed by an Iranian adventurer, Mir Jumla, who had become the mayor of the palace of the sultan of Golconda, Abdullah Qutb Shah. Both a trader and a warlord, Mir Jumla had carved a principality out for himself on the east coast and had his own army, with European artillerymen. Threatened by his sovereign who wanted to take back control of affairs, he went over to the Mogul side and helped Aurangzeb conquer Hyderabad, which was pillaged, and then lay siege to the fortified city of Golconda: only an order from Shah Jahan forced Aurangzeb to withdraw after increasing the tribute money exacted from the sultan.

Taking advantage of the problematic succession of Muhammad Adil Khan, who died in 1656, Aurangzeb undertook the conquest of Bijapur with the help of Mir Jumla. Again, the intervention of Shah Jahan, under pressure from Dara Shukoh, saved Bijapur, whose sultan had to sign a new treaty of vassalage in 1657. Aurangzeb had, in the course of this war, his first skirmishes with the new chief of the Marathas, Shivaji.

Bijapur and Golconda gained a respite. However, during his second and brief viceroyalty, Aurangzeb had unveiled the policy that he would pursue once he acceded to the throne and which would lead, thirty years later, to the annexation of the two last sultanates of the Deccan.

A tragic war of succession (1657–8)

The intrigues of Aurangzeb in the Deccan were interrupted by the outbreak of the war of succession. In November 1657, Shah Jahan fell seriously ill. His four sons had gained a seasoned experience in political and military affairs. The first son, Dara Shukoh, who was residing in the capital, had been designated by his father as his successor because he had been closely associated in the affairs of the empire. The other three were in the provinces (Aurangzeb in the Deccan, Shuja in Bengal and Murad Bakhsh in Gujarat), where they had at their disposal a considerable number of contingents, and they joined forces against Dara Shukoh.

Shuja and Murad Bakhsh took the first step by proclaiming themselves as kings each in his own province; Aurangzeb followed suit in the Deccan where he was in a position of force and where he could count on the army and the artillery of Mir Jumla. In April 1653, he advanced towards the north and joined Murad Bakhsh. The two brothers fought the first imperial army in Dharmat, near Ujjain. The following month, in Samugarh, near Agra, they repulsed a more powerful army commanded by Dara Shukoh in person.

The war of succession swung from then on in their favour, or rather in favour of Aurangzeb, who, henceforth in a position to call the tune, set his mind on eliminating his father and his brothers. He first forced the capitulation of the fort of Agra, where he consigned Shah Jahan to imprisonment, then succeeded in condemning Murad Bakhsh to death for the murder of his 'finance minister' in Gujarat (he would be executed in 1661). Shuja was pursued across Bengal as far as Dacca by Mir Jumla, who forced him to take refuge on the Burmese coast of Arakan, where he died under mysterious circumstances; Aurangzeb's first son, Muhammad Sultan, who had rallied to his cause, was imprisoned; he would eventually be executed in 1676.

As for Dara Shukoh, Aurangzeb, then his officers pursued him across Delhi, Lahore and Multan, as far as the Indus Valley, Gujarat and Rajasthan, where he was defeated in April 1659. He was captured following an act of treachery in Sind, while he was attempting to escape to Iran. He was brought to Delhi, paraded around the city; Aurangzeb obtained against him a death penalty in due form on the charges of heresy and executed him in 1659.

Some historians have interpreted this conflict of succession as a war of religion that opposed, in the person of Aurangzeb, a pure Islam, allowing no concession to Hinduism, and a syncretic religion favourable to Hinduism, epitomized in the person of Dara Shukoh: the latter had in effect meditated at length on the Hindu scriptures and had written works on the 'convergence' of Hinduism and of Islam. But the issues at stake were not that simple: Dara Shukoh was condemned on the charges of heresy (*ilhad*) and not of apostasy (*irtidad*); his condemnation was grounded in reasons internal to the Muslim community and not related to his relations with Hinduism. The factions that supported Dara and Aurangzeb did not align on the basis of religious divides and there were as many Hindus on one side as the other. What spelt the doom of Dara Shukoh in the final analysis was his reputation as a very poor politician; he did not inspire confidence. We must therefore not project into such a distant past modern religious divides; in this war of succession, as in so many others, divides were above all motivated by political expediency, while personal charisma played a vital role.

An appraisal of the reign

After pathetic protestations against his imprisonment, Shah Jahan had to resign himself to living in the seraglio of the palace of Agra, where he spent the final eight years of his life under strict surveillance, with his letters censored. Cared for by his highly cultured daughter Jahanara, he shared his time between his devotions and the women of his harem. He breathed his last in 1666 and was hastily buried near his favourite wife in the Taj Mahal.

Notwithstanding the failure of his unrealistic Central Asian policy, Shah Jahan extended Mogul power by forcing its sovereignty on the Deccan. By the sumptuousness of his reign, he revived the tradition of Akbar: like him, he was a great constructor and encouraged all the arts, in particular music. He also perpetuated his policy of tolerance and his alliance with the Hindu aristocracy: like his favourite son Dara Shukoh, he showed a great interest for the cultures and religions of India.

He nevertheless deemed it fitting at times to underline Islamic orthodoxy (as had Akbar and Jahangir on certain occasions). Projecting himself as a staunch defender of the Law, he ordered the destruction of recently constructed Hindu temples and posed as a renovator of Islam by the constructing of new mosques.

Aurangzeb (1658–1707): a controversial figure

As the restorer of Islamic orthodoxy and the saviour of the Muslim community in the eyes of Muslim fundamentalists, Aurangzeb (1658–1707) attracted the hatred of militant Hindus who attributed to him the systematic destruction of temples and large-scale forced conversions. According to a tenacious legend, he filled seventy-four and a half chariots (*sic*) with the sacred threads torn away from the shoulders of Brahmins, whom he forced to embrace Islam. Many have construed this return to orthodoxy as the principal cause of the decline of the Mogul Empire. This Manichean image needs radical correction.

The early conquests (1658–66)

During the first eight years of his reign, while his father was still alive, Aurangzeb pursued a policy not very different from that of his predecessors. Wary of altering the *modus vivendi* established with the various stakeholders of the empire, he exerted himself to justify his seizure of power by proving his capacity as a conqueror. He launched offensives on several fronts and expanded the territory by bringing Rajasthan and Bihar under Mogul control.

First, in the northeast, his astute general Mir Jumla conquered in 1661 the kingdom of Cooch Bihar; he navigated the Brahmaputra River against the current with an imposing fleet and in the spring of 1662 subdued Assam; this campaign brought enormous spoils, but the Moguls had to relinquish Assam after four years. In Bengal, they had more enduring successes: Shayista Khan, the son of Asaf Khan, was appointed its governor in 1664 and swept the region clean of Portuguese and Arakanese pirates, who were engaged in slave trade; in 1666, he recaptured the port of Chittagong (a Burmese coastal province, bordering Bengal) from the king of Arakan. A strategic outpost, Chittagong would remain the principal commercial port of call before entering the waters of the delta.

In Deccan, the results were more equivocal. Prior to his campaign in Bengal, Shayista Khan had been despatched to this region to face the threat of the Maratha chief, Shivaji. The latter succeeded in penetrating Shayista Khan's camp under cover of darkness. He cut off three of his fingers and killed his son. Shayista Khan, recalled to the north, was replaced by Aurangzeb's son, Muazzam. Accompanied by the Rajput Jaisingh, he succeeded through diplomacy in convincing Shivaji to sign a treaty of vassalage (1665). But the Maratha appeared in the hall of public audience in Agra in 1666, where, discontent with the humble rank granted to him in the Mogul hierarchy, he refused to submit himself to the etiquette: it is even said that he sat in the presence of the emperor. Imprisoned in the fort of Gwalior, he succeeded in escaping and resumed guerrilla warfare in the Deccan.

Shivaji and the power of the Marathas

The Marathas, a peasant caste of the region of Maharashtra, in the southwest of the peninsula, were subject to the sultanates of Ahmadnagar and Bijapur and constituted support troops for the sultanates in their fight against the Moguls. They soon rallied under their own banner under the leadership of Shivaji (1630–80). This young charismatic chief, who was to distinguish himself by his ability to incite his troops to action, was the son of a high official of Ahmadnagar who had entered the service of Bijapur. He started his career as a warlord when he was only an adolescent, annexing forts, recruiting an army of infantrymen and then of cavalry-men, and built an important principality. In 1659, by treachery, he routed the army of Bijapur sent to defeat him under the direction of general Afzal Khan; the latter was assassinated and four thousand horses captured. In 1664, after getting rid of the Mogul governor Shayistha Khan, he launched his first audacious raid in Gujarat to plunder with complete impunity the port of Surat, then the most important port of India.

In 1670, following his deceptive submission to Aurangzeb, he began to extort money from the Mogul territory. In Khandesh, he exacted one quarter of the rev-enue (*chauth*) in exchange for his protection; in the event of non-compliance, he reserved himself the right to pillage the recalcitrant villages; the *chauth* was to become the instrument for establishing his power all over India. In the same year, he sacked Surat a second time.

It was then that Shivaji revived the ancient Hindu ceremony of coronation in 1674 to legitimise his power. This happened concurrently with the upsurge of Aurangzeb's push towards orthodoxy (the two phenomena were perhaps linked to each other). Proclaiming the reign of Hinduism (*hindu padshahi*) in the territories under his control, he declared himself the protector of cows, Brahmins and gods. He relentlessly extended his supremacy over the south of the peninsula until his death in 1680. His son Sambhaji succeeded him.

The revolt of Shivaji was only one among the numerous rebellions that shook the empire from 1666 onwards.

A series of rebellions (1666–81)

Revolts were endemic in the Mogul Empire where the aristocracy, few in number and for the most part of foreign stock, was always obliged to display its strength in order to ensure obedience and the levy of taxes. However, the great revolts that flared up after 1666 were considered atypical by the chroniclers of the age.

Even as Shivaji was flouting the Moguls in the Deccan, in their own territory and plundered Surat with impunity, in the very heart of the empire, between Agra and Delhi, the Jats of the region of Mathura spurred a mass revolt in 1669, then in 1681 and 1688. They would continue to pose a threat to the security of the great Mogul capitals until the end of the reign and even further. The popular imagination was particularly shocked by a revolt of rogues in the region of Narnaul, about a hundred kilometres to the southwest of Delhi: the incident involved the Satnamis, a mystical sect of 'miserable rebels: goldsmiths, carpenters, sweepers, tanners and other igno-ble beings', in the words of a chronicler. It is one of the rare occasions when the Mogul chroniclers portray artisans: and needless to say, the revolt was drowned in blood.

Dissidence was also endemic in the northwest of the empire for nearly ten years: Aurangzeb had to come in person to Peshawar in 1674 and appointed an iron-fisted governor in Kabul in order to restore peace in Afghanistan. The Sikhs of the Punjab were outraged by the execution of their guru Tegh Bahadur in 1675; an attempted assassination against Aurangzeb was committed in the great mosque of Lahore.

The crisis that shook the empire the most was the revolt of Marwar, in Rajasthan. Its prince, Jaswant Singh, who was also a Mogul high official, died childless in 1678. Aurangzeb wanted to take advantage of this situation to annex the greater part of the principality and place on the throne a man of straw, Indar Singh. On the other hand, the Rajputs asserted the rights of a posthumous son of the prince, Ajit Singh. A war ensued, dragging on until 1681, and which was marked by the rebellion of one of Aurangzeb's sons, Akbar: despatched to subdue the revolts, he went over to the side of the enemy and had to seek refuge with the Marathas and from there fled to Iran, where he died.

A lot of ink has been spilled over this Rajput war, as it was at this juncture that the religious reforms of Aurangzeb came into force.

Reaffirmation of religious orthodoxy

As early as 1662 Aurangzeb commissioned a bureau of ulemas to compile a monumental compendium of Islamic law in Arabic entitled *Al-fatawa al-alamgiriyya* (or *Al fatawa al-Hindiyya*), which remains authoritative even today throughout the Muslim world.

From 1669, the emperor took a series of measures destined to bring the law in force closer to the ideal of the Islamic Law; he interdicted the construction of new temples and ordered the destruction of recent temples, discouraged the teaching of Hinduism and encouraged conversions to Islam. The emperor even put an end to a certain number of rites revolving around his own person that had overtones of idolatry. He stopped appearing before the crowd in the morning at the window of his palace and having himself weighed against gold or silver on the occasion of his birthdays. He forbade the writing of the chronicles of his reign and he discouraged music and painting. Non-Muslims had to pay higher customs duties than those imposed on Muslims. The move that sparked off the most vehement protests was the reimposition in 1679 of the *jizya*, the discriminatory poll tax on non-Muslims (*dhimmi*), which Akbar had abolished. Aurangzeb thus reinstated the Islamic ideal of discrimination between Muslims and non-Muslims.

The reasons and the aims of measures like these are not always very apparent.[4] In fact, they were part of the typical arsenal of the ulemas and the Sufis, who were the most concerned about compliance with the Law. Akbar could reduce them to silence because he was in a position of force. But the spate of rebellions had placed Aurangzeb in a difficult situation, and religious reforms presented a means of rallying the Muslim Sunnite population to present a united front against the Hindu rebels and the Shiite sultans of the Deccan.[5] These reforms were introduced only in the second decade of his reign, and were rescinded during the closing years. In fact, they were only a measure of expediency. In the same way, it is incorrect to make the conflict with the Rajputs into a religious war. Hostilities were limited to the principalities of Marwar and Mewar; the other Rajputs remained loyal to the emperor. The reaffirmation of orthodoxy was therefore primarily aimed at mobilizing the favour of the ulemas (who, by the way, were also beneficiaries of the profits derived from the *jizya*): we must not make Aurangzeb out to be more devout than he was.

Imbroglio in the Deccan

After the conclusion of the Rajput conflict, Aurangzeb turned his attention exclusively towards the Deccan, where he stayed until his death, residing in his new capital of Aurangabad or in camps during his numerous campaigns. In order to situate these campaigns in the international context, it is worthwhile to recapitulate the development of trading companies under the reign of Aurangzeb.

The Portuguese lost all importance in the second half of the seventeenth century. The sphere of the Danish was confined to their trading post of Tranquebar, on the east coast; the French established themselves in Pondicherry only in 1674 and had hardly any weight before the following century. The two most important companies were therefore those of the Dutch and the English.

Apart from the rise to prominence of the English, what marked the end of the seventeenth century was a shift in the centre of gravity of international commerce from the west to the east. By way of sea around the peninsula, just as overland through Agra, Delhi and the Ganges Valley, merchants traded increasingly with the Coromandel coast (which would be integrated into the Mogul empire at the end of the seventeenth century) and with Bengal, which became one of the richest provinces of the empire; inland cities, in particular Patna, became important for textiles and saltpetre. Thus emerged the configuration that would pave the way for the British conquest with Bengal as its base.

In his long campaigns in the Deccan, Aurangzeb no doubt pursued a two-fold objective. It is certain that he wanted firstly to destroy the rising power of the Marathas. But it is not impossible that he also wanted to appropriate the agrarian revenues as well as the commercial revenues of the Coromandel ports that were then experiencing spectacular growth. Until 1684, he employed modest means, hesitating to embark on the conquest of the sultanates of Bijapur and Golconda, as he had done under the reign of his father. He used diplomacy and attempted to join forces with them to present a united front against the Marathas. He did not succeed, however. Subsequently, Aurangzeb decided to employ considerable resources to subjugate the sultanates in order to fight the Marathas later. Bijapur capitulated without offering any resistance in 1686, but despite a protracted siege, the Moguls could not make a breach into the formidable fortress of Golconda: they had to bribe some of its defenders into opening the city for them.

In the wake of this twin victory, the Moguls found themselves alone against the Marathas, who henceforth formed the principal political force of the Deccan. Was it expedient to provoke them into war or to cajole them by diplomacy? Many high officials, like the Hindu Bhimsen, were favourable to the latter solution; Aurangzeb opted for the former. He believed that he had achieved his goal in 1689 when his troops captured Sambhaji, the son and successor of Shivaji; he ordered his execution and kept his son Shahu as hostage, thereby hoping to control the Marathas. In fact, in 1691, he levied tribute as far as Tanjore and Trichinopoly, in the extreme southeast of the subcontinent. This was the apogee of Mogul power.

However, this victory was illusory, as the Marathas had not given up their fight. After the death of Sambhaji, his brother Rajaram, and subsequently his sister-in-law,

Tara Bai, ruled as regents. Their relentless attacks demoralized the Moguls, whose administration deteriorated. Far from bringing wealth, the conquest of the Deccan proved to be a drain on the imperial finances. Aurangzeb simultaneously employed persuasion and force: he recruited the Muslims of the Deccan and Marathas en masse, appointing them as high officials with a view to forging loyalty to his dynasty, as Akbar had done with the Rajputs. They swept up the administration and there were no more lands to grant them as assignments, or *jagirs*.

Aurangzeb was obstinate in his desire to reduce all the recalcitrant forces to submission and to destroy their forts. For nearly fifteen years, he moved his camp the length and breadth of the Deccan without the power to subjugate his elusive enemies. Though old and ailing, he never gave up pursuing his adversaries, while pathetically maintaining the decorum of his mobile court. In his death throes, he moved to Ahmadnagar to die. In accordance with his will, he was buried in the cemetery of the Sufis of Khuldabad, a great centre of mysticism near Aurangabad, under a simple burial stone, without a mausoleum.

The process of the disintegration of the empire had already commenced.

The testament of Aurangzeb

Aurangzeb's intransigence was only apparent. The decisions he took after the execution of Sambhaji in 1689 and the testament he left to his descendants in the form of letters shed light on a change in the hardline religious policy that he had formulated in the middle of his reign.

He did not implement the policy of systematically destroying temples in the Deccan, as he had done in Rajasthan. Incitement to the conversion of Hindus to Islam was no longer the order of the day. On the contrary, he tried to entice them by the mass recruitment of Hindu Marathas to high positions in the administration. In the entire Mogul history, the proportion of Hindus among the high officials had never been higher than in the second half of the reign of Aurangzeb: 31.6 per cent against 22.5 per cent under Akbar (this discredits a widespread preconception according to which Hindus had been disadvantaged). Finally, the emperor suspended the collection of the jizya in the Deccan from 1704 onwards. His testament does not give religion a predominant place. It contains many references to Shah Jahan and even to Akbar, and advises to follow their conciliatory policy. Aurangzeb thus emphasizes continuity with his predecessors and not the rupture that had marked the middle of his reign: this religious upsurge was therefore a measure of expediency reflecting a strategy of confrontation: when this strategy did not produce the desired result, he returned to the policy of his predecessors.

Besides, innumerable anecdotes concerning the religious life of Aurangzeb reveal a complex personality. Even though he was well versed in the religious sciences and led an austere life, he did not allow religion to encroach on the interests of the empire, and even went against the letter of the law when the reasons of the state demanded it. Far from being the fundamentalist he is described as today, he appreciated Persian mystic literature, frequented numerous Sufis, and did not hesitate to discuss religion with Hindu sages.

VII

THE EMPIRE IN ITS PROSPERITY

The chronicles accurately record how the empire should have functioned, but it is impossible for us to know exactly to what extent these norms were applied. Similarly, the figures that we have at our disposal were tax bases that show what the empire intended to collect, while we are unable to determine to what extent production and collection corresponded to this claim. Furthermore, the richest source of information dates from the beginning of the empire, from the reign of Akbar (1556–1605): but this was apparently a period of prosperity. All these uncertainties have given rise to sharply conflicting interpretations.[1]

There is yet another difficulty: all the central archives and almost all the regional archives having disappeared, quantitative sources are limited to the figures recorded by the official historians in the Indo-Persian chronicles; these data are essentially taxation statistics on the basis of which the other data needs to be reconstituted.[2]

The greatest unknown concerns the population. Akbar ordered a census around 1580, the result of which – if it was in fact carried out – has not come down to us. Several estimates of the population have been made on the basis of diverse indicators, like the area under cultivation, agricultural produce, the number of soldiers (which is known). The discrepancy between the various estimations is to the tune of fifty per cent, going from 100 to 145 million for India as a whole.[3] Nevertheless, even if we keep to the lowest estimate, the mass is considerable; the estimated population of the Ottoman Empire during the same period rises to around twenty-two million. As for population development, the estimates range from a nil growth for the period 1600–1800 to an annual growth of 0.21per cent.

The composition of this population has given rise to the same uncertainties. Estimates concerning the proportion of the urban population vary from fifteen to twenty per cent, and the ratio of Muslims to Hindus remains unknown. We know that the Muslims were aware that they represented a small minority (Abduqadir Badauni commented on that at the time of Akbar); we also know that when the first census was carried out by the British, in 1872–1874, their proportion compared to the total population was slightly less than twenty per cent. We can reasonably suppose that the proportion of Muslims kept growing throughout the Mogul period (just as it continues to do so even today), and was therefore certainly less than twenty per cent in the sixteenth and seventeenth centuries. To venture beyond this as far as estimations are concerned would be risky. Mogul India represented one of

the largest populations of the globe, and this mass was to an overwhelming majority rural and Hindu.

The emperor and the imperial household

The emperor had to be recruited from among the descendants of Babur, therefore
from the dynasty of the Timurids, in the lineage of Timur and, on the women's side,
in the lineage of Genghis Khan. This rule would never be contested, even in the
eighteenth century, when the emperors had lost all their power and were at the
mercy of the factions of the court. This rule also declares one of the dynasty's
sources of legitimacy: the emperors were, through the ancestor Genghis Khan,
born out of the divine light, reminiscent of their name 'Moguls', which means
'Mongols'.

But even then it was imperative that every generation of the dynasty produced
sons in order to ensure its continuity: the Moguls had this luck, or rather this grace,
which had been granted to them since the time of Akbar by the saints of the
Chishtiyya brotherhood. Sufism was in effect a second source of legitimacy.

There was no specific rule however on which of the heirs of the dynasty could
accede to the throne and when. Succession therefore appeared as a sort of divine
judgement that sometimes pitted father against son when the latter wanted to come
to power prematurely, or more often sparked off disputes among the brothers when
the father had relinquished the throne: the winner being considered the elect of God
and becoming the legitimate sovereign.

The figure of the Mogul emperor – until Aurangzeb who endeavoured to restore
the simplicity of primitive Islam – was in effect larger than life. Favoured by the
saints or himself a saint as Akbar had been, he reigned by divine favour and played
the role of a spiritual guide for the nobles, at least until Aurangzeb. On this image
intended for the Muslim minority superposed another image, that of the Hindu
majority that considered the emperor a legitimate king.

All power emanated from the emperor. The 'ministers' and the governors of
provinces who exercised a part of this power in the capital or in the provinces did so
only on the expressed authority of the emperor and were liable to dismissal at any
moment. The omnipotence of the emperor manifested itself in two different ways:
not subject to the division of powers, he exercised absolute control on military,
financial, religious and legal affairs (for instance, his judgements on litigious trials
were final, without possible appeal); second, he supervised in person all the important affairs of the kingdom that he dealt with every day in court. No position in the
Mogul central administration resembles that of a defence minister or a commander
of the armed forces: the emperor himself organized and conducted wars.

In theory, the emperor could delegate his eminent powers to a 'representative'
(wakil), who, in his absence, was authorized to govern the empire. But during the
golden age of the Moguls, except during the regency of Bairam Khan in Akbar's
youth and when Itimaduddaula and Asaf Khan played an influential role under
Jahangir and Shah Jahan, the post was honorary and eventually remained vacant.
Most often, the Mogul emperors effectively administrated all political affairs.

The capital and the camp

The treasure of the emperor was synonymous with that of the empire: there was no clear-cut distinction between the private domain and the domain of the State. The functionaries of the imperial household also had a role in the administration of the empire and vice versa.

The site where they performed their functions was where the emperor was, in other words it was mobile. The Moguls – contrary to the Ottomans but like the Safavids – were itinerant. The seat of their government moved between the successive capitals of Agra, Fatehpur Sikri, Lahore, Delhi and Aurangabad. Even so, they did not reside there all the time because in the summer they lived in their gardens, in Delhi, Lahore or in Kashmir. When they were on the move between the various capitals and during their military campaigns, they lived primarily in camps, veritable cities of canvas, which at times accommodated hundreds of thousands of people: the same Turkish word, *urdu*, denotes both the capital and the camp.

Whether it was made of stone or canvas, the imperial city always rested on the combination of three constituents. In the first place, everything converged on the emperor, who resided in his fortified citadel (which in the camp was reduced to a simple enclosure of tents). Here, there was a clear dividing line between a public domain where the affairs of State were transacted and a private domain reserved for the harem, guarded by slaves and eunuchs. Second, there were bazaars: closely associated with the citadel, they converged on it in Delhi, and surrounded it in the camp. In the third place came religious edifices like mosques. The space between the citadels, the bazaars and the mosques was occupied by the houses of nobles (miniature replicas of the royal citadel) with their servants' huts clustered around them.

It is hardly possible to find a more extensive imperial household. It was a city within a city, with its menageries, its stables for horse and elephants, its barracks and its arsenals, its royal manufactories (*karkhana*), each with an official manager; the *mir saman*, a sort of superintendent of the imperial household, headed the entire set-up.

The citadel housed the personal army of the emperor comprising three branches: a cavalry of around four thousand men, a royal guard of approximately twenty thousand soldiers, armed with muskets, swords or bows, and lastly, his own contingents distinct from those of the nobles, paid in cash by the treasury, and who represented all the arms (with, in particular, an artillery and sappers). In the camp as in the city, the citadel was guarded by rotation by contingents that every noble was in charge of maintaining.

At the end of Akbar's reign, the total expenditure of the household of the king, including the maintenance of his troops, was estimated at 13.7 per cent of the revenue of the empire.

The court ritual

The court ritual, whose rigid order impressed western travellers, governed the relation between the imperial household, the nobles who administered the empire and the people. It was pervasively authoritative even to the point of determining the layout of the buildings (or tents).

The ritual of Akbar's court that was described earlier has remained famous. Let us briefly describe Shah Jahan's court ritual at Delhi, the most sumptuously planned of the Mogul capitals. Shah Jahan woke up before sunrise, performed his ablutions then went to recite prayers in the mosque of the citadel (now known as the Red Fort). Thereafter, he appeared standing on the balcony (*jharoka-i darshan*), specially built for this purpose, to receive the adoration of the people who had gathered at the foot of the fort, on the bank of the Jamuna. He then proceeded to the public audience hall where, surrounded by his chief 'ministers', he sat on the throne facing a crowd of courtiers standing by order of precedence: it was there, in public, generally in the presence of the principal stakeholders, that most of the affairs of the central and provincial administration were transacted. Afterwards, the emperor retired to the private audience hall to deal with confidential matters, always with his important ministers, in particular to examine the reports despatched by the imperial spies. Another meeting for the discussion of classified issues was held in the tower called Shah Burj. Then followed a period of rest in the harem where the emperor had lunch and a siesta. He devoted the end of the afternoon and the beginning of the evening to finish, if necessary, examining the affairs of the State in the two audience halls and in the Shah Burj, and to inspect the troops: the rest of the time was spent on discussions and entertainment. Towards midnight, the emperor retired to the zenana where he spent the night.

The nobility and the *mansabdaris*

The essential task, namely the administration of the empire, was in the hands of a handpicked elite, conventionally called 'nobles'. Indian historians have used the word 'nobility' to translate the Arabo-Persian term *umara* (singular: *amir*), which denoted armed high officials. Contrary to European nobles, this was an open cosmopolitan class, composed of individuals recruited by the emperor and subjected to his good will.

The Mogul Empire organized its nobility into a hierarchic body according to a numerical gradation, expressed by two numbers: the higher the number, the higher the grade was. The grade or title was called *mansab*; the holder of the grade was the *mansabdar*. The first number defined the personal rank, the *zat*, of the noble concerned: it determined his salary. Once the number was fixed by the emperor, the administration could exactly calculate his emoluments according to meticulously established rules. It was in other words a salary index. The second number defined the military obligations of the noble and the remuneration that he earned in this capacity. It was called *sawar*, literally: 'cavalry.' It determined the size of the contingent of cavalrymen and horses that the noble had to recruit and keep constantly available for the service of the emperor.

Under Akbar, strictly speaking, only those whose grade (in the *mansabdari* system) was equal or higher than five hundred were considered as nobles: in the seventeenth century, the limit was raised to one thousand.

The nobility represents a small minority in Mogul history. At the end of the reign of Akbar, there were 122 nobles; when Aurangzeb acceded to the throne, in 1658, there were 248; their number increased with the expansion of the empire under Aurangzeb, to exceed the 500 mark in 1707: very few indeed for an empire that had between 100 and 150 million subjects at the time.

The officials whose grade was less than 500 under Akbar (and later, less than a thousand) did not have the right, strictly speaking, to the title of nobles. Nevertheless, they were recruited according to the same principles and were subjected to the same obligations as the nobles, and they were also called *mansabdars*. They were around 1,649 at the end of Akbar's reign and around 8,000 at the end of Aurangzeb's rule.

Owing to the diversity of its origins, the nobility formed a heterogeneous entity. Recent immigrants, all of Islamic faith, had precedence: the Turks of Central Asia, collectively called Turanians (*Turani*), the first among whom were the royal princes, also subjected to the inflexible authority of the emperor; then came the Iranians (*Irani*) and the Afghans. In the second place were the officials of Indian stock, whether Hindus or Muslims (Indian Muslims had less consideration than recent immigrants): they formed various groups like Indian Muslims, the Rajputs, the Marathas and other Hindus (in particular those who belonged to the caste of scholars and who were employed in the tax services). The proportion of these constituents varied in keeping with the policies of the emperors: Shah Jahan, obsessed with Central Asia, favoured the recruitment of Turanians for the highest grades. These variations call into question certain preconceived ideas: under Akbar, who has the reputation of being very pro-Indian, apart from the spectacular recruitment of a limited number of Rajputs and of some scribes, it was primarily immigrants who were favoured; under Aurangzeb, who is presumed to have been hostile to Hindus, the proportion of the latter kept growing, rising from 21.16 per cent to 31 per cent, notably owing to the massive recruitment of Marathas after the conquest of the Deccan.

There was no fixed procedure for recruitment. The nobility was not hereditary and if the sons of nobles had more chances to accede to this status, success was not guaranteed: more than half of those recruited were not descendents of nobles. It was the prerogative of the emperor to decide in the last instance who could be admitted to the court: Indians potentates whose allegiance he wanted to secure, defectors of enemy state. In fact, the recruitment of nobles enabled him to adapt the domestic and foreign policies of the empire.

Once inducted into the administration, the nobles, both themselves and their possessions, were in the hands of the emperor. In the hall of public audience, after consulting the *mir bakshi* seated next to him, it was he who decided on their recruitment, their grade and their salary or their promotion or their removal from office (even royal princes could be dismissed). The nobles owed absolute obedience to the king. They were obliged to go without demur where they were posted, often to the four corners of the empire, because the emperor constantly transferred them to prevent them from forming a power base in the provinces. The refusal of the post was paramount to treason. They were also expected to appear as often as possible at the court, bearing gifts as tokens of the renewal of their personal allegiance. Lastly, they had to ensure the guard of the palace by rotation.

The properties of the noble, often of considerable value, were subjected post mortem to a control of the tax administration. The moment he breathed his last, all his possessions were sequestered. The administration first had to recover all payments due to him. However, the emperor also took possession of what appeared to him to be a dubious accumulation of wealth and finally gave the inheritors only what he wanted to. It is only from Aurangzeb's time that in the name of orthodoxy the Islamic laws of inheritance were rigorously applied.

Even though formed of free men, the corps of nobles thus retained certain servile features – like absolute obedience and the control of properties – reminiscent of the role of slaves in the Sultanate of Delhi, or in the Ottoman Empire.

To maintain their armed contingents, the nobles received remuneration distinct from their salary. These provisions throw light on the indirect nature of the Mogul government. We had seen earlier that the personal army of the emperor was limited: the great armies of the campaigns of conquest were constituted by mustering the contingents of the nobles who participated in them; they were commanded by the emperor in person, or the official he delegated.

The payment of this two-fold remuneration was also indirect: the personal troops of the emperor were paid directly by the exchequer; the nobles, on the contrary, did not receive money directly. The tax administration granted them assignments of land called *jagir* (a Persian term that, under the Moguls, replaced the Arabic term *iqta*, in use under the sultanate of Delhi). The nobles were granted the right to collect taxes on their allotted lands, the amount of which varied according to its quality, no matter which part of the empire. The responsibility for recruiting tax collectors was theirs. These concessions were purely fiscal, and did not imply the right either of administration or of justice. To prevent nobles from forming fiefs, the lands of these *jagirs* were often situated in a region far from their place of residence and were changed periodically. The *mansabdars* absorbed the greatest part of the riches of the empire,[4] but in return, they had to bear the largest part of the expenses incurred in the collection of taxes as well in the recruitment and equipment of the army.

Central and provincial administration

The Mogul government was a military empire, because the nobles who ran it were military leaders commanding armed contingents.

The administration was divided into independent branches, each being accountable directly to the emperor. This division was not a separation of powers, in the modern sense of the term, destined to preserve the rights of the subjects, but an application of the maxim: 'divide and rule'. The government could not cast a shadow on the power of the emperor as long as these different structures were isolated and controlled one by the other.

These principles, which have an ancient Islamic origin, led to the constitution of three principle branches. The first branch, the administration of justice and the financing of the religious institutions, was the preserve of the religious experts, the ulemas, where, in principle, the Islamic Law (*sharia*) reigned supreme. The other two branches, finance and the management of personnel, came under the purview of the arbitrary regulations (*zabita*, plural *zawabit*) of the emperor.

Justice and religion were considered inseparable because both of these necessitated experts in religious sciences whose language was Arabic; this role was often played by the so-called Indian Muslims, who actually belonged to ancient lineages of Arab origin, and who maintained the tradition of Arabic study in India. The function could be split into its two components, but this was rare.

The role of the chief official of the religious department (*sadr as-sudur*) was in particular to distribute imperial charities among the most meritorious with the aim of developing the religious sciences. These endowments generally were made in the form of lands exempted from taxes called 'benefits' (*suyurghal* or *madad-i maash*); under Akbar, it is estimated that 3.5 per cent of the potential revenue of the empire was absorbed by these donations.

The role of the chief of the judicial apparatus, was to oversee that part of the law that fell under the purview of the Islamic Law, therefore essentially family law and only a part of criminal law (but a great part of the civil and criminal affairs, exempt from the application of the Islamic Law, was subjected to the arbitrary power of the administration and of the sovereign). The *sadr*, at the time the chief qadi (*qazi*), himself judged the cases that were brought before him and was in charge of appointing the qadis who officiated in all the subdivisions of the empire down to the level of cantons (*pargana*).

In all the Islamic regimes, the chief tax official (*amil*) was distinct from the military commander (*amir*). From Akbar's time, the administration of finances had always produced a very motivated elite group, in which Hindus from the castes of scholars and scribes were particularly numerous, especially in the lower echelons. The official in charge of administration at the central level had the title of *wazir-i mamalik* (minister of the kingdom) or *diwan-i kull* (chief minister of finances). He had three subordinates responsible for *jagirs*, *khalisa* lands (where taxes were levied directly by the treasury) and for the management of the imperial household. These four men controlled all the finances of the empire: they were charged with the task of determining the tax base on the basis of appropriate inquiries and surveys, of ensuring the collection of taxes and of accounting for the expenditures.

The third great figure of the empire, the *bakhshi*, was not a commander of the armies, but rather a chief of personnel. With the help of several assistants, he was responsible for controlling the recruitment and promotion of all the *mansabdars*, whether they served in the army, in the administration of provinces or in the finances: he was also in charge of supervising their appointment to such and such a post; finally he had to control the maintenance of the armed contingents of each noble through periodic musters of men and horses, the latter being branded to avoid fraud.

The *bakhshi* also had the duty of coordinating the espionage department. In every provincial city and in the administrative centres the 'news writers' (*waqia nawis*) were posted who sent their reports every day through very sophisticated postal system (*dak*) that functioned by relays: these reports were centralized by the provincial *bakhshi* who

despatched them to the capital. The emperor was thus informed of all that happened in the empire within a few days.

The provincial administration was a replica of the central administration. The
same division of powers was prevalent. The governor (*subadar, nazim* or *nawab*) was
the official representative of the emperor, a viceroy so to speak, who took ultimate
decisions with respect to the management of the province. His power was, however,
not absolute, because he had to give account to the emperor and he did not have
direct authority on his closest collaborators. The officials had an eye on each other,
reinforcing the power of the emperor: the *sadr*, the chief of justice and religious
endowments, *diwan*, the chief of finances, *bakhshi*, chief of personnel, as well as military governors (*faujdars*) posted in the principal districts (*sarkars*) of the province, were
appointed by the emperor: they were accountable to him and to their counterparts
in the central government and not to the governor of the province.

The exercise of power did not stop with the administrative centre of the province.
Since the time of the sultanate of Delhi, there had existed a smaller administrative
subdivision: a sort of canton, the *pargana*, or *mahall*, a group of several villages containing the smallest Muslim towns, the *qasbas*, where were stationed the humblest
functionaries of the empire: here, a qadi (*qazi*) dispensed justice, an *amil* supervised
the fixation of the tax base and the collection of taxes (from Shah Jahan, he was
assisted in this functions by an *amin*).

Below the level of the *pargana* there were no imperial functionaries. In the regions
of direct administration, the chieftains of villages and principalities (*muqaddam,
zamindar*) served as intermediaries for the collection of taxes, of which they pocketed
about 25 per cent; Hindu scribes maintained the tax registers at the village level. In
the marches of the empire, for example in the Himalayas, the principalities that did
not fall under direct administration continued to be governed by their kinglets, who
paid only a tribute, often in kind: the kinglets of Nepal sent elephants. Besides, the
emperor maintained fortresses in the major strategic points situated on the frontiers,
for which he directly appointed commanders.

The intermediate subdivisions between the administrative centre of the province
and the *pargana* varied in the course of the Mogul period. The largest, since the time
of Akbar, was the *sarkar*; it was above all a military subdivision managed by a *faujdar*
but it was also utilized intermittently by the tax authorities. The *cakla*, an intermediate unit between the *sarkar* and the *pargana*, was created under Shah Jahan. Other
officials had more circumscribed functions at the provincial level. We have already
mentioned the commanders of fortresses; we can also cite *kotwals*, chiefs of police in
the principal cities, *mir bahrs*, admirals of maritime and especially riverine fleets.

Mogul administration therefore had functions of control rather than of management, but it would be misleading to discern in it a sort of prefiguration of a modern
centralized state.

The efficiency of the administration was not negligible. It is remarkable that, until
the end of the reign of Aurangzeb, it continued to increase the area of registered
lands, that it followed up (and often caused) the extension of clearings and that it
could derive profit from the growth in production by more than doubling the tax
base. The empire was solidly implanted till the level of the *pargana*, and control on

the rural world – still loose under Akbar who is erroneously reputed to have definitively fixed the administrative structure – had progressively consolidated itself under the reigns of Shah Jahan and Aurangzeb, the period in which were written the principal administration manuals.

Currency and bills of exchange

The empire put its currency in circulation, destined to facilitate not only commerce but also the collection of taxes. One of the characteristics of the Mogul Empire was in effect to have regularized the collection of taxes in cash (not in kind, as was customary in India). For this purpose, it developed and controlled the mint of a single currency all over the empire, which progressively supplanted the local currencies, even that of Gujarat that had been so long in demand. Renewing a tradition going back, beyond the period of the sultanates, to the beginning of the Delhi sultanate, the Mogul Empire produced abundant good quality coinage which had currency as late as the first decades of British rule. British coinage did not mark a definitive break from the past: the silver rupee of Queen Victoria, hoarded and mounted on jewels even today, was the last version of the Mogul rupee.

The production of this coinage was spread out all across the empire.[5] The administration fixed uniform standards and controlled the application of these: the workshops received demonetized coins and metal as ingots, and minted them for which they took a percentage for themselves: 10.77 per cent for copper and 5.3 per cent for silver at the end of Akbar's reign.

Akbar introduced the policy of trimetallism: gold, silver and copper. Gold coins of 11 grams were called *mohr* or *ashrafi*. However, gold was never a common medium of exchange. Gold coins were offered to a superior, like the emperor, as a mark of renewing one's personal allegiance to him or else it was hoarded.

As for the rest, Akbar adopted and adapted the monetary system inherited from the Sur interregnum. During his long reign, copper coins (a locally produced metal) were the most common medium of exchange and currency of account.[6] Minting workshops scattered all over the empire manufactured in abundance coins of this type that were used for minor transactions.

However, with the expansion of trade and the massive arrival of the silver-metal from the New World, the medium of exchange and the currency of account in the seventeenth century became the silver rupee, *rupiya* (from *rup*, silver) or *sikka*. The coin minted by the Moguls generally had a diameter of 25 millimetre and weighed 11.50 grams. The accounts of the empire were henceforth expressed in rupees.

The evolution of currency and prices over a period as long as the Mogul Empire can only be conjectural. Copper coinage seems to have retained its value, because this metal was highly in demand, notably for the artillery. The evolution of silver is remarkable: its value diminished in comparison with copper and there was net growth (despite highs and lows) in the issue of silver coins in the course of the seventeenth century. Furthermore, we know that the total amount of taxes levied in cash more than doubled between the end of the sixteenth century and the beginning of the eighteenth century. But was this due to inflation or, on the contrary, did the growth in money supply correspond to a real growth in production that precluded inflation? The general economic trend seems to lend credence to the second hypothesis.

The Mogul period witnessed the development of another means of payment, the bill of exchange (*hundi*), which heralded the beginning of a banking system almost entirely in the hands of Hindu castes of merchants and moneychangers. Its use was possible owing to the existence of a network of correspondents scattered all over India (and even abroad for foreign trade). Against the remittance of a sum in cash in a given city, the changer issued a bill payable by a correspondent in another city in return for a small commission (1 per cent during the belle epoque). The usage of the bill of exchange continued to develop: it was adopted by traders, the Mogul administration (for the transfer of revenue from the provinces to the centre) and by nobles (for transferring revenues from their assigned lands). Bankers and changers also provided loans to merchants and, if necessary, even to the Mogul administration when short of liquid funds: according to the English traders of the seventeenth century, the annual rates ranged from 8 to 9 per cent (the rate was 4 per cent at the time in England).

The budget of the empire

The revenue of the empire in 1595–6, according to *Ain-i Akbari* as it has been interpreted by Shireen Moosvi, amounted to 3,680 million *dams*, that is 99.01 million rupees. Its distribution is as shown in the table below, which makes it clear that the bulk of the revenues of the State went to the *mansabdars* for their personal expenses and particularly for the maintenance of their cavalry (the biggest item): this budget was above all a military budget; second, it financed the pomp of the emperor and the nobles.

Agrarian production was certainly the major component of the Indian economy, but extant records are not sufficient to enable us to quantify its value as compared with the urban economy.[7] Even though the state exacted the equivalent of half of the agricultural production in cash, the sums effectively collected, given the deductions made by intermediaries and the collection costs, accounted at the most for only 30 per cent of agricultural production, the value of which would therefore stand at 297 million rupees. It is not known what this sum represents with respect to production.

Budget of the empire (1595–6)[8]
(in millions of rupees)

Expenditures for the *mansabdars* 80.95
which can be broken down to:

- personal salaries (*zat*) 20.69
- maintenance of horses 9.29
- remuneration of cavalrymen 50.97

Expenditures for the troops of the emperor 8.97
which can be broken down to:

— wages 3.57
— horses and elephants 4.85
— weapons 0.55

Expenditures for the imperial household 4.69
Surplus hoarded 4.41
Total 99.02

Rural society and the agrarian economy

In theory, the Mogul administration claimed to negotiate the tax amount directly with the producer after measuring his lands and estimating his average production. However, under Akbar less than half of the empire had been registered with the land registry. For the rest, estimations of production remained approximate and the tax amount was negotiated with intermediaries, denoted by the general term of *zamindars*.

Rural India, that had remained Hindu in majority, had been characterized since time immemorial by a tiering of land rights. Generally, a given piece of land was cleared and colonized by clans belonging to one or more dominant castes. If these clans were well organized, their local chieftains, remaining close to their dependants, acted as intermediaries for the administration. Sometimes, the chiefs of principalities had acquired eminent rights on a peasantry without any hold over them. Whatever the scenario might be, a small minority of *zamindars* dominated the mass of farmers: below the latter came a disadvantaged army of workers who had an even lower status and who provided seasonal labour for farming operations.

Agricultural production was governed by the monsoons but in general there were two harvests a year. Crops sown in autumn, which benefitted from the reserves of water accumulated during the monsoon and from the meagre spring rains, were reaped during the spring harvest (*rabi*): these crops included cereals like wheat, oats, barley; oilseeds like mustard; sugar cane, etc. During the monsoon that fell from June or July to October cultivated crops were grown in flooded lands, in particular rice and others that required a lot of water, like millet and Indian millet; cotton was also cultivated during this season; these crops were harvested in autumn (*kharif*). Each region had its specialities: some arid areas, like the Punjab, produced especially wheat; hot and humid regions, like the delta of the Ganges or Kerala, yielded several rice harvests per year. India had for a long time used diverse methods of irrigation: wells, reservoirs or canals distributing river water by gravity. The Muslims developed canals and introduced the technique of chain pumps.

Although the texts written during the reign of Akbar compile a list of these various harvests, and of the revenue that the State derived from them in the form of taxes, production estimation seems to have been a challenge. The latest studies have proved that crop distribution and productivity at the end of the sixteenth century were comparable to those at the end of the nineteenth century, while cultivated acreage was less as well as (consequently) total production.

Agriculture did not remain static during the Mogul era, which saw the introduction of new crops: tobacco spread all over India between 1600 and 1650; there is evidence of the cultivation of maize in Rajasthan and Maharashtra from the middle of the eighteenth century; the culture of silk, newly introduced in Bengal, underwent dramatic expansion. Horticulture, promoted by the nobles, also developed in this region: new plants were introduced, like the grapevine (the Moguls were great drinkers of wine), as well as new techniques like grafting.

The total cultivated area increased all through the Mogul period. It was the constant policy of the dynasty to promote clearing; there is abundant historical evidence on the breaking of new lands for agriculture in Oudh or in Bengal (the lands of present Bangladesh were opened for cultivation during this time). We know that taxes levied had multiplied by two and half between the end of the sixteenth century and the beginning of the eighteenth; it is true that administrative controls had been tightened from the reign of Shah Jahan, but it would be erroneous to attribute this increase in taxes solely to an enhancement of the efficiency of the administrative machinery. There were evidently more farmers cultivating vaster areas and it was the growth in production that had engendered the increase in the taxes levied.

Apart from periods of famine caused by adverse weather or war, foreign testimonies as well as archives give the impression of a population that was still sparse (the dearth of agricultural labour posed a problem) and that lived on the land and produced surpluses marketed in part to pay the taxes (assessed in cash), and in part to accumulate wealth.

The increase in the marketing of agricultural products is another hallmark of the Mogul Empire. Besides the surpluses of subsistence corps, farmers put commercial agricultural products on the market: cotton, indigo, oilseed, etc. Numerous market towns (*ganj*) developed to absorb the growing commercialization.

The handicraft industry and the urban economy

New needs, new networks

The seventeenth century was marked simultaneously by the hegemony of the Mogul Empire, which encompassed almost the entire subcontinent and by the second phase of European expansion – with the growing influence of the Dutch and the British -which modified the networks of international commerce. By creating new needs, this two-fold trend considerably increased the demand for manufactured products and gave a decisive fillip to the entire economic process.

With the advent of the Moguls, a military society of Islamic origin took command of the greater part of the country. This was not a new phenomenon because powerful sultanates had emerged since the twelfth century, but for the first time a lifestyle left its mark almost everywhere because it was that of a triumphant minority, even if a Hindu majority remained attached to its traditions. Mogul society lived, ate and dressed differently. The Mogul peace, which succeeded in the wake of the cruellest wars of conquest, was propitious to the expansion of productivity. The ruling dynasty's links with Central Asia opened new markets in the region, and new roads leading to it were built. The subcontinent itself was criss-crossed with routes, and cities emerged at the crossroads. It was discovered that jungles and forests were no longer impenetrable and that overland routes were swifter than the coastal shipping that had earlier connected the ports with each other. Some of these ports were abandoned in favour of those situated at the end of a route, others developed near European factories.

Opened by conquerors long ago, the existing routes were widened and enhanced. The economy of the Gangetic plain hinged on the Lahore-Patna artery from which the roads that penetrated the South branched off at Agra. One of these routes led to Surat via Ajmer, Jaisalmer, Ahmadabad and Cambay, the other connected Golconda and the Coromandel Coast, engendering a maze of minor roads linking Mandu, Aurangabad, Dabul, Bijapur and Goa, Masulipatnam and Pulicut. It was around Burhanpur that this impressive network centred. Thus, the cities of the Deccan could send their products to Bengal, Agra, Lahore and Kandahar, as far as the markets of Central Asia where caravans coming from the borders of China and the Ottoman Empire waited to take the merchandise onwards. Regional frontiers crumbled, most border taxes were abolished, freeing provinces that had never before communicated with each other. To this day, vast areas, such as Orissa and Mysore, remain dependent on ancient routes. In the far south, the accessibility of maritime links and the extensive network of rivers and the lagoons continued to meet the requirements of trade activities.

Mogul road networks attracted products and people. The roadways, usually following a straight line, were raised and lined with trees. On these roads, in a cloud of dust, pedestrians and herds walked, chariots and the long train that followed the movements of military camps, escorted by horses and elephants. In the crossroads, at the confluents of waterways and land routes, houses of brick and stone and newly created towns rose above the grass huts.

The interior of India was animated. The Mogul presence shook up the rigidity of Brahminical customs; the Islamic nobility effortlessly changed their posts and their domains. An imposing bureaucracy emerged, leading to the birth of a hitherto non-existent middle class. Towards 1665, this new class was still so discreet that the voyager François Bernier believed that it was absent. These new consumers, these new modes of consumption and distribution would hardly affect the structures of rural areas, where the Hindus perpetuated the same needs, the same habits and the same rhythms of work. The impetus given by the Mogul expansion to the economic process would however bring about significant modifications in production and in markets.

The evolution of the traditional handicraft industry

The Florentine trader Filippo Sassetti made this observation at the end of the sixteenth century: 'The Great Mogul consumes everything'. The court and the military camps in fact swallowed up a very large part of handicraft production.

Nobles and rich merchants made it a point of honour to imitate the style of living of the imperial household.

The demand for textiles was considerable. It was necessary to meet the needs of the harems – at least four women and at times several hundreds, around whom thronged thousands of maids and slaves. Cotton fabrics and more particularly muslins fulfilled their traditional role, but silk goods experienced an increasing demand that India endeavoured to meet. Hitherto reserved for local use, the shawls of Kashmir began to be marketed. If women remained loyal to draped clothes, the men adopted tunics and underpants cut in Mogul fashion. The wearing of turbans became widespread. Fabrics were embroidered, flecked with gold, inset with pearls and precious stones, mobilizing an army of artisans. Life in harems lent itself to the enhancement of comforts and interior decoration, to the display of carpets, wall hangings, bed hangings, cushions and comforters.

The large textile-producing regions – Gujarat, Bengal, the Coromandel coast – continued to meet a growing demand that also stimulated other centres scattered in the subcontinent. The array of cotton goods seems infinite. The Portuguese and the British classified more than one hundred, sometimes very difficult to identify. We can nevertheless distinguish a few categories: calicos – *bafta* of Gujarat and *ambati* of Bihar – which were sold raw and whose relatively rough texture made it ideal for the making of packaging materials, sail-cloth and especially tents, extensively used owing to the prevalence of war camps; other cotton goods, also raw, were exported to Africa or to the East Indies where the natives decorated them according to their style; there were still others, more finely woven, like cambric (*parkala*), which were bleached and used to make shirts, or else were painted or printed; the range of muslins was very varied – some had the reputation of being more transparent 'than slivers of the moon', in the words of the poet Amir Khusrau.

The conquests of Akbar, who annexed Gujarat in 1572, in the wake of a cruel war, and Bengal in 1592, had only little impact on production, which was curtailed only for a few months and which staged an immediate recovery, stimulated by an even higher demand. More serious were the consequences of the famine of 1630–2, the brunt of which was borne by Gujarat. Entire villages were depopulated, people displaced, while specialists fled towards other centres of production. Asiatic merchants and European companies then turned towards Bengal and the Coromandel, which would retain their clientele. This trend would contribute to the prosperity of Patna where calicos were manufactured and muslins were imported from nearby Bengal. This proximity would soon make Patna the largest market for silk, produced since the fifteenth century in the region of Kasimbazar, but the manufacture of which had hitherto been limited. The Mogul court and the aristocracy highly prized this precious material. In order to avoid the costly imports of Chinese silk goods from Central Asia, the emperor Akbar encouraged the planting of mulberry trees and the breeding of silkworms, which found favourable conditions in Bengal. He employed the services of foreign specialists, Persians and Chinese, to work on silk. Soon a large quantity of pieces came out of imperial workshops and manufactories – raw silks, brocades, velvets, satins brocaded with gold or silver.

The producers and merchants of Gujarat would succeed in overcoming the difficulties posed by the political situation. Conquests and famine were succeeded by the raids of the Marathas who ravaged Surat periodically. Seaborne commerce was curtailed by the insecurity of the western seas of the Indian Ocean, scoured by the pirates of Konkan and Muscat. Sunk in the sands, the ancient port of Cambay was eclipsed by Surat and Ahmadabad, which undertook both the production and distribution of textiles. The fabrication of cotton fabrics, adorned with blocks to cover the surfaces rapidly, reached the stage of pre-industrialization. Producers were above all keen on diversifying materials in an effort to meet the competition of the countries of the Bay of Bengal. Silk was worked on in Bharuch, Surat and Ahmadabad, skilfully dyed or mixed with cotton. Skeins of raw thread were most often imported from Central Asia, Balasore and Kasimbazar, or from the northern ports of Sumatra.

The rapid expansion of the textile industry gave a boost to the fabrication of dyes. Formerly confined to Gujarat, the indigo industry declined after the famine of 1630 in favour of cereal crops and spread to other regions, like Bihar and the environs of Agra. Obtained by the fermentation of the leaves of *indigofera tinctoria* in huge vats, indigo, skilfully dosed, dyed all shades of blue until it appeared almost black on the roughest cotton fabrics. *Morinda citrifolia* was used in Gujarat for red colour, but could not rival *oldenandia umbellata*, the famous *chay* painted on the fabrics of the Coromandel. Madder mixed with tannin gave a black or deep red colour when it was applied on cloth soaked in alum. The dried flowers of *terminalia chabula*, crushed in pots of stone, then diluted, and boiled, gave a yellow colour brighter than ochre. All these dyes were applied with the help of mordants discovered long before by the artisans of India – alum, tannin or pastes of myrobalans.

The military character of the Mogul Empire spurred the activity of all sectors related to arms and equipment. Used since the beginning of the sixteenth century and constantly improved since then, artillery imposed itself definitively as the principal force of combat. Metallurgy flourished around iron mines, especially in Assam, in the Khasi mounts, Mysore, Gujarat, Berar and in Kashmir, processed in small clay furnaces. Guns of all sorts, cannonball, iron bars and nails were forged according to rudimentary procedures while Golconda produced the best steel in India.

The chief component of gunpowder, saltpetre was exploited everywhere, all the more because it was also used to cool water. The Portuguese had discovered the profits they could draw from its presence in Konkan, on the Karnataka coast where Honavar was the principal distributor. The reinforcement of artillery, both Mogul and European, brought in its train an increase in demand. Saltpetre was collected in abandoned villages where it was refined in situ by decoction and dried in the sun. It was found in plenty in the coastal regions of the peninsula, in Bihar, around Patna, and in Rajasthan, near Ajmer.

The production of spears and bladed weapons, javelins and daggers mobilised a large number of specialists, all the more as a collection of luxurious arms contributed to the prestige of the Mogul lord. Already of repute in medieval Europe, the famous swords 'of Damascus', as they were called, were in reality hardened most often in Golconda, their hilts wrought like jewels by goldsmiths, their blades sheathed in velvet by skilful makers of scabbards with tips of gold or silver. The city of Indelwai, near Nizamabad, was home to ordnance factories the quality of whose arms would appeal to the Dutch company. Military gear demanded constant renewal. It was necessary to equip the camps with tents, chariots, pots and tools, to provide the cavalry with saddles, harnesses and straps. The stables of the emperor Shah Jahan had not less than two hundred thousand horses and eight thousand elephants. Harnesses, boots and leather sandals were widely used in Islamic society, by both soldiers and civilians. Thanks to their increased needs, merchants of leather goods, particularly in Lahore, made their fortune.

The reconstruction of cities destroyed by conquests and the creation of new cities changed the face of urban landscape. Rural populations, the majority of them Hindu, were satisfied with more or less sizeable huts with walls of adobe or woven palms, and always attached more value to jewels and clothes than to their habitat. On the contrary, for the Moguls, the home had an importance hitherto unknown in India, except in princely families. Edifices of bricks and stones dominated by the high terraces of the *havelis* of nobles or merchants, caravanserais, mosques and mausoleums rose in the entire northern half of the country. Mogul style became predominant. The architectural structures of Turko-Persian origin were modelled by the skilfulness of Indian artisans and modified by regional influences, like on the west coast where doors, balconies and windows of sculpted wood adorned the facades.

On the imperial construction site, transfers of technology occurred between the artisans who came from all over the Indian world and foreign specialists, hired by the emperor – Persian architects, Italian master workers specialized in the inlay of coloured marbles. Indian techniques of stone sculpting, used in the past for decorating the walls of Hindu temples with a profusion of idols, were applied to the chiselling of trellises and lintels. Wood was gilded or lacquered; large quantities of bricks were moulded then varnished and enamelled. Thrones and columns were inlaid with agate, cornelians and even precious stones. The famous Taj Mahal of Agra is the most striking example of the perfection reached by the artisans at the service of the Moguls.

Other talents were at work in the large-scale projects of land use planning: construction of routes, bridges, fortifications, aqueducts and dams. The development of the hydrographical network led to the growth of river shipping. Construction sites bustled with activity on the banks of watercourses in order to increase the number of local boats, at times hauled by hand on the riverside paths. Certain lords possessed fleets of more than a hundred barges with painted and gilded fittings, cabins stretched with silks. For deep-sea navigation, India used rot-proof materials – teak wood from the forests of the South and ropes from the Maldives. As early as the opening years of the sixteenth century, the Portuguese had exploited these advantages to construct some of their own vessels in Malabar, thus enhancing the local techniques. Since then, an increasing number of ships of the European type set sail from the construction sites of Surat, Narasapur, Masulipatnam, Pulicat, Cranganore and Cochin.

It is impossible to list the multitudinous manufactured goods whose fabrication was accelerated by Mogul demand. Semi-precious stones from Gujarat, diamonds from Bijapur and Golconda, precious stones imported from Ceylon and rubies from Burma were purified, cut and mounted by an infinite number of jewellers. The jewels of the poorest, made of pewter or of bell metal, bear testimony to the expertise of village artisans.

The fabrication and conditioning of food products remained traditional – oils, butters, *ghee*, arrack and *toddy*, conserves made of sugar sold as powder or as pieces (candy). Till then concentrated in the south, the market for drugs, balms and perfumes spread all across the country. Of Egyptian origin and distributed by the Arabs during the medieval age, opium began to be extracted from poppies of Gujarat and Bihar, and widely marketed as analgesics, sedatives and at times as narcotics. Tobacco, introduced to India by the Portuguese, was increasingly popular. The harems were great consumers of perfumes skilfully prepared with jasmine, amber and musk. Even the horses of the imperial stable were anointed with essence of roses.

Paper was a newcomer to India. It appeared in Gujarat only in the thirteenth century, in Delhi in the fifteenth century and would have to wait until the seventeenth century to become an object of common use. It was produced for the most part at Junnar in Maharashtra. The popularization of this medium was concomitant with the appearance of the first printing presses and the recovery in the activities of print manufacturers and miniaturists.

If the making of utensils, tools, pots of mud and copper remained traditional and hardly went beyond the scope of the needs of local consumption, the manufacture of decorated objects grew and became widespread, owing to urbanization and the demand of European companies. What in the past had brought prosperity to Cambay – luxurious and cheap ornaments, jewellery of semi-precious stones and glass, small furniture inlaid with pearl or ivory, carafes and ewers of tin and silver – flooded the Old World and soon penetrated the New World. These articles accompanied caravans and cargoes. The extension of the road network also stimulated the fabrication of chariots, litters and palanquins.

The organization of artisans' societies

Agricultural and handicraft activities coexisted in rural areas, the former enjoying more prestige than the latter. The unit of production was the artisan's family where ancestral techniques were ingrained during childhood. This tradition made it possible to reach a high level of skill while using very simple instruments. The hierarchy of tasks, which was determined by one's birth, was governed by the caste system.

Village production was specialized in the food industry, the processing of salt, saltpetre, indigo, and other dyes, in small-scale metallurgy and in textiles. The textile industry was present in almost all rural communities where men, most often Muslims, wove while women spun and embroidered. In Gujarat, each village was specialized in a different technique.

Artisans were generally remunerated according to the *jajmani* system: in self-sufficient villages, they received a part of the resources, occasionally even the enjoyment of land ownership, more rarely a sum of money. The principle was based on an exchange of services between farmers and artisans according to arrangements specific to each region. Certain villages also worked for the market, a trend that grew in the course of the seventeenth century. The artisans then made contact with intermediaries, who acted on behalf of a local *bania*. They were remunerated according to the *dadni* system, that is, by advances in cash or in kind. When the village artisan produced the raw material, he enjoyed more liberty with regard to the trader than when the latter supplied it to him.

This same system functioned in cities, where there were not less than sixty-six known castes of artisans, multiplied by an infinite number of sub-castes. Each of these groups lived in their own block of houses. In certain emporiums frequented by the agents of European companies, there were *aurangs*, that is, centres that consolidated specialized workshops and their shops. These centres were also prevalent in the proximity of sources of raw materials – in Kasimbazar for silk, Masulipatnam for cotton, Golconda for diamonds. Wages were generally low, except for goldsmiths, carpenters, jewellers and firework manufacturers. These artisans, even as they increasingly perfected their specialization, tended to climb up the social ladder and to join the nascent middle class. In fact, the fact of belonging to a low caste was not an obstacle to the accumulation of wealth.

All manufactured goods as well as certain work tools were subjected to taxes that went into the imperial treasury. Whether Hindu, Jain or Muslim, the families of *banias*, on whom heavy taxes were imposed, perpetuated the strict traditions of parsimony. They amassed precious stones and metals in their houses. This was the contemporary form of saving, investment being practically unknown. Tax pressure was aggravated by the currency of bribes and the universal practice of usury.

The artisan thrived only by peacefully accomplishing his hereditary vocation and remained resistant to the incitement of traders to negotiate greater profitability. The weight of tradition often prevailed over financial interests. In villages, a change of residence was synonymous with alienation. The secrets of fabrication were not to be divulged in foreign provinces, even when artisans were forced to move in the wake of wars or famines. Nevertheless, there emerged a movement towards cities, where manufactories were more and more numerous and dynamic, such was extent of domestic and foreign demand. Some of these factories belonged to the emperor, who allocated the profits earned to public works. Created by Akbar, the carpet factory was managed by Persian specialists.

If the Hindu rajah showed reticence in interfering in the world of business, from which he contented himself with receiving the taxes, the Muslim monarch had no such qualms and took initiatives in the economic world whose management he organized. Monopolies were not unknown in the world of medieval India where the *zamorins* of Calicut had the monopoly of pepper and the king of Ceylon controlled the markets of cinnamon and precious stones. The Moguls would arrogate the monopoly of indigo, saltpetre and lead, which would result in discouraging the operators.

The intervention of the emperor, even when it was beneficial, disturbed established conventions and displaced people. He recruited specialists from distant provinces to work in *karkhanas*, workshops where those who worked on costly materials assembled. The Moguls set up these establishments in their principal cities where they functioned for them, whether it was for the equipment of the army, public works, the faceting of diamonds or the composition of miniatures. The *karkhanas* were melting pots where Mogul civilization crystallized, where technical and artistic initiatives were born out of the innovations of foreign specialists and the expertise of the best artisans of the Indian world.

The rapid expansion of urbanization

The emperor Babur writes in his memoirs that the cities of India 'become depopulated or established in an instant' and that if there were 'the reasons for fleeing from them, then, in a day or a day and a half, there no longer remained any trace of the vestiges of the great cities that had been populated for years and years.'[9] This remark made towards 1529 by the first of the Moguls enables us to gauge the extent of the transformations that had come about since then, as they have been observed by European voyagers under the reign of his successors.

We must be cautious not to generalize Babur's statement, which concerns only the north of India, but which brings to light the fragility of the urban fabric, made of hovels and the grass huts dominated by a few sanctuaries of stone or brick. By reinforcing the economic and architectural structures of ancient cities and by creating new cities, the Mogul Empire was to bring about a remarkable development of urbanisation and a relative stability. Epidemics, famines and wars continued to depopulate cities temporarily, like Surat, which had to brave simultaneously the famine of 1630 and the devastating raids of the Marathas.

The information that we have at our disposal cannot be exhaustive, because it emanates for the most part from European travellers who had only a limited vision of urban life. Besides, we lack accurate statistical and demographic data, while we cannot consider the estimates put forward by Abul-Fazl in *Ain-i-Akbari* as reliable facts.

With the exception of Fatehpur Sikri, the imperial city that was soon abandoned, there exists no prototype of the Mogul city. The ruling Muslim class reigned over a population of Hindu majority. Consequently, the new architectural landscapes – fortifications, mosques, outdoor arenas for equestrian exercise – superimposed or juxtaposed the structures of ancient cities. These structures corresponded to an age-old social organization, which succeeded in dominating even the new cities. All the same, city dwellers were more affected by the Islamic way of life than others were, especially when they worked in the imperial manufactories and *karkhanas*, where the rhythm of everyday life was governed by the calls to prayer and the Muslim calendar.

The administrative divisions of the territory led to the development of certain cities, which had become the centres of *subas* or *sarkars*. Others emerged at the junction of road networks, thanks to the impetus given by a few business-minded *jagirdars*; they thrived around forts, caravanserais and mosques. The ever-growing demand, of both the Moguls and Europeans, gave a fillip to the manufacturing traditions of cities like Ahmadabad for textiles, or incited other cities, like Patna, to diversify their production. These avenues for development sometimes concurred to bring prosperity to cities like Agra and Lahore, or crowned the fame of pilgrimage centres like Benares, Puri or Ujjain. The activities of European companies favoured the emergence of emporiums in coastal areas.

Rather than founding an entire city for their glory, the Moguls preferred to edify twin or satellite cities bearing the stamp of their style adjacent to ancient urban centres – like Shahjahanabad, at the gates of Delhi, or Hyderabad, under the walls of Golconda. However great these cities might have been, none of them could claim the status of a capital. The Mogul Empire only had capitals of a day, or of a few months, there where the emperor resided, be it in Agra, Delhi or Lahore, or else the tents of a military camp. Camps in fact attracted a crowd of artisans, merchants, servants and strolling players. The largest of them accommodated, according to François Bernier, three to four hundred thousand people and sometimes gave the neighbouring city a boost for its future prosperity. It was only in the eighteenth century that Delhi became the de facto capital.

Almost always fortified, the cities sprawled beyond the walls. The prevalence of suburbs is a typically Indian phenomenon, observed in Gaur or in Vijayanagar a long time before the Mogul period. Here, vegetable field crops alternated with Muslim tombs and small Hindu temples. It was here that a semi-rural population bustled around the fires of its villages and that the members of the impure castes were relegated – butchers, tanners, launderers; it was also here that those who were unable to reintegrate after being displaced by wars or famines assembled. Sometimes, suburbs gained significance thanks to their proximity with a military camp or the sepulchre of a Sufi saint.

Dominated by the citadel, the city centre was divided into quarters (*mahals*) closed by gates, and characterized by the geographical origin, religion or function of those who lived there. The city was a juxtaposition of *mahals* where everybody lived side by side, yet without mixing with each other. Municipal bodies were non-existent, a number of *mahals* being governed by their own caste-based assemblies that dispensed justice concurrent with their customary law. The only relations of dependency were those that bound certain artisans to imperial *karkhanas* or to powerful patron-clients who guaranteed them opportunities for employment but who did not refrain from harassing them.

The city came under the authority of the local *subadar* and did not have any other governor than the governor of the citadel whose prerogatives were limited to military affairs. Order was ensured by notables who may have been elected or chosen by the provincial authorities. The qadi was charged with the task of applying the Koranic Law. The *kotwal*, initially the commander of the stronghold, was a sort of chief commissioner of police, already present in pre-Mogul cities, and whose role became increasingly important. Assisted by a militia, he ordered patrols, imprisoned delinquents, supervised the closing of the gates, monitored weights and measures and collected certain taxes. He would gradually become the eyes and ears of the emperor, for whom he organized espionage activities in the area under his control. His multitudinous duties sometimes overlapped those of the *muhtasib*, in charge of inspecting the markets and of ensuring the probity of transactions. In the big cities of the north of the peninsula, primarily in Gujarat and Rajasthan, merchant communities were congregated within a *mahajan*, a representative body placed under the authority of a *nagarseth*, generally a *bania* or a Jain, sometimes a Parsi. The *mahajan* was free from all political obligations and was linked to the central power only by financial servitudes. Taxes, customs and transit duties were levied and transmitted by the *nagarseth* to the imperial authorities.

At the end of the seventeenth century, Kabul, Lahore, Delhi, Agra, Benares, Patna, Ahmadabad, Surat, Ajmer and Burhanpur were the great cities of the empire. They prospered while, on the fringes of the subcontinent, the warehouses and forts of European companies developed in Madras, Calcutta and Bombay. No one suspected at the time that these new agglomerations were to become the metropolises of the future.

VIII

THE MARITIME ECONOMY
AND THE TRADING COMPANIES

From the fall of Vijayanagar until the arrival
of European companies (1565–1600)

The turn of the sixteenth century had been marked by the domination of oceanic commerce by Indian-born Muslim sea traders. In the course of the years that followed, the mounting power of the Gujaratis clashed with the maritime expansion of the Portuguese, but the fortunes of these rivals soon began to wane. The tide had turned, in Asia as well as in Europe. Annexed by Akbar to the Mogul Empire in 1573 in the wake of a gruelling war, Gujarat had rapidly recovered its economic growth under the impetus given by the conquering emperor, but was never to attain the glory of bygone days. Previously, the Gujarati merchants had transferred a part of their activities to Diu and Goa, bringing the Portuguese State of India a recurrence of prosperity. United with the Spain of Philippe II of Habsburg in 1580, Portugal retained control of its overseas possessions, but with reduced resources. The setbacks encountered by the Portuguese India Company, incorporated in 1628, were to bring Portuguese expansion in India to a halt.

The networks of Indian maritime traders suffered the backlash of these fluctuations in the balance of power. While the old ports of Vijayanagar, Pulicat and Bhatkal entered a course of decline, the fortune of Golconda contributed to the prosperity of Nagapattinam and gave Masulipatnam a spectacular economic fillip as early as 1560. In Malabar, the revitalization of Cochin meant it eclipsed all the other ports, which had been weakened by the new circuits of distribution of pepper to the domestic market, and by competition from Sumatra whose long pepper was increasingly in demand. With Cambay sinking deeper and deeper into the sands, Surat asserted itself as the largest port of Gujarat, stimulated by Mogul demand and by the growth of the Ottoman Empire, a great consumer of textiles.

A century after the arrival of the Portuguese, the almost simultaneous birth of the Dutch and English East India Companies would have far-reaching repercussions on the entire seafaring life of the seventeenth century. It would bring about a transformation in the nature of commerce, the appearance of new types of merchants and the emergence of new ports. The success of the two companies soon served as a model: a Danish company was founded as early as 1616, which had to restrict its expansion to the trading post of Tranquebar, more famous for its missionary activities than for its commercial performances. A Swedish company was incorporated in 1617 only to disappear almost immediately.

European conflicts, carried to Asia, fuelled mercantile rivalries, all the more with the French company entering the fray (1719). The Anglo-French wars went beyond economics and were not without consequence on the political power balance of the subcontinent.

For those interested in the history of modern India, Europe is too often the tree that hides the forest. However significant the Dutch, English or French interventions might have been, these must not overshadow the economic activity of Indian business circles, which remained considerable in the course of the seventeenth and eighteenth centuries.

The decline of the Portuguese, Indian alliances and European rivalries. Portuguese Asia at the dawn of the seventeenth century

Let us make a brief review of a century of Portuguese presence. They had created an immense maritime network, sustained by about fifty bases of operations around the Indian Ocean and the China Sea, particularly in Ormuz, Colombo, Malacca, Macao and Nagasaki. In India itself, they had established a capital, Goa, the seat of the State of India (*estado da India*) that encompassed all their Asian possessions. The trading posts and fortresses implanted on the coasts of Malabar – Cannanore, Cochin, Quilon – dated from the early years of Portuguese expansion, while the strongholds of the North – Diu, Daman, Bassein, Chaul – and the trading posts of San Thome and Pipli, on the Bay of Bengal, had been founded more recently.

The Portuguese Crown had arrogated the monopoly over the pepper trade and had to face the hostile reactions of Muslim communities who had previously cornered the profits from it. The conflicts began to abate at the beginning of the seventeenth century, perhaps owing to the new order that emerged on the subcontinent. Earlier, the Portuguese had taken advantage of the disarray caused by the wars of Mogul conquest in order to consolidate their positions, but it was not long before they felt the effects of the disorganization of trade in the Deccan, then of the trend that diverted commerce towards Delhi and to the countries of the Bay of Bengal.

In 1580, the year in which Portugal was united with the Spanish Crown, what did commerce in India represent for the Habsburgs of Madrid? Essentially, the loads of spice on vessels that set sail for Lisbon every year in January. However, these cargoes did not amount to more than 6–7 per cent of the trade of the *estado da India*, which had entered the more lucrative channels of inter-Asian trade a long time ago. As early as 1513, Albuquerque declared that it was more profitable to distribute spices in Asia than to transport them to Lisbon. The pepper crisis only intensified this trend. Poorly paid, and more interested in the incomes offered by private traffic than in the profits of the Crown, the royal functionaries had no concern for fighting administrative corruption and nonchalance.

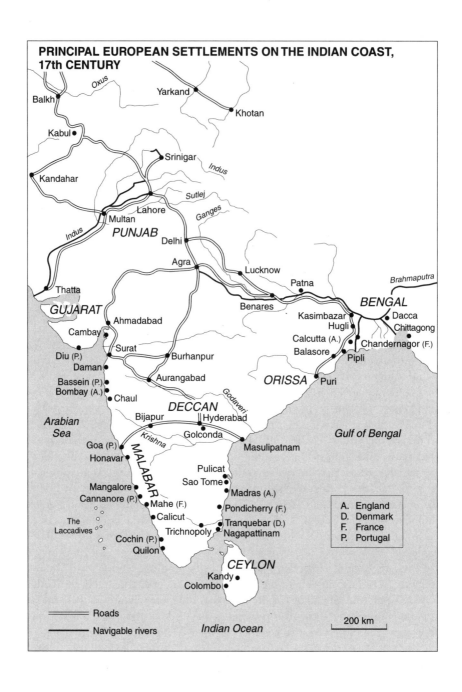

PRINCIPAL EUROPEAN SETTLEMENTS ON THE INDIAN COAST, 17th CENTURY

Oxus

Balkh

Yarkand

Khotan

Kabul

Srinigar

Indus

Kandahar

Sutlej

Lahore

Ganges

Multan

PUNJAB

Delhi

Indus

Agra

Lucknow

Patna

Benares

BENGAL

Brahmaputra

Thatta

Kasimbazar

Dacca

Chittagong

GUJARAT

Ahmadabad

Hugli

Cambay

Surat

Calcutta (A.)

Chandernagor (F.)

Diu (P.)

Balasore

Daman

Burhanpur

Pipli

Bassein (P.)

Aurangabad

ORISSA

Puri

Bombay (A.)

Chaul

Godaveri

Arabian
Sea

DECCAN

Bijapur

Hyderabad

Golconda

Gulf of Bengal

Goa (P.)

Krishna

Masulipatnam

Honavar

MALABAR

Pulicat

Mangalore

Sao Tome

Cannanore (P.)

Mahe (F.)

Madras (A.)

The
Laccadives

Calicut

Pondicherry (F.)

Trichnopoly

Tranquebar (D.)

Cochin (P.)

Nagapattinam

Quilon

CEYLON

Kandy

Colombo

A.	England
D.	Denmark
F.	France
P.	Portugal

Indian Ocean

Roads

Navigable rivers

200 km

Despite these signs of decadence, the prestige of Portugal remained intact during the early years of the seventeenth century, as reported by the Frenchman François Pyrard de Laval.[1] It was in no way eclipsed by that of Spain whose king was only a name in the diplomatic protocol and whose currency, the silver real, was much better known because its value attracted merchants and financiers to Goa. India was acquainted only with the Portuguese of Goa whom Akbar and his successor treated with deference. The respect that the Moguls showed earned them also that of sultans and rajahs, who, almost all, sent ambassadors to Goa and permitted the Portuguese to trade in their ports. In Malabar, Calicut kept its distance, but Cochin prospered and created fruitful relations with Bengal where a large number of Portuguese lived on private trading, the profitability of which adversely affected the official commerce. Pyrard affirms that the Portuguese language was understood in most of the coastal regions of the eastern seas. Goa offered the safety of its port from where armadas in charge of escorting Indian merchant ships set sail two or three times a year – from fifty to hundred ships for each convoy (*cafila*), thus protected from the attacks of pirates.

Mogul policy contributed to moderating the attitude of the Portuguese towards Islam. The enemy was no longer the 'Moor,' but the 'other European', whether English or Dutch. In fact, Portugal was to pay the price for its association with the crown of the Habsburgs, which forced it to become entangled in the quarrels of Spain and to compromise its age-old alliance with Flanders and England. Transposed to the Indian seas, Spain's European contention would further endanger a policy that was perhaps already doomed to failure.

The Portuguese India Company

The profits that the Dutch and the English began to amass gave the leaders in Madrid and Lisbon food for thought. With the advantage of their relations and their experience, should not the Portuguese be faring better? It was only in 1624 that the Portuguese India Company crystallized and forthwith became a part of the 'grand project' of the Spanish minister, the count-duke of Olivares, designed to strike at the nascent power of the Dutch and to expand Hispanic commerce worldwide. Nothing of this inordinately ambitious design was to be successful, except for the official incorporation of the Portuguese India Company.

The company caused more mistrust than enthusiasm. The board of directors had its headquarters in Lisbon and its directors were members of the Business Council of Madrid, which added fuel to the anti-Spanish prejudice of a fraction of public opinion. The Council of Goa functioned under the command of Lisbon, but distance conferred a relative autonomy. In fact, it was directly subjected to the authority of the viceroy Count Linhares, an indefatigable worker to whom the Company owed its brief existence. The company, however, deserves to be mentioned because the changes effected by the adaptation of new structures to the routines of the *estado da India* throw light on the profound causes of its failure.

Lack of funds prevented the Company from endowing itself with powers sufficiently great to overcome the difficulties that were in store for it. One of the most redoubtable of these was the opposition of the municipal authorities of Goa. Jealous of its privileges, the municipality obliged the company to confine its activities to the trade in spices with Lisbon and to give up the lucrative inter-Asian commerce, which extended as far as the China Sea. A prisoner of its prejudices, it could not suffer the presence of 'new Christians'[2] among the company's directors, which discredited the entire enterprise. The Company could lay claim only to the monopoly of pepper, coral and ebony, and to some profits earned from the export of indigo, saltpetre and cinnamon. It committed a spate of errors and never advanced funds necessary for buying pepper during the high season, as did the Dutch who swept up almost all the production of Malabar at cheap rates. No arrangement had been made for the maintenance of barques, which set sail without having been repaired, with ailing crews, bitter biscuits and rotten provisions. Consequently, only sailors of fortune, often adolescents, could be recruited. Adult and physically fit men turned their back on India and preferred the promising future offered by the Americas.

Though certain agreements had been signed with the English, the tenacity of the Dutch remained unshakeable and increasingly restricted the field of supplies for the Company. Soon deprived of the spices of the Moluccas, it strove to obtain the monopoly on cinnamon by clinging on to Ceylon, where the uprising in Kandy, in 1630, completely shattered its hopes. In Goa, the viceroy could no longer hide his scepticism with regard to the future. At the end of 1632, the company was reviewed, and a few years later liquidated. In 1641, the Dutch fleet seized Malacca, dealing the death blow to Portuguese hegemony over the spice trade.

The Companies of Northern Europe

The companies of the United Provinces

Flanders, more than any other country in northern Europe, had been associated with Portuguese expansion in Asia. From the early years of the sixteenth century, the names of Flemish artillerymen, recruited for their skills by the Portuguese Crown, appear in wage rolls.

We can trace the career of some of these men, like Rutger de Gueldre, *condestabre*[3] of the fortress of Cannanore, who returned to Europe and who was one of those who frequented the Portuguese trading post of Antwerp. In this connection, we need to highlight the role played by this commercial establishment, which also doubled as a cultural centre frequented by Erasmus, Thomas More and Albert Dürer, and from where news from India was disseminated to Great Britain and to the Germanic world. It was here, among the bundles of spices, the jewels and the textiles, that an interest in India awakened in Europe, an interest that would grow unceasingly. Thanks to the close ties between Lisbon, Flanders and Holland – these last two countries were in fact unified under the sceptre of the Habsburgs – Dutch agents were numerous in the Iberian ports. Some of them embarked on armadas and gained knowledge of the customs of eastern commerce.

Even as the Mogul order was establishing itself in India, Europe became embroiled in religious wars, adding fuel to the competition between Catholic Spain and Protestant England. The northern provinces of the Netherlands revolted against the domination of the Habsburgs and founded in Utrecht the Republic of the United Provinces in 1579, a year before the accession of Portugal to Spain. Philippe II immediately prohibited Dutch access to the Iberian ports. The Dutch then decided to break the Hispanic monopoly over the spice trade. They had a choice informer at their disposal: Jan Huygen van Linschoten, who was at the time on a short stay in Seville, embarked for Goa, where he served several years under the archbishop of the city. He gathered a wealth of information that he pertinently exposed in the report that he published after his return (1592).[4] On reading of this text, we are no longer surprised at the rapidity with which the Dutch adapted themselves to the world of Asian business.

In 1594, the Company of distant lands was born in Amsterdam. It raised capital of 290,000 florins and fitted out four vessels that set sail the following year under the command of Cornelius Houtman. In order to keep clear of the Portuguese patrols, he navigated directly from the Cape to Java, where he succeeded in gaining from the sultan of Bantam the same privileges as those granted to the Portuguese. Houtman's fleet would not however reach the Molucca Islands. It would return to Amsterdam with a meagre cargo of spices and with crews reduced by half. In spite of a few signs of discouragement, other companies were incorporated in Zealand, Rotterdam and Amsterdam. A second expedition, undertaken in 1600 by the companies based in Amsterdam, would earn profits of about 400 per cent.

The leaders of the United Provinces then decided to consolidate the companies with a view to optimizing their efficiency. The charter of 20 March 1602 recorded the creation of the Vereenigde Ooste Indische Compagnie (VOC) under the aegis of the Republic and under the authority of seventeen directors, the famous Heeren XVII. Under the control of the Admiralty and of the central government, it nevertheless enjoyed a relative autonomy. The economy of the company and that of the Republic would not be confused with each other. In a country where land was rare and land tax high, a large number of people wanted to invest in seaborne commerce. The entire nation participated in an enterprise that would make the United Provinces a world power.

Taking advantage of the Portuguese experience, the Dutch were wary of projecting any ideology and aspired only to the prosperity of their trade. Pragmatically, they went to the very source of the most precious spices, the Indonesian Archipelago and especially the Moluccas where clove and nutmeg grew. From the Cape to Java, they used a straight route that touched Ceylon where they got supplies of cinnamon. Nevertheless, payment for spices in silver coinage proved to be costly, and they could no longer deny the facts: it was not possible to dissociate the commerce of the Archipelago from that of India, whose cotton goods were the base of all trade. Thus, they would not be able to avoid India, where they would have to brave the hostility of the Portuguese. The Zamorin of Calicut and the *ali rajah* of Cannanore sought to forge ties with them but the Portuguese tracked down these heretic *luteranos* (Lutherans) who sought to seize the monopoly of the spice trade from them. In Cochin as in Goa, the local judicial authorities did not hesitate to carry out sentences in anticipation of the verdict of the Inquisition: any foreigner whose origin was dubious was clapped in irons and hung if he was proved to be Dutch.

As early as 1605, the VOC confirmed its determination by asserting its supremacy in the spice market and sent its agents to Masulipatnam, where, the following year, they obtained tax benefits from the sultan of Golconda and the authorization to establish a trading post. From Masulipatnam, the finest cloths were exported to Bantam and Atjeh, in the East Indian Spice Islands, but the Dutch soon discovered that the cheapest cotton goods were produced in the south of Coromandel, outside the limits of Mogul taxation. Furthermore, these were the cotton goods that met the demand of the inhabitants of the Moluccas. The VOC opened its factories in Tenganapatnam (1609) and Pulicat (1610), which would soon become the hub of a prosperous activity. It was at this juncture that Hendrik Brouwer declared that Coromandel was the left arm of the Moluccas.

The other great textile-producing region, Gujarat, was more difficult to penetrate. The Portuguese held strongholds here and patrolled the length of the coasts with the assent of the Moguls. The first Dutch agent reached Surat and died in 1607. A small trading post would stagnate until 1619, the year in which Pieter van den Broeke established a permanent factory.

From their bridgeheads on the Javanese coast, the Dutch harassed and pillaged Portuguese vessels, which could no longer leave Malacca without peril. Malacca remained prosperous and continued to distribute textiles in many ports in the archipelago, thanks to the Indo-Portuguese Coromandel network, based in San Thome. The Dutch established themselves in Jakarta, which they re-named Batavia (1619) making it their capital, and seized control of the island of Amboyna with a view to impeding the meeting of the Portuguese fleet of Malacca with the armada of the Spanish established in Manila. In these early years of the seventeenth century, they had to brave the counter-attacks of the Portuguese and the Spanish while simultaneously tackling the enterprises of new European competitors, the agents of the English East India Company.

The East India Company

The same motivation, the same design, had driven the Dutch and the English on the route to Asia, both making the most of the same initiation, that of the Portuguese experience. The coastal trade on the Atlantic had forged age-old ties between the Portuguese ports and those of the British Isles. The English merchants had already begun to show an interest in the East, motivated by the profits amassed in Lisbon, and even more by the valuable captures of English corsairs who swooped down on the barques en route to Antwerp.

Since the beginning of the sixteenth century, merchants and navigators had striven to reach Asia by the northern seas. Later, the agents of the Turkey Company tried to reach India overland. This was achieved by John Newberry, who was received in 1584 in the court of Akbar before disappearing. His companion Ralph Fitch pursued this voyage, reaching as far as Bengal, and later visiting Burma, Siam and the Malay Peninsula. On his return (1591), the movement that urged the English towards India reached a turning point. The state of war with Spain closed the Iberian ports to British ships and merchants. This was neither the time for futile attempts to find a route to India other than by way of the Cape. England had been fortified by the recent successes of Francis Drake and his henchmen, which had proved the quality of its ships and its sailors. In 1599, a group of London-based merchants requested authorization from Queen Elizabeth I to start a private company. Incorporated in the last days of the year 1600, the East India Company inaugurated its first trading post in Bantam two years later.

Like the Dutch and for the same reasons, the English had headed for the East Indian Spice Islands. The intransigence of their competitors on the question of monopoly had shattered their hopes. The solidarity of the Protestants against the Catholic powers could not prevail over the stakes of the spice trade, all the more so, as England, since the advent of James Stuart (1603), had become a 'Papist' nation. The East India Company, which had only one-tenth of VOC's capital, had to be satisfied with playing second fiddle or had to hunt on other grounds. That is why the English turned towards India, not only to acquire the indispensable textiles, but also to scout for new markets. It was an arduous task: the Portuguese controlled the west coast where they vied for the pepper-producing lands with the local rajahs, the Dutch had already entrenched themselves in the Coromandel, and buying the connivance of local merchants and notables was onerous.

What assets could they have if they could no longer count on spices? Sugar, textiles and saltpetre were less lucrative as they were more cumbersome in the holds. After vegetating for a few years, the English chose to establish themselves in Gujarat, at the source of textiles, and to forge diplomatic relations at the highest levels, that is with the Moguls. By doing so, they played two winning cards.

In 1607, Captain William Hawkins reached Surat and soon earned the friendship of Jahangir, who made him a *mansabdar*. The favours he received there were personal privileges and not rights granted to the Company. During the four years that Hawkins spent in the royal entourage, the groundwork was laid and the image of the European changed. Indians discovered that the Portuguese were not the only people to rule over the seas and that, even if they were the best pilots, they had less patience and less business acumen than the traders of northern Europe. The latter refrained from interfering in political or religious affairs. The Moguls were growing increasingly intolerant towards the constant attacks that the Portuguese mounted on vessels carrying pilgrims to Mecca. When, in 1612, Captain Best meted out a crushing defeat on the Portuguese fleet off the coast of Gujarat, the tide began to turn in favour of the English. An imperial *farman* granted them the right to trade in Surat the following year. This city would from then on be the seat of the presidency of the East India Company. In London, the government, formerly sceptical, would extend its support to its enterprises.

The Company established trading posts in Siam (1612), in Macassar (1613), in Sumatra (1615) and entrenched itself solidly in Masulipatnam where it had started a factory[5] in 1611 through the good offices of a Dutch agent. In 1615, a diplomatic mission from James I led by the ambassador Thomas Roe, obtained important privileges. In return, an English squadron escorted the vessels of Muslim pilgrims and the merchant ships that accompanied them. This agreement, faithfully abided by, would safeguard the enterprises of the East India Company until the end of the eighteenth century.

The establishment of the British in Surat hailed the beginning of their fortunes. They took control of the route through the Persian Gulf, which the Portuguese fleet based in Diu disputed to their own great cost. In 1622, they laid siege to Ormuz, which they captured after furious resistance, with the help of Persian troops. In the Spice Archipelago, the rupture with the VOC was complete when Dutch agents pillaged a British factory on the island of Amboyna and massacred its occupants (1623).

Portuguese supremacy collapsed while the Dutch asserted their presence in the south and the English in the north. A new scenario was taking shape, where the strategies of these two new powers would be deployed with the collusion or otherwise of Indian maritime traders.

The economic policy of the companies

In the course of the seventeenth century, the English and the Dutch would succeed the Portuguese in the markets of the Indian Ocean, a political context marked by the ascension of three great powers: the Ottoman Empire, present on the Indian Ocean since 1517, the Persian Empire of the Safavids, and the Mogul Empire. All these three powers were Islamic; they actively encouraged commerce; they constructed and protected transport links that connected the ports to increasingly distant continental cities. The naval power of the Ottomans declined following the loss of Yemen (1636), but they retained possession of a part of the Iraqi coast, at the head of the Persian Gulf. On the Iranian coastline, Bandar Abbas thrived at the end of the caravanserai route that served Chiraz and Ispahan.

The new economic circumstances in the western seas of the Indian Ocean opened the road for the East India Company, all the more as the defeat of the Portuguese was rapidly reaching its culmination. Ousted from Bahrain in 1602, they lost Ormuz in 1622, Suhar (Oman) in 1643 and Muscat in 1650; they nevertheless maintained their presence in Diu, notwithstanding the assaults of the Ottoman fleet. Diu had to face relentless competition from Surat where the English had obtained from the Moguls the same import entitlements as those granted to Asian merchants. Fortified by their mission of protecting the Indian Muslim ships sailing to Mecca, the English deployed their activities in the ports of the Middle East, the length of the sea route linking Surat to Moka. They stood their ground in spite of the attacks of the Marathas and the great famine of 1630, which threw the production of textiles into disarray. Even though the English compensated their losses by transferring a part of their purchases to the markets of Coromandel and Bengal, they secured the respect of the Gujarati merchants, who would always prefer them to the Dutch.

As for the Dutch, they pursued their conquest of markets in the South Seas, as it was easier to exert pressure on the local kinglets than on the sovereigns of great empires. Their aim was the total control of the spice trade. Their bases grew in number in the Indonesian Archipelago where they consolidated their monopoly of cloves, nuts and mace. They carved out their place in the Southeast Asian networks controlled by the Chinese and the Japanese. After driving the Portuguese out of Malacca (1641), they succeeded in less than ten years in eliminating them from the South Seas, deprived them of cinnamon by taking over Colombo (1656), then of pepper by capturing Cochin (1663) and the other strongholds of Malabar from them. This loss was a disaster to Goa, already subjected to a Dutch blockade for the preceding thirty years. As the absolute masters of the spice trade, the Dutch would quote their prices, in Asia as well as in Europe.

However impressive these advances might have been, they have to be placed in the context of the great Asian trade in order to understand that the commercial activity of the Europeans was still a marginal element, confined to the coastal regions, and vulnerable since it was far from its bases. There is no doubt that their survival in Asia owed much to the discovery of America and its silver mines. The appearance of the Spanish real on the markets of Goa had played a decisive role in the maintenance of its prosperity. Henceforth, more prized than gold, silver came from all quarters: from Acapulco by the galleon of Manila,[6] from Spain through the Middle East for the purchase of silk, indigo and spices. It also came from Japan through Batavia. But to be exchanged on the Indian markets, silver had to be melted, then minted into the local currency, which incurred additional expenses.

Between 1650 and 1750, the volume of trade grew at a constant pace. Dutch expenses were multiplied ten-fold. Even though the profits of the VOC were considerable in Amsterdam, the company had to reduce the draining of silver into Asia and find new resources by distributing spices in India where consumption was greater than in Europe. It established warehouses in Agra, Bengal and even in Surat, where it sought in vain to supplant the British company in the textiles market.

Practically excluded from the spice-growing lands, the East India Company had to buy them second hand. Since its beginning, the Dutch monopoly had forced it exploit other resources and to imagine other trades. Why not offer Europe these textiles so appreciated in Asia? English ships took to London the calico of Gujarat, the demand for which would only grow. In 1614, 12,000 pieces were loaded in Surat and more than 220,000 in 1625. Not content with flooding the market in London, the British carried muslins, light cotton goods and painted fabrics to the Near East.

The movement gained momentum in the second half of the seventeenth century, all the more as the English had established since 1640 a small coastal enclave in Madras obtained as a lease from a neighbouring rajah, where they traded in complete independence. On the Bay of Bengal, where their trading post of Amagaon functioned since 1625, they settled down in 1690 in Calcutta, on the banks of the Hoogly, on the oldest arm of the Ganges. With the same concern for autonomy, they would build a fortress around this city. A third important place fell to their share in 1674 in the west coast, following the marriage of Charles II and Catherine of Braganza, a Portuguese princess, of whom it is said that she introduced the use of tea to Britain and who brought the territory of Bombay as dowry.

The European clientele developed an unprecedented craze for textiles from India. Sold at affordable prices (manpower in India was five to ten times cheaper than in Britain), white cotton fabrics, striped or checked, spread everywhere. Chintzes from

Coromandel, embroidered pieces and taffetas from Bengal, were soon more in demand than the silks of Persia, France and Italy. The East India Company – which became in 1708 the United Company of Merchants of England – did not content itself with the European market, it distributed calicos of low quality (Negro's cloth) in the ports of Africa and sold striped and checked fabrics called 'madras' as far as America. To cite just one example, it exported 750,000 pieces from India in 1664, representing 75 per cent of its turnover. In the meanwhile, the Company began to take an interest in other products, like indigo and especially saltpetre, the demand for which was high in England owing to the development of artillery.

The Dutch used textiles as a trading currency for obtaining spices rather than for marketing them all over the world. Their business activities were in no way less remarkable to those of the British, but focused on other trades. But before the English, they had engaged in the inter-Asian commerce and had developed their own network thanks to the solid positions they had conquered in the Spice Islands and to their intermediaries in Bengal, Malabar and the Persian Gulf. The trade that they carried on on a large scale allowed them not only to gain substantial profits, but also to obtain silver from Japan, which they added to the silver they continued to bring from the United Provinces. If the Indonesian Archipelago and Malabar supplied spices to them, it was in Bengal that they concentrated their inter-Asian commercial activities. With abundant supplies of food, textiles and saltpetre, this region provided them with most of the merchandize required for lucrative trading. At the beginning of the eighteenth century, while British commerce spanned the north and the west of the Indian Ocean, Dutch trade activities, based in the south, extended to the Far East.

In exploiting the market by activities that went beyond the scope of traditional trades, the companies of northern Europe triggered off an evolution laden with consequences for the Indian economy. For instance, the Dutch brought tea from China and copper from Japan to Surat, cheaper than European copper. They brought porcelain, ruining the port of Rander in Gujarat, which had specialized for centuries in its distribution. In the Persian Gulf, the British preferred to barter Indian sugar for silk to bartering rice for horses. They would soon take up the sale of horses to the Moguls through the ports of Gujarat. On top of that, the Europeans ushered in new modes of transaction, particularly in the field of textiles. After presenting a certain number of samples in the market places in London or in Amsterdam, the companies placed orders with the Indian brokers for prices that pleased their clients and that they were sure to dispose of.

Everything was done on the basis of contracts negotiated several months before the arrival of their ships in India. The quality of the fabrics, their dimensions, colours and prices were recorded, along with the name of the supplier and the date of delivery. Procedures like these led to a standardization of production. It was difficult for the broker to obtain from the artisans mass produced pieces which were exactly the same and in sufficient quantities. The companies advanced money that the producers transmitted to the weavers, but they were demanding and rejected pieces that did not conform to the order. Thus, with a view to limiting losses, Indian merchants deferred deliveries until the last minute, so that the Europeans, in a hurry to set sail, did not have the time to carry out thorough inspections before their scheduled departure.

If the companies' business flourished, the balance of trade always tipped in favour of India, whose consumption of European goods, though it was growing rapidly, remained meagre. The companies still brought in silver in abundance, lead, coral and mercury, and also luxury products that were highly prized by Mogul nobles: tapestries and mirrors, clocks, amber from the Baltic, velvet and woollens, Spanish swords and coins pirated on the galleons.

At the dawn of the eighteenth century, the prosperity of Indian trade continued to be such that there was no suspicion of these European traders with their modest lifestyles and crude manners. The exasperation that their business demands some-times caused was compensated by the profits that their activities produced: an influx of silver coinage, the augmentation of taxes, the increase in customs revenues owing to the volume of exports. The unprecedented growth of the textile industry ensured full employment and enriched the brokers, even if the producers suffered from the fall in prices and the weavers from the constraints of a large-scale production.

The English and the Dutch succeeded there where the Portuguese had failed, no doubt because their methods were more efficient and because they were not impeded by administrative bottlenecks imposed by distant national bodies. The northern Europeans acted on behalf of private interests that placed great emphasis on initiative and never bound the political authorities of England or the United Provinces. Contrary to the Portuguese who had infiltrated into already existing net-works, they had to innovate, obliged by the pressure of the already established powers to imagine strategies, to export to Europe products other than spices, to keep in tune with the evolution of the Asian demand. Thus, the English overcame their initial shortcoming by a minute observation of the local economic scene and by a prudent adaptation. They acquired a certain expertise in bargaining and a patient tenacity in negotiations. The Mogul hegemony forbade all political or religious interferences, even if the successes of the East India Company in Bengal gave its governor, Sir John Child, a glimpse of the possibility of dominating India and urged him to make war with the Moguls (1687–9). This vain adventure, which only resulted in the retreat of the British into their strongholds, henceforth fortified, did not shake the power of the Mogul Empire.

The French Companies

The early expeditions

'The abundance of all sorts of goods that France produces . . . can be the reason why the French have for a long time neglected the navy. As the land . . . faithfully supplied them with goods in sufficiency, they felt no need to look for any other among the dangers of the infidelity of the seas,' wrote François Pyrard de Laval in 1615.[7] This explanation is perhaps not totally devoid of truth, but it does not satis-factorily explain why so few French had ventured onto the recently discovered route to India. It is true that some pirates, lured by the captures made on the Portuguese barques off the coasts of Brittany, had set sail to India, but no one knew what had become of them.

In 1528, the *Marie du Bon Secours*, fitted out by the merchants of Rouen, had run aground off Diu where its crew was sold by the Portuguese in the slave market. Other expeditions with only one or two vessels had not been followed up by a coherent project. Thus, in 1601, a company of the merchants of Saint-Malo, Laval and Vitré had reached Sumatra and carried Pyrard to the Indian seas. The account that Pyrard and his companion François Martin de Vitré made of their experience incited the king to create a company in the image of that of the United Provinces, which had become the model of success in a few short years. The hostility of the Dutch and the reticence of business circles to concur in investing in an enterprise like this only produced unsatisfactory results. A succession of ill-fated companies came into being only to die out almost immediately, but not without having brought several cargoes of pepper, indigo, cotton fabrics and a few caskets of precious stones.

A little later, in 1626, Cardinal Richelieu, who had succeeded in neutralizing the Dutch opposition for some time, encouraged the creation of a powerful company, the *Cent Associés pour le Commerce*, and subsequently the *Nacelle de Saint-Pierre Fleurdelysée*. The call for capital for both the companies met with failure, so great was the scepticism towards a project without clearly defined structures. 'Everyone wants to keep to himself,' observed King Louis XIII, on witnessing the inextricable rivalries between the Breton and Norman ship-owners. Besides, the complexities of the customs and taxation systems of the kingdom made the financing of private associations difficult.

However, sustained commercial relations with the ports of the Indian Ocean began to crystallize as early as 1635, thanks to the initiatives of small Dieppe-based companies, backed by Parisian financers, including Nicolas Fouquet. But they restricted their activities to the exploitation of Madagascar and the Mascareignes, which the French wanted to establish as the base for their ventures, as Java was for the Dutch. The continuity of these trade exchanges was to contribute to the implementation of the project that Colbert launched in 1664, the creation of a general Company destined to 'procure the kingdom the activity of commerce and to prevent the English and the Dutch from profiting from it alone, as they had done up to then.'[8]

The French East India Company and the Saint-Malo associations

Among the associations consolidated within the General Company, the *Compagnie des Indes Orientales* in particular attracted the attention of Colbert. Advised by François Caron, a Huguenot who had worked for the VOC, he studied the Dutch model at great length before nominating twenty-one directors, spread out over six autonomous provincial chambers who sent their delegates to a general chamber based in Paris. All these directors had the right to fit out ships, to undertake and to invest in projects. Colbert bestowed the Company with substantial funds. The registered capital was fixed at 15 million pounds in part raised with the support of the royal exchequer. This financing method, unfamiliar to the companies of northern Europe, would give the French enterprise a political dimension. It would guarantee a constant supply of resources, the support of the navy and the arbitrage of the State for resolving internal quarrels. The possible intervention of political authorities, however, put off the merchants who subscribed to only 16 per cent of the capital and deprived the chambers of the advantage of their business acumen.

Led by Admiral de la Haye, nine armed vessels stopped over in Surat in 1671. If we are to believe the testimony of Abbot Carré, dissensions among the French which were aired openly discredited them in the eyes of the Gujarati traders, to the great satisfaction of their English and Dutch competitors. On the Coromandel coast, the French seized San Thomé, the former Portuguese port recaptured by the sultan of Golconda, who, with the help of the Dutch, drove them out two years later. Distraught, de la Haye's squadron wandered the length of the coast until the admiral sent an emissary to the village of Pondicherry, ruled at the time by a kinglet, a vassal of the sultan of Bijapur. He received authorization to settle down there on the condition that he protected its sanctuaries.

Doomed to failure by the scarcity of subscribers and the inexperience of its managers, the first French East India Company hardly survived more than twenty years, despite the manna of royal subsidies. During this period, however, the French asserted their presence in the sea of Bengal, for which we have to give due credit to François Martin. Appointed director of Coromandel in 1685 after having served at Surat and Masulipatnam, he cultivated the alliance of the local princes and fortified Pondicherry. The small town had to simultaneously withstand the attacks of the English and Dutch naval forces and the disarray of a hinterland troubled by Maratha conquests. At the time of the death of François Martin (1709), the territory of Pondicherry had extended to include five other villages, and the Company had obtained the right to mint coins. The trading post of Chandernagore, founded in 1688 by François Martin's son-in-law, Boureau-Deslandes, prospered in Bengal.

Following its liquidation in 1706, the French East India Company was taken over by a group of ship-owners based in Saint-Malo who ferociously defended the local character of their company. They succeeded in what the royal company could not accomplish, with a smaller capital and a greater freedom for initiative. The competence of their navigators, the dynamism of their businessmen, the discernment of their buyers enabled the Saint-Malo companies to figure among the most successful enterprises and to dominate the markets for Asian goods in Europe.

The nature of the Saint-Malo trade was hardly any different from that of its competitors: in Pondicherry, as elsewhere, silver of Spanish origin, iron and lead were exchanged for saltpetre, dyewood, raw silk, cotton goods and large quantities of pepper. But its volume was much smaller: between 1711 and 1716, for instance, the Saint-Malo merchants despatched to India more than thirty vessels, in other words half of the strength of the East India Company, and one-fifth of that of the VOC. That said, and despite the tribulations of the companies, French positions had been consolidated in the sea of Bengal during the early years of the eighteenth century, while France became increasingly enmeshed in the disasters of the war of the Spanish succession.

The rebirth of the Compagnie des Indes (1719)

The financier John Law proposed to the ruined country a system wherein all the businesses of the kingdom were taken back, including the *Compagnie des Indes*, which alone survived the collapse of the enterprise. It had been equipped with new organizational structures designed to prevent it from becoming the stake of the clans of Saint-Malo and Nantes. Its management was shared among shareholders, six or eight directors and the commissioner of the king, who was in reality the true master and the executor of the governmental directives. In 1721, the Company received a new regulation codifying the previous texts, and which specified the hierarchy of the 'men of letters and soldiers'. On the field, the staff was few in number – about one hundred Europeans, all over India – assisted by native labourers and brokers. The military force included three hundred garrisoned soldiers who came to swell the ranks of a troop of Indian soldiers that at times numbered several thousand men.

Every year, after a stopover in Cadiz where Spanish silver piastres were bargained, the Company's squadron set sail from Lorient for the Mascarenes and the Coromandel coast. Pondicherry thrived under the authority of Beauvilliers de Courchant and especially Pierre-Christophe Lenoir, appointed governor in 1726, and president of the councils of all the provinces of the Indian Ocean: île de France and the Bourbon island, Chandernagore in Bengal, and Mahé on the Malabar coast, acquired in 1725. French factories were established in Calicut and Surat.

A skilful administrator, Lenoir settled the debts of the Company and attracted the Indian traders by the rigour of his management. He maintained cordial relations with the other European companies and succeeded in winning the favour of neighbouring Indian princes. At the same time, he built dissuasive fortifications around Pondicherry. Inside the enclosure wall, the city was constructed in the fashion of bastides, according to a plan of perpendicular roads. 'Like a gardener, Monsieur Lenoir enriched, ploughed, manured and prepared the soil for cultivation,' the Tamil broker Ananda Ranga Pillai would write later. When Lenoir returned to Paris in 1735, the Company was ready for more daring enterprises.

Indian merchants and new trends in seaborne commerce

It is difficult to measure the real impact of the activity of European companies on Indian commerce in the course of the seventeenth century. The great amount of documentation of the former too often masks the unknowns of the latter, even if it throws light on a few significant traits of Indian trade. Entire branches of Asian trade remain shrouded in obscurity, as the Europeans at that time had only limited contacts with merchant society. They could have access to the business world only through the mediation of a broker – *dubash, mudaliyar* or *banyan* – whom they had to choose with the utmost care. Indispensable for all trade negotiations, this character had to be rich enough to be creditworthy, competent enough to act as banker, money-changer and sometimes interpreter, and influential enough in the court to ensure his clients the favour of those in power. A failure could plunge them into misery or even cost them their lives.

In the wake of the changes that occurred in the course of the sixteenth and seventeenth centuries, what had become of the merchant societies that we had encountered at the dawn of the sixteenth century? The Gujaratis were no longer all-powerful in the western seas of the Indian Ocean, where Turkish naval forces were present, though the economic role of the Ottoman Empire was extremely limited. The *sharifs* of Mecca were the true masters of the Red Sea. The Persian Gulf witnessed a spurt of commercial activities under the impetus given by the Safavids, especially after the fall of Ormuz. The new port of Bandar Abbas attracted traders from the Middle East, India and Europe. Persian merchants, who had been present in the ports of the Deccan for a long time, reinforced their influence, often in liaison with the Armenians. The latter spread out all across India, working within an international network that, with Persia as its base, extended from Eastern Europe to the Far East. In 1562, they obtained from Akbar the authorization to settle down in Agra. At the beginning of the seventeenth century, they were present in Madras, Hoogly, Batavia, Manila, Burma and especially Surat. Christians without a state and without any will to dominate or to proselytize, they had integrated perfectly into the Asian economy thanks to the rapid coordination of their commercial intelligences. The English would make use of their services as those of the Parsi community, which was to take charge of trade in Bombay.

Spurred by the activity of new competitors, the Gujaratis no longer aspired to hegemony, but did not cease their wealth seeking. They took advantage of new trades, as in Moka, where the coffee market attracted an influx of Spanish piastres that the Gujarati merchants bartered for cotton goods. The ordeals that came down upon Gujarat – Mogul wars of conquest, famine, epidemics, Maratha raids – did not prevent Surat from being the most active port on the west coast, the one that met the combined demand for textiles of the Ottoman Empire, the Mogul court and the European companies. As we saw earlier, the East India Company occupied a privileged place in this city, even though it was consolidating its positions in Bengal and the Coromandel; the Portuguese ports of Diu and Goa hosted the negotiations of Gujarati merchants, who thus escaped the constraints of Mogul taxation. Indeed, so heavy were taxes in the middle of the seventeenth century that they forced a few important traders to exile. Focused on the western seas of the Indian Ocean, the Gujarati network fell to pieces in the South Seas, where Tamil merchants, who had supplanted them in Malacca during the Portuguese era, dominated Southeast Asian commerce. The Gujaratis also lost their positions in the Spice Islands, where the Dutch preferred the Chinese to them.

These new circumstances made the fortune of mercantile societies of the eastern Indian Ocean, where the situation was still influenced by the reactions provoked by Portuguese naval power. Under their protection, the Tamil merchants of Malacca had fitted out huge junks up until the middle of the seventeenth century. Other traders on the Coromandel coast escaped Portuguese control by resorting to smaller and more mobile ships and established a network of permanent trade with the ports of Irrawaddy and with Atjeh, to the north of Sumatra. These links were consolidated by the growing prosperity of Masulipatnam, enriched by both the power of Golconda and the revival of the maritime commerce of Arakan and Siam. At the beginning of the seventeenth century, Masulipatnam was the most important port on the east coast, the market where merchants exchanged rice, saltpetre, textiles, diamonds and weapons for horses from the Persian Gulf, elephants from Siam, rubies from Burma and spices from the Moluccas, the latter being brought by the Dutch. The Europeans were at the time just foreigners among others. Even while retaining their position in Masulipatnam, they preferred to it the ports of the small kingdoms of the South, where trade negotiations were less costly and where they could acquire their own territory. This shift would stimulate economic life around Madras and Pondicherry and give their chance to local traders.

The business circles of Bengal also experienced a recrudescence in commercial activity. Foreign trade was still based on food supplies and luxury textiles, but the increase in the production of silk and saltpetre guaranteed new profits. Too often devastated by hydrographical modifications, the cities of the eastern delta of the Ganges were soon abandoned in favour of those in the West that punctuated the banks of the Hoogly. It was here that Mogul notables and local dignitaries engaged in trade. And it was here that the Armenians fitted out their ships, the Europeans opened their factories, the English fort at Calcutta flourished.

The most significant feature of the economic scene in the seventeenth century was the concentration of commercial circuits catering to domestic markets. Oceanic and continental trades had deeper ramifications than in the medieval age. They appear intimately linked with each other operating within networks encompassing village economies, financial operations based on land revenues and the emporiums of coastal cities. A trend like this brought into contact social groups freshly integrated into the business world, who established new branches of trade.

In the present state of our knowledge, it is difficult to know to what extent traditional merchant society was affected by such transformations. It underwent a period of transition wherein the development of the state-production-foreign trade triangle depended both on structures peculiar to the Indian world and on opportunities offered by the activities of foreign economies. The guilds of the medieval age, on the path to extinction, survived in the form of family-owned enterprises that still imposed their presence in the distribution circuits of coastal trade. The character of the big trader, who already made his appearance in the sixteenth century, henceforth occupied a prominent place. The career of some of them even transcended the barriers of the caste system.

The separation of economic and political powers became less and less evident. In Bengal, seaborne commerce was dominated by the Mogul nobility before it fell into the hands of civil or military officials – *diwans* or *faujdars* – who collaborated with Armenian and English ship-owners. In Golconda, the merchant princes ruled over transoceanic trade, like Mir Jumla, governor of the capital, or the governor of Narsapur, who fitted out vessels for the sultan. If the sixteenth century offered numerous examples of religious leaders or officials of the state involved in commerce, like the *ali rajah* of Cannanore or Malik Gopi of Surat, they enjoyed complete freedom in business circles, but this was not true in the case of Mogul functionaries whose status made them vulnerable to governmental pressures. On the western front of the peninsula, Gujarati merchant society seemed, on the contrary, to have retained its traditional structures organised around the *mahajan*, which conferred them a greater autonomy. The astute strategy of the merchants of Surat enabled them to rise again into prominence at the close of the seventeenth century and to fit out huge vessels, comparable to those of a Mogul emperor.

At the beginning of the eighteenth century, the increase in imports to imperial cities and the growth in exports spurred by European demand ensured the prosperity of seaborne trade, in spite of the constraints imposed by the Mogul bureaucracy. But the leeway for the expansion of Indian maritime traders began to shrink: the Chinese staged a comeback in the eastern seas of the Indian Ocean and the Arabs in the Arabian Sea, and all the while European companies were establishing their own distribution networks.

IX

SOCIETY AND CULTURE

The Moguls and the sultans who had immediately preceded them were contemporary with the Renaissance and the century of Louis XIV, but they lived in an
intellectual and economic universe far removed from that of our European ancestors.
In spite of the presence of European travellers, ambassadors, merchants, artillerymen and missionaries, Indians were not really interested in the thought and
techniques of the West, not even in firearms. Athough they borrowed a few curious
or useful objects, like the swivel gun or hand pump for bailing out ships, they had
adopted neither printing nor the clock. Nor did they show the slightest curiosity for
the development of scientific thought that had followed in the wake of the
Copernican revolution in Europe. They would develop a modern mentality only
slowly, in the course of the nineteenth century: scholars like Sayyid Ahmad Khan
(1817–98) would write treatises as late as the middle of the nineteenth century to
defend the geocentric vision of the world. In India, the Middle Ages lasted until the
dawn of the nineteenth century.

Since the arrival of the Portuguese, India had maintained ties with Europe and
the development of its commerce, of its craft industry and no doubt of its money
supply was linked to these new trades. But for all that, mentalities did not change.
The horizon of the merchant remained limited to the closed communities of the
ports and the large inland cities. The vision of the rulers did not go beyond the
Muslim world, especially Iran and Central Asia, and at its best, their distant rival, the
Ottoman Empire.

Understanding Mogul culture is all the more difficult as generations of Indians,
and presently Pakistanis, have tried to revive the anachronisms created by their
British masters and to consider the past through the preoccupations of a nascent
nationalism. Instead of viewing the Mogul Empire as the last medieval empire
founded on the allegiance of heterogeneous territories and populations to a single
dynasty, they have seen in it a prototype of a bureaucratic modern state resting on
a national consensus. But, whatever the loyalty of the servants of the empire might
have been – and it was often great – we must not forget that it was based on a personal relation with a dynasty, and not on the abstract service rendered to the state
and to the nation.

Among these anachronisms, there is one specific to the Indian context, and which
consists of projecting into history the ideological opposition of the religious

communities, the consequences of which have so tragically marked modern history. In this regard, Indian nationalists, both Hindu and Muslim, (as well as a number of Western publicists, even scholars) espouse views contrary to those held by Pakistani ideologists, who are by definition of the Islamic faith. Underpinning their reasoning on common presuppositions, both these opposing schools of thought reduce the Mogul Empire to a Manichean struggle between two cultures and two religious communities. They even establish a chronology: until the end of Akbar's reign, harmony prevailed between the two communities, resulting in a limitless syncretism; in the seventeenth century, from Jahangir and especially under Aurangzeb, the trend was reversed with the Muslims reasserting their distinct identity, announcing the beginning of an inexorable movement the logical consequence of which was the partition of 1947.

Particularly dangerous is the interpretation that, projecting the modern ideals of egalitarianism on the Islam of that age, sees in this conflict the clash of two civilizations founded on diametrically opposed worldviews and values. This was formulated in the famous Lahore resolution of 1940 and attributed to Jinnah (1876–1948). It laid claim to a separate state for Muslims, and is a remarkable piece of political propaganda.[1]

Indeed, under the Moguls, the oppositions between Hinduism and Islam were sometimes great, and the maintenance of the marks of difference between the two religious communities had perhaps been a constant preoccupation for a small number of medieval Muslim theologians and jurists. However, these trees should not hide the forest: Hindus and Muslims shared the same vision of the world and of society. And it is these analogies that render Mogul history intelligible: how else can one explain the fact that a minority of Muslims could durably establish their authority over a Hindu majority?

An almost immobile world: the cosmos, space and time

The here and now had only a minor importance for these men whose inclinations were often towards the mystical. The universe in which they lived was an emanation of an unknowable Absolute that could be approached only by death, or mystical ecstasy, a prefiguration of death. They were moreover not certain whether the present was anything more than an appearance, whether it had a real existence distinct from the principle from which it emanated. Their vision of the world was above all religious.

It was also resolutely geocentric. Around the earth revolved the planets (these were gods for the Hindus, whereas, for the Muslims, they were moved by a spirit of the world), which influenced the course of human lives. The rulers, Hindu or Muslim, had their official astrologers and did not distinguish between astrology and astronomy: the same person calculated the date of eclipses and predicted the future. The Muslims had a science of heavenly bodies, derived from the Greeks and distinct from the Hindu tradition, but it rested on analogous principles.

Esoteric sciences and divination were the order of the day everywhere, even among the Muslims: in the sixteenth century, a famous Sufi saint of the Shattariyya brotherhood, Muhammad Ghauth of Gwalior – brother of the official magician of the emperor Humayun, Shaikh Bahlul – wrote a treatise on esotericism in two versions, Arabic and Persian, where he insisted on the magical use of the names of Allah: this work, still in use in India, was also printed in the Arab countries.

To live in harmony with the cosmos, and not to transform it, was the ideal sought after. This is evident in traditional medicine: the Hindu *ayurvedic*[2] tradition, like the Muslim *yunani* tradition (*yunani* means Greek), seeks to maintain the balance of the humours and to keep the body and the soul in harmony with the places and the seasons in which one lives. Today both these religious traditions have become manifestly differentiated, but the dividing line was not so clear-cut during the Mogul age when it was often believed that there was only one medicine just like there was only one astrology. India was the Muslim country where *yunani* medicine witnessed its highest development.

Despite all this, Hindus and Muslims did not share an identical perception of earthly existence. Largely apathetic to history, the Hindus were also indifferent to geography and showed no interest for distant lands: they had no memory of the people who had created the civilization of Southeast Asia, from Indonesia to Vietnam, of the preachers who had propagated Buddhism as far as China, of the merchants who had ventured as far as the Red Sea and eastern Africa. They conceived the universe as a sacred diagram, a *mandala*, of which India obviously occupied the centre; the other continents were arranged geometrically around it, like the petals of a flower. The world was, in the final analysis, a great temple dedicated to the worship of the 33 million gods who populated it.

As for the Muslims, they had perfected the sound geographical tradition inherited from the Greeks and the ancient Iranians and which divided the known world into seven 'climates'. One of the earliest scholars to have been interested in India, Al-Biruni (973 – *c.* 1050), was also its first great geographer. Thanks to his works, the Muslims had precise knowledge not only of India, of the Arab, Turkish and Iranian world, but also of Europe and China. Their world vision was centred on Mecca and not on India. This geography written for the sake of pilgrims, merchants and conquerors did not for that matter form a realistic vision of the world within the meaning that we give to that expression.

However little Mogul India was open to the outside world, it could not hide its own insufficiencies from itself with respect to the tools that the Westerners then had at their disposal. François Bernier reports that Aurangzeb was one day furious with his preceptor, blaming him for having taught him inadequate notions on the kingdoms of Europe which had trade relations with India. It was only after the seventeenth century that Indian geographers, like Sadiq Isfahani (Jaunpur, 1647), substantially improved the world maps established by their Arab and Iranian predecessors, though it is impossible for us to say whether they drew inspiration from local bodies of knowledge or whether they fell under the influence of Europeans.

Were there similar rationalizations with regard to the concept of time? Two different manners of envisaging time co-existed: the first, that of eternal recurrence, was cyclic, whereas the second was messianic centred on the wait for the end of the world. Both these approaches rested on a pessimistic conception of time, considered as doomed to deteriorate after a golden age situated in the past. It is interesting to note that the dividing line between the followers of either of these conceptions of time did not coincide with that of the religious communities in question.

In traditional India (as in ancient Greece), history was a succession of cosmic periods, each of which, spanning several thousand years, recurred identical to itself, as days and years form cycles that followed on indefinitely. The world, every time it was born again from the primordial divinity, was totally perfect; in the course of each of the four 'ages of the world' that together constituted a period, it lost a quarter of its splendour; such that in the fourth age (in which we presently live), the remaining quarter of perfection vanished; the world plunged into chaos and dissolved in the ultimate deluge, only to start all over again. . . . In this system, only the individual soul had the possibility of change: in the course of reincarnations, it could regress, or progress towards a definitive 'deliverance' and break free from the wheel of existences.

Muslims were not strangers to this belief: heterodox circles, especially the Ismaili Shiites and certain Sufi saints in and outside India espoused it. Shah Waliullah, who is today considered a paragon of orthodoxy, believed in the eternal recurrence; his master Muhammad Afzal Siyalkoti (died 1733) did not consider the belief in reincarnation as heterodox.

There is, however, another vision of time specific to Islam, that of a single time punctuated by a succession of revelations and culminating in the perfect epoch of the Prophet Muhammad who recreated a golden age. The world then deteriorated inexorably until the end of the world, which would witness, after the appearance of a sort of Antichrist called Dajjal, the return of Jesus and a figure called, depending on the sects, the *mahdi* or the hidden Imam (for the Shiites): the latter would re-establish a new golden age before the ultimate end of the universe.

These messianic beliefs roused passions in times of crisis, because, as the date of the end of the world was unknown, any ambitious reformer could claim to be the *mahdi*. The beginning of the sixteenth century had witnessed the rise of the *mahdi* of Jaunpur, Sayyid Muhammad Kazimi; another messianic movement appeared a little later among the Afghan tribes of the northwest, the Raushaniyya founded by Bayazid Ansari, which symbolized the resistance of the Afghans against Mogul domination. The fever of mahdism never really subsided during the sixteenth century, especially with the approach of the year one thousand of the hegira, which coincided with the peak of Akbar's reign. Akbar, as we have pointed out, commissioned the writing of a *Tarikh-i alfi* ('History of the millennium') in order to mark this date. At the time, contradictory events were expected to occur: some maintained that the world would cease to deteriorate thanks to the arrival of a 'renovator' (*mujaddid*) who would reform it: Ahmad Sirhindi (1564–1624) was believed to be such a renovator by his disciples; others, on the contrary, thought that the end of the world was near: Akbar, it was presumed, could well be the *mahdi*.

More often, however, Muslims lived in a more mundane time, which put off the end of the world to an indeterminate future. Since the advent of Islam, the chronological milestones had been signalled by the great dynasties that left their stamp on it. This age was that of the chronicles, the speciality of the Indian Muslims who constituted a gigantic historiographical corpus in Persian. The most ambitious of these works deal with Islam as a whole; others speak only of Muslims in India, of Timurids or of regional sultanates. The most detailed works, generally official chronicles, are devoted to a single reign year after year, like Abul-Fazl's *Akbar nama*. An ambitious ruler in fact had a tendency to concentrate time around his person, just as he reorganised space by constructing capitals: Akbar established a new era, the 'divine' era (*ilahi*), and a new solar calendar that replaced the lunar time of the Islamic calendar in administration and chronicles.

A hierarchical and militarized society

The world was almost immobile, threatened by the end of time or by an end of the cycle that called for a radical reconstruction; it was not believed to evolve towards any kind of maturity. The same was true of society, which was construed as a static whole; the obsession was to preserve it from disorder, the evil par excellence.

The metaphor that dominates Hindu and Muslim texts (like the texts of the European Middle Ages) is that of the body. Society is a great body whose parts have to be organized into a hierarchy in order to preserve the equilibrium. The Hindu vision of the social order finds expression in legal texts called *Dharmashastra*, or 'Treatises on the cosmic order.' Society was born out of the dismemberment of the primitive 'Person,' a figure of divinity:

> In order to protect this universe the Lord assigned distinct duties and functions to those that were born out of his mouth, his arms, his thighs and his feet. To the Brahmins he assigned the teaching and the study of the Vedas; sacrifice for themselves and for the others, the donation and acceptance of alms; he commanded the *kshatriyas*, to protect the people [. . .]; he charged the *vaishyas* to pasture the cattle, to trade, to lend money and to cultivate the land. He prescribed only one function to the *shudras*: to serve the other three orders with humility' (The Laws of Manu, I/87 *sq*).

This metaphor of the body is found in Muslim texts, notably in the 'Mirrors of Princes,' compiled in Iran and widely read and imitated in India.[3]

Social hierarchy is presented in these texts as a divine institution perpetuated by heredity and whose order resembles the one described in the Hindu texts: men of letters; warriors or soldiers; merchants and artisans; farmers.

According to the Muslim tradition, these four 'orders' correspond to parts of the body, but also to the elements that make up the universe (water, fire, air and earth respectively). This provides the most apt expression of the ideal of these medieval traditions – to maintain harmony between the human body or the social body and the universe itself, conceived as a great organism. This ideal was the cornerstone of the esoteric speculations that were so important during this age.

The obsession of the theoreticians and the political leaders was to maintain the equilibrium between these different parts of the social body, especially by the mechanism of heredity: justice, the principal function of the ruler did not consist of promoting equality, but to render to each what was due to him in accordance with the rank in which God had placed him. In particular, social mobility towards the top was construed as a source of danger and had to be meticulously checked in order to preclude too many people from rising to the high classes. Shah Waliullah – who, in a gross anachronism, is sometimes considered a precursor of socialism – vehemently protested against the dangers that threatened the social order when too many people abandoned agriculture to enter the craft industry, the bureaucracy or the army.

Some have construed this insistence on social hierarchy expressed by Indian Muslims as being the influence of the Hindu context. This is a misinterpretation, which arises from the idea that egalitarianism was a key concept of Islam. This was not the case. The texts written in India only reaffirm a recurrent doctrine of the Persian classics. In the legal texts written in Arabic, social inequality, especially with regard to marriage, is constantly reiterated: men of letters and warriors are superior to farmers and artisans; some occupations considered as vile, like that of weavers or sweepers, are on the borderline of untouchability. As in the Hindu texts, the ideal of marriage is hypergamy: a man may, if he absolutely must, take a woman of inferior category, but the inverse is forbidden – a woman may not marry into a lower class. This hierarchical doctrine was reaffirmed in the last great legal compendium compiled at the behest of the very orthodox Aurangzeb under the name of *Al-fatawa al-alamgiriyya*.

Did caste exist?

It is not possible to ignore the question of caste, a term that we have so far studiously avoided in this chapter. We have evoked the principal divisions of the categories of people that the Hindu and Muslim normative texts have organized into a hierarchy on the basis of the function they perform in society; we translate the terms that they use (Sanskrit, *varna*, and Arabic, *tabaqat*) as 'class', an unfortunate rendition as it causes confusion with modern issues arising from Marxism; the medieval ideal of 'order' would be a better approximation.

These major orders in fact included numerous subdivisions.[4] With the Hindus, these were, from top to bottom of the social ladder, castes (*jati*), in theory endogamous, organized into a hierarchy and often characterized by a hereditary occupation: thus there were several castes of Brahmins, *kshatriyas* (warriors) or farmers. At the lower level, however, a caste generally corresponded to a professional specialization: weavers, curriers, sweepers, etc. Among the Muslims, the higher levels – scholars and warriors (most often of foreign stock, Arabs, Turks, Iranians, Afghans) – were subdivided not according to the paradigm of castes, but according to that of ethnic groups and lineages; the smallest endogamous unit often constituted a lineage within an ethnic group (marriage among cousins was not infrequent in the higher Muslim orders). But in the inferior orders of farmers and artisans, composed of local converts, the caste structure remained after conversion.

We must keep a vital fact in mind: this social structure was not frozen; constantly fluctuating, it fixed a hierarchical ladder that remained relatively stable through the generations, but which offered individuals and groups the possibility to move. British descriptions have tended to freeze a moving structure; we must not mistake something that was immediately dated for a portrait of eternal India.

Despite all this, it was a very compartmentalized and hierarchized society, where even among Muslims (at least in the lower echelons), it is justifiable to speak of castes. This complexity did not exclude mobility to a certain extent. Nor does it rule out polyvalence: the portraits that we have sketched above are ideal prototypes that we rarely find in their pure state, even among Hindus: many Brahmins were soldiers by profession; among Muslims, the warrior was also generally a scholar and often did not consider it beneath his dignity to undertake commercial investments.

The primacy of the warrior

Hindu and Muslim scholars, when they wanted to exalt themselves, placed men of letters in the highest ranks of society. But authors like Abul-Fazl who were associated with power conferred this honour on warriors. In the perspective of social and political history, the latter view seems more realistic, as the power of ultimate decision belonged to the victorious rulers who were also military entrepreneurs. In the final analysis, the sovereigns fixed their own rank and that of their subordinates. A Hindu king could even change the status of his Brahmins.

While reading the texts dating from this period, it is striking to note the place held by the military ethos. A man of quality – whether a scholar or a mystic – had not only to know Persian literature, but also to be a good horseman and know the art of handling a sword; at all the echelons of the society, martial arts were highly prized.

Those who were engaged directly or indirectly in the professions of arms numbered in the millions according to Mogul statistics: nearly five million under Akbar. Mogul administration, highly militarized, absorbed only a small part of it, but it was a vital part as it laid down the law in the subcontinent: mainly, it was an aristocracy of foreign stock, administering troops for the most part composed of locals. If the bulk of these warriors hailed from the populace, the backbone was the former local aristocracy, of Hindu majority, which had become part of the empire, those that the Mogul texts call with contempt the *zamindars*, in other words, the masters of the land. The necessary intermediaries between the empire and the peasantry – who regrouped in ethnic confederacies like the Rajputs or the Jats – or later the Marathas, they possessed their own armies that terrorized the countryside and occasionally defeated the imperial forces.

All these men constituted an inexhaustible pool of military labour on which the empire and the *zamindars* drew indefinitely: the British would do the same to consolidate their power. Only at the end of the British conquest in 1818 would the demilitarization of India truly commence.

Warriors, ascetics and vagrants

Another figure, not always distinct from the warrior, but idealized in the Hindu tradition, was the ascetic. Having given up life in the world, he was initiated into a mystical fraternity and led a life of celibacy (in theory) with his fellows, organized around the monasteries of his order – certain orders were Saivaites, like the Sanyasis, or the Kanphatta Yogis, whereas others were Vaishnavites, like the Bairagis.

Unmistakable in their saffron costumes (or the lack of costume, as some of them went around nude), they are those who are today called the *sadhus*, the 'men of benevolence'. They represented an important moral pressure group to the rulers, whom they often served as spies. They generally succeeded in securing a considerable territorial and financial base. They could also be well-organized traders, in which case they competed with the merchant classes. Finally, each of these orders possessed its own armed unit.

Islam also had its form of asceticism: the one who renounced the world was called a dervish (Persian: *darvesh*) or more often a fakir (*faqir*): this Arabic term, which has passed into our language with the narrow meaning of an illusionist, included during the Mogul period all ascetics, both Hindu and Muslim. The ascetics had close or remote ties with a mystical order or a Sufi fraternity, and had their own distinct costumes in the past. The majority of them led a discreet existence (as members of a sort of third order rather than as full-time ascetics) in liaison with hospices and shrines of saints. On the other hand, a sizeable number of them, of whom European travellers have left picturesque descriptions, led the life of wandering true ascetics, often affiliated to the so-called heterodox orders (like the Qalandaryyas or later the Rifaiyyas in the west and the south, and the Madariyyas and the Jalaliyyas in the north; these two orders had an armed branch).

Armed ascetics were active players in the political scenario: they confronted the Mogul troops or the local rajahs and, should the occasion arise, waged war with each other: in the seventeenth century, a pitched battle between the Muslim Jalalis and Madaris on the one side and the Hindu Sanyasis on the other, left several hundred dead. At the end of the eighteenth century, the British had to fight an actual war to disarm the last bands of fakirs. The spectacular figure of the armed ascetic was not the only link between asceticism and the profession of arms: we often have the tendency to conceive these roles as incompatible, but among the Hindus, the same man can perform both these functions alternately – in his youth, when he goes in search of an occupation as soldier, he willingly assumes the identity of an ascetic (folklore in fact presents the two roles as interchangeable); with age, he returns to live like a family man, becoming a lay person again.[5]

In general, identities were not as stable as in the British age. And the population was not as sedentary as it was to become after the institution of the *pax britannica*. Large sections of the population adopted a nomadic existence, under religious pretexts or otherwise. Long distance transport was the monopoly of nomadic caravanners, the Banjaras. Peasants often changed their masters: when the taxes increased too much, they fled their lands to sell themselves to the highest bidder, which was possible at the time given the relative scarcity of labour. Misfits often turned themselves into fakirs. Peasants ruined by famines became brigands . . . not to mention the fact that there were probably castes, as today, where brigandage was a hereditary profession. These people posed problems to the authorities who sometimes deforested the environs of the dangerous routes. The emperor Jahangir, notorious for his cruel games, organized hunts to capture refugee wanderers in the forests and sold them as slaves. Under Akbar there are reports of roundups of fakirs, who were deported to Afghanistan to be bartered for horses.

The subordination of men of letters

There was widespread confusion between the roles of scholars and the specialists of the sacred. The identification was almost total in the Hindu tradition where the Brahmin simultaneously had the monopoly of rites, study and teaching. It was the Brahmins who transmitted the high culture of India, in Sanskrit, and this they did without discontinuity until the modern age. In relation to Hindu monarchs, they had to remain in subordinate positions as counsellors, ministers, even scribes, in which case they competed with the scribe castes such as the Khatris or the Kayasthas. Brahmins and Hindu scribes occupied a prominent place in the tax administration of the Mogul Empire, as in the Deccan sultanates.

Among Muslims, the religious scholars, the *ulemas*, did not form a closed caste, even though they generally came from insular scholarly and religious lineages, most of whom claimed Arab descent – those who are today called the *Sayyids* (descendants of the Prophet) and the *Shaikhs* (from the other Arab tribes). These so-called Arab lineages had often lived in the subcontinent for generations, and the high Mogul officials, the majority of whom were recent arrivals in India of foreign stock, regarded them with contempt as Indian Muslims.

The ulemas kept alive the tradition of Arab culture that formed the basis of the education of religious dignitaries. They had control over the big mosques and over religious education through the seminaries that they managed. Finally, as we saw earlier, they had the monopoly of posts in the department of justice and religion under the direction of the *sadr as-sudur*. These functions placed them under the authority of the rulers and the warriors who appointed them and who bestowed on them the gifts and 'benefits' on which they lived.

The ulemas were often initiated into one or more mystical orders – Sufism had been for a long time accepted by the orthodoxy. Passionately fond of mystical literature, they read it in Arabic, but especially in Persian (the language specific to Sufism in India). Thus Abdulhaqq Muhaddith Dihlawi (1551–1642), who had studied in Mecca and popularized the study of the traditions of the Prophet in the subcontinent, wrote a biography in Persian of Abdulqadir Jilani (died 1196), the founder of the Qadiriyya brotherhood, and a biographical dictionary of Indian Sufi saints. Shah Waliullah, another great Sufi, wrote mystical treatises that are still read.

Ulemas and Sufis constituted in fact a single religious class. Like the Brahmins, they were in the final analysis subordinated to the warriors who wielded power: they were vital for the performance of rites, the management of religious affairs; and more generally, they were indispensable to the rulers in order to endorse their legitimacy in the eyes of the believing masses.

The ubiquitous merchant

The merchant appears in the limelight in the accounts of voyagers, themselves often traders, but is barely present in the literature bequeathed to us by the Moguls. Trade had never been very prestigious for these conquerors hungry for worldly power, and when the high officials of the empire invested in commercial enterprises or cargoes of vessels (which was frequent owing to the prevalent polyvalence), they did not boast of it; the merchant himself generally concealed his profession under a religious title like *hajji*, a pilgrim to Mecca.

The ethnic groups composing the merchant classes were in fact very heterogeneous. First, like the scribes of the Mogul administration, the typical merchant of the period was a non-Muslim; in western India, he belonged in general to the merchant castes, the majority of whom were members of the ascetic sect of the Jains, the famous Marwaris; similarly, among the Muslims, merchants were of local extraction and often converted to the heterodox Shiite sect of Ismailis: they were the Khojas, today forming a group under the leadership of the Agha Khan, and the Bohras. In Kerala and the Coromandel coast, there were also merchant castes of the Sunnite sect, while the Deccan had always been the preferred place of settlement for the Twelver Iranian Shiites. Finally, the merchant class was the most cosmopolitan, with the presence of numerous Armenians and the continuous arrival of Europeans, interlopers or attached to big trading companies, not to speak of the more ancient presences of Jews, Christians of Saint Thomas and Zoroastrian Parsis.

The term 'merchants' in fact encompassed very diverse activities. Merchants did not content themselves with exchanging merchandise, they also commissioned its production from artisans; they were lenders, bankers and changers, soon even leaseholders of taxes on behalf of the failing Mogul administration. In short, they formed a small but powerful class, on whom the survival of the administration itself hinged.

Artisans and servants

As for those who came after the merchants in the social hierarchy, data from the time is very fragmentary. It was very probable that expertise was transmitted hereditarily within the framework of Hindu or Muslim castes: for instance, the caste of Muslim glassmakers, manufacturers of glass bracelets, has been attested since the fourteenth century. Artisans worked either for individual households, or for merchants who ordered stocks for domestic trade or for export. A number of them were employees in manufactures (*karkhana*) that belonged to the emperor or the high officials of the empire. Their remuneration, in kind or in cash, was the object of erudite speculation. The same was true for the army of servants, some of whom, like the sweepers, no doubt belonged to the lowest castes of untouchables.

The peasantry

Notwithstanding the mass of documentation that has come down to us on agrarian administration, it is difficult to know the real living conditions of peasants, as the administrative presence of the Moguls reached at its best the *qasba*, or small town, the administrative centre of a *pargana* or canton: here, it had to deal not with individual peasants, but with intermediaries who formed the local aristocracy and were overwhelmingly Hindu. The peasants (from the Persian *raiyat*, that became *ryot* in Anglo-Indian) are mentioned only in events of crises, when they deserted villages and needed to be replaced, which happened very frequently, or when they revolted.

Repression could then be severe: men were massacred, women and children sold as slaves in the thousands. Thus Abdullah Firoz Jang, an Uzbek high official at the service of Jahangir and Shah Jahan, boasted of having killed more than two hundred thousand men between 1620 and 1640 and having made about five hundred thousand slaves. We must also keep in mind that this peasantry, partly armed, could be brought to heel only by terror, which Abul-Fazl and Jahangir deplore in their writings, but justify as a state necessity.

Daily life in Indian villages barely appears in these sources. The social structure of villages probably differed little from the one that the British discovered: a small world rigorously organized into a hierarchy and dominated by one or more landowning castes of higher status. These rich peasants cultivated their lands themselves, or by hiring poor or landless peasants or untouchables and even slaves. These peasants had priests and artisans, such as carpenters and blacksmiths, in their service, and untouchables, such as tanners. They remunerated these workers most often in kind on the basis of annual contracts that guaranteed them a fixed share in each harvest: this is what is called today the *jajmani* system, derived from the name of the relation binding the Brahmin and the landowners for whom he officiated. Contrary to a theory invented in the Romantic age, these village communities did not live in autarchy: the peasants had to resell between a third and half of their produce on the market in order to pay their taxes. Village artisans like weavers also often worked for merchants of the cities.

What do we know about conversions?

The sources are almost silent about the religious affiliation of the people, except that they express the constant sentiment of Muslim governors of being a minority. We do not have any statistics dated from before 1872. All that has been written about earlier periods is therefore pure speculation.

Nothing for instance corroborates the theory that conversions were often due to the pacific persuasion of Sufis. Did Aurangzeb resort to mass conversions by force? This is certainly false. Is it true that egalitarian Islam particularly attracted the lowest of castes who thus liberated themselves from untouchability? This is also false, as the statistical distribution of converts by castes contradicts this hypothesis grounded on the idea, disputable as we saw, of the egalitarianism of Islam. Conversions concerned merchants, peasants and primarily respectable artisans who supplied luxury products to the courts: the untouchables just as much as the Brahmins rebuffed Islam. Groups rather than individuals seem to have opted for conversions: a single caste often split into two segments, one remaining Hindu, and the other converted to Islam. In 1872–4, the population of Muslims compared with the total population was a little less than 20 per cent: in the Mogul period, it was certainly less, even though we cannot put forward any figures to prove this. We know that during the British age, the majority of weavers were Muslims, but no extant source enables us to affirm that that was the case during the Mogul period.

What about slavery?

Hinduism and Islam traditionally authorized slavery. This institution had played a vital role under the sultanate of Delhi, whose army consisted of Turkish slaves; moreover, the manufactures of the state employed servile labour in the thousands at the time. The tendency had, however, reversed as early as the foundation of the Mogul Empire, which, in any case, employed free military and administrative staff; and only free artisans worked for the imperial manufactures.

Nevertheless, slavery persisted even though it was of no capital importance for the empire; it would be abolished in India by the British only in 1843 and in Nepal in 1925. The data that we have in this regard is disparate, as there was no specific regulation in Muslim India. The practice of slavery survived, it appears, for reasons of prestige: people in high ranks, especially in the imperial family, had to possess slaves in their personal service in the palace or as bodyguards: it was evidently a residual domestic slavery. There was, however, a recrudescence of military and agricultural slavery in the eighteenth century, notably in the principalities founded by the Afghans in the upper valley of the Ganges.

Trade in slaves did not cease under the Moguls. In India itself, the majority of the slaves were probably of local origin: enslaved rebels, people condemned for misdemeanours or debts, children sold by their families in times of famine, and more simply victims of the raids of traffickers: was not the empire an inexhaustible source of manpower? Though it appears that at the time only free workers came from Central Asia, Africa remained an ancient source of slaves that never dried up: the black slave (*habshi*, 'Abyssinian') continued to be highly in demand and regularly arrived in Gujarat and in the Deccan. On the other hand, India remained a large exporter of slaves towards Central Asia (where they served in particular as trading currency for horses or dogs) and perhaps also towards the Middle East and Southeast Asia. It should be remembered that the Portuguese, especially in Bengal, were also involved in the slave trade.

Classical cultures

These working masses maintained an erudite elite class that was the custodian of a refined and highly sophisticated culture, or rather cultures. Mogul Indian culture presented a stratification of genres that we shall now run through, from classical literature to oral epics. These genres include vernacular literature, partly oral and partly written. There was no clear dividing line between the oral and the written at the time and it is not rare even today to hear an illiterate peasant quote verses written by a famous poet centuries ago that he had heard from a itinerant singer. Poetry was essentially meant to be sung.

High culture, which hinged on dead languages and ancient classical texts, was subdivided on the basis of religious affiliation. The Muslims had three languages of culture: Persian, Arabic and Turkish, the mother tongue of the founder of the dynasty that a minority of scholars would cultivate until the eighteenth century. Persian was the language of reference; it was the lingua franca of travellers, merchants and administrators, it had a status comparable to that of Latin in Europe until the sixteenth century: all the elites, from Istanbul to Golconda, read it and often spoke it but it was rarely their mother tongue.

The educational system illustrates the importance of Persian. The young child first learnt to read (and at best, memorized) the Arabic text of the Koran, without translation, under the supervision of a preceptor, male or female. Formal education came later, under his parents or his preceptors, invariably began with a Persian text of the thirteenth century, written in simple beautiful language, partly in prose and partly in poetry, by Saadi of Chiraz (born 1193), the *Gulistan*, or *Garden of Roses*: from this text or others that were progressively more complex, the young boy (or more rarely the young girl) learnt to read and to write Persian. He was also required to memorize innumerable classical verses, with which he would sprinkle all his compositions, written or oral. He also learnt very early to versify – any educated man had to be capable of composing poetry. This early education aimed at inculcating what the Muslim authors call the *adab* – 'etiquette' in its widest sense – in order to maintain self-control and to know what to say and do in all circumstances.

Subsequent to this core training, education diversified. Only a minority of young men destined to maintain the religious and judicial institutions undertook the study of Arabic classics. Mogul India did not have many seminaries (*madrasa*) –places devoted to study – as they were so numerous in Central Asia; the few well known *madrasa*s, like the one constructed at Delhi by Ghazi Khan at the close of the seventeenth century, which the British would call Delhi College at the beginning of the nineteenth century, were exceptions rather than the rule. Education was therefore dispensed in mosques or more often, in the houses of masters belonging to erudite lineages: for instance, the family of Shah Waliullah, or the clan of Farangi Mahal in Lucknow, which ensured the continuity of religious education from the end of the seventeenth century to the middle of the twentieth. The content of education was based on a small number of Arabic texts, written for the most part between the tenth and the fifteenth centuries: they perpetuated the so-called Timurid culture, developed in Central Asia under Timur and his descendants. Education remained personal: each student read and commented on these texts under the supervision of several masters, each then conferring a *ijaza*, or 'licence', so that the student could in his turn teach that text. The syllabus started with Arabic grammar and literature; then came the exegesis of the Koran and the study of the traditions of the Prophet, and finally came Islamic law. Besides these scriptural sciences and the rudiments of theology, the Timurid culture attached importance to the sciences of reason: mathematics and logic (both of which remained Greek to the letter), then speculative philosophy in the Iranian fashion. Mystical authors, Arab and Persian, were also evidently widely read.

Such was the education of the ulemas of Sunnism of the Hanafi law school, which dominated the whole of India. The Twelver Shiites – present particularly in the Deccan, and who grew stronger in the eighteenth century in the Ganges Valley, in Oudh and Bengal – proposed a similar curriculum; education was based on common texts, except for theology and law. As a minority, they depended on the large Shiite centres of Iran and Iraq, but the minorities of coastal merchants, who had settled down there a long time ago, had different intellectual traditions: the Sunnites of Kerala and the Coromandel coast, more in touch with the Arab world, followed the school of Shafi'i law. Finally, there existed a specific Ismaili culture: very distinctly influenced by the Arabic legal texts of Fatimid Egypt, it abided by the gnosis established in Arabic and Persian by the great heterodox thinkers of the Abbasid period (750–1258); their devotional texts were for the most part in the Gujarati language.

Apart from the ulemas, other Muslim scholars had an essentially Persian culture. The courtiers perfected themselves especially in the study of historians and moralists, and invariably in poetry. Disciplines of scientific knowledge, especially medicine, even though they make reference to classical Arab authors like Avicenne (980–1037), seem also to have drawn particularly on Persian texts. Excepting religious sciences, one could be a great scholar in India without knowing Arabic.

For Hindus, classical culture, in Sanskrit, was dispensed in temples and monasteries, and particularly at the house of the masters. This culture remained alive under the Moguls: classical texts of the Vedas and the Upanishads were still committed to memory. The great mythological tales or epics (*Ramayana* and *Mahabharata*) and the *Puranas* continued to be transmitted through writing in distinct regional versions. There was no end to commentaries on texts. The great works of Sanskrit literature had been written during an earlier epoch, but the production of literary and especially scientific texts from the sixteenth century onwards remained substantial. What was new in the Mogul period was the emergence of a syncretic erudite literature, an upshot of the development of a dual culture, Sanskrit and Persian, among Hindu scholars who worked for the Mogul administration.

Urban space and architecture

In architecture as in the courtly arts, the Mogul era was not, as it is widely believed, the beginning. Akbar did not invent Mogul culture, no more than he created an imperial administration out of nothing. The precedents from which he drew inspiration are especially found in western India, particularly in Gujarat and in Malwa: it is to this architecture that the Moguls owe their most graceful monuments, which used entablature instead of the arch and the vault, Islamic specifications in the Indian context. The Moguls also built on the imperial innovations of their predecessors, in particular the Lodis and the Surs; they retained, especially in gates and mosques, the inspiration of the Timurids, to whom certain monuments owe the grandiose appearance that renders them truly imperial. Similarly, the Deccan also produced its own syncretic elaborations that evolved concurrently in the South. If Mogul architecture is better known, it is no doubt because its works have been better preserved and better studied, and because, backed by the imperial power, they have been largely imitated all over the subcontinent, in a trend towards a uniformity of styles.

The appropriation of space: the cities

Like all the great Muslim conquerors, the Moguls were keen to punctuate space with monuments in testimony of their splendour and their power: this preoccupation is explicitly stated in their writings. The major trunk roads completely rebuilt were marked out with milestones and caravanserais: the most elaborate road stretch, the main Delhi-Agra road, was entirely remodelled under Jahangir. They also built victory towers, in which they had no qualms over embedding the skulls of vanquished rebels.

The monuments had to be equal to the grandeur of the dynasty. Babur and Humayun, too preoccupied with their conquests, did not leave behind any monument in a unique style. Only from the reign of Akbar and the construction at Delhi of the tomb of Humayun can we talk of Mogul architecture. Unfavourably received by the people of Delhi, Akbar left his stamp especially in the other capitals where he lived in succession. At Agra, the capital inherited from the Lodi dynasty, he contented himself with reconstructing the fort. It was with the construction of a palace in Ajmer, followed by that of the city of Fatehpur Sikri from 1571 onwards that Akbar fully expressed his conception of the imperial order in the city-palace, which was organized around imperial halls of audience and a mosque that was also the tomb of a saint. Fatehpur Sikri, quickly abandoned, expressed above all the enshrining of power: by appropriating the *baraka* of the saint Salim Chishti, Akbar concentrated all political and religious powers on his person and projected himself as the uncontested centre of religious and cultural life. The relatively brief reign of Jahangir left its mark on the cities of Lahore (in present Pakistan) and Dacca (in present Bangladesh).

It was under Shah Jahan that the Mogul conceptions of urban space attained their maturity. He remodelled Lahore and Agra; and in particular, he designed, from scratch, the plans of the new capital of Shahjahanabad in Delhi (today called Old Delhi). Like the Mogul camps that served him as models, it was grounded on the fusion of an imperial citadel and bazaars. In accordance with a structure that is prevalent in the other Mogul capitals, everything converged on the citadel-palace situated in the northeast, near the Jamuna river; it marked the upper part of the city where the houses of the nobles stood: two great perpendicular bazaars (east-west and north-south) led to the citadel and organized the city. The mosque, on the highest hill, was the geometric centre, but not the true heart of the city, which beat in the citadel; the working-class districts were relegated to the southwest. The ramparts and the gates, which did not have any real strategic utility – they had never stopped any invasion – rather marked a sort of ritual shutting of the city, outside of which were rejected impure activities, as well as the rituals of the great Muslim festivals: these took place, in accordance with the canonical rules, in the great prayer area (*id-gah*), situated outside the walls in the west, in the direction of Mecca; most of the feasts of saints took place on the tombs also situated outside the walls and provided an occasion for weekly meetings and great annual fairs.

Aurangzeb, more preoccupied with forts and mosques than cities, nevertheless constructed a new capital in Aurangabad, in the Deccan, where his campaigns retained him. This was the last great urbanization project of the dynasty. The fever of construction, which never abated, then passed on to the dynasties of the successor states that again diversified the regional styles.

The palaces

In the imperial capitals, the palace-citadels, true cities within cities, were the primary object of the emperors' solicitude. Too often built and rebuilt to keep in tune with the art historians, their traces have sometimes been obliterated. Of the palatial architecture of Akbar, characterized by the predominance of pink sandstone and occasionally offset by lines or panels of white stone, only the buildings of Fatehpur Sikri have survived almost intact, the interpretation of which has given rise to endless speculation. The edifices built by Jahangir suffered from Shah Jahan's zeal for construction.

It is to Shah Jahan that we owe the Red Fort of Delhi, as the citadel of Shahjahanabad was called, where the palatial architecture of the Moguls has been best preserved. There, in the centre of the citadel, after traversing the gardens, bazaars and manufactures, we enter the holy of holies through a monumental gate; the upper floor consists of a hall of orchestra, the *naubat-khana*: musicians, with kettledrums and long trumpets, marked the various moments of the day as well as the arrival of great personalities (this orchestra was an imperial privilege that only the saints shared, as we shall see). We then enter the palace, formed of a succession of courtyards where stand the buildings of white marble (the favourite material of the Moguls since Shah Jahan) inlaid with semi-precious stones forming motifs according to the Italian technique called *pietra dura*. The prime area of the palace was the public audience hall: it was here that the emperor received the nobles and the ambassadors, himself seated on the famous throne in the shape of a peacock that was placed on a raised platform surmounted on a dais.

This platform and its decoration provide the key to the imperial symbolism of the Moguls. The ruler was presented as a semi-divine figure, seated in the east, like the rising sun; the ornate *pietra dura* panels– some of which were imported from Europe, others made locally – depict floral and animal motifs; on the top, in the centre, Orpheus plays his lute in the midst of wild animals: this Italian panel was chosen and placed above the head of the emperor to illustrate (in a conscious reinterpretation) the mythical role of the ruler, the new Solomon who re-establishes justice and peace on earth, as much among men as among animals: the lion no longer attacks the lamb. This example shows the eclecticism of western motifs borrowed and re-used in Mogul art; as in science and technology, what was borrowed was adapted to a traditional universe, without bringing about any revolution in a mentality that remained that of the medieval East.

The mosques

The mosque was a potent symbol in the architecture of the Moguls, who were above all Muslim rulers: this was particularly true of the mosque-cathedrals of the capitals; better preserved than the palaces, they are even today the most telling testimonies of the dynasty. High officials, and even princesses, vied with the emperors to have their name attached to monumental mosques. The religious style of the Moguls, which revived the Indian traditions through Timurid inspiration, took shape from the mosque-cathedral of Fatehpur Sikri onwards. It would evolve until the reign of Aurangzeb, to whom we owe several edifices: on the one hand, the intimiste-style jewel of white marble, the pearl mosque (*Moti masjid*) that he constructed for his personal use in the Red Fort of Delhi; on the other, the Imperial mosque (*Shahi masjid*), that dominates the city of Lahore. This mosque, the biggest in the entire subcontinent, carries to a grandiose level the style popularized by Shah Jahan particularly in Delhi, but its decoration is more refined, with the sandstone and marble complemented by floral motifs in stucco. Its exceptional dimensions (the courtyard can contain sixty thousand people) is due to the fact that it served both as the mosque-cathedral for the Friday prayer and as the *id-gah* or 'place of festival' for celebrating solemn prayers during the two great festivals.

Gardens and tombs

The Moguls have remained famous in Western eyes for their tombs and their gardens. In tune with an Islamic tradition revived in India by Babur, the rulers showed a predilection for creating oases of peace for themselves, in deserts as well as in the luxuriant vegetation of tropical India. In these geometrically planned gardens divided into rectangles by canals that symbolized the four rivers of paradise, a pavilion served as the summer palace. Gardens like these marked the environs of the capitals of the Moguls, Agra, Delhi, Lahore and their summer resorts in Kashmir.

The tomb, a funerary monument aimed at immortalizing emperors and their dignitaries, was often constructed in a garden, could be inhabited, serve as a holiday resort, or as a university, and be fortified, as the case may be. The tomb of Humayun at Delhi, the first example of the Mogul architecture, marvellously illustrates these multiple usages: situated in one of the earliest Mogul gardens, it served as a place of prayer and study; it was also the refuge for the last Mogul emperor besieged by the British following the defeat of the revolt of 1857 – it was here that he was taken prisoner before being sent to Rangoon. In Sikandara, near Agra, the tomb of Akbar, who was considered a saint, was also an object of worship. All the emperors had their tomb-garden, except the austere Aurangzeb who wanted to rest among the Sufis of Khuldabad, in the Deccan, and had his sepulchre marked with just a slab of stone. The most famous tomb-garden is evidently the one that Shah Jahan constructed for his favourite wife, the Taj Mahal, entirely of white marble, reflected in the canals of paradise.

The courtly arts

The sumptuousness of the courts of the Moguls as those of their predecessors and their successors is also evident in painting, music and the minor arts. Thanks to the splendid collections that have come down to us, painting alone can give us a glimpse of this splendour.

Here again, the Moguls did not start from scratch. There was a genre of Muslim painting under the Delhi sultanate, today almost completely lost; there were also regional schools in the sultanates that followed it, especially in the sultanate of Malwa, several specimens of which have survived. Besides, India had its own age-old pictorial traditions; Hindu and Jain artists who worked for Muslim rulers were not without influence in the development of Islamic painting in India.

Humayun, following his exile in Iran, brought back to Delhi new Persian master painters and reorganized the imperial workshop. Under the impetus given by the young Akbar, this breeding-ground for imported and local artists gave rise to a new style that was largely imitated all over India.

Painting during the Mogul era consisted originally of miniatures which ornamented books and became also a complement to calligraphy. Apart from the classical texts of Persian culture, it illustrated the historiography of the dynasty: it was most certainly an instrument of propaganda abroad. It also exceeded the scope of the purely Islamic civilization inasmuch as Hindu religious texts, which were profusely translated at the time, were also embellished with pictorial illustrations. Finally, Christian scenes, objects and motifs were reinterpreted in tune with Islamic thought.

The novelty of the Moguls was in making miniature painting an independent art, primarily in the form of albums of pictures that retained the format of a book. There were even independent paintings of a larger format, notably representing emperors or the entire Timurid dynasty. The preferred subjects of Mogul painters were portraits and scenes depicting nature. Mogul painting survived brilliantly in the courts of the Rajputs and the *nawabs*.

Music during the Mogul era was an important melting pot where pre-Mogul Hindu and Islamic traditions blended to give rise to a new style. Akbar gave it impetus by paying huge prices to attract famous artists from rival courts, for example the celebrated Tansen. These artists played a crucial role in the diffusion of a cosmopolitan pan-Indian culture, instrumental music being inseparable from a chant that transmitted poems in vernacular languages, sometimes secular, most often sacred.

We have come to know the music of this age essentially through the descriptions and reviews of texts given by Muslim scholars attached to the courts, notably under the encouragement of Shah Jahan. A ruler of the Deccan, Ibrahim Adil Shah of Bijapur (1580–1627), was himself the author of a book on music, the *Kitab-i nauras*, or the *Book of Nine Emotions*.

As for Mogul monuments, today we can only see walls and bare and cold floors. We have to imagine, with the aid of miniatures, the settings in which emperors and high officials lived: colourful carpets, richly embroidered brocade draperies, the multi-coloured costumes of the nobles, often tailored in the royal workshops (as the emperors regularly gratified them with robes of honour) are reminiscent more of the *Drap d'or* camp with its mobile draperies than of the Versailles palace, where the decorations are part of the building.

The confluent of the two seas: erudite encounters

We have made several allusions to the convergences of Hindu and Muslim traditions during the pre-Mogul or Mogul periods. It is now time to look at the complete picture. Mogul achievement in this domain is not an innovation either. From time immemorial, Muslims had been interested in Indian civilization. The first translations of Sanskrit into Arabic were undertaken under the Abbasids in Baghdad. A turning point in the exact knowledge of India and its religions was marked in the eleventh century by Al-Biruni, whose *Book of India*, compiled in Lahore and in

Ghazni, remains an indispensable reference to today's orientalists. Though lacking the genius and the freedom of thought of this exceptional scholar in the history of Islam, the Mogul authors of the sixteenth and seventeenth century accomplished a work comparable in its boldness and much more substantial in its volume. They had the advantage of a cumulated experience, almost uninterrupted since Al-Biruni: the second half of the fourteenth century, under Firoz Shah Tughluq (1351–88), had in fact witnessed the first wave of systematic translation. Furthermore, the Timurids had inherited from the Mongols an ecumenical tradition with a comparative study of religions. The reciprocal knowledge of the two traditions was also facilitated by the growth of a class of Hindu scribes well versed in Persian.

The definitive impetus emanated from Akbar who, alongside organizing debates on religions, established a translation bureau. Brahmin and Muslim scholars worked side by side to render into literal and then into literary Persian the great works of Hinduism, in particular the *Yoga Vashishta*, the *Ramayana* and, especially the immense encyclopaedia of Hindu beliefs that is the epic of *Mahabharata*. Abul-Fazl wrote a long preface for the translation of the *Mahabharata* entitled *Razm-nama*, illustrated manuscripts of which have survived. The Al-Biruni of his times, by ambition if not by genius, he referred to this prestigious model and devoted a part of the third book of *Ain-i Akbari* to describing Hinduism and the other religions of India.

This movement continued throughout the seventeenth century, which saw the elaboration of an astounding encyclopaedia of religious beliefs entitled *Dabistan al-madhahib* (*The School of Religions*), written towards 1655, no doubt by a Zoroastrian living in India. But the most audacious attempt was that of Dara Shukoh, brother and unhappy rival of Aurangzeb. He translated the *Upanishads* into Persian in 1657 under the title *Sirr-i Akbar* (The Great Secret); he formulated an exegetical theory according to which Hindu scriptures contained an ancient revelation the knowledge of which was indispensable to interpret the Koran accurately; his theories find expression in his commentary of the *Upanishads* as well as in a work whose title is drawn from a Koran verse, *Majma al-bahrain* (The Confluent of the Two Seas). His Persian version of the *Upanishads*, translated into Latin and published in Strasburg in 1801–02 by A H Anquetil-Duperron (1731–1805), heralded the starting point for studies in Europe on the ancient religions of India.

The dominance of Aurangzeb did not dissuade these quests for convergence: right in the middle of the eighteenth century, a Naqshbandi, reputed to be orthodox, Mirza Mazhar Jan-i Janan (1698–1781), was initiating Hindu ascetics into his mystical order and proclaiming that Krishna and Rama, the avatars of the god Vishnu, had been authentic prophets in their times.

The court of the saints: Sufism, *Bhakti*, Sikhism

Concurrent with these discourses in Arabic and in Persian, which were accessible only to elite scholars, was a much richer tradition of convergences through the vernacular literatures, that thrived in the market for mysticism that was highly popular at the time. As Al-Biruni had pointed out as early as the eleventh century, it was in mysticism that Hinduism and Islam presented analogies that could serve as a bridge between the two. Here, we have to leave the courts of the kings for another rival court, that of the ascetics. For though the warrior was supreme among the men of this world, he had a contender beyond reach among those who had renounced the world. Just as in Christianity since Saint Paul true sovereignty belonged to the Christ-King, for the Muslims and Hindus, it belonged to the saints; invested with royal titles (*sultans, maharajahs*), these saints were the true masters of the land, on whose authority the kings reigned.

Sufism in India participates in this royal symbolism. It was already well represented under the Delhi sultanate, notably by the favourite fraternity of the Moguls, the Chishtiyya, and by the Suhrawardiyya. In the fifteenth century the Qadiriyya appeared which regained its popularity in the first half of the seventeenth century, particularly with Dara Shukoh. Under the Moguls a new brotherhood from Central Asia, the Naqshbandiyya, was introduced which remained influential in Delhi until the fall of the empire. Gujarat and the Deccan witnessed the arrival by sea of the Rifaiyya (Sunnite) and the Nimatullahiyya (Shiite).

The great Sufi saints were especially influential with the elites. After their death, they began a royal career that was at times spectacular. Their tomb (*dargah*, that is 'palace') was then served by a minister (*diwan*), who had the right to an imperial orchestra. The emperor himself, as we saw with Akbar, was his humble supplicant and came on foot to prostrate himself in front of his tomb.

The mausoleums of the saints and the buildings that surrounded them provide further examples of Mogul architecture. The great sanctuaries of the Chishti saints at Delhi, Ajmer and Pak-Pattan date from the Mogul era: the mausoleum is surmounted by a dome; inside, an ambulatory was built around the tomb so that the faithful could come and bring their offerings; besides the mosque and often a school, the building included hospices for pilgrims. The tombs were served by the descendants of the saints who formed a veritable caste, living on the offerings of the faithful whom they guided in their devotions.

Adjacent to these buildings, there is sometimes, notably in Ajmer, a concert hall, *mahfil khana*, where musicians belonging to a low Muslim caste, the *qawwals*, themselves in the service of those who served the tomb, performed mystical chants in Persian and especially in vernacular languages, in order to provoke ecstasy and spontaneous dance in the devotees present: to die in a trance – of which numerous examples have been attested – was the most beautiful of deaths.

These chants were the starting point for a Muslim mystical literature in vernacular languages, from as early as the sixteenth century. The Sufis thus joined the movements of medieval Hindu devotion known under the name of *bhakti*. Abdulquddus Gangohi (1456–1537), of the Sabiri branch of the Chishtiyya, has recorded the memory of a spell with Hindu devotion: writing sometimes in Persian and sometimes in Hindi, he frequented the Kan-phatta Yogis (the privileged interlocutors of the Sufis), used Indian techniques of yoga to arrive at ecstasy and composed mystical poems in old Hindi.

These Yogis were not the only Hindu mystics. There were at the time an entire series of Saivaite and Vaishnavite saints under the name of *sants*, who, in the name of the virtue of renunciation, called into question the potentates of this world, particularly the kings. The most famous of them was the weaver Kabir (*c.* 1440–1518); we do not know whether he was a Hindu or a Muslim, but his chants, made public orally for a long time, are predominantly of Hindu inspiration. The whole of India, from the South where the movement started, to the North where it eventually reached, provides similar examples. In many respects, the true living culture in India is the one that developed in the Middle Ages, in the vernacular languages, under the impetus given by the *sants*.

The interpretation of these devotional movements has given rise to two misconceptions. Some have seen in them a revolutionary literature, because these vernacular texts often emanated from milieus more modest than those from which Sanskrit authors hailed and because they challenge the hierarchy of castes. But this was not the case: the questioning of castes, also asserted in Buddhism, was only a logical consequence of the renunciation of the world; we are here in the universe of mysticism and not that of social reforms. Others have discerned in these movements the influence of Muslim civilization, in this respect construed as egalitarian. This theory, dear to Indian nationalists, does not hold true either: this was not an influence but a coincidence. This literature illustrates the profound analogies that exist between the two religious trends.

Closely attached to these Hindu movements were also the Ismaili merchants of the west coast, the Khojas and the Bohras; they have left behind a remarkable corpus of devotional literature in the Gujarati language that employs the terminology and the symbolism of Hindu poems.

It was in this context that the new religion of the Sikhs developed, founded by Guru Nanak (1469–1539), who was initially a *sant* among others in the Punjab: their sacred book, the *Guru Granth*, is a collection of poems composed by Hindu and even Muslim devotees: its symbols and its terminology were drawn from both these religions. The conflicts of this new sect with the Moguls and its growing influence in the peasantry of the Jat caste transformed it into a socially distinct community that soon assumed the status of a separate religion; its doctrine is closer to Hinduism than to Islam, especially from the eighteenth century onwards, when the rupture with the Moguls was complete.

The development of vernacular literatures

Vernacular literatures are very ancient in India. Even in Buddha's time Sanskrit was already a dead language; and certain regions in India, like Tamilnadu and Bengal, had age-old literatures. At the dawn of the period in which we are interested, texts in vernacular languages acquired their prestige all over India and began to be produced profusely: these new literatures went well beyond the scope of devotional poems, to include narrative poems, poetry and even prose. The great texts in Hindi, generally in the Awadhi dialect, as the *Ramayana* of Tulsi Das, a contemporary of Akbar, date from this period. Though it is not possible here to narrate the history of these literatures, to which Muslims often contributed, we must underline the importance of vernacular languages for the Muslims.

The Hindi dialect of the Delhi region, the Khari Boli, gave rise as early as the Delhi sultanate to a common language that was written in Arabo-Persian script and which was disseminated all across India by Muslims; it would be called Hindustani or Urdu during the British era; until the nineteenth century, it was simply called Hindi. This was the language of the soldiers and the merchants. It acquired its prestige in the sultanates of the Deccan in the sixteenth and seventeenth centuries. It is this that the textbooks call, anachronistically, the beginnings of Urdu literature. The literary use of this language was introduced in North India only in the eighteenth century for poetry and in the nineteenth century for prose. Urdu, today a potent symbol of Islam, is therefore a relatively young language. In South India, Urdu competed with another supra-regional language,[6] Tamil, which gave rise to a specific Muslim literature read not only in Tamilnadu, but also in all the regions speaking Dravidian languages, like Kerala and Sri Lanka.

Apart from these common languages, all the regions in India also witnessed in the age of the sultanates and in the Mogul era, the development of profuse and original local literatures, written either in the Arabic script, such as Awadhi, or in local alphabets, such as Gujarati and Bengali. We have already mentioned the birth in North India of a Muslim literature in the Awadhi dialect of Hindi (thus different from Urdu of the Deccan). Bengal, a region of great creativity, from both Hindus and Muslims, has particularly fascinated specialists. Gujarati has become the object of thorough studies today. Further to the northwest, Sindhi literature was born; and among Afghan tribes, Pashto acquired a literary recognition thanks to the millenarianist movement of the Raushaniyya.

The devotional literature of Sufis and *sants*, transmitted orally for a long time before being recorded in writing, was no less an erudite literature. To have an idea of what was happening at a more humble level, we must study the works of folk-lorists in the last century: here we find an echo, perhaps distorted with the passage of time, of immemorial traditions transmitted by untouchable bards and by women. Sometimes, we encounter stunning syncretic figures, like that of the Muslim saint Ghazi Miyan, whose name means 'Lord of the holy war [against the Hindus]' (died 1033): in the Ganges Valley, he became a sort of deity of rain and vegetation, a new avatar of the god Indra; he was simultaneously the healer of lepers. Both Hindus and Muslims flocked to his tomb. The chants of supplication that Muslim women sang on his tomb draw on the terms that the Hindus used to address their tutelary goddesses. His legend has been transmitted orally by bards of a Muslim caste of untouchable musicians, the Dafalis.[7]

X

THE DISINTEGRATION OF THE MOGUL EMPIRE

(1707–39)

A controversial period

In the space of about thirty years, from 1707 to 1739, the Mogul Empire underwent a radical transformation. At the death of Aurangzeb, in 1707, the central institutions were apparently intact and the empire still had reserves in the treasury at the fort in Agra; in 1739, the pillage of Delhi by the Persian emperor Nadir Shah (1736–47) portended the ultimate collapse of an empire incapable of defending itself and henceforth in a state of insolvency.[1]

Until the 1970s, the theme of decline dominated the interpretation of the eighteenth century. Indo-Persian chronicles archived by the Mogul court, which at the time had lost all its powers, could only adopt a tone of disillusionment; the traditionalist religious authors continued to express these lamentations on the collapse of the last Muslim empire. It was in the best interests of the British who followed to reiterate the same analysis, as the decline of the Moguls justified their conquest of India as an initiative to re-establish peace and prosperity. Early modern historians have echoed this theme.[2]

This 'decadence' has been interpreted differently according to period and context. Some have put forward psychological and moral explanations: the later Moguls failed owing to their lack of character, their depravity, or because they forsook Islamic orthodoxy. But two explanations are predominant in modern historiography. The first is religious: it attributes the decline of the empire to the revolt of the Hindus, triggered by the orthodox policy of Aurangzeb's reign; the rebellions of the end of the seventeenth century and the beginning of the eighteenth reflected the insurgency of the Hindu majority to shake off a six-hundred-year-old Muslim domination. The second, more recent explanation[3], still prevails in academic circles. It construes the decline as the outcome of the excessive exploitation of the peasantry by the nobility.

There is a third, more partial explanation[4] that imputes the Mogul decline to the role of bankers, for the most part Hindus, who were indispensable intermediaries in the management of the finances of the empire: they dealt the deathblow to the

Mogul dynasty by withdrawing their confidence in the emperor to enter the service of regional potentates and foreign trading companies.

Finally, there are those who concede that there was a 'crisis' at the turn of the eighteenth century, but that it was essentially political and that it took place against a backdrop of sustained economic growth.[5] The revolts that broke out were then the price of prosperity. It was an unprecedented economic development that enabled the provinces to gain their independence and to transform the institutions of a centralized empire into a very loose federal structure.

The crisis of the imperial institutions

The imperial court at the beginning of the eighteenth century presented, in truth, an often deplorable spectacle. The first two decades witnessed a spate of wars of succession, before the longevity of Muhammad Shah (1719–48) brought back a semblance of stability. However, in the course of this long reign, as in the preceding ones, the court and the person of the emperor were undermined by factional disputes.

A classic rule: Bahadur Shah I (1707–12)

In accordance with the Mogul tradition, the death of Aurangzeb, on 3 March 1707, triggered a war of succession among his three surviving sons. The first to gain knowledge of the news, the second son, Azam Shah, who was present in the camp of his father in the Deccan, proclaimed himself king with the support of the *wazir*, Asad Khan; he marched towards Agra to take possession of the treasury. But his designs clashed with the ambitions of his elder brother Muazzam. The latter, posted to the other end of the empire, in the Hindu Kush, inside the fortress of Jamrud, made haste to Agra after messengers had brought him the report of the death of his father, in less than just twenty days. Meanwhile he proclaimed himself emperor in Lahore, had himself crowned in Delhi, and succeeded in taking possession of the treasury in Agra before his brother. He was joined by his son Muhammad Azim, who brought him funds from Bengal. The two brothers confronted each other in the middle of June in Jajau, to the south of Agra, near the site where Aurangzeb had fought with Dara Shukoh: Azam Shah and his sons were killed; their troops dispersed. But the youngest of Aurangzeb's sons, Muhammad Kham Bakhsh, had also proclaimed himself king in the Deccan in Bijapur: a strong army had to be despatched to defeat him (he was eventually defeated and killed in Hyderabad). The nobles who had sided with the vanquished brothers were reintegrated into the Mogul administration by the new emperor. Muazzam reigned, henceforth uncontested, under the name of Bahadur Shah I (or Shah Alam I). He died of ill health in Lahore in 1712, at the age of seventy.

Muazzam left behind an apparently intact empire; however, difficulties began to emerge during his reign. With little trust in the nobles of Aurangzeb's entourage, he appointed to high positions a large number of newcomers whom he recruited from among Muslims of Indian origin. Iranian and Turkish families, thus sidelined, began to see their personal interests as distinct from those of the imperial dynasty: this marked the beginning of factional disputes that were to mark subsequent reigns. This trend could only be aggravated by the financial crisis that manifested itself at the same time.

It was also under Bahadur Shah I that revolts, which resumed and magnified those that had troubled the reign of Aurangzeb and which were to smoulder on under the following reigns, broke out all across western India: between 1707 and 1709, the empire witnessed the successive insurgency of the Jats around Delhi and Agra, the Rajputs and the Sikhs. Then, from 1713, the Marathas, pacified for a short period in the Deccan, recommenced their murderous depredations. Furthermore, the war of succession and the endemic revolts in western India had endangered the finances of the empire. Bahadur Shah I had inherited almost intact reserves. On his death, the empire could not longer defray the expenses of its military expeditions.

A turbulent interregnum: Jahandar Shah (1712–13)

The four sons of Bahadur Shah I were present in his camp near Lahore at the time of his death. The second son, Azim, seemed to have the best chances of winning the throne: a close advisor to his father, he had made his fortune in Bengal and possessed a large army. In an effort to resist him, his three brothers (Jahandar Shah, Rafiushshan and Jahan Shah) forged an agreement with the *mir bakhshi* of the empire, Zulfiqar Khan: in the event of victory, they were to divide the empire amongst themselves, while the *mir bakhshi* was to be the key figure in the loose federal structure that would then be instituted. The war of succession broke out while Bahadur Shah I was in his death throes and lasted three months. Eventually, the eldest son, Jahandar Shah, eliminated not only Azim, but also his two other brothers in violation of their agreement.

Jahandar Shah definitively re-established the court in Delhi. During his brief reign, the Mogul institutions began to deteriorate visibly. For the first time, the nobles who had supported the defeated princes were punished. They were imprisoned or divested of their properties, two of them were actually killed. For the first time also, the emperor relinquished his absolute power in favour of his supporter, Zulfiqar Khan, who became the *wazir* (finance minister), and in favour of the right arm of the latter, Davud Khan Panni. The *wazir* acted henceforth as a kingmaker and took all the important decisions in place of the emperor. At this time began a factional dispute for the control of positions in the court.

The new *wazir* tried to restore peace in the empire by adopting a conciliatory policy towards the Rajputs, the Sikhs and the Marathas. This brief respite was, however, marred by institutional mayhem. The emperor himself began to conspire against his excessively powerful minister, and brought discredit upon himself even further in the eyes of his nobles; he took as his main wife the daughter of a court minstrel, ennobled her family and ruined himself by indulging in feasts. The tax administration continued to deteriorate: the nobles had more and more difficulty in earning revenues from their *jagirs*; functionaries, powerless, had to lease taxes, while soldiers were no longer paid their wages. The empire was in a situation of national insolvency.

The situation was propitious for a claimant from the new generation. Farrukhsiyar, the son of the defeated Azim, had consolidated his positions in Bengal in the former fief of his father. He had himself crowned in Patna and forged an alliance with a family of Indian Muslims, the Sayyids of Baraha, Husain Ali Khan, governor of Bihar, and Abdullah Khan, governor of Allahabad. He promised them to spearhead a new faction and to confer the offices of *bakhshi* and *wazir* on them. When Farrukhsiyar marched on Delhi, the imperial troops, who had not been paid for a long time, dispersed, and most of the nobles rallied to his cause. Reaching Delhi, he had Jahandar Shah and Zulfiqar Khan executed, and blinded and imprisoned all potential rivals among the Mogul princes. He infringed tradition once again by ordering the execution of other nobles belonging to the party of the fallen emperor.

Farrukhsiyar (1713–19) and the reign of the Sayyids of Baraha (1713–20)

An atmosphere of terror shrouded the entire court where even the most loyal of nobles feared to appear. More seriously, an open and armed conflict flared up between the emperor and the two Sayyid brothers, whose personal armies paraded even in the Red Fort of Delhi. The tumultuous story of this reign is that of a protracted conflict, unresolved for a long time, each party trying in vain to eliminate the other. It was only in 1719 that the Sayyids succeeded in deposing and then assassinating Farrukhsiyar. He was successively replaced by two young princes, who died of tuberculosis in a space of a few weeks. The crown then passed to a cousin of Farrukhsiyar, Muhammad Shah, who would reign for more than thirty years.

During these seven years of conflict, the imperial authority continued to decline. The two parties, swayed by their fluctuating alliances, had to make unprecedented concessions to the Rajputs, the Jats and especially the Marathas. Meanwhile Mogul control over western India became increasingly tenuous. Tax administration was collapsing and the emperor could no longer pay his functionaries. Several famines added to the desolation and spurred the revolts of peasants.

The long reign of Muhammad Shah (1719–48)

The culmination of the struggle was played with the new emperor. In 1720, Muhammad Shah forged an alliance with a Turkish noble, Nizamulmulk, who rallied the Turkish and Iranian nobles; with his support, he succeeded in eliminating the armies of the Sayyids and the Sayyid brothers themselves. In fact, all he accomplished was replacing one faction with another and he could not re-establish the imperial authority. The post of *wazir* was first conferred on the chief of the new faction, Muhammad Amin Khan, then on Nizamulmulk, and finally on Qamaruddin Khan, the son of the former; it became a sort of hereditary transmission.

Muhammad Shah did not leave behind the impression of a competent ruler. Even though he preserved the façade of the imperial routine, he fell under the influence of favourites, both male and female, who squandered the rest of the imperial finances and sought to recruit nobles who offered the fattest bribes. In the provinces, as we will see later, the central administration was nothing more than an empty shell, a formal source of legitimacy; the various factions were keen on holding on to high positions in the court that enabled them to consolidate their authority and to increase the powers that they were carving out for themselves in the provinces.

The collapse: Nadir Shah at Delhi (1739)

The ultimate proof of the impotence of Muhammad Shah was offered in 1739 by the Iranian sovereign Nadir Shah (1736–47). Of Afghan origin, Nadir Shah had supplanted the Safavid dynasty in Iran, definitively ousted the Moguls from their rampart of Afghanistan and reduced the Punjab to submission. He routed a Mogul army that had been hastily mustered at Karnal, about a hundred and sixty kilometres to the north of Delhi. The emperor was forced to surrender and to receive Nadir Shah in Delhi. An uprising of the people of Delhi against the Persian soldiers sparked off a terrible revenge: for nine hours, the Persian army massacred thousands of people, then systematically pillaged the city; it went home two months later, loaded with a fabulous plunder, including among others, the peacock throne, the symbol of the Mogul Empire.

The Mogul emperor had become nothing more than a symbol: Afghanistan and the territories to the west of the Indus were definitively lost and the imperial finances ruined.

Rebellions and autonomy in the western provinces

Was the situation any better in the provinces? We are above all struck by the extent of peasant rebellions, the revolts of non-Muslim ethnic groups and the disaffection of provincial authorities for Mogul authority. But were not these phenomena the indicators of a new prosperity and an entirely new type of political formation better adapted to the needs of the provinces?

The western provinces had a more tumultuous history: they had already witnessed numerous revolts under Aurangzeb; the weakening of the emperor paved the way for former rebels to strike again. Thus local chieftains arrived on the scene who were not Muslims and who often did not belong to the usual cadres of the nobility. All the same, they did not break away from the Mogul Empire; they remained vassals of the emperor and paid him a nominal tribute in return for their legitimacy.

The Jat insurrections were the most spectacular because they erupted close to the capital. The Jats took advantage of the wars of succession of 1701 and 1712 to indiscriminately plunder various camps and to exact money from merchants. Neither negotiations, nor corruption, nor the threat of a Rajput army could break down their resistance bolstered by the fortress of Thun. Farruhksiyar had to admit their chief Churaman into the nobility of the empire in order to gain his submission.

The Rajputs also made the most of the weakening of the empire to assert their

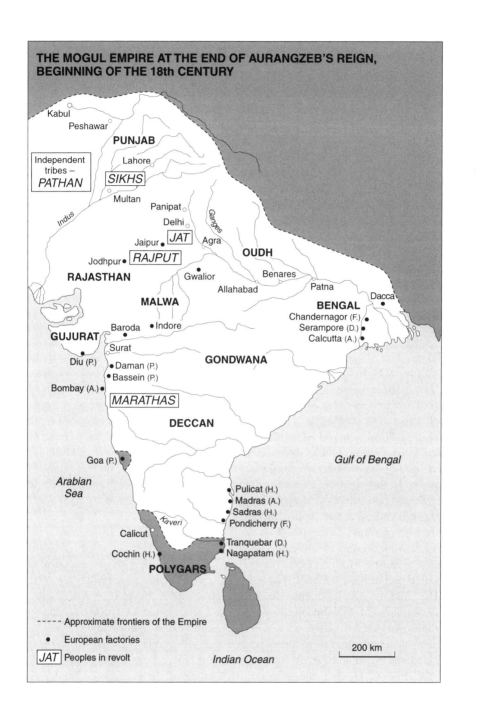

THE MOGUL EMPIRE AT THE END OF AURANGZEB'S REIGN, BEGINNING OF THE 18th CENTURY

Kabul

Peshawar

PUNJAB

Independent
tribes –
PATHAN

SIKHS

Lahore

Multan

Panipat

Delhi

Indus

Ganges

Jaipur   *JAT*   Agra

OUDH

Jodhpur   *RAJPUT*

Gwalior

Benares

RAJASTHAN

Allahabad

Patna

Dacca

MALWA

BENGAL

Baroda   ● Indore

Chandernagor (F.)
Serampore (D.)
Calcutta (A.)

GUJURAT

Surat

Diu (P.)

● Daman (P.)
● Bassein (P.)

GONDWANA

Bombay (A.) ●

MARATHAS

DECCAN

Goa (P.) ●

Gulf of Bengal

*Arabian
Sea*

● Pulicat (H.)
● Madras (A.)
● Sadras (H.)
● Pondicherry (F.)

Kaveri

Calicut

● Tranquebar (D.)
● Nagapatam (H.)

Cochin (H.) ●

POLYGARS

- - - - Approximate frontiers of the Empire

● European factories

JAT Peoples in revolt

Indian Ocean

200 km

power. From the death of Aurangzeb, Ajit Singh took back possession of his capital Jodhpur, from where he ousted the Mogul functionaries. Jai Singh Kacchwaha of Amber revolted in his turn. In 1708, a Mogul army had to be despatched to re-conquer Amber and Jodhpur; after a second revolt, the emperor brought the recalcitrant rajahs to submission through conciliation, and reintegrated them into the nobility of the empire in 1709.

This first revolt was the beginning of a process of autonomization of the Rajput principalities that had been integrated into the empire since the reign of Akbar. Under the Moguls, the Rajputs controlled only a limited region around their capital, the *watan jagir*, the other parts of Rajasthan being administered by Mogul functionaries. Even while retaining their nominal functions in the nobility of the empire, they gradually re-appropriated their territories by resorting to two methods: either they caused other lands in the proximity to be attributed to them officially as *jagirs*, or they offered their good offices to the functionaries in order to lease the revenues of the adjoining regions. With the weakening of the empire, they ceased to pay the revenues to Delhi. As early as 1726, eastern Rajasthan had become independent; the remaining territories were to follow suit.

The emergence of the Sikhs and the decline of the Punjab

The revolts of the Sikhs and the Marathas had another significance, as they were not simply a return to the past, but reflected new religious and political phenomena.

The Sikhs were the only rebels that the Mogul archives define by their religion, while the others, even the Marathas, were simply referred to as belonging to such and such a region or ethnic group. Initially nothing more than a heterodox sect on the fringes of Hinduism and Islam, the Sikhs had acquired under their tenth and last guru, Guru Gobind Singh (1666–1708) a religious personality closer to Hinduism; they had also built a militarized organization that was to establish their reputation to this day. In the eighteenth century, they recruited members increasingly from the middle and poor classes of the peasantry and focused the feelings of rural discontent against the urban classes, both Hindu and Muslim.

In 1708, Gobind Singh, who had sided with Bahadur Shah I in the war of succession, was present in the camp of the latter in the Deccan in order to seek justice against a Muslim noble, Wazir Khan, who had killed his two sons. But the accused had him assassinated. This event triggered the first important revolt of the Sikhs. The majority of them rallied themselves under the banner of the official representative of Gobind Singh, Banda. In 1710, armed bands of peasants and artisans plundered the cities situated between Lahore and Delhi. Bahadur Shah had to send an army against them: the campaign dragged on until 1715 and into the reigns of Jahandar Shah and Farrukhsiyar, as the Sikhs enjoyed the support and collusion of the chiefs of Hindu principalities in the foothills of the Himalayas. Banda, who had proclaimed himself the guru, was betrayed by a sector of the Sikh community, which earned the favour of the emperor. Taken prisoner, Banda was publicly executed in Delhi with seven hundred of his disciples. The agitation of the Sikhs in the countryside was to remain endemic, however, with the complicity of the chiefs of Hindu principalities.

This instability was aggravated by external threats. The contemporaneous upheavals in Afghanistan and in Iran gravely perturbed international commerce, which was one of the sources of wealth for the Punjab. This province, situated on the route of invasions, suffered from 1739 onwards from the campaigns of Nadir Shah and his successors.

In the face of this two-fold adversity, the Mogul administration could find support only in the cities: there, it could rely not only on Muslims, but also on Hindu merchants, especially the Khatris, who remained loyal to it. The Punjab nevertheless continued to deteriorate; only in 1799 with the creation by Ranjit Singh of a Sikh state would the province recover its former glory.

The rise to supremacy of the Marathas

The principal adversaries of the Moguls in western India were the Marathas, who were seen as a threat and feared from the far South to the gates of Delhi and Calcutta.

Immediately after the death of Aurangzeb, Azam Shah, the unhappy protagonist of the war of succession, had liberated the heir to the throne, Shahu, until then held prisoner. Azam, subsequently Bahadur Shah and his *bakhshi* (chief of personnel) Zulfiqar, who was also governor of the Deccan, strove to pacify the new king, as well as the rival claimant Tara Bai, in an effort to reintegrate them into the empire and to put an end to the imbroglio in the Deccan. Their demands, unacceptable to the Moguls, brought about the failure of the negotiations: in exchange for peace, Shahu claimed 25 per cent of the revenue (*chauth*) of the Deccan, plus 10 per cent of the costs of collection (*sardeshmukhi*). The incursions of the Marathas from all quarters into the Deccan and as far as Malwa forced the Mogul vice-governor of the Deccan, Daud Khan Panni, to compromise and to concede to the pecuniary demands of the Marathas, who henceforth swallowed up to 35 per cent of the revenue. This pact was violated under Farrukhsiyar by the Sayyid Husain Ali Khan; the raids of the Marathas were resumed, fuelled by the intrigues of the emperor against the Sayyid brothers. Eventually, the latter concluded an alliance with the Marathas against the emperor, and definitively granted them political supremacy in the Deccan, by leaving them 35 per cent of the revenue. This pact, ratified by Muhammad Shah in 1720, became permanent.

From that year onwards, the Maratha kingdom took shape as a loose confederacy. Firstly, the power passed from the king to a hereditary prime Minister, called *peshwa*, belonging to a Brahmin family: the first *peshwa*, Balaji Bishwanath, occupied the post from 1714 onwards, his son Baji Rao took over from him in 1720 and gained full powers in 1727; and his son Balaji Baji Rao succeeded him in 1740. The dynasty of the *peshwas* was to endure until the English conquest in 1818.

Subsequently, the Marathas added to these domains in the Deccan new territories, conquered in the north in the provinces of Malwa, Gujarat and Bundelkhand, the annexation of which was officially ratified by the emperor after 1740. Maratha chiefs of war established subaltern dynasties in western India, like the Gaekwars of Baroda, the Sindhias of Gwalior and the Holkars of Indore. Their predatory raids extended even further, practically all over India: to the gates of Delhi, in the Punjab, then towards Oudh, Bengal and Orissa. The whole of western India, including Gujarat, was henceforth under their control. The port of Surat, until then the largest port of India, declined while Bombay and ports of the eastern coast rose to prominence.

The emergence of the *nawabs* in the eastern provinces

In eastern India, the reorganization of Mogul institutions did not involve the interference of foreign elements. It was the governors of provinces themselves, the *nawabs* (honorific plural of *naib*), 'representatives' of the emperor, who, without breaking their bond of allegiance with Delhi, became the masters of their provinces and founded local dynasties.

To arrive at this point, they first had to infringe a certain number of rules laid down by the Mogul administration. Firstly, the precariousness of office: to preclude the constitution of fiefs, the nobles were frequently transferred from one corner of the empire to the other; the *nawabs*, however, succeeded in establishing themselves in their own territories, if necessary, disobeying orders from Delhi. Next, the separation of powers: the governor, the *diwan* (revenue-chief), the provincial *bakhshi* (chief of personnel) and the high functionaries of the judicial machinery – who all fell under the direct authority of Delhi – were independent of each other and kept an eye on each other; but gradually, the *nawabs* succeeded in concentrating in their hands most of these civil and military powers, and in warding off all interference from the capital in the provincial administration. Finally, the revenues from the provinces, after the deduction of the costs of local administration, were payable to Delhi; the *nawabs* began to appropriate these revenues for themselves and thus progressively acquired sovereignty in their domain. Nevertheless, to be able to maintain themselves in their territories, they had to obtain the consent of their subjects by strategies that varied in the different major provinces.

It was in Bengal that this trend towards autonomy encountered the least resistance. This prosperous province was experiencing sustained growth and agriculture and trade were expanding rapidly, attracting foreign merchants. It was fortunate to have as its head an astute *diwan* appointed by Aurangzeb, Murshid Quli Khan, a Shiite Muslim who was presumably of Brahmin origin: confirmed in his office by Bahadur Shah, he maintained his post until his deposition in 1727. To replace Dacca, situated too far away in eastern Bengal, he created on the Ganges, in western Bengal, a new capital that bore his name, Murshidabad. Little by little, he succeeded in taking over the posts of governor and *diwan* of the provinces of both Bengal and Orissa; in 1719, he also became the master of Bihar.

Far from the intrigues of the court, Murshid Quli Khan surrounded himself with a competent staff, especially Hindu. He regularly collected revenues that he promptly sent to the capital where he proved to be a valuable contributor in these times of financial crises. He could maintain his authority thanks to the prosperity of the provinces that he administered, the rigour of his administration and his integrity towards the emperor. Even though autonomous, Bengal remained within the sphere of influence of the empire. But in 1727, the son-in-law of Murshid Quli Khan, Shuja Khan (1727–1738) seized power by a coup and stopped sending revenue to Delhi: his only official link with the court was the title of investiture and a large annual tribute. He acted until his death in 1738 as a *nawab*. His son Sarfaraz (1738–40) succeeded him and was himself supplanted in 1740 by Alivardi Khan (1740–56).

The province of Oudh had a more turbulent history. The changes in appointees were very frequent until 1722, the year in which Burhanulmulk was appointed governor and who was succeeded in 1739 by Safdar Jang: these two figures, who founded the famous dynasty of Oudh that was to endure until 1857, were Iranians; they made their province a great centre for the Shiah sect, with close ties to Iran and Iraq.

The administration of this province was not without imposing difficulties. Oudh had benefited, like Bengal, from a continuous agricultural and urban expansion, but it was also the scene of repeated peasant revolts which threw the administration out of gear. The *nawab*s succeeded in consolidating their domination and in fending off the threat of the Marathas. They offered advantages to their constituents, for instance by transforming *jagir*s into permanent fiefs; above all, they had to win over, by consolidating their agricultural positions, the various wealthy classes – Hindu and Muslim *zamindar*s, religious dignitaries, whose 'benefits' were transformed into private domains, and finally, merchants, who were mostly Hindu. Oudh became a model of prosperity and tolerance: Muslim sovereigns of the Shiah sect ruled over Sunnite subjects, and notably over a Hindu majority.

Another haven of peace emerged in Hyderabad, in the eastern Deccan, on the ruins of the ancient Golconda. This region, laid to waste by the Marathas, inhabited by a Hindu majority speaking Telugu, did not seem destined to become the seat of a prosperous Muslim State. In effect, anarchy reigned supreme until the arrival in 1713 of a governor who re-established order, Mubariz Khan, appointed by Farrukhsiyar. In 1715, when Sayyid Husain Ali Khan was appointed governor of all the Deccan provinces, Mubariz Khan succeeded in having himself confirmed in his dual office of governor and *diwan* of Hyderabad. Disregarding the pact concluded with Delhi by the Marathas, he refused to concede to the latter the right to collect, as they did elsewhere, 35 per cent of the revenue in his province, which could as a result recover its prosperity. His relations with Delhi were limited to a formal allegiance: as the absolute master of Hyderabad, he withheld all the revenue for himself.

A newcomer reaped the fruit of this labour. Nizamulmulk, of a Sunnite Turkish family, chief of the Turanian faction that had propelled Muhammad Shah to the throne, was looking for a base in the Deccan. He succeeded Sayyid Husain Ali Khan as governor; thereafter he sought to dismiss Mubariz Khan, who refused and had to defend his position by arms. Mubariz Khan perished in 1724 at the Battle of Shakar Kheda. This marked the beginning of the *nizam* dynasty, which was to reign over the richest Muslim princely state of India until 1948.

Decadence or a new political order?

Such is the outline of the key events that marked the disintegration of the Mogul Empire into a number of successor states. There were many other episodes, of lesser importance, several of which had Muslims as protagonists, as in Bahawalpur in the Punjab, Rampur in Rohilkhand, to the north of Delhi, in Bhopal, in central India, or as the *nawab* of the Carnatic, on the Coromandel coast. A number of Hindu principalities, following the example set by the Rajput states, also came into existence.

The dismemberment of the Mogul Empire occurred in a rapidly changing context. Firstly, the central empires of Islam, the Ottomans and more particularly the Safavids, were themselves undergoing significant changes. The collapse of the Safavids and their replacement, in 1736, by the Afghan Nadir Shah completely changed the picture in northwest India and in Afghanistan. The Moguls lost their political control over these regions. Above all, they lost the profits derived from the trade that passed through these regions in transit. Mogul Punjab suffered from this loss, but successor states, like those of the Afghans of Rohilkhand, benefited.

The encirclement of India by the networks of trading companies probably also played a role. The openings offered to artisans and merchants, and the consequent accumulation of wealth in the regions, must have reinforced centrifugal tendencies. However, the companies did not yet interfere in politics directly.

The Mogul Empire was therefore caught in a changing international scene that was beyond its control. It is nevertheless beyond doubt that the predominant factors were internal. To assess them, we need to make short work of several current interpretations.

First, the disintegration of the empire cannot be understood in terms of the resurgence of Hinduism after five centuries of Muslim domination. The political use of religious slogans that we encounter very occasionally in the seventeenth century under Aurangzeb and under Shivaji was equally uncommon in the eighteenth century. Only the Sikhs resorted to it, and even they would achieve their goals only much later, in 1799. The uprisings between Hindus and Muslims, while attested by evidence, were rare. Neither the Rajputs nor the Marathas put forward the idea of a 'Hindu royalty'; they continued to draw their legitimacy from the investiture of the emperor. They also continued to use Mogul administrative structures and retained Persian as the technical administrative language. Particularly under the *nawabs*, a close political and administrative cooperation between Hindus and Muslims exsisted, a collaboration without which none of the successor states could have been viable.

The theory that imputes the fall of the Mogul Empire to the poverty resulting from the over-exploitation of the peasants does not stand up any better than the religious explanation. The peasant insurrections of the closing years of the seventeenth century and of the eighteenth century were not the revolts of beggars acting out of misery. Whatever the regional variations might be, they were most often the doing of *zamindars* who had accumulated wealth thanks to more than a century of Mogul peace, and who had the means to arm themselves. Their aim was two-fold. Of course they sought to take advantage of the weakness of the empire to evade payment of taxes; but they also fought amongst themselves to consolidate their territorial gains.

In fact, the political mayhem did not signify in any way an economic decline. There were of course, especially in western India, regions that were devastated and ruined, but this picture must not be generalized to describe the whole of India.

The growth of agricultural production was continuous as late as the first half of the eighteenth century; peasants were still considered as solvent. The collection of taxes, which was increasingly leased, was thought to be profitable: there was a market for *zamindaris*, that is, offices of tax collectors. The same was true for handicraft production. In the course of the eighteenth century, market towns continued to emerge and flourish, testifying to the expansion of trade. Communication links remained intact, financial institutions as well: it was possible to make financial transfers from Bengal to Delhi; bills of exchange continued to be honoured in the entire subcontinent. Except for the political instability, the uprisings that flared up were the reuslt of prosperity rather than misery.

What had changed in reality was the distribution of power and wealth. The empire in its grandeur made the emperor the source of all powers and the point on which all the riches converged, which he then re-distributed sumptuously. Now the power had slipped out of his fingers; it had passed from the capital to the regions, where it had fallen into the hands of the *nawabs* and non-Muslim chiefs of the other successor states. These were henceforth masters in their territories. They were also masters of the court, as, through the factions that they supported, it was they who made and unmade emperors.

The emperor had also lost his wealth. If the central administration was in a state of insolvency, it did not signify that India was ruined. It only meant that the surplus collected by the tax collectors did not arrive at the capital; it was withheld at the provincial level, not going beyond the new heads of states, who constructed sumptuous capitals for themselves.

In a certain way, a new cycle was complete. There was a return to the plurality of prosperous sultanates that was prevalent before the advent of the Moguls. There was however a difference: at the end of the fourteenth century, after the collapse of the sultanate of Delhi, there was no common institution encompassing the sultanates. In the eighteenth century, the successor states maintained an organic link with the empire out of which they had emerged. They owed allegiance and tribute to the emperor who conferred their legitimacy on them. This situation was to endure until 1857, when, following the deposition of the last Mogul, Queen Victoria would become their new source of legitimacy.

PART THREE

INDIA BETWEEN TWO EMPIRES
(1739–1818)

The year 1739 marked the end of the existence of the Mogul Empire as a relatively centralized political structure. All over the empire, new states came into existence (Chapter XI). Although they continued to claim their legitimacy from the emperor, they enjoyed complete independence with respect to Delhi, whether they were Muslim states like Hyderabad, Oudh and Bengal, or non-Muslim states created by the Maratha, Rajput or Sikh chiefs. The Marathas seemed in a position to exercise a certain hegemony, but their defeat at Panipat in 1761 by the Afghans brought their momentum to an abrupt end. The date of 1761 is of more import to the history of India than that of the Battle of Plassey (1757), which enabled the English to gain control over Bengal, because it created in North India a political vacuum of which the East India Company would finally be able to take full advantage.

At the same time, in South India, the East India Company and the French Indian Company were locked in a struggle for commercial and political supremacy (Chapter XII). The consequences of the Franco-English conflict of the years 1761–74 were not circumscribed to the defeat of the French, because Dupleix, as the pioneer, imagined modes of intervention in the politics of Indian States, modes that the British would pursue and that would finally lead to the conquest of India (Chapter XII).

However, it was in the rich province of Bengal that the East India Company undertook their first widespread territorial annexation. The complex history of the British conquest of Bengal culminated in 1765 in the acquisition by the Company of the diwani, which invested it with the right to collect taxes, to administer civil justice and therefore with the real control of Bengal (Chapter XIII).

Between the acquisition of Bengal and the establishment of British supremacy, more than half a century elapsed, during which time the Company entered into conflict with the most of the Indian powers. Its two principal rivals were on the one hand Mysore, a Muslim state endowed with a formidable army, under the rule of Sultan Haidar Ali and his son Tipu, and on the other hand, the Marathas, a warring Hindu 'confederacy' made up of five principalities each of which theoretically acknowledged the suzerainty of the peshwa (a sort of prime minister) whose seat was in Poona. Luckily for the Company its two principal rivals never formed a durable alliance. During Lord Wellesley's office as proconsul (1798–1804), it could thus liquidate Mysore and deal decisive blows on the Marathas whose final defeat in 1818 was nothing more than a formality, to such an extent had they become weak and divided. Eighty years after the collapse of the Mogul Empire, the greatest part of India found itself unified once again under another imperial domination (Chapter XIV).

XI

THE SUCCESSOR STATES
(1739–61)

The accession to autonomy, even to independence, of the principal provinces of the moribund Mogul Empire, the emergence of new non-Muslim powers, the Sikhs, the Jats, the Marathas, and above all the British domination of Bengal, following the elimination of the French threat were the events that marked eighteenth-century India.

These upheavals were the consequences of the decline of the Mogul Empire, which had been perceptible by the end of the reign of Aurangzeb, evident under his immediate successors and irremediable by mid-century. The collapse of central power, from 1739 onwards, was precipitated by the political crises that rocked Iran and Afghanistan but also by the grave mayhem caused in Delhi itself by a nobility that was militarily humiliated, materially weakened and morally distressed.

If the head betrayed signs of weakness, the body remained solid. Driven by economic growth, though irregular and unequal from one region to another, certain social classes, like the merchants, who had been for long time confined to the service of the empire, asserted their presence and contributed to the emancipation of the regional States and to the political and military advance of the European companies.

The Afghan invasions

India appeared particularly vulnerable while the central power was falling to pieces. Between 1739 and 1769, the northwest of the country was to face not less than eleven invasions. After Nadir Shah's incursion into the north of India, it was from Afghanistan that the danger loomed. In 1747, on the death of the Persian sovereign, a brilliant captain of his guard, Ahmad Khan, member of the Abdali tribe, marched on Kandahar, at the head of a Pathan army and proclaimed himself sovereign of a new dynasty that he named Durrani. By the end of the year, he had gained control over territories that extended from the gates of Herat to the Indus. The war of conquest, besides the enormous plunder that it brought, cleared the way for him to control the Afghan nobility and to unite the various tribes under his authority. Thus, he would annex a part of Iran and territories extending from the Hindu Kush to Amou-Daria. Above all, it was towards India that he turned his attention: into this country, he would lead over ten expeditions.

His first expedition saw the Mogul Empire in its last throes. Ahmad Shah Abdali, after defeating the governor of Lahore, was checked by the Mogul army on 11 March 1748 at Manipur. Thereafter, under the iron rule of the new and energetic viceroy of the Punjab, Muinulmulk, the imperial troops regained the four districts of the Punjab that Nadir Shah had restored to the empire, crossed the Indus and threatened Peshawar and Kabul.

The personal rivalries and factional disputes that agitated the higher echelons of the Mogul Empire, however, would soon play into the hands of Ahmad Shah Abdali. The *wazir* Safdar Jang, chief of the Iranian party, was envious of the success of viceroy of the Punjab, Muinulmulk, a strong personality of the Turanian party. He refused to lend him his assistance during the second and the third Afghan invasions, at the end of 1749 and at the end of 1751.

Abandoned by Delhi and routed by the Afghan army on 5 March 1752, Muinulmulk was driven to accept the proposition of Ahmad Shah Abdali, who, won over by his tough character, asked him to continue as the head of the Punjab, but as a representative of the king of Kandahar and no longer that of the Mogul emperor at Delhi. With the provinces of Multan and Kashmir also annexed to Afghanistan, Delhi lost, in April 1752, all its frontier provinces, without ever engaging in a battle or in negotiations.

At the same time, it is true, the Mogul court was paralysed by a terrible civil war between the Iranian clan of the Shiite *wazir* Safdar Jang and the Sunnite Turanian clan led by the debauched emperor Ahmad Shah, the eunuch Javid Khan and the mother queen Udham Bai, who was as incompetent as she was extravagant with public money. Defeated in November 1753, Safdar Jang sought refuge in his lands in the kingdom of Oudh.

His departure did not bring to an end the internecine fights that continued to rage between the new *wazir* Intizamuddaula, supported by the emperor, and the *mir bakshi*, Imadulmulk. In alliance with the Marathas, the latter asserted his ascendancy, made Ahmad Shah recognize him as *wazir* before proclaiming his deposition and establishing in his place on the throne a puppet, Alamgir II.

In the wake of this palace revolution, the position of Imad, even though he concurrently held the offices of *wazir* and *mir bakshi*, remained most precarious. His Maratha allies, whom he could not afford to pay, pillaged the environs of Delhi, where famine was rampant. The Jat warriors of the region of Agra took advantage of the disintegration of the Mogul power to extend their domain at the expense of that of the emperor. The Rohillas (Pathan warriors of North India) followed suit and occupied the districts of Meerut, Panipat and Sirhind.

Soon threatened by the Marathas, whom Imad pressed to interfere, the Rohillas solicited the aid of the king of Afghanistan. They were supported by numerous defenders of Islam, including Shah Waliullah, who implored the master of Kandahar to deliver Delhi from this Hindu Raj – the Hindu rule – of which Imad was only an instrument.

In August 1756, Ahmad Shah Abdali arrived in India. Najib Khan, the chief of the Rohillas, offered him the support of his army. In January 1757, Ahmad Shah was in Delhi. He ousted Imad, and replaced him with Intizamuddaula, who had offered him twenty million rupees to take the reins of a State without territory, without revenue, and without an army. For one month, the city of Delhi was subjected to looting, but the atrocities committed here are not comparable to those endured in February and March by the Jat country, where Ahmad Shah offered five rupees for every head of a Hindu delivered by his soldiers. More cities, Mathura, Vrindavan and Agra were looted and their Hindu sanctuaries desecrated. Only an epidemic of cholera in the Afghan army put an end to the carnage.

Before returning to his mountains, master of an enormous plunder loaded on 28,000 animals, Ahmad Shah pronounced the annexation of the region of Sirhind, appointed his son Timur Shah viceroy of the Punjab and left Delhi to his loyal ally, Najib Khan Rohilla. The reign of the latter was as brutal as it was ephemeral: Imadulmulk, no sooner had the Afghans left, appealed to his Maratha ally, Raghunath Rao who, in September 1757, entered Delhi and reinstated him in his feeble powers. A few months later, the Marathas occupied Lahore, from where they chased Timur Shah.

Reduced to insignificance, the Moguls were henceforth condemned to see the troops of new powers march one after another on the roads of their capital, troops that took advantage of their disunity and prospered at their expense. Nevertheless, despite the collapse of his powers, the emperor remained a 'fountain of authority': 'The value of the royal charisma increased even when the royal Treasury was getting exhausted.'[1] The *nawabs* of Bengal, Oudh and the Carnatic, as well as the *nizam* (sovereign) of Hyderabad, who all encroached on his powers, respected his status and the eminent character of the person, and did not seek either the imperial title or the quasi-religious functions attached thereto. The Sikhs and the Marathas themselves aspired to become the agents of the Mogul sovereignty. The Marathas even attempted to appropriate the person of the emperor, a source of legitimacy and authority.

The successor states: The new Muslim powers

The transfer of power, if not of authority, from the centre to the periphery is not specific to India. During the same period, an identical process was at work in the Ottoman Empire, where diverse local powers, even while claiming to owe their allegiance to Istanbul, founded in effect veritable regional dynasties.

In India, the first half of the eighteenth century was marked by the evolution towards autonomy of the ancient historical regions that possessed a certain geographic, linguistic and cultural unity. These were the regions which the Moguls had made their principal administrative entities. At Hyderabad, in Oudh and in Bengal, the governors broke away from the central power by using almost identical methods: 1) the governor (*subadar*) or, sometimes in the secondary entities, an officer of inferior rank, appointed his functionaries, notably those in charge of finances, without consulting with Delhi. 2) He designated his successor. Nonetheless, anxious to establish the legitimacy of his dynasty, he endeavoured to obtain confirmation from the emperor. He generally achieved his ends by offering cash in return. 3) He desisted thereafter from paying even a single rupee to the imperial treasury, cornering for himself all the revenues of the state, which he then led to autonomy. 4) He pursued an independent foreign policy. He launched military campaigns that enabled him, thanks to the annexations that they resulted in, to increase his economic and politic resources. 5) He established a capital for the embellishment of which he devoted considerable sums of money. 6) He struck his own coins, in his name. 7) He ordered that the Friday prayer be recited in his name, not in the name of the emperor.

However, in the former Mogul provinces, as in the Ottoman world, the local and regional sovereigns remained respectful for a long time of the moral authority of the emperor, from whom they derived their legitimacy, and generally did not take the last two steps of this process of decentralization.[2]

Hyderabad

In 1713, Nizamulmulk was appointed viceroy of the six provinces (*subas*) of the Deccan (Khandesh, Berar, Aurangabad, Bidar, Hyderabad, and Bijapur) and military deputy governor (*faujdar*) of the Carnatic. He appeared at the time as the only person capable of liberating the Deccan from the Maratha tutelage and of re-establishing order. In effect, taking full advantage of the dissensions among the Marathas, he contested the right to levy tribute that they had arrogated for themselves. Concerned about the welfare of the peasantry, who had suffered for a long time from Maratha incursions and tax exactions, he also endeavoured to put in place a system of uniform and equitable taxation.

Recalled in 1715, Nizamulmulk could resume his work only eight years later. Appointed *wazir*, he was unable to enforce his reformist policies. Disheartened by the inertia of the emperor and the court, he decided after several years of vain attempts to retire to the Deccan. His departure provoked the ire of the emperor Muhammad Shah, who ordered the *faujdar* of Chicacole, Mubriaz Khan, to drive him out of the Deccan. His arrival also caused anxiety to the *peshwa* Baji Rao, who was afraid that henceforth the right that had been granted to him to collect *chauth* (a quarter of the land taxes) in these regions might be contested. With astuteness, Nizamulmulk negotiated a treaty of 'mutual friendship' with the Marathas and turned his army against Mubariz Khan, who was routed and killed at Shakar-Keda, in Berar, in October 1724. Thereafter, Nizamulmulk's hegemony in Hyderabad was no further challenged by Delhi. When, in wake of his victory, he proclaimed his attachment and his loyalty to the Mogul dynasty, Muhammad Shah recognized him as viceroy of the Deccan.

From then on and until his death, in 1748, Nizamulmulk governed as an independent sovereign. He declared wars and negotiated peace without consulting with Delhi, did not pay a single rupee to the imperial treasury and organised according to his wish the administration and the finances of his kingdom, which was divided into three parts: the *jagirs*, bestowed on the partisans of the sovereign, the *sarf-i-khas*, a domain that was reserved for him, and the *diwani*, the revenues of which were allocated for the expenditures of the administration.

Sovereign in his states, Nizamulmulk remained attached to the Mogul dynasty and to the person of the emperor, whose name was engraved on the coins of Hyderabad and mentioned in the mosques on Fridays. He was indeed the most faithful servant of the empire during its phase of dismemberment: in 1738, he undertook, though unsuccessfully, the task of chasing the Marathas out of Malwa, at the behest of Muhammad Shah. One year later, during the invasion of the shah of Persia, Nadir Shah, he distinguished himself by his military and diplomatic qualities and above all by his loyalty: when, shortly after the betrayal of the *nawab* of Oudh, Nadir Shah asked him to govern the empire instead of Muhammad Shah, he reminded him that, like all his forefathers, he had always been loyal to the Moguls and assured him that he intended to remain so.

Oudh

Throughout the Mogul period, the administration of Oudh was identical to that of other provinces. At the head of the province, a governor (*subadar* or *nazim*) was in charge of maintaining law and order. The *diwan*, responsible for the tax and financial services, was also appointed by the emperor. The province was made up of five administrative districts (*sarkars*) (Oudh, Gorakhpur, Bahraich, Khairabad and Lucknow), each of which was subdivided into *parganas*.

Fallen into disgrace at the court in Delhi, Saadat Khan was appointed *subadar* of Oudh by the emperor in 1722. From then on, his policy consisted of compensating for the weakening of his positions at Delhi with the extension of his powers in Oudh. He first appointed his son-in-law, Safdar Jang, as his successor. Thereafter, he abolished the office of the imperial *diwan* and from 1725 onwards, he suspended his payments to the treasury of Delhi. Simultaneously, he extended his possessions towards the east by annexing Benares, Jaunpur, Chunargarh and Ghazipur.

For all this, Saadat Khan did not break away from Muhamad Shah, but sought to take advantage of his interventions in favour of the empire. Thus, after a campaign against the Marathas in 1737, he demanded the provinces of Agra, Malwa, Gujarat, Bihar and Ajmer, which would have made him the most powerful sovereign of India. Despite the refusal of the emperor, he joined two years later with the Mogul coalition that had been formed to curb the Persian invasion. But, when the post of *mir bakshi*, which he coveted, was offered to Nizamulmulk, he did not hesitate to betray the empire and to seek from the king of Persia the political leverage that the court of Delhi had denied him. Contemptuously rebutted by Nadir Shah, he committed suicide two days before the sack of Delhi.

Saadat Khan bequeathed to his successor, Safdar Jang, an autonomous kingdom, prosperous and powerful, with an army of 50,000 men and a treasury containing over one hundred million rupees. The new *nawab* could without any difficulty pay the viceroy of Persia the sum he demanded as tribute for acknowledging him as the ruler of Oudh. He could even afford to recruit into his army 6,000 to 7,000 Persian cavalrymen by offering them fifty rupees per month, while the pay of the mercenaries of Oudh added up to only thirty rupees.

Pursuing the policies of Saadat, Safdar Jang extended his power by demanding a price for his support to the empire. Promising to intervene in favour of the *nawab* of Bengal, who was then threatened by the Marathas, a promise that he would eventually dishonour, he received, for instance, the forts of Rohtas and Chunar. Despite

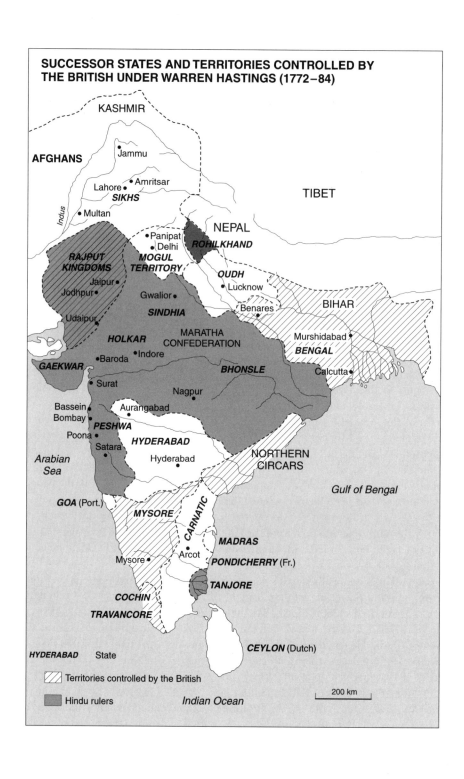

SUCCESSOR STATES AND TERRITORIES CONTROLLED BY THE BRITISH UNDER WARREN HASTINGS (1772–84)

KASHMIR

AFGHANS

• Jammu

Lahore • • Amritsar

SIKHS

Indus

• Multan

TIBET

• Panipat

• Delhi

NEPAL

ROHILKHAND

RAJPUT KINGDOMS

MOGUL TERRITORY

Jaipur •

Jodhpur •

OUDH

• Lucknow

Gwalior •

Udaipur •

• Benares

BIHAR

SINDHIA

MARATHA CONFEDERATION

Murshidabad •

HOLKAR

BENGAL

GAEKWAR

• Baroda • Indore

BHONSLE

Calcutta •

• Surat

Nagpur •

Bassein •

• Aurangabad

Bombay •

PESHWA

Poona •

HYDERABAD

Satara •

Hyderabad •

Arabian Sea

NORTHERN CIRCARS

Gulf of Bengal

GOA (Port.)

MYSORE

CARNATIC

MADRAS

Mysore •

• Arcot

PONDICHERRY (Fr.)

TANJORE

COCHIN

TRAVANCORE

CEYLON (Dutch)

HYDERABAD   State

Territories controlled by the British

Hindu rulers   *Indian Ocean*

200 km

the ambivalence of his relations with the empire, he relentlessly reinforced his positions at the court, no doubt because he was the most powerful of Mogul princes. In 1743, he was appointed *mir atish* (chief of artillery) and *subadar* of Kashmir. In 1748, on the death of Muhammad Shah, he obtained from the new emperor, Ahmad Shah, the *suba* of Allahabad, which cleared the road for him to expand his territorial possessions considerably, as well as gain the post of *wazir*. On the strength of the authority that this office conferred on him, he could ensure the continuity of his dynasty, designating his son, Shujauddaula, as his heir. He placed, on the other hand, the Mogul army at the service of Oudh, and as its head, wrested from his neighbour, the Pathan *nawab* Ahmad Khan Bangash of Farrukhabad, thirty three *parganas* that he annexed.

In 1750, a powerful coalition was formed against Safdar Jang, rallying the ambitions thwarted and interests wronged by his omnipotence: it assembled Nazir Jang (the successor of Nizamulmulk), Intizamuddaula, Javid Khan, the Bangashes of Farrukhabad and the Rohillas of Rohilkhand. Threatened, Safdar Jang had no other recourse but to turn to the Hindu powers, the Jats and the Marathas, to save the situation temporarily. The assassination of Javid Khan and the civil war of 1753, however, precipitated his fall at Delhi: he retired to Oudh where he died in 1754.

It was under Shujauddaula that the first centrifugal forces became obvious in Oudh. Even as the *nawabs* progressively increased their economic, financial, military and political powers at the expense of the centre, they themselves had to brave the ambitions of some of their vassals who did not hesitate to resort to the same strategies to increase their resources and to gain autonomy. The rajah of Benares, Bhalwant Singh, who claimed the fort of Chunar, was all the more formidable because he protected a holy place that all the Hindus, and notably the Marathas, were ready to defend. In 1757, Shuja occupied Chunar and Benares, but he had the wisdom to maintain the rajah and contented himself with demanding an indemnity from him.

After the assassination of his father Alamgir II, the emperor Mogul Shah Alam II fled from the court of Delhi regimented by Imadulmulk. In exile, he made Shujauddaula his *wazir*. It was, however, without the support of the latter that he embarked in 1760 and 1761 on two hazardous expeditions against the English in Bihar. Finally defeated and captured, he was handed over by the British to Shujauddaula who offered him a safe asylum. The *nawab* was henceforth the master of the person of the emperor, the principal source of legitimacy in India. This was the apogee of the independent state of Oudh.

Bengal[3]

Attempts at autonomy were also manifest in Bengal under the government of Murshid Quli Khan (1716–27). Appointed by the emperor to restore the fiscal health of the country, he imposed his authority on the *zamindars*, and embarked on his personal politics, taking advantage of the mayhem that reigned at the time in Delhi; he concurrently held the offices of *subadar* and *wazir*, appointed and revoked administrative and financial staff and designated as his successor, his son-in-law Sarfaraz Khan.

Sarfaraz Khan almost never governed: he was deposed for the first time, in 1727, by his father Shuja Khan, and a second time in 1740, by Alivardi Khan, the representative of the *nawab* in Bihar, two years after the death of his father.

Alivardi Khan had his coup d'état legitimized by the emperor and resumed the policies of Murshid Quli Khan. Concurrently holding the functions of *nazim* and *diwan*, he filled all the important positions, choosing notably representatives or *naibs* from among his relations for the cities of Patna, Dacca (eastern Bengal) and Cuttack (Orissa), as well as the *faujdars* of the frontier districts. Lastly, he organized a powerful army around a core of Pathan warriors.

During the years that followed his accession to power, Alivardi Khan suspended his payments to Delhi, which amounted to around ten million rupees per year under Murshid Quli Khan. In 1758, the total remittance made in the fifteen preceding years did not exceed five million rupees, whereas the revenues of the *nawab* added up to more than fifteen million per year. To justify this retention of funds, Alivardi Khan could invoke the perpetual wars that he had to confront. Indeed, much more than Oudh, Bengal was under the threat of the Marathas from the outside and of powerful centrifugal forces from the inside.

In 1742, the Maratha Raghuji Bhonsle, solicited by the unfortunate rival of Alivardi Khan, Sarfaraz Khan, invaded Orissa and western Bengal and pillaged the vicinity of the capital, Murshidabad, and of Calcutta where the British hastily dug the 'Maratha ditch'. One year later, two Maratha armies made a foray into Bengal, one led by Bhonsle and the other by the *peshwa* Balaji Rao. Alivardi Khan bought their departure by promising to pay them *chauth*. Nonetheless, he had to brave fresh incursions, in 1744, 1745, 1748 and in 1751 when the Marathas were once again at the gates of Murshidabad. Alivardi Khan then had to undertake to pay an annual *chauth* of 1,200,000 rupees and to cede Orissa to the invaders.

From the inside, the *nawab* had to fight against the separatist tendencies of his nobles, some of whom were lying in wait for an occasion to return in kind the treatment he had inflicted on Sarfaraz Khan, and of a part of his army, which was admittedly powerful, but also heterogeneous. In 1748, for instance, Pathan soldiers revolted and seized Patna, which they controlled for a period of time. Contrary to these mutineers who would be brought to submission, the *faujdar* of Purnea liberated himself from the tutelage of Alivardi Khan and succeed in creating a small autonomous state.

The influential Hindu *zamindars* also posed a potential threat. Such was their power that the *nawab* could only compromise with them: on the death of Murshid Quli Khan, the *zamindars* of Burdwan and of Rajshahi procured a quarter of the revenues of Bengal: some decades later, it is estimated that 60 per cent of the resources of the *nawab* came from only fifteen *zamindari* domains. To ensure the maintenance of order in their domains, each of these rajahs possessed an army, thanks to which he could certainly, if need be, defy the authority of the *nawab*: the army of the *zamindar* of Burdwan had not less than 30,000 men.

Even at the time of the Maratha incursions, when circumstances drove him to ask for an exceptional contribution of ten millions rupees from the rajah of Burdwan alone and when the *peshwa*, in the name of Hinduism, called for a revolt and a secession, Alivardi Khan succeeded in imposing his authority over these powerful vassals. No doubt, the atrocities committed by the Maratha warriors explain the loyalty of these powerful *zamindars*. Perhaps we can also discern in their attitude the manifestation of a Bengali solidarity that, at the elite level, transcended religious solidarity.

The rajahs of Bihar were much more recalcitrant: those of Darbhanga and of Champaran made vague attempts at autonomy. Between Patna and Gaya, two kinglets, Khamgar Khan of Hasua and Sundar Singh of Tikari, tore each other apart on a regular basis and came to an agreement only to resist the tax requirements of Murshidabad, making the intervention of the *nawab*'s army necessary. It appears that the revenues that the *nawab* derived from Bihar were very modest.

Lastly, the *nawab* had to appease the dominant bankers and notably the Jagat Seths, veritable pillars of the state. In 1742, as they fled before the Marathas, Alivardi Khan employed all his influence to retain them at Murshidabad, 'their presence being as necessary for governments as for merchants.'[4]

Social harmony and religious and cultural development

As has been made evident by the role of the Jagat Seths, Hindus were indispensable to the Muslim sovereigns of the successor states. They were present everywhere in the highest spheres. When he decided to establish himself in the Deccan, Nizamulmulk surrounded himself with Hindus, as much as with Muslims, and conferred on them eminent positions, following in this regard the example set by the Qutb Shahis of Golconda and the Adil Shahis of Bijapur. In Bengal, Alivardi Khan, who appointed his close relatives to all the high offices, made sure that they were surrounded by competent Hindu functionaries. His Treasury (or *khalisa*) was managed by Hindus who bore the title *mutaseddi*. In Oudh too, Saadat Khan assigned the administration of the finances to a Hindu of the merchant caste of the Khatri, Atma Ram. The son and grandson of the latter, Ram Narayan and Maha Narayan, were to fill the same positions under Safdar Jang and Shujauddaula respectively. The prime minister and the secretary of Shujauddaula were Brahmins. From 1750, a contingent of Naga Sanyasi soldiers, who fought entirely nude with their bodies covered in ashes, constituted the jewel of the army of Oudh. They numbered 12,000 towards 1760.

A scandal sparked off by Shujauddaula, in the beginning of his reign, reveals the importance of Hindus in his states. The new *nawab*, had violated a Khatri woman, which gave rise to resentment and agitation among the Hindus, and a conspiracy was devised against him under the leadership of the Hindu Ram Narayan and the Muslim Ismail Khan. These two loyal servants of the state planned to dethrone Shujauddaula and to replace him with Muhammad Kuli Khan of Allahabad. The influential queen mother Sadrunnisa Begam finally dissuaded the conspirators and calmed the situation. The affair is none the less a pointer to the precariousness of the position of the sovereigns, whose survival 'depended on the care that they exercised for the needs and susceptibilities of their subjects',[5] particularly when they were of an origin different from that of the ruling family.

Simultaneously a certain religious and cultural intermingling became evident, as much at the popular as the elite level. In the eighteenth century, an English observer, Buchanan, signalled the existence of a great number of cults in eastern Bengal in which Hindus and Muslims participated. At Rangpur, for example, the two communities worshiped the same deity, which the Hindus called Satya Narayan and the Muslims Satya Pir. On the occasion of great festivals in which the *nawab* took part at Murshidabad and his representative (*naib*) at Dacca, both the religious groups venerated with the same fervour Kwajah Khizir, the protector of sailors.

Similar phenomena were observed in certain states of the south: the Maratha rajahs of Tanjore and the Danish merchants of Tranquebar maintained the mosque at Nagore; Jews and Christians participated in the ceremonies of the coronation of the rajah of Cochin. In northwest India, the Marathas protected the sanctuary of Shaikh Muinuddin at Ajmer, which attracted the Hindus of Rajasthan.

Was political decentralization a reflection of the emergence of cultural identities? This is a controversial question. The attachment of the *nawabs* to the Mogul tradition is certainly evident; it is hardly probable on the other hand that they were interested in local traditions. In Bengal, the *nawabs* were tolerant towards the Hindus, but tolerance signifies neither syncretism nor ecumenism. Their concern seems to have been primarily to maintain a Mogul order in which the Hindus had their place.[6]

On the other hand, the debate on the supposed cultural decline of India in the eighteenth century is closed. The harsh judgements of certain Europeans had supported for a long time the thesis of a spiritual and intellectual vacuum during this period. On the contrary, todays historians concede the emergence, in the successor states, of profound religious movements and artistic trends that were vigorous, if not markedly innovative.

In Bengal, for example, Hinduism experienced a revival. The worship of the Goddess, or Shakti, the feminine energy of the great gods, and the devotional cults of Rama and more particularly Krishna developed as early as the eighteenth century. Rajahs and *zamindars* but also simple *faujdars* and village notables constructed temples dedicated to Durga and to Kali or to the major avatars of Vishnu. In this manner, they converted their financial resources into prestige and social recognition. Certain castes of wealthy farmers or of rich merchants devoted themselves also to patronage, in which they saw a means of climbing a hierarchical ladder that was never static.

While the rajahs of Vishnupur edified pagodas, the *rani* of Rajshahi and the *zamindar* of Nadia opened schools and encouraged Sanskrit studies. Towards 1780, the Sanskrit scholar William Jones celebrated the quality of teaching of the Brahmins of Nadia. It is with the assistance of one of them that Henry Colebrook compiled his *Code of Hindoo Law*. In Bihar, the rajahs of Darbhanga protected Brahmins and poets. The region of Mithila, which fell under their jurisdiction, became a great literary centre where Maithili flourished, a language derived from Bihari and spoken in the north of the Ganges. Other regional languages and literatures developed rapidly: it was the case with Oriya, for example, which gained ground in certain parts of southern Bengal.

Patronage of the arts was not the prerogative of the rajahs of the north. In South

India, in the first half of the eighteenth century, the Maratha rajah Sufoji of Tanjore protected literature and the arts: in his small state, Carnatic music experienced a remarkable development. Following the example of the Hindu patrons, certain Muslim sovereigns encouraged the letters and the arts: this was the case in the south with the *nawab* of Arcot and the Afghan princes of Nellore. At Lucknow and Murshidabad, the Shiite *nawabs* of Oudh and of Bengal contributed to the progress of their sect. Even at Delhi, the Sufi brotherhood Naqshbandiyya established teaching institutions and endeavoured to bridge the gap between the scholarly and mystical traditions.

However, the malaise of the Sunnite Muslim world reverberated in India. In the middle of the century, the fundamentalist Shah Waliullah vehemently denounced the fossilization of Islam and the compromises of a number of his coreligionists. Eschewing the out of date teaching of the ulemas in the *madrasas* of Delhi, he advocated critical thinking. He was the voice of an Islam that aspired to a renewal indispensable for checking the progress of Sikhism and Hinduism.

The non-Muslim states

Mogul principles and practices were less perceptible in the non-Muslim states than in the successor states, no doubt because, in the former, what occurred was not just a seizure of the centre's powers by a regional elite, but rather the affirmation of an identity that crystallized around a language, a faith and common interests. The Maratha confederacy, the largest of these political formations, has often been described as a Brahmin kingdom where cows and Hindu holy places were protected, the Sikh confederation as an egalitarian peasant state, born out of the struggle against the Indo-Muslim aristocracy that supported the Mogul Empire. With the exception of the Sikhs perhaps, who were intransigent with respect to the Muslim power, whether it was Mogul or Afghan, these states did not seek the destruction of the empire. On the contrary, they depended on Delhi for the legitimization of their ambitions and their annexations.

The birth and the affirmation of the Sikh power

Confrontations between the Sikhs and the Moguls had commenced as early as the reign of Jahangir. It was, however, in the first half of the eighteenth century that the disciples of Guru Nanak acquired a true military organization and succeeded in braving the *subadars* and the *faujdars* of the Punjab.

The *Khalsa* or 'gathering of the pure', an armed and egalitarian brotherhood, was founded by the tenth and last guru, Gobind Singh (1666–1708). It did not gather all the Sikhs: the *sahajdhari* or 'upholders of facility', who were not part of it, were nonetheless considered members of the Sikh community (*panth*). The members of the *Khalsa* distinguished themselves by wearing the five 'K's: *kes* (uncut hair and beard); *kangha* (comb); *kirpan* (sword); *kara* (metal bracelet) and *kacch* (short pants). The men of the brotherhood added *Singh* (lion) to their name and the women *Kaur* (princess).

His four sons having been killed by the Moguls, Gobind Singh decided to put an end to the authority of the 'personal guru' and to transfer it to the Book, called *Guru Granth Sahib*, and to the assembled *Khalsa* or *guru panth*. Every year, the Sikhs congregated (*sarbat Khalsa*) in April, on the occasion of the new year celebration (*Baisakhi*), and in October, for *Diwali*. The *Guru Granth* was then placed in the centre of the assembly, which deliberated on questions of common interest. The resolutions that it adopted (*gurmatta*) were sacred.

On the death of Gobind Singh, the leadership of the community was entrusted to Banda Bahadur (1670–1716), who embarked on a ruthless fight against the Moguls. In 1710, he took over the fort of Sirhind and established a truly independent state. He eliminated the Mogul functionaries and abolished the *zamindari* system. He promised lands to those who did not have any and introduced peasant ownership. He struck his own coins and imposed a new calendar. He rallied to his cause Hindus and Muslims who were allowed to practise their religions even within his army. The egalitarian ideal of the Sikhs and his policy on the redistribution of wealth earned him the support of individuals from disadvantaged castes.

This independent state was ephemeral. As early as the end of 1710, Banda Bahadur suffered his first setback. Routed by the imperial army in December 1715, he was eventually executed at Delhi in March 1716. The emperor Farrukhsiyar then ordered the execution of all Sikhs who refused to convert to Islam. To escape the massacres, the disciples of Nanak fled towards the mountains: it was their first experience of wandering in the political wilderness.

Spearheaded from Lahore by Zakariya Khan and from Multan by Abdussamad Khan, the repression produced only mediocre results: the raids by Sikhs descending from the mountains increased in number. In sheer desperation, Zakariya Khan decided to negotiate: in 1733, he conferred on the Sikh chief, Kapur Singh, the title of *nawab* as well as a *jagir*. The truce was short-lived: divided into the *Taruna Dal*, the army of the young and *Budha Dal*, the army of the veterans, and under the leadership of Kapur Singh, Sikh warriors resumed their war of liberation.

Victorious in 1736, the year in which they took control of Amritsar, the Sikhs subsequently suffered fresh repression and serious setbacks. In March 1746, under Yahiya Khan, the successor of Zakariya Khan, the Sikhs of the region of Lahore were massacred, the temple of Amritsar desecrated and the reading of Sikh books rendered punishable by death. In June, the first *ghalughara* or 'holocaust' took place, in the course of which around 10,000 Sikhs were massacred.

However, less than a year later, the ruthless Yahiya Khan was chased out by his young brother Shah Nawaz Khan, who was much more favourable towards the Sikhs: in fact, he chose as the *diwan* a *sahajdhari*, Kaura Mal. Ahmad Shah Abdali's first invasion also contributed to the Sikh renaissance: in March 1748 while the Mogul army confronted the Afghan invader, Jassa Singh Ahluwalia seized Amritsar.

On 29 March 1748, the day of *Baisakhi*, the *Khasla*, assembled at Amritsar, designated Jassa Singh the supreme commander of the Sikhs and decided on the organization of a true state. Jassa Singh forthwith ordered the construction of a vast fort, Ram Rauni, at Amritsar, not far from the Golden Temple. He extended his authority little by little all over central Punjab, rallying under his banner populations weary of Mogul rule.

Charged with the task of resolving the Sikh problem once and for all, the *faujdar* of Jullundur, Adina Beg, preferred to negotiate with Jassa Singh whom he invited to govern, in the name of the emperor, all the territories that he controlled. The supreme commander rejected this peace proposal, declaring to Adina Beg that the mission entrusted by God to the Sikhs was the destruction of Mogul power, the outcome of which could only be war. The *Khalsa*, he added, should govern with sovereignty and not as a vassal of a foreign prince. His arrogant words aside, he had the astuteness to form an alliance with the governor of Lahore, Muinulmulk, during the second and third Afghan invasions. Thanks to the benevolent attitude of Kaura Mal, whom Muin had maintained in his post of *diwan*, the Sikhs gained a respite that enabled them to organize the structures of their state.

It was during this period that the Sikh confederation was created, by the establishment of the *misldari* system: the *Khalsa* was divided into twelve *misls*, equal warrior bands each with a territorial base. The goal of the reform was to create local powers equipped with the greatest initiative to brave the three-fold threat posed by the Moguls, Afghans and Marathas. Decisions concerning the entire *Khalsa* were henceforth taken by delegates of the *misls*. The climate of insecurity engendered by the Afghan invasions explains the institution of the *rakhi* system: in exchange for one fifth of their harvests or their revenues, peasants and *zamindars*, regardless of their religion, enjoyed the protection (*rakhi*) of the *Khalsa*. Almost everywhere in the Punjab, Sikh *sardars* actively supervised the construction of powerful forts.

When the Punjab came under the sovereignty of the Durrani dynasty, in April 1752, in the wake of the third invasion of Ahmad Shah, the Sikhs, refractory to all forms of domination, embarked on a new war of liberation. They scored numerous successes, notably in 1757, when they humiliated Timur Shah, son of the king of Afghanistan and engaged in pillaging at the very gates of Lahore. Shortly afterwards, they formed a coalition with Adina Beg of Jullunder and the Maratha Raghunath Rao. In April 1758, the coalition entered Lahore, from where Timur Shah had just enough time to flee. The return of the Marathas to their country and the sudden death of Adina Beg left the Sikhs the sole masters of the Punjab. In 1761, Jassa Singh was proclaimed king in Lahore, and like Banda Bahadur a few decades ago he struck his own coins.

His supremacy was momentarily jeopardized at the time of the sixth Afghan invasion: on 5th February 1762, the Sikhs suffered a crushing defeat and became the victims of a veritable massacre: this was the *wadda ghalughara*, or 'the second great holocaust.' Fifty chariots were necessary to transport the heads of the victims to Lahore. Ahmad Shah ordered the walls of the mosques desecrated by the Sikhs to be washed with their blood.

From the month of October 1762, however, the *Budha Dal* and the *Taruna Dal* regained the upper hand, inflicting a severe defeat on Ahmad Shah. Between this date and October 1764, they imposed their authority on Amritsar, Sialkot, Sirhind and Multan. In April 1765, in the wake of the defeat of Ahmad Shah Abdali's seventh expedition, they recaptured Lahore. The later Afghan invasions, in 1766–7, 1768 and 1769, could not succeed in posing a threat to the domination of the Sikhs in the Punjab. As early as the end of 1767, they invaded the Doab and reached the gates of Delhi. When Ahmad Shah Abdali died, in 1772, the Sikh confederation exercised absolute domination from Saharanpur in the east to Attock in the west and from Multan in the south to Jammu in the north. True to what Bussy wrote in 1784, they were the masters of the vast spaces that sprawled between Delhi and the Persian Empire.

To a large extent, the Sikhs owed their victories to the military fraternity of the *Khalsa*. This solidarity soon formed cracks following the elimination of the Afghan threat. Incessant quarrels flared up among the *misls*, notably the Bhangi Misl founded by Chhaja Singh and the Sukarchakia Misl of Charat Singh. It would be up to be the grandson of the latter, Ranjit Singh, to put an end to these quarrels, reunifying the *misls* and proclaiming himself maharajah in 1800.

The small Hindu states

The Rajput states

The weakness of the Rajput states of the northwest of India was the result of their disunities. At no time did they envisage uniting in order to take advantage of the disintegration of Mogul power. Their sovereigns, mediocre as they were, perhaps with the exception of Sawai Jai Singh of Jaipur, still seemed dazzled by the Mogul splendour of the seventeenth century and were incapable of gauging the import of the decline of the empire. Furthermore, clannish fights that ravaged each of these kingdoms rendered any alliance between the states impossible.

The decline of Mewar (Udaipur) was irremediable. It can no doubt be attributed to the isolationist policy of the *rana* Sangaram Singh II who, contrary to his neighbours, did not nurture any territorial ambitions, but also to the rivalry of the two main clans of the Saktawats and the Chundawats. Moreover the chief of the latter clan possessed sweeping powers that enabled him to paralyze the action of the *rana*. The endemic state of anarchy in which Mewar was bogged down in the eighteenth century, in fact, made it an easy prey for the Marathas.

Marwar (Jodhpur), on the contrary, drew substantial advantages from the interventionist policies of Ajit Singh and Abhai Singh (1724–49), who projected themselves as the defenders of the Mogul Empire. Ajmer, Nagore and even Gujarat were for some time administered by the Rathore dynasty of Jodhpur.

A passionate amateur of astronomy and mathematics, the builder of the city of Jaipur, Sawai Jai Singh of Amber (1699–1743), chief of the Kachhwa clan, rival of the Rathores, pursued a similar policy in his states. Appointed *subadar* of Agra in 1712 and of Malwa in 1713, he defended without great enthusiasm or success these territories against his Maratha coreligionists, for whom he harboured some sympathy. He did not hesitate, on the other hand, to employ, to the greatest advantage of his own states, both his influence at Delhi and the money that the emperor paid him to fight against the *peshwa*: he annexed in particular the small state of Bundi that Jaipur would control between 1729 and 1748.

However cultured and skilful he might have been, Jai Singh proved to be incapable of federating the Rajputs. On the contrary, he let himself become embroiled, in 1741, in a fratricidal and disastrous war against the Rathores. Jaipur and Jodhpur suffered severe losses in the Battle of Gangwana (28 Mai 1741), in the course of which the two principalities sacrificed their best warriors.

The wars of succession that shook Jaipur after the death of Jai Singh and Marwar from 1749 consummated the ruin of Rajasthan. The Marathas, solicited sometimes by a contested prince, sometimes by an evicted pretender, took advantage of the situation and became the true masters of the region between 1750 and 1760.

The Jats

While the star of the proud Rajput nobles was waning, that of the modest Jat farmers began to shine with ever-increasing brilliance. It was to the west of Agra, around the city of Bharatpur, that the embryo of the first Jat state was created by the village chieftain Churaman, who conducted numerous guerrilla operations against the troops of Aurangzeb.

Ultimately defeated by Sawai Jai Singh, who was commanding the army of the Mogul emperor, Churaman committed suicide in 1721. His nephew Badan Singh was the true founder of an independent Jat kingdom, emancipated from the tutelage of Jaipur. He constructed the four formidable fortresses of Dig, Khumber, Bharatpur and Ver that protected the territory extending between Rajasthan and the Jamuna.

In reality, Badan Singh, suffering from blindness, relinquished most of his powers around 1745 to his adopted son, Suraj Mal. An audacious general and a consummate statesman, the latter concluded an alliance with Safdar Jang, who, concurrently holding the functions of *nawab* of Oudh and *wazir* of the empire, was, between 1748 and 1752, the most powerful man in northern India. The victories he scored against the Afghans of Rohilkhand and Farrukhabad, two *faujdaris* that had become independent, earned Suraj Mal the recognition of the *nawab* of Oudh. As a reward, he received the position of *faujdar* of Mathura and obtained for Badan Singh the title of rajah.

When, after falling into disgrace in Delhi, Safdar Jang retired to Lucknow, his Jat allies had to confront the new strong man, Imadulmulk. With the help of the Maratha Malhar Rao Holkar, and at the head of an army of 80,000 men, Imadulmulk laid siege to Khumber. He was defeated and the Jats, pressing their advantage to the full, got away with pillaging the environs of Delhi. The Marathas acknowledged Suraj Mal, who succeeded Badan Singh in 1756, as the master of the entire region of Agra.

Nevertheless, no solidarity gelled between the two Hindu powers. The Brahmins who governed the Maratha confederation showed a sovereign contempt for the Jats who were peasants of low extraction. They did not offer any support when their territory was devastated in 1757 by the Afghans of Ahmad Shah Abdali. However, they were soon to pay a heavy price for this political error.

The Maratha confederation

The rise to ascendancy of Maratha power was one of the crucial events of the first few decades of the eighteenth century. Nevertheless, despite a series of impressive victories, Maratha cavalrymen, who since Shivaji had been the unrivalled masters of guerrilla warfare and of an early form of lightning warfare, could establish only partial and ephemeral domination over the territories that they devastated, so obvious were the shortcomings of their administration. Their collapse, in 1761, was also the outcome of the two chronic evils of the Maratha State: the dilapidation of their finances and internecine dissensions.

The First Two Peshwas

In May 1707, the Mogul emperor Bahadur Shah liberated Shahu, grandson of Shivaji and the son of Shambaji, who had been captured by Aurangzeb in 1689. The *swarajya*, the heart of Maratha country, was promised to him, as well as the *chauth* (a quarter of the land revenue) from the *subas* of the Deccan. These lavish offers were not disinterested. At Delhi, it was firmly believed that this liberation would divide and weaken the Marathas. The prediction proved well founded: Shahu effectively clashed with Tara Bai, wife of the king Ram Raja, who had ascended to the throne in 1689 following his capture. Against him, Tara Bai supported the claims of her son, another Shivaji. It was only at the end of a civil war that had lasted seven years (1707–1714) that Shahu succeeded in bringing all the Maratha *sardars* and feudatories to recognize his authority.

Shahu's policy towards the Moguls was far from being as radical as that of his predecessors: he even seemed disposed to support the empire against its internal and external enemies. On the other hand, he intended to be the sole master of the Deccan and sought to be recognised in this capacity by all the *subadars* and by the emperor himself. It was thanks to the military and diplomatic aptitude of his *peshwa* or prime minister, Balaji Vishwanath (1660?–1720) that he achieved his ends. In effect, the *peshwa* wrested three *firmans* in March 1719, securing for his king, in addition to the full and undiminished sovereignty in the *swarajya*, the right to levy *chauth* and *sardeshmukhi* (one tenth of the revenue) in the six *subas* of the Deccan, as well as in Mysore, Trichinopoly and Tanjore. In exchange for the 180 million rupees that thus became their due, the Marathas were required to maintain 15,000 cavalrymen for the service of the empire and to pay the imperial treasury the petty sum of a million rupees per year. These *firmans*, which brought the *chhattrapathi* (the king) authority and resources, indubitably contributed to the revival of the Marathas.

However, neither Balaji Vishwanath nor his son, Balaji Rao, who replaced him in 1720, could succeed in creating a united and centralized state. A central administration did exist. It was headed by the *peshwa*, assisted by an assembly of eight ministers, or *ashtapradhan*. Each *pradhan*, appointed by the king, managed a department consisting of finances, archives, correspondence, diplomacy, army, religious affairs and justice. With the exception of the last two, they also exercised military responsibilities. They were assisted by subaltern functionaries, *chitnis* (correspondence), *fadnis* (accounting) and *potnis* (treasury).

In fact, the authority of this administration hardly went beyond the *swarajya*. The king, who granted immense *jagirs* to his best *sardars*, in accordance with the rule 'conquer and rule,' thus contributed to the creation of regional entities and the weakening of his own powers. The *jagirdars*, concurrently collectors of taxes, civil administrators and military officers, enjoyed substantial room for manoeuvre that they could be tempted to abuse. However, they had responsibilities with respect to the centre: they could neither declare war nor sue for peace without the consent of the sovereign. They also had to ensure the prosperity of sanctuaries, maintain their army for the service of the *peshwa*, despatch the archives and accounts of their domain regularly to Poona and remit the share of revenues due to the king.

The revenues were distributed as follows: the total amount of the *sardeshmukhi* was payable to the sovereign, who also received the *rajbati*, that is the quarter of the *chauth* and the revenues of the *swarajya*. From the three quarters that remained, which formed the *mokasa*, he had a further share of 9 per cent. The greatest part of the *mokasa* was left at the disposal of the *sardars* administrating the conquered territories. In the *swarajya*, tax was collected directly from the tenants by *patels* (village chieftains). It depended on the fertility of the lands, which were divided into four categories. The *chauth* was simultaneously the end and the means of the wars of conquest, but it also resulted in making the Maratha regime unbearable and thus hindered the formation of a vast Hindu solidarity under their aegis.

A series of impressive victories marked the governance of Baji Rao, between 1720 and 1740. Nizamulmulk, who contested the right of the Marathas to collect *chauth* that had nevertheless been conceded to them in 1719, met with a defeat in February 1728. On 6 March of the same year, he was forced to sign the treaty of Mungi Sheogaon, by virtue of which he undertook to pay the arrears of *chauth* and *sardeshmukhi*, which was tantamount to the recognition of Maratha supremacy in the Deccan.

In February 1729, Baji Rao arrived in Bundelkhand on the request of the bundela Rajput chief Chattra Sal, who had refused to submit to the Moguls. Under the command of Muhammad Khan Bangash, the Moguls suffered a defeat and had to withdraw from the region. A short while before his death, in 1731, Chattra Sal relinquished one third of his states to Baji Rao.

Even as Baji Rao was waging a war in Bundelkhand, the Maratha *sardar* Chimnaji devastated Malwa, without, however, being able to capture the capital, Ujjain. Appointed *subadar* of Malwa in 1730, the Rajput Sawai Jai Singh ceded a *jagir* of one million rupees to Baji Rao.

Simultaneously, another Maratha, Trimbak Rao Dabhade, obtained the rights of *chauth* and *sardeshmukhi* in Gujarat. In return, the *peshwa* was to maintain 2,500 cavalrymen to uphold peace and imperial authority in the province. Trimbak Rao Dhabade, who harboured a vague desire for independence, going as far as to renew his contacts with Nizamulmulk, was defeated by Baji Rao and killed on 1 April 1731. The secessionist tendencies of certain *sardars* were for some time checked.

For Shahu and Baji Rao the elimination of the Sidis of Janjira was an urgent necessity. They were the admirals of the Mogul emperor, whose fiefs extended from the district of Kolaba in Bombay as far as Anjanwel. The Sidis were on the western coast what the *nizam* was to the east of the Deccan. In the wake of a three-year war, in April 1736, Sidi Sat and Sidi Yaqut were defeated and killed. Sidi Abdur Rahman of Janjira was forced to sign a treaty that put an end to the maritime power of the Mogul emperor's admirals.

Between 1737 and 1739, the Marathas consolidated their control of the western coast to the detriment of the Portuguese, whose domination extended to two provinces, that of the north with Bassein as capital and that of the south around Goa. Solicited by the local Hindu population, who were suffering from the religious intolerance of the Portuguese, the troops of the *peshwa* seized Bassein on 4 March 1739. The treaty that was signed subsequently granted them the entire province of the north, the revenue of which amounted to 2,500,000 rupees.

After this resounding victory over a European power, Baji Rao was at the pinnacle of his glory. All the more because two years earlier, making light work of four Mogul armies, he had reached as far as the gates of Delhi. He had spared the capital after obtaining, on 31 March 1737, the government of Malwa and the promise of an annual tribute of 1,300,000 rupees.

On his death, on 28 April 1740, Baji Rao's achievements were impressive. Nevertheless, he had not followed through his intentions, checked as he was by the moderate Shahu, who did not seek the destruction of the Mogul Empire in the north and of the *nizam*'s states in the south. On the domestic front, the chief feudatories were waiting for an occasion to raise their head once again. Lastly, in the absence of coherent tax organization, the state of the finances remained precarious.

Balaji Baji Rao (1740–61)

The distinctive quality of Balaji Baji Rao, the son of Baji Rao, whom Shahu, giving force of law to the hereditary nature of the office, appointed *peshwa* at Satara on 25 June 1740, was, in the opinion of certain historians, his constant concern for ensuring regular revenues and for maintaining fiscal balance. His twenty-one-year government was characterized by brilliant successes that poorly concealed the weakness of the Maratha system, errors in judgement with far-reaching consequences and the creation of a succession of threats.

On the domestic front, Balaji certainly succeeded in consolidating his power at the expense of the king, the *chhattrapati*, but he had to confront an increasing number of separatist forces that jeopardized the Maratha unity.

The first decade of his government was marked by the problem of the succession of Shahu, who did not have any heir. With great tact, Balaji approved the proposal of the king to adopt Ram Raja, whom the aged Tara Bai claimed to be her grandson. Out of gratitude, Shahu then granted him the supreme military command and confirmed the hereditary nature of the title of *peshwa*. Following the death of the old king, on 15 December 1749, he obtained from his heir, Ram Raja, the confirmation of all his rights and powers. Tara Bai, who was hoping to govern in the name of her grandson, had no other recourse but to stir up an uprising against the *peshwa*. Eventually defeated, she admitted in 1752 that Ram Raja was just an impostor she had manipulated. That was the end of the authority and the prestige of the *chattrapati* who would henceforth live as a '*roi fainéant*' loafing in his fortress at Satara. Poona was thereafter the true capital of the confederacy and the *peshwa* its sole master, in theory at least.

Balaji Rao had come up against the ambitions of the powerful feudal lords before this war of succession that in effect crystallized general dissatisfaction. Right from the beginning of his government, his chief adversary was Raghuji Bhonsle, who had covered himself with glory in the Carnatic in 1739 and 1740, successively defeating the *nawabs* of Kandanur, Cudappah and Arcot and taking over Trichinopoly.

The latent conflict between two men flared up when Bhonsle launched his troops against Bengal. At the behest of the emperor, Balaji Rao negotiated with the *nawab* Alivardi Khan, who offered him the *chauth* of his *suba* and an indemnity of 2,200,000 rupees, in exchange for an intervention against the aggressor. In the wake of his defeat in April 1743, Raghuji Bhonsle recognised the supremacy of the *peshwa* within the confederacy. In September, Shahu, who had always feared a schism, imposed his arbitration: the zone of influence of Balaji was to extend between the Narmada, the Ganges and the Son; that of Bhonsle was to spread out to the east of the river Son. This was an attempt at conciliation, which evidently concealed the seeds of separatism. Nevertheless, during the war of succession, Bhonsle, caught up in serious financial problems and under the threat of powerful neighbours, the *nizam* in the south and Alivardi Khan in the northeast, maintained a prudent reserve. He even signed a new agreement with the *peshwa* that renewed his recognition of the latter's rights on Gondwana, Orissa and Bihar.

Shortly after the accession of Ram Raja, Balaji negotiated the agreements of Sangola with him, which defined the rights, responsibilities and spheres of influence of the principal *sardars*. Thus took shape the outlines of the future Maratha 'pentarchy' that was to be composed of the states of the *peshwa* (Poona), of Holkar (Indore), Sindhia (Gwalior), Gaekwar (Baroda) and Bhonsle (Nagpur). For the time being, Balaji succeeded in having his prerogatives respected: Damaji Gaekwar, who, discontented with the lot that the agreements of Sangola granted him, had allied himself with Tara Bai, was severely sanctioned.

Tulaji Angria, was, on the strength of his sixty warships with which he imposed his law on the west coast and the waters of the Arabian Sea, another partisan of Tara Bai. His audacity and his power drove Balaji to commit his first political error, in this case, an alliance with the English whose maritime commerce had been adversely affected by Tulaji's fleet. While the *peshwa* was leading the terrestrial operations, Admiral Watson, who commanded the British squadron, seized the fort of Gheria and its fabulous riches. The treaty of 12 March 1756 brought the territories of the Angrias under the sovereignty of Poona, but for the *peshwa*, who had not gauged the depth of the potential danger that his allies represented, it was a Pyrrhic victory: whereas the British had succeeded in neutralizing a formidable enemy, the Marathas had lost all their warships. The successes that Balaji had scored against the traditional enemies of the Marathas were too often jeopardized by his errors in judgement.

Contrary to his father, Balaji gave priority to an expansion towards the south, where, on many an occasion, he demonstrated the military superiority of the Marathas. In 1756 and 1757, he crushed the Afghan *nawabs* of Kurnool, Cuddapah and Savanur, whom a Maratha chief, Murar Rao Ghorpade, had set against him. Thereafter, he captured fourteen districts in Mysore. In the occupied territories, he strove to establish an administration, a taxation system and troops on a permanent basis, conscious that Maratha conquests were often lost because of a lack of durable organization.

On the other hand, he was for long time helpless against the *nizam*, his all-time enemy. Salabat Jang, the successor of Nizamulmulk, was in fact a French protégé. It was only after Bussy was recalled that he could inflict a crushing defeat on the troops of the *nizam* at Udgir (February 1760). The conditions that were then imposed on Salabat Jang were draconian: he had to cede in particular the forts of Asirgarh, Daulatabad, Bijapur, Ahmadnagar and Burhanpur, territories worth over two *lakhs*, and to pay *chauth*. Henceforth, he controlled only Hyderabad and some parts of the provinces of Bijapur and Bidar. Humiliated, the *nizam* would relentlessly strive to obtain a revision of the treaty of Udgir. By his intransigence, Balajo Rao literally handed him to the British on a plate.

On top of that, a great part of the Maratha forces was retained in the south at a time when perils loomed large in the north. As he was not really interested in these regions, Balaji failed to fully appreciate the gravity of the situation. He abandoned them to his powerful vassals, like the Bhonsles, who snatched away Orissa from Bengal in 1751.

Malhar Rao Holkar and Raghunath Rao, the brother of the *peshwa*, might well be calling the tune in Delhi, successively supporting Safdar Jang and Imadulmulk, but their policies did not follow any guideline. What is more, they could obtain nothing more than mere promises of tribute, promises that were rarely kept.

The depredatory raids that were rampant in these regions similarly procured only mediocre spoils, inadequate to resolve the permanent difficulties of Maratha finances. They only resulted in alienating the populations and their sovereigns. The incursions of Maratha cavalrymen ravaged not only Muslim states, like Farrukhabad and Rohilkhand, which were defeated in 1752, but it also devastated the Hindu States of Rajasthan and the Jat kingdom of Bharatpur at regular intervals. When in their turn the Marathas would be threatened, these states understandably did not offer any help.

The Disaster of Panipat

From 1757 onwards, Raghunath Rao and Malhar Rao Holkar set their eyes on the rich Punjab. They joined the coalition that the Sikhs and Adina Beg of Jullunder formed and that ousted, on 20 April 1758, Timur Shah, the son of Ahmad Shah Abdali, from Lahore. This expedition did nothing towards establishing their domination in the Punjab, from where they withdrew as soon as they had obtained the promise of an annual tribute from Adina Beg. It resulted, on the other hand, in consolidating the power of the Sikhs in this region and in kindling the fury of the king of Afghanistan. After the capture of Lahore, a confrontation between the two greatest powers of the region was inevitable.

In December 1759, while he was ravaging Rajputana yet again, Holkar received the news that the Afghan army was marching on Delhi and was threatening the Maratha chief Dattaji Sindhia. He arrived too late to save the latter, who was defeated and killed on 9 January 1760.

Balaji Rao then decided to mobilize all the forces that he possessed and to designate as the supreme commander Sadashiv Rao, who had recently distinguished himself at Udagir against the *nizam*. This proved to be an unfortunate choice, because, contrary to a Ragthunath Rao or a Holkar, Sadashiv Rao was completely ignorant of the political and military situation of North India. The capture of Delhi, on 2 August 1760 and of Kunjpura in October contributed only to the nurturing of the illusion: Sadashiv was alone, the Jats and the Rajputs hiding behind prudent neutrality, while Ahmad Shah Abdali, on the other hand, had the support of Shujauddaula, Najib Khan Rohilla and Ahmad Khan Bangash of Farrukhabad. Above all, the Maratha general was desperately short of money: between March 1760 and January 1761, he received only a quarter of the sum that he needed to feed the half million people that formed the army and its following.

Because famine had begun to decimate his troops Sadashiv, abandoning the traditional strategy of guerrilla warfare and harassment, plunged into a pitched battle in Panipat, to the north of Delhi, on 14 January 1761. The disaster was complete: nearly thirty thousand Marathas died on the battlefield. The main chiefs, including Sadashiv, were killed. Only Malhar Rao Holkar and Mahaji Sindhia escaped the massacre.

Ahmad Shah could not take full advantage of his victory. Urged by his troops, he returned to his mountains after recognizing Shah Alam II, son of Alamgir II, as emperor of India and entrusting the government of Delhi to his loyal ally, Rohilla Najib Khan. For the Marathas, the repercussions of the disaster were aggravated by the death of Balaji Rao, in June 1761, and by the conflict between his young son Madhav Rao, the new *peshwa*, and Raghunath Rao who believed the time had come to make his own claims.

No sooner had Maratha prestige been dealt a severe blow than the neighbours, who had been docile for long a time – the Rajputs, Jats, Rohillas and Bangashes – raised their heads once more. As early as 1761, the states of the south that had been defeated by Balaji tried to regain their territorial integrity. Nevertheless, neither Mysore nor Hyderabad, which had fallen in 1762, achieved their ends: the Maratha confederacy was weakened but not annihilated by the defeat of Panipat.

In the wake of the battle, no Indian power seemed capable any longer of exercising any sort of hegemony. The political situation in India was propitious to the British, who, at the same time, succeeded in finally eliminating the French threat and in consolidating their influence over Bengal.

XII

FRENCH INDIA
AND FRANCO-BRITISH RIVALRY
(UNTIL 1761)

While the powerful Dutch Company (VOC) concentrated its commercial operations in Indonesia and while the other European companies, particularly the Swedish (incorporated in 1731) and the Danish (1732) companies, were chiefly interested in Chinese trade, only the French company seemed capable of competing with the East India Company. At Pondicherry, talented governors, Lenoir (1721–35), then Dumas (1735–41) in particular, gave a new impetus to business and considerably consolidated their territorial, political and military power, laying the groundwork for Dupleix. The latter made Chandernagore a prosperous city, between 1731 and 1741, before becoming the chief of the colony. However, the French adventure in India was to be brief, and the capture of Pondicherry by the British in 1761 brought it to an abrupt end.

The affirmation of French power

The growth of trade

Most Anglo-Saxon and Indian works dealing with commerce in India in the eighteenth century make only a passing mention of the French India Company.[1] One author declares it bankrupt as soon as it was incorporated.[2] In fact, contrary to this prejudiced account, the French company was a lucrative enterprise.[3] The number of ships fitted out is significant, as early as the 1720s, French shipping resources were greater than those of the East India Company (see table at the end of this chapter).

Shipments of precious metals, and especially of silver, without which trade was not possible beyond the Cape, continued to increase in the eighteenth century. Amounting to a value of more than ten million *livres tournois*, the quantities sent by the French were almost equal to those sent by the English between 1735 and 1740. They reached thirteen million *livres* between 1750 and 1755. It is true that during this period the East India Company had regained its edge with more than twenty million *livres*,[4] however, the Indian trade of the French Company expanded constantly from the arrival of Lenoir as governor in 1721 until the departure of Dupleix, excepting the five years corresponding to the War of Austrian Succession (see table at the end of the chapter).

The growth in the commercial activities of the East India Company was equally spectacular, especially in Bengal (see table at the end of the chapter). The total amount of sales of goods bought beyond the Cape by the French Company, which varied from twenty to twenty-seven million pounds between 1749 and 1755, almost equalled that of the East India Company at the time. Furthermore, as early as the 1730s, the profit earned by the French reached 25 per cent per year, while that of the British Company was less than 10 per cent.[5]

The two companies, despite the expansion in the volume of their trade, came up against certain difficulties, which did not fail to have an impact on their relations. After the continuous growth experienced during the seventeenth century, they had to brave, in particular, the stagnation, even recession, of the prices of goods consigned from Asia, owing to the narrowness and the saturation of the European market.

In effect, European traders, whose ever-increasing demands contributed to the economic boom of certain productive regions,[6] were dependent on Indian merchants and bankers, without whom their operations would be practically nil. While in the past French historians did not take Indian merchants, weavers, artisans, soldiers and sailors into consideration, today they concede that the survival of the French Company, more than that of the East India Company, depended on them. Until the middle of the eighteenth century at least, it was Indian merchants who supplied the two companies with saltpetre and opium from Bihar, silk goods from Kazimbazar, muslins from Dacca and cotton goods from the Carnatic. Thus the broker of the French Company met with Indian merchants in May every year at Pondicherry, informed them of the quantities of fabrics required and accordingly made monetary advances. The merchants then charged their agents to place orders with the weavers, to whom deposits were paid. An inspection of the fabrics delivered took place in October. Because of the care taken in Pondicherry, French fabrics were always of excellent quality and were preferred in the European markets.

As Indian merchants were indispensable, it is understandable that Dupleix was eager to draw traders from Madras to Pondicherry, especially at the time of the siege of the former city in 1746. Because of the difficulties in the procurement of supplies, it not surprising that he granted substantial benefits to weavers with a view to urging them to settle down in French territory. There is no doubt that the control of the zones of production and of the major roadways partly motivated the intervention of Dumas, governor of Pondicherry from 1735 to 1741, and of Dupleix in Indian affairs.

Territorial expansion also offered the advantage of bringing in new revenues to a company that was often short of funds. This was the case in 1727, 1729, 1730, 1750 and 1754, when the precious metals sent from Europe arrived too late for commercial operations to be carried out normally. Under these circumstances, or when funds were not sufficient, the agents of the Company had no other recourse but to borrow money from Indian bankers at rates in the region of 10 per cent. So large was the debt incurred by the French Company to Bengal's powerful bankers, the Jagat Seths, that it had little chance of ever being discharged.[7]

Trading posts

Trading posts swallowed up half the colonial budget of the Company. Their expenditures, which exceeded the one million *livres* mark every year, were not covered by their own revenues (these amounted only to 108,000 *livres* in 1725, 350,000 in 1738 and 650,000 in 1754). The greater part of the financial resources was devoted to Chandernagore and Pondicherry, which respectively took up 49 per cent and 30 per cent of the resources of the colony.

Dupleix pulled Chandernagore out of its state of lethargy – he was its administrator from 1731 and 1741. Thanks to its location in the heart of prosperous Bengal, it was the premier French commercial centre in India: while this trading post had, for its commercial operations, the same sum as Pondicherry (from 1.5 to 2 million *livres* per year), it shipped 3.6 to 4.7 million *livres* worth of merchandise annually, against less than 3 million by the metropolis on the Coromandel coast.[8] Five factories, consisting of one or more domains of a few hectares, a residence and some shops depended on the pleasant city of Chandernagore, which had 25,000 inhabitants in the middle of the century. The factories can be summarized as follows:

– Kasimbazar was an excellent centre of observation at the gates of the capital of Bengal, Murshidabad. Situated in the heart of the silk belt, this factory supplied cargoes of silk goods.
– Dacca, where the factory was founded in 1722, exported muslins for a value of 400,000 rupees per year in the middle of the century.
– The factory of Jougdia, founded by Dupleix in 1735, supplied ordinary fabrics to the French Company (which bought from it goods for a value of nearly 100,000 rupees per year).
– In Patna, in Bihar, where the factory was founded in 1727, the Company sold drapes from Europe and bought saltpetre and opium.
– Lastly, the factory of Balasore, founded in the confines of Orissa and Bengal at the close of the seventeenth century, suffered from the inadequacy of its road connections and disappeared from the commercial scene in the eighteenth century.

Further to the south, the French had settled in Masulipatnam. In 1731, the chief of this factory gained the concession of a domain in Yanaon, which produced the finest white fabrics, the canjun.

Pondicherry had become the capital of the colony since the time of François Martin. Protected by powerful fortifications, the construction of which had been completed in 1735, the city 'benefited a lot under the government of M Lenoir'. Along the streets, 'perfectly straight and planted with trees on either side, which was of a charming aspect'[9] stood in a line, at least in the white town, sumptuous residences built with bricks and tiles. Its churches, its public buildings and in particular

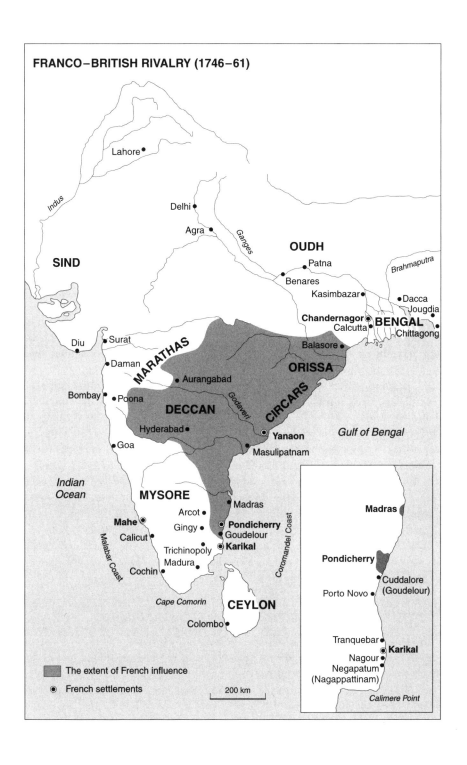

FRANCO–BRITISH RIVALRY (1746–61)

Lahore

Delhi

Agra

SIND

Ganges

OUDH

Patna

Benares

Kasimbazar

Brahmaputra

Dacca

Jougdia

Chandernagor

BENGAL

Calcutta

Chittagong

Indus

Diu

Surat

Balasore

MARATHAS

ORISSA

Daman

Aurangabad

Bombay

Poona

Godaveri

CIRCARS

DECCAN

Hyderabad

Yanaon

Goa

Masulipatnam

Gulf of Bengal

*Indian
Ocean*

MYSORE

Madras

Arcot

Mahe

Gingy

Pondicherry

Calicut

Goudelour

Karikal

Trichinopoly

Madura

Cochin

Coromandel Coast

Malabar Coast

Cape Comorin

CEYLON

Colombo

Inset map

Madras

Pondicherry

Cuddalore
(Goudelour)

Porto Novo

Tranquebar

Karikal

Nagour

Negapatum
(Nagappattinam)

Calimere Point

The extent of French influence

French settlements

200 km

its governor's palace, built between 1738 and 1752, embellished the city, which, if we are to believe the broker of the French Company Ananda Ranga Pillai, dominated 'like Mount Meru, [. . .] Delhi, Agra and the other great cities'.[10] The setting was no doubt less impressive in the black city, where the Indians lived.

The Europeans, who numbered from 1,500 to 2,000, represented only a small fraction of the population, which probably exceeded the 100,000 mark towards 1740. 'According to the census carried out in the last few years,' wrote the abbot Guyon, 'there are in Pondicherry 120,000 inhabitants, Christians, Mohammedans or Gentiles.'[11] Until 1740, the city did not have a hinterland, its territory extending to the west only by a few kilometres.

On the west coast, France possessed factories at Calicut and Surat, where trade activities were almost nil in the eighteenth century. It possessed in particular the trading post of Mahé, ceded in 1721 by one of the numerous kinglets of Malabar, Bayanor, who expected to increase the revenues of his customs by this cession to a commercial power. Remarkably situated in the heart of a pepper-producing region, Mahé was both a source of wealth and trouble. The English, who had established themselves in Tellicherry, a neighbouring port, set the local sovereigns against their French rivals from the beginning. In 1724, a naval expedition launched from Pondicherry re-established the rights of France in the trading post and order in its environs. An accord was signed on 20 March 1728 between the chiefs of Mahé and Tellicherry by virtue of which they promised to eschew all military actions 'even should there be a war in Europe between the two crowns'.[12]

No confrontation broke out openly between the two powers in Kerala until 1760. Nevertheless, tension was high, as testified in a letter addressed by the Council of Mahé on 6 August 1740 to his counterpart in Pondicherry: 'The safety of this establishment and the commercial interest of the Company require absolutely that we prohibit the English and all foreigners from entering the river [through which we transport our pepper] [. . .] and should we lack the right and the reasons, we ought to look for pretexts. They set us an example every day.' The next year, a new expedition, led by La Bourdonnais, the governor of the Isles of France and Bourbon, was necessary to prevail over the local princes, no doubt set against the French by the agents of the East India Company. In spite of these skirmishes, the British and the French pursued a very prudent policy in the first few decades of the eighteenth century. It was under the new governor of Pondicherry, Benoît Dumas, that the French began to interfere effectively in Indian affairs.

The interventionist policy of Benoît Dumas

At the end of the seventeenth century, the most influential of the directors of the English Company, Josiah Child, was in favour of increasing the military power and the revenues of his company in view of establishing a vast English dominion in India. Nevertheless, except for the incidents in Kerala, the British did not intrude on the politics of the country before 1732, the year in which they formed an alliance with Indian merchants to oust the governor of Surat. Again in 1738, the Court of the directors of the East India Company reminded its agents in Bombay that the company they served was a company of merchants, not of warriors.[13] The administrators of the French Company shared the views of their counterparts. However, in India itself, Benoît Dumas came to the understanding that astute diplomacy could gain significant advantages for his country.

Until 1736, imported precious metals were melted and struck at the mint of the nawab of Arcot, under whose authority Pondicherry came, and who collected an *ad valorem* duty of 7 per cent. Dumas, in exchange for 20,000 rupees, obtained the right to strike gold coins (pagodas), rupees and silver coins (fanams) in Pondicherry. The profit resulting from this concession was to the tune of 400,000 rupees per year for the Company. In 1738, Dupleix, the administrator of Chandernagore at the time, and Volton, physician at the court in Delhi, brought the work of Dumas to fruition: they ensured that the coins struck in Pondicherry had currency in Bengal, where they had hitherto been refused.

In 1738, the Maratha rajah of Tanjore, Shahuji, keen to eliminate a rival, solicited Dumas's financial support. In return, he ceded Karikal to him, which, situated in the heart a very rich rice-growing region of the Cauvery Delta, was to become the granary of Pondicherry. But the rajah of Tanjore backtracked on his promise. Eventually, the French succeeded in establishing themselves in Karikal in February 1739 thanks to the support of Chanda Sahib, the sovereign of Trichinopoly and son-in-law of the nawab of Arcot, Dost Muhammad. This marked the beginning of an enduring alliance between France and the Navaiyits, a princely family of Arab origin.

Thus dispossessed, the rajah of Tanjore called upon the support of the Maratha Raghuji Bhonsle, who was then plundering the south of the Deccan. On 9 May 1740, in Damalcherry, Dumas's ally, Dost Muhammad, was killed while he was attempting to resist the invasion of his states. His son, Safdar Ali, succeeded him and agreed to pay an indemnity immediately to the Marathas. His widow and what remained of his army took refuge in Pondicherry, 'which they regarded as the safest place on the coast because of the fortress and the walls and bastions that surrounded the city, and which were in good condition and equipped with more than adequate artillery, and because of the great reputation for valour that the nation had acquired in these countries.'[14] Dumas granted hospitality to these Muslims, which earned him the gratitude of Safdar Ali, of Nizamulmulk, the sovereign of Hyderabad and of the emperor Muhammad Shah, but also the hostility of the Marathas. When the latter demanded that he hand over the widow and pay a tribute, the governor proudly replied: 'France, our country, produces neither gold nor silver; that which we bring to this country to buy goods comes to us from foreign countries. Ours produces but iron and soldiers that we employ against those who attack us unjustly.'[15] Raghuji spared Pondicherry: more than the determination of its leader, the might of its walls and the superiority of its artillery, it was the impossibility of conducting two sieges simultaneously that persuaded him not to attack it. The Maratha army besieged Trichinopoly with the support of Safdar Ali, who had crossed over to their side because of his hatred for Chanda Sahib. The city capitulated in March 1741 and Chanda was taken captive to the capital of the Maratha kings, Satara.

Dumas, despite the loss of this ally, made the most of these events: Safdar Ali ceded to him the important town (aldee) of Archiwack, to the south of Pondicherry, which would be attached to the Company's domain in 1742. A little later, Muhammad Shah granted Dumas and his successors the title of nawab 'for life.' Henceforth, the trading Company was also a political and military power, a vassal of the Mogul emperor. The benefits from the elevation of the governor to the rank of *nawab* were evident to many who desired to exploit them immediately. According to a contemporary, Charpentier de Cossigny, 'it would be [. . .] by the extension of its domain to embrace a number of places, and should it be possible, these vast countries, that the Company would be above the events of the sea, that it would be able to load as many ships as it pleased it to send to Europe.'[16] This plan was to come to fruition about ten years later under the leadership of Dupleix.

Dupleix: the pinnacle of French India

The sieges of Madras and Pondicherry

The commercial and diplomatic successes of the French under Dumas caused apprehension among the directors of the East India Company, who, as early as 1737, began to gather information on these 'powerful competitors' and their trade.

To such an extent had the rivalry between the two powers been exacerbated that, in 1740, when the War of Austrian Succession broke out, Mahé de La Bourdonnais, governor of the Isles of France and Bourbon since 1734, foresaw that Britain would sooner or later take part in it and that the Franco-British conflict would spread to the Indian Ocean. He obtained authorization from the Controller General of Finance Orry and his brother, Orry de Fulvy, commissioner to the king, to arm five vessels for this region. The instructions that were given to him stipulated that 'all the officers of the Company, both on land and at sea, shall forthwith execute the orders that [he] shall give them [. . .]. With the understanding that in case the action should take place in any government other than that of the Isles, the Councils should grant him prior authorization to give orders on land, as with respect to maritime forces, he was required under all circumstances to command them.' Confidential directives expressly prohibited him 'from seizing any establishment or trading post belonging to the enemies with a view to conserving them'.[17]

However, owing to the delay in the breakout of hostilities between France and England, La Bourdonnais was forced to send back his squadron, following his demonstration before Mahé, in December 1741. With the result that when the war was declared on 15 March 1744 France did not have any naval force in the Indian Ocean, while its rival despatched Admiral Barnett's fleet to the scene. Dupleix, aware of this disadvantage and concerned for the interests of trade, offered a neutrality agreement to the authorities of Bombay, Tellicherry, Madras and Calcutta. The capture of several French ships, including three sailing from Canton with cargoes worth nearly 7,500,000 pounds, however, soon made these proposals void.

In January 1746, after countless delays, La Bourdonnais finally received reinforcements from France. He then had at his disposal 10 vessels, 406 canons, 2,350 white soldiers and 700 black soldiers. He arrived within sight of Pondicherry on 8 July 1746, after a bloody and indecisive naval battle off Nagapattinam, against the squadron of Barnett's successor, Peyton.

His relations with Dupleix, who had become the governor of Pondicherry on 14 January 1742, soon began to deteriorate over issues of precedence. La Bourdonnais was determined to act with complete independence, while the governor of the city considered himself the sole master of the lands. The recognition, under Dumas, of the right of jurisdiction of the Supreme council of Pondicherry over the Isles and the instructions given to La Bourdonnais gave a certain weight to Dupleix's arguments. What is more, La Bourdonnais seemed implicitly to agree with him. In effect, he hesitated to attack Madras, as had been planned, for fear of Peyton's fleet that was cruising in the Bay of Bengal, and finally accepted the decision of the Supreme council. Meeting no resistance, the French captured Madras on 21 September 1746. The mediocrity of the fortifications, the feeble determination of the garrison and of the British governor Morse, the timidity of Peyton, whose squadron had not arrived, explain the ease with which the victory was won by the French, who counted only nine wounded.

Paradoxically, the successes of the French only worsened the relation between the two men. La Bourdonnais considered Madras a prize which conferred the greatest possible advantage, while Dupleix sought to use the victory to weaken if not ruin the British rivals and to extend the commercial, territorial and political power of France in Asia. More than the opposition of two personalities, it was two divergent policies that were at issue: for the sailor, hegemony could be acquired by a privateering cruise, the capture and the destruction of enemy ships; it presupposed mastery on the seas. For the colonial, it hinged on a solid territorial base and a network of reliable alliances. Dupleix thus envisaged razing Madras to the ground, after evacuating the population of the city to Pondicherry, and returning the site to the *nawab* of Arcot, indisposed by this European war within his sphere of sovereignty, in exchange for the rich district of Valdavur, adjacent to Pondicherry.

It was not long before conflict flared up. La Bourdonnais, acting in compliance with his instructions, now five years old, that stipulated that he should not retain any foreign establishment, negotiated the restoration of Madras in return for a ransom. When Dupleix heard of these talks, he sent councillors to prevent what some considered a felony. Turning a deaf ear to all arguments, the Saint Malo sailor responded by another act of insubordination and placed the deputies of the governor of Pondicherry under confinement. His intransigence is in part understandable given the '*douceur*' that the British offered him, amounting to 100,000 *pagodas*, in other words 975,000 *livres tournois*. This was undoubtedly a bribe, but it must be added in La Bourdonnais's defence that he gave his officers a share in it.

On 13 October 1746, a terrible storm caused the wreck of two French ships and forced La Bourdonnais to return to his islands, putting an end to what was the beginning of a civil war. On the eve of his departure, on 21 October, La Bourdonnais signed the treaty with Morse that gave Madras back to the British with effect from January 1747, in exchange for 600,000 *pagodas* payable in India and a further 500,000 in Europe. Nonetheless, as early as 7 November, the treaty was revoked by Dupleix, whose attitude would be approved by the authorities in France. Indicted for treason, La Bourdonnais would eventually be acquitted, thanks to a pertinent defence. As for the city of Madras, it would remain under French administration until 1749.

It is hardly probable that a good understanding between the sailor and the colonialist could have resulted in French domination of India as early as this period: the Mogul emperor, the *subadar* of the Deccan, the *nawab* of Arcot, who all took a dim view of Franco-British conflicts, would not have suffered it. Moreover, the French lacked the means, both financial and military, in particular when their fleet was anchored in Mauritius, too far from the scene of operations. In this regard, the helplessness of Dupleix's troops before Fort Saint-David of Cuddalore, shortly after the capture of Madras, is significant. *A fortiori*, any attempt against Bombay or Calcutta was doomed to fail, all the more given that, as early as 1747, England despatched to the Indian Ocean a powerful squadron of thirteen men-of-war and eleven transport ships, under the command of Boscawen.

Pondicherry was in its turn besieged from 6 September to 15 October 1748. Despite an intensive bombardment of the city, the siege soon caused the discomfiture of the English admiral: while his troops were suffering from hunger, the besieged seemed to lack nothing thanks to the wise precautions taken by Dupleix. When Boscawen ordered the retreat, on the fortieth day, he had lost 1,675 men including 1,317 dead, while the French recorded only 393 dead and wounded. The triumphant resistance of Pondicherry caused a great sensation in the Indian courts. Dupleix appeared increasingly as a *nawab* whose alliance was sought after.

In the wake of the siege, the fate of Madras remained unresolved, as it became difficult to keep the city while the defence of Pondicherry required the largest part of the available forces. As early as the beginning of the year, the directors of the Company rejected the idea of retroceding Madras for a ransom, or of exchanging it for Louisbourg, the most powerful French fortress in Canada, taken in 1745 by the British. The latter solution perhaps being the most advantageous for the state, but not for the Company, which had spent substantially for the wars in India. The directors finally voted in favour of the destruction of the city and the exchange of the site for the districts of Villenur and Valdavur, in accordance with Dupleix's wishes.

As early as 1748 however, the French government concurred with the idea of an exchange for Louisbourg. The Treaty of Aix-la-Chapelle containing a clause relative to this exchange came to be known in Pondicherry in January 1749 and Madras was restored to the British in September of the same year. 'The Madras affair illustrates well the state of dependency in which the Company found itself with respect to the political power. Forced to protect itself by its own means owing to the limitations of the navy, and having scored fine military successes, it saw them being sacrificed to interests arising out of necessities more important for the government, but irrelevant to the Company'.[18] From this time onwards, Paris had chosen its American interests in preference to the assets of India.

Dupleix's Indian policy

Dupleix on the other hand seemed to have already formulated a clear-cut policy for that country. Notwithstanding the preoccupations of France, he decided to prolong, through the intermediary of Indian princes, the struggle against the British. Thus the French and the British, who 'fought each other in Europe before entering into war, [. . .] are going to fight in India after concluding peace'.[19]

Unusually for a European, Dupleix, who had been living in India since 1720, had perfect knowledge of the country, as readily testified by his broker, Ananda Ranga Pillai. The study of the political scenario in which he engaged himself while he was administering the trading post of Chandernagore enabled him to form, right from that time, a personal idea of the future of the Company and to chart the outlines of a project that he was to progressively refine, in tune with the changing circumstances. He understood that the commercial interest of the Company and his own interest demanded an intervention in Indian politics, but the form that this was to take remained vague: in 1732 and 1739, he advocated the use of force against the arrogance of the 'Moors' and their exactions; in 1743, on the other hand, he informed Orry about a new conviction at which he had arrived after a 'special study' that he had undertaken in Bengal: the necessity of 'cultivating the friendship of these princes.' The advantages that the title of *nawab* would give the governor of Pondicherry became evident to him as early as 1739, perhaps even before. On 10 January 1740, he wrote to Dumas that 'the title of five *hazari* [*nawab* commanding five thousand horses] would preclude, particularly in Bengal, many a humiliation; it is the greatest mark of distinction and protection that one can obtain from the Mogul, which, in many cases, would curb the avidity of the miserable government with which we have to deal.'[20] Dupleix seems to have understood even at that time that the smooth functioning of business demanded that the representative of the king of France, the '*fétor*,' also became *nabab*, in other words, the representative of the Mogul emperor. Invested with a measure of authority by the one who was the source of all authority in India, the '*fétor-nabab*' shielded the commerce of his nation against the habitual 'humiliations.'

Eager to facilitate the procurement of supplies, which could not be done without interference and to which the title of *nawab* was expected to contribute, Dupleix was anxious about the trade imbalance of the Company. He explained, in his memoir dated 16 October 1753, that 'any trading company must shun, when it is possible, the export of gold and silver; this is a time-honoured maxim that more these materials are common in a State, more prosperous it is.' As early as 1737, he advocated the export of French manufactured goods to India, a solution doomed to failure given the low demand in India. Later, observing that 'the Dutch Company supported itself only with its resources in India,' he envisaged 'to earn 600,000 *livres* as revenue in countries that a handful of people was sufficient to keep.' The leasing of Crown lands and the collection of various duties on a sufficiently extended territory would procure 'this constant and abundant revenue'.[21]

In effect, interference in the politics of the Carnatic very soon gave Dupleix much more than a modest *jagir* of the size of Villenur and Valdavur. The aggressiveness of his policy enabled him to establish in a few months his influence over the entire Deccan, something he had neither truly planned, nor perhaps wished.

The situation in the Carnatic had become propitious for intrigues of all kinds since the battle of Damalcherry. Safdar Ali, the *nawab* of Arcot, and subsequently his young son, were assassinated by the governor of Vellore, Murtaz Ali. In March 1744, Nizamulmulk, who despised the Navaiyit family, to which the *nawabs* of Arcot belonged, placed at the head of this region Anwaruddin Khan, who belonged to the rival family of the Wallajahs. But Chanda Sahib, Dumas's ally in the Karikal affair, still held a prisoner in Satara, denounced this nomination and laid claim to the Carnatic.

For a long time, Dupleix played a double game: he maintained the most cordial relations with Anwaruddin even while supporting with his rupees and pagodas the machinations of Chanda, the long-standing ally of France. While he promised Madras to the former, he wished to see the latter sweeping through the Carnatic at the head of 100,000 Maratha cavalrymen, and exerted himself to bring this project to fruition, from which the Company would not fail to draw numerous benefits.

His relations with Anwaruddin deteriorated by the end of October 1746, when the latter's son, Mafuz Khan, exasperated with the Franco-British war and the delays that the French caused in the cession of Madras, marched on this city. He was routed, on 24 October 1746, near Adyar, by the troops of the engineering officer Paradis. This was a decisive victory, which showed for the first time that European troops, disciplined, trained and operating their weapons with more efficacy, could defeat Indian armies that were ten times more numerous but fighting without order or method. It did not come as a surprise to Dupleix: some time before the capture of Madras, when his broker Ananda declared to him that 'a thousand French soldiers, with mortars and a hundred bombs, could conquer Arcot and the entire Carnatic as far as the banks of the Krishna,' he replied that five hundred Frenchmen and two mortars would be sufficient.[22]

Dupleix however did not nurture such a design. In the wake of the siege of Pondicherry, his concern was to occupy the troops who could not be repatriated. He sought to do so in the best interests of France, but apparently without envisaging any territorial conquests. In February 1749, he resumed his relations with Chanda Sahib, finally liberated and still resolved to overthrow Anwaruddin. In the beginning of the summer, Chanda allied himself also with Muzaffar Jang, who coveted the throne of Hyderabad, on which Nazir Jang had established himself on the death of Nizamulmulk, in 1748. On 13 July, Dupleix explained to the Supreme Council that the two pretenders would cede the district of Villenur to the company in exchange for its support. The Company authorized him to help Chanda, and consequently, Muzaffar, 'until he was established and the tranquil possessor of his government'.

On 3 August 1749, in Ambur, 420 French soldiers and 2,000 sepoys (native soldiers) from Pondicherry routed the army of Arcot. Anwaruddin was killed; his elder son Mafuz Khan was captured, but his younger son, Muhammad Ali Khan Wallajah, could flee to Trichinopoly. Out of gratitude, Muzaffar Jang ceded to France, apart from the district of Villenur, the district of Bahur, about twenty kilometres to the south of Pondicherry, as well as the full and undivided enjoyment of Masulipatnam and the island of Divy, at the mouth of the Krishna. To all this, Chanda Sahib added lands in the environs of Karikal.

By accepting these territories, Dupleix allowed himself to be caught up in a spiral and took the risk of exasperating the Company, which wanted to make profits and not conquests. If Chanda Sahib's rival has been eliminated, Muzaffir Jang's was still well established on his throne; Nazir Jang even swept through the Carnatic in 1750 at the head of an army, according to certain estimations, of 300,000 men. He enjoyed, as did Muhammad Ali, who had entrenched himself in Trichinopoly, the discreet support of the British, apprehensive in the wake of the initial victories of the French.

While Dupleix's officers, Latouche and Bussy, distinguished themselves in audacious hit-and-run raids, the latter for instance seizing the fortress of Gingy, reputedly impregnable, the governor of Pondicherry conspired with those close to Nazir Jang. On 16 December 1750, while the battle was raging in the environs of Chettipett, Nazir Jang was assassinated by a conspirator. Muzaffar Jang forthwith proclaimed himself *subadar* of the Deccan and conferred on Dupleix the command of the territories extending from the Cape Comorin to the Krishna, as well as the *jagir* of Valdavur, worth 100,000 rupees. At Pondicherry, the 'white Jaipur', then at its apogee, grandiose feasts celebrated the accession of the new sovereigns of Hyderabad and Arcot, through whose intermediary Dupleix could henceforth exercise a certain influence in the south of the peninsula.

However, Muzaffar's power was precarious and Dupleix had to consent to have Bussy escort him to his capital, precisely when Muhammad Ali, from Trichinopoly, rose up against Chanda Sahib. While Bussy imposed his protectorate over the Deccan, mediocre officers caused the French forces to become bogged down before Trichy, sounding the death knell for Dupleix's daring policy.

Bussy in the Deccan

The *nawab* Dupleix was conscious of the precariousness of his domination of the Carnatic, gained by the use of arms. In his effort to consolidate his position vis-à-vis the Indian powers and to give a better account of his policy in France, he understood the importance 'of covering himself with the authority of the legitimate sovereign of the country.' However, 'to be able to confer *de jure* authority on him over the Carnatic, this sovereign, in this case Muzaffar Jang, had to be master of his states.'[23] This was the result that Bussy, leading a force of 300 French soldiers and 2,000 sepoys, was charged with achieving.

The precariousness of Muzaffar Jang's position, which justified Bussy's mission, was indeed real: on 14 February, shortly after their departure from Pondicherry, the *subadar* of the Deccan and his protector had to brave a revolt of three *nawabs* (Cuddappah, Savanur and Kurnool). Muzaffar was killed in the battle. Bussy, who did not lack decisiveness, replaced him immediately with Salabat Jang, his brother. By doing so, he ensured continuity at the head of the 'Moor' state and army, but he committed an abuse of power, the appointment of the *subadar* being the prerogative of the emperor, and consequently took a real risk: Salabat had an elder brother, Ghaziuddin, then in Delhi, who, wronged, was sure to claim a throne that was his by right.

On 12 April 1751, Salabat and Bussy entered Hyderabad. On 18 June, they were at Aurangabad. Intoxicated by these easy successes, Dupleix believed that Bengal was already within the hold of Bussy, who would have no difficulty in defeating Alivardi Khan's modest army. Perhaps Dupleix had the presentiment that the domination of India could be gained by that of rich Bengal, as the British would later prove. It is more plausible that he was thinking of the profits that French trade could earn from the control of this region, once it had been liberated from the exaction of the agents of the *nawab*. Whatever the case might have been, the project, unrealistic given the weakness of Bussy's troops, was largely the result of the limitations in the political analysis of the governor of Pondicherry, who spurned the consolidation of advantages already acquired for new gains that were only hypothetical and illusory.

Bussy was 'confident that he could place the French in possession of all the countries as far as the Krishna by the emperor himself,' but he required new 'forces from Europe'. For the time being, he was content to remind the Controller of Finance Machault, on 15 September 1751, that his presence at the heart of India had no other objective than to serve the commercial interests of the Company: 'I am endeavouring [. . .] to liberate the French from all the duties within the span of the domination of the Mogul emperor. As it is necessary here more than anywhere else to combine trade and war, I have focused all my attention on earning the friendship of the lords who are in command of places adjoining our concessions so that they favour our trade.'[24]

In reality, the friendship of the lords of the court was not easy to earn: not all tolerated the rule of 'infidels' over their state and Salabat, too subservient to Bussy, was far from enjoying unanimity. Ghaziuddin did not lack partisans at Aurangabad and Hyderabad, which pushed him to seize the power. Having mustered 150,000 men in Delhi and having gained the support of the *peshwa* Balaji Rao, he decided to march on the Deccan in September 1751.

The prospect of a new war did not alarm Dupleix, who opened negotiations with the regent of the Maratha states, the aged Tara Bai, the enemy of the *peshwa*, and the Angrias. Apart from a victory over the coalition that threatened Bussy, he hoped to gain from this alliance the port of Bassein, to the north of Bombay, and in particular the cession to the Company of the *chauth* collected by the Marathas from Cuddapah, Kurnool, the Carantic, Trichinopoly, Mysore and Tanjore. Thus could be resolved the financial crisis that undermined the French position both in the Coromandel and in the Deccan.

Even as Dupleix pursued his negotiations and his dreams of grandeur, Bussy scored his first diplomatic success by obtaining from the emperor the *firman* that confirmed Salabat as the ruler of the Deccan. Thereafter, he proceeded to meet Balaji Rao, and taking advantage of a lunar eclipse on the night of 3 to 4 December 1751, inflicted a crushing defeat on the Maratha who 'used to make the emperor himself tremble'. On 17 January 1752, the *peshwa* accepted the Peace of Ahmadnagar, which forced him in particular to restore to Salabat all the territories that he had conquered at the expense of the viceroys of the Deccan since the death of Nizamulmulk. For all this, Ghaziuddin did not give up. Allying himself with other Marathas, the Bhonsles and the Holkars, he arrived in Aurangabad in the end of September 1752 and there he obtained the support of numerous lords.

Bussy's situation was all the more fragile because, owing to the shortage of funds, his troops were no longer paid. What saved him was the sudden death of Ghaziuddin, poisoned, on 25 October, by a woman of his suite. Notwithstanding this coup de theatre, Bussy thought henceforth of only 'extricating himself from this labyrinth': the coffers were empty, Salabat was so weak and so undecided that he could at any moment turn against his protector, and lastly, countless machinations brewed around Ghaziuddin's son and the *diwan* Sayyid Lashkar Khan, who, in order to liberate the state from French tutelage, successively negotiated with the Marathas, Muhammad Ali and the English. 'Deceitfulness and duplicity are as if natural' to Indians, wrote Bussy to Dupleix on 28 November 1752, 'and we shall always be the dupe of the relationships that we have with them. I thought I had observed a few vestiges of probity and good faith among the Marathas and, should we have to choose, I would place my trust more in them than in the Moguls; but the safest policy is not to trust any of them and not to interfere in their affairs in any way.'[25] This opinion was not shared by Dupleix, who was convinced that the British would not fail to establish their influence in Aurangabad as soon as Bussy left, unless Balaji Rao outstripped them.

Bussy's illness, which obliged him to retire to Masulipatnam in January 1753, put an end to his disagreement with Dupleix. The poor management of Goupil, to whom he had entrusted the command, and the fresh conspiracies of Sayyid Lashkar Khan, on the verge of defeating the French, made him realize that it was his duty and his honour to prevent the destruction of his work. On his return to Hyderabad, he threatened to ally himself with the Marathas if the four Circars (or *sarkars*) of Rajahmundry, Ellore, Chicacole and Mustafanagar were not ceded to France. The revenue that he could thus earn would enable him to strengthen his authority once again over his army and consequently, over the Deccan. With no difficulty, he ensured that Lashkar Khan was dismissed and replaced with Chanavas Khan, who was favourable to the French cause, and also that equally loyal provincial governors were appointed. The victory that he won over Raghuji Bhonsle, who posed a threat to Hyderabad in April 1754, brought him to the walls of Nagpur, in Berar, and proved yet again to Salabat that he was the providential man.

Despite this confrontation, and even though his position was stronger than ever from Aurangabad to Hyderabad, Bussy was henceforth convinced that France needed to modify its Indian policy and let 'the Maratha rule succeed the Mogul government in the Deccan'. The alliance with a rapidly expanding power would be more profitable to his country than the support that it gave to a decadent and corrupt state, where politics was reduced to an endless series of palace intrigues. Dupleix, who conceded 'that with such deceitful people, we have to be more deceitful than them', that they would find 'always more good faith among the Marathas' and that 'we will be obliged to come to that,' however did not dare to effect this change in alliances. The prestige of the Mogul emperor was still such that the *nawab* of Pondicherry could not envisage a rupture that would be tantamount to putting an end to the advantages legitimized by Delhi. It is probable that he also considered the Maratha alliance too capricious and risky even as events took a turn for the worse in the Carnatic.

At a time when Dupleix's policy was being called into question, Bussy's achievements seemed considerable. He himself gives an account of it, without modesty no doubt, but also without great exaggeration: 'Kings placed on the throne by my hands, supported by my forces, armies routed, cities taken by storm by a handful of my men, peace treaties concluded by my sole mediation, guaranteed, respected and renewed by just the fear of displeasing me, my alliance sought after by all the powers of the Mogul Empire, my friendship bought with the price of riches and vast domains that the Company possesses [. . .] the honour of my nation elevated to a point of glory that has made it preferred until now over all the others nations of Europe and the horizon of the interest of the Company extended beyond its hopes and even its desires.'

Certain historians affirm that 'it was Bussy who, very consciously, discovered, developed these methods of protectorate, to which tiny Europe owed its easy expansion all across the world. Methods to which the greatest, a Gallieni, a Lyautey would be unable to add anything.'[26] Bussy is credited in particular with having paved the way by forming within the country itself a force sufficiently redoubtable that he did not have to resort to it.

Others, on the contrary,[27] object to the term 'protectorate' with regard to the Carnatic, preferring to speak more simply of a control relying on alliances and the occupation of a few fortresses. This control was furthermore fragile, on the one hand because Dupleix, far removed from the scene of operations and from his allies, could act only through the intermediary of a recognized sovereign, as did Bussy, and on the other hand precisely because he did not have a second Bussy in the Carnatic, where the British at Madras had more reason to intervene, and more means to do so, than in the distant Deccan.

The end of French India

The recall of Dupleix

On the very day of the Battle of Ambur, the Carnatic, which Dupleix believed they held, was in fact lost. By renouncing it to pursue Muhammad Ali, the son of Anwaruddin, the French committed an error the consequences of which would soon prove to be disastrous. Taking refuge in the impregnable citadel of Trichinopoly, this Wallajah prince proclaimed himself the *nawab* of Arcot and received at once the support of the British at Madras.

Even as the French officer Jacques Law and Chanda Sahib exerted themselves to establish a blockade of Trichinopoly, a young English officer, Robert Clive, seized Arcot, on 11 September 1751, with 200 European soldiers and 300 sepoys. For 50 days, he resisted Chanda, who strove to recapture his capital, and was finally saved by Raghuji Bhonsle, whom the authorities of Madras and Muhammad Ali had rallied to their cause.

Law's situation, before Trichinopoly, became untenable, as the rajah of Mysore, Nandi Raja, had also declared war against France in January 1752. In April, he retreated to the island of Sri Rangam, where, from then on, he was the one besieged. On 11 June 1752, he capitulated to Major Stringer Lawrence: 35 officers, 785 French soldiers and 2,000 sepoys were made prisoners. On the same day, Chanda Sahib was assassinated and Muhammad Ali became the de facto sovereign of the Carnatic.

This disaster was to have more repercussions in Paris than in India where the situation of the French was far from being hopeless. Pondicherry was not in any way under threat, as the British were not officially in a state of war against France, and because their Indian allies were incapable of conducting a siege of the city. Moreover, these allies were too engrossed in their own quarrels, in the wake of the victory, to think of pressing their advantage to the full: Nandi Raja in particular demanded Trichinopoly as the price for his intervention, which Muhammad Ali refused to relinquish.

Dupleix astutely took advantage of these dissensions. In December 1752, he came to an agreement with the Marathas, to whom he would pay 125,000 *livres* per month in exchange for 4,000 cavalrymen and 2,000 infantrymen. In February of the following year, he signed an agreement with Nandi Raja, promising him the cession of Trichinopoly after the victory. These diplomatic successes however did not produce any effect on the field: the Hindu allies proved to be more interested in Dupleix's rupees than in the outcome of battles. Furthermore, the French officers who succeeded Law were not of Bussy's calibre, not by a long shot: Bernier, Maissin and Astruc failed one after another before Trichinopoly, and Mainville, though more talented, could do no better. The conflict dragged on.

In January 1754, negotiations were opened in Sadras between the governor of Madras, Saunders, and Dupleix. The former demanded the recognition of Muhammad Ali as a precondition to all discussion, and the latter retorted that the designation of the successor to Chanda Sahib was solely the prerogative of Salabat Jang, the sovereign of the Carnatic. The conference came to a sudden halt. By this time, moreover, the recall of Dupleix had already been decided, which was no doubt suspected in India.

Favouring the strictest neutrality, the French Company received the resounding victories of 1749 and 1750 half-heartedly. The directors no doubt congratulated Dupleix, but they added, 'we can regard these advantages as perfectly real only when they lead you to a solid peace, which alone is capable of working for the good of commercial affairs, which the ministry and the Company desire that you be essentially concerned with.' And the minister Machault concurred, on 5 May 1751: 'You must use all means not only to make peace but also to avoid with great care any occasion to enter into war again.'[28]

With the pursuit of war, stalemate and reverses, reticence became reprobation. More than ever India was a 'drain on the finances', but henceforth, it was military action, more than trade, that swallowed up millions of pounds. The expenses incurred by Dupleix for his operations are estimated at more than 66 million *livres*[29] for the period from June 1748 to February 1754, an amount that revenues from India were far from being able to make good. Owing to the insufficiency of revenues, Dupleix, in view of covering his war expenditures, would take 7,200,000 *livres* out of his own income and in particular 20,924,000 *livres* out of the money sent by the Company for other, especially mercantile, purposes.

As early as 1751, even while the amount of money taken out of the Company funds by Dupleix was still not known, and not without reason, the shareholders were convinced that the government of Pondicherry was converting the sums reserved for commerce into sovereignty expenditure. During their meeting on 24 December, they already demanded the recall of Dupleix. Their exasperation grew a year later, when the news of the capitulation of Law coincided with the poor earnings from sales in October 1752. A letter, despatched from Pondicherry in February 1753, announcing that it had become necessary to borrow 300,000 rupees at 20 per cent in order to send two ships to procure their load of pepper from Mahé, persuaded the government and the Company to come to a decision. Thus, it was the repeated injunctions of the shareholders that led to the recall of Dupleix, which became official in September 1753.[30]

Dupleix himself would attribute his recall to the pressures of the cabinet at London on the ministers of Louis XV. It is true that in January 1753, the directors of the East India Company informed the Secretary of State Holderness of the prejudices occasioned by the French governor to their activities on the Coromandel Coast. On the other hand, it is quite improbable that the simultaneous recall of both Dupleix and Saunders was discussed during the negotiations that took place in London that year between the Duke of Newcastle and Holderness on the one hand, and the director Duvelaer and the Duc de Mirepoix on the other. It was certainly decided then to send to India two commissioners, one French and the other British, 'in charge of establishing the affairs on a footing that rendered war impossible as long as the governments of the two countries were at peace,' but at that date, it had already been decided in Paris to replace Dupleix. We cannot therefore say, concludes the historian Philippe Haudrère, that Dupleix 'was recalled following the injunction of the British government. Quite simply, it appears that the protection of British interests in Asia and the criticisms of French shareholders converged on a common point.'[31]

From Godeheu to Lally-Tollendal

The commissioner chosen by the French authorities was the director from Lorient, Charles Godeheu, who had known Dupleix in Chandernagore nearly twenty years earlier. He arrived in Pondicherry on 1 August 1754 invested with the title of commissioner to the king and commander of all the French establishments on the African coast and beyond the Cape of Good Hope.

As early as the month of October, Godeheu had executed to a large extent the instructions of the government: Dupleix boarded for France, the siege of Trichinopoly was raised, a truce of three months was concluded and negotiations were opened with Saunders. A treaty was finally signed on 11 January 1755, by virtue of which both the companies undertook not to interfere in Indian politics in particular, which was tantamount for France to the surrender of the Carnatic and to an implicit recognition of Muhammad Ali. On the other hand, the French retained possession of Karikal and Pondicherry on the Coromandel, and the British held Madras, Fort Saint David and Devicotta, between Pondicherry and Karikal.

Godeheu returned to France as early as February 1755, transferring the government of Pondicherry to Duval de Leyrit. In Paris, the terms of his treaty with the governor of Madras were adjudged 'good and honourable'. In Pondicherry, some considered on the contrary that this agreement was only 'the preamble to the superiority of the English'. From the distant Deccan, Bussy saw this commitment to neutrality as 'a chimera that will never become reality.' Effectively, the British 'will always agree to everything and will do only what concurs with their interests'.[32]

The effect produced in Hyderabad was disastrous, all the more, as Godeheu apparently told Salabat's ambassadors: 'Declare to the soubab, your master, that I have been sent on behalf of my king who has forbidden me from interfering in the Mogul government. Let him fend for himself as he pleases.' British propaganda aggravated the disarray of Dupleix's allies: 'The King of France, asserted the agents of the East India Company, is a small prince without ships, without money, whose subjects are poor and who fears the King of England, a very powerful prince, possessed of a lot of ships, lot of money and whose subjects are rich.'[33]

Echoing Dupleix's accusations, certain historians have reproved Godeheu not only for not using the troops that disembarked with him against Trichinopoly, but also for undoing the work of his predecessor. In his *Histoire des Français dans l'Inde*, Lieutenant-Colonel Malleson states that, 'the conditions of the treaty that Godeheu signed [. . .] were not only disadvantageous to French interests, but degrading to the honour of France.' At the most, his detractors give him the credit for not recalling Bussy, enabling the latter to continue to interfere in the politics of the Deccan princes. In view of the depressed state of the finances and the inferiority of the French troops, which, according to the Supreme Council of Pondicherry, numbered only 1,150 men against the 2,500 that their adversaries had, Godeheu might very well have saved what was essential. Edward Ives, who arrived in India in 1754, even believed that he had achieved 'a masterstroke'. Admirals Watson and Pocock deplored the treaty of 11 January 1755, which deprived them of a sure victory.[34]

This debate has no doubt been blown out of proportion: the Saunders-Godeheu treaty was in effect never executed. It was to enter into force only after ratification in Europe. But, since a mission of the director of the Company, Duvelaer, in charge of proposing to the British government a perpetual neutrality agreement beyond the Cape had failed, there was no longer any question of ratifying the treaty. Consequently, the French positions in India after the departure of Godeheu were to remain what they had been upon his arrival. Godeheu is therefore not directly responsible for the destruction of Dupleix's work, which was in fact the result of the Seven Years' War. This conflict gave the British the opportunity that they had been waiting for to eliminate the trade and influence of the French in India. Their opposition to the treaty of perpetual neutrality reveals their intentions in this matter.

The breakout of hostilities

The war was declared on 17 May 1756. The news reached Bombay on 6 October of the same year. Chandernagore, which fell on 23 March 1757, was the first establishment to bear the brunt of the opening of hostilities. Its chief, Renault de Saint-Germain, committed the mistake of rejecting the alliance proposals of the *nawab* Sirajuddaula, who was also at war with the British, and of believing that a neutrality treaty could be signed with Clive and Watson.

The loss was considerable, since French trade in Bengal amounted to 23,220,000 *livres* between 1749 and 1754 against 16,697,000 *livres* between 1739 and 1744. It was nevertheless compensated by fresh feats performed by Bussy, who, no sooner had he heard of the fall of Chandernagore, swooped down on the British factories on the coast of Orissa. From Ganjam in the north to Masulipatnam in the south, the French henceforth controlled 600 kilometres of the coastline.

In Paris, the authorities decided to entrust the Comte de Lally-Tollendal with the task of driving the British out of India. This Jacobite of Irish origin, who had distinguished himself in the War of Austrian Succession, did not know anything about India, which did not prevent him from severely denouncing the interventionist policy of Dupleix. He was equally ignorant of trade, but was convinced that Pondicherry had the potential of becoming the warehouse of this part of the world. Brave, intelligent and above all incorruptible, he was also pretentious, intransigent and disdainful. His lack of diplomacy would lead Pondicherry to its ruin, prophesied the Marquis d'Argenson: 'On the first negligence that compromises the arms of the king, on the first semblance of insubordination, M. de Lally will thunder, if he does not penalize heavily. His officers will cause his operations to fail in order to take vengeance on him. Pondicherry will have a civil war within its walls with an external war at its gates.'[35]

None of his predecessors had ever had at their disposal means as considerable as he had. Lally-Tollendal was to have under his orders thirty officers, including 'the jewel of the French youth', the likes of Soupire, d'Estaing, Landivisiau, Conflans, La Tour du Pin . . . and 5,500 soldiers. He was to be supported by the eleven vessels of Admiral d'Aché's squadron and six million *livres* in cash.[36]

But, there was the other side of the coin. In spite of holding the titles of lieutenant general of the armies of the king, commander of the troops of India, commissioner to the king and commander general of all the French establishments in the East Indies and lastly of trustee of the Company, Lally-Tollendal had to share his powers: he commanded only on land, d'Aché being the sole master of naval operations, which made him run the risk of coming up against the same difficulties that Dupleix faced with La Bourdonnais. Furthermore, he was not authorized to administer the finances, as the management of revenues has been entrusted jointly with the commissioner Clouet and the governor of Pondicherry, Duval de Leyrit.

His mission consisted in attacking the establishments of the enemy 'as much as his forces and the circumstances allowed' and in 'razing to the ground the fortifications of coastal sites.' As for French possessions, they had 'to be restricted to mercantile establishments on the coasts and to a territory circumscribed around these establishments.' In Pondicherry, he was charged 'with eradicating the spirit of cupidity' of the employees and 'with re-establishing order, discipline and military spirit in the troops of the Company of the Indies.'[37]

The chevalier de Soupire arrived in Pondicherry as early as September 1757, but did not seek in any way to take advantage of the weakness of the defences of Madras, as the British troops were then mobilized in Bengal. Lally-Tollendal arrived only in April 1758, after a voyage of one year. In spite of the coldness of the first contact, he succeeded in taking Cuddalore and Fort Saint-David after meeting no resistance. This was his first and last victory.

Since the departure of Dupleix, Pondicherry had continuously deteriorated, appearing as 'a business under liquidation in which everyone was seeking a profit'. Voltaire would denounce its population, who 'gleaned in the field of the public that had become sterile for the Company [. . .]. The colony of Pondicherry resembles a dying man whose furniture is plundered before he expires.'[38] The trading post owed not less than 14 million in 1758 and its discredit was such that when the Supreme council offered 100 per cent interest to the Dutch for a loan of 240,000 *livres*, the latter declined.

With a view to replenishing the coffers of the Company, Lally-Tollendal decided to march on Tanjore, a kingdom that owed a 550,000 rupee debt to France. Poorly prepared, the expedition resulted in a bitter defeat. This mistake was followed by others, the greatest of which was certainly the recall of Bussy, ordered in June 1758. Clive understood that the time had come to destroy the French protectorate on the Deccan: at his behest, Forde invaded the Circars in October 1758, routed Conflans, Bussy's successor, in December, and seized Masulipatnam in April 1759. Salabat Jang, passing from one tutelage to another, ceded to the British considerable territories around this city and promised never again to negotiate with the French.

While Admiral d'Aché, after two indecisive battles, had just returned to the islands, Lally-Tollendal decided to lay siege to Madras. He lacked, apart from the support of the fleet, the confidence of the soldiers, who were no longer paid. His men affirmed that they were fighting only because it was better to die of a bullet under the walls of Madras than of hunger within the protection of those of Pondicherry. It was in fact as much the insubordination of his troops as the arrival of Pocock's fleet, in the middle of February, that urged Lally to give up his plan of taking Fort Saint-George by storm and to raise the siege.

From then on, time was in favour of the British, who, being masters of Bengal, could concentrate their forces on the Coromandel. Admiral d'Aché reappeared in September, but brought only meagre subsidies and Lally-Tollendal had to pay the mutinous regiments out of his own funds. After an indecisive but bloody naval battle, off Cuddalore, the admiral sailed again back to Mauritius, leaving Pondicherry to its sad fate.

As the situation worsened, Lally-Tollendal had to accept the resumption of Dupleix's policy and to seek help from the Indian princes. He appealed without success to the Moguls of the Deccan, the Marathas and the new strong man of Mysore, Haidar Ali. Furthermore, the French strategy was confused: whereas the threat loomed from the north, the lieutenant general thinned out his defence by sending

Crillon to the south to capture Sri Rangam. Sir Eyre Coote took advantage of the occasion and seized Vandavashy. On 20 January 1760, in his attempt to recapture this site, Lally-Tollendal suffered a complete disaster: Bussy himself was captured and two months later, Pondicherry was occupied.

In accordance with the predictions of Marquis d'Argenson, Dupleix's capital suffered simultaneously from internecine struggles and British assaults. To the inhabitants who blamed him for reducing them to 'beggars', Lally-Tollendal replied that their city was a 'Sodom that will be inevitably destroyed sooner or later by the fire of the English, if not that of Heaven.' The British, however, made no haste, leaving famine to complete its work: by the end of December, 'dogs, cats, boiled leather, anything was fine. A rat costs 2 rupees.'[39] Lally-Tollendal capitulated on 17 January 1761, and while the Pondicherrians exiled themselves to Tranquebar, he was taken in captivity to England.

The Treaty of Paris, signed on 10 February 1763, restored to France its five trading posts and its various factories, but at a time when India was not yet British, it was lost to France, reduced to an insignificant role.

On his return to France, Lally-Tollendal was accused of treason and executed. He thus paid the price of not only his errors, but also those of the Company and the government, which, thinking only of procuring supplies for the French market and of making profits, refused to take into account the highly complex political situation of India, on which, however, hinged the achievement of their objectives. The attitude of the French reveals 'the continuity of a strictly mercantile economic philosophy and [. . .] the complete lack of interest for distant lands in their relations with Europe.' In brief, the priority for France, a continental power, remained Europe, whereas Britain, a maritime power, turned increasingly towards to the oceans and distant lands.[40] During the Seven Years' War, Britain was mistress of the seas. The British admiral Pocock, who dissuaded d'Aché from venturing beyond Mauritius, played a crucial role in the collapse of the French power.

The triumph of the British was perhaps also due to the difference in the structures, even in the nature, of the two companies. The East India Company was a private undertaking; based on free enterprise and individual initiative, it lived on the profits of Asian commerce and did not depend in any way on the State, on which it was able to exert a great influence, at least through the intermediary of its directors who took their seats in the Parliament. The French Company was, on the other hand, a State undertaking the directors of which were appointed by the Crown; it received subsidies from the government and received revenues not exclusively accruing from trade in India, like those derived from the lease of tobacco. The characteristic lethargy of its departments and its establishments in India seems to be a result of this bureaucratic control.[41] Subjected to the shortsighted policy of the state, paralysed in its initiatives, the French Company had no chance of succeeding. The British victory was, as it were, that of free enterprise over a nationalized economy.

Companies and European trade
In the eighteenth century

Trend of the number of ships fitted out from 1701 to 1770[42]

Decades	VOC	EIC	French armaments
1701–1710	271	143	38
1711–1720	323	132	100
1721–1730	396	141	210
1731–1740	372	162	181
1741–1750	315	184	177
1751–1760	272	188	151
1761–1770	303	259	113

(VOC: The Dutch Company; EIC: East India Company).

Purchases in India, sales revenues and profits of the French Company between 1726 and 1760 (annual averages expressed in livres tournois)[43]

Five-year periods	Value of purchases in India	Value of sales in France	Profit
1726–1730	3,200,232	6,990,065	3,789,833
1731–1735	5,496,191	10,611,339	5,115,148
1736–1740	6,078,709	11,298,767	5,220,058
1741–1745	7,216,579	13,316,752	6,100,177
1746–1750	984,628	2,011,605	1,026,977
1751–1755	7,723,916	15,025,543	7,301,627
1756–1760	4,908,455	7,173,652	2,264,197

Imports of the East India Company between 1701 and 1760 (annual averages expressed in sterling pounds)[44]

Decades	From Bombay	From Madras	From Bengal	Totals
1701–1710	42,763	71,180	115,047	288,970
	18.6 per cent	31 per cent	50.2 per cent	100 per cent
1711–1720	67,758	108,943	231,274	408,475
	16.6 per cent	26.7 per cent	56.7 per cent	100 per cent
1721–1730	56,549	125,413	318,791	500,753
	11.3 per cent	25 per cent	63.7 per cent	100 per cent
1731–1740	53,335	81,671	409,090	544,096
	9.8 per cent	15 per cent	75.2 per cent	100 per cent
1741–1750	62,357	105,877	457,530	625,764
	10 per cent	17 per cent	73.1 per cent	100 per cent
1751–1760	54,518	95,925	353,924	504,367
	10.8 per cent	19 per cent	70.2 per cent	100 per cent

XIII

THE BRITISH CONQUEST
OF BENGAL

(1757–84)

In 1756, the East India Company was yet to become a territorial power. The three 'Presidencies' – Fort William (Calcutta) in Bengal, Bombay and Fort Saint-George (Madras) – were but trading posts and forts, encircled by native states and connected to each other only by sea. Each presidency had a governor who corresponded directly with the East India Company in London and deputy governors were placed at the head of less important trading posts, but this did not form even an embryo of a state.

The wars with the French in South India, however, had led the Company to equip itself with a proper army, composed in the main of indigenous soldiers (*sepoys*); it would not be long before it used it in Bengal for territorial conquests.

The collapse of the Mogul Empire in effect paved the way for the British company to gradually lay the foundation for its future domination. Its naval and military supremacy would enable it to rally to its cause the bone and sinew of the society: warrior castes, lured by the high salaries that it distributed, bankers and merchants, whose trade benefited from the protection of its flag and its squadrons. Its respect for the customs, practices, cultures and laws of the country earned it the esteem of functionaries and scholars. With their support, sometimes at their instigation, as in Surat, where Hindu merchants and Muslim notables pressed it to capture the castle that controlled the port in the interest of their operations, the East India Company became part of the new order and consolidated its positions, accumulating rights and powers. Having attained the same status as the *nawabs* or *subadars*, it showed, following the example of the latter, the greatest deference to Delhi, with a view to drawing the indispensable legitimacy from it.

Notwithstanding the recommendations from London, hardly favourable to interference, the managers of the Company in Calcutta, Bombay and Madras would be sucked into the 'military bazaar' that was India in the eighteenth century. Acting as *nawabs*, the governors of the presidencies exacted a price for their military support and manipulated their allies, whose conquests eventually became theirs, thus becoming 'the great beneficiaries of this age of war'.[1]

Control over Bengal

An Anglo-Indian enterprise: Plassey

The *nawab* Alivardi Khan died in April 1756. In conformity with his wishes, his grandson, Sirajuddaula, succeeded him. Impetuous and jealous of his authority, the latter inaugurated his reign by an astounding victory over his cousin Shaukat Jang, who had elevated his *faujdari* of Purnea into an independent state. In his effort to consolidate his control over the administration and the armed forces, he got rid of Alivardi's right-hand men and replaced them with his own. Victims of these purges, Mir Jafar, the supreme commander of the armies of the previous *nawab*, and Rai Durlabh, the Hindu chief of administration, were henceforth ready for conspiracies of all kinds. As were the powerful zamindars of Burdwan and Nadia, as well as a large number of bankers and merchants from whom Sirajuddaula had exacted substantial sums of money in particular to finance his war against Purnea. The Jagat Seths, the leading bankers of Murshidabad, thus had to pay 30 million rupees; their chief, who had protested against the enormity of the amount, was beaten up.

As avaricious as he was tactless, the new *nawab* of Bengal also earned the hostility of Europeans – French and Dutch, from whom he demanded 350,000 and 450,000 rupees respectively, and more particularly the British. On 20 June 1756, meeting no resistance, he seized Calcutta, whose governor, Roger Drake, had fled at the first gunshot. The following night, several dozen British subjects perished in the 'black hole' where they had been crammed. Sirajuddaula was probably not directly responsible for this tragedy, but even today facts remain shrouded in countless conjectures as to the reasons that pushed him to sack Calcutta: did he seek only to exact money from the city or did he intend to put an end to the commercial privileges enjoyed by the Europeans, or even to their companies? Was his objective to destroy the fortifications that had been constructed recently by the British without his authorization? In any case, it seems that the *nawab*, jealous of his independence, did not tolerate these enclaves under foreign sovereignty that the European trading posts were.

For big landowners (*zamindars*), who sold the products of their domains to the East India Company, for merchants who transacted with it, for the entire corporate world of Bengal, which, in one way or another, benefited from its imports of precious metals, its ruin would also be theirs. The capture of Calcutta was, in their eyes, a new humiliation, with more far-reaching consequences than the exactions that they already suffered. The Company reacted with promptness. As it did not have any troops in Bengal, it called for reinforcements from South India.

In October 1756, Clive, the then deputy governor of Fort Saint-David, left Madras with 900 European soldiers and 1,500 sepoys. Buttressed by the squadron led by Watson, he recaptured Fort William of Calcutta in January 1757. In February, Siraj was forced to restore to the Company all its privileges. After the capture of Chandernagore, in March, Clive decided to join the conspiracy fomented by the Indian notables under the leadership of the 'bankers of the world', the Jagat Seths, with a view to replacing Siraj with Mir Jafar. The latter promised to grant new privileges to the British, once he was established on the throne with the force of their arms. The Jagat Seths promised on their part substantial recompense for the functionaries and soldiers of the East India Company who would contribute to the overthrowing of the tyrant (it would rise to a total amount of more than 1,250,000 pounds). Their rupees would furthermore serve to buy off enemy troops.

On 23 June 1757, at Plassey, between Calcutta and Murshidabad, Sirajuddaula was vanquished and killed. A week later, Mir Jafar entered Murshidabad, where he was proclaimed *nawab* of Bengal. Traditional historiography presents these events as the starting point of a new era, that of the domination of the British over India. In fact, in the wake of Plassey, no one suspected that the battle would lead to the domination of the entire subcontinent[2]: for the Indian elite, on the contrary, the defeat of Siraj marked a return to the order that had prevailed under the previous *nawab*. Even the British themselves believed that their victory did nothing but re-establish the situation prior to the capture of Calcutta. They had no doubt gained new privileges, like the right to strike rupees in their own mint and in particular, the revenues of the twenty-four *parganas* extending to the south of Calcutta. Nevertheless, neither the directors in London, nor Clive himself, who was eager to return to the south, envisaged venturing any further. There was no question of disparaging the powers of Mir Jafar, whom London considered as an independent ally. The role of the resident established in Murshidabad was confined to the maintenance of the most cordial relations with the *nawab*.

The Battle of Buxar

Little by little, however, the British, whose trade demanded a certain political stability, were dragged into the internal affairs of Bengal. Clive, anxious about the disarray caused by factional disputes, thus strove, in the wake of Plassey, to preclude a rupture between the Hindu chief of administration, Rai Durlabh, and Mir Jafar, who seemed to be infuriated with the tactlessness of the latter. He also endeavoured to reconcile the *nawab* and his representative in Bihar, Ram Narayan.

As arbitrators of internecine quarrels, the British acted as a bastion against foreign aggressions. The victories that they won successively against the Marathas and the emperor Shah Alam, supported by some powerful zamindars of Bihar, mitigated the shortcomings of the army of the *nawab* and saved Bengal. But they also proved fatal for the independence of Mir Jafar, whose destiny was increasingly at the mercy of the Company. The latter could henceforth demand that most of the troops of Bengal, who had demonstrated their inefficiency, be demobilized and that the sums that had been earmarked for them serve hereafter the maintenance of its own soldiers.

These successes incited the Company in particular to boost its financial demands. Since Plassey, in effect, its needs had continued to increase: with the decrease in the shipments of precious metals, the revenues of Bengal henceforth financed its commercial operations in India and in Canton. They also went into the budget of the Presidency of Madras and enabled to defray fresh expenses, such as the construction of the fort of Calcutta.

As early as 1758, Clive had obtained that the revenues of certain districts be allocated temporarily to the Company. In January 1760, he left Bengal to return to England. The new governor of Bengal, Vansittart, believed that only definitive annexations could allow the Company to meet the needs of its troops, of its establishments and its trade. He turned his attention to the rich districts of Burdwan, Midnapur and Chittagong.

Already drained by Clive, and heavily indebted to the Jagat Seths, faced with the hostility of his relations, who did not tolerate his complacency towards the British, Mir Jafar, in an élan of national pride, refused to accede to the demands of the Company. In October 1760, he was forced to abdicate to give way to his son-in-law, Mir Kasim, who promised the British, apart from the three districts of Burdwan, Midnapur and Chittagong, the reimbursement of the debts of his predecessor and a 'donation' of two million rupees to the Council of Calcutta. A military expedition was of course necessary to bring the *zamindar* of Burdwan into submission, but as early as the end of 1760, the three districts came under British sovereignty, ensuring the Company a supplementary annual income of 500,000 pounds (that is about 4,600,000 rupees).

Mir Kasim, the new *nawab*, who lacked neither character nor political ambitions, proved less complaisant than hoped by Vansittart and his council. Abandoning lower Bengal and the capital of his predecessors, Murshidabad, as too close to the regions under British influence, he established his court in Monghyr, in Bihar. He refused to receive any resident, thereby expressing his desire for independence. The allies of the Company were either eliminated – like Ram Narayan, the *naib* of Bihar, who was relieved of his office and later assassinated – or placed under surveillance, like the Jagat Seths. Lastly, whereas Mir Jafar had sacrificed his army, Mir Kasim exerted himself to create a new one, organized according to the European model. In order to finance it, he did not hesitate to substantially increase the tax amounts, which came close to twenty-one million rupees, against less that nineteen million under Alivardi Khan.

The increasing participation in the domestic trade of Bengal of Englishmen acting on their own behalf particularly exasperated Mir Kasim. Their rapacity and the abuses that they were guilty of were prejudicial to his Treasury as much as to his subjects. Some individual traders, for example, seized control of the manufacture of salt in the districts of Dacca and Lakshmipur, which came under the sovereignty of the *nawab*. Others were interested in the trade of saltpetre and opium from Bihar, muslins from Dacca, silk goods from lower Bengal, even tobacco, betel and rice. In 1763, British merchants invested around 500,000 pounds in these various commercial operations. Three partners alone – John Johnstone, William Hay and William Bolts – contributed to the tune of 67,000 pounds. Vansittart himself made a huge fortune thanks to his investments in domestic trade.

Profits were all the greater as these individuals did not hesitate to use any means necessary – furthermore enjoying at times the support of the sepoys of the Company and backed by this protection, they could force Indian producers to sell at rates that were suitable for them and their customers, and force them to buy up to 50 per cent above current prices; they did not refrain either from granting themselves the privileges of the Company and especially from exempting themselves from paying the customs duties demanded by Mir Kasim; they even made a fray into the *nawab*'s traditional monopolies, which henceforth had no takers.

In an effort to put an end to these abuses and perhaps to trigger a war that could liberate Bengal from British domination, Mir Kasim decided, in October 1762, to intercept ships sailing under the British flag. Vansittart, who made haste to Monghyr and accepted that the domestic trade by the British be subjected to a duty of 9 per cent within the *nawab*'s territories, was disowned by his council. From then on, war was inevitable. It broke out in June 1763 at Patna, where some British traders, including William Hay, were massacred.

From July onwards, Mir Kasim, defeated, had to seek refuge in Oudh, at the court of Shujauddaula. Mir Jafar was reinstated on his throne, but he had to pay the Company a sum of 4,800,000 rupees in lieu of damages and to exempt trade activities carried out by individuals, except for salt, subjected to a duty of 25 per cent.

Mir Kasim, however, succeeded in mobilizing a large anti-British coalition at Lucknow, rallying to his case the *nawab* of Oudh, the emperor Shah Alam and the Rohilla chiefs. The coalition army, which invaded Bihar in the beginning of 1764, had the advantage of numbers, but suffered from a lack of cohesion that the British strived to exploit. Some Mogul contingents were ready to change sides with arms and baggage for material benefits; the emperor himself, who had misgivings about the victory of the coalition, negotiated with the British and seemed inclined to recognize Mir Jafar on the condition that the Company helped him to consolidate his authority over Delhi; Beni Bahadur, the prime minister of Oudh, also played a double game; as for Shuja, he fell out with Mir Kasim, whom he even arrested under the pretext that Bengal had not paid any tribute to the emperor for years; when Mir Kasim paid up his debt, he cornered the largest share for himself, leaving Shah Alam only a symbolic amount.

Under these circumstances, there was little doubt as to the outcome of the war. However, on 23 October 1764, at Buxar (or Baksar), between Benares and Patna, the troops of Major Hector Munro won the victory only with great difficulty. In spite of the defections of Beni Bahadur and a part of the Mogul and Rohilla forces, the troops that had remained loyal to Shujauddaula and Mir Kasim had fought with new ardour.

Though limited in scope, the victory of Buxar was no doubt more decisive than that of Plassey, as it had been won against a coalition mobilizing all the Mogul forces capable of checking British hegemony in the northeast of the country. No sovereign was any longer in a position to contend with the East India Company for Bengal and Bihar.

This hegemony appeared almost fortuitous, events dictating for the most part the conduct of the British authorities between 1756 and 1764. The assault delivered by Sirajuddaula had forced them into a war into which they entered all the more resolutely because they enjoyed the support of the Indian elite groups. As Mir Kasim's vague desire to be independent posed a threat to their interests, the British had become embroiled in a new conflict that they had not expected.

We probably cannot underestimate the influence of the profit-mindedness of the business world and a part of the Council of Calcutta on the course of events and on the attitude of *nawabs*, but no coherent policy aimed at the conquest of Bengal was formulated either in India or in England. If we may be justified in speaking of 'sub-imperialism' inasmuch as the authorities of Calcutta took advantage of the events to extend the interests of their nation, the hegemony over Bengal was not in any way the fruit of a deliberate policy of the home country. The thesis according to which the conquest of Bengal was to contribute to meeting the needs of the British economy has been proved wrong.[3]

In May 1765, Clive, who had been appointed governor and commander-in-chief of Bengal in 1764, returned to Calcutta. He declared himself to be against fresh military interventions that would annoy the local population and would end up being fatal to the Company. As the brutal seizure of all powers by the British was liable to exacerbate the resentment of the elites, he declared himself in favour of a protectorate, the effectiveness of which had been demonstrated by Bussy in the Deccan.

However, progressively, all the branches of the administration passed under British control, the *nawab* being henceforth but a puppet in their hands.

The diwani

In exchange for the throne, Mir Jafar had promised to add a monthly indemnity of 5,000,000 rupees to the revenues of the districts ceded in 1760. Though advantageous, this solution did not satisfy Clive. He wanted a change in the previous settlements by virtue of which the *nawab* collected the revenues and paid an indemnity to the Company. In accordance with his wishes, the Treaty of Allahabad, which he obtained from the new emperor Shah Alam II on 2 August 1765, conferred on the Company the *diwani* of the provinces of Bengal, Bihar and Orissa. In exchange for the collection of taxes and the administration of finances, it was to pay the emperor an annual sum of 2,600,000 rupees.

With the *nawab* Mir Jafar retaining the office of *nazim* (or *subadar*), which included defence, maintenance of order and justice, the Treaty of Allahabad apparently marked a return to the situation that prevailed before the advent of Murshid Quli Khan, in 1716, when the *diwani* and the *nizamat* were separate. It also perpetuated the fiction of the subordination of the Company to the emperor, concurrent with the wishes of the Council of Calcutta, which was keen to proclaim the legitimacy and the legality of its powers in the eyes of European powers, Indian sovereigns and public opinion in the home country.

The Treaty of Allahabad did not give India to the East India Company, not any more than the victories of Plassey and Buxar. It nevertheless conceded to it a power that soon became absolute in one of the most powerful successor states. Immediately after the death of Mir Jafar, in 1765, the Company, on the grounds of the youth of the new *nawab*, conferred the *nizamat* to a *naib suba* of its choice. Through the latter and its resident at Murshidabad, the Company defined the politics of Bengal. As early as 1765, it exercised the functions of defence and maintenance of order that normally fell on the *nazim*. Furthermore, in 1766, the last troops of the *nawab*, and especially his cavalry, were demobilized. On the other hand, the strength of the British army kept increasing, the number of sepoys rising from 25,000 in 1768 to 40,000 in 1784. Military expenditures, which amounted to 9,700,000 sterling pounds between 1761–2 and 1770–1, accounted for 44 per cent of the budget of the Company (which stood at 22,000,000) and were largely responsible for its financial difficulties.

British Bengal

The British administration

An oppressive taxation

Though the Company held all power in its hands, Clive believed that it must not exercise it nor interfere in the minutiae of the administration of Bengal and Bihar. He therefore entrusted the management with the *naib diwan* Muhammad Reza Khan and with an army of Indian functionaries. This 'dual system' was to have disastrous effects. It proved to be on the one hand incapable of generating the revenues necessary for financing trade, for supporting the presidencies of Bombay and Madras and for maintaining the army. On the other hand, it reduced the already stressed population to misery. Richard Becher, counsellor to Harry Verelst (who succeeded Clive as governor in 1767), observed on 24 May 1769 that 'since the accession to the *diwani*, the condition of the people [. . .] has become worse than before [. . .]. This fine country, which prospered under the most despotic and arbitrary governments, is on the verge of ruin.'[4]

This situation, aggravated by the drought of 1769 and the famine of 1770, which killed a quarter or even a third of Bengali peasants, was all the more shocking as Indian tax agents, lease-holders of taxes and the functionaries of the East India Company were making huge fortunes. The luxuries that the Company's servants paraded insolently on their return to England contrasted sharply with the financial difficulties of their Company, which was incapable, in 1767, of paying the annual tribute of 400,000 pounds to the Treasury.

While the system put in place by Clive was unanimously condemned, opinions diverged as to the reforms that needed to be introduced. Some, believing Bengal to an exceptionally rich country, advocated the increase of tax pressure. Others, like Verelst and Becher, convinced that the country was facing a serious economic crisis, suggested the enhancement of productive capacities before intensifying tax pressure.

Two principles rapidly became obvious to all: Indian agents, rapacious and cruel as were the servants of all 'Eastern despotisms', had to be, if not replaced, at least controlled by Europeans imbued with the principles of honour, good faith, rectitude and humanity, which, if we are to believe Verelst, characterized the English nation. What is more, the powerful magnates who collected and paid taxes to the Company must find an interest in the long run in the development of the region under their influence and should no longer be tempted to amass a fortune during their often brief stay in office. 'The security of private property, it was reiterated in Calcutta, was the foremost incitement to assiduity at work on which hinged the prosperity of each State.'[5] These principles began to be recognized towards 1770.

Tax reforms

As early as the end of the 1760s, British functionaries, invested with the title of 'supervisors', were placed at the head of tax authorities, which until then had been under the absolute control of *zamindars, faujdars*, or *amils*. As early as 1770, they were charged with the task of collecting taxes instead of the latter who were relieved of their offices. From 1772 onwards, they carried the title of 'collectors'.

This policy was pursued by Warren Hastings, appointed governor of Bengal on 13 April 1772. The *diwani* of the Company was immediately reaffirmed by the dismissal of Muhammad Reza Khan and the scrapping of the post of *naib diwan* that he occupied. The governor and the council henceforth directly controlled the collection of taxes and the management of finances, a special department ('Board of Revenue') being entrusted with the minutiae of this administration. The *nawab*'s Treasury (*khalisa*) was transferred from Murshidabad to Calcutta and placed under the control of the high officials of the Company. From then on, the British managed taxation and finances both at the central and local levels.

British intervention did not signify the end of all Indian influence: lacking experience, the collectors had to place their trust in Hindu and Muslim *diwans* and *sherestadars* who, very often, were the true administrators of the districts. Warren Hastings himself soon fell under the influence of his counsellor, Ganga Govind Singh, whom Indians considered 'the second most important person in the government, if not the foremost.'[6]

Hastings also took a series of measures in order to boost savings, the primary victims of which were his suzerains. Thus, he suspended the payment of the sum that the Treaty of Allahabad promised the emperor. As regards the share of the *nawab* in the revenues, already cut down on several occasions (5,300,000 rupees in 1765 to 4,100,000 rupees in 1766 and 3,200,000 rupees in 1769), it was further divided by two, and amounted henceforth only to 1,600,000 rupees per year.

As the savings of 500,000 pounds that resulted from these measures did not satisfy the Parliament at London, new tax reforms became indispensable. Persuaded that only long-term leases would urge their holders to invest in view of the enhancement of agriculture and long-term profits, Hastings decided to put an end to the practice of renewing contracts on an annual basis and to lease taxes for five years to the highest bidders.

The new regulation, applied as early as 1772, produced disappointing results. Most of the *zamindars* could retain possession of their lease of taxes only by making a higher bid in order to eliminate their competitors. Some of them, like the *zamindars* of Nadia and Vishnupur, lost at this time their traditional rights to collect revenues. The increase in tax collections resulting from higher bids was only theoretical and the new system soon began to produce serious setbacks.

Administrative reforms and tax policy discussions

In 1773, the head of the British government, Lord North, granted the Company a loan of 1.5 million pounds to help it to overcome its chronic deficit. In return, a law limited the dividends of the shareholders to 6 per cent until the complete reimbursement of the loan. Simultaneously, the term of office of the directors was restricted to four years, one-fourth of them being renewed every year. In India, the governor of Bengal assumed the title of 'governor general of the Presidency of Fort William in Bengal', which conferred on him, if not true supremacy, at least moral authority over the presidencies of Bombay and Madras. His council was also renewed.

Three of the four new councillors, General Clavering, Colonel Monson and in particular the ambitious Philip Francis soon proved to be antagonistic towards Warren Hastings and notably towards his tax reforms. The failure of the regulation of 1772 armed them with solid arguments: not only did revenues not come in, but leaseholders, who affirmed that they were unable to honour the clauses of their lease, pressurised the peasants, as they had done at the time of annual renewals.

The councillor Philip Francis affirmed that in keeping with the law of the country British law must recognize that land was the hereditary property of the *zamindar* who paid his contribution regularly to the government. Along with this recognition, the establishment of a fixed charge that the government refused to increase, whatever the circumstances might be, would give the *zamindar* the security that was necessary to urge him to undertake the development of his domains.

Influenced by the theories of the Physiocrats and Adam Smith, Francis's propositions met with a favourable response in England. They were, however, opposed by Warren Hastings who could not bring himself to confer the status of proprietors to local potentates, who would always favour their interests at the expense of the general interest. He was particularly loath to limit the tax requirements of the Company to their profit. In 1777, on the expiry of the regulation of five years, he decided that the tax leases would be renewed and adjusted annually. However, this was only a stopgap measure, which satisfied neither the Company nor the leaseholders.

In 1784, following the complaints formulated by certain 'rajahs, zamindars and other native proprietors', Pitt's *India Act* stipulated the establishment of 'permanent rules', for example that the collection of revenues was henceforth carried out according to 'the principles of moderation and justice'. It would be the task of Lord Cornwallis, the successor of Warren Hastings, to resolve the issue in harmony with the principles advocated by Philip Francis.

Apart from affirming the *diwani* and seeking to strike a balance between the interests of the Company, the leaseholders and the tax payers, the government of Warren Hastings was characterized by a reorganization of justice, which was not however unconnected to tax administration.

British justice

Much in the same manner as they seized, as early as 1765, the functions of defence and maintenance of order theoretically vested in the *nazim*, the British infringed on the latter's judicial attributes too. They asserted, in the wake of the Treaty of Allahabad, that civil justice fell under the jurisdiction of the *diwan*. Concurrent with this principle, Hastings created in 1772 the first civil courts of the Company, the *diwani adalats*, presided by the collectors. Appeal proceedings were heard by a supreme civil court, the *sadr diwani adalat*, presided by the governor general, assisted by two members of his council. Hindu and Koranic laws were applied in these tribunals, which was indispensable to gain the acceptance of the people, but they were sometimes interpreted by magistrates imbued with ideas foreign to India, like equality before the law, such that there appeared 'a new form of law with roots in both the cultures'.[7]

Criminal justice came under the jurisdiction of the *nazim*, and Indian magistrates under his authority presided over his courts. However, as early as 1765, the British acquired a right to review in these proceedings through the *naib nazim*, who could not be appointed without their consent. From 1772 onwards, their control was reinforced, as the *sadr nizamat adalat* or the supreme civil court, even though presided by an Indian, was transferred to Calcutta and subjected to the surveillance of the governor and his council. As early as 1781, British magistrates dispensed penal justice, and in 1790, the function of *naib nazim* was scrapped, the courts henceforth passing into the hands of European judges. With this ultimate usurpation of the prerogatives of the *nizamat* the last vestiges of the authority of the *nawabs* in Bengal were obliterated.

The limits of British rule

The affirmation of British sovereignty, the increase in tax pressure, foreign interference in civil and criminal justice, and consequently in the affairs of family, caste and religion, did not rouse any general hostility, nor any uprising worthy of note, which perhaps proves that in the eyes of the people, the government of the Company, comparable to that of the other successor states, did not mark a rupture, but on the contrary fell in line with the general process of the decentralization of the Mogul Empire.

The revolt of the rajah of Benares, the subsequent revolt of the *zamindars* of Bihar in 1781 and the uprisings in the districts of Birbhum and Rangpur in 1783, were no doubt little more than a disorganized attempt to coerce the Company to mitigate its tax requirements. There is no proof either that the *dacoits*, the brigands who scoured the region of Bengal, were motivated by any determination to resist foreign domination: in effect, they rarely attacked European possessions and persons.

If we cannot speak of a precocious opposition to the British rule, the traditional image of a central power pacifying an unstable society does not correspond to the facts either. The control of the British over Bengal coincided on the contrary with a recrudescence of violence and insecurity, no doubt owing to a profound economic and social crisis, aggravated by the intensification of tax pressure and certain despoliations. The helplessness of the police and the law against the *dacoits* underlines the limits of British rule in Bengal a long time after Plassey.

The exploitation of the riches of Bengal

The regulation of domestic trade

In the wake of the Battle of Buxar, the authorities in London were more than ever determined to put an end to the abusive trade practices that had triggered the war. Such was the objective that Clive claimed to pursue, when, as soon as he returned to Calcutta, in 1765, he ordered the cessation of trade in Oudh and in Benares, prohibited the British from carrying out transactions on certain products, like lime and timber wood and founded a society of trade. Composed of the most senior functionaries of the East India Company, it was placed in charge of controlling the production of salt, betel and tobacco that it resold to Indian wholesalers at prices set by the government of Bengal. It paid a part of its profits to the Company.

Of of the society's three objectives, namely to ensure a revenue to the functionaries of the Company, fill its treasury and provide the population with subsistence foodstuffs at realistic prices, only the first was reached, with the result that it was condemned as early as December 1766 and ceased all activities two years later.

Functionaries were thereafter prohibited from trading. Clive himself had to take an oath not to engage in such activities. The governors who succeeded him would have to follow suit. The *Regulating Act* of 1773 renewed the interdiction for the members of the Council and the functionaries in charge of the collection of revenues and the administration of justice. It was more tolerant towards the other agents, notably the employees of the offices in Calcutta, who would enjoy this lucrative privilege until 1789.

Certain transactions were however prohibited to all Europeans, either because they were reserved for Indian merchants, or because they were subject to the monopoly of the Company. In October 1772, for instance, Warren Hastings transferred to the East Indian Company the monopoly of salt that certain British functionaries had arrogated for themselves. Henceforth, brine fields belonged to the Company, which sold to the highest Indian bidder the right to manufacture salt for five years. It bought the total production that it subsequently auctioned, exclusively to Indian merchants. These merchants, who formed veritable cartels, made substantial profits at the expense of the consumers. The Company nevertheless would spare itself the trouble of making far-reaching reforms in a system that guaranteed it a considerable income, to the tune of seven to eight million rupees in 1793 and double that amount in 1827.[8]

In 1773, Warren Hastings granted the Company the monopoly of the production of poppies in Bihar, thereby ruining the few functionaries of Patna who were making huge fortunes by trafficking opium. Produced by the East India Company, this narcotic was sold by auction in Calcutta to individual merchants who exported it to China. In exchange for bills of exchange payable at London, these merchants handed over the proceeds from their sales in Canton to agents of the Company who used these funds to buy cargoes of tea destined for the British market.

Apart from salt and opium, Hastings granted the Company other monopolies, like that of saltpetre, putting an end to many an abuse, though he failed in effecting a complete reorganization of the market. He also took a series of measures destined to facilitate domestic trade: abolition of laissez-passers (*dastak*), of customs and tax exemptions and privileges, of taxes collected by *zamindars* and others magnates of rural areas, and the adoption of a uniform duty of 2.5 per cent imposable, in a number of customs offices, on all the merchants, both Indian and European, including those functionaries authorized to carry out trade.

It is not easy to assess the results of the attempts made at regulating domestic trade. The purchases of the Company in Bengal increased significantly between 1765 to 1780, growing from 400,000 pounds to more than a million, but this increase resulted no doubt more from the acquisition of the *diwani* and the consequent increase in resources than from the organization of production and commerce.

The growth of foreign trade.

In spite of the dire economic situation at the end of the 1760s and the beginning of the next decade, owing to the growing shortage of silver, the import of which from Europe had ceased as early as 1757, to the famine of 1770, which threw the economy of Bengal out of gear, and to the predations of *dacoits*, the turnover of the port of Calcutta was constantly on the rise, as Warren Hastings was fond of pointing out.

The turnover of the port of Calcutta[9]

Years	Number of ships anchored at Calcutta	Tonnage	
1716		1,320	20 to 40 ships per year between 1714 and 1760
1735		7,901	
1770	88	22,475	
1771	101	24,140	Figures put forward
1772	119	26,184	by Hastings
1773	161	37,187	
1783	128		The war of American Independence
1791	575		

The Company retained its monopoly of exports bound for England, which were primarily made up of cotton goods. Between 1777 and 1786, 550,790 pieces per year on an average were sold at London and 777,237 between 1792 and 1801. This increase was brutally interrupted in 1802, the year in which the British government, in an effort to protect the cotton industry of Lancashire, imposed heavy customs duties on textiles imported from Bengal.

As opposed to cotton weaving, which in certain regions seemed to have regressed, the cultivation of silk continued to progress, driven by the high demand for raw silk in England. This growth was all the more remarkable as the Silk Belt was particularly affected by the Maratha invasions and the great famine of 1770. It was in part due to the introduction, in 1769, of Italian techniques of reeling. The construction, a few years later, of modern yarn mills belonging both to the Company and to individuals, Indian and European, does not seem to have affected the traditional craft industry.

The spectacular expansion of the export of sugar and indigo towards Britain was due to the War of American Independence, which interrupted supplies from this continent. From 1778 onwards, Indians began to engage in the cultivation of indigo, to the north of the Ganges in particular, while individuals, British for the most part, invested in the manufacture of dyes. This was the proof of the vitality of private enterprise in Bengal and the sign of a certain decline of the East India Company, incapable of producing on its own so indispensable an article for its export trade. The first indigo factory was opened in Bihar in 1783. Two years later, the number grew to fourteen.[10]

Capitalists keen to invest in the manufacture of silk or indigo could procure funds by applying to banking institutions, the 'houses of agency', which received the savings of Europeans and financed inter-Asian trade carried out by private individuals.[11]

Until about 1770, 'country trade' – the trading of local products – was principally oriented towards the Arabian Sea, the Persian Gulf and the Red Sea. Each year, about a dozen vessels of a consortium run by the governor and the Council, the 'freight ships', on which any functionary could load his own merchandise, transported raw silk to Surat and brought back cotton from Gujarat. At Tatta, in Sind, in Bandar Abbas, Bassora, Moka or Jedda, where they introduced rice, sugar and silk, the 'Calcutta Ships' could on the contrary find a back freight only with the greatest difficulty. They completed their cargo with pepper from Malabar – 700 tonnes per year between 1760 and 1770 – cardamom, cinnamon and sandalwood.

The growing shortage of connections with the ports of the western India Ocean as early as 1735–40 dealt a severe blow to the entire economy of Bengal. External factors, the decline of Surat, and piracy in the Arabian Sea, the Maratha raids in Gujarat, the instability of Iran, the Turco-Persian and Arabo-Turkish conflicts and civil wars in Yemen contributed to this decline compounded by internal factors, especially the increase of prices in Bengal. Raw silk and cotton goods, which increased respectively by 40 per cent between 1756 and 1780 and 30 per cent in the 1770s, were supplanted on the coasts of the Red Sea and the Persian Gulf with similar products, imported for instance from China.

However, from 1770 onwards, commerce in Bengal began to turn towards the east: Coromandel, Burma, the Strait of Malacca and China. This rapid expansion of exports towards the Far East put an end to the depression of more than thirty years consequential on the shrinkage of the Persian and Arabian markets. In 1777, even as this new trend was only beginning to crystallize, the far-eastern regions already absorbed nearly 25 per cent of the exports from Calcutta.

Inter-Asian Trade from Calcutta
(exports in 1777[12])

Destinations	Value of exports (in rupees)	Percentage	
Suez	21,000	0.8	
		} 4.9	
Bassora and Muscat	107,100	4.1	
Western coast	828,149	32.3	
Coromandel	980,254	38.2	
Penang and the East Coast	289,900	11.3	
Pegu	23,180	0.9 }	23.3
China	283,500	11.1	
Total	2,533,083	100	

This shift is probably indicative of British trade hegemony, incontestable from the 1760s. In the beginning of the eighteenth century, the operations of British traders were determined by the needs of the Asian people. They only followed the established routes and exploited the traditional markets. In the wake of Plassey, their domination of Bengal and its products, opium for instance, enabled them to chart out their own routes in keeping with their needs and interests. The spectacular growth of commerce between Calcutta and Canton was thus 'a British creation meeting a British need', in this case, the procuring of supplies of tea from China.[13]

Incapable of adapting to the new conditions and of meeting British competition, the Indian ship owners and merchants, who had played a non-negligible role in the relations with the western Indian Ocean, were from then on ousted even as trade shifted to the east. They were not the only ones to disappear. After the dislocation of the society of 'freight ships', in the beginning of the 1770s, the functionaries of the Company turned away from inter-Asian trade to invest in industries or domestic trade. They left the road open for independent entrepreneurs, the 'free mariners' and the 'free merchants,' who cornered the profits made from trade with Burma, Malay, Indonesia and China.

Though non-negligible, these transformations did not have the same scope as those that would engulf Bengal in the nineteenth century. In the second half of the eighteenth century, this region remained a small importer of British goods, a small exporter of raw materials and a large exporter of manufactured goods that the Company and the 'free merchants' distributed all across the world.

The British community and its relations with Indians

The population of Calcutta expanded in the eighteenth century, even as British supremacy consolidated itself in Bengal. According to commonly cited figures, it grew from 300,000 in 1739 to 400,000 in 1759 and 600,000 at the close of the century. According to some, these statistics are exaggerated, the city having not more than 120,000 inhabitants in 1750, which in itself is a remarkable figure.[14]

The British, even though their community was expanding, were only a minority. The functionaries or contractual agents of the Company, the 'covenanted servants', were 50 in number in 1710, 70 in 1750 and 250 in 1773. After the *Regulating Act*, there were 400 of them. Soldiers were more numerous, especially in the wake of Plassey: there were only 250 to 300 in the middle of the eighteenth century, but their number grew to more than 3,000 in the beginning of the 1760s. The increase in the number of officers is indicative of the growth in strength: 114 in 1763, 500 in 1769 and 1,069 in 1784.

The 'free merchants, 'in order to be authorized to live and trade in Bengal, had to enter into an agreement with the Company and post a substantial bond'. Fifty-nine of them were officially recorded between 1736 and 1756, in which year they represented only 7.5 per cent of the British nationals living in Bengal, whose number is estimated at 751. In 1766, there were 232 in Calcutta, including 64 foreigners (19 Germans, 16 Dutchmen, 13 Frenchmen). At the same time, 70 'free merchants' resided in other regions of Bengal. Their number kept increasing at the close of the eighteenth century: they were slightly less than a thousand in 1800[15]. At this time, 3,000 to 4,000 Armenians are believed to have settled in Bengal, as well as a non-negligible number of Greek and Portuguese merchants.

Missionaries were almost absent in Calcutta, whereas they continued to be numerous and influential in the Portuguese, Danish and French trading posts. They were of course tolerated in Bengal, but they were subjected to the nit-picking sur-veillance of the Company, which saw in their presence a possible cause for social instability. It was only in 1793 that the Baptist William Carey arrived in Bengal and only from 1813 onwards, when the role of the Company was on the wane, that Bengal became a land of mission.

The Company exercised a real dictatorship over the British community in India. It had the right to deport anyone who infringed its laws; it subjected the press to strict censorship and did not allow the creation of any representative institution. No one could seriously contest the order that it imposed. People came to Bengal to make a fortune and not to enjoy liberties, which were still very limited even in Europe. Consequently, there was more opposition to the monopolies of the East India Company than to its government.

It was possible to build solid fortunes, thanks both to inter-Asian trade and to domestic trade. Towards 1767, domestic trade earned a profit to the order of 20 to 30 per cent against 8 to 10 per cent in Europe, according to Adam Smith.[16] In the 1770s, Robert Lindsay, leaseholder of the taxes of the district of Sylhet, for instance, acquired a colossal fortune thanks to two small monopolies, those of the capture of elephants and the sale of oranges in the bazaar of Calcutta.[17]

Even though Indian merchants and bankers were on the decline, either because they had not resisted the turmoil caused by the conflicts between the English and the *nawab* Mir Kasim, as was the case with the Jagat Seths, or because they had been ousted from the most lucrative markets, the Europeans could not yet dispense with their services and their experience. They continued to borrow considerable sums, sometimes from the big bankers of Benares, who, from 1765 onwards, played the role held earlier by the Jagat Seths, sometimes from usurers and changers, the *mahajans*. On his death, in 1771, the councillor Francis Hare owed 640,000 rupees to several creditors, Indians for the most part, who would be reimbursed without difficulty. Those who lent to Samuel Middleton, deceased in 1775, were less fortunate: their losses would rise to one and a half million rupees.

More than their money, British businessmen needed the experience of Indians, their knowledge of the country, of its languages, its customs and practices. They therefore relied on the services of a rich *banyan*, who became their interpreter, their designated representative, even their moneylender. Thus associated with an Englishman, the *banyan* benefited from his protection and the advantages and privileges enjoyed by the masters of the land. The master–*banyan* relation was probably not a new fact in the wake of Plassey, but it was to become widespread. A man as powerful as Krishna Kanta Nandi, called Cantoo Babu, who had made a fortune in the trade of silk, did not hesitate to enter the service of Warren Hastings, whose *banyan* he became.

This type of relations tended to fade out from 1780 onwards, when the increase in the 'houses of agency' made Indian moneylenders less indispensable. At the same time, the British, who had accumulated wealth from their commercial businesses, ventured into banking activities, loaned money to their compatriots and supplanted the *mahajans* and the *banyans*. This two-fold process of accumulation of European capital and the creation of powerful business houses appeared as the sign of a new dimension in private British enterprise, henceforth capable of shaping the commercial conditions of Bengal in tune with its own needs.

XIV

THE BIRTH OF THE BRITISH
EMPIRE IN INDIA

(1765–1818)

Once it had established its rule in Bengal in 1765, the East India Company did not immediately embark on the conquest of the rest of India. In fact, nothing proves that the conquest of the subcontinent figured among the plans of its representatives in Bengal. As for the British government, it certainly did not dream as yet of getting its hands on the whole of India. But the domination of Bengal made the Company one of the major territorial powers of the subcontinent. Little by little, it was to become embroiled in the complicated and multifarious conflicts of post-Mogul India. The first important state whose politics it was led to interfere in was Oudh, its neighbour, which made the mistake of trying to support the *nawab* of Bengal.

Factors leading to British supremacy

In retrospect, the English conquest appears to be a natural development within the framework of 'European expansion'. But the end of the eighteenth century and the beginning of the nineteenth was a period when this expansion stopped, with the loss of the American colonies of England, France, Spain and Portugal. From 1760 to 1830, leaving aside the Russian advance into the Caucasus, India was one of the two cases of overseas expansion by a European state, the other being the Dutch conquest of Java. European expansion therefore has little relevance to an understanding of the British conquest of India. Must we then link the conquest of India to the emergence of Great Britain as the largest industrial power in the world and to the industrial revolution? It is doubtful because the instrument of this conquest, the East India Company, was itself a classic example of a mercantilist organization, the favourite target of the invectives of Adam Smith and the liberals. We must also keep in mind that the Company exported fabrics to England at the same time as the cotton industry of Lancashire, the driving force behind the Industrial Revolution, achieved formidable growth.

In fact, it is in the Indian context that we have to look for the key to the territorial expansion of the Company. This company of merchants transformed itself into a 'military despotism', whose dynamics, while remaining linked to trade, assumed an increasingly territorial and political dimension. For all this, its economic motivations were far from negligible: the growing interpenetration between the interests of the Company and British private interests gave these motivations increasing weight. For instance, the importance of interests involved in the lucrative trade with Oudh was certainly not irrelevant to the decision taken by Governor General Wellesley in 1801 to annex the richest part of the kingdom. At the same time, the British vision of India underwent a transformation, with the appearance of ideas of racial superiority, completely unknown in the eighteenth century. It was in the circle of Wellesley that these ideas, which could be used justify the conquest, came into the open.

Lastly, it is certain that the great European conflict of 1792–1815 had significant repercussions in India, though these were indirect. A French 'threat', largely a figment of the imagination, thus gave Wellesley an excellent pretext for his final assault against Mysore. Despite all this, no truly coherent imperialist ideology was at work before the second half of the nineteenth century. Conquest would not be the object of any comprehensive rationalization until the Victorian age, marked by a triumphant imperialism. Therefore, it should not be interpreted mainly as a stage in the overseas expansion of Britain or Europe, but viewed in the local context.

There remains the question as to how a handful of Europeans succeeded in subjugating in so short a period such a vast and populated subcontinent. Here as well, there is no easy answer. Europe had not yet acquired the technological superiority that explains in part its stunning colonial conquests of the end of the nineteenth century. It is certain that European military technology had the edge over Asian military technology, in particular in the field of artillery, but the Indian states, thanks to specialists, including Frenchmen among others, had access to this technology, and their dependence vis-à-vis these specialists, who were above all motivated by considerations of personal gain, was an important reason for their weakness. The army of the Maratha prince Sindhia, once it was deprived of the services of De Boigne, the brilliant Savoyard officer who created and commanded it for ten years, rapidly lost his efficiency: the successor of De Boigne, the Frenchman Perron, dealt it the death blow in 1803, when he capitulated without really putting up a fight. In the final analysis, it is not so much technological superiority that enabled the Company's army to defeat those of the Indian states as its more effective organization.

From the 1760s onwards, the Company's army became in effect increasingly efficient. The combination of an essentially indigenous troop with a corps of British officers and British methods had produced a military machine of great efficacy, at least in the Indian context. In the absence of rigorous studies, this alchemy remains somewhat of a mystery: nevertheless, the valour of the Bengal army, which by far constituted the core of the Company's army, seemed partly linked to its mode of recruitment. The Company continued to recruit from among the high castes of Oudh, which traditionally formed the great pool of soldiers for all the North Indian states.

What incited the Brahmins and the Rajputs of this region to enter into the service of *Company Bahadur* (the Indian title for the Company)? First, without doubt was the pay, which was good and, contrary to what happened in most of the Indian armies, paid regularly. Second, the decline in the prospects of employment in other armies, as Indian states, which drifted into the sphere of influence of the Company, were driven either to downsize or dismiss their troops. At the beginning of the nineteenth century, thanks to the success of its recruitment campaigns in North India, the Company possessed one of the largest European-style armies in the world (155,000 men in 1805). The indigenous soldiers, the *sepoys* (from the Persian *sipahi*, which has given the French '*spahi*'), adapted themselves without apparent difficulties to the fairly strict discipline that reigned in the British army and spread fear among their adversaries who were wont to more laxity. It is not possible to overestimate the advantage that the Company drew from the existence of this army recruited on the spot, on the one hand because it cost less than British soldiers and on the other hand because it was accustomed to the climate and familiar with the terrain. The Company recruited, admittedly, a few regiments from among the floating European population in India, which had a very bad reputation. It also employed a certain number of royal regiments, placed at its disposal by the British government, and which played a not negligible role in several engagements, but on the whole, it was with an Indian army that the Company conquered India.

This Indian army was commanded by British officers and leadership skills also contributed to its success. Admittedly, the corps of officers was of uneven worth: primarily made up of the younger sons, often Scottish, who had come to India at a very young age (thirteen or fourteen years old), attracted by the adventure and the lucre, it included without any doubt a good many incompetent individuals, but a sufficient number of talented men to make the difference with the generally mediocre leadership of the Indian armies of the time. We only need to think of men like Elphinstone, Munro or Malcolm, the future administrators of colonial India, representative of this group of conquerors with the multifaceted talents of litterateurs, historians and men of war who were the veritable founders of the Indian Empire. The fact is that the Indian adventure attracted some of the best (as well as some of the worst) sons of Great Britain, which is probably explained by the romantic aura that surrounded the subcontinent during this period.

However, if the army of the Company finally conquered India, it is above all because it never encountered a sufficiently unified and determined opposition to impede it. British historians of the nineteenth century construed this lack as a confirmation of one of their favourites theses, that of the inferiority of Asian political systems in comparison with European ones. The reality is more prosaic. The two Indian states that were capable of offering a protracted resistance to the Company, Mysore and the Maratha confederacy were ill-equipped to head 'national' resistance, supposing the term made sense at the time.

The Maratha confederacy took shape towards 1720 and even during the period of its greatest expansion, that is, until 1761, it had always had a weak structure. Its defeat in that year by the Afghans at Panipat, exacerbated the tensions between the different social groups and the different clans and factions. Even though it still possessed sufficient dynamism, it could no more lay claim to the domination of the subcontinent. The rivalry between the two greatest Maratha princely houses, the

Sindhias and the Holkars, constantly kindled by the intrigues of the chief minister of the *peshwas*, Nana Fadnavis, was a debilitating factor. As regards Mysore, a more recent creation by a Muslim adventurer who had descended from the Punjab, Haidar Ali, it was also a fragile construction. Haidar Ali's son, Tipu, who acceded to the throne in 1782, extended his conquests to establish a vast state, relying on the exploitation of rich agricultural lands, but it was ethnically very heterogeneous.

If Mysore like the Marathas entered into conflict with the Company on numerous occasions, these two powers could not put up a common front. Tipu, a very pious Muslim, dreamt of establishing a Muslim state in South India on the model of the Mogul Empire, even while pursuing a policy of conciliation with his subjects, the majority of whom were Hindus. The Marathas, for their part, who had emerged from a long fight against the Moguls, posed themselves as the protectors of Hinduism, though they had numerous Muslim soldiers in their army. Tipu perceived early enough the threat that the East India Company posed for the Indian rulers, but his diplomacy was not of the same calibre as his military talents. The great British historian James Mill, writing a few years after the events, attributed the largest share of responsibility for the dissension between the two principal Indian powers to Sindhia. The latter seems to have above all feared that a rapprochement between the *peshwa* and Tipu might be to his disadvantage.

Whatever the case might have been, each fought on his own. Mysore was the first to fall, a victim of Wellesley's vindictiveness and desire for glory. The Governor-General made the attempted formation of an alliance between Tipu and France under the 'Directoire', a pretext to get rid of an adversary who was already weakened but who still inspired fear. Nevertheless, Tipu had embarked on the only course that could have saved the Indian states that were still independent: an attempt at the 'Europeanization' of his regime through the implementation of a sort of state mercantilism. He instituted monopolies on spices and other products, enabling the state to muster increased financial resources. Tipu endeavoured likewise to create a disciplined army in the European manner, recruiting mercenaries of diverse origins. But the advance of the armies of the Company left him no time to bring his plans to fruition. In any case, his control over the diverse regions that constituted his kingdom was probably too weak to give him a chance to succeed. India at the end of the eighteenth century was not ripe for a Meiji.

The sultan of Mysore was the only one who attempted to fight European mercantilism with its own weapons. The Marathas, who reigned over poorer territories, were not in a position to follow the same policy. On the contrary, the links between the various territorial components of the Maratha confederacy had a tendency to weaken, as each princely house attempted to consolidate its power at the expense of its rivals. Sindhia, who was the most powerful Maratha chief at the end of the eighteenth century, concentrated his efforts on his army, whose discipline and efficiency he reinforced by engaging the services of French and English officers. But, for financing it, he had recourse to a Mogul-inspired tax system that was poorly adapted to the circumstances.

The absence of sufficient resources was no doubt the principal reason for the weakness of Indian states in the face of the East India Company. The latter had succeeded in increasing the financial returns of its territories of Bengal, already considered the richest province in India. Its Indian rivals did not possess comparable resources and therefore the pressure of war weighed down more heavily on their societies, causing turmoil and scissions that weakened them even further. On the other hand, the Company, despite the ferocious rivalries between individuals, maintained a united front and could count on the support of the British government. The triumph of a small group of European traders and administrators over a more numerous Indian elite class therefore is primarily due to the capacity of this group to mobilize more efficiently human and material resources of both Indian and British origin.

As regards Indians in general, apart from the ruling elite classes, it is difficult to know their reactions to the conquest. Research underway tends to show that the phenomena of resistance were more widespread than hitherto believed. After the armies of Indian rulers had been defeated or neutralized, an armed resistance continued at the local level, at times for a fairly long period. It could be led by local notables, like the chiefs (*polygar*) who fiercely fought the troops of the Company in the Tamil country in 1799–1801, or Maratha and Nayar chiefs, like Daundia Waugh or the rajah of Piche, who, between 1799 and 1806, fought Wellesley and Munro in the Canara country that had just been annexed. Often, these notables were capable of rallying to their cause a considerable part of the peasantry. There were also some cases of more specific peasant resistance in regions where the social structure was less hierarchical. These resistances, however dogged they might have been, were nevertheless too scattered to pose a threat to the British conquest. They succeeded only in delaying the outcome.

The absence of an Indian national spirit at the beginning of the nineteenth century is incontestable and was at times used by the British to legitimize the conquest. However, this argument has only limited value because, even in Great Britain at that time, the national spirit, although fuelled by the Napoleonic wars, existed only in an embryonic state. Other forms of loyalty could have inspired a more unrelenting resistance: after all, even Tipu, the sultan of Mysore, who preferred to die fighting rather than be captured, could not be called an Indian 'nationalist'.

In fact, certain factions of the Indian elite openly played the British card, though their motivations are not always very clear. We have mentioned the role of the great family of Marwari bankers, the Jagat Seths, in the victory of Colonel Clive at Plassey, in 1757. In the course of the following half-century, other native bankers granted advances to the East India Company that enabled it to finance its armies in part. One important section of the merchant world, primarily Hindu, no doubt welcomed the perspective of a rule by the Company because it brought a certain security and a legal environment conducive to business. Given the importance of merchant castes in the Indian society of the eighteenth century, this support was one of the reasons for the success of the British conquest. The merchant-bankers were not the only local support that the Company enjoyed: a certain number of rural magnates were also quite favourable to its enterprises. The British could thus take full advantage of a fracture within the Indian elite itself.

The stages of the conquest

From 1765 to 1790, the East India Company sought above all to guarantee the safety of its possessions in Bengal and South India, which led it to enter into contractual or conflicting relations with number of Indian States. It succeeded in integrating most of them into its system of alliances, except for the Marathas and Mysore, but did not launch into any fresh territorial annexations. The second war with Tipu (1790–92) brought in its train the resumption of the territorial expansion of the Company, but it was only an episode in a period of relative peace. It was only after the arrival of Governor-General Wellesley in 1798 that the Company embarked on a systematic policy of territorial annexations. The recall, in 1804, of this remarkably energetic proconsul led to a respite of ten years, before the wars of 1814–18 that would definitively establish British supremacy in the subcontinent.

The subjugation of Oudh

In the wake of the defeat of the combined forces of Oudh and the Marathas by the British, on 3 May 1765, the East India Company decided not to annex Oudh, but to make it a buffer state to protect Bengal from the Maratha incursions. By the Treaty of Benares, the *nawab* of Oudh, Shujauddaula, retained his sovereignty in exchange for an indemnity of five million rupees. The troops of the Company had to evacuate his territories with the exception of a garrison – which was to guard the fort of Chunar until the complete payment of the indemnity – and of the troops in charge of the protection of the emperor Shah Alam, who was granted the revenues of Kora and Allahabad.

One year after the treaty, Shujauddaula reimbursed almost the entire sum due, in *sikka* rupees (that is, struck in the same year and consequently not depreciated). Clive (Governor of Bengal) decided to recompense this mark of good will: he persuaded the emperor to elevate Shuja to the dignity of *wazir*.

Nevertheless, this entente was ephemeral. While he honoured his commitments of Benares, Shujauddaula reconstituted a powerful army, trained in the European style, which numbered 48,770 men in 1768. The Council of Calcutta then became aware of the danger that it posed and signed a new treaty that limited the army of Oudh to 30,000 men (of whom not more than 10,000 could be initiated into European techniques and organization). The consequences of such an agreement were more political than military: it constituted a case of British interference in the politics of Oudh and a defiance of the sovereignty of this state.

Article 8 of the Treaty of Benares, which granted English merchants the right to engage in trade in Oudh and to enjoy substantial customs privileges, triggered yet another conflict. As in Bengal in effect, the free merchants did not satisfy themselves with these advantages and committed an increasing number of abuses: they imposed their prices, exempted themselves from paying transit duties, monopolised certain trades, like iron, lead and saltpetre and violated the monopolies of the *nawab*.

So vehement and legitimate were the protestations of the latter that in May 1768 the Council of Calcutta forbade all the civil servants of the Company from trading

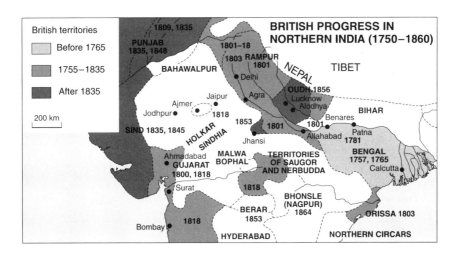

BRITISH PROGRESS IN NORTHERN INDIA (1750–1860)

British territories

- Before 1765
- 1755–1835
- After 1835

200 km

1809, 1835

PUNJAB 1835, 1848

1801–18

1803 RAMPUR 1801

BAHAWALPUR

Delhi

NEPAL

TIBET

OUDH 1856
Lucknow
Alodhya

Ajmer   Jaipur

Jodhpur   1818

Agra

SIND 1835, 1845

HOLKAR   SINDHIA

BIHAR

Benares
Patna

1853   1801   1801

Allahabad   1781

Jhansi

BENGAL 1757, 1765

Calcutta

Ahmadabad
GUJARAT 1800, 1818

MALWA BOPHAL

TERRITORIES OF SAUGOR AND NERBUDDA

Surat

1818

BHONSLE (NAGPUR) 1864

ORISSA 1803

Bombay   1818

BERAR 1853

HYDERABAD

NORTHERN CIRCARS

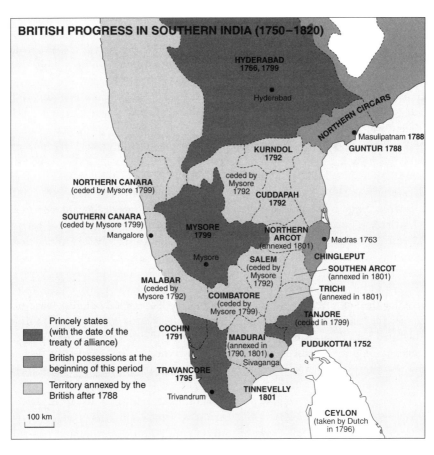

BRITISH PROGRESS IN SOUTHERN INDIA (1750–1820)

HYDERABAD 1766, 1799

Hyderabad

NORTHERN CIRCARS

Masulipatnam 1788

GUNTUR 1788

KURNDOL 1792

NORTHERN CANARA (ceded by Mysore 1799)

ceded by Mysore 1792

CUDDAPAH 1792

SOUTHERN CANARA (ceded by Mysore 1799)
Mangalore

MYSORE 1799

NORTHERN ARCOT (annexed 1801)

Madras 1763

Mysore

SALEM (ceded by Mysore 1792)

CHINGLEPUT

SOUTHEN ARCOT (annexed in 1801)

MALABAR (ceded by Mysore 1792)

COIMBATORE (ceded by Mysore 1799)

TRICHI (annexed in 1801)

TANJORE (ceded in 1799)

Princely states (with the date of the treaty of alliance)

COCHIN 1791

MADURAI (annexed in 1790, 1801)
Sivaganga

PUDUKOTTAI 1752

British possessions at the beginning of this period

Territory annexed by the British after 1788

TRAVANCORE 1795

Trivandrum

TINNEVELLY 1801

CEYLON (taken by Dutch in 1796)

100 km

in Oudh and withdrew its protection to free merchants. This decision was revoked in 1771 before being definitively confirmed by Warren Hastings, Governor-General from 1772.

It is also with the consent of Hastings that Shujauddaula embarked on a certain number of territorial annexations, Rohilkhand, Kora and Allahabad relinquished by Shah Alam, and lastly Etawah on the Jamuna. The *nawab* also reinforced his western and northern frontiers by reducing to subjection Muzaffar Jang, the heir of the Bangash dynasty of Farrukhabad. In exchange for the recognition of these annexations, he had to accept in 1773 the presence of British troops in his territory and the payment of an indemnity for their maintenance. On his death, he bequeathed to his successor, Asafuddaula, a considerably extended and wealthier kingdom, freed from the invading presence of British trade and, despite the Treaty of 1768, fortified with an army of 100,000 men supervised by 150 European officers, including the Frenchmen Madec and Gentil.

However, the new *nawab* was, even less than his father, master in his own house. It was to his mother Bahu Begam that the deceased *nawab* had entrusted the management of the Treasury and, to break free from her control, the new ruler decided to transfer the seat of his capital from Faizabad to Lucknow. In reality, the splendour of power interested Asaf more than the exercise thereof, which he relinquished to his favourite, Mukhtaruddaula, of mediocre ability, under whose administration the state quickly began to disintegrate. Mukhtar practised nepotism on a large scale, appointing his son treasurer and his brother governor of Allahabad. He placed at the head of the best troops men who had never held a weapon and elevated to the highest dignities barbers, butchers, sweepers and tanners.

The disintegration of power encouraged longings for independence amid the local notables. Tax leaseholders stopped their payments to the Treasury; mutinies shook the army, like the rebellion of the powerful general Gosain Rajah Anup Giri. In the face of the hostility of all the dynamic forces of the country, the threat of the Marathas looming large on the frontiers, Asaf could count henceforth only on the help of the English, who exerted themselves to use this tumultuous situation to the full. In exchange for their military protection, the *nawab* granted them as early as 1775 the control of the region of Benares, in addition to a substantial increase in the indemnity devoted to the maintenance of their troops. The resident, Bristow, increasingly influential in Lucknow, also obtained the dismissal of French instructor officers and their replacement by British officers invested with far-reaching powers, including the authority, if necessary, to summon Indian officers before a court martial. Furthermore, the resident persuaded the *nawab* to reinstate the minister Muhamad Ilish Khan, whom he had previously dismissed. In short, the Company henceforth enjoyed a right of inspection and in certain cases the power of decision with respect to the defence of frontiers, the maintenance of order and the administration of the state.

For all this, the country experienced a political instability that taxed the patience of Warren Hastings. The Governor-General overtly intervened in the internal affairs of Oudh and persuaded the *nawab* to banish Imam Baksh, the commander-in-chief of his troops, who was hostile to the British. The growing political control exercised by the British enabled them to reinforce their economic hold over the country. Convinced that the indemnity paid for the maintenance of troops was insufficient and its payment highly irregular, Bristow demanded that the cash payments be replaced by *tankwahs*, in other words, that the revenues of certain regions, in this case the Doab and Rohilkhand, be allocated to the Company. The share that the British exacted from the overall revenue of the State thus soared vertiginously, rising from 16.5 per cent in 1774 to 52.7 per cent in 1777. Eventually, it stabilised at 45 per cent of the *jama*, which was considerable.

Private individuals also stood to gain from the control of the Company on the finances of Oudh: Major Hannay, a protégé of Warren Hastings, became in 1778, one of the most important *mustajirs*, or holders of *ijarah*. The *ijarahdari* system, adopted in Rohilkhand as early as 1727, consisted of selling to the highest bidders leases (*ijarah*), the holders of which could retain the surpluses of the land revenues that they collected in exchange for a lump sum paid to the government. Some *mustajirs*, like Almas Ali Khan, became as powerful as the *nawab* himself, and possessed considerable armies. This nouveau riche constructed a capital, Mianganj, which claimed to rival Lucknow. During this time, the military aristocracy of great *jagirdars* weakened: Asafuddaula did not hesitate to accelerate this trend by dispossessing some of them of their domains, while granting small *jagirs* to his favourites, Hindus for the most part, which modified the balance of power between the communities.

These socio-religious transformations compounded with the growing tax demands of the Company sparked off grave events. Their immediate cause was the refusal of the rajah of Benares, Chait Singh, to pay a subsidy of 500,000 rupees, for the fourth year consecutively, towards financing the war against Mysore and to supply the Company with two thousand cavalrymen. Warren Hastings, the Governor-General of India, construed this double refusal a 'criminal disobedience' and proceeded to Benares where he ordered the arrest of Chait Singh. This arrest poured oil on the fire. On 16 August 1781, the rajah's troops massacred the detachment of the Company that had seized the person of the sovereign. Hastings succeeded in fleeing and found refuge in the fort of Chunar, while the revolt spread to the immense territories that sprawled from Farrukhabad to Patna. The insurrection, in which the peasants participated, was encouraged by Bahu Begum, who, from her stronghold of Faizabad, waged a veritable war against Major Hannay whose domains were adjacent to hers.

Asafuddaula did not use this rebellion, which could appear as a movement of the peasants directed against an oppressive taxation, to emancipate themselves from British tutelage. On the contrary, in mid-September, he marched to Chunar at the head of his troops, which he offered to Hastings. Thanks to reinforcements arriving from Allahabad, Cawnpore and Lucknow, the Governor-General re-established order in October 1781.

The Anglo-Maratha conflict

After the disaster of Panipat, in 1761, the death of the *peshwa* Balaji Rao and the civil war between his young sixteen-year old son, Madhav Rao and his brother, the ambitious Raghunath Rao, had weakened the Maratha confederacy. After gaining victory over his uncle, thanks to the support of loyal Mahaji Sindhia and to the counsel of the Brahmin chief minister Nana Fadnavis, Madhav Rao strove immediately to restore cohesion and prestige to this pentarchy. As early as September 1763, he imposed the Treaty of Aurangabad on the *nizam* of Hyderabad, who had to return territories producing an income of more than eight million rupees per year. In 1770, he seized Agra and Mathura. A year later Mahaji Sindhia was at Delhi, where he re-established the emperor Shah Alam on his throne. After an eclipse of ten years, Maratha power affirmed itself once again in North India.

However, Madhav Rao died in 1772, without having been able to consolidate his power, and other Maratha princely houses continued with their intrigues. Holkar and Bhonsle still harboured a desire for independence. Raghunath Rao was waiting for an occasion to seize power: in August 1773, he instigated the assassination of Narayan Rao, who succeeded his brother Madhav Rao. However, he could not benefit from his heinous crime because the Brahmins, the council led by Nana Fadnavis and the rajah of Satara obliged him to leave Poona in 1774.

It was then that the East India Company found itself directly caught up in Maratha politics. Raghunath succeeded in opening negotiations with the Council of Bombay, which, without referring to Calcutta, signed the Treaty of Surat in March 1775, by virtue of which it undertook to provide 2,500 soldiers, including 700 Europeans, to Raghunath in exchange for the island of Salsette and the port of Bassein, to the north of Bombay.

Confronted by this *fait accompli*, Governor-General Hastings denounced the treaty as 'impolitic, dangerous, devoid of legal base, and unjust', but nevertheless believed that Britain ought to honour its commitments. Such was not the opinion of the majority of his Council, which charged Colonel Upton with the task of negotiating with the authorities of Poona in order to return to the *status quo ante*. In March 1776, Upton signed the Treaty of Purandhar, by which the British, in exchange for Salsette, undertook not to support Raghunath Rao. Curiously, the directors of the East India Company condemned this treaty, which they construed as interference in the politics of the Indian states. Hastings took advantage of their stance to resume relations with Raghunath and to advocate the course of war with the Marathas on the pretext of the presence of French counsellors at Poona.

The first Anglo-Maratha War did not produce the results anticipated by the Governor-General. In 1778, the army of Nana Fadnavis posed a threat even to Bombay, which was finally saved by Upton. In January 1779, the British had to sign the Convention of Wargan, which caused them to lose the meagre advantages that they had gained through their unwarranted interference in Maratha politics. What is more, the war resumed after a very short time. The English generals Goddard and Popham initially scored a few sensational successes, seizing Allahabad, Bassein and even Gwalior, the capital of Sindhia, but Goddard, who advanced towards Poona, was soon checked. A year later, the Treaty of Salbai, signed through the intermediary of Mahaji Sindhia, re-established the status quo, apart from Salsette, which was definitively ceded to the Company. Raghunath Rao had to renounce his claims to the title of *peshwa*. In the final analysis, the Anglo-Maratha War cost a heavy price to the Company and marred the prestige of Warren Hastings, who, placed before the *fait accompli* by the authorities of Bombay, made the mistake of obstinately supporting the lost cause of Raghunath Rao. In South India too, he found himself in a tricky situation.

The difficulties of the Company in South India

The rich regions of the Circars, situated immediately to the south of Orissa, whose littoral produced fine printed fabrics greatly in demand and whose hinterland yielded teak, saltpetre and iron, aroused the cupidity of the agents of the East India Company and of the free merchants. In liaison with Indian capitalists like the powerful Jogi Pantalu of Rajahmundry, they had arrogated highly lucrative monopolies. The political and the military difficulties of Nizam Ali, brother and successor of Salabat Jang on the throne of Hyderabad, enabled the British to increase their economic privileges and to penetrate ever deeper into the interior. In November 1776, while the *nizam* was at war with Haidar Ali of Mysore, the government in Madras offered him troops in exchange for commercial advantages in the Circars. In their correspondences with the Court of Directors and the governments of the other Presidencies, the authorities of Madras justified their intervention in favour of the *nizam* more by strategic considerations than by arguments of an economic nature. They asserted that, just as Oudh was a defensive bastion for Bengal, Hyderabad had to stand as a buffer state protecting the Circars and the Carnatic from the formidable powers that were the Maratha confederacy and Mysore.

From January to March 1767, Haidar, despite his qualities as a strategist, was defeated by Madhav Rao, whose troops invaded Mysore. Nizam Ali, who had cautiously not interfered, decided to join the peace negotiations that took place in May. The treaty signed was advantageous for the Marathas and Hyderabad without being oppressive for Haidar Ali, so much so that the British found themselves brutally isolated in the face of these three great native powers of the South. Confronted with this triple alliance, Colonel Smith won a number of successes in September 1767 at Changama and Trinomali, but the treaty that the Company signed in 1768 with Nizam Ali in Masulipatnam contained humiliating clauses for it, and was disadvantageous for the other powers of the Deccan, which was likely to bring new complications in its train in the short run.

'You have brought us into such a labyrinth of difficulties,' wrote the Court of Directors to the government of Madras, 'that we do not see how we shall be extricated from them.'[1] Indeed, as early as 1769, Haidar Ali, dissatisfied with the Treaty of Masulipatnam, was under the walls of Madras. He withdrew only after obtaining the solemn undertaking that the troops of the Company would interfere in his favour should he fall victim to aggression. Yet, two years later, when the Marathas launched new raids against Mysore, his calls remained unanswered, which contributed to further discredit the authorities of Fort Saint George.

The atmosphere that reigned in Madras was 'pestilential'.[2] Almost all the functionaries and officers and a good number of free merchants indulged in the most audacious speculations. A large number of them even played against the interests of their own nation by lending huge sums of money to the *nawab* of Arcot, Muhammad Ali, the victor of Chanda Sahib, who reinforced his army to consolidate his authority in the region and eventually to liberate himself from the crushing British tutelage. With great sagacity, the *nawab* had relied on British financers with a view to securing, in the highest spheres of Madras and Calcutta, support for his cause. Some of these creditors of Arcot, after advancing a part of their gains and profits in the 'country trade', did not hesitate to borrow themselves from Indian bankers and usurers to meet the demands of the *nawab*. Their fortune henceforth hinged on that of the latter.

Yet, in 1776, Muhammad Ali invaded the lands of the rajah of Tanjore without any other justification than the need for fresh resources. The Governor of Madras, Pigot, immediately denounced this act of aggression and decided to reinstate the rajah in his rights. He was then disowned by the majority of his Council, within which the group of creditors led by the architect Paul Benfield enjoyed considerable sympathy. Arrested, Pigot died in 1777 in captivity. The scandalous circumstances surrounding his death brought the government of the Company even more disrepute and tarnished the reputation of Warren Hastings, despite the fact that he was not involved in these events.

After falling under the control of Paul Benfield 'and company', who were impatient to cash the return on their investments in the court of Arcot, the Council of Madras incited Muhammad Ali to engage in the looting of the rich land of Mysore. Haidar Ali's response was not long in coming: in July 1780, his troops ravaged the Carnatic as far as the immediate environs of Madras. Munro, the victor at Buxar, suffered a crushing defeat and fled. He was killed soon after in Madras where he had taken refuge.

In the end of 1780 and in the beginning of 1781, the situation of the English in India seemed desperate. In the west, they were caught up in an uncertain fight against the Marathas; at the gates of their stronghold, Bengal, they had to confront the rebellion of Benares; in the South, they were assailed by an exceptional general, who, having understood that only the alliance of Hindus and Muslims could check the Company, had opened negotiations with Poona and Hyderabad. The French themselves, ousted as they were from Chandernagore and Pondicherry, emerged as a threat once again: a squadron commanded by the bailli of Suffren was announced in the Indian ocean and already an emissary of Vicomte de Souillac, governor of the Isle of France, negotiated with Haidar Ali.

Confronted with these numerous adversaries, the representatives of the Company could only count on themselves: no help could be hoped for from the home country, which was focusing its efforts on the American continent, nor from Muhammad Ali, who increasingly shared the Anglophobia of his son Umdatulumara. Warren Hastings nevertheless found the necessary resources in this time of adversity. Sir Eyre Coote, whom he sent to rescue Madras in 1780, proved equal to the occasion. With the reinforcements brought by Pearce in January 1781, he contained the army of Mysore. Simultaneously, Hastings entered into negotiations with Bhonsle and Sindhia: they resulted in May 1782 in the Treaty of Salbai, which stole the Maratha alliance from Haidar.

On the Coromandel coast, the errors made by the French and a combination of circumstances served the British interest. General Duchemin, who landed in May 1782, restricted himself to a prudent wait and see policy and Bussy, on whom the hopes of the French rested, arrived only in March 1783 after an interminable voyage. In the meanwhile, in December 1782, Haidar Ali died brutally and his son Tipu Sultan, exasperated by the French equivocation, proceeded to Malabar where a confused situation reigned. The French could not take advantage of the replacement of Eyre Coote, deceased in April 1783, by the incompetent Stuart. The negotiations opened in Europe resulted in the signature of the Treaty of Versailles in September 1783 and brought the hostilities to an end.

Despite the loss of his French allies, Tipu pursued the fight until the beginning of 1784, when he seized Mangalore to the north of Malabar. The treaty that he signed in this city in March 1784, which put an end to the First Anglo-Mysore War, was so favourable to him that Warren Hastings disapproved of its terms. However, at this point in time, all danger had been averted and the Company was at peace with all the Indian powers. On the other hand, it was far from having established its ascendancy in South India.

The primary consequence of these events was a radical reorganization of British India and the departure of Warren Hastings. The *India Act* of 1784, adopted by the Parliament on the initiative of Pitt, transferred the greater part of the power of decision from the Court of Directors of the East India Company to a 'Board of Control' that functioned under the authority of the Crown and consisted of three to six members. Its first President, Henry Dundas, would remain in office for eighteen years. The Board could send to India confidential orders through the intermediary of a 'Secret Committee' of not more than three members. These orders related to declarations of war and peace negotiations as well as to all issues concerning relations with Indian princes, matters that largely escaped the jurisdiction of the authorities of the three presidencies. Deprived of a part of their attributions, the directors nonetheless retained, in addition to the management of commercial affairs, the authority to appoint to civil, military and judicial positions. They continued above all to designate the governors of the Presidencies of Bombay and Madras, as well as the Governor-General. However, the Crown, on the advice of the president of the Board of Control, could recall all persons in the service of the Company, including the Governor-General. The latter, whose authority over the governors of Madras and Bombay was re-affirmed, could also command the army and had the freedom to disregard the opinions of his Council.

This reorganization was followed by the departure of Warren Hastings in 1785. Accused, in particular by Edmund Burke, of having emptied the coffers of the Treasury and of having extorted considerable sums from the rulers of Benares and Oudh, he answered his detractors: 'I extended your dominion and gave it form and consistency. I protected it. I sent, with efficacy and economy, its armies across regions unknown and hostile in order give assistance to your other possessions; I gave you every thing and you have rewarded me with confiscation, disgrace and impeachment.'

The successor of Hastings was the Marquis Cornwallis, who had met with defeat at Yorktown at the hands of the American insurgents. This soldier could not nurse the hope of restoring in the battlefields of India his image tarnished in America. The *India Act* reiterated in effect that all plans of conquest and territorial expansion would be adverse to the wishes, honour and policies of Great Britain. Chosen by the directors for his profound integrity, Cornwallis was assigned the task of stabilizing the financial situation in India and of implementing the fiscal reforms that his predecessor could not put into effect.

The establishment of British ascendancy in South India (1790–1801)

The treaty of 1784 was followed by a period of relative peace in South India. A precarious balance had been struck between the Marathas, Mysore, Hyderabad and the East India Company. Tipu took advantage of this respite to consolidate his force against his rivals. A war with the Marathas ended with the Treaty of Gajendragarh (February 1787), which maintained the status quo. But the confrontation had weakened the two Indian states, tilting the balance in favour of the Company, which was biding its time.

The pretext for the second war against Tipu was an attack of the latter against the Hindu Kingdom of Travancore, a state on the Malabar coast, which maintained good relations with the Company. The Company enjoyed the support of the Marathas and of the *nizam* of Hyderabad, both of whom were anxious about the expansionism of Mysore. Faced with such a coalition, Tipu owed his survival only to the rapidity of manoeuvre of his cavalry, which enabled him to thwart the first offensive launched by Cornwallis against Seringapatnam in 1791. But the Governor-General returned the following year with additional forces and Tipu, who found himself in a difficult position, was driven to accept his terms. Cornwallis did not seek to annex Mysore, but to weaken it. Tipu was then forced to cede almost half of his territories, which were shared among the Company and its two allies, the *nizam* and the Marathas. The Company received a certain number of districts to the east of Mysore bordering the Carnatic, as well as the northern part of Malabar, rich in spices. Its position in South India was thereby reinforced, all the more so as in the wake of the conflict, it was in a position to impose a treaty of subsidiary alliance on the rajah of Cochin, the state situated to the north of Travancore. Nevertheless, the Marathas used the defeat of Tipu to extend their power and the Company still had to reckon with them. As regards Tipu, his dreams of expansion had been shattered forever; he had to withdraw to the heart of his kingdom. He ceased to pose a real threat to the Company, but his name continued to provoke terror, which was to prove fatal to him.

In the course of the following five years, under the governorship of Sir John Shore, the Company returned to its traditional policy of giving priority to diplomacy over warfare. A treaty of alliance was concluded in 1795 with Travancore, which definitively placed this state within the sphere of influence of the British. The only episode of belligerence was a direct consequence of the conflicts that were taking place then in Europe: as Holland found itself allied with revolutionary France, an army from Madras embarked in 1795 on the occupation of Dutch possessions in the Island of Ceylon, at the very time when an expedition from Britain seized the Cape, a crucial step on the route to India. Even when a conflict broke out, in 1795, between the Marathas and the *nizam*, an ally of the Company, Shore chose to remain neutral. The *nizam* was defeated and had to cede to the Marathas a part of its territories. However, the aggravation of internecine dissensions among the Marathas, subsequent to the accession of Baji Rao II to the throne of Poona in 1796, limited the consequences of this victory, which could have weakened the Company.

The situation appeared to have relatively stabilized in 1798, when Shore was succeeded by the flamboyant Richard Wellesley, who, more than Clive, merits the title of conqueror of India. This aristocrat, an ardent counter-revolutionary, arrived in India at the age of thirty-eight after a political career that had led him in 1793 to the Board of Control of the East India Company, where he established close relations with the president, Henry Dundas, and with William Pitt the younger. The two men sent him to India in 1798 not ignoring that he was resolved to break away from Shore's inertia and to make the Company the dominant power in the subcontinent. To bring this plan to fruition, Wellesley had considerable astuteness and determination, all the more as he enjoyed the support of a circle of equally determined counsellors, among whom figured his two brothers Henry and Arthur (who was none other than the future Duke of Wellington, the victor of Napoleon).

The first victim of the new Governor-General was Tipu, who no longer represented a true danger, but of whom he decided to make an example. The necessary *casus belli* presented itself in the form of a document that seemed to indicate the existence of contacts between the sovereign of Mysore and the French authorities of the island of Mauritius (Isle de France).

England was then at war with revolutionary France allied with Holland and Spain, and its only European ally, Austria, had just been defeated by Bonaparte; mutinies broke out in the English fleet, that were imputed to a 'Jacobin' conspiracy. In this climate of crisis, accusing Tipu of collusion with the French (an accusation against which he protested) was tantamount to condemning him in the eyes of the British government, which was particularly apprehensive about Bonaparte's expedition in Egypt, since it seemed to imply designs on India. Their traditional reticence regarding a policy of annexation was consequently swept aside. Wellesley gradually began to close in on Tipu, leaving him no way out. He started by renewing the treaty of alliance with the *nizam* and convinced the latter to get rid off a few battalions of his troops commanded by French officers and to replace them with troops of the Company. In February 1799, he girded himself for action and an army of 40,000 men marched on Seringapatnam. Tipu tried courageously to resist but the fortress fell on 5 May and the ruler, true to his legend, preferred death to capitulation. In a letter to the directors of the Company, Wellesley did not hide the fact that he expected that the fate of Tipu would be 'a salutary lesson for the Indian princes'.[3]

After the death of Tipu, Mysore was divided into three: the former Hindu dynasty was re-established in the central region, the heart of the kingdom until 1761, but this reconstituted Mysore was a vassal state of the Company, which directly annexed

Canara, the coastal region situated immediately to the north of Malabar, as well as the southern districts situated around Coimbatore; certain territories of the north-east were ceded to the *nizam* of Hyderabad. But the following year the *nizam* had to restore them to the Company, in addition to the territories he had acquired from Mysore in 1792. By virtue of a new treaty, the Company took control of the foreign affairs of Hyderabad; in return, it granted the *nizam* the guarantee of its protection and gave up the annual subsidy paid by the latter towards the maintenance of British forces stationed in his territory. Also in 1799, the small Hindu kingdom of Tanjore was placed under the protection of the Company. Lastly, in 1801, the Carnatic, controlled de facto since 1781, was annexed under the pretext of a secret collusion between the *nawab* and Tipu. The Company's domination in South India was total from then on.

Having reached his objectives in the south, Wellesley turned his attention towards the north of the subcontinent, where the situation was particularly favourable to English intrigues.

The second Maratha expansion in North India: Mahaji Sindhia's hour of glory (1784–94)

The Maratha chief Mahaji Sindhia had taken advantage of the civil war that had been ravaging the heart of the former Mogul Empire to force the emperor Shah Alam to grant him in November 1784 the title of plenipotentiary regent (*wakil-i-mutlaq*). Sindhia had become the holder of authority with the emperor a docile instrument in his hands. However, power without resources was nothing. The principal feudal lords of the emperor, in particular the rajah of Jaipur, refused to pay him tribute. Sindhia launched an expedition against the Rajput state, but could not obtain the results he had hoped for: after an indecisive engagement at Lalsot between the Maratha and Rajput forces, he withdrew. Then followed an eclipse of Maratha power in the north of India for one year, a period of anarchy and chaos. At last, on 17 June 1788, Sindhia re-established his supremacy by his victory over Ismail Beg, a Mogul noble who had attempted to fight the Marathas. The Afghan chief Ghulam Qadir, Ismail Beg's ally, took over Delhi and terrorized the imperial court: he deposed Shah Alam and blinded him, then established in his place a puppet. But his bloody excesses soon became wearisome: on 2 October, the forces of Sindhia occupied Delhi and reinstated Shah Alam on the throne.

Even though Mahaji Sindhia had once again become the strong man of North India, he encountered numerous obstacles; the major threat came from the inside. Tukaji Holkar, the Maratha prince of Indore, encouraged underhandedly by the *peshwa*'s minister, Nana Fadnavis, did everything to bring about his fall and the Rajputs continued to obstinately defy him. Sindhia despatched De Boigne to crush the forces of Jaipur at Patan (20 June 1790) and those of Marwar (another Rajput state) at Merta (10 September): the Savoyard general showed in these battles the true worth of his talent as a strategist, and Rajasthan was once again brought into sub-mission. Despite all his efforts, Sindhia could not arrive at a compromise with Holkar. The latter was defeated by De Boigne in the Battle of Lakheri (1 June 1793).

Sindhia seemed to have asserted himself once again as the master of North India, but he had exhausted all his strength and his death, at the beginning of 1794, jeopardized all his achievements.

In fact, the foundations of Maratha domination in North India were extremely fragile.[4] They would not survive the death of Mahaji Sindhia.

Anarchy in North India and the emergence of Jaswant Rao Holkar (1794–1802)

After the death of Mahaji and of the *peshwa* Madhav Rao (October 1795), a complex situation emerged in North India. The heir of Mahaji, Daulat Rao Sindhia, rapidly succeeded in consolidating his ascendancy over the feeble successor of Madhav, Baji Rao, but he came up against the opposition of the widows of Mahaji. On the other hand, the departure of General De Boigne in January 1796 and his replacement by the mediocre and scheming Frenchman Perron considerably weakened the army of Sindhia. The latter did not fully support his viceroy in North India, the honest Lakhwa Dada, and preferred to rely on Perron.

The meteoric rise of Jaswant Rao Holkar took place against this confused backdrop. After the death of Tukaji Holkar, his father, in August 1797, he led the life of a fugitive, before crowning himself the sovereign of Indore in June 1799. He then took the side of the widows against Daulat Rao Sindhia by forming an alliance with Lakhwa Dada. Thereafter, he changed sides and abandoned Lakhwa to confront Perron alone. The champion of the widows was defeated by the Frenchman at Seondha in May 1801. But, Jaswant Rao then turned against his short-lived ally Daulat Rao Sindhia. The *peshwa* having taken Sindhia's side, it was the entire Maratha camp that was to soon plunge into a civil war. After several successes, Holkar suffered defeat in front of Indore at the hands of Sindhia's generals (14 October 1801). Giving up open confrontations, he launched guerrilla operations, moving with great rapidity from one place to another. In May 1802, he embarked on the invasion of the Deccan; the decisive battle took place near Poona on 25 October 1802: the combined forces of the *peshwa* and Sindhia were defeated by Holkar.

This Maratha civil war left the country devastated and favoured the enterprises of the British. The fruit was ripe: Wellesley had but to pick it. What is more, Perron, appointed chief general of the armies of Sindhia, had only one plan in mind: to betray at the right time so that he could enjoy his fortune.

In the meanwhile, the Governor-General used the threat of the establishment of a 'French State' on the banks of the Jamuna to convince the authorities in London about the necessity for a decisive action. He intensified the pressure on Oudh, the *nawab* had to accept, in February 1800, the demobilization of his army and an increase in British military staff in his territory. In November 1801, he was forced to cede the richest region, Rohilkhand and a part of the Doab (which bordered Maratha territories) to the Company. Wellesley would have wished to annex the whole of Oudh, but he had to curb his ambitions. The position of the Company in North India was nevertheless considerably reinforced by this annexation.

Wellesley's insatiable craving for territories started to cause serious concern amid the authorities in London. This did not preclude the impetuous proconsul from pursuing his expansionist policy. A confrontation with the Marathas, the last important native power had become inevitable. The Maratha civil war offered him the pretext anticipated: the *peshwa*, driven out of Poona, accepted by the Treaty of Bassein to come under the protection of the Company. He was re-established on his throne by the troops of the Company under the command of Arthur Wellesley.

The Second Maratha War

The Second Maratha War broke out in 1803: only Sindhia and the rajah of Berar proceeded to meet the British in battle. The war took place on two fronts: in the Deccan, where the forces of Sindhia were defeated at Assaye by Arthur Wellesley, at the cost of heavy losses, and those of the rajah of Berar at Argaon; in North India, where the bulk of Sindhia's forces, commanded by Perron, confronted the *sepoys* of the formidable General Lake. The latter inflicted a severe defeat on Perron's army at Koil on 29 August 1803 and captured the powerful fortifications of Aligarh on 4 September, which led to the capitulation of Perron, who had only been eagerly expecting this occasion to abandon the lost cause of the Marathas. Thereafter, on 11 September, Lake defeated Perron's lieutenant, Bourquien, before Delhi and on 16 September, Shah Alam placed himself under British protection.

The final clash took place at Laswari, where the army created by General De Boigne was definitively wiped out by Lake at the cost of heavy losses. This victory was decisive: the two Maratha chiefs had to accept Wellesley's terms. British residents established themselves in their capitals and they ceded large territories to the Company. The Company thus acquired Orissa from Berar, which enabled it to connect its possessions in Bengal with those in Madras, and from Sindhia, Delhi and Agra, as well as Gujarat and a part of the Deccan. With the fall of Delhi, it was the Mogul emperor, a figure without effective power but whose symbolic role remained considerable, who came under the protection of the Company.

Wellesley's victory was nevertheless not total, since Holkar was still undefeated. An attempt to begin negotiations failed and the war resumed in April 1804. The British General Monson was defeated at Kotah, Holkar laid siege to Delhi, while Lake failed to take the strategic position of Bharatpur. These failures were exploited by Wellesley's opponents in London who obtained his recall.

Even though he did not achieve his objective of controlling the whole of India, Wellesley had come close to it. In the space of a few years, the extent of the direct possessions of the Company had doubled and numerous Indian states had been forced to accept treaties of subsidiary alliances that created de facto protectorates.

Sikhs and Gurkhas

The Company was not the only power in the subcontinent to experience territorial expansion. In North India, two states in particular, the Sikh kingdom of the Punjab and the kingdom of Nepal, were also on a course of rapid expansion. In the Punjab, Ranjit Singh, whose father, at the head of *misl* of the Sukurcharias, had become the most powerful chief of the region, took advantage of the decline of the Durrani empire of Afghanistan to gain recognition, in 1799, of his claims on Lahore. At war against other Sikh chiefs, he invested in 1802 the holy city of Amritsar and in 1805, he was recognized by most of the Sikh chiefs as the legitimate sovereign of the Punjab. Even though he was supported primarily by the members of the sect, he had the wisdom to resist the extremists, the Akalis, who were seeking to establish a theocracy. The Sikhs represented not more than ten per cent of population of the province, in which the peasantry was in majority Muslim, while Hindus formed the largest part of the urban population. Therefore, Ranjit Singh always took great care to associate as much as possible Hindu and Muslim notables in the administration of the affairs of the state and also mitigated the burden of land taxes. This policy contributed powerfully to the stability of his regime and to the relative prosperity of the province. Yet, since the capture of Delhi in 1803, the Company was directly interested in the political developments in the Punjab and a sort of informal alliance was concluded with Ranjit Singh. For the British, a strong power in Punjab represented a buttress against a possible French threat, via Persia and Afghanistan.

While the Sikhs were consolidating their power, the kings of Nepal, from the valley of Kathmandu, extended their domination to embrace the numerous small principalities of the Himalayan region.

An interlude of ten years (1804–14)

Wellesley's successors – for some months an aged Cornwallis, then the insignificant Barlow and lastly Lord Minto (1807–13) – exerted themselves above all to consolidate their gains. The policy of expansion at all costs was therefore suspended for some years. But the British had the good fortune of getting rid of their most dangerous adversary, Holkar, without having to fire a single shot. The formidable Maratha chief, whose mental condition worsened from 1808 on, died in 1811, and his successor proved to be incompetent.

The only territorial advance happened in the Punjab: a crisis broke out in 1808 between Ranjit Singh and the Company regarding the fate of a certain number of principalities situated on the southern side of the Sutlej river. A conflict seemed imminent but Ranjit Singh backed out and, by the Treaty of Amritsar in 1809, recognized the protectorate of the British in this region. The Sutlej was to form the frontier between the Punjab and British India for more than thirty years. Ranjit Singh, blocked in the east, continued his conquests towards the North and the West: after several campaigns in the mountainous region of the Punjab, he occupied Jammu in 1812, and the strategic crossing point of Attock, on the Indus, in 1813. Multan, in the confines of Sind, fell into his hands in 1818, then he headed towards Kashmir, which he snatched definitively from the Afghans in 1819. This great conqueror built a formidable empire in the northwest of India, without ever suspecting that he was working for the Company.

The authorities of Calcutta were more active outside India, and the country contributed to Britain's fight against Napoleon and his allies: in 1810, Indian troops invested the Dutch possessions of Ambonya and the Moluccas, in the East Indian

Spice Islands, as well as French islands like Reunion and Mauritius; the following year, the island of Java was occupied. Thus was established the role of India as England's base of operations in Asia and in the Indian Ocean.

The Third Maratha War and the definitive establishment of British supremacy (1814–18)

The arrival of Lord Hastings as governor (1813–22), which coincided more or less with the end of the Napoleonic wars in Europe, marked the return to a more expansionist policy in India itself. In 1814, a cross-border conflict with the rulers of Nepal became a veritable war and enabled the Company to stabilize the northern frontier of its territories by the annexation of a part of the Himalayas. After two years of warfare that was sometimes difficult, the Hindu kingdom of the Himalayas had to sign a treaty by which it ceded to the Company Kumaon and Gahrwal, and accepted the presence of an English resident at his court. Nepal, subjected from 1846 onwards to the domination of the Ranas, was to serve as a buffer state between China and India and to provide the English with the famous *gurkha* regiments, the jewel of the armies of India.

However, Hastings's main preoccupation was central India, where bands of marauders, the Pindaris, had unleashed a reign of widespread insecurity and conducted increasingly audacious raids in the territories of the Company, as the Maratha princes were unable to control them. An extermination campaign was launched against them in 1817: they were to be sandwiched between two armies from the north and the south. The Company demanded the cooperation of the Maratha princes: Sindhia had to provide troops and Baji Rao to sign a new treaty, with terms humiliating for him (June 1817). However, the *peshwa* attempted to take advantage of the initial difficulties encountered by the English in their campaign and in November, the English residence at Poona was attacked. This was more an act of despair than a rational decision: the troops of the Company promptly recaptured the city, while Baji Rao fled. The rajah of Berar attempted the same thing in Nagpur but failed in his turn. The only important engagement of this Third Maratha War occurred between the British and the forces of Holkar, which were easily defeated. The operations against the Pindaris continued without difficulty. There remained only the *peshwa*: he was captured in June 1818.

The campaign ended in complete success: the Pindari bands had been destroyed, the Marathas no longer existed as a politico-military force and the Company annexed a large part of their territories, including almost all territories of the *peshwa* and a part of those belonging to Holkar and to the rajah of Berar. What remained of the Maratha states – Baroda, Gwalior, Indore, Satara and a few small principalities – was controlled through treaties of subsidiary alliance. Furthermore, in the wake of the collapse of the Marathas, the representative of the Company at Delhi, Sir Charles Metcalfe, succeeded in persuading the principal Rajput states to conclude treaties of alliance. The Company had no more rivals in the subcontinent. The only important Indian state that it did not control was the Punjab, but it was situated at the periphery and in any case, its relations with the Company were amicable. In less than thirty years, almost the whole of India had fallen under the control of the East India Company, which itself was increasingly becoming a direct emanation of the British government.

Without having really desired it, Great Britain found itself at the head of an immense empire in Asia. This conquest had not cost a single penny to the British taxpayer, since it was financed firstly by the revenues of Bengal, thereafter, with the victories won, by those of other territories. The Company had to put in place an efficient system of administration for so vast a domain. Should it apply to the entire country the system adopted in Bengal? This question would give rise to contradictory answers. However, more and more, the very existence of the Company would be called into question. The East India Company was to survive for forty years more: four decades, which would be a period of transition towards the British Indian Empire in its 'classical' form. Before that, the great revolt of 1857 came dangerously close to bringing everything down.

PART FOUR

INDIA IN TRANSITION

(from the end of the eighteenth century to
the middle of the nineteenth century)

Between 1818 and 1857, the East India Company put a state in place. Relations between this state and Indian society were far from harmonious, leading to a crisis in its legitimacy, which culminated in 1857 in widespread revolt. This so-called Sepoy Revolt almost put an end to British rule. But eventually it only modified its form: the Company was abolished and India passed directly under the Crown (Chapter XV).

In the first half of the nineteenth century, society and economy underwent several transformations, but the changes did not follow the calendar of political events. In the villages, the agrarian economy showed a certain dynamism, owing to a demographic growth that was fairly constant, though limited in magnitude. While no technological innovation had been introduced by the conquest, the period witnessed an expansion in the cultivated area and a development of commercial crops, such as cotton or indigo. The impact of English colonization was especially obvious in the area of production relations, with the attempt at the stabilization of land ownership as embodied in the permanent settlement in Bengal. The zamindars, those intermediaries between state and peasant, became landowners with full rights, and the tax amount that they must pay the state was fixed once and for all. For all this, an endemic agrarian agitation kept brewing; it was to culminate in the great revolt of 1857 (Chapter XVI).

Trade hardly progressed, but British businessmen seized control of financial and commercial circuits: the long-term consequences of this domination would be considerable. For the time being, the non-agricultural economy experienced only a very modest growth and cities, with the exception of port-cities like Bombay or Calcutta, developed only slowly (Chapter XVII).

This half-century witnessed significant cultural transformations, in which religious questions played an increasingly important role, as Hindus and Muslims were confronted with the colonial challenge and the preaching of Christian missionaries. It was also during this time that orientalism was born and that vernacular literatures flourished (Chapter XVIII).

XV

THE BEGINNINGS OF THE RAJ

(1818–58)

Even though the East India Company remained in theory the ruler of India (while hiding behind the ambiguous fiction of the continuation of the Mogul Empire) and despite the fact that the British Crown was not officially involved in Indian affairs, we can speak of a British Indian Empire from 1818 onwards. Comparable to the Russian and Chinese empires, it was without doubt the foremost political construction of the nineteenth century. In the course of the four decades that followed the defeat of the Marathas, the English extended the boundaries of this empire. Above all, they established and consolidated an administrative system and a judicial-legal framework, which were to endure until 1947 and even thereafter.

The consolidation of British India from 1818 to 1857

In 1818, in the wake of the defeat of the Marathas, no native power represented a threat for the Company any longer, but the situation that reigned in the confines of India in those zones that escaped British control caused apprehension among the rulers in Calcutta. In the northwest, the traditional route for invasions, the English feared a possible advance of Russia towards Central Asia. In the northeast, the expansion of Burma forced the Company to interfere actively. Between 1818 and 1857, the Company therefore found itself embroiled in several conflicts in these peripheral regions. From 1840 onwards, Calcutta changed its attitude towards the Indian princes and annexed a certain number of protected states. Thus, the political map of India would be redrawn.

The Burmese War and the Afghan expedition

The conflict between the Company and the Burmese kingdom appears as rather a marginal episode in the history of the subcontinent, but it resulted in the annexation of the entire northeast of India, in particular Assam, which was to play an important role in the colonial economy. The roots for this conflict reside in the expansionist policy of Burma at the close of the eighteenth century, exemplified by the conquest of an independent kingdom, Arakan, a neighbour of Bengal, in 1784. Thirty years later, the Burmese annexed the small Hindu kingdom of Manipur (1813), and thereafter in 1818, obtained the recognition of their suzerainty over Assam, the ancient Ahom kingdom conquered by the Moguls at the end of the sixteenth century. With these turbulent neighbours, border skirmishes were not long in flaring up.

The advance of the Burmese troops from Manipur towards Cachar, a principality allied to the Company, was the pretext for the First Burmese War (1824–26). The operations took place on several fronts and the English suffered heavy casualties; the expeditionary corps that landed at Rangoon was decimated by illnesses and did not gain any decisive success, but the Burmese, under pressure from all sides, ended up by accepting the English terms. Burma renounced all its claims on Assam, Manipur and Cachar and ceded to the Company the coastal provinces of Arakan and Tenasserim. It also had to pay a huge indemnity, to accept an English resident at its court and to conclude a commercial treaty. This war, in which the territorial gains appeared limited, was the first of several to come. The age of easy conquests of rich territories had ended.

Assam was annexed little by little because the Company did not have any clear policy regarding this territory with which it was rather unfamiliar: the conquest was completed only in 1838. Cachar was annexed as early as 1832, the rajah having died without any heir. The territories of the Jaintia and Khasi tribes were also placed under the protection of the Company. The British possessions therefore embraced the entire northeast.

Unfortunate strategic considerations triggered the disastrous Afghan expedition in 1842. This military operation was motivated by a fear of a Russian expansion across Central Asia towards India which was widespread in certain Whig circles. The failure of an English diplomatic mission sent to the ruler of Afghanistan, Dost Muhammad, raised the fear of Russian domination and the Governor-General Lord Auckland (1836–42) was led to grant his support to the claims of the former ruler Shah Shujah, overthrown in 1810, who had found refuge in the Punjab at the court of Ranjit Singh. Allying himself with the latter, Lord Auckland organized an expedition to restore Shah Shujah to the throne of Kabul. His advisors, underestimating the difficulties of an expedition in mountainous terrain as well as the military capacity of the Afghan tribes, had imagined that it would be just a pleasure trip.

Nevertheless, the campaign started rather well: on the approach of the British troops, Dost Muhammad fled from Kabul and Shah Shujah acceded again to the throne. Even though the objective of the expedition had apparently been attained, it was decided to leave behind a garrison of nearly ten thousand men of the Bengal army in Afghanistan. Thus, the Company found itself forced to maintain substantial forces far from their bases and with unreliable means of communication. But, the presence of a foreign army of occupation became increasingly offensive to the Afghans. The British soon had to face a general insurrection and decided to withdraw. This retreat degenerated into a rout, only a few survivors crossed the Khyber Pass to announce it. Even though a punitive expedition was thereafter despatched by the successor of Auckland, Lord Ellenborough, to avenge this defeat, it withdrew quite speedily after seizing Kabul and inflicting severe reprisals. The overall outcome of the First Afghan War was calamitous: human and financial losses were considerable and the morale of the Indian army was seriously shaken.

This disastrous adventure directly resulted in the annexation of Sind in 1843 on the initiative of Sir Charles Napier, who forced the hand of the Company with the complicity of Ellenborough. This province, for a long time subject to Islamic influences and governed since the end of the eighteenth century by the dynasty of the *mirs* of Talpur, had attracted the attention of the British who overestimated the commercial possibilities offered by the navigation on the Indus. This was in fact a poor territory, inhabited by a turbulent population.

The Sikh Wars

The annexation of Sind intensified the involvement of the Company in the affairs of the Punjab. In the course of the last twenty years of his reign, Ranjit Singh had succeeded in creating a European-type army with the help of experts like the Frenchman Court and the Italians Ventura and Avitabile, all of whom were veterans of the Napoleonic wars, and had used it to advance towards the Khyber Pass, annexing Peshawar to his kingdom in 1834. His feudatory lord Gulab Singh, from his fief in Jammu, had extended Sikh domination into the heart of the Himalayas, bringing Tibetan Ladakh to submission in 1835. But in his attempts to make inroads into Sind, Ranjit Singh came up against the resistance of the Company, which wanted to secure its control over navigation on the Indus, and in 1839, despite his reticence, he had to lend assistance to the expedition towards Kabul. His death the same year triggered an acute crisis in a state that, despite its territorial expansion, or because of it, remained fragile. Complicated struggles for succession, marked by the bloody palace revolutions of 1841 and 1843, gave rise to a state of almost complete chaos in 1844.

Yet, the prolonged instability of the Punjab – a rich agricultural region occupying a strategic position halfway between the Khyber Pass and Delhi – inevitably had an effect on British India. The new Governor-General, Lord Hardinge (1844–8), rapidly won over to the idea of a direct military intervention, began to mobilize troops on the frontier of the Sutlej River. One of the factions of the court of Lahore made contact with the British and, with its help, the Sikh state was projected as the aggressor. The Sikhs themselves crossed the Sutlej on 11 December 1845; two days later, Hardinge declared war against them.

The Sikh army was a formidable adversary and the conflict was bloody. According to a contemporary observer, the Sikh army was composed of around 70,000 regular troops, of which 13,000 belonged to the cavalry, in addition to about 40,000 irregular soldiers; it possessed nearly 800 pieces of artillery. The regular troops received a relatively high salary and even though their discipline left much to be desired and their locally manufactured guns were of inferior quality in comparison with the guns used by the *sepoys* of the East India Company, they were capable of well-coordinated movements. They showed great courage in combat, all the more so as they fought for their land, unlike a number of Indian armies composed of recruits from different regions, and for their religion. But the treason of two of the principal military chiefs considerably facilitated the task of the British.

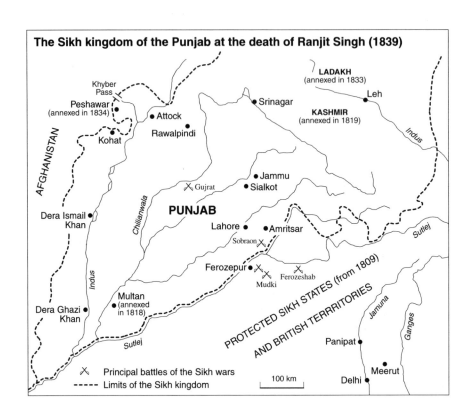

The Sikh kingdom of the Punjab at the death of Ranjit Singh (1839)

LADAKH
(annexed in 1833)

Khyber
Pass

Peshawar
(annexed in 1834)

Leh

● Srinagar

KASHMIR
(annexed in 1819)

● Attock

AFGHANISTAN

Kohat ●

● Rawalpindi

Indus

✕ Gujrat

● Jammu
● Sialkot

Dera Ismail ●
Khan

PUNJAB

Chilianwala

Lahore ●

● Amritsar

Indus

Sobraon ✕

Ferozepur ● ✕ ✕
Mudki

✕
Ferozeshab

Multan
● (annexed
in 1818)

PROTECTED SIKH STATES (from 1809)

Sutlej

Dera Ghazi ●
Khan

AND BRITISH TERRITORIES

Jamuna

Ganges

Sutlej

Panipat ●

● Meerut

Delhi ●

✕   Principal battles of the Sikh wars

- - - -   Limits of the Sikh kingdom

100 km

After a first indecisive engagement at Mudki, the Battle of Pherushahr in December 1845, resulted in a partial victory for the British, who suffered considerable losses: 2,400 killed and wounded (including 1,600 British and 800 Indian *sepoys*) of a total of 17,000 men. A second victory at Sobraon, in February 1846, equally costly in terms of human loss, was more decisive. The route to Lahore lay open to the British, but the Governor-General preferred to negotiate. Part of the Punjab was annexed directly by the Company while Kashmir was attached to Jammu to form a semi-independent state under the leadership of Gulab Singh, who had helped the British in their campaign. The rest of the State of Punjab retained its independence; not, however, for long.

A British resident, Henry Lawrence, settled in Lahore, was in charge of controlling the administration with a view to ensuring that the indemnity owed to the Company would be duly settled. This energetic man, who subsequently played a significant role, acted like a governor. The days of the Sikh state seemed numbered. All the more so as the new governor-general, Lord Dalhousie, who succeeded Lord Hardinge in 1848, was of the same stuff as Wellesley, an imperial aristocrat convinced of the superiority of the British system and contemptuous towards Indians. He soon found an opportunity for translating his ideas into practice, when an incident in a peripheral province of the Punjab, in the course of which some British officers were killed, degenerated into the second Anglo-Sikh War.

Dalhousie did not hide his intention to teach the Sikhs a severe lesson and an army advanced into Punjabi territory. The British forces first met with a defeat at Ramnagar, on 22 November 1848. Another engagement, at Chillianwalla, claimed from the British camp nearly 3,000 killed and wounded (14 January 1849) and ended without a clear outcome. The decisive battle took place at Gujarat on 21 February: in the face of the firepower of the British artillery, the Sikhs had to retreat. On 14 March, they capitulated. Dalhousie, opposed to the policy of conciliation with the Sikhs recommended by the resident, annexed what remained of the Sikh state. Henry Lawrence nevertheless remained in place, but as a member of the 'council of three', which also included his brother John, who was more hostile towards the Sikhs. This council succeeded rapidly in equipping the province with an efficient administration and undertook large-scale works, of irrigation in particular. The Punjab was to become, in the course of the following period, the granary of India. During the revolt of 1857, it would serve as the base for the reconquest of North India by the British.

The Sikh wars were unquestionably the bloodiest of all the wars of colonial conquest and never, since Tipu, the sultan of Mysore, had the British encountered so great a resistance. However, once it was conquered, the Punjab proved to be on the whole loyal towards British authorities. From a strategic point of view, the annexation resulted in pushing back the frontier to the foot of the Khyber.

The Second Burmese War and the annexation
of Indian princely states

After a few years of peace, a new conflict broke out with Burma in 1852. Once again, the Indian army crossed the sea and after a rather brief campaign, annexed lower Burma. In the course of the second half of the century, this region would become a rice bowl for India.

Dalhousie also annexed several princely states without firing a single canon shot. The new governor had instituted the ingenious *doctrine of lapse*, according to which, should a ruler bound to the East India Company by a treaty (as they were all now) die without a male heir, his territory would be annexed by the Company. Formerly, the custom was to hastily adopt a boy, a practice sanctioned by the Hindu religion, but which Dalhousie prohibited in this precise case. Thanks to the application of this providential doctrine, several Indian states fell into the hands of the Company: Satara, a small Maratha principality, which was all that remained of the former territories of the *peshwa*; Nagpur, also in Maratha country; Jhansi, in Bundelkhand; Tanjore, in South India. This policy culminated in the annexation, in 1856, of Oudh, the most important surviving state in North India. This act, the last under the governorship of Dalhousie, provoked a great outrage in the entire country and was one of the causes of the revolt of 1857.

Nevertheless, in 1857, at the time of the departure of Dalhousie, the country appeared calm and British domination more solidly established than ever before. The state into which the Company had transformed itself seemed to be a durable political construction. It was referred to by the Anglo-Indian term Raj (literally: 'rule').

The rule of the East India Company: The beginning of the Company Raj

After the abolition, in 1813, of its commercial monopoly, already in fact diminished, the East India Company found itself confined to its political, administrative and military functions (its principal commercial function remained the lucrative commerce with China that it lost only in 1833). Increasingly, it appeared as just a facade behind which loomed the British government and Parliament. Because the Board of Control of the Company was in fact a sort of ministry and its president generally an influential politician, there was a fairly rapid rotation in this post in tune with the changes in the government in London. Rotation was also quite rapid in the post of governor-general – in forty years eight men had assumed this office. Nevertheless, the enormous distance that separated Calcutta from London, before the era of the telegraph and the piercing of the Suez Canal, conferred on the representative of London in the field a considerable leeway, which the succeeding proconsuls did not fail to use to the full.

In the wake of the reforms implemented at the close of the eighteenth century, the governor-general was also invested with a greater authority over the governors of the two other Presidencies, Madras and Bombay. He was therefore a sort of autocrat, subject during his stay in office to the distant control of London and exercising almost unlimited power, including the authority to declare war. The paradox represented by this more or less absolute monarchy, even while in the home country the Parliament was playing an increasingly important role, did not escape the attention of British observers of the period. However, India was considered a special case, a spoil of war as it were, which was not subject to the general laws of the British political system. This strange Anglo-Indian hybrid that was the Company Raj thus persisted, despite the loss of its commercial monopoly, in 1813, and despite the acerbic critics to which it became increasingly subject.

What were the characteristics of this state and to what extent did it evolve after 1813? It had taken shape in Bengal between 1765 and 1790 and the legacy of these beginnings continued to weigh on it. The Company then had objectives that were above all of a commercial nature and it was in this perspective that it envisaged extending its control over the land revenues of Bengal. The Company Raj was therefore conceived above all as a tax machine on the model of the Mogul Empire. British influence was principally manifest in the structure of the state: a patrimonial-type bureaucracy instituted by the Moguls and the *nawabi* regime progressively gave way to a bureaucracy formed of high functionaries, the covenanted civil servants, recruited by the Company in England, in principle on merit, even though, in practice, patronage played an essential role in appointments and promotions. The main differences between the Company Raj and the Indian kingdoms were that the state maintained a strict religious neutrality (in this regard it was also different from the British state), which exposed it to the criticisms of the evangelical circles in England, and that it arrogated a veritable monopoly of the use of armed force, which the Indian states had never claimed. Therefore, in the effort to achieve the goals that were those of all Indian states since the sixteenth century, it adopted methods that were on the whole more efficient. This made the Company Raj perhaps the most powerful state that India had ever known, but at the same time, the one that was the most cut off from Indian society, because the Company very rapidly sought to reduce the role of Indians in its functioning. The principal justification of this objective was their 'corruption'. We must, however, concede that from this point of view the British were no better.

The growing exclusion of Indians from all responsible positions, even if it did open up opportunities for the employment of a number of younger sons of English or Scottish families of the small nobility, had the disadvantage of largely cutting off the state from the most active elements of society, which would prove to be very dangerous. The only social group on which the Company Raj could totally rely was the British population, insignificant in number (a few thousand excluding soldiers), though rapidly growing and above all, living more and more without any contact with the outside world, isolated from the local elite classes. In fact, the state drew its support essentially from the army and the bureaucracy, the police still being at that time an embryonic institution. The army, which remained the *ultima ratio* of British rule, continued to be reinforced, but its loyalty posed a problem. As regards the administration, its control was largely sufficient to ensure the regular collection of land revenue, which still constituted the financial base of the state.

The crucial role of the army, which has led certain historians to consider the Company Raj as a military despotism, was above all the corollary of the weak links that bound the state with society. The loyalty of the local elites, which had not been secured by any mechanism comparable to those to which the Moguls had resorted (matrimonial alliances with the princely lineages, honours conferred on local notables, participation in military campaigns), rested in the last analysis on the conviction that the British Raj possessed an invincible military force. This invincibility had to be demonstrated at regular intervals, which explains the frequent use of the army in functions that fell rather under the purview of the police (the latter being not very efficient). The army thus intervened not only in the numerous 'border' conflicts with the neighbours of British India (Sikhs of the Punjab, Burmese, Afghans) but it was also systematically resorted to in the suppression of recalcitrant forces at work inside the country ('tribal' uprisings in certain regions), and was even present to prevent any reaction to such and such *fiat* of the Company (as the entry of its troops in Oudh in 1856, even though there were no troubles).

Nevertheless, this army on which the British rulers relied and which swallowed nearly half of the budget expenses was the source of many a worry. Mutinies broke out as early as the beginning of the nineteenth century – the most serious of these occurred in Vellore in 1806 and in Barrackpur in 1824 – and at regular intervals, the high command became apprehensive about the loyalty of the *sepoys*. It was the Bengal army, by far the biggest of the three armies of the Company, that caused the greatest anxiety. Recruited, as we have seen, from among the Brahmins and the Rajputs of North India, from Oudh in particular, it was very sensitive to anything that appeared to undermine the Hindu religion (or Muslim religion, because it also included Muslim *sepoys*). The British officers who commanded the army (very few Indians were elevated above the grade of non-commissioned officer) showed themselves increasingly hostile to the native religions, reflecting the general change in attitude among their compatriots in India. The tension continued to mount, even as certain officers did not hesitate to try to convert recruits to Christianity.

In the face of the *sepoy* regiments, the Company could line up only a small number of European regiments, even if we take in account the royal troops placed at its disposal. All in all, it seems surprising that this army revolted only in 1857, and not earlier. The decline in the morale of the *sepoys* had become perceptible from the Afghan expedition onwards, and during the Sikh Wars, the high command had to place European regiments on the frontline, which explains the higher percentage of loss among the British troops. This latent crisis of the military institution, a cause for great anxiety for the Company Raj, was the reflection of a deeper crisis of legitimacy, which we shall discuss later.

The administration of the East India Company received contradictory assessments. In Britain, where it was often severely criticized, it was blamed for the uprising of 1857. On the other hand, it was generally considered to be much superior to the Indian administrations that had preceded it, which demonstrates the poor idea that was entertained of the latter. Recently, some historians have insisted on the fragility of its local implantation and have underlined the decisive role that the local elites continued to play in the districts. This ignores the limited nature of the goals that the Company had imparted to its administration: it wanted above all to ensure the collection of land revenue and was hardly concerned about controlling society in its totality, leaving it to the local elites to maintain order in day-to-day life.

The East India Company strove to ensure the liaison between the local level, where its intervention remained discreet, and the higher levels. The crucial echelon was that of the district, an administrative unit comparable to a French department. In Bengal, under Cornwallis, it had been decided to separate the functions of the collector from those of the judge at the district level. However, at the time of the annexation of a part of Mysore, in 1799, Munro declared himself in favour of the concurrent holding of more than one office and each district therefore had a magistrate responsible at the same time for the collection of taxes and for justice. This principle, which Munro considered more compatible with Indian practices, was adopted in most of the territories annexed in the course of the following period, thereafter extended to Bengal under the governorship of Lord William Bentinck (1828–35). The 'district magistrate', who continued to be referred to by his former name of 'collector', has therefore been sometimes described as a sort of small kinglet or as a puppet manipulated by local notables.

The reality is probably somewhere midway between these two stereotypes. The collector needed the collaboration of the local notables to ensure the collection of land revenues and had at his service an entire corps of small Indian functionaries sensitive to the pressures of local society. For all this, he was but a cog in a great administrative machinery, susceptible at any moment to be called to order by his superiors. The room for manoeuvre that he enjoyed was quite limited: his competence was in effect defined by a code of regulations, adopted in 1793, which applied to the three Presidencies. A certain number of territories annexed from 1803 onwards were nevertheless not subject to these regulations, hence their name of 'non-regulation provinces.' In these provinces, the collector was called the deputy commissioner and the officers of the army could exercise this function. The collector, who, in most of the regions, embodied the state for the rural masses, was probably not the romantic figure that some have made him out to be, but rather the local representative of an increasingly bureaucratized administration. Even though their profile tended to become standardized, these men nonetheless had different competencies, in particular a varying degree of linguistic skills. Some of them took an interest in learning the local language and showed themselves keen observers of society; others stood on the notion of cultural superiority and made no effort to understand those under their administration.

Between the district, the basic administrative unit, and the apex of the administration, represented by the central authorities in Calcutta, there existed an intermediary echelon, the province. Originally, the administrative division of British India comprised only the three Presidencies of Bengal, Madras and Bombay. But with the succession of conquests, several provinces were added such as Assam or the Punjab, the governor of which had an inferior rank compared to the governors of the Presidencies. These Presidencies enjoyed a relative autonomy with respect to Calcutta and their governors had the right to correspond directly with London. Furthermore they had their own army, distinct from that of Bengal. Nevertheless, their governors contented themselves with executing the directives of Calcutta and neither Bombay nor Madras formed rival centres of power. All the more so as most of the annexed territories were attached to Bengal and the governor-general supervised the relations with all the princely states.

In brief, despite the slowness of internal communications prior to the advent of the telegraph and the railways, British India was a relatively unified political entity. The political situation of the princely states linked to the Company by various treaties was even more diverse but the British were in a position to control them quite closely thanks to the establishment of relations with the *diwans* who were at the head of the financial administration of the different states. With the exception of Mysore, which the Company administrated directly from 1831 to 1881, these states nevertheless retained their own institutions and did not become subject to administrative reforms.

The Company Raj and Indian society

If Hindus and Muslims had distinct conceptions about politics, both communities did not envisage it as the mainspring of society. The scriptures gave a general definition of the ideal sovereign but hardly ventured any further. Hence, in practice, there existed a degree of pragmatism that, in the course of the centuries, paved the way for a certain political collaboration between Hindus and Muslims. Some key ideas were nevertheless deeply entrenched. Even though there had taken place in India, as some believe, a 'secularization' of the royal function the equivalent of which could be found in the systems that came from Central Asia with the Muslim conquerors, the king was nevertheless perceived as bound to the accomplishment of certain religious duties. For the Hindus the good ruler was the one who maintained the *dharma* (the socio-cosmic order), who protected the cows and the Brahmins, while for the Muslims he was the one who established the reign of the *shariah*. A 'secular' state, in the modern sense of the term, did not yet have a place in the mental universe of the Indian population.

Yet the Company, which was the emanation of a state the secular character of which was not very clear – the legal emancipation of Catholics in Britain occurred only in the 1820s – adopted a perfect religious neutrality with a view to averting any suspicion of favouring the Christian religion. This attitude did not allay all the fears, particularly when, under the pressure of the evangelical circles in Britain, the arrival of missionaries and the establishment of a local Anglican Church were authorized. Even though the Company had taken on itself some of the functions of religious patronage exercised by its predecessors (intervention in the administration of Hindu temples, grants for charity institutions), it was nonetheless considered rather hostile to the religions of the country. So ineffectually was the colonial state rooted in the society that it found it difficult to arouse sentiments of loyalty among the population. It was therefore a state in a perpetual legitimacy crisis, which explains why it was careful not to abolish the Mogul Empire when the British army took over Delhi in 1803. Because, by setting itself up as the protector of the Mogul emperor, following the example of the Maratha chief Sindhia, the Company hoped that part of the prestige and the legitimacy attached to the person of the emperor would reflect back onto it.

It succeeded in this attempt, at least partially, since Muslim theologians were divided on the question of whether the Muslims could or could not legally live under British rule, with always only a minority espousing the extremist position. But the lower classes, both Muslim and Hindu, persisted in seeing the Company as an impious power and increasingly suspected it of supporting the proselytizing activities of Christian missions. All the more so, as under the growing influence of the liberal doctrines of Manchester, the Company limited its intervention in the economic life, in particular in the case of famine, under the pretext that any food crisis would be better resolved by allowing the free play of market mechanisms. This policy placed the Company in direct conflict with what may be called the ideas of a 'moral economy.' For the Indian population, like for many others of the pre-industrial world, the ruler had the duty to guarantee the subsistence of his subjects and, in the event of a disaster, to come to their aid.

The Company strove to hide behind the fiction of a continuity with the Mogul Empire, but the state that it had instituted was radically different, its guiding principles as well as its mode of functioning being foreign to Indian traditions. Hence, a perpetual legitimacy crisis, which was reflected in particular in resistance taking various forms. During the colonial period, the dominant historiography underlined the beneficial effects of the *pax Britannica* and treated the phenomena of resistance as residual or marginal. If the stereotype of an appeased India won over by the positive effects of colonization no longer has currency, we should not fall into the opposite stereotype of an India in perpetual rebellion. The *pax Britannica* was indeed a reality: in comparison with the turbulent situation that reigned in numerous regions after 1730, the safety of communications had been ensured on the whole towards 1830 and no armed dissidence of significance prevented the execution of the directives of the central government.

For all this, British law and order did not effectively prevail everywhere. The existing statistics on criminality are hardly usable, but the allusions to rural criminality (*dacoity*) were constant in official correspondence. This kind of criminality was rife, especially in Central and North India. The Indian dacoits hardly resembled the 'social bandits' of Europe described by Eric Hobsbawm. Nevertheless, the persistence of the phenomenon over a long period (it has not totally disappeared to this day) reveals the limits of state control in the countryside. The urban revolts also seem to have been endemic in nature. Classic 'grain riots', revolts of artisans affected by competition from English products and agitations of a 'communal' nature (conflicts between Hindus and Muslims) were the most widespread. Among the affected cities, were Benares (1809–18, and then in the 1830s), Delhi (1833–8), but also Madras (1803, 1833, 1854). In Surat, in 1844, the rise in salt tax led to a widespread protest: a mob of thirty thousand protestors marched towards the court in order to demand from the British magistrate the annulment of the rise. This was a truly popular agitation, as the local urban elite found itself completely bypassed. The urban lower classes formed a very restless section of the population that overtly expressed anti-British sentiments.

In the absence of organized political movements, unknown in India during this period, opposition to colonial rule manifested itself through these sporadic revolts the target of which was never the colonial government itself, which was too far removed, but such and such a measure taken by the administration at the local level. The year 1857 was to reveal the true extent of the potential for revolt. In what measure did the reforms undertaken by the colonial government from the 1820s onwards contribute to the nurturing and strengthening of that potential?

The reforms and their limits

If the colonial government set limited objectives for itself and did not claim to regiment society, even less to change it, from the 1820s onwards, it became vulnerable to growing pressures from various circles in Britain that pressed it to adopt a more interventionist policy in the social sphere.

The beginning of a 'reformist' phase in the administration of the East India Company is generally linked to the person of the governor-general, Lord William Bentinck (1828–35). Bentinck was sent to India primarily to restore a financial situation compromized by the increase in military expenses due to the Burmese campaign and by the inflation of administrative expenses. By imposing severe cuts in the budgets and by downsizing the administrative staff, he succeeded in creating a surplus. But this financial restoration, accomplished largely at the expense of efficiency, was soon compromized by the resumption of military adventures at the frontiers. The 'modernizing' component in Bentinck's programme, in particular the projects aiming at the development of irrigation and the improvement of means of communication, could not be implemented owing to economic difficulties and the insufficiency of state resources. From this period remain only a few 'social' reforms, the importance of which was above all symbolic, but which, in a liberal perspective, appeared as significant progress. If these reforms testify to a change in the Company's policy of non-intervention in matters related to social life, they only had a very limited impact.

The most famous example was of course the prohibition, in 1829, of *sati*, a custom according to which widows immolated themselves on the funeral pyre of their husbands. In fact, *sati* was a practice that was not sanctioned by the scriptures, and its resurgence in Calcutta at the beginning of the nineteenth century seemed a classic case of the 'reinvention of tradition' by an elite faced with the cultural challenge of the colonial power. Its interdiction hardly changed the status of women in India. The fight against the 'thugs', this sect that indulged in the ritual sacrifices of voyagers, has become shrouded in romantic mystification, but it seems that it was a marginal custom. As for the measures taken in the field of education, that went in tandem with the replacement of Persian by English as the language of the courts in 1835, they only accelerated a trend that already existed among the elites of Bengal towards the acquisition of 'western' knowledge (the first teaching institution of the 'modern' type in India, the Hindu College, was created without any official intervention).

Other attempts to modernize the economy were made, with more success this time, in the course of the 1840s and the 1850s. The new spirit of the administration was particularly evident in tax adjustments that tended to distribute the burden more equitably by taxing poor and marginal lands less heavily (in the Bombay Presidency in 1847). Fundamentally, the 'predatory' conception of the state that had been that of the Company since 1765 was little by little replaced with the idea that the prosperity of the peasantry was a precondition of political and social stability. At the same time, technological advances, with the advent in India of the telegraph and the railways, gave more consistency to the project of modernization. The ruling circles started to envisage India as a great exporter of raw materials (cotton in particular) towards the home country and as a large market for British manufactured goods (above all, the cotton fabrics of Lancashire). The plan for the railway network, bequeathed by Dalhousie to his successors, drew its inspiration from this idea. But purely strategic considerations also played a role. Because in the minds of the British, the modernization of India depended on the consolidation of the colonial state and the progressive annexation of territories that had remained independent or placed under the indirect control of the Company.

In this project of modernization, which marked the transition to the Victorian era of triumphant imperialism, the role allotted to Indians was that of docile subjects. They were not considered mature enough to participate actively in political life. But the Anglo-Indian version of 'enlightened despotism' was becoming more and more unacceptable to the Indian elites, who, already dispossessed of their power, had the impression that their way of life and their religion were now under threat.

The Great Revolt of 1857 (The Sepoy Revolt)

Even though the Company had been reduced since 1833 to only a fiction, the reality of power belonging to the British government and Parliament, the mutiny of 1857 nevertheless marked an important rupture in the history of colonial India. Nationalist history has interpreted it as the beginning of the struggle for independence. Even though this idea is debatable, it remains that the great rebellion brought the age of conquests to a close: except for a few frontier adjustments, British India was not to undergo any further territorial expansion and the policy of annexing princely states was to come to an end.

A century of expansion since the Battle of Plassey had resulted in creating a vast Empire, a unique political construction in the world at the time. It came dangerously close to being swept away in 1857, but the mobilization of a part of British military power saved it and it maintained itself, almost without having to modify its form, for nearly another century. Nevertheless, the context had been radically changed: a century of industrial revolution had made Britain the largest world power, endowed with the most advanced technology. What had started as an episode in Indian history had become a chapter in the history of the world.

The mutiny of 1857 effectively dominates the entire history of colonial India. So totally unexpected a jolt, eventually without any durable repercussion, and which rapidly acquired a mythical dimension both for the English and for the Indians, it was part of the revolutionary wave[1] that, at the time of the European revolutions of 1848–49, rocked Asia in the middle of the nineteenth century, marked by the revolt of the Taipings and the Niens in China (1858–61). All these revolts were repressed and hardly had any direct consequences on the political order.

For more than a century, the mutiny of the *sepoys* of the Bengal army has provoked the curiosity of historians and its bibliography swells each year. Some historians have interpreted it as the symptom of a more profound crisis in Indian society, resulting from the policies of the colonial government, and in particular from the measures that jeopardized the interests of the elites classes.[2] Others have described it as an organized uprising, the work of a few leaders, the premature breakout of which spelt its failure.[3] This thesis, revived and turned around in 1907 by the nationalist pamphleteer Savarkar,[4] forms the basis for the official Indian interpretation, that of the first war of independence, highlighting its proto-nationalist nature. Lastly, there are those who analyse it as a Muslim uprising sparked by the determination of the Muslim elites to regain the dominant place that they had lost in the wake of the establishment of the British rule. These interpretations have for a long time fuelled the historiographical debate, and it was only towards the end of the twentieth century that the role of the participation of the common people, of the peasants in particular, in the uprising began to be taken into account.

The events

The uprising started from the Bengal army, the largest of the three armies of the East India Company. Discontentment in the ranks, simmering since the disastrous Afghan expedition of 1842, had further intensified: in effect, rumour had it that the colonial authorities had the intention of making native soldiers lose their caste, before forcing them to convert to Christianity. Two decisions taken by the British military authorities in 1856 seemed to give a certain credence to these rumours. The first, the *General Service Enlistment Act*, motivated by a shortage of troops for the garrison of Burma, took away a privilege enjoyed by the *sepoys* of the Bengal army in comparison to those in the armies of Bombay and Madras, that of being exempted from serving overseas, thus enabling them to avert the violation of a religious prohibition to which they were very attached. The second decision was the introduction of the new Enfield gun, of more rapid fire, but whose cartridges the soldiers had to take out from their cases with their teeth, which aroused in them the fear of being sullied by the contact with impure substances (cow grease for the Hindus, pig grease for the Muslims).

Compounded with what was the beginning of a regional diversification in the recruitment of the army (with the formation of the first units recruited in the Punjab and in Nepal) that seemed to threaten the quasi-monopoly of employment enjoyed by the high castes of the North-Western Provinces, these measures unleashed a wave of panic among the *sepoys*, who had furthermore been appalled by the annexation, in 1856, of the princely state of Oudh, which was the native country of many of them and with which they maintained close contacts. In January 1857, at Dumdum, near Calcutta, the men rejected the new cartridges even though the authorities, backtracking, had abandoned the idea of demanding that they be torn with the teeth. The first to openly brandish the flag of revolt was Mangal Pande, a *sepoy* who, on 29 March, attempted to trigger a mutiny at Barrackpur; he was not followed by the majority of his comrades, but the authorities deemed it prudent to dissolve the 34th regiment to which he belonged. During the weeks that followed, the authorities, alternating between threats and concessions, only aggravated the exasperation of the *sepoys*. The explosion had become inevitable.

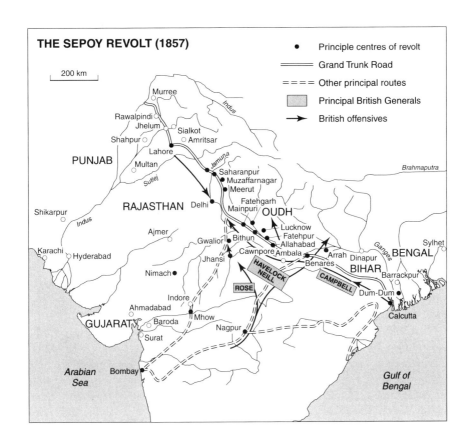

THE SEPOY REVOLT (1857)

200 km

● Principle centres of revolt
══ Grand Trunk Road
= = = = Other principal routes
▨ Principal British Generals
→ British offensives

Murree
Rawalpindi
Jhelum
Sialkot
Shahpur
Amritsar
Lahore
PUNJAB
Multan
Indus
Jamuna
Saharanpur
Muzaffarnagar
Meerut
Sutlej
RAJASTHAN   Delhi   Fatehgarh
Shikarpur   Mainpuri   OUDH
Ajmer
Indus   Lucknow
Karachi   Gwalior   Bithun   Fatehpur
Hyderabad   Jhansi   Allahabad
Nimach   Cawnpore   Ambala   Arrah   Dinapur   BENGAL   Sylhet
HAVELOCK   Benares   BIHAR   Ganges
NEILL   Barrackpur
ROSE   CAMPBELL
Indore   Dum-Dum
Ahmadabad   Mhow   Calcutta
GUJARAT   Baroda   Nagpur
Surat
Brahmaputra
Arabian   Bombay
Sea
Gulf of
Bengal

The revolt, strictly speaking, broke out at Meerut, near Delhi, on 10 May 1857. That day, three *sepoy* regiments of the Bengal army mutinied because eighty-five of their comrades who had refused the new cartridges had been clapped in irons. In fear of being attacked by the European troops that shared their quarters, which was one of the largest in India, the soldiers of 3rd regiment of cavalry and the 11th and 20th regiments of infantry marched on the prison where their comrades had been incarcerated, freed them and massacred their officers. Taking advantage of the inertia of the European troops, due to the surprise element and to a wrong appreciation of the situation by those in command, the mutineers left Meerut without difficulty and marched on Delhi, where the *sepoys* of the local garrison joined them. As Delhi did not have any European troops, they easily captured the city and placed as their head the aged Mogul emperor Bahadur Shah, whom the British had maintained in a purely honorary function. By doing so, the mutineers hoped to draw on the feelings of loyalty that were still alive among the population towards the Mogul dynasty.

The mutiny spread like wild fire. The active mutineers were no doubt only a minority, but they were determined, and by resorting to violent and symbolic acts, like the massacre of British officers and their families, they created the irreparable; not leaving their comrades any illusion as to their lot in the event of the re-establishment of British authority, they succeeded in mobilizing the bulk of the soldiery. To resist mutinous units, the British command could only count on the European regiments. But the strength of European soldiers in the Bengal army was at its lowest: 23,000 men against 128,000 in the *sepoy* regiments, and the majority of these forces were concentrated in the Punjab, a province that had been recently annexed; between Meerut and Bengal itself, there were practically no European troops. British rule being fundamentally a military despotism, the loss of its armed branch was tantamount to a political revolution.

Nevertheless, the uprising was confined primarily to the north and the centre of India. In the rest of the subcontinent, in particular in the presidencies of Madras and of Bombay, the mutiny was limited. This was because the armies of the other two presidencies, the total strength of which was less than 90,000 men (including 15,000 Europeans), unlike the Bengal army, lacked homogeneity. Furthermore, the mutiny did not meet with a great response among the civil populations. The uprising was thus rapidly limited to the Presidency of Bengal and to certain bordering princely states.

Even inside the Bengal Presidency, the mutinies failed in two key regions: first in the Punjab, where the authorities entrusted the young and formidable General Nicholson, leading his famous 'mobile column', with the task of disarming the rebellious units before the contagion could infect the entire army and where the Sikhs, likely be the most dangerous element, remained on the whole loyal; then in Bengal proper, where, despite a few serious alerts, the mutinous regiments were also fairly rapidly neutralized. From these two points, the British, who received reinforcements from June onwards, closed in on the mutineers and finally defeated them.

But for some months, British authority over the greater part of North India was almost completely overturned. With the exception of the main cities and a few important lines of communication that were controlled precariously, the British had lost their hold over the country. The concentration of the available forces in Delhi aggravated the situation in the countryside. The power vacuum thus created was in part filled by the emergence of indigenous local powers in places where there existed leaders invested with a recognized authority. Thus, in the region of Allahabad, an Islamic religious leader, the *maulvi* Liaqat Ali, established an independent regime for a few weeks, before being defeated by the British on 17 July 1857. In the district of Meerut, the *nawab* Walidad Khan, who had come from Delhi, exercised a sort of authority for some months, and thereafter met with defeat in turn. In other regions, as the district of Muzaffarnagar, no recognized authority supplanted the faltering British administration and a certain anarchy prevailed.

The rapidity with which the colonial administration disappeared in vast regions in North India points to the fragility of British rule in the countryside. The British could maintain their control only where the local magnates remained loyal, in other words, where they had allowed them to accumulate wealth; elsewhere, the powerful landlords (*taluqdars*) joined the rebellion or observed a prudent neutrality. In fact, hatred for the *Firinghi*[147] was rife in all sections of society. The urban lower classes expressed it by participating with enthusiasm in the actions of the mutineers against the British population living in small garrisons. British authors have attributed these anti-British manifestations to the desire for loot, but they also had more noble motivations, a profound attachment to the Hindu or Muslim religions, which seemed threatened by Christian missionaries. On the other hand, the attitude of the merchants of the cities was more ambiguous: the disorders caused by the mutiny were not good for business and the commercial circles in general showed some prudence, waiting to see how things would turn out. Yet it became clear quite rapidly that the mutiny was doomed to failure.

The military operations themselves took place in three stages. First, the British concentrated their efforts on the re-conquest of Delhi, and elsewhere they contented themselves with defending certain crucial points. While the *sepoy* regiments were rising up in rebellion in the North of India and massacring their officers as well as the European residents of numerous small garrisons, the commander-in-chief, Anson, mobilized his troops and service corps at Ambala in the Punjab. At the beginning of June, the British controlled not more than three points between Rajasthan and Benares; the fort of Agra, some positions at Cawnpore (where a descendant of the *peshwas*, Nana Sahib, had become the leader of the mutineers) and the residence of Lucknow. Absolute priority was given by the general staff to the reconquest of Delhi over the mutineers. On 11 June, a column that had come from Madras under the command of Neil seized the fort of Allahabad and thus secured a strategic position. However, failures followed. At the end of the month, Wheeler capitulated at Cawnpore, which was followed by the massacre of British prisoners, including women and children, which earned Nana Sahib first place in Victorian demonology. As for the army camped by Delhi, it was not long before it found itself in the position of the besieged rather than the besieger in the face of *sepoys* who clearly outnumbered it.

The situation of the English, already precarious, was aggravated by the failure of an attempt at the disarmament of three mutinous regiments at Dinapur, near Patna, in Bihar (25 July). The mutineers succeeded in escaping, and under the command of the Rajput chief Kunwar Singh, they inflicted a severe defeat on the British forces at Arrah on 29 July. The Great Trunk Road, which connected the Khyber Pass with Bengal, was cut off and the safety of the entire region was jeopardized. Nevertheless, as early as 12 August, the British ousted Kunwar Singh from his hideout in Jagdishpur and reopened the Great Trunk Road to the circulation of convoys. In September, the arrival of reinforcements from the Punjab commanded by the famous Nicholson enabled them to take over Delhi after six days of fierce street fighting. The city was abandoned to looting and a part of the population massacred. This first success was symbolically important because of the still immense prestige of the imperial throne of Delhi, but did not have far-reaching consequences on the military situation, as the rebellion, deprived of its head, tended to develop further.

A few days later, on 25 September, General Havelock, who had left Allahabad on 7 July to deliver the besieged garrison in the residence of Lucknow (where Henry Lawrence had died on 4 July succumbing to the injuries received in combat), succeeded, following ferocious engagements, in entering what was little more than a pile of rubble. He was, however, besieged in his turn. The operations thereafter were concentrated around Lucknow. The second siege of the residence came to an end only in November, after the arrival of Sir Colin Campbell leading considerable reinforcements. This was a turning point that modified the balance of power, because an increasing number of British troops taken from various scenes of operations (Crimea, Persia, China) rejoined him. Campbell completed his success by inflicting a severe defeat on the troops of Gwalior, commanded by the best rebel chief, Tantia Topi. Nevertheless, in Oudh, the population had risen up in revolt under the leadership of the *taluqdars* and the British had to wage three months of very violent combat before capturing the city of Lucknow on 1 March 1858. This British victory brought the second phase of the uprising to an end.

The last phase of operations took place in Central India, where the *rani* of Jhansi, a small princely state, and Tantia Topi continued the fight despite the evident superiority of the British forces. In March, Sir Hugh Rose seized Jhansi after defeating the rescue force commanded by Tantia Topi. The *rani* fled and resumed the fight alongside the general: defeated at Kunch in May, the two rebel chiefs succeeded in capturing the fortress of Gwalior thanks to the complicity of the troops of the Maratha prince Sindhia. Two engagements were necessary to break their resistance and on 20 June the fortress was taken, the *rani* choosing to die fighting. Tantia escaped the British and waged guerrilla operations along the Nepalese border, which stopped only after his capture and his execution in April 1859. The fall of Gwalior put an end to the military phase of the uprising. As early as 8 July 1858 the Governor-General Lord Canning proclaimed the re-establishment of peace.

In fact, fighting persisted in several regions for nearly another year, but the spine of the uprising had been broken. British forces controlled the principal lines of communication and courts everywhere rendered summary justice against all those who were suspected of having participated in the revolt, even of simply showing sympathy for the mutineers and ordered thousands of executions. The victims of the British repression were nevertheless much more numerous; British columns at times systematically burned the villages and massacred the male population. In addition to the human losses that no doubt numbered in the hundreds of thousands, the uprising brought in its train a wave of destruction in villages and cities: official buildings and residential bungalows set ablaze by rebels, numerous houses razed to the ground by British troops. Not to mention the properties confiscated by the British authorities, some of which were given as a reward to those who had remained loyal. A number of present day Indian fortunes have their origin in the collaboration in the repression of the uprising.

Controversies surrounding the uprising

Several myths rapidly sprung up around this tragic episode. First, British myths, which transformed the mutiny into a great test aimed at showing the superiority of the Anglo-Saxon race. Which explains the emphasis laid, on the one hand, on the atrocities committed by the mutineers, in particular on the massacre of Cawnpore, and on the other, on the heroism of a handful of British who resisted the barbaric multitudes (Henry Lawrence at Lucknow). The hero worship that developed around military chiefs like Havelock, Campbell, Neil or Nicholson provided Victorian Britain with the pantheon that it needed to nurture its dreams of glory. A pilgrimage was organized around the important sites of the mutiny: any Briton visiting India at the end of the nineteenth century stopped compulsorily at Cawnpore to pay homage to the victims of Nana Sahib at a monument built on the site of the well where the bodies of the victims of the butchery were thrown, as well as at the residence of Lucknow, deliberately left in the state in which it had been found by Campbell, the only place in the entire empire where the Union Jack was never lowered. This imperialist imagery of course glossed over the atrocities committed by the British: the alleys of gallows that lined the march of Neil's column, the hundreds of villages razed to the ground, the prisoners attached to the mouths of canons, Delhi abandoned to the looting and rape perpetrated by the British soldiery.

The Indian myths highlight a generalized uprising against the *Firinghis*, uniting princes, soldiers, peasants, artisans, and merchants, Hindus and Muslims; a cult developed around two figures of legend, Lakshmibhai, the *rani* of Jhansi, who has become a symbol of the heroism of the Indian woman, as the guardian of values, and Tantia Topi, the elusive rebel who taunted the British; these myths were created by the nationalists who sought to transform retrospectively a large-scale regional uprising into a national war of independence in an effort to base the legitimacy of the national movement on a past that was still fresh in the collective memory. In this perspective too, the massacres committed by the rebels have been obscured.

All these myths have a long life and the passage of time does not seem to have toned down the emotional charge that they still possess among both the British and Indian public. However, the historian has to examine this painful episode with detachment. Firstly, he must strive to put in perspective the acts of violence, even the atrocities, committed by the two camps. These acts of violence, which could appear as gratuitous, even useless, are explicable above all in reference to a symbolic logic, which has been at work, at all times and in all places, in revolutionary moments.

From the point of view of the rebels, the systematic massacre of the British, including women and children, was justified by the necessity to wash in blood the shame and the pollution represented by the conquest of India by infidels or the *mleccha*[6] (according to whether it was from the point of view of Muslims or of Hindus); the recourse to extreme measures is also understandable by the fear, amplified by rumour, and by the desire of the chiefs to compromise all the participants to the maximum. We must not forget that British rule was built on the constant and calculated use of controlled violence: the *sepoys* had perfectly imbibed the lesson of their masters. The controlled nature of their violence is evident in the absence of rape, which at first sight seems surprising – it has been rarely acknowledged by the British, despite the lack of official testimonies: this was because, in the minds of the rebels, such an act would have meant serious pollution for the ones who committed it (and not for the victims). On the side of the British, the harshness of the repression seemed justified by the need to make the repetition of such a revolt impossible forever, by making its price appear disproportionate. Of course, fear played its role, as well as a feeling of racial superiority that nurtured the belief that an Indian life was worth markedly less than a British life. But here too, even if certain military chiefs showed real sadism, violence was of a deliberate and a very political nature.

Even though the armies in presence numbered several dozens of thousands of men, the fight consisted above all of innumerable skirmishes between small groups and there were very few large-scale engagements. The fiercest fighting took place in Delhi and in Lucknow, where the two camps engaged in assaults of gallantry. We ought to do away with the calumnies hurled by most of the British authors on the mutineers, generally described as scum driven by the desire to loot and incapable of fighting once they were deprived of their British officers. In fact, wherever the mutineers maintained a certain cohesion, they gave a hard time to their adversaries. The precision and the constancy of the fire of their artillery often elicited admiring remarks from the British. On the other hand, they were rarely capable of facing the fire of the enemy without scattering: the absence of effective supervision was cruelly felt. As regards tactics and logistics, they were also at a disadvantage. However, they fought with courage, in particular in hand to hand combat and did not hesitate to brave markedly superior forces.

Their defeat was primarily due to the lack of clear objectives and the absence of a unified command. The pure and simple reestablishment of the Mogul Empire was not realistic and it is in any case doubtful whether the mutineers, in majority Hindu, wanted this. But, no other political institution inspired a comparable loyalty that went beyond the limits of a small region. No other Indian prince enjoyed a prestige sufficient to be recognized as the leader of all the rebels, except in Oudh, where there was consensus on the restoration of the fallen dynasty: it is therefore not surprising that the uprising was more important in this region, uniting the Shiites, the Sunnites and the Hindus, powerful landlords (*taluqdars*) and peasants in a shared execration of the *Firinghi* usurper. As for the British, they had their back to the wall and knew that they were fighting to maintain their dominant position in India, under threat for the first time. However, certain native elements, the Sikhs and the Gurkhas (Nepali soldiers) in particular, fought on their side and played a significant role in the final victory.

Nevertheless, unlike in numerous colonial wars waged by the British in India, the civil population participated sometimes in the fighting on the side of the mutineers and of the contingents of certain princely states. The mutiny of soldiers transformed itself into a generalized uprising where two conditions were met: the absence of European contingents or other troops loyal to the government to defend the administrative centre of the district and the existence of local magnates rallied to the rebel cause and capable of exercising a certain political authority. This was the case in part of the North-Western Provinces and of Oudh, where the mutineers could easily seize the treasury and establish a sort of parallel government before joining the great centres of revolt, like Delhi, Cawnpore and Lucknow.

We thus come to the question of the nature, of the intensity and the reasons of the participation of the common people. For British historians of the nineteenth century, the question was posed in simple terms: once British authority had disappeared, the looting instincts of the lower classes were given free rein, but the masses did not have at any moment the least autonomy of action. For these historians, the only thing that counted was the attitude of the elites: some have discerned in their alienation the fundamental cause of the uprising and showed some sympathy for their point of view[7], while others underscored the desire for revenge among elements that had lost their power and prestige. For the early 'nationalist' historians, the masses could only follow their 'natural' leaders and the attitude of the latter was therefore decisive. Among the Indian historians of Marxist inspiration, some endorse the thesis of a proto-nationalist uprising and highlight the unity between different social classes in their opposition to British rule and others underline the popular and peasant participation in the revolt. There are in effect numerous examples of the mobilization of armed peasants and of raids conducted by them against government buildings but also against village moneylenders and wealthy classes. Nevertheless, the participation, however important it might have been, of peasants in an uprising is not sufficient to make it a peasant uprising. The question gets further complicated when we consider the fact that the *sepoys* for the most part were of rural origin but, as they belonged in general to the upper land-owning castes, did not cultivate their farms themselves. Admittedly the mutineers were a rural army, the attachment of the *sepoys* to their territories being a powerful cause for dissolution, once the time of the first success had passed, but were they a peasant army? The question remains to be answered.

The 'colonial impact' was far from being uniform in the plains of North India.[8] Certain groups of the rural population, especially in the zones situated away from the great lines of communication, had suffered enormously from the rise in taxes after 1818 and had even lost lands; they found in the rebellion an opportunity to settle their score with the British and the nouveau riches who were associated with them. On the other hand, near the great lines of communication, where commerce was most developed, a new class of magnates had taken advantage of British rule to extend their influence and were hostile to the uprising. Their attitude was nevertheless not always decisive because the peasantry forced them at times to side with the rebellion. The revolt in the countryside cannot therefore be reduced to simple economic motivations. In fact, the bulk of the rebels were motivated above all by the feeling of a threat against their religion and their way of life. Whether this threat was real or largely imaginary matters very little in the final analysis.

Nothing illustrates this better than Oudh, where the British found themselves confronted with an uprising of the entire population, the magnitude of which can be explained by several factors: a state tradition more than a century old, represented by a Muslim dynasty of the Shiite faith that, in perpetual conflict with the local Sunnite Muslims, had always pursued a policy of conciliation towards the Hindu majority; the brutality of the agrarian measures taken by the British in 1856–57 after the annexation, measures that alienated the *taluqdars*, without satisfying the peasants; lastly, the close relations between the mutinous *sepoys* and the state of Oudh, which was the native land of most of them. The insurgent troops, regiments of the Bengal army mingled with local troops, thus enjoyed not only the active complicity of the lower classes of Lucknow, but also after, their victory over the British at Chinhat on 30 June 1857, the support of numerous *taluqdars*. Some of them had, however, helped British officials to escape from the mutineers during the first phase of the uprising. That they went over to the side of 'rebels' (in British terminology) was felt by the British as betrayal. The reasons for the volte-face of the *taluqdars* become evident in the words spoken by one of the greatest among them, Hanwant Singh, to Captain Barrow: '*Sahib*, your compatriots came to this country and chased our king. You sent your officers to scour the country to examine the validity of the titles of ownership of the domains. All at once, you deprived me of lands that had belonged to my family since time immemorial. I acquiesced. Suddenly, misfortune has struck you. The people of the country have risen up in revolt against you. You came to me whom you had dispossessed. I saved you. But, now I am marching on Lucknow leading my men in order to try to chase you out of the country.'[9]

The forces mobilized by the *taluqdars* in the villages represented the majority of the 53,000 armed 'rebels', counted by the British on the arrival of Campbell at Lucknow. It was above all these forces that pursued the fight after 1 March 1858, forcing the British to fight until the end of the year. In certain districts, there was a mass mobilization of peasants in response to the call of the *taluqdars*. Eventually, several thousand men crossed the Nepalese border rather than surrender. This fierce resistance in a desperate situation shows the determination of the mutineers. Their bitter hatred for the Firinghi can be explained by their attachment to an order that the British had so brutally upset. They did not simply seek to restore the legitimate dynasty, but more radically, to put an end to what they perceived as a concerted attack against religion in its dimension as socio-cosmic order (*dharma*). Hindus and Muslims likewise, *taluqdars* as well as peasants, everyone resisted such an attack. In Oudh, there developed a veritable war of independence, supported by a large part of the population.

If we cannot generalize it to the whole of India, the magnitude of the uprising nevertheless reveals the fragility of the colonial political construction: deprived of its armed branch, it vacillated, coming under the threat of a collapse. For the first time British troops had to intervene, at a very high price that was to weigh heavily, and for a long time, on the finances of India. All the more so as the authorities, learning a lesson from these events, decided that a substantial British garrison should remain permanently in India in order to guarantee the security of this crucial possession for British power in the world. Another lesson that the British learnt from this episode was the necessity to conciliate the Indian princes, which led them to modify their policy regarding the princely states.

The first victim of 1857 was the honourable East India Company, which terminated its two-and-a-half-century career quite unceremoniously. In fact, the passage of India under the direct administration of the Crown represented but a formal change: the British found themselves confronted with the necessity of reorganizing the entire structure of the colonial state. They would have to confer on it a legitimacy that the fiction, maintained with great difficulty, of a continuity of the Mogul Empire could no longer provide. Thus, they would strive to personalize power by organizing a cult around Queen Victoria.

As for Indian society, it could only lick its wounds in the hope of better days. But the severity of the British repression of the uprising widened the gulf between the colonizers and the colonized, even if the Indians, all of whom were *a priori* suspected of harbouring sympathy for the revolt, ostensibly flaunted their loyalty.

XVI

THE AGRARIAN ECONOMY AND RURAL SOCIETY

(1790–1860)

Indian countryside at the end of the eighteenth century

An contrasted conjuncture

Historians have for a long time painted a dramatic picture of the Indian country-side towards of the end of the eighteenth century. It was characterized by depopulation, regression of cultivation and rural trade, widespread insecurity, and autarchic withdrawal in village communities. This stereotype accords itself with the historiographical tradition born during the colonial period, which projected the Indian eighteenth century as a long phase of anarchy and decadence, brought to an end by the installation of benevolent British rule. Recent research suggests, how-ever, that the political and military history of India in the eighteenth century, tumultuous though it may have been, nevertheless witnessed phenomena of urban and commercial growth, and did not dim the brilliance of Indian civilization. It did not lead either to the general and uniform deterioration of rural life, even if the tones in certain parts of the picture were unquestionably very dark during the later decades.

The secular demographical trend was by and large positive. The first two-thirds of the eighteenth century seems to have been relatively free from large-scale famine. The population of the subcontinent probably stood at 180 million as early as 1750. There is evidence to show that the cultivated area recorded a constant expansion following clearings not only in Bengal and in the Gangetic Plain, but also in the Deccan, at a time when the irrigated coastal plains and lower valleys of rice-pro-ducing peninsular India were already densely populated. This slow rise was, however, interrupted by major economic accidents (famines and epidemics) in the course of the last three decades of the century. The great Bengal famine that struck in 1769–70 killed from a quarter to a third of the population of eastern India. It was followed by a serious crisis of the same nature that hit a great part of North India, from the middle valley of the Ganges to Kashmir and Rajasthan, from

1783–84, then by another that raged, though less severely, across the Deccan from 1790 to 1792. Demographic recovery, however, occurred rapidly, if we are to believe the first censuses carried out by the British in the regions concerned at the beginning of the next century, even if some regions here and there were dotted with deserted villages.

The miseries of war

We must also take into consideration the havoc wreaked on rural populations and agriculture by the ever-present bane of war. Not all wars were equally bloody and ruinous for the rural world. Conflicts that centred on the sieges of fortified positions (the wars of the Carnatic) were comparatively less destructive outside the site of combat, even if the people necessarily suffered from the movement of armies. On the contrary, incessant wars at the heart of the Mogul political space (in the region of Delhi and Agra), the devastating incursions of the Marathas in eastern India (which came to a definitive end only in 1803), the four wars waged by the English against Mysore between 1767 and 1800, the internecine wars of the Maratha confederacy in the west of the Deccan left profound scars. In the affected regions, mortality imputable to combats, pillages, shortages, epidemics propagated by armies was often considerable. It is estimated that the district of Tanjore alone lost 200,000 people (20 per cent of the population) due to the second conflict with Mysore (1780–4). These deaths, compounded by abductions and other forced displacements of population, collective migrations, requisitions of agricultural products, cattle and means of transport, as well as by increased extortion of money by war chiefs, led to a severe contraction of cultivated space.

Despite these regressions at the end of the century, pre-1760s agricultural growth continued in numerous regions. The sources that we have at our disposal are certainly heterogeneous, incomplete and at time ambiguous or partial: travellers accounts of the second half of the century, reports of the first British administrators of conquered regions, statistics on the proceeds from land taxation. The indications that these supply are sufficiently clear to preclude the idea of a general agrarian regression.

The situation was certainly critical in numerous regions. Agriculture, formerly so productive in the central regions of the Mogul Empire, clearly declined between Agra and Delhi, a zone rife with banditry, as it did in Rohilkhand, in the Doab between the Ganges and the Jamuna, where irrigation was in jeopardy, and lastly in Rajasthan, Haryana and the south of the Punjab, where cattle-breeding pastoral tribes regained ground over cultivated areas. In East India, the western districts of Bengal were periodically ravaged until the end of the century by the raids of the Marathas (notably the district of Midnapur, the depopulation of which was spectacular), while in Orissa, which was under Maratha control until the British conquest in 1803, the peasants of the plains were systematically ransomed and deserted hundreds of villages. The situation was no better in Assam, in the Ahom kingdom, which plunged into anarchy after 1780, and where the constant mobilization of peasants by rival war chiefs seriously disorganized agriculture. In western India, the

north and south confines of the Maratha country were ravaged and depopulated by
marauding armies, the depredatory raids of the Pindaris, the endemic banditry (in
Khandesh, the upper valley of the Godavery, parts of Karnataka and the countries
of Ahmadnagar). Further to the south, the picture that Thomas Munro, the first collector in Canara, and after him, Francis Buchanan, the investigator despatched to
the field by the East India Company, painted of the village of the midwestern part
of the Deccan in the wake of the defeat of Tipu Sultan (1799) is likewise that of a
drained agrarian economy. Last, in Tamil country, deeply affected by the wars
against Mysore, the pointers to an agricultural crisis are legion: countless deserted
villages, deterioration of irrigation, regression of cultivated space, stagnation of the
production of rice and of the proceeds from land taxes.

The foundations of economic recovery

In a certain number of cases, however, we have reason to suspect that the picture has
been deliberately blackened by the authors of the early colonial reports, in order to
highlight by contrast the benefits of the British regime.

At the turn of the century, the agricultural slump was far from being universal.
The miseries of war did not uniformly affect all the villages: adjacent to a devastated
village, another, protected by some local chief, safeguarded its prosperity intact. In
the ravaged zones at the heart of the former Mogul Empire, the villages that formed
the hinterland to the principal agglomerations (Delhi, Agra, Rampur, Bharatpur,
etc.) formed important enclaves of prosperous agriculture. The same was true across
the Gangetic Plain, of the countryside that surrounded the regional metropolises of
Cawnpore, Allahabad, Lucknow, Benares. The kingdom of Oudh, where the population was dense and the area of cultivated space under constant expansion, had
continued to witness agricultural development since the middle of the century, with
the exception of its easternmost regions. Descriptions dating from this period also
highlight the uninterrupted dynamism of the central regions of Maratha country, to
the northwest of the Deccan, the triggering factor of which had been the initial
moderation in the collection of land revenues. In various regions of the subcontinent, at the end of this century reputed to be disastrous, clearings continue on the
fringes of the cultivated space (the frontiers of the Western Ghats, the north and
south boundaries of the Ganges Valley). On the whole, the demand for agricultural
products did not diminish, even if the local commercial situations often had their
vicissitudes. The available data (fragmentary, it is true) on the evolution of agricultural prices do not point to a clear downward trend before the beginning of the
nineteenth century.

The best sign that the vast agricultural economy of India resisted the widespread
political upheavals is that land tax, in the second half of the eighteenth century, continued to be levied in cash, which evidently implies that peasants continued to
produce for sale, even if the products that they sold were not strictly speaking a surplus. Which also implies that the trade in agricultural products, especially trade at
medium or short distance towards rural fairs and markets and towards neighbouring towns, remained pretty vibrant. Permanent rural markets emerged well beyond

1750 in the kingdom of Oudh, in the Maratha territories of the *peshwas* in the south of the peninsula. And we also know that merchant bankers continued to invest in land in Rajasthan and in western India during this period.

The relative autonomy of the agrarian economy in relation to the vicissitudes of political and military history and in any case its capacity for recovery when it was locally affected by them seem evident. The agricultural regions that were the most durably affected by war and banditry were those where agriculture, owing to climatic conditions, was the most fragile and depended on artificial systems of irrigation (such as countries situated to the north and west of Delhi). But, on the whole, these localized declines were by and large offset by phenomena of agricultural growth observed in the zones that were spared. These regional tendencies towards expansion were pre-existent to the instauration of the 'colonial peace' to the stability of which they contributed.

Myths and realities of the Indian village community

British administrators, during the early days of colonization, imagined the Indian village as a miniature of the Greek city, and the whole of India as a sort of cellular fabric of rural communities that were self-managed, cohesive and impermeable to the vicissitudes of history. In a report of 1806 relative to the 'ceded districts' at the time recently conquered by the English in the centre of the Deccan, Thomas Munro wrote: "Every village, with its twelve Ayangadees [municipal officers] as they are called, is a kind of little republic, with the Potail [village chief] at the head of it; and India is a mass of such republics. The inhabitants, during war, look chiefly to their own Potail. They give themselves no trouble about the breaking up and division of kingdoms; while the village remains entire, they care not to what power it is transferred: wherever it goes the internal management remains unaltered; the Potail is still the collector and magistrate, and head farmer. From the age of Menu until this day the settlements have been made either with or through the Potails"[1]

This mythical image of the Indian village was to enjoy a long life, as, after emerging into the nineteenth century as one of the hallmarks of the colonial interpretation of Indian society, it was revived by Indian nationalists as a symbol of the pre-colonial 'golden age'.

This cliché, we must concede, was not totally without truth in those regions of India where traditions of clan solidarity were particularly vigorous, and where rural communities, often fortified and armed, represented small political entities on their own scale: as could be seen in the region around Delhi, domain of the Jat peasantry, or in the villages in eastern Oudh. This image of a cohesive community reflected on the other hand a very widespread social fact in the Indian world, namely, the interdependence of castes within the local community. This was a customary system of reciprocal services, often hereditary, which linked, within each village, families of different professional specializations (and of varying ritual status), a network of relations of a religious nature that modern ethnologists have described under the name of *jajmani* system.

To construct on these facts a vision of the Indian village as a harmonious microcosm, and in the strict sense, without history, was evidently an indulgence in romantic idealization. Two essential aspects of rural life were therein eclipsed: on the one hand, the presence of social inequalities and the central role of conflicts in the village universe; and on the other, the existence of very real relations of power that placed the village under the domination of the higher echelons of the political system. This original British image of the Indian village community is, however, historically important due to the role it played, as we shall subsequently see, in the birth of the colonial agrarian regimes.

The peasants and the land on the eve of the conquest

Before the British conquest, there were two main kinds of villages, called *taalluqa* villages and *raiyati* villages in North India, according to the administrative terminology derived from the Mogul Empire. The term *taalluqa* denoted a village conceded by the imperial power to a *zamindar* (literally, 'holder of land'), authorized to collect rent from peasants in exchange for the regular obligation of remitting a tribute or of providing a military contribution. A *raiyati* village, on the other hand, transacted without intermediary with the representatives of the state for the payment of agrarian taxes, the burden of which rested individually on the farmers, or at least on the most important of them. In each village, whether *taalluqa* or *raiyati*, two main categories of cultivators coexisted: on the one hand, the minority elite class of farmers who held hereditary rights of occupation, generally belonging to a high caste, and who paid the revenue charges directly, and on the other, those, often more numerous, who did not enjoy guaranteed land rights, and who paid their dues through the intermediary of the former. The government in power, moreover, customarily conceded entire villages, or in each village specific lands, to religious institutions or personalities, who collected rents from these domains but were not subject to taxes, and who in effect could lease them or even alienate them as if they were the owners. At the lower level of the village population, were first the tenants and sub-tenants of the chief farmers, and then the agricultural labour force, made essentially of landless peasants of very low castes, like the Chamars of the Gangetic India and the Paraiyars of the Tamil South (from whose name came the English 'pariah'). Serfdom and domestic slavery were present in diverse forms in most of the regions.

This schema, valid in its salient features from the north to the south of India, presented countless regional variants. As for the amount of land dues, it also differed considerably from place to place and in accordance with the prevalent political circumstances. In most of the agricultural regions, there was a tax base well known by the peasantry, fixed on the basis of the productive capacities of the land, and which had often been subject, in a more or less ancient periods, to an official regulation (Mogul, Maratha or any other). In the provinces of the former Mogul Empire, the level of taxation generally stood between the third and the half of the gross product of the land, but could descend in the poorest regions to one ninth of this product. In the course of the eighteenth century, in the wake of the decline of the central authorities and the insatiable financial needs of war chiefs, these basic taxes almost everywhere had been increased, or compounded with supplementary taxes, in a way that the peasant populations deemed illegitimate. Taxation could amount to two-thirds of the total agricultural income in the richest irrigated regions.

There were, however, limits to the tax demands of the powerful. A village had more than one means of concealing its true capacity for payment, or to forge at the local level advantageous alliances with the tax agents. Furthermore, armed peasant communities were often in a position to negotiate the amount of their contributions. Lastly, in an overall context of low density of population, where land was more abundant than labour for cultivation, any overexploited peasant was liable to flee and enter the services of a kinder master ready to welcome him. There were thus safety nets, and limits that the masters of the land refrained from crossing for the sake of their own interests.

Rural society and the market

The detailed description of land rights and land rents in each village was extremely complicated, and irreducible to a purely economic logic. Thus, the amount of rent and taxes varied both in inverse proportion to the rank of the caste of the payer as well as in function of the local demand for land or of the productive capacity of the agricultural area in question. A parcel of land rarely had a single owner, but generally, several right-holders, each of whom could lay claim to a part of the produce and none to full and undivided ownership. Most often, the access of a peasant to one form or another of land occupation depended on the personal relation that he maintained with the member of the local elite, however modest he might be, who exercised the eminent right over this land. Economic relations, in effect, were only one aspect of social relations, in the broader sense, that bonded men in function of their kinship, caste, profession. For this reason, the mode of functioning of the rural economy could not be brought down solely to the laws of the market. There was, strictly speaking, no integrated land market, as land was not in general personal property and was not dissociated from the social relations (nonetheless, the right to a share in the income from the land could be sold). Agricultural remunerations, essentially customary, were not wages in the true sense of the word.

On the other hand, as we have mentioned, there was a market for agricultural products, because farmers had to sell a fraction of their produce to pay their dues in cash. It would be an exaggeration to conclude from this that Indian agriculture was, as early as this period, largely commercialised. The ideal for the ordinary cultivator was still to draw all the elements of his subsistence from his land, and to sell in the neighbouring rural market only to pay his dues. His marketing activity was thus marginal and represented a constraint more than an economic choice. In certain regions however, especially at the periphery of cities, in the irrigated rice-producing basins and in the zones that produced for exports, the trend towards the specialization of agriculture for the market was a widespread phenomenon. But, owing to the difficulties in communication, the market for agricultural products remained highly compartmentalized, and prices could differ in significant proportions between neighbouring regions in keeping with local fluctuations in the economic situation. The state of the techniques thus combined with the state of the mentalities to limit the influence of the market, which was present in the economic sphere, but did not form the organizing principle of rural life.

The setting up of the colonial agrarian order

The British and the establishment of land revenue

One of the first tasks of the British government in India was to levy what we shall call land revenue in the territories that, with the succession of conquests, passed under their control. In doing so, they merely imitated the Indian administrators that they had supplanted, as the taxation on the produce of the land represented in the India of this period, as in all agrarian civilizations, the greatest part of the revenue of the state. They brought to bear new economic and judicial concepts on this task, those that accompanied, at the close of the eighteenth century and the dawn of the nineteenth century, the advent of the modern age in the West. The objective of the East India Company in the beginning was admittedly not to effect radical reforms in India, but to administer it at the least cost, and for achieving this, to draw from it adequate tax revenue.

It soon became evident, however, that, in order to gain satisfactory and stable tax revenue, it would not be sufficient for a minority of foreigners to delegate to self-interested intermediaries the task of centralizing the collection of dues, without controlling the tax base and the mechanism of collection. It was therefore necessary for the early administrators of the Company, in each of the conquered territories, to strive to understand the system of land tenure and taxation locally in force to attempt to adapt it to the objective pursued by the colonial power and to the conception that it had of a modern and equitable government. It was a colossal task, undertaken from village to village and year after year all across the subcontinent. From one region to another, empirically and at the price of inevitable errors, the British advanced in their understanding of the modes of agrarian organization in India and exerted themselves to retain the features thereof in their land legislation, though the gulf between local customs and modern notions of ownership, of contract and of market that they brought with them was not bridged to a large extent. The place that land occupied in social relations did not change overnight. Rural society simply appropriated the new rules of the game by adapting its customary practices to the colonial law. The influence of modern values that this law conveyed could evidently become manifest only in the long run.

Historians have written a lot about the schools of thought (conservative or paternalist on the one side, liberal or utilitarian on the other) that could have influenced the agrarian policies successively implemented by the administrators of the East India Company as the conquest of India gained ground. These theories are in effect apparent in the correspondence of the most highly placed officers, who had to constantly justify the policies pursued and those that they proposed to adopt. But the practice of the administrators in the field was more empirical than doctrinaire. Elphinstone, governor of the Presidency of Bombay, wrote in 1819: "[The greatest difficulty in governing a newly counquered country] originate in the impossibility of standing still and of pausing while you consider what is best to be done [. . .]. Thus rules are made, not deliberately and systematically, but merely in the operation of despatching current business"[2]

In effect, the land systems of colonial India, as described in the official literature of the time, were primarily formal systematizations of diverse arrangements, concluded pragmatically in the field in tune with the local realities.

The aristocratic experience in Bengal

It was in Bengal that the first trial was carried out. Most of the villages in this region were dominated by *zamindars*, local chiefs or tax-farmers who had become hereditary. The East India Company, by becoming the *diwan* of the kingdom in 1765, assumed the charge of the settlement and collection of the land revenue. Its agents, not knowing anything about the modes of taxation and the taxation practices in use, contented themselves initially with allowing the Indian intermediaries to act, to the detriment both of the level of proceeds and of the interest of the peasants, who were taxed abusively for the sole profit of these tax agents. The Company decided in 1772 to assume its responsibilities fully, and to build its own system for the settlement. But to do so on solid foundations, it first had to start by establishing who, in Bengal, was the owner of the lands, and according to which principle the tax amount ought to be calculated. Long discussions followed in the government circles. They however were unable to determine if it was traditionally the state that possessed the land in Bengal, the *zamindars* being just agents responsible for the collection of charges or if the latter were the true masters of the land. They could not find anybody in the field, in any case, who corresponded exactly to the western definition of a proprietor, even if the *zamindar* and the farmers of his villages presented a few superficial resemblances with the English landlord and his tenants.

After years of trial and error, the necessity to obtain regular and sufficient tax proceeds, compounded with the desire to stimulate the development of agriculture, the condition for the prosperity of the Company's commerce, forced them to arrive at a conclusion. Three elements played an important role in the choice of the solution adopted: the model of the dynamic landlord, the architect of the English agricultural revolution, that the officials had in mind; the liberal conception of ownership as a sacred right of the individual; lastly, the economic ideas, then in vogue, of the French physiocrats, who considered agriculture as the source of all wealth. It was decided to formally recognize the *zamindars* as owners, and it was established that the tax amount that they would have to pay should be fixed by the State once and for all. This measure, it was hoped, would incite the landowners to develop the production of their domains rapidly, since any surplus in revenue thus obtained would remain integrally in their hands. This taxation system at a fixed rate ('permanent settlement') was officially promulgated in 1793, under the government of Lord Cornwallis.

The *zamindari* system thereby created, if it partly embodied doctrinal convictions, also represented an effort toward pragmatic adaptation to local traditions. On the one hand, the *zamindars* were the dominant figures who ruled effectively in the countryside, and it was easier and more economical to maintain cordial relations with them, on the condition that they be controlled by the British collector posted by the Company in their district, rather than to deal directly with the multitude of farmers.

At the same time, it was a means of linking the destiny of these dominant elements with the stability of British rule, the efficient intermediaries of which they actually became. Furthermore, this permanent settlement was not an absolute innovation. Under the previous Muslim regime, the tribute demanded from the *zamindars* was also in principle invariable, even if it was periodically burdened with additional taxes officially alleged to be exceptional.

In any event, from the perspective of the economic and social effects of the new system, the British administrators were soon brought down to earth. They realized too late that they had deprived the state, in advance and without due consideration, of the principal source of expansion of its budgetary revenue. Second, the *zamindars* did not abandon their ostentatious and parasitic mode of management to adopt the enterprizing agriculture modelled on the English. It was by increasing the rents of their tenants more than by investing in agriculture that they would eventually increase their revenues. Furthermore, most of them, far from personally investing in the improvement of their lands following the example of English landlords, lived as absentee landlords, as those in Ireland, and delegated the management of their domains in fragments to intermediaries in charge of collecting rents and charges on their behalf in exchange for a commission. With these intermediaries soon sub-contracting their office in a similar manner, there grew progressively between the actual cultivators and their estate-owners an entire hierarchy of right-holders, among whom the land revenue was scattered without any benefit for agriculture.

In the years that followed the promulgation of the Permanent Settlement, the tax amount having been fixed very high (90 per cent of the total revenue of the land rents) and exacted without any room for flexibility, a large number of *zamindars* had to resign themselves to seeing their domains confiscated and sold by public auction, most often in portions. A third of the lands in Bengal thus seem to have changed hands within a space of twenty years, and nearly half in five years (1801–06) in the kingdom of Benares, which was in its turn subjected to a permanent settlement in 1795. The purchasers of these lands often hailed from the literate high castes that the *zamindars* employed as managers, or from the circle of Indian brokers who had accumulated wealth in the service of British traders. They formed the new class of great landowners, more unscrupulous than the former, but for the most part belonging to the same upper castes. Thereafter, in the course of the nineteenth century, the gradual rise of prices brought in its train a relative decrease in the fixed amount of land revenue, which ended up becoming exceptionally low, to the greatest advantage of the landlords.

The peasants, on the other hand, henceforth defined as tenants, had not received since 1793 any guarantee capable of protecting their rights effectively against the arbitrary power of their masters, to whom the law, in application of the modern principle of proprietorship, conferred total and exclusive authority over the land within the limits of their domains. Not all the peasants, however, suffered in the same way under the new judicial order. The minority of powerful cultivators in each village (often called *jotedars* in the delta of Bengal) could maintain their positions to a large extent, thanks to their relative wealth, to their local influence and to their capacity to resist exactions and threats of eviction. The condition of the rest of the peasantry was becoming increasingly precarious, while the foreign characters of the new British judicial system made it in practice inaccessible to the majority of the rural population. What is more the system was paralyzed by the abundance of cases.

The colonial state, not much inclined on principle to encroach on the prerogatives of the proprietors and to hamper the freedom of enterprise, would nonetheless be obliged to legislate constantly, in the nineteenth and twentieth centuries, to try to put an end to the most flagrant abuses of the powerful landlords of the plains, who were always strong enough in their villages to circumvent or infringe the law with impunity and whose local power it had itself reinforced.

In the Deccan: the recognition of peasant ownership

In the first territories brought to subjection by the East India Company in South India from 1765 onwards (the hinterland of Madras and the Northern Circars), it was also the *zamindari* type of system that was put in place, and a permanent settlement was instituted between 1802 and 1805. The evolution was different in the vast conquests made in the southern Deccan during the decade 1792–1802, which, with the previous territories, formed the Presidency of Madras. Alexander Read, then Thomas Munro, in charge of the revenue settlement in the various regions of central (Baramahal, 'Ceded Districts') and western (Canara) Deccan, did not encounter, except for a part of Canara, intermediary powers comparable to the *zamindars* of Bengal. Anxious not to disturb the rural social order, they chose almost everywhere to recognize the right of ownership of the local village elite groups, by dealing individually with the farmers concerned. Thus emerged the so-called *raiyatwari* system (from *raiyat*, 'cultivator'). In several other conquered regions (Malabar, the kingdom of Tanjore, the Carnatic), there was a landed gentry, but the leaders of the Company, as early as the dawn of the nineteenth century, were already resolutely disposed in favour of the new *raiyatwari* model, and the local chiefs were mostly eliminated or reduced to insignificance, to the advantage of the *raiyats*. This *raiyatwari* system was extended to all the other parts of the Presidency of Madras in 1820.

The preference for the new system was due to several reasons, in fact more pragmatic than doctrinal. The defects of the *zamindari* system in Bengal had begun to become patent. The contact of the administration with each individual farmer, implied in the *raiyatwari* system, appeared more conducive to the interests of the state, assess the cultivated area and the income of the taxpayer, and which could itself carry out the collection of taxes. This system also had advantages for the peasant, who was spared the oppressive domination of a big landowner. Lastly, even though prejudicial to the landed gentry where it existed, this system perturbed less, apparently at least, the customs and social balances of the rural world. Without any doubt, the ideas in vogue in Great Britain at the time also played a certain role in this choice. They echoed in effect the growing intellectual influence of utilitarian philosophers, whose aversion to landlordism was marked; perhaps it also reflected, at the dawn of European romanticism, the idealization of rustic values that had currency in the home country.

Behind apparent differences, the *raiyatwari* system and the *zamindari* system shared certain fundamental similarities. In both cases, the British had favoured certain categories of right-holders to the detriment of others by conferring on them full and undivided proprietorship of the land. The *raiyats* of South India were dominant peasants with whom, in each village, the agents of the Company had deemed it expedient to negotiate and under whom subsisted other categories of subordinate right-holders. As the customary organization of land rights often varied considerably from one region to another, the standard term of 'raiyatwari system' in effect embraced a variety of different configurations.

In both the systems, the spirit of the law tended towards the institution of proprietorship in the modern sense of the word, and with it, of a mode of agrarian relations whose logic was contractual and commercial, even if in practice, the evolution of mentalities towards this direction proved to be very slow. The very dissimilar land stratifications that both the systems seemed to announce (landlordising on the one hand, peasant ownership on the other) gradually turned out to look alike. Owing to the practise of the judicial sale of the properties of defaulting taxpayers, on the one hand the domains of *zamindars* were divided into medium and small properties, and on the other, *raiyats* became medium or big owners by successive acquisitions.

Under both the systems, the place of the land in social life remained unchanged. Enjoying a preponderant right on land, in the Indian society, was at the same time drawing the revenue that this land produced and exercising power over dependents who drew from it the whole or part of their subsistence (and it was, complementarily, assuming certain responsibilities towards them). The relation to the land was, as it were, encompassed in social relations. The introduction of proprietorship – and of a contractual conception of agrarian relations – initially only reinforced in the villages the local power of the already dominant individuals or groups, who were to become the first users or the principal beneficiaries of the colonial legislative and legal machinery. The seeds of a modern conception of the relations between owners and tenants or labourers were sowed in the minds, but they would produce a perceptible effect in mentalities only in the long run.

In North India: the regime of village communities

It was the land system of the *raiyatwari* type that was extended, with the necessary adaptation to local conditions, to the territories conquered from the Marathas in 1818 which, along with a few other territories acquired previously, formed the Presidency of Bombay. In the conquered regions of North India denoted by the term 'Ceded and Conquered Provinces' (acquired for the most part between 1801 and 1803), which sprawled between Benares and the Sikh kingdom of the Punjab, it was a third system, called *mahalwari* (from *mahal*, 'domain'), that eventually prevailed.

In the wake of the conquest, in these regions that still formed, from the administrative point of view, only extensions of Bengal, the government started by transacting with local chiefs, tax-farmers and other established notabilities, as it had done formerly in Bengal, and it even envisaged a permanent settlement in favour of the big proprietors. With the passage of time, however, the administrators understood gradually that a regime of the *zamindari* type would totally disrupt local traditions. The romantic idea of the village community as the basic unit of Indian society also gained ground in their minds. Under the impetus given by Holt Mackenzie, on the basis of methodical and detailed investigations carried out in the field, they undertook the registration of land rights village by village from 1822 onwards.

In a certain number of cases, the local chiefs with whom they had hitherto negotiated (rajahs, *zamindars*, *taluqdars*), being of ancient stock or firmly established, were confirmed as owners. But most often, it transpired that the mastery over village cultivated lands, in these regions, traditionally belonged to the undivided community of farmers, in general represented by the village headman. Consequently, it was the village community that was declared jointly and severally owner and taxpayer, its members being left to distribute among themselves the tax charges. Here, as elsewhere, the group of powerful individuals who became full-fledged proprietors did not include all the cultivators. It consisted of a peasant elite that employed agricultural labour, and whose lands were often cultivated by tenants. This system served a model for the land system that was adopted subsequently in the Punjab (conquered in 1849), as well as in the central provinces after 1863 (the *malguzari* system). In Oudh, annexed in 1856, a system of manorial property (instituted for the benefit of the local aristocracy of *taluqdars*) and a village system of the *mahalwari* type coexisted. The colonial administration had come through the phase of familiarizing itself with local realities and simply adapted the models elaborated in the course of the conquest to the diverse regional contexts, with the two-fold objective of ensuring sufficient tax revenues and of gaining the support of the rural elites.

The tax burden

An essential trait common to all the land taxation systems imposed after the permanent settlements of Bengal and the Northern Circars was that the settlements were subject to periodic revisions generally at intervals of twenty to thirty years. The revisions of the tax base presupposed a detailed knowledge of the taxation units (holdings, estates, villages) and of their revenues. In all the British territories under the *raiyatwari* or *mahalwari* systems, codified methods and specialized administrations were gradually put in place for the surveying of lands and for the settlement of land rights, rents and charges. The same work had to be undertaken in the regions under the *zamindari* system, not for the assessment of the land revenue 'which was fixed' but for the protection of the rights of tenants and for the requirements of justice. Thus came into existence, little by little, the immense, and regularly updated, corpus of the modern land records of modern India.

Under the *mahalwari* system, the standard for tax assessment was generally fixed at half of the rental value of the land, including ancillary dues. Under the *raiyatwari* system, the taxation standard represented half of the gross income of the land. The modes of computation (always complicated) of these taxation bases, in an economy that was still only partially governed by the laws of the market and the system of pricing, inevitably included a substantial element of approximation and arbitrariness, and they varied in effect from one district to another in keeping with the conditions of agriculture. As earlier in the countries of permanent settlement, land revenue in these provinces was generally fixed too high in order to meet the tax demands of the East India Company, and its integral and punctual payment was enforced with inflexible rigour. There followed in many regions, in the course of the first few decades of the nineteenth century, an important trend of land alienations, as the farmers, especially in times of economic crisis, were forced to sell due to excessive indebtedness, or their lands were confiscated and sold by auction on the grounds of a tax default.

It is not certain, however, that the social stratification of the villages underwent a radical metamorphosis, as in the second half of the century, the same dominant groups endured as at the beginning of the colonial era. There was in any case a tendency, beyond the middle of the century, towards the reduction of the tax charge weighing on the land, or at least towards greater flexibility in the modalities of collection. Thus in the Presidency of Madras, the tax standard was scaled down in 1822 to 33 per cent of the gross produce (instead of 50 per cent) in non-irrigated regions, then it was decided in 1864 to fix it at 50 per cent of the net produce (after deduction of the operating costs). On the one hand, the crushing nature of the initial demand was recognized, and on the other, it was understood that a more flexible and moderate demand favoured the clearing of new lands, thereby augmenting the revenues of the state.

Rural growth during the first century of colonization

The expansion of cultivated land

Recent estimates of the population of the Indian subcontinent as it stood in 1800 vary, according to demographers, from 160 to 214 million. At the first general census undertaken by the British in 1871, this population was probably close to (in adjusted figures) 255 million. India therefore experienced, during the first two-thirds of the nineteenth century, an unquestionable, though modest, demographic growth (in any event, less than 1 per cent per year). With a death rate of around 45 per thousand (the severity of which was largely imputable to famines and epidemics), a life expectancy at birth that did not exceed twenty-five years, a fertility rate maintained below the biological maximum owing to diverse social and institutional factors, the rise in population could not have been higher. The growth was furthermore very unevenly distributed in space, always mercurial in time, and its chronology varied considerably from one region to another: thus the population increased probably by more than 2 per cent per year in the northwest of the Deccan between 1825 and 1850 and soared likewise in Haryana and North Bihar during the second third of the century, even as it plunged dramatically in vast regions in the Presidency of Madras in the course of the 1830s.

Demographic growth was not an automatic cause for agricultural expansion in traditional economies, far from it, but it represented a necessary precondition for it. It played a vital role in the increase in the cultivated area that followed, in a large part of India, the establishment of British rule. This increase was not a general and immediate fact. Agriculture in Bengal underwent a major regression in the course of the 1770s and 1780s in the wake of the great famine of 1769–70. In Vidarbha (Maratha country), villages continued to be deserted after the colonial conquest owing to banditry, floods, famines. The initial heavy burden of British taxation led to a decline in the cultivated areas in certain regions of Haryana, of the Presidency of Bombay, etc. When ownership rights granted by the British to farmers or land-lords included fallow lands, these were put into cultivation by their owners in order to meet the tax demand. If it were otherwise, as it was the case under the *raiyatwari* system, clearings were far from active, all the more so as cultivators lacked the nec-essary capital owing to the high rate of land tax.

In general, nevertheless, in zones of anciently settled and dense population, and notably in the plains, the abandoned areas were speedily reoccupied after the con-quest, and clearings were pursued thereafter, though at a variable rhythm. In Bengal, the agricultural recovery after the famine of 1769–70 was initially slow owing to the shortage of labour, but it greatly accelerated from the end of the century onwards. HT Colebrooke, a keen observer of rural life in this region, wrote as early as 1813: 'Increase of agriculture has proceeded with rapidity surpassing expectation and the greatest part of the country has already reached its limit.'[3] The first half of the nine-teenth century was the period of the greatest advance of land colonization in North Bihar. The progress made beyond 1860 was slower and affected marginal lands. In these *zamindari* regions of eastern India, the *zamindars* played a significant role in the growth of the cultivated area, by granting incentive rent rates, even credit facilities, to tenants who undertook clearings.

Growth was no less marked in the rest of the Gangetic Plain. Thus in the district of Gorakhpur, which included vast forests in the beginning of the century, the cul-tivated area doubled between 1801 and 1821, and the district became a large rice-exporting region, thanks to a successful policy of tax incentives. The same policy was implemented, with the same results, in other districts of the Himalayan piedmont. In the central Doab, as in the region of Agra and in Haryana, agriculture had regained, as early as the 1820s, the ground lost in the course of the preceding decades.

The course of events was slightly different in western India. Gradual but real rural growth had marked the reign of the Marathas in this region, where the administra-tors, who were of the same ethnic and cultural stock as the farmers, had promoted agriculture. This expansion was seriously compromised by the turmoil that eventu-ally caused the political decline of the Marathas. The agricultural stagnation dragged on for more than fifteen years after the installation of British rule, in spite of the increase in population, owing to the initial harshness of colonial taxation. The cultivated area began to expand markedly only towards the middle of the century, after the land revenue assessment had been revised downwards (it rose by more than 60 per cent between 1840 and 1870, mainly during the 1850s). In the Madras Presidency, the area under cultivation did not increase during the first half of the nineteenth century, even where the population grew rapidly. It increased manifestly only in the districts of Malabar and Canara, along the west coast, where the rate of land tax was the lowest. It appears that, on the contrary, it had diminished during the second third of the century in the parts of the Telugu country where this rate was the highest.

The structural fragilities of the agrarian economy

That rural growth was considerable between 1800 and 1860, particularly rapid during the 1840s and 1850s, is beyond doubt. In the greater part of India, it was in the course of the second third of the century that there was a changeover from a situation of abundant land and rare labour to a situation where the demand for land exceeded the supply (Bengal was probably the region where this threshold was first reached). It was also the period when the colonial government decided, in various provinces, to lower the assessment of the land revenue with a view to regularizing its proceeds. Despite this trend towards an expansion of the cultivated area, the agricultural economy suffered from serious structural inadequacies. First, growth did not occur in tandem with any notable advance in agricultural techniques. The ordinary wooden country plough, with or without an iron share, and unsuitable in both cases for deep ploughing, remained in use everywhere. The wooden harrow and hand tools (hoe, spud and sickle) formed for the most part the rest of the tools of the ordinary peasant. The cart was still an onerous equipment reserved for a well-to-do minority. The quality of cattle, whose grazing space grew smaller and whose fodder was often deficient, compounded with the absence of effective selection, tended to deteriorate. This lack of technical means was logical in an agrarian economy characterized by shortage of capital and low cost of labour, where all attempted investment moreover carried a high risk due to the irregularity of climate and the high cost of credit.

Agricultural practices were also stagnant. The use of dung as manure was limited to the most fertile patches of land near inhabited sites, where valuable market crops were grown on a small scale. Its use as domestic fuel, which became more widespread with the increase in population and the regression of fallows, reduced its use for agriculture. Agricultural specialization was rare but for localized exceptions, as the cultivator had to think first of guaranteeing his subsistence and the payment of dues, and thus had to vary his crops to the maximum with a view to minimizing the impact of the vagaries of nature. There was no other means of increasing the production of his farming operations than practising, if it were possible, two crops per year, even three in the best of cases, within the limits imposed by the capacities of the natural regeneration of the soil.

The only way to overcome this system of constraints was the development of perennial irrigation. Small-scale private irrigation by wells, tanks or canals locally improved the yields in normal years, and enabled the practice of double or triple crops, but its efficiency became minimal or even nil during times of drought. The great pre-British perennial canal systems had often deteriorated in the eighteenth century, as for instance the sophisticated Grand Anicut of the Cauvery delta, the dams of the Tungabhadra constructed during the Vijayanagar period in the six-teenth century, the western and eastern canals of the Jamuna, respectively built in the fourteenth and eighteenth centuries. The government of the East India Company endeavoured to repair these canals, both for the good of the people and for the proceeds of the land tax, at the cost of modest investments. The renovation of the Cauvery system and of the Jamuna canals was completed in the 1830s. The immediate economic and tax advantages that resulted from it in the beneficiary regions, as well as the disastrous famine of 1837 to 1838, urged the government to launch in 1841 the construction of the monumental Ganges canal, 1,400 kilometres long and capable of irrigating 600,000 hectares across the Doab, which was completed in 1854. Lastly, it reconstructed and enlarged the canal systems of the deltas of the Godavery and the Krishna in the 1850s. A large number of small-scale structures were also restored or created. This was the only technical advance that marked agriculture in the course of the first century of colonization, but it benefited only certain favoured regions (and it did not exclude certain ecological and sanitary disadvantages, such as the sterilization of soil by saline deposits, or the propagation of malaria in the zones where the canals obstructed drainage).

In general, the expansion of the cultivated area occurred in lands of mediocre quality. This fact, coupled with the quasi absence of technical progress (outside the few regions recently irrigated), and despite the effort towards intensification that locally accompanied the rise in rural densities, leaves the impression that the output curve could not have followed the curve of the cultivated area. As early as the 1860s, the limits of expansion of the primordial factor of production, namely land, began to be reached. The quality of the primary technical factor, cattle, declined owing to the limitation of grazing space. The rural population, however, increased – though still modestly and in spurts. The tendency of the average per capita production, outside the most dynamic regions and the last pioneer zones, started henceforth in all probability to incline downwards. The stage was set for the great famines of the end of the nineteenth century.

Owing to the poor integration of the Indian economy, despite the gradual progress in inland communications, agricultural prices varied in considerable proportions within a same region. They were also subject to mercurial seasonal and annual fluctuations, determined by the movement of production, itself inseparable from the vagaries of the climate (primarily of rainfall). At the beginning of the colonial period, in economic situations marked by acute crises caused by climatic variations, aggravated by the inflexible harshness of tax collection, it was not rare that a peasant deserted his land to settle down elsewhere. Towards the middle of the nineteenth century, as land was becoming scarce, desertions and migrations became more difficult.

The classic repercussions of these periods of crisis were henceforth the accumulation of arrears in the payment of dues, increased indebtedness, distress sales of land rights. In the wake of the great famine that struck North India in 1837–8, one of the most terrible of the century, the district of Agra lost 20 per cent of its population, the district of Etawah 15 per cent. The recovery, however, was generally rapid. In the district of Agra, the population, fifteen years after the calamity, was

50 per cent higher than its previous total. When the colonial state, after 1840, took charge of seriously organizing the fight against famine, and undertook to develop for each province a 'Famine Code' that laid down the instructions for famine prevention and relief, deaths due to these crises abated. During the great famine of 1860–1 in North India, the surplus mortality imputable to the crisis in the most affected regions culminated at 10 per cent.

Commercial Agriculture

India before 1860 was still too insufficiently integrated with the world economy, and its agrarian economy was still too compartmentalized for fluctuations of the international market to affect its agriculture in a uniform way. There was nothing comparable here with the economies dominated by monoculture that were prevalent during the same period in Latin America or in West Africa.

The development of export crops was particularly notable in eastern India (Bengal and Bihar), even though the agricultural area in question was too limited compared to the total for this development to significantly affect the regional rural economy as a whole. This region had an ancient tradition of exporting silk and cotton fabrics. The East India Company encouraged the production of raw silk for the English textile industry. The cultivation of sugarcane, also a local tradition, grew considerably to meet the European demand for sugar, but this time primarily under native control. The major export crops of eastern India after the English conquest, nevertheless, were indigo, opium and tea. The entry of European capital in the production of indigo was determined at the close of the eighteenth century by the crisis faced by the European markets in the procurement of supplies of indigo from North America and from the West Indies (as a consequence of American independence, the conversion of West Indian planters to the cultivation of coffee and sugar and the Black rebellions in Santo Domingo).

This speculation was encouraged in Bengal and Bihar by the East India Company as early as the close of the eighteenth century. The initiative was taken by private European entrepreneurs who induced peasants to cultivate indigo by granting them advances of money. This type of enterprise had fragile financial bases, as the entrepreneurs generally launched out into indigo with borrowed capital, and were consequently very vulnerable to the strong variations in indigo prices in the international market. Bankruptcies were therefore numerous, although there were spectacular successes. The cutthroat competition that these entrepreneurs practised brought into this activity a lot of violence and abuse, of which the peasants were the principal victims. In 1859–60 these abuses resulted in a wave of serious disorder in the villages in the delta of Bengal, which forced the migration of most of the European enterprises towards the regions of Tirhut, to the north of Bihar. The production of eastern India was to the tune of 4,500 tonnes of indigo in the 1850s. It had succeeded, as it was at the time the best in the world, in largely supplanting the traditional native production of the upper Gangetic plains and of the Madras region, on foreign markets.

As regards the cultivation of opium in eastern India, it was entirely controlled by the colonial government. The East India Company promoted this production with a view to exporting it to the Chinese market and to finance by this means the British imports of silk and tea from China (the demand for products manufactured in Great Britain was very poor in the Chinese market). This cultivation of opium was practised not in virgin lands and by European entrepreneurs, as was tea, but by local peasants, on patches of land belonging to their own farms. These peasants operated within the framework of contracts of cultivation accompanied by advances of cash money concluded with the Opium Department of the colonial government. At the end of the 1830s, Indian opium experienced a crisis in market opportunities provoked by the hostility of the Chinese government towards the entry of the drug into its territory, a crisis that culminated in the breakout of the Opium War in 1840. The British victory over China restored the status quo and spurred cultivation into new advances. The production of opium in eastern India, which did not exceed 4,000 chests in 1789, reached 50,000 chests in the 1860s. It competed victoriously from then on in the Chinese market with opium of lesser quality called 'Malwa opium' that the princely states of central India and Rajasthan produced.

Tea was a plantation crop established in virgin lands, and exclusively employed wage labour. It owed its development in India after 1840 solely to European private entrepreneurs (employees of the government of the East India Company in particular). The principal difficulty was the procurement of labour for these plantations. However, a breakthrough occurred as the quantity of tea produced by Bengal rose from 144,000 to more than 3,000,000 pounds between 1847 and 1864 and towards 1860 began to make inroads into the monopoly of Chinese tea in certain markets.

The common features of these speculative crops were the dominant role played by European capital, the fact that they were under the sometimes perilous dependence of volatile international markets, and especially their nature as a graft or an enclave without any spread effect over the local rural economy. This last trait, particularly evident in the production of tea, which was but an overseas extension of the British economy, was also manifest in the sectors of indigo and opium, although they were produced within the framework of the peasant economy. This was because the peasant producers received, in exchange for the product that they delivered, compensation only as salary, without any relation to the value of this product in the market, and because European capital used the traditional peasant mode of production as it was, owing to its low cost, without investing in it or modernizing its operations. The fact that these crops were not very lucrative often led the peasants to attempt to resist their cultivation, as was the case especially with indigo, which caused the European entrepreneurs to resort to more or less disguised forms of constraint. The primary advantage that the peasants drew from this was the availability of very cheap, even free, credit by way of annual advances on the harvest, granted by the European employer, and the receipt of liquid money that enabled them to settle at least a part of their taxes and rent charges.

In North India, where the native production of indigo was an ancient tradition, European capital was also interested, but without being as closely involved in the peasant economy as in Bengal and Bihar. The raw material (the indigo plant) was bought for industrial processing from small-scale Indian entrepreneurs who transacted directly with the cultivators. In the trade of sugar, cotton and opium, native capital was similarly active alongside the capital of Europeans. As early as the 1820s, regional agricultural specializations began to take shape in the cultivation of cotton and indigo in the riparian districts of the Ganges, from where it was easy to transport the production towards Calcutta. This concurrently resulted in the growth of the grain trade, as the exporting regions no longer produced to cater entirely to their subsistence, as well as in the impetus given to investment in agriculture (irrigation, equipment). Nevertheless, in the whole of North India (the United Provinces,[4] the Punjab), it was the production of food that continued to dominate almost everywhere, market crops representing only very rarely more than 15 per cent of the total cultivated area of a district. The recurrence of drought, as well as the poor state of communications, made it a priority for peasants to ensure the subsistence of their households. Moreover, only those farmers whose economic base was substantial enough could brave the short-term fluctuations of the economic conjuncture of commercial crops.

In western India, the chief commercial crop was cotton. The region, however, was not the largest supplier of cotton to the British textile industry, as the colonial government would have wished, because the fibres of the local varieties were too short, the efforts toward the acclimatization of American varieties failed and the lack of adequate measures of communication impeded the transport of harvests from the hinterland towards the coasts. There should have been a sufficiently high and constant foreign demand for cultivators to opt for the large-scale cultivation of varieties that did not cater to the local demand. Lastly, in South India, the development of cotton, which accounted in 1857 for a twelfth of the total cultivated area of the Presidency of Madras, was curbed by similar difficulties. The traditional native production of pepper and other spices for export in Mysore and the coastal regions of the southwest remained active. The production of raw silk, launched as in Bengal by the East India Company at the end of the eighteenth century, experienced a rapid expansion in Malabar and in Mysore. Coffee plantations also made their appearance on the hills of the south from the 1830s onwards.

Commercial agriculture, it goes without saying, was not limited to export crops. But the domestic market for agricultural products at this time is much less well known than the export market, as the local foodgrain trade, which was in the hands of the natives and was infinitely fragmented, was little controlled by the colonial State, and documents dealing with it are comparatively less abundant. It is clear that the severity of the British tax demands until the 1840s had considerably increased the forced commercialization of agricultural products. The rapid growth of metropolises (Calcutta, Bombay, Madras) had brought in its train new regional polarizations in foodgrain trade. This commerce, carried out by carts, boats, or in the most remote regions, by pack animals, was mainly a short distance trade. It was subject to the seasonal and climatic fluctuations of agricultural economies of the ancient type. Only large-scale cultivators, who had surpluses, could afford to stock their produce in order to await circumstances favourable for sale. More than an export-oriented agriculture controlled by European capital, less lucrative for the native producer, it was this form of speculation that gave an impetus to social mobility in the Indian countryside.

Social dynamics and resistance movements in villages

Indian rural society, faced with the ordeal of the wars and calamities of the late eighteenth and early nineteenth centuries, showed a remarkable capacity for recovery and adaptation, and its structure was not fundamentally modified. The peasant world, as we mentioned earlier, was markedly stratified before the advent of the British. Each village had its families of notables, generally from the dominant land-owning castes of the regions (Jats, Rajput or Bhumihar of North India, Kamma or Reddi of mid-eastern Deccan, Nayyar of the far Southwest, etc.). In certain regions, these peasant elite groups did not manage to safeguard their local influence when put to the test of the turmoil and trauma of the first century of colonization. But in other regions, their dominant situation was consolidated further in the course of the nineteenth century, when the gaps between the poor masses and the affluent minorities tended to widen owing to the rise in population and to the growing commercialisation of agriculture. During the same period, new peasant elite groups began their ascendancy, such as the Patidars of Gujarat, the Vellalars of Kongunad in the Tamil-speaking South, the Mahishyas of Midnapur (Bengal) etc.

The first century of colonization did not bring about any sweeping changes at the other end of the village social ladder either. Rural society included even before the conquest a substantial minority of landless peasants belonging to the menial castes, often untouchable, who were employed as agricultural workers. This category probably represented about one-fifth of the total peasant population. Its existence was the logical corollary of the existence of the stratum of substantial labour-employing peasants that employed labour. This labour force, if not servile, was to a large extent unfree. Slavery was widespread in India during the time of colonial conquest, but it was essentially domestic slavery. However, there is evidence to prove the presence of a servile agricultural labour in the beginning of the nineteenth century in eastern India (*kamiyans* of Bihar), in Gujarat (*hali* labour), in various regions in southern Deccan (*adimais* of Malabar, *pannaiyals* of the Tamil country). Apart from slavery in its strict sense, agricultural workers could be tied to their master in numerous ways, of which debt-bondage was one of the most common. Despite the initial harshness of the British taxation authorities, there is nothing to indicate that the size of this disinherited population underwent a spectacular rise. There was thus continuity, from the point of view of the stratification of rural society, between the first colonial age and the preceding era.

Peasant resistance nonetheless remained a chronic phenomenon during this entire period, as in the past. It expressed itself through various forms of protest of very ancient origin, of which the Revolt of 1857–8 was the last far-reaching manifestation. No year passed without agrarian disorders breaking out in one region or the other in the subcontinent. It took the form sometimes of revolts of *zamindars* or other local chiefs, exasperated by the demands of the tax authorities or by the amputation of their local sovereignty; sometimes of movements of tribes driven to revolt by the exploitation of the inhabitants of the plains and by the progressive disintegration of their traditional ways of life; sometimes of subsistence riots, often accompanied by looting of markets and attacks on merchants; sometimes of conflicts between masters of the land and dependents on matters relating to dues, labour-services and extra collections in kind; sometimes of outbursts of collective violence between the farmers and the pastoral and nomadic groups that existed on the margins of sedentary society, eruptions sparked off by the delinquency of the nomads or by competition between cattle breeders and peasants for the use of grazing grounds and clearings.

The last three types of protest were part of the ordinary chronicle of agrarian turbulence at the local level. The first two, on the contrary, could take the form of sweeping conflagrations. The armed resistance of local chiefs against a European conqueror who sought to liquidate them or to subjugate them was a permanent feature of the history of the penetration and of the 'pacification' of India by the British. These rebels – *poligars* of the Tamil South, Nayyar chiefs of Kerala, Maratha chiefs of West Deccan, Rajput chiefs of central India, rajahs of Oudh, of the Himalayan confines and elsewhere – often fought with peasant troops recruited from their rural sphere of influence by village chieftains and dominant cultivators, to whom they were themselves linked by allegiances of caste or clan solidarity. After the inevitable defeat of these chiefs, the local tradition often preserved their memory – and certain of these popular heroes are still commemorated today.

Tribal movements of protest were principally directed against the encroachments and the exactions of moneylenders and merchants, of the *zamindars*, of the colonial forest authorities, of the police, who expropriated them, harassed them, exploited their labour force, taxed the use of forest produce and of grazing grounds and hampered their shifting cultivation. Complex phenomena, generally irreducible to a single cause, and in which symbolic factors played an essential role, these uprisings often gave rise to pathetic guerrillas, with millenarian connotations, and finally to massacres of primitives doomed to failure in advance. The rebellions of the Bhils of central India in the 1820s, of various tribes of Chota Nagpur (Kol, Bhumij, Chero, Kharwar) in the beginning of the 1830s, of the Santals of west Bengal in 1855–6 were the most notable among the protest movements in this category.

Lastly, the frequent tensions between dominants and dependents resulted sometimes in mass agitation, particularly in cases where economic antagonisms were superimposed on religious divides. It was against such a backdrop that the agitation of the Faraizis flared in Bengal in the 1820s. In this fundamentalist Islamic movement, merged a reformist religious aim and the hostility of Muslim cultivators against Hindu merchants-moneylenders and the British indigo planters of the region. The trouble lasted for three decades. Such was also the general configuration of the repetitive uprisings of the Mappilais (Moplahs) of Malabar, Muslim tenants of Hindu landowners consolidated by the colonial regime, who punctuated the history of this region for more than a century from 1802 with acts of insurgence (there were twenty-two eruptions of collective violence between 1836 and 1854, then fresh outbursts between 1882 and 1885 and in 1896, before the great rebellion of 1921, all of which were severely repressed).

These mass movements were spearheaded by political or religious leaders or notables (rajahs, tribal chiefs, religious leaders), and they had a fundamentally conservative perspective. They aimed at the restoration of the former order, and notably at the restoration of the local powers dispossessed or destroyed by colonial intervention. Popular mobilization took place through the network of ordinary solidarities (kinship, clientele, caste, tribe, religious community), whose symbols the leaders manipulated and whose sanctions they used. Even when the agitation was primarily motivated by grievances of an economic nature, the structure of popular participation was not reduced to a schema of clear-cut oppositions between classes in the economic sense of the word.

Roughly the same characteristics can be found in the Revolt of 1857–58, which appeared as a peasant war in vast regions of Gangetic and central India. The precise modalities of the intervention of peasants in the uprising varied from region to region. In the countries of the Ganges and the Jamuna, insurrection was the action of the closely-knit Jat and Rajput peasant communities ruined by debts and the harshness of land taxes. In the region of Delhi and in Haryana, the impetus for the revolt came from nomadic groups (Gujar, Bhatti) who had been ousted from grazing grounds by the expansion of agriculture. In Oudh, the peasants rallied under their dispossessed lords, the *taluqdars*, who formed the aristocracy of the kingdom of Oudh annexed in 1856. Almost everywhere, and notably in central India, rajahs and tribal chiefs, who had been impoverished, deposed or threatened by the colonial administrative and tax systems, called upon their dependents to take up arms to combat the foreign oppressor. The ultimate defeat of the rebels in 1858 marked the end (except in tribal or very remote areas) of a model of agrarian protest.

British policy towards the princely and landowning elite underwent a radical change as soon as these troubles were brought to an end, resolutely tending towards conciliation. This self-interested clemency in the wake of defeat transformed the Indian princely and landowning class into a solid, though at times skittish, ally of British rule in the countryside. In the economic situation of the last colonial century that dawned at the time, it was from within the peasant world itself that agrarian protest was to appear and the leaders were to emerge, with the support of new intellectual and urban elite groups.

XVII

MERCHANTS AND CITIES
(1760–1860)

The uniformly blackened picture painted by colonial historiography of the state of the Indian economy in the mid-eighteenth century needs to be nuanced. In North India, the decline of the Mogul Empire, from 1707 onwards, was not synonymous with economic collapse: the successor states that emerged in the 1730s, especially Oudh and Bengal, showed a certain vitality.

The dynamism of trade

In North India, political decentralization seemed to occur as a corollary to economic dynamism.[1] In the entire Gangetic Plain, commerce intensified: cities played an increasingly important economic role, by the advances that their merchants and bankers granted to landowners; land revenues were more and more leased to merchants and paid in cash, no longer in kind; the consequent increase in the circulation of cash money irrigated the entire economic circuit. Lastly, the burgeoning of princely courts in the wake of the weakening of the Mogul Empire, led to a rise in the consumption of luxury products, which offered opportunities for employment to numerous artisans in the cities. The cities were in effect the hub of extremely active business networks that increasingly penetrated the countryside and housed the residences of a 'service' gentry, which occupied an essential place in the administrative structure of the various states. The frequent wars between these states following the end of the Mogul peace were themselves conducive to dynamism insofar as the armies and their dependants formed an important clientele for a number of commercial and industrial activities. Similar phenomena occurred in South India.

However, the prevalent insecurity had negative effects on inter-regional and international commerce. The principal trade route of Mogul India that connected the port of Surat, on the Arabian Sea, with the port of Hoogly, on the Bay of Bengal, via Agra, the starting point of the caravan route towards Central Asia and Persia, was greatly affected by the impact of the Maratha tumults, while the port of Surat itself suffered from the interruption of maritime trade with the Middle-East in the wake of the collapse of the Safavid Empire of Persia. Between 1701 and 1750, its fleet plummeted from 112 to 20 ships. On the contrary, political upheavals hardly had an effect on trade inside the country, which formed the major part of trade in India in terms of volume, if not of value. These exchanges relied essentially on credit. There was in effect a complex financial system controlled in particular by communities native to Rajasthan (the Marwaris) and which covered the greater part of the subcontinent. The Indian business world in the middle of the eighteenth century thus took the form of a pyramid. At the summit were enthroned the powerful merchant bankers, established in the capitals of states (the Jagat Seths in Murshidabad in Bengal, Gopal Das or Monohar Das in Benares). Below them, operating in smaller cities, were big merchants (*saudagars*). In the smallest towns functioned wholesalers (the *goldars*) whose range of action was more limited. Then, in the non-permanent village markets, the *beparis*, most often rich farmers, marketed agricultural products. Lastly, at the bottom of the ladder, itinerant traders (the *phiriwaras*) scoured the countryside.

In the absence of censuses before 1872, we are restricted to hypotheses concerning the percentage of urban population. In the Gangetic region – covering an area equal to more than half of France – there were about sixty centres having a population of not less than 10,000.[2] To these, we must add a great number of smaller agglomerations, often with a population of 2,000 to 3,000, but having a marked urban character (the *qasbahs*, an Arabic term denoting an agglomeration where an essentially Muslim gentry lived).

Among these large agglomerations, Lucknow and Benares had a special place with respect to their population (more than 100,000 inhabitants). Lucknow, the capital of the principal successor state of the Moguls, Oudh, had a primarily political role; Benares, whose banks and business houses extended their influence over a vast region, a religious and economic role.

In the other regions of India, the density of the urban network was unequal: comparable to the density of the Gangetic region in the Tamil country, it seems to have been much lower in Central and East India. On the other hand, Gujarat, which had a longstanding urban tradition, had numerous active centres. If the urban mosaic in India presented varied nuances, the urban fabric on the whole was dense enough for a pre-industrial economy.

Indian nationalist historiography has held British colonization responsible for a process of 'de-urbanization,' which it has interpreted as both a symptom and a cause of economic stagnation. In the absence of reliable statistics, this question has become the subject of debates that are more political than scientific in nature. It is certain that colonization modified the hierarchy of urban centres, without radically perturbing it. In fact, the impact of colonization on the Indian economy was not the same before and after 1813, the year of the abolition of the monopoly of the East India Company.

Trade in India under the monopoly of the East India Company

From 1765 onwards, the East India Company concurrently performed the functions of the ruler of Bengal and of a trading company. Its role in the Indian economy was consequently both weakened and strengthened. Weakened, because it had to make more and more room for English private traders, who had been tolerated in India since 1667, but whose activities developed considerably in the course of the second half of the eighteenth century. Strengthened, because the acquisition of political supremacy over one of the richest provinces of the subcontinent opened new trade opportunities for the Company. In the beginning, in effect, its functionaries, free from all impediments, could take control of all the economic activities of Bengal. In the space of a few years, they thus dominated the trade in opium, tobacco, salt and betel nut, and radically reorganized the textile industry of the province. Furthermore, the transition from the *nawabi* regime to the government of the Company favoured corruption on a large scale, of which the agents of the Company were the largest beneficiaries. Employing all means, legal and illegal, and with the collusion of the authorities of Calcutta, who had become intoxicated with this sudden and excessive accumulation of wealth, a certain number of servants of the Company amassed substantial fortunes within just a few years.

At the same time, the Company could use the considerable resources of Bengal to finance its purchases in India of merchandise destined for export. This the British called 'investment'. Until 1765, these purchases necessitated every year the import from Great Britain of significant quantities of precious metals, as the sales by the Company of imported goods in India could cover only a small fraction of its purchases. After 1765, this outflow of precious metals from Britain to India ceased and was progressively replaced by an inverse movement. The export of capital brought the economy of Bengal under threat of serious demonetization.

Those responsible for this transformation, which was perceptible as early as the 1760s, were the British of Bengal. The great majority of them worked for the Company and were migratory birds destined for a short life – the average life expectancy of Europeans in Bengal at the time was forty years. Only the prospect of a rapid return to Britain, once their fortune had been made, motivated them to brave the perils of a stay in India. They were hardly inclined to invest their money there, except in very speculative investments, and sought to transfer the greatest part of it to Britain to acquire lands and to live the life of a 'nabob' after returning from India. They therefore had to find a quick and discreet way to carry out these transfers of funds (remittances) towards Britain. Because the legal mechanism – the purchase of Company bonds payable at London – was considered inconvenient and not sufficiently discreet, parallel circuits came into existence, using non-British trading companies that were still present in India, in particular the Dutch, French and Danish companies. Between 1757 and 1784, fifteen million sterling pounds are estimated to have been transferred in this way from Bengal to Britain, in other words, an average of 500,000 pounds per year. It was partly for the remittance of these funds that private companies known as 'agency houses' were created in Calcutta from the 1770s. These companies that were constituted by the partnership of several individuals, generally private traders, rapidly extended their activities towards trade.

The 1770s in effect witnessed the beginning of a significant change in the direction of trade outside India[3] with the development of the 'country trade' (inter-Asian trade) towards the Far East. The Indonesian archipelago, China and the Philippines progressively replaced the Middle East as the preferred outlet for a certain number of Indian products, particularly for textiles.

Trade with China was promoted by the *Commutation Act* of 1784. This act, which appreciably reduced duties on the entry of teas into Britain, resulted in the increase of purchases of tea by the Company at Canton. In order to finance these purchases, in the absence of a market in China for British goods, and with a view to precluding the outflow of precious metals, the Company encouraged the sale of Indian products in China, especially of opium and cotton. A triangular system of trade thus emerged between Britain, India and China, the export of Indian goods to China financing the purchase of Chinese tea by Britain. This system relied on an association between the Company, which had the monopoly of the trade in Chinese tea, and private traders, who were in charge of selling opium and cotton. The vessels that transported merchandise from India to China, particularly from Bombay, belonged most often to the agency houses.

A growing symbiosis became evident between the activities of the Company and those of the private traders. It was facilitated by the reorganization of the Company whereby the administrative and financial branch was separated from the commercial branch. In 1786, in effect, Cornwallis prohibited the functionaries of the Company from trading on their own behalf and these men had to depend more on the services of the private traders. Around 1790, there existed in Calcutta about fifteen British agency houses (Ferguson, Fairlie & Co., Lambert & Ross, Graham & Co., etc.) and there were also some in Bombay and Madras. These companies possessed most of the vessels by which inter-Asian trade was carried out – vessels, usually of low tonnage, which were constructed in the shipyards of Calcutta and Bombay. They had become a power comparable to the Company in the commercial sphere, as their activities also encompassed banking, insurance and the financing of indigo plantations.

The private traders led an episodic struggle against the monopoly of the Company, which was challenged officially for the first time. In 1793, at the time of the renewal of the Charter of the Company, a new clause was introduced stipulating that each year a tonnage of 3,000 tons on the vessels of the Company was to be allotted for private trade. The revolutionary and Napoleonic wars relegated the question of monopoly to oblivion and twenty years would pass before it was abolished (except for trade with China). These twenty years witnessed the consolidation of private interests both in India and in Great Britain where the impact of the Industrial Revolution was becoming increasingly palpable. With the restoration of peace, in 1815, India was to become the target of a British commercial offensive of great magnitude, which it was not ready to resist.

What assessment can we make of this half-century? Nationalist historiography[4] considers it disastrous, marked by impoverishment for the artisans of Bengal, serious difficulties for merchants and, more generally, the beginning of a drain of wealth from India towards Britain, which is supposed to be largely responsible for the current economic backwardness of India. It is unquestionable that the political domination of the Company in Bengal had adverse consequences on the textile industry. This activity, essential for the regional economic balance, was particularly prosperous at the time of the conquest: cotton goods represented half of the total exports from Bengal until towards 1800. Textile production employed a substantial labour force, especially of rural origin, women for the spinning and men for the weaving and the 'finishing' operations. Though organized as a cottage industry (except for the finishing, carried out in larger workshops), it necessitated nearly twenty operations, each being executed by a different artisan. Moreover, there were several qualities of cotton goods, one destined for the local market, another for the court and the aristocracy, and lastly a third one for foreign markets, both in Europe and Asia. Besides a considerable population of artisans, numerous merchants and various middlemen depended on the industry for their subsistence. The combination of low costs of production and very high quality of products gave the textile industry of Bengal an obvious competitive edge.

The Company used its power to the full to reorganize the regional textile industry to the detriment of Indian producers and merchants. The essential tool for doing so was the *arang*, a collection centre for textiles, which consisted of several villages, and which enabled it to reinforce its control over the artisans and thus to circumvent private Indian traders. A series of regulations passed between 1773 and 1793 imposed very strict obligations on the producers, all dereliction being severely sanctioned. The artisans were gradually transformed into quasi-salaried employees, and thereby lost the opportunity to negotiate with their employer, the Company.

Between 1750 and 1800, the real income of the artisans no doubt tended to decrease, though this did not increase the competitiveness of the textiles of Bengal in foreign markets. After reaching a peak towards 1801–02, the export of textiles began to dwindle rapidly owing to the increased competition from English fabrics in the main foreign markets. Indian textiles, already excluded from the British market by a series of customs measures taken at the instigation of English textile interests (the Manchester lobby), no longer had outlets in Europe and in America, and were even under threat in the Asian markets. The re-conversion of Indian artisans and merchants was painful: a number of the former returned to agriculture while the latter had to be satisfied with less lucrative activities. The decline of the textile industry reinforced the agricultural nature of the economy of Bengal and prepared the ground for its transformation into a market for English cotton goods.

The establishment of monopolies by the Company on opium and salt also had adverse consequences on Indian producers and middlemen. The primary victims of the ascendancy of English companies were the *banyans*, whose role as middlemen between the international network and the local network had been crucial for nearly two centuries, and who had lost much of their prestige by 1810.

If the conquest of Bengal by the British impoverished native merchant communities, in other regions that had entered the sphere of influence of the Company subsequently, there were some positive upshots, particularly the development of the trade in opium and cotton with China that enabled a number of Parsis of Bombay to accumulate veritable fortunes, the huge orders placed with local shipyards, lucrative contracts concluded by the army of the Company with local suppliers.

From the abolition of monopoly to the abolition of the East India Company (1813–58)

Though sometimes described in ideological terms as a victory of the free traders, over the advocates of the evil monopoly, the reform of 1813 that abolished the commercial monopoly of the East India Company rather embodied the triumph of a coalition of interest groups, some of which had in fact made the best of monopoly for a long time. Among these stakeholders, the most powerful were on the one hand the agency houses, which operated both in London and in India, and on the other, the cotton producers of Lancashire, who saw the Indian market as an enormous potential outlet for their growing production. These two influences henceforth guided the economic policy of the Company, which had become nothing more than a facade behind which loomed the British government.

In the years 1813 to 1858, India witnessed a sharp rise in imports, which increased tenfold in value between 1814–15, and 1854–5, whereas exports hardly multiplied threefold. The composition of exports changed with the significant growth of cotton (16 per cent of sales in 1857–8 against 8 per cent in 1814–15) and of opium (which reached 33 per cent of the total exports in 1857–8), and a marked drop in raw silk (from 13 to 3 per cent) and especially in textiles (from 14 to 3 per cent), which confirmed the trend towards the loss of foreign outlets for the Indian craft industry in the face of competition from the products of English factories. China remained the major market with its purchases of cotton and opium, but Great Britain was a large buyer of indigo (26 per cent of the exports in 1839–40, only 6 per cent in 1857–8) and more importantly the largest supplier to India, textiles being by far the most important export. Despite the rise in imports, India still earned a substantial surplus in its commercial transactions, particularly with China, a surplus that continued to compensate the structural deficit in the trade between Great Britain and China. India thus played an important role in the British balance of payments: every year, transfers of money from India to Great Britain amounted to four to five million pounds sterling.

What is more, India transformed itself little by little into an important market for British industries. The shipping of cotton goods from Liverpool started as early as 1814: that year, cotton goods represented 6 per cent of British sales in India, to reach 20 per cent four years later and 50 per cent in 1828. From 1843 until 1939, India was the major foreign outlet for the British cotton industry. In terms of quantity, the sale of British fabrics to India grew from one million yards in 1815 to 25 million in 1824, more than 50 million in 1835, 230 million in 1845, and more than 450 million in 1855. These exports consisted essentially of ordinary fabrics, and before the advent of the railways, their distribution was largely confined to the coastal regions.

Until 1850, the Indian textile industry seemed to have suffered more from the closing down of its traditional export markets than from direct competition from imported English cotton goods. Those artisans who worked for the luxury market, as the producers of the famous muslin of Dacca, were the most adversely affected, reduced to unemployment and destitution. The phrase attributed to Governor-General Lord Bentinck and repeated by Marx in *Das Kapital* regarding the 'bones of

the weavers that bleached the plains of India' probably refers to this category of artisans. Those who worked for the local market were less affected as the high costs of
transport to the interior of India constituted a certain form of protection. If local
production of cotton thread could not sustain itself in the face of competition from
the thread produced by English factories, the local fabrics offered better resistance.
Indian artisans switched to the use of imported thread, which enabled them to
minimize their costs. At the price of a spectacular decrease in their standard of
living, the weavers were in a position in certain regions, particularly in South India,
to remain competitive.

The employment scenario seems to have varied from one region to another. In
Bihar,[5] the number of artisans decreased considerably, and the cotton industry
became impoverished. In South India, the loss of the principal foreign outlets in
America and Southeast Asia, compounded with the restrictions on sale in the markets of Europe and the Middle East brought about a very great distress in several
districts and weavers emigrated in vast numbers to Ceylon, Burma, the Reunion and
Mauritius.[6] Other branches of the craft industry, such as metalwork, were also considerably affected by competition from imported British goods. If we cannot speak
of the 'deindustrialization' of India in the course of the first half of the nineteenth
century, it is nonetheless unquestionable that the production of the traditional industry recorded a decline. The few attempts to create modern factories before the
1850s all ended in failure.

The British conquest also had the paradoxical effect of reinforcing the domestic customs barriers. Before colonization, the merchants had to pay numerous grant duties
and other taxes, but their amount was variable. In Bengal, the British imposed in 1810
a unification of town and transit duties, giving rise to a significant increase that seriously penalized domestic trade for a quarter of a century. It was only in 1836 that the
domestic customs barriers were abolished in Bengal – Bombay and Madras followed
suit in 1844 – which stimulated domestic trade. The state of the communication network, however, remained a black point: the road network, in particular, was deplorable,
in spite of the establishment in 1842 of the first link between Calcutta and Bombay.

From the time of the abolition of the monopoly of the East India Company, the
economy of North India was to witness three successive trends. After a period of
commercial expansion spurred by the boom of cotton and indigo, it faced an acute
crisis between 1825 and 1845, which was followed by a marked recovery until 1857,
the year of the great revolt.

The expansion in cotton cultivation in Bundelkhand and in Central India, in
order to meet a growing Chinese demand, commenced during the decade 1800 to
1810 and was spurred on by the increase in land revenue from 1818 onwards. The
financing, the transport and the first transformation (ginning) of the harvest were
carried out by a complex network, comprising both Indian merchants, particularly
the *gosains*, belonging to a warring monastic order that had been very active since the
eighteenth century, and European merchants. This network, centred around the city
of Mirzapur, rested on a whole hierarchy of primary and secondary markets. The
latter, which were formerly oriented towards local trade, easily turned towards the
Chinese market. It was at Mirzapur that the agents of the large European firms with

their headquarters in Calcutta came to get supplies of cotton, which they first transported to this city and thereafter to Canton. This export-oriented trading economy,
despite a rapid expansion, remained fragile.

The depression of the years 1825–45 was caused by the combination of several
factors: a shortage of liquidities, a series of bad harvests due to exceptional droughts,
an increased competition in foreign markets for certain export products like indigo
or cotton, a contraction in the domestic demand for luxury goods owing to the
decline of native princely courts; it brought in its train a serious crisis in the financial system marked by the collapse of most of the agency houses.

At the same time, the export-oriented trading economy suffered serious setbacks.
Thus the sale of cotton in China, after experiencing a short-lived boom subsequent
to the abolition of the monopoly of trade with China by the Company in 1833,
began to drop from 1838 onwards. Difficulties accumulated in the course of the
1840s in all the foreign markets, affecting a crucial section of the export-oriented
trading economy. The decline of cotton was in part offset by advances in the export
of sugar; those increased rapidly in the course of the 1840s, but decreased after
1850. If we add that the production of indigo never got over the crisis of 1827 and
that opium also faced serious difficulties, the overall balance sheet of agricultural
productions destined for exports seems quite dismal.

These negative trends were further reinforced by several measures taken by the
Company, like the closing down of the mints of Farrukhabad (in 1824) and of
Benares (in 1829). Driven by a desire for centralization, this closing affected the
entire credit structure of North India. Likewise, the greater security offered to
investors in territories placed under the direct control of the Company resulted in an
outflow of capital from the princely states. The state of Oudh, which embraced a
large part of the region, was particularly affected by these trends, which resulted in
economic stagnation after 1830. Similar phenomena occurred in the princely states
of Rajasthan, from whence the exodus of Marwaris towards British territories of
North India, and increasingly towards Calcutta, gained momentum. Was the Indian
economy the loser in this game of internal transfers? The answer seems to be in the
affirmative, because the increased dynamism of the beneficiary regions did not
compensate the loss caused by the decapitalization suffered by the other regions.

This scenario was further aggravated by the crisis faced by the agency houses. We
have seen the predominant role played by these companies based in Calcutta or in
Bombay in the trading economy of India. They were also very actively involved in
the development of the sale of British goods, especially textiles, in the Indian market.
But their role was equally vital in the export economy. Their activities had a strongly
speculative nature, because, in order to attract capital, they had to offer a rate of
return higher than the one offered by government bonds. The speculation on indigo,
which could produce very high profits, but whose market was subject to sudden fluctuations of great amplitude, led to a certain number of bankruptcies as early as
1826–7, like that of Mercer & Co at Calcutta. The First Anglo-Burmese War of
1826 resulted in a shortage of liquidities, obliging the agency houses to borrow at
exorbitant rates, which only aggravated their difficulties. The bankruptcy, in 1830,
of the best-known house, Palmer & Co, brought about by particularly imprudent

speculations, sparked off a chain of consequences. A wave of panic seized the business circles of Calcutta, which demanded the intervention of the government. The latter, aware of the calamitous effects of the impending collapse of the agency houses over the economy of Bengal and even of the entire Gangetic region, granted them advantageous loans, but this was not sufficient to bring about their recovery. In 1833, the collapse of the indigo market caused the fall of the six largest houses that still survived.

The crisis of the agency houses paradoxically had a more adverse effect on Indian merchants than on European businessmen. An act passed in 1828 by the British Parliament (*Relief of Insolvent Debtors in the East Indies Act*) enabled in effect the British insolvent debtors, and not the Indians, to circumvent the very stringent provisions of English law on bankruptcies. Most of the European partners of the bankrupt agency houses were treated with indulgence and could rapidly take back their place in the commercial world under a new corporate name, while the *banyans* – the Indian collaborators of the big firms – obliged to reimburse enormous sums, disappeared from the scene. The crisis thus resulted in further consolidating the European supremacy in the commercial life of Calcutta. The second grade agency houses that had escaped bankruptcy, and were reinforced by new firms from Britain, in particular from Liverpool, thus formed the core of the managing agencies (sort of trusts). This system was to dominate the business world of India until independence. For the time being, the disappearance of the most dynamic commercial firms evidently had negative consequences, especially on the trade in indigo, and several years would elapse before a recovery could occur.

However, the crisis of the North Indian economy had deeper roots and resulted also from social transformations that testified to the growing impact of colonization. The most spectacular was perhaps the brutal demilitarization of society from the 1820s onwards. Thus the redundancy of the Maratha armies, which numbered 150,000 men before 1818 (to whom should be added camp followers), dealt a severe blow to the commercial economy of the Deccan as well as of North India, as the maintenance of these vast armies offered employment to countless artisans and merchants. The decline of the Jat states of Deig and Bharatpur, which, towards 1816, maintained 25,000 men permanently in their armies, had similar effects on a part of Rajasthan. The increase in the strength of the armies of the Company was not sufficient to compensate these mass redundancies, as this army imported the bulk of its equipment from Britain, which reduced outlets for the local production of weapons, uniforms, etc. The decline, if not the disappearance, of a certain number of princely courts had the same consequences on several branches of the luxury craft industry. The impact of these readjustments, often painful, compounded with a stagnant economic situation to engender a cycle of depression in the economy of North India.

From the middle of the 1840s onwards, the return of better climatic conditions favoured a certain recovery, but export crops could not regain their level of the 1820s and the craft industry felt the growing competition of imported goods. In the course of the 1850s, the recovery was confirmed and the dawn of a true modernization became apparent with the beginning of the construction of railways.

However, this process was temporarily interrupted by the outbreak of the Sepoy Revolt of 1857.

Economic fluctuations along with social transformations in North India resulted in a deterioration in the position of big native merchants, though there was no notable penetration of British capital that dominated the coastal regions. There was a contrast between the west and the east of the subcontinent. In Calcutta and in the entire East India, where the depression of 1825–45 seemed to have been less marked than in North India despite the difficulties of the traditional textile industry, British firms controlled all the most lucrative sectors of the economy. In the 1850s, native capital was clearly reduced to a secondary role.

The failure of Bengali businessmen in the course of the first half of the nineteenth century has given rise to many questions. In effect, after the fall of the agency houses, a few firms founded with the collaboration of English and Indian partners played an important role in Calcutta: the most famous, Carr Tagore, had as its principal partner Dwarkanath Tagore, belonging to one of the most illustrious *zamindari* families of Bengal. This firm, which was the driving force behind the creation of mining and navigation companies, as well as the firms of Rustomji Turner (Rustomji Cowasji) and Oswald Seal (Motilal Seal) fell victim to a new financial crisis that struck Calcutta in 1848, in consequence to the fall of the Union Bank. This bank, created in 1829, even though closely linked to the Carr Tagore firm, was managed by the British; its bankruptcy, due to imprudent operations, caused Indian businessmen to lose their confidence in collaboration with Europeans; Indian shareholders were actually the primary victims of the bank's liquidation by order of the court, whereas the British who were responsible for the bulk of the difficulties came through rather comfortably. After 1848, the rich *zamindars* of Bengal no longer ventured into commercial and industrial enterprises whose risks they had come to gauge and contented themselves with exploiting their lands. Their conduct, which has often been explained in 'culturalist' terms (excessive attachment to tradition and values inhibiting the spirit of enterprise), seems rational when we take into account the setbacks suffered. There was no room in the Calcutta of that time for a true partnership between Indian and British businessmen.

In Western India, particularly in Bombay, Indian capitalists played a significant role, including in the flourishing cotton trade. The quantities of cotton exported towards China from Bombay were much higher than the volume shipped from Calcutta. Cotton came from Gujarat and the Deccan, and its trade was in the hands of Indian merchant communities, particularly the Gujaratis and the Marwaris of Rajasthan. But the influence of Indian merchants was markedly felt in Bombay itself. The presence of Parsis, precociously 'westernized' and particularly open to the outside world (their religion did not impose any taboo on overseas travel) was perhaps one of the reasons. Numerous Parsi businessmen were involved in the trade with China; it was also Parsis, the Wadias, who owned the most important Indian shipyard in Bombay, then very active. Other communities, both Hindu (Vani of Gujarat, Bhatia of Kutch) and Muslim (Bohra, Khoja), played an important role in the commercial life of Bombay. Differences of a political nature perhaps explain the contrast between Bombay and Calcutta: the survival of powerful native states

(Marathas) in Western India forced the British merchants for a long time to seek the collaboration of Indian merchants, whom they could dispense with in Bengal. It was Indian businessmen who, from 1854 onwards, opened the first modern cotton factories in India, while in Calcutta, the first jute factories were created by Scottish capitalists.

The abolition, complete from 1834 onwards, of the monopoly of the East India Company, produced certain repercussions in the British business circles that had instigated it. India became a growing market for British manufactured goods, particularly for cotton goods, and to a lesser extent, a source of cheap raw materials for British industries. However, Indian cotton was not suitable for the cotton industries of Manchester, which preferred the fibre produced by the south of America, and neither could sugar from Bengal overcome the competition from the West Indies. Despite the creation of tea plantations in Assam, Great Britain continued to import the bulk of its tea from China. The low competitiveness of Indian goods in the British market – the most open in the world since the abolition in 1846 of the *Navigation Acts* – explains why the role of India was primarily to finance the purchases of Great Britain in China and in America. This relation between India and Great Britain, inherited from the time of the monopoly of the East India Company, was to prove extremely durable: India was to remain a capital-exporting country, which evidently was not conducive to a process of local accumulation.

The cities

Between 1810 and 1850, the population of the cities of North India did not experience any significant rise. The percentage of the population residing in agglomerations of more than 5,000 inhabitants maintained itself at around 10–11 per cent. This stability embraces very different trends, with the proportion of the population residing in agglomeration of more than 10,000 inhabitants tending to decline, while that of the category of 5,000–10,000 was rather on a rise. On the other hand, numerous small agglomerations – the *qasbahs* – lost their urban character due to the difficulties faced by the small administrative nobility that controlled them. The decline of numerous centres with administrative and military functions, owing to the political reorganization of the region, was offset by the development of market towns that functioned as warehouses. Furthermore, cities suffered fluctuations due to the demographic evolution: a series of bad harvests causing famines accompanied by epidemics could bring about a sharp fall in the population of an agglomeration, a fall that was at times durable.

Cities nonetheless continued to absorb migrants from the villages. The higher mortality rate in urban areas, due to defective living and hygiene conditions, explains why these migrations did not lead to a growth in urbanization. There were also movements in the opposite direction, in particular the return of ruined artisans towards their ancestral villages.

The study of urbanization in colonial countries has for a long time revolved around the sole question of the impact of urban forms introduced by colonization, such as the famous 'colonial port-city', without being concerned about the internal dynamics of urbanization. In India, colonial urban creations certainly developed in the course of the first half of the nineteenth century, but their number was much too limited for them to be characteristic of the fate of the entire urban network.

Thus in Calcutta, towards the middle of the nineteenth century, the 'European city' (white town), constructed in accordance with the urbanistic principles then in vogue in England in affluent neighbourhoods, only encompassed a small fraction of the agglomeration around Fort William, the headquarters of the East India Company. With its wide avenues, its green spaces (*maidans*) used for riding by horsemen, its vast houses with a colonial appearance, the city formed as it were a protected oasis that was home, in 1837, to 3,000 British residents. But the majority of some 230,000 residents counted during the same period lived in the Indian city (black town) that sprawled to the north of the agglomeration. The black town, though created more recently, was made up a number of localities (*paras*) that had most often developed around the domain of a family, sometimes of merchants in the service of the Company, each having its own bazaar and all the services necessary for its functioning. The feeling of belonging to a locality was very strong, as the locality was the basis of the system of factions (*dals*) whose rivalry formed the best part of politics in the agglomeration. The elite classes, essentially Hindu, that reigned here, though thirsty for western knowledge, did not seek to imitate British urban models, and hardly bothered to equip them with roads. Between these two poles, there was a 'grey' zone inhabited by a heterogeneous group of communities of various origins (Eurasians, 'Portuguese', in fact Catholics who were often Indians, Armenians, Jews, altogether not less than 10,000 residents) that often played an important role in the administrative and commercial life of the city. If the Europeans formed the dominant community, their influence on life in the agglomeration was nevertheless quite restricted: the city was, in many respects, still very close to the countryside. Functionally, it was above all an emporium, a vast warehouse that received from the hinterland goods destined for export and redistributed imported goods. But it was its administrative functions as the capital of the Bengal Presidency and of the whole of British India that made it truly important. For the Bengali elite, overwhelmingly Hindu, it was 'the city' par excellence, the centre of social and cultural life, and all the great *zamindar* families had a residence there, where they spent part of the year.

Towards 1850, the population of Bombay, which had experienced a very rapid growth in the course of the preceding three decades, exceeded that of Calcutta and reached 500,000 inhabitants. Its sharp rise reflected a commercial prosperity that was deeply interlinked with the development of the cotton trade. But the annexation in 1818 of the territories of the *peshwa* had made it the capital of a vast administrative unit. However, its political functions were less important that those of Calcutta and it did not play the role of a cultural centre for Maharashtra as Calcutta did for Bengal. This was because its population was of more diverse origin than that of the metropolis of the East. The Parsis and Gujaratis played a vital role in the commercial sphere, while Maharashtrians, who were more numerous, were primarily employees of the administration and manual workers. As in Calcutta, there was divide between the European city built around the fort and the native city. The native city had a more 'urban' character than in Calcutta due to the higher density of population, and the influence of European architectural models was more visible, for instance in the sumptuous houses built by rich Parsis. The same features were present in the third of the great port-cities of India, Madras.

In effect, the only urban form that was purely a colonial creation was the 'hill station', to which flocked the European population of the plains during the hottest months of the year: Simla, developed in the pre-Himalayan hills from the 1840s onwards and which had become the summer residence of the governor-generals, was the model, reproduced in several copies all across the subcontinent (Darjeeling, in Bengal, Nainital, in the United Provinces, Ootacamund in the Madras Presidency, etc.). In the rest of India, the British contented themselves with lining the 'native' cities by a cantonment in which they concentrated. Among them were mainly administrators, but also missionaries and a few traders.

Among the 'native' cities that experienced a certain growth during this period figure Ahmadabad and Benares. Their relative dynamism testifies to the resilience of the pre-colonial urban culture and the limited attraction exerted by the urban models introduced by colonization. After its annexation by the Company, in 1817, Ahmadabad did not witness any notable inflow of European population, and despite the edification of a cantonment situated three kilometres to the north of the fortified wall, and which housed a few functionaries and European missionaries, the centre of the agglomeration remained the old city with the houses of the traders and the *pols*, where members of the same caste packed together in unhygienic conditions. The powerful trader-bankers of Ahmadabad, the Seths, found in the financing of the trade in Malwa opium, a very lucrative sphere of activity, while the traditional textile industry, which for several centuries had formed the basis for the prosperity of the city, continued to flourish, as the high costs of transport from the ports protected it from competition from English fabrics. Similar phenomena occurred in Benares whose large banking houses extended their range of action and whose traditional silk industry maintained itself, before entering another phase of expansion in the twentieth century. Here again, the British presence remained minimal.

The colonial impact on urban India was therefore quite limited in the first half of the nineteenth century. The British did not seek to create a new urban landscape and contented themselves with ad hoc adjustments. The big cities developed without any comprehensive plan, in the most complete anarchy. The insignificance of colonial achievements with regard to urbanism reflects both a financial prudence, justified by the chronic difficulties of the government in balancing its budget, and the absence of a true imperial vision.

Indian cities were largely left to themselves. The British administration did not go further than to control them through the intermediary of civil courts and of the *kotwal*, whose role was reduced to the rank of just a commissioner of police; for the rest, the local notables took care of maintaining law and order in the *mohallas* (localities). In reality, the urban community disintegrated, as the decline of certain controlling bodies (*qadi*, judge) was not offset by the emergence of elected municipal authorities. In North India, during the revolt of 1857, cities often proved to be the weakest links in the edifice of British rule.

Cities were also the cradle of the growth of associations, which had a vital role in the genesis of Indian nationalism. The early 'modern' associations were student clubs, such as the Society for the Acquisition of General Knowledge, founded in Calcutta in 1838, and which numbered 200 members in 1843. But it was the perspective of the renewal of the Charter of the East India Company in 1853 that led the members of the trading elite classes and of the nascent intelligentsia to create the first associations with truly 'political' objectives. Calcutta set the example with the British Indian Association, founded in 1851, which had the aim of influencing discussions on the mode of governance and working towards the improvement of the local administration. Bombay followed suit in 1852 with the Bombay Association, while a little later, the Native Association was created in Madras. These associations, which affected only an infinitesimal elite, hardly played any role before the 1870s. They reflected the aspirations of a thin section of society in the capitals of the Presidencies, but could not claim to speak on behalf of urban India, which remained on the whole resistant to British influences.

XVIII

CULTURAL AND RELIGIOUS TRANSFORMATIONS

(1780–1857)

In the cultural arena, India at the close of the eighteenth century presented a picture full of contrasts. The early English orientalists, who marvelled at the splendour of the literary creations of ancient India, asserted that Indian culture was at that time in the process of a rapid decline into decadence.

In the sphere of the fine arts, which was of little interest to them, this impression admittedly seemed to find corroboration in the comparison between the architectural achievements of the great century of the Moguls, the seventeenth century, and those of the following century. In comparison with the Taj Mahal, the tomb of Safdar Jang in Delhi or the monuments raised by the *nawabs* of Oudh in Lucknow (Imambara) seem to point, despite their charm, to a loss in vigour and in impact. However, in the art of painting, the miniatures of the Pahari style executed in the Hindu principalities of the pre-Himalayan hills (Basohli and Kangra styles) and of Rajasthan were not inferior in quality to the most exquisite Mogul works.

In the literary field, there was admittedly no creation of major works. Poetry remained by far the dominant genre. Devotional literature of the *bakhti* movement and of Sufi mysticism continued to be the mainspring of poetic inspiration. Prose as a genre was still little developed. However, in a society where only a very small minority could read or write, forms of oral literature were those that reached the largest audience and they remained vigorous.

In the absence of interest for western science, and in spite of a certain renaissance of traditional astronomy through borrowings from the Islamic world and from Europe, intellectual life was dominated by the speculations of Brahmins and Muslim theologians. The most important centre of Brahminic knowledge was in Nadia in Bengal, where in the course of the eighteenth century *pandits* were engaged in an incessant production of commentaries of the great Sanskrit treatises and of the already existing commentaries. This is revelatory of an intellectual tradition that was still alive, though it did not experience any revival. Islamic sciences remained vigorous, especially in Lucknow and Delhi.

The intrusion of the British was to have dissimilar consequences among the Hindus and Muslims. Its principal effect would be a redefinition of Hinduism, this cluster of rites and beliefs that made up a system but were not unified by a body of central doctrine, as a fully-fledged religion, akin to Christianity and Islam. This redefinition was to occur in two 'phases,' the 'Orientalist phase' and the 'missionary phase.'

The Orientalist phase in Bengal

When the East India Company established its political supremacy over Bengal in 1765, it began a drive among its employees to encourage a better knowledge of local culture and society. Very pragmatic considerations explained this new preoccupation. In order to exploit the province more rationally and in particular to increase the return of land revenue, it was necessary to understand the manner in which land rights were organized. This presupposed knowledge of the judicial and legal systems in force in the province. But the agents of the Company were handicapped by their ignorance of languages, particularly of Sanskrit, in which the principal treatises (*Mitakshara, Dayabagha*) were written. Warren Hastings, governor-general of India from 1772, was the first to have a true understanding of the problem and to strive to overcome it.

The birth of Indology, and more generally of Orientalism, as a field of scientific knowledge, at the close of the eighteenth century, thus fell in line with political expediency. Does this mean that Orientalism must be understood as an instrument used in an endeavour to consolidate the political domination of Europe over the East? [162] At the least, this thesis has the defect of denying the role of the intellectual elites of the Eastern countries and of making them the passive spectators of their own reification. To keep to the case of Bengal during this period, the birth of Orientalism or, more specifically, of 'Indology' was the fruit of the action on the one side of the East India Company and on the other of a certain number of British scholars who worked for it but who were stirred by intellectual curiosity, directly inspired by the spirit of Enlightenment, and lastly of Indian scholarly circles.

Warren Hastings combined political vista and intellectual curiosity. This astute statesman wanted to institute in Bengal a true partnership with the local elite groups. It was largely thanks to him that scholars like Sir William Jones enjoyed the collaboration of Indian scholars. Because Hastings was perfectly conscious of the fact that the native intelligentsia had a role to play and that, without it, the British would not be able to acquire the knowledge indispensable for the comprehension of Indian society. In fact, a number of Hindu *pandits* and Muslim legal scholars offered their assistance to the British scholars. Their contribution to the cultural blossoming that Calcutta experienced between 1780 and 1830 cannot be overestimated.

Admittedly, and partly due to political circumstances, it was above all the English Orientalists who have left their stamp on posterity. The name of Sir William Jones is linked to this 'Oriental Renaissance' of which he was the greatest precursor. Sir William was not the first 'Orientalist'; we must not forget the important contribution of the Frenchman Anquetil-Duperron, the first translator of the *Avesta*, the sacred book of Zoroastrians, and of several Upanishads. We owe to Sir William the popularization among erudite circles of the hypothesis of the common origins of Indo-European languages, which was so fraught with consequences. We also owe to him the establishment of the first chronology of the history of ancient India (thanks to the definitive identification of Chandra Gupta Maurya with the Sandracottus mentioned by the Greek authors), the resurrection of the ancient theatrical literature of India (by his translation of Kalidasa's *Sakuntala*) and especially the foundation of the Asiatic Society of Bengal, in 1784, a year after his arrival in Calcutta to assume the post of judge at the Supreme Court. This first scholarly society of India, one of the most ancient in the world, became, for half a century, the great centre for Indological studies.

Among the other British scholars who participated actively in the works of the Asiatic Society, we can cite Charles Wilkins, the actual founder of Indian epigraphy, HT Colebrooke, who was the first to undertake the critical study of the *Vedas* and who carried out a comparative study of the texts and practices of Hindus, HH Wilson, a remarkable Sanskritist who laid the foundation for the social history of India though his study of religious sects, and lastly, James Prinsep, who, being the first to crack the secret of the Asoka inscriptions, until then undecipherable, opened up an immense historiographical field of research.

The Orientalists were all great admirers of ancient India, which they believed had a 'classical' civilization comparable, though inferior, to Greek civilization. They maintained that this civilization had been destroyed by the Muslim invasions, which in their view marked the beginning of a profound decadence. These ideas had lasting currency in India. The thesis of a Hindu golden age that prevailed in the distant past and that fell victim to Islamic intrusion appealed much to the *pandits*, who embraced it with great enthusiasm. Even today, it is the cornerstone of the conception of Indian history advocated by Hindu nationalists. \

This intellectual effervescence led to the swelling of the ranks of the Indian intelligentsia. Even as a number of *pandits*, whose patrons, the *zamindars*, had become the victims of the upheavals that attended the implementation of the Permanent Settlement, were leaving their province to settle down in Calcutta, the ushering in of new techniques from Europe, in particular printing, began to produce its effects. The first modern presses, established by the Baptist missionary William Carey in 1801 in Serampore (in Danish territory), published, apart from translations of the Bible, the first works in modern Bengali prose, and a little later, the first newspaper (the *Samachar Darpan* in 1818).

A new type of intellectual was born in Bengal. Belonging to the upper castes that had traditionally enjoyed the monopoly of knowledge (especially, Brahmins and Kayasths), he was characterized by his two-fold education, Indian and European. Ram Camul Sen, one of the earliest Indian members of the Asiatic Society, was well versed in English, besides his knowledge of Persian and Sanskrit, which enabled him to find employment in the colonial administration before being engaged by the Hindustani Press, a printing press of which he soon became the director. Other Bengali intellectuals taught in the Fort William College, founded in 1800, by Wellesley with a view to training the functionaries of the East India Company. A new social class of men, financially independent of the *zamindars* and other local magnates, thus began to crystallize. Though it rarely produced original works, it played an important role.

The development of this group was considerably spurred on by the creation in 1816 of the first modern educational institution, the Hindu College. The fruit of a purely private initiative, essentially that of a few Calcutta nouveau riche families, it dispensed an education that was strongly oriented towards European literature and science. The designation 'Hindu' reflected the composition of the group of founders, all of whom were Hindus (an indication of the gulf that began to appear in Bengal between the Hindu elite and the Muslim elite). Despite the emphasis laid on European disciplines, the Bengali language and traditional arithmetic figured in the programmes. The College was very soon equipped with a laboratory, built thanks to a grant from the government. The Hindu College, that numbered four hundred students at the end of the 1820s, was to remain the best educational institution of Bengal for a long time. We must also mention the Sanskrit College, created at the initiative of the colonial authorities, where traditional disciplines (sacred scriptures, Hindu Law, Sanskrit grammar) coexisted in harmony with modern scientific disciplines.

The birth of this intelligentsia was retrospectively interpreted as the beginning of a movement called, in analogy with the Europe of the sixteenth century, the Renaissance of Bengal, a movement that blossomed in the second half of the century and which bequeathed major literary works in the Bengali language. Today, it is fashionable among Bengali intellectuals to be dismissive of their achievments, under the pretext that they were but pale imitations of European models. It is nevertheless unquestionable that it was an important landmark in the intellectual history of colonial India. Largely similar phenomena occurred in most of the regions of the subcontinent. Everywhere, literatures in vernacular languages emerged, which facilitated the dissemination of new ideas.

The development of vernacular languages

It was at the beginning of the nineteenth century that modern vernacular literatures flourished, especially in Hindi and Urdu, which supplanted both the erudite literatures in Sanskrit and Persian and the medieval religious literatures written in dialects, often different from the standard languages. The East India Company created and encouraged this trend; the Fort William College, founded in 1800 with the aim of training the high functionaries of the Company, promoted the writing and publication of texts in vernacular languages (which were often translations and adaptations of Sanskrit or Persian texts). By doing so, it encouraged the diversification of the two standard languages of North India. The common language of the bazaars was until then Hindustani, Hindi crossed with Arabo-Persian words, written most often in the Arabic script, as was Persian.

In the first decade of the nineteenth century, thanks to Fort William, two series of works appeared. Firstly, those that remained in the Arabo-Persian script and would retain preference among the Muslims: their language, which retained a high proportion of Arabo-Persian words, would soon be called Urdu (the term was not yet in use). First used in the eighteenth century, especially in Delhi and Lucknow for poetic compositions, then at the end of the eighteenth century for the translations of the Koran at Delhi, Urdu gradually became the language of prose and replaced Persian: an early history of India in Urdu, entitled *Araish-i mahfil*, was written as early as 1805 in Calcutta. The Delhi College, founded in 1825, with a view to marrying eastern knowledge with western civilization, promoted the translation of numerous western scientific works into Urdu. More importantly, Urdu became the language of religious education and theological debates, henceforth one of the potent symbols of Indian Islam. Secondly, the most recent texts were written in the Devanagiri script, just as Sanskrit. Arabo-Persian loan words were replaced by terms derived from Sanskrit. This latter language, which would have the preference of the Hindus and which would become their symbol, would be called Hindi: at the time, the term was still used as a synonym of Hindustani and denoted either Urdu or Hindi. From 1802 onwards, Fort William commissioned the writing and publication of works in Hindi. Hindi and Urdu, already loaded with religious affects, would be the idioms used in the preaching and controversies of the reform movements.

Christian missions and the policy of Anglicization

The beginning of the nineteenth century witnessed the emergence of Christian proselytizing, another intervening factor that was to occupy an increasingly important place in the debates.

Christianity had existed in India since the fifth century (the so-called 'Saint-Thomas' Christians following the Syrian rites on the Malabar coast). With the arrival of the Portuguese, the majority of these Syrian Christians passed under the authority of Rome, while on the western coast, fishermen and members of other low Hindu castes converted to Catholicism. A Catholic church closely linked with the Portuguese *Estado do India* was thus established in the sixteenth century. The Portuguese were joined by Jesuits and Franciscans of various nationalities; they were particularly active in South India, predominantly in the famous Madura mission, from where were written the *Lettres Édifiantes et Curieuses*. Catholic and Protestant missionaries – the latter arrived in the seventeenth century – played a vital role in the beginnings of Indology by producing the first translations of Sanskrit works and the first dictionaries. However, in India itself, except in Goa, their influence remained confined to poor and isolated communities, to which belonged the majority of the 800,000 or so Christians who lived in India towards 1800 (of whom 750,000 were Catholics).

With the establishment of British rule in Bengal, missionaries, primarily Protestants, hitherto concentrated in western and southern India, began to spread out in North India. However, the East India Company was mistrustful of these Christian missionaries. The Baptists, who were the most active, under the remarkable leadership of William Carey, who had arrived in Calcutta in 1793, decided in 1800 to establish themselves in Bengal at Serampore, in the Danish territory. They were followed by the Anglicans of the London Missionary Society, who arrived in North India in 1798, and by the Scottish Presbyterians. In South India, the Anglicans took over the Danish mission at Tanjore, established by German Lutherans from the neighbouring Danish trading post of Tranquebar.

More than in conversions, which remained limited in number, the influence of the missions was evident in schools and publications. The Baptists of Serampore created several primary schools and an intermediary school. Even though the great majority of their students were Hindus, they introduced in their programmes the rudiments of the teaching of Christianity, and through this medium, exercised a certain influence on their minds. But their efforts were above all focused on the propagation of the Christian message by the publication of translations of the Bible in Indian languages. William Carey completed the first translation of the Bible into Bengali before 1800; a revised version appeared in 1832. Between 1808 and 1820, the Baptists translated the Gospels into Sanskrit, Oriya, Hindi, Marathi, Punjabi, Assamese and Gujarati. On the death of Carey, in 1833, they had established nineteen missions in India, in Bengal, Assam, in the North-Western Provinces and in Delhi. At the same time, there were twenty-eight Anglican missionaries in the north of India. Their work in the British territories was greatly facilitated by the amendments introduced in 1813 in the Charter of the East India Company.

In effect, under the influence of a powerful evangelical movement, the British Parliament imposed measures on the Company conducive to the development of Christianity. An Anglican church was established in India, under the authority of a bishop residing in Calcutta, and the missionaries had the right to settle down in British territory.

The rise in evangelist influence led to a decline in orientalist ideas. The positive appreciation that Sir William Jones and his colleagues had given of Hindu civilization was increasingly called into question. The representatives of the evangelical movement, the most prominent of whom was Charles Grant, inveighed violently against Hinduism, presenting it as a body of superstitions, and they asserted that only a mass conversion of Hindus to Christianity could save India from barbarism. In tune with this evolution of ideas in England, the missionaries who had settled down in India hardened their attitude towards the beliefs of the people. While the early missionaries showed respect and strove to avoid direct invectives, the new generation did not hesitate to thunder from their pulpits against the degradation of the mores of the 'pagans'.

Even while tolerating the proselytizing of Christian missionaries, the East India Company did not wish to encourage it, as it feared to arouse hostile reactions from the local population. In effect, these reactions were not directed so much against the missionaries themselves, as against the Hindu converts, who fell victims to ostracism from members of their caste, and even to acts of violence.

The intellectual influence of the missionaries, however, continued to grow, as they benefited from the growing prestige acquired by England and European science in Indian scholarly circles. It was in the course of the 1830s that the first conversions among the intelligentsia of Calcutta took place. In an effort to reach scholarly circles, the missionaries did not hesitate to express themselves in Sanskrit, the language of the *pandits*. Thus, the Scottish Presbyterian missionary John Muir composed in 1839 a treatise in Sanskrit, the *Matapariksha* or 'Comparative study of religions', in which he formulated an apologia of Christianity and a systematic criticism of Hinduism. To refute his arguments, not less than three *pandits* took up their pens. One of them,

Nilakanta Goreh, retaliated with a treatise entitled *A verdict on the verity of the Shastras*, which embodied an attempt to put European rationalism at the service of the defence of Hinduism. Subsequently, the same Goreh was nevertheless to convert to Christianity.

Christian preaching thus forced the *pandits* to develop an argument in order to defend what they considered as the *dharma*, and that the missionaries denounced as a particularly perverse form of paganism. Hence, the necessity for them to define in more precise terms what they upheld. It was in the course of the 1830s that the terms 'Hindu' and 'Hinduism', hitherto used in competition with others, finally found currency. The long-term effect of the action of the missionaries was thus, paradoxically, the transformation of Hinduism into a fully-fledged religion. However, this transformation did not occur only as a reaction to the missionary intrusion: we must also keep in mind the remarkable capacity that the Brahmins have always had to assimilate external elements and to appropriate them.

For the time being, the growing hostility of the British against the culture and religions of India led them to want to create an Anglicized class in the country. A debate raged for about twenty years between the 'Orientalists' led by HH Wilson, who championed the development of teaching in the vernacular language, and the 'Anglicists,' favourable to the use of English. Eventually, the latter prevailed. Thomas Babington Macaulay, historian and brilliant Parliamentarian, one of the most illustrious representatives of English liberalism, appointed in 1834 member of the Council of the Governor-General, published in 1835 a report ('minute') in which he recommended the adoption of English as the medium of secondary and higher education in India. In this famous text, Macaulay, after declaring his disdain for oriental knowledge, advocated the formation of an 'anglicized' middle class, 'a class of persons Indian in blood and colour, but English in tastes, in opinions, in morals, and in intellect.' The same year, the government decided to make English the language of the courts instead of Persian. However, it did not take any concrete step before 1854 to create educational institutions. The anglicized middle class that Macaulay wished for would come into existence only about twenty years later. But a direction had been set, and there was no room for turning back. It was against this backdrop that Hindus and Muslims were led to look for ways towards modernity that enabled them not to relinquish what made up their particularity. Several religious reform movements emerged from this perspective.

Hindu reform: Brahmo Sabha and Brahmo Samaj

Among the Hindus, the first socio-religious reform movement was the Brahmo Sabha, which took shape in the late 1820s in Bengal. Calcutta was then caught up in intellectual and social transformations that would soon extend to the other large cities of India. The penetration of western values initially gave rise to two sorts of reactions: on the one hand, it was concurrent with the emergence of a group called 'Young Bengal', whose leader, the Eurasian Derozio (1809–31) taught at the Hindu College; this movement adopted the rationalism and certain practices, especially food habits, of the English; on the other hand, it provoked a rejection from the partisans of tradition, of which the Hindu Dharma Sabha (Association of Hindu Dharma) would be the leading institutional embodiment from 1830 onwards.

The Brahmo Sabha apparently occupied an intermediate position between these two reactions, as suggested by the personality and ideas of its founder, Rammohun Roy (1772–1833). Hailing from a Brahmin family that was relatively persianized, having served Muslim power, he was himself employed by the East India Company for nine years, until his retirement in 1814, and spoke excellent English. This cosmopolitan background partly explains his capacity to analyse Hindu society in terms comparable to those used by its detractors. He endorsed the criticisms that the missionaries directed against the inhuman custom of *sati* (by which widows immolated themselves on the funeral pyre of their husbands), against the hierarchical and hereditary logic of castes, which alienated the individual, and especially against idol worship, the symbol of 'superstitious polytheism'. The missionaries with whom Rammohun Roy had contacts were particularly the Baptists of Serampore, a locality in the vicinity of Calcutta. He was also associated with certain Unitarians, with whom he formed a Unitarian Committee in 1821. Roy further claimed that Christianity constituted a higher moral code.

Having been personally shocked by the sacrifice of a relative according to the ritual of *sati*, Roy militated from 1818 onwards for its abolition by law, which the authorities effected in 1829 despite the opposition of the traditionalists. In his concern for the condition of women in India, he denounced the polygamy of certain Brahmin *jatis* and became the advocate of their right to education. Driven by the desire to promote the education of Indians in general, he believed that public instruction must give a large place to western knowledge. In 1823, he also rose up against the British project of establishing a Sanskrit College in Calcutta, contending that a more imperative need for India was the teaching of European sciences. Colonization was for him revelatory of the backwardness of India and a providential opportunity for progress. But he interpreted this backwardness in terms of a decline from a resplendent Indian past and thus precluded a radical repudiation of his culture.

His efforts to reform Hindu society were firstly focused on the question of idol worship, which he made the subject of a tract in Persian as early as 1804. In his opinion, this practice was a perversion – imputable to Brahmin priests – of the Vedic religion, which was purely monotheistic, centred as it was, as attested by the *Upanishads* to which he referred primarily, on the *Brahman*, spiritual substance sustaining all beings, both animate and inanimate. Roy's attempt to rehabilitate this form of worship however betrays Christian influences: his conception of God as 'an eternal Being, unknowable and immutable, who was the Author and the Preserver of the universe' effectively displays theistic connotations.[2]

If Roy perceived the British presence as a 'providential fact', he also saw in it a cultural challenge. This cultural challenge was primarily embodied by the missionaries, whose propaganda he eventually sought to defuse by claiming to find in a Vedic golden age the same values that were the cornerstone of their proselytizing, namely monotheism and a form of equality in the path to salvation. He devoted a lot of energy to translating the *Upanishads* and emphasized, in contrast with the 'pure

Vedic monotheism,' the limits of Christian monotheism that allowed the Trinity! In 1821, he would even found a bilingual *Brahmminical Magazine* with a view to disseminating his ideas among the Bengali intelligentsia and the missionaries of Serampore, with whom he entered into a lively debate. Apart from his activities as a publicist, he founded in 1815 the Atmya Sabha (Association of Friends), where debates were held every week on religious issues, and in 1828, the Brahmo Sabha (Association of Brahma), the members of which met every Saturday to chant theistic hymns often drawn from the *Upanishads*.

On the other hand, Roy's knowledge of the Vedas seems to be limited to the *Upanishads*. Max Muller would say that 'he had no idea of what the Vedas really were.'[3] In effect, it appears that Roy selected and highlighted those texts that enabled him to challenge most effectively the monotheistic propaganda of the missionaries. This choice would not be devoid of consequences, as reformed Hinduism, especially in Bengal, was to remain associated with the *Upanishads* until the beginning of the twentieth century.

In 1830, the Brahmo Sabha acquired a building in Chitpur, a neighbourhood in Calcutta. The responsibility for the entire organization then fell on Roy's shoulders. However, he died in 1833 in London where he had gone to represent Indians at the time of the revision of the Charter of the Company. His final voyage confirms the fundamental ambiguity of his defence of a reformed Hinduism, as, in London, he reiterated his attachment to utilitarian ideals, especially during his meeting with the philosopher Jeremy Bentham.

Roy was succeeded as the head of the Brahmo Sabha by the members of a rich Brahmin family of Calcutta, Dwarkanath Tagore (who had financed the organization in its infancy), then by his son, Debendranath Tagore. The latter had become a member of the Brahmo Sabha in 1842, after having founded a Tattvabadhini Sabha in 1839 which aimed at refuting the accusations of missionaries against Hindu polytheism. In 1844, he sent a few disciples to Benares to get from the *pandits* a copy of the Vedas with a view to bolstering this counter-argumentation. When he discovered the highly heterogeneous nature of these scriptures, he experienced a profound crisis. In 1850, he renounced the idea that the Vedas were infallible and returned to more orthodox Hindu practices: the Brahmo Samaj (the new name that the Brahmo Sabha was given) henceforth tended to be reabsorbed by Hinduism as had been so many other heterodox sects that had preceded it.

The movement then expanded beyond the confines of Calcutta (a branch was opened at Dacca in 1846) but involved only a minority of the intelligentsia, as being a member of the Brahmo Samaj was generally tantamount to breaking with one's community by a reformist ideal. The Brahmos, often from the high castes, were in effect ostracized by coreligionists of the same status, owing to the heterodoxy that was manifest, for instance, in the rejection of the sacred thread.

The radiating influence of the Brahmo Samaj was nevertheless not in proportion with the small number of its partisans. It formed a true seminal movement, as attested by the title of 'father of modern India' often conferred on Rammohun Roy. This movement primarily ushered in a Hindu method of adjusting to western intervention: on the one hand, its leaders showed themselves open-minded to certain features of western modernity and strove to reform their society; on the other hand, they took up the cultural challenge posed by the missions by contending that Hinduism, in his original form, already incorporated the values in the name of which their propaganda was deployed. The invention of a Vedic golden age that crystallized in this context laid the foundation for an ideological discourse of resistance to the colonizer.

Muslim reforms

In the religious movements of the beginning of the nineteenth century, Muslims were the most active and the most ostentatious. These movements began in 1818: it is no accident, because this year that marked the defeat of the Marathas coincided with the demilitarisation of India. Rather than fighting against the British, the time had come to reform the Muslim community.

Muslim doctrine and institutions had hardly changed since the Mogul Empire: the timid revival ushered in by Shah Waliullah in the eighteenth century in Delhi was pursued by his son, particularly by the eldest, Shah Abdulaziz, without fundamentally altering the medieval balance. The ulemas remained faithful to the medieval order taught in the *madrasas* that maintained an Arab and Persian culture and restricted themselves to submission (*taqlid*) to the schools of Law.[4] Sufism impregnated both scholarly and popular spirituality: all Muslims believed in the intercession of the saints.

Wahhabism

Muslim India, even after the British conquest, had always been largely open to the rest of the Muslim world by land and sea routes. People travelled from India towards Central Asia and Arabia, as the scholar and lexicographer Murtaza Zabidi (1732–91), a student of Shah Waliullah, who settled down in Yemen; Indians on the route of pilgrimage and studies or of trade generally integrated a prolonged stay in Yemen. In the opposite direction, subjects of the Ottoman Empire – as the famous reformer of Kurdish origin Maulana Khalid Baghdadi – came to study Sufism in Delhi, which remained a cosmopolitan city. The events that transpired at the time in Arabia were not unknown to Indian scholars. The eighteenth century had witnessed the birth of a puritanical movement called Wahhabism, from the name of its founder, Muhammad Ibn Abdulwahhab (1703–92).

Drawing inspiration from the great theologian of Damascus Ibn Taimiyya (1263–1328), Ibn Abdulwahhab elaborated a doctrine that laid emphasis on divine unity. Proscribing all cults and beliefs that attributed to creatures powers that only belonged to God, he forbade the veneration of pagan divinities and even the worship of saints; he enjoined Muslims to distinguish themselves in all possible ways from non-Muslims. Ibn Abdulwahhab forged an alliance with the family of the Sauds, who, after his death, founded in the Arabian peninsula the First Wahhabite Empire (the second, which lasts even today, would be established in 1926). They conquered Medina and Mecca in 1804. They were ousted from there in 1814, then definitively defeated in 1818 by a expedition of the Viceroy of Egypt, Muhammad Ali, who was acting at the behest of the Ottoman Empire. On this occasion, the British fleet at Bombay made a demonstration of force in the waters of the Arabian Sea: this proves that these events did not pass unnoticed in India. And in effect, in the Indian subcontinent, a militant minority broke away from the tradition from 1818 onwards. It was spurred on by two movements: the Faraizis of Bengal and the Mujahidinns of the Tariqa-i Muhammadiyya order.

The Faraizis

This movement, limited in space and in the social hierarchy, was of immediate concern for the British, as it affected the small farmers and artisans of eastern Bengal, not far from Calcutta, the capital of the empire.

Its initiator was a modest scholar of rural origin, Hajji Shariatullah (1780–1840), who had gone on pilgrimage to Mecca, and had remained there to study for nearly twenty years with a master called Tahir Sambhal. On his return, he undertook the reform of the religious practices of his coreligionists in Bengal. Without opposing Sufism per se, but only its excesses, he allowed his enlightened disciples to practice the *dhikr* of the Qadiriyya brotherhood – even while prohibiting the mass of the peasants to take saints as intercessors – and banned the worship of pagan deities. He exhorted his followers to distinguish themselves from non-Muslims by their dress. More than any other movement in India, the Faraizis laid emphasis on Muslim solidarity and the equality of its members: peasants and artisans mingled in it. The teaching of the master was recorded in poems composed in Bengali. The movement, at a very potent time in eastern Bengal, was centralized: disciples entered the sect through an initiation with the founder or with his representatives, who scoured the territory.

Very exclusive, the Faraizis distinguished themselves from Hindus but also from non-reformed Muslims – who in general were richer – with whom they refused to eat and whom they refused to marry. The son of Shariatullah, Dudhu Miyan (1819–62), who was to succeed him as the leader of the movement, organized a militia trained and armed with bludgeons. Their principal adversaries were the powerful landowners, the *zamindars* or landlords, who were in the majority Hindu in this region; the Faraizis on the contrary were small farmers who worked for them. This class conflict assumed a religious dimension owing to the circumstances.

Another particularity of the Faraizis was that they refused to recite the solemn prayer of the two important festivals because India was no longer governed by Muslims. Some have interpreted this refusal as a declaration of war against the British presence. In reality, the Faraizis did nothing but draw the legal consequences of a matter of fact. They preferred the British administration to the authority of the Hindu *zamindars* and urged the peasants to leave the land of the latter to settle down in lands administered by the functionaries of the East India Company.

The Faraizi movement was therefore not a revolutionary and anti-British uprising, as some have maintained. In its social and political dimensions, it enabled a small Muslim peasantry to take advantage of the *pax Britannica* in its struggle against

Hindu landowners. This movement, initially religious in nature, drew its inspiration from Arabia: if British colonization gave it a chance to develop, it did not cause it.

The Tariqa-i Muhammadiyya of Sayyid Ahmad Barelwi

The same is true of this movement, which in the eyes of its adversaries represented Indian Wahhabism par excellence. Of much greater scope, it embraced the whole of India, and its influence has endured to this day.

Its founder was one of the most extraordinary figures of Muslim India, Sayyid Ahmad Barelwi (1786–1831). In an apparent paradox, this reformer who was to crusade against the worship of saints was born in a rather modest family that hereditarily served at the tombs of saints, at Rae Bareilly, in the middle valley of the Ganges, near Lucknow. Educated in the religious sciences but also in martial arts as most of the men of his time, he tried to become a mercenary at the beginning of the nineteenth century; out of desperation, he went to Delhi to pursue his studies under Shah Abdulaziz. He was a strange student, rebellious and not gifted. Hagiography has it that he refused to prostrate himself in front of his master as was required by the medieval practice, because this honour, in his opinion, was reserved for God alone. He then proved himself incapable of learning: which, in traditional thought, was a sign of divine election, as the saint, like the Prophet, was an 'illiterate', *ummi*, who learnt directly from God without needing the screen of human knowledge. He then enrolled himself in the army of an Afghan adventurer, Amir Khan, who, in the wake of the Marathas, had cornered a fief in Rajasthan. After the defeat of the Marathas and the demilitarization of India, Amir Khan made peace with the British who allowed him to form a princely state in Tonk, in Rajasthan. After returning to civil life, Sayyid Ahmad Barelwi definitively opted for a career as a religious reformer.

On his return to Delhi in 1817 to 1818, Ahmad Barelwi first lived as a recluse in the Akbarabadi mosque where he had visions. Founding a neo-Sufi order, the Tariqa-i Muhammadiyya, a synthesis of all the preceding orders, he initiated disciples: the most famous of these, the one who was to accompany him until his death, was Shah Waliullah's grandson, Muhammad Ismail Shahid, who would become the brains behind the movement. Towards, 1818, he wrote in Persian its first manifesto, *Sirat al-mustaqim*, 'The Straight Way', in which he recorded the words and visions of his master. The latter, reviving the terminology of the Naqshbandis, laid claim to a superior form of Sufism, the 'way of prophecy,' which placed him in direct communion with God and made him a representative of the Prophet. He thus had the responsibility of re-establishing the prophetic message in its purity and its religious, social and political entirety, through preaching and example.

Sayyid Ahmad Barelwi, Muhammad Ismail Shahid and their disciples set out on preaching tours in the Ganges Valley, reaching out to all sections of the population. Like the Faraizis, they preached against pagan rites, the worship of saints and the imitation of Hindus: this teaching is summarized in what remains to this day the model of fundamentalist catechisms in India, the *Taqwiyyat al-iman*, the 'fortification of faith'. This early doctrinal work written in Urdu was completed in 1824, and soon after published: Muslim reformers, vying with the missionaries, began to publish an abundant literature on religious education in Urdu.

The social reform that they advocated did not at all aim at abolishing existing hierarchies, but at reintroducing the primeval simplicity of Islam by eliminating expensive and ostentatious ceremonies, and at encouraging the remarriage of widows. The emphasis was laid on the compulsory practices of Islam, including especially those that were believed to have fallen into disuse: pilgrimage and holy war. From 1821 to 1823, Sayyid Ahmad Barelwi went on a pilgrimage to Mecca with more than six hundred disciples. In 1826, he started the holy war: with thousands of disciples, henceforth called Mujahidins, he left Delhi, marching across Rajasthan, Sind, Afghanistan, to attack the Sikhs from Peshawar. He founded in this region a short-lived theocratic state, where he proclaimed himself the commander of the faithful (*amir al-muminin*), a title traditionally reserved for the caliph; it was with the spiritual authority of a caliph that he wrote to the heads of states of India and Central Asia. This state was financed by the collection of funds and the mobilization of volunteers from all over North India as far as Bengal. But the grandiose dream would soon be shattered: betrayed by the Afghan tribes, who did not endorse his reforms, pursued by the Sikh armies, Sayyid Ahmad Barelwi fled to Kashmir: his army was decimated by the Sikhs at the Battle of Balakot, to the north of present Pakisthan, in 1831: he died a martyr (*shahid*) at the same time as Muhammad Ismail Shahid.

His career however did not come to a close, as a fraction of his disciples, refusing to believe in his death, continued to maintain an army in the rear of the Sikhs. For them, he was the *mahdi* whose advent at the end of times had been announced by Muslim traditions: he was not dead, but only occulted and must therefore come back to lead the faithful to victory. In effect, this figure did not have any realistic political project, he was above all the visionary founder of a Messianic movement.

This belief led to a schism. The more radical of the disciples, who preached and pursued armed conflict as late as the 1860s, assembled in the Patna school around Wilayat Ali. The others abandoned the armed fight and devoted themselves to religious reform like Karamat Ali Jaunpuri, who vied with the Faraizis for the Islamization of Bengal, or the scholarly circles of Delhi, from where the modernist Sayyid Ahmad Khan (1817–98) would emerge.

But, whether partisans or not of armed struggle, the disciples of Sayyid Ahmad Barelwi, who remained a minority at the time, distinguished themselves henceforth from the mass of Muslims by their spirit of reform that questioned traditional mystical religiosity, the worship of saints and immemorial social customs of Indian Islam; their proselytizing zeal was a form of *jihad*.

Their traditionalist opponents would call them as early as the 1820s 'Wahhabites.' From the Wahhabites of Arabia, they had certainly embraced the fundamentalist beliefs in divine unity. There is not doubt that this movement drew its inspiration from the reformers of the Arabian peninsula, but for this, they were not the blind disciples of Muhammad Ibn Abdulwahhab: the indications of hagiography on the contrary point to an indirect inspiration drawn from the reformers of the time in Yemen, particularly from Muhammad ibn Ali Al-Shaukani (died in 1834), whom several Indian reformers, including Sayyid Ahmad Barelwi himself, had met during their pilgrimage. An intermediary like this explains the frame of mind of the Indian reformers, who, like Al-Shaukani and unlike the Wahhabites would always retain a mystical dimension. This exogenous movement was thus favoured by the *pax Britannica* but not caused by it.

The adversary of these movements was not exclusively, not even primarily, the British presence. These early Muslim movements were above all a debate among Muslims, wherein the British were not specifically targeted. Fraught with far-reaching consequences for the future, they marked for a zealous minority an adaptation to both the reforms underway elsewhere in the Muslim world and to the loss of their power in India.

PART FIVE

FROM THE BRITISH INDIAN
EMPIRE TO INDEPENDENCE
(1858–1950)

The second century of colonial rule (1858–1947) witnessed the apogee, the decline and the fall of the British Empire in India. After the crushing of the Sepoy Revolt, the colonial state reorganized itself and became the embryo of a modern bureaucratic state. British rule was soon contested by a nationalist movement, which was embodied by the Indian National Congress, founded in 1885. From 1905 onwards, a protest movement developed but on the eve of First World War, British domination in India still seemed firmly entrenched (Chapter XIX).

After the First World War, Indian nationalism acquired a popular dimension as evident in the three great anti-British movements: in 1919 ('Rowlett Satyagraha'), in 1920–2 ('Non-Cooperation') and in 1930–4 ('Civil Disobedience'). In the face of the magnitude of these movements, the British were constrained to make political reforms: in 1937, Congress governments could thus come to power in most of the provinces of British India. A very progressive transfer of power to Indians then seemed possible, but in the course of the Second World War, a rupture appeared between the colonial government and Congress, which led to a violent confrontation in 1942 (Chapter XX).

A quarter of the population of India lived at the time in hundreds of princely states. These were not strictly speaking part of the provinces of British India and were subjected to the authority of princes on whom the colonial power retained a right of control. The size of their states varied greatly: about a dozen states embraced a large share of the population of princely India. Between Hyderabad, the largest of them, where absolute despotism prevailed, and Mysore or Baroda, where enlightened rulers encouraged economic and social progress, the contrast was considerable. All these states were to disappear as sovereign entities at the time of Independence (Chapter XXI).

From 1860 to 1950, the countryside and the cities underwent several transformations. Until towards 1920, the rural world, where demographic growth remained very moderate, had witnessed a certain agricultural prosperity, but it suffered a wave of famines in the last quarter of the nineteenth century; from the 1920s onwards, the demographic growth accelerated while agricultural production made hardly any progress, even if there were great disparities from one region to another. Peasant movements, at times on a vast scale, multiplied but their impact remained limited (Chapter XXII).

The evolution of the non-agricultural economy was of course closely linked to the situation in the countryside, as India remained overwhelmingly rural and agriculture. After 1920, modern industries recorded regular, though modest, growth. The country was still little urbanized but some cities grew into 'imperial metropolises.' Nevertheless, against the backdrop of economic stagnation, India already assumed the image of an under-developed country (Chapter XXIII).

Hindu and Muslim religious reforms continued and became one of the catalysts for the emergence of Indian nationalism from the 1870s. Hindu 'revivalism' that expressed the affirmation of a Hindu identity, at times aggressively, would lead to a minority political trend – Hindu nationalism. The Muslim movements, whether modernist or fundamentalist in nature, would contribute to the rapid growth of Indian nationalism before fostering separatism, which would be embodied from 1940 onwards in the Muslim League.

In 1942 the Congress triggered the anti-colonial Quit India movement, which was repressed by the use of force leaving profound scars. The desertion of a number of the soldiers of the Indian Army who joined the Indian National Army created by Subash Chandra Bose and who fought on the Japanese side dealt a blow to British power. In 1945, London was forced to open negotiations with the Congress and the Muslim League, but was unable to come to an agreement on the maintenance of a united India. A year later, the British envisaged a partition between an India with a Hindu majority and a Pakistan with a Muslim majority. This partition occurred in 1947 in haste and unleashed tragic acts of violence in the Punjab. The two new states, faced with serious internal problems, entered into conflict regarding Kashmir (Chapter XXV). This was only the beginning of a difficult coexistence.

XIX

THE COLONIAL STATE AND INDIAN SOCIETY

(1858–1914)

The disappearance of the East India Company and the passage of India under the direct sovereignty of the British Crown were the principal immediate consequences of the Sepoy Revolt. However, this was but a change in outward appearances, as the Company had been, since 1813, only a facade behind which the British government called the tune. In 1858, after taking back Delhi, the British put the Mogul emperor Bahadur Shah on trial for treason and deported the old man to Burma, where he was to die a few years later; his descendants were all executed. The extinction of the dynasty offered them a good pretext to abolish definitively the Mogul Empire, which for a long time, had been nothing but a political cadaver.

Deprived of the fiction of Mogul suzerainty behind which they had sheltered, the British had to find a new legitimacy in order to be recognized by their two hundred million Indian subjects. No political regime can survive very long if it rests on pure force. A mixture of conservative British ideas and orientalist views on the nature of power in Asia gave rise to the project of making Queen Victoria the direct sovereign of India.[1] It would take twenty years for this project to come to fruition, owing to the opposition of influential circles in Britain that believed that it was too favourable to Indians and detrimental to Her Majesty's British subjects resident in India.

The reorganization of the colonial state

The colonial government endeavoured firstly to reinforce the bonds between the sovereign and her Indian subjects – especially the elite, from where the attachment of the masses was supposed to follow. The British experts of India maintained that the new western-educated intelligentsia was negligible in number and suspected it of lack of loyalty. In their opinion, only the landed aristocracy, and in particular princes, constituted the 'natural' elite of the country. As early as 8 November 1858, a royal proclamation (the Queen's proclamation) thus promised the Indian princes that 'their rights, their dignity and their honour' would be respected, as well as the integrity of their territorial possessions, thereby signalling a complete break from the systematic policy of annexation of princely states pursued by Lord Dalhousie. The creation of the order of the *Star of India*, in 1861, led to the integration of powerful Indian princes into a purely British system of honours. Visits of members of the royal family were organized with a view to arousing feelings of loyalty towards the Crown.

This policy culminated in the *Royal Titles Act*, passed by the British Parliament in 1876, which made Queen Victoria the Empress of India. In a great *durbar* organized in Delhi in 1877 by the Viceroy Lord Lytton, the Queen (who was not present in person) was solemnly proclaimed Empress before an assembly of the principal notables and princes of India. The British monarch became the 'fountain of all honours', while the governor-general was invested with the title of viceroy in order to highlight his role as the personal representative of the Crown in its relations with the Indian princes. Yet, if the princes were to show themselves on the whole loyal to the British Raj until the eve of independence, they represented a feudal nobility only in the imagination of the British. Many princely dynasties had emerged only recently and enjoyed only a limited prestige among their subjects. The measures taken by the British to appease the princes and the big landowners, notably by the reinstatement of the *taluqdars* of Oudh to the fullness of their prerogatives, would fail to resolve the political problems. It would not be long before the British realized this.

The Sepoy Revolt had laid bare the fragility of administrative structures, which could not be palliated by a mere change of name. The *India Act* of 1858 in effect transferred to the secretary of state for India, who was a member of the British Cabinet, all powers hitherto enjoyed by the president of the Board of Control of the East India Company. The secretary of state for India, who had his office in London, thus became the head of a 'ministry of India', the India Office, as distinct from the ministry of colonies (the Colonial Office), under which came, for instance, the colony of Ceylon. The secretary of state was assisted by a council of fifteen members, who had an essentially advisory role. In India, the governor-general and viceroy's powers were confirmed with regard to the governors of the Presidencies of Bombay and Madras, but he was placed under the authority of the India Office and of the secretary of state for India. This control was consolidated by the spectacular advances in communication between England and India (telegraph by land in 1868, the opening of the Suez Canal in 1869, submarine cables in 1870). The government of India was henceforth subjected to the nit-picking surveillance of the London bureaucracy of the India Office.

In India itself, the structure of the government was also revamped. From 1861 onwards, the executive council that surrounded the viceroy tended more and more to become a full-fledged ministry, each member of the council being responsible for a department. All this contributed to favour the emergence of a true despotism, which was not always enlightened. In effect, the prerogatives of the government extended to new areas (public health and hygiene, labour legalization, etc.), even as the possibilities of action multiplied thanks to an increased specialization of functions within the bureaucracy. The senior administration, constituted by the Indian Civil Service, a body of civil servants recruited in England among the graduates of the best universities, also played an increasingly significant role and formed the 'steel frame' of British rule.

Yet, at the same time, representative institutions remained extremely embryonic.

The Central Legislative Council, created by Dalhousie in 1853, renamed in 1861 as the Imperial Legislative Council, as well as the provincial legislative councils, instituted in 1861, were composed exclusively of appointed members and played the role of chambers of records. As long as the viceroy enjoyed the confidence of the secretary of state for India in London, he had the possibility of pursuing a personal policy. Inasmuch as his appointment was increasingly dependent on partisan considerations within the British political system, he generally enjoyed the support of influential people in London. The manner in which the representative of the Crown employed his immense powers consequently varied considerably in accordance with circumstances and personalities. Whereas Mayo (1869–72) or Lytton (1876–80) demonstrated an unbridled activism, Northbrook (1872–6) or Dufferin (1884–8) were champions of inertia.

Financial policy

The principal impediment to the despotic power of the viceroy was the often difficult financial situation of the government of India. Nevertheless, a series of financial reforms was implemented after the mutiny of 1857, which played a great role in the transformation of British Raj into an embryonic modern bureaucratic state.

The financial difficulties of the colonial state were not a novelty, but they were particularly acute after 1858. The repression of the Sepoy Revolt in effect had caused government expenditure to soar from 132 million rupees in 1856–7 to 247 million rupees in 1858–9, in other words to multiply two-fold, while revenues stagnated, thus resulting in a sharp rise in public debt (plus 36 per cent in the course of the same period). This sudden surge was due to the inflation of military expenses; the transport and maintenance of the great expeditionary corps despatched to India was entirely defrayed by the government of India, in other words the Indian taxpayer. It was of course out of the question for the English taxpayer to disburse a single penny for the defence of the most important overseas possession of Great Britain. At that time, there was not yet talk of the 'white man's burden' and the colonies were not expected to cost anything to the home country.

The emergence of a substantial deficit in the accounts of the colonial government became a cause for concern for the British government, which was increasingly anxious to ensure fiscal balance and to restore the financial situation in India. James Wilson, the founder of the famous newspaper *The Economist* and one of the most vocal advocates of the new liberal orthodoxy in financial questions, was appointed to the newly created post of finance member of the government of India, the equivalent of a minister of finance. He was in office for only two years, but had the time to lay the groundwork for a new financial system that his successors, in particular Laing and Trevelyan, consolidated. Wilson adopted an annual budget from 1860 onwards – earlier the government had only an approximate idea of its revenues and its expenditures. This reform led to a better control of financial flows, but did not resolve the problem of deficit.

Military expenditure represented on an average a quarter of the budget, the remaining being distributed between administrative expenses (35 per cent), public works (15 per cent) and the reimbursement of interests on the public debt (10 per cent). On the side of revenues, land taxes contributed to the tune of 40 per cent, the other receipts being the tax on opium (15 per cent), the tax on salt (10 per cent), customs duties (5 to 9 per cent) and the tax on alcohol (5 per cent).

Given the stability of the taxes on opium or alcohol, the government could only raise the salt tax or customs duties. But an increase in the former, the only one that affected the mass of the population, was fraught with political risks; as regards customs duties, an increase might be objectionable to the partisans of free trade and to the powerful lobbies that supported them, in particular the lobby of the cotton manufacturers of Manchester. There remained the solution of introducing new taxes: in 1861 a licence tax and an income tax were established, but they sparked off violent protests, notably in business circles, both British and Indian. In consequence, income tax was abandoned in 1865, reinstated in 1869, again abandoned and reintroduced definitively in the 1880s. These difficulties reveal the precarious foundation of colonial rule and the passive resistance of Indian society to the encroachments of a state that it looked upon as predatory.

On the other hand, the colonial government was more successful in it efforts at lowering its expenses. It succeeded in particular in bringing down the level of military expenditure from 299 million rupees in 1859–60 to 145 million rupees in 1862–3. The strength of the native troops, renamed the Indian Army in 1893 after the fusion of the armies of the three presidencies, dropped from 213,000 in 1859–60 to 121,000 in 1862–3. At the same time, the strength of the European troops was downscaled from 106,000 to 76,000; eventually stabilizing around this figure.

A plan for financial decentralization was moreover adopted in 1870 at the initiative of Viceroy Lord Mayo. It provided for the transfer to the provincial governments of the responsibilities of the central government in the fields of education, construction and maintenance of roadways, as well as urban works. Nevertheless, as the revenues of the provincial governments were greatly limited (and these governments were reticent to introduce supplementary provincial taxes in the fear of adverse reactions from the population), the plan also implied a transfer of resources from Calcutta towards the provinces in the form of an annual allocation. The provincial governments thus received nearly 10 per cent of the total income of the State: the net gain for the central finances was therefore quite limited.

Despite the adoption of annual budgets, which were generally balanced, the State did not truly succeed in restoring the financial health of the country. Public debt, which had surged from 59.4 million sterling pounds in 1857–8 to 107.5 million in 1861–2, after recording a slight decrease for a few years, resumed its upward trend from 1866 onwards, to reach a total of 121.7 million in 1871–2, due to the continuous rise in the 'Home Charges'. These 'Home Charges' represented the expenses that the government of India had to defray each year in London in sterling pounds; they covered interests on the debt contracted in England, the payment of supplies bought every year in the country (for the army and the administration), the cost of the maintenance of British forces in India, including the cost of transport of troops from England to India and vice versa, the pensions paid to the retired staff of the army and the colonial administration and lastly, guaranteed interests paid each year to the holders of Indian railway bonds. These Home Charges being paid in sterling pounds, their amount depended on the fluctuations in the parity between the value of the rupee, a silver currency, and the sterling pound, a gold currency, i.e., in the final analysis, on the parity between gold and silver. But, the value of silver markedly depreciated with respect to that of gold from 1873 onwards with the beginning of the Great Depression that followed the crash of the Kredit Anstalt of Vienna. The burden of the Home Charges consequently intensified further for the government of India. Thus, the financial reform implemented in the 1860s could not prevent a certain fragility from becoming a chronic aspect of the financial situation until the end of the nineteenth century.

The army and the stabilization of the frontiers

British rule after 1858, relied more than ever on the existence of a powerful military instrument, but this was rarely resorted to within the subcontinent. The bitter memory of the crushing of the revolt of 1857, as well as the significant rise in the British military presence in India remained the major guarantee for the survival of the colonial order, despite the attempts to create affective bonds between the Queen and her Indian subjects. Hence, the attention devoted by the authorities in London and Calcutta to military questions.

The authorities in effect endeavoured to reorganize the 'native' military forces: the Indian Army, the strength of which had been markedly reduced, and also concurrently suffered a reduction of its military capacity, by the abolition of the artillery, which became an entirely European branch. The English had not forgotten the skill that the mutinous *sepoys* had demonstrated in the handling of canons and were eager not take any risk in this regard. They reinforced the supervisory role of Europeans – Indians no longer had the possibility of being elevated to grades higher than that of a non-commissioned officer – and modified the recruitment of the army: the Brahmins and Rajputs of Oudh and the neighbouring regions were replaced by the members of the so-called 'martial races', in particular Muslims and Sikhs of the Punjab, as well as the Gurkhas recruited from Nepal following an accord with the ruler of this country. The quasi-elimination of 'orthodox' Hindus facilitated the transformation of this army into a sort of imperial reserve force available for overseas expeditions. Great Britain employed it on numerous occasions in its wars of colonial expansion at the end of the nineteenth century.

Within the subcontinent, the maintenance of the colonial order henceforth hinged on the European forces, the British Army in India. If its strength was not very considerable – it nevertheless represented the bulk of the ground forces maintained permanently by Great Britain – its reputation and the equipment that it had at its disposal sufficed to dampen any desire for revolt.

From the British point of view, the principal threat to the security of India came from the instability that reigned on the northwest frontier. The Russian advance in Turkestan (the occupation of Khiva in 1873) revived the question of Afghanistan. The excessive zeal of the Viceroy Lord Lytton plunged India into the Second Afghan War in 1879. Its result was no more conclusive than the first: after sending an expeditionary corps that did not score any significant success, the British had to recognize Abdurrahman, who they feared was a Russophile, as the *amir* of Kabul in 1880, and to renounce the presence of an English resident in his court. After a new conflict consequent on the Russian advance on Merv in 1881, Anglo–Afghan relations stabilized and a border agreement was concluded in 1887.

There remained the problem of the frontier zone that extended between Afghanistan and the British districts of the northwest. This zone was populated by turbulent Baluch and Pashtun tribes which frequently conducted raids into British territory. The question arose as to whether it was necessary to occupy it or just control it from the plains. The partisans of occupation initially seemed to prevail: in 1876, Quetta, in Baluchistan, was annexed and in 1893, in the wake of an accord between the Afghan and British governments, the 'Durand line' divided the tribal zone into two, Afghan territory and British territory. However, the attempts to occupy the land effectively triggered in 1897 a general insurrection of the tribes. To suppress it, it was necessary to engage 35,000 men, who suffered heavy losses without scoring any lasting success. Lord Curzon learnt the lesson from these events and from 1899 onwards, renounced the policy of effective occupation (the 'forward policy'). This zone was to remain in peace until the end of the First World War. With a view to consolidating its administration, five districts as well as the tribal zone were dissociated from the Punjab to form the North-West Frontier Province.

In the northeast, the British, anxious about the advance of the French in Indochina, launched the Third Burmese War ending in the occupation of upper Burma (1885). The whole of Burma was attached to the Indian Empire until 1937. In 1904, Viceroy Curzon sent an expedition into Tibet, but this Himalayan country, protected by its isolation, remained outside the sphere of influence of the British.

The considerable rise in British military staff stationed in India after 1857 led to a militarization of British society in India. In the informal system of caste that ranked this society according to a strict hierarchy, the officers of the British Army in India occupied the top of the ladder along with members of the Indian Civil Service; at a lower echelon, came the officers of the Indian Army, followed by the engineers of the Public Works Department and of the railways, the missionaries, the *boxwallahs* (employees of English trading houses), technicians and qualified workers; the bottom of the ladder was occupied by the BORs (British other ranks), British soldiers and non-commissioned officers (most often Welsh, Scottish or Irish), who were held in great contempt, particularly because they indulged in sexual relations with the natives.

The militarization of society was accomplished by the growing affirmation of an imperialist ideology. The idea, already widespread, of the intrinsic racial superiority of the British over the Indians, as well as that of the providential nature of British rule in India had been definitively confirmed by the Mutiny. From then onwards, the British increasingly tended to live in an insular society and avoided all the contacts with Indians that were not strictly necessary. This closure was certainly facilitated by the inprovement in sanitary conditions and in communications with Britain, which enabled a growing number of Britons to return regularly to their home country on leave and to bring their wives to India.

The influx of British women has often been cited as the reason for the growing racial exclusivism of British society in India, but there is no doubt that it was responsible for the quasi-interruption of relations between British men and Indian women, as well as for the contempt shown to the 'Eurasians', the population of mixed blood born out of a more liberal period. These people, who were not yet called 'Anglo-Indians' (this term was at the time reserved for those Britons born in India), nevertheless represented a group that was greatly attached to British rule and was employed in intermediary positions, particularly in the railways.

Lord Curzon and the high noon of Empire

It was at the close of the nineteenth century that British rule assumed its 'classical' form, the most imposing reflection of which remains the grand and often extravagant architectural productions that marked in Calcutta as in Bombay and Madras the brief apogee of a Raj at the zenith of its power. No figure can incarnate this 'high noon of Empire' better than the flamboyant Lord Curzon, Viceroy of India from 1899 to 1905, imbued with the importance of his mission, as testified by the statement attributed to him: 'As long as we govern India, we shall be the greatest power in the world. If we lose it, we shall fall forthwith to the rank of a third rate power.' The whole of Britain at the time shared in the new religion of the empire, the most spectacular manifestation of which was the grand jubilee festival of Queen Victoria in 1897.

In this empire 'on which the sun never set', India was unquestionably the most resplendent jewel. The central place of the subcontinent in the entire imperial construction of the British is a known fact. We must keep in mind that it was with a view to ensuring the security of the route to India that the British annexed Malta, Cyprus, Egypt, Aden, Somaliland, Socotra, the Island of Ascension, Saint Helena, the Cape and Mauritius (which was conquered by Indian troops). It is with Indian troops that they conquered Burma, Ceylon, Singapore, (which was administratively a part of India until 1867), Nyassaland and Anglo-Egyptian Sudan. It was Indian coolies who constructed the railways of Kenya and Uganda. It was Indian traders from Gujarat (Muslim Bohras and Khojas, Hindu Patidars and Lohanas) and from Tamil Nadu (Nattukottai Chettiars) who opened up Burma and eastern Africa to extensive British trade by serving as middlemen in the financing and commercialization of the rice, cotton and coffee harvests. The considerable human resources of the subcontinent favoured the economic profitability of colonial enterprises, because Indian soldiers and traders worked for a lesser cost than their British counterparts.

Lord Curzon was therefore not wrong when he made the possession of India the basis for the grandeur of the British Empire. However, the worm had already eaten into the fruit, because Indian society, far from being the formless clay waiting to be moulded by an imperial artist such as Curzon, was experiencing profound changes. On the facade of imperial splendour and tranquillity that impressed visitors, large fissures started to form.

The birth of a political life

The Sepoy Revolt has often been considered a watershed in the history of colonial India. For some historians, it was the fulfilment and the conclusion of a period of so-called primary resistance to British rule, with the mutiny heralding the beginning of modern nationalism. In reality, this break seems rather artificial because movements of primary resistance persisted until the 1920s. It is from the 1870s that we may speak of the emergence of Indian nationalism. This period witnessed the birth of a true challenge to colonial power, not as much on its principle as on its modalities, a challenge that would abruptly turn radical in the years 1895 to 1905. If a small educated elite group was at the origin of the rise of nationalism, popular movements also played an important role. Nevertheless, both elite protestation and popular resistance drew their inspiration from a common springhead, the rise of communitarian sentiment among the Hindus.

This was because the government itself encouraged the affirmation of supra-local identities, in particular caste identities. The censuses – the first of which took place in 1872 – were accompanied by a classification of the population according to castes and religious communities, which promoted the appearance of 'horizontal' solidarities. Little by little, a sentiment, which admittedly had been very diffuse, of belonging to a pan-Indian Hindu community crystallized among many. This feeling, which had probably never existed in the past, was not in contradiction with the increasing affirmation of caste identities, in as much as caste presupposed the existence of hierarchy. The lowest castes seemed to aspire to conform with the practices of the upper castes, in particular the Brahmins (vegetarianism notably), a trend that is called 'Sanskritization'. They did not seek to call into question the hierarchy, but to establish themselves in a better position within it. It was largely with this objective in mind that numerous caste associations came into existence, especially in the urban milieu where it was more difficult than in villages to observe ritualistic prescriptions and to avoid the pollution that resulted from contacts with the impure.

At the same time, there was an assertion of regional identities that were more precisely delineated. The dynamic development of a press and of literatures in the principal vernacular languages contributed powerfully to this. However, the feeling of belonging to a Bengali or Marathi linguistic group did not contradict the affirmation of a larger Hindu or Indian identity. The region often appeared as a specific avatar of the nation and conflicts of loyalty were rare. It was only in South India that a 'Dravidian' movement developed in opposition to 'Aryanism', which would lead in the twentieth century to a strong Tamil nationalist movement.

The political translation of this Hindu communal affirmation was far from immediate. It nevertheless began to exert a growing influence on political life. Similar phenomena occurred among the Muslims and among the Sikhs – we shall deal with these in Chapter XXIV. The nascent nationalist movement therefore soon found itself in the face of a serious dilemma: to define identity above all as Indian or as Hindu? And if, as many believed, the two terms were in principle synonymous, what place ought to be reserved for non-Hindus, in particular for Muslims?

Nevertheless, the educated elite that was the spearhead of the movement, notably in Bengal and in Maharashtra, seemed hardly preoccupied with questions of religious and communal identity. They seemed to concur with the criticism that Christian missionaries directed against the evils of Hindu society and were on the whole favourable to social reforms. A Calcutta Brahmin, Pandit Iswarchandra Vidyasagar, thus played an essential role in the legalisation of widow remarriage, adopted in 1856, and in the passing of first *Age of Consent Bill* in 1860, fixing the legal age of marriage at ten years.

This elite, whose members continued to come from the upper castes of Hindu society, had started to learn Western sciences and English as early as 1817, with the creation of the Hindu college at Calcutta. The adoption of English in 1835 as the official language instead of Persian, in the wake of the Macaulay Report, gave a new impetus to the development of westernized education. Macaulay, in 1835, nevertheless foresaw the formation of a class of Indians educated in the English style, apt only for filling positions of clerks in the colonial government. The development of a veritable native intelligentsia was not part of the British plans.

It was only in 1854 and with report of Sir Charles Wood that the colonial government adopted a coherent plan aimed at developing education. Thus were born, in 1857, the first three Indian universities at Calcutta, Bombay and Madras. Thereafter, the trend gained momentum. Between 1864 and 1885, nearly fifty thousand candidates passed the entrance exam to the university and some eighteen thousand of them earned a university degree. Others undertook specialized courses in institutions independent of the universities, such as medical colleges and engineering schools. It is undeniable that, in a country with a population of 250 million, the production of about a thousand graduates a year could appear paltry. However, we need to appreciate this figure in relation to the capacity of the Indian economy for the absorption of qualified Indians at a time when the most prestigious and the most highly remunerated posts in the administration as in the railways, public works, university and judiciary were de facto reserved for Britons. In the administration, the most coveted positions, those of the Covenanted Civil Service (Indian Civil Service) were filled on the basis of an examination, in principle open to all, but the final tests of which were conducted in England, which prevented Indians from taking them (except if they belonged to an extremely affluent family and were free from all religious taboo against overseas travel). Consequently, it is hardly surprising to observe that in 1887 only a dozen Indians had passed the entrance exam to the Covenanted Service (which numbered around a thousand employees). The creation by Lord Mayo of a parallel way in the form of a recruitment that did not include any exam had hardly any practical consequences, because the rare Indians who had opted for this line of action soon discovered that they were being shunted onto the sidelines. Only the Uncovenanted Service (the inferior echelons of the administration) offered posts to Indians, but these were not very prestigious and carried only a modest remuneration. The administration therefore did not open any real employment opportunities for the new graduates with ambition.

In reality, it was the bar and the judiciary that formed the principal source of employment: at the end of the nineteenth century, in the three Presidencies, nearly fourteen thousand Indians were employed in legal professions: among them, there were a certain number of advocates earning considerable incomes. The other prospects for employment were the press (with the growing number of newspapers in English and in vernacular languages) and the medical profession. However, in all these fields, the labour supply tended rapidly to exceed the demand, which resulted in a decrease in average incomes and the emergence of masked unemployment.

On the basis of these facts, some had attempted to find an explanation for the genesis of Indian nationalism: the new elite, frustrated by the absence of satisfactory employment opportunities, would have turned against the English. It is undoubtable that this frustration can explain certain individual behaviours – and there is no dearth of examples to show the humiliations suffered by nationalist leaders at the hands of colonial bureaucrats – but it seems hazardous, to say the least, to interpret the evolution of an entire social class in these terms. Among those who played an important role in the new political associations, many had succeeded spectacularly in their professional lives.

Elite protest

The change in the attitude of the intelligentsia towards British rule, which became perceptible during the 1870s, without doubt had causes that were far more complex. Western intellectual influence, conveyed by the new educational institutions, had significant effects on the literary production in vernacular languages. New genres appeared during this period, such as the pamphlet and the historical novel, and a new interest for the history of India emerged. Thus, in Maharashtra, the articles and pamphlets of Lokahitawadi aroused an interest in the Maratha period and awakened strong nostalgia for the time of the *peshwas*. In Bengal, the historic novels written by Bankimcandra Chatterji, which had an enormous impact, posed the question of the foundations of nationalism, in particular of the role of Muslims, of whom the author painted a very negative picture.

The rediscovery of the grandeur of the Indian past, largely identified with a golden age that preceded the Muslim invasions, was spurred on by the researches carried out by European Orientalists (particularly, Max Muller) and inspired in the members of the new intelligentsia a pride that led them to view the legitimacy of British rule in a different perspective, without calling it fundamentally into question. Their enthusiasm for social reform, supposed to cure Hindu society of its evils, markedly abated. Their confidence in the Raj was also rudely shaken by the appearance, between 1875 and 1880, of several severe famines that the colonial government did nothing to stop. These famines on their turn encouraged a number of researches on the economic history of India, which gave rise at the close of the nineteenth century to a caustic criticism of the economic aspects of British rule, among others by Dadabhai Naoroji and Romesh Chunder Dutt.

This new state of mind prevailed in an important sector of the intelligentsia and resulted in the formation of associations that were the first to adopt openly political standpoints. The best known and the most active of these, the Indian Association, was created in 1876 in Calcutta, the spearhead of which was the advocate Surendranath Banerji, a good organizer and a talented orator. In the Bengal

Presidency, the Indian Association rapidly supplanted the old British Indian Association, the mouthpiece of the *zamindars*, which had been practically inactive since the end of the 1860s. In the course of its early years, it fought for the opening to Indians of the Indian Civil Service, a cause that concerned only a small privileged group. Thereafter, it spread to the principal cities of Bengal and equipped itself with an embryonic organization that enabled it to conduct propaganda activities reaching beyond the intelligentsia. It could thus attract a larger public by demanding the institution of elections in municipalities, the members of which had so far been appointed by the government. It also organized the first pan-Indian protest campaigns against the *Vernacular Press Act* of 1878, by which Viceroy Lord Lytton attempted to muzzle a thriving vernacular press that was more and more critical of the government.

In the Bombay Presidency, at Poona, the great intellectual centre of Maharashtra, another association, the Sarvajanik Sabha, was created in 1870 at the initiative of the one of the most brilliant representatives of the new intelligentsia, Mahadev Govind Ranade. It first aimed at making progress in social reforms, and then increasingly asserted its political positions and pursued actions parallel to the Indian Association. In the course of the following decade, similar associations appeared in Madras (the Mahajana Sabha, 1884) and in Bombay (the Bombay Presidency Association, 1885).

The members of the new intelligentsia played a pre-eminent role in these associations. For all this, the link between the existence of a Western educated elite fashion and the rise of nationalism does not seem as evident as it has been believed for a long time. If Calcutta and Poona, the cradles of the first two associations, had an important concentration of graduates, the 1891 census shows that it was in the Madras Presidency that the greatest number of Indians with a knowledge of English lived (nearly 70,000 against 60,000 in Bengal and a little more than 40,000 in the Bombay Presidency); yet, in the political arena, Madras had always lagged behind Calcutta and Bombay.

Two historians[2] have suggested that in the Presidency of Madras and the city of Allahabad (United Provinces) Indian nationalism was a consequence of the decentralizing reforms of centralization implemented by Viceroy Mayo and pursued by his successors. The transfer of certain central government responsibilities such as maintenance of roads, public buildings, to local institutions, the district boards, led in effect to the election of a part of their members from 1882 onwards. To avoid an excessive intervention of the colonial authorities in local affairs, the magnates strove to have themselves elected. As they did not themselves possess the necessary talents (in particular of oration) to make a good impression, they solicited representatives of the intelligentsia, publicists, whom they financed but on whom they maintained a close control. Thus, in Allahabad, as in the Madras Presidency, members of the intelligentsia intervened in the political scene not as the representatives of their own social class, but as the agents of rural magnates or of the powerful banker-traders of the cities.

This thesis, which provoked an interminable controversy, has the merit of drawing attention to the regional diversity of the genesis in the nationalist movement, but it underestimates the weight of ideological considerations in the growing political mobilization of the Indian intelligentsia. Nonetheless, the socio-economic context within which this intelligentsia operated, a context marked by the overwhelming predominance of landed wealth over movable wealth, was not conducive to the development of truly bourgeois movements: this fact has been too often neglected by Indian Marxists in their quest for a class-based explanation of the rise of nationalism. Most of the members of the intelligentsia, especially in Bengal, belonged to landowning families (*zamindars*), which without doubt explains the timidity of their agrarian programme. The crystallization of what was still just an unorganized current of opinion and its transformation into an embryonic political movement owed much to the attitude of the British authorities.

In this regard, the viceroyalty of Lord Ripon (1880–4) formed a watershed. Succeeding the brilliant but very conservative Lord Lytton, Ripon arrived in India preceded by a flattering reputation for being a liberal. He strove to appease the new intelligentsia by repealing the *Vernacular Press Act* and by taking measures aimed at encouraging the development of primary and secondary education. However, the consent that he gave to the *Ilbert Bill*, which allowed an Indian magistrate to judge a European, earned him violent criticism from the British population in India. A campaign was organized for the revocation of the bill and in the face of the violence of attacks that assumed openly racist overtones, the viceroy preferred to backtrack: finally, the bill was amended to include the possibility of a jury half the members of which would be European. This half-measure did not give satisfaction to any of the two camps and ruined the credit of Ripon among the Indian intelligentsia. Nevertheless, when Ripon left India, at the end of 1884, Indians acclaimed him all along his route from Calcutta to Bombay. This was the first great political demonstration that India had known; on this occasion, Indian opinion clearly expressed its hope for a liberal turnaround in British politics.

However, this hope would soon meet with disappointment. Lord Dufferin, who succeeded Ripon, adopted a policy of extreme prudence and did not take any concrete measure to satisfy the expectations, however modest, of Indian opinion, such as opening employment opportunities in the upper echelons of the civil service for Indians. It was under his viceroyalty that there occurred an event that is traditionally portrayed as the birth of the nationalist movement and more generally, of modern politics in India, namely the first session of the Indian National Congress, which was held in Bombay in December 1885.

Popular movements

Simultaneously, mass agitation developed. The most violent protests flared up in 1879 in the hills of the Rampa country of the Godavari (the present state of Andhra Pradesh); there, tribal peasants under the leadership of their local chieftains, revolted against the suzerain (*mansabadar*) placed by the British with a view to extending their control over the forests of the region. It took eighteen months for the British and six infantry regiments to break the resistance of these rebels who controlled a zone covering 13,000 square kilometres. The best-known tribal upsurge, however, was the

Ulgulan (the Great Tumult) that broke out in 1899–1900 and that had the same causes: a part of the Mundas of Bihar (in the district of Ranchi) revolted at the call of Birsa, a prophet who preached a religion stamped with Christian influences, and wanted to put an end to the oppression of the moneylenders and usurpers of land who came from the plains, who were supported by British power.

The tribal populations were not the only ones to rise up in revolt. In 1875, in Maharashtra, in the regions of Poona and Ahmadnagar, moneylenders (*sowcars*), most often Marwaris, became the object of coordinated attacks by the local peasantry of the Maratha caste: this episode, known as the Deccan riots, obliged the colonial government in 1879 to take measures aimed at protecting farmers (*Deccan Agriculturists' Relief Act*). Similar movements, though pacific, occurred in several districts of eastern Bengal. The same year, another significant uprising was launched by Vasudeo Balvant Phadke, a Maharashtrian Brahmin and a low ranked civil servant of the colonial administration, who wanted to proclaim a Hindu Raj and restore the glory of the *peshwas*.

These revolts, even though too dispersed to pose a threat to British rule, laid bare the growing malaise in the subcontinent. The development of an organized nationalist movement was to give it an occasion to express itself more openly.

The rise of nationalism (1885–1914)

The Indian National Congress has for a long time dominated political life in India, which has led to exaggeration of the importance of its actual historical role. The year 1885, when the Congress was founded, was certainly not a major turning point in the history of India, even thought its centenary was marked by grandiose celebrations in 1985.

The seventy-two delegates who met at Bombay in December 1885 adopted the pompous name of 'Indian National Congress,' but in reality represented only themselves. All of them belonged to the educated class living in big cities (Calcutta, Bombay, Madras, Poona) and most of them played an active role in local associations. Nevertheless, it was not from the associations that the initiative for the meeting came, but from an Englishman, Allan Octavian Hume, a retired member of the Indian Civil Service.

That an Englishman was the founder of the principal Indian 'nationalist' movement is only apparently paradoxical. The Congress at its inception was not a subversive organization that sought to overthrow colonial rule, but a debating club, where gentlemen could exchange urbane views on current affairs, in which an Englishman could feel perfectly at ease. Some have interpreted the role played by Hume as a clue to a conspiracy by the colonial government to create a sort of safety valve allowing the feeling of discontent among Indians to express itself without jeopardizing British rule. In fact, the private correspondence of Viceroy Lord Dufferin shows that the colonial authorities never took Hume seriously. If the Indians who attended Congress meetings accepted the leadership of a Briton, it was because they profoundly admired Britain and the British; they wished above all to see British constitutional principles applied in India. Furthermore, the fact that Hume was British placed him above regional rivalries.

From its foundation onwards, the Congress met every year in a different city. These sessions became a political and society event, and anyone claiming to some notoriety had to take part in them. They were organized according to a well-established ritual; after listening to a long introductive discourse from the president and to other speeches generally made in English, the only language understood by all participants, the delegates adopted a certain number of resolutions, and thereafter separated. Between sessions, there was no permanent organization. During these early years, the Congress therefore was not a political party, but a sort of informal movement.

The principal demands of the Congress concerned the reform of the central and provincial legislative councils (they demanded that these should have greater powers and that they should be composed at least partly of elected members), the Indianization of the top-level administration by the simultaneous organization in India and in Britain of the entrance exam to the Indian Civil Service, judicial reforms, the access of Indians to high ranks in the army. Their other demands were economic in nature: the reduction of the Home Charges and of military expenditure, the encouragement of technical education with a view to facilitating the industrial development of the country, the abolition of the duty on alcohol, the extension of the permanent settlement. These questions were of interest only to a small minority of privileged individuals, but there were other demands that reflected more the preoccupations of the masses: thus, the Congress adopted numerous resolutions demanding the reduction of the salt tax, the betterment of the conditions of Indian coolies working in colonial plantations, the revocation of the forest laws. The Congress members did not call for agitations and devoted themselves to writing petitions, speeches and articles with soundly constructed arguments (many of them were advocates) in the hope of convincing English liberal opinion of the necessity for reforms.

During the years when the Congress was led by Hume (1885–92), it nevertheless showed a dynamism that contrasts with the relative inertia that crept into it in the subsequent years. The number of delegates rose rapidly to reach two thousand in 1889 and substantial funds were collected though public subscription; they served to finance propaganda activities, like the publication, in 1887, of two pamphlets on the agrarian question that were translated into a dozen Indian languages. The Congress strove to extend the movement towards the Muslim elite that had tended to keep its distance, as encouraged by the great reformer Sir Syed Ahmad Khan. These attempts nonetheless produced only limited results, and when the government began to show some impatience toward the activities of what the Viceroy Dufferin called a 'microscopic minority,' the other influential Congress members, taking fright, exerted pressure on Hume to abandon his demands in favour of the peasantry. Increasingly frustrated, Hume left India in 1892, predicting serious troubles if the Congress did not show itself more energetic and the government more conscious of the necessity for reforms. He was never to come back to India.

After the departure of Hume, the Congress functioned for some years under the leadership of a small informal group, from which emerged the two strong personalities of Surendranath Banerji from Calcutta and Pherozeshah Mehta, a Parsi advocate from Bombay. Thereafter, the Congress devoted the best part of its efforts to try to influence British opinion; in England, the economist Dadabhai Naoroji, William Wedderburn, a liberal won over to the Indian cause, and Hume were charged with the mission of popularizing the Indian cause. Nevertheless, changes began to take shape, changes that were to lead to a phase of greater dynamism within the Congress. One of the decisive factors was the change in the intellectual climate, marked by a regression of reformist tendencies and the rise of 'Hindu' revivalism.

Nothing illustrates this change better than the debate that was sparked off by a new bill relative to family law, the *Age of Consent Bill* of 1891. The initiative came from a partisan of social reform, Behramji Malabari, who launched a campaign against early marriage so as to reduce the number of very young widows in which it resulted. He succeeded in persuading the authorities to pass a law raising the legal minimum age of marriage from ten to twelve years. Yet, enlightened Hindu opinion, far from being carried away by the cause of the reform as it had been in 1860, divided, itself with an important faction openly opposing the bill. In addition to arguments of a religious nature, some of them, in particular a young Maharashtrian advocate from Poona, Bal Gangadhar Tilak, put forward a nationalist argument, denying the colonizers the right to interfere in questions related to the beliefs of the native population.

The years 1890 saw the entry of religion, particulary of Hinduism, into the political arena. Outside the capitals of the Presidencies and a few big cities where the new intelligentsia was concentrated, the political discourse changed and preoccupations of a religious nature became predominant. In North India in particular, a Hindu elite that drew on a double culture, Sanskrit and Persian, began to feel threatened by the administrative reforms and the ascension of a new anglicized intelligentsia. After having sought the alliance of the Muslim elite that shared the same culture and the same preoccupations, it found a way to defend its positions by the affirmation of a Hindu identity. The propaganda of the Arya Samaj, the revivalist Hindu sect influential in the Punjab, thus evoked a favourable response in the entire Gangetic Valley. In 1893, in North India, a movement against the slaughter of cows (Cow Protection Agitation) mobilized hundreds of thousands of Hindus in hundreds of small and medium localities, leading to physical confrontations with the Muslims. This type of conflict was not unknown in India. However, for the first time, confrontations took place simultaneously across a vast region, bringing to light new solidarities and the influence of the Arya Samaj propaganda. The Hindu community, that disparate collection of castes, sects, local cults, manifested itself, if not at the national level, at least in the whole of North India, the 'Hindi belt', which accounted for nearly half the total population of the country. Admittedly, this agitation was not directed against the colonial government, but it had indirect political implications. It established a network of local associations and cadres, which was to devote its efforts above all to 'social' missions (assistance to victims of calamities, charity), and which could lend itself to political actions. What was also new was that this movement concerned strata of the population that had hitherto remained aloof from the public arena, in particular the merchant castes.

The affirmation of a Hindu identity led some to oppose the colonial government directly. When the latter took the first public health measures at the time of epidemics, and when health inspectors penetrated houses, they often met with hostile reactions. This was because all that concerned the body brought into play notions of the pure and the impure. The growing interventionism of the colonial authorities in the socio-economic sphere, in the name of a modernization that was often authoritarian, led them, for the first time since the Sepoy Revolt, to clash head on with the beliefs of the majority of the population.

The Congress leaders, who belonged to the most liberal fraction of the Indian intelligentsia, were not inclined to exploit this opposition. On the contrary, they subscribed to the modernistic credo and would rather tend to criticize the authorities for their excessive prudence. Refusing to make social reform an objective of their political action, they did not tackle social issues directly during the annual sessions of the Congress: these questions were debated in an Indian Social Conference that met outside the framework of the Congress, forming a distinct forum. However, within the movement, a group of activists belonging to a new generation was willing to exploit the potential for the mobilization of the Hindu community that was revealed by the Cow Protection Agitation. Seeing here an opportunity for extending the movement and for going beyond the limited core of the small anglicized elite that formed the social base of the Congress, they set out to address in priority traders, artisans and wealthy cultivators. They criticized the Congress leadership for its methods that they believed were too timorous: for them petitions were insufficient and it was necessary to organize systematic agitations, but they had not yet reached the stage of advocating violence.

The principal figures of this so-called extremist movement, in opposition to the dominant moderates, were Aurobindo Ghosh and Bipin Chandra Pal in Bengal, and Lala Lajpat Rai in the Punjab, where the Arya Samaj, the revivalist Hindu organization, offered an efficient relay, and, in Maharashtra, Bal Gangadhar Tilak who was to gradually become a national leader. Tilak was the first to understand the use to which religion could be put to achieve political ends. This Brahmin, author of scholarly works on the Vedas, was himself very familiar with popular religiosity in his region of Maharashtra, where he organized each year, from 1894 onwards, a Ganapati festival (in the honour of the god Ganesh, worshipped with particular fervour in this region); he was also the founder of a festival in honour of the Maharashtrian national hero Shivaji, in which religious and 'patriotic' themes were interwined.

The extremists, for whom Indian and Hindu identities were one and the same, were not aggressive towards Muslims, but believed that the latter had to shed their 'cultural' particularities (and not their religious practices) if they desired to participate in the national movement. As early as this period, the themes that would be the hallmarks of 'Hindu nationalism' in the twentieth century already began to take shape.

While the extremists in the Congress advocated mass actions, others, who did not belong to the movement, ventured on the path of individual terrorism. Here again, Maharashtra set the example: the first terrorist attack took place in 1897 in Poona.

Revolted by the manner in which the British authorities had violated certain prescriptions of the *Shastras* (Hindu normative texts) while they were fighting a plague epidemic, two Brahmins, the Chapekar brothers, assassinated two British civil servants. The government reacted by putting Tilak on trial on charges of sedition: an article published in the newspaper *Kesari* that could be interpreted as a justification of terrorism gave them grounds to sentence him to deportation. The departure of its most active leader left the extremist movement without a leader for a few years and the moderates came once again to the forefront of the Congress.

The only success that the Congress could claim in the years 1885–95 was the passing of the *Indian Council's Act* of 1892, which opened the way for a certain number of members who did not belong to the administration to enter the central and provincial legislative councils, but without yet acknowledging the principle of election. Despite this law, the number of Indians elected to the corporation of Calcutta was reduced in 1899, which constituted a step backward for Indian aspirations in the capital of the country.

From 1899 to 1904, the moderate leadership of the Congress, in which Gopal Krishna Gokhale, a Maharashtrian Brahmin who proved to be particularly active, played a growing role, came up against the implacable opposition of Lord Curzon. This viceroy, so representative of Victorian imperialism, was resolved not to pay the slightest regard to the opinion of the Indian intelligentsia that he profoundly disdained. He took several measures to fight nationalist agitation: thus, in 1902 and 1903, the strength and the salaries of the police were reinforced and a special department was created to deal with political crimes, while the control of the authorities over the universities was also consolidated (*Universities Act*, 1904).

However, the showdown with the nationalists took place in connection with the administrative division of Bengal, in 1904, and had several motivations. The Bengal Presidency was a territory that was too vast and too heterogeneous (it embraced four principal linguistic regions, Bengal proper, Bihar, Orissa and Assam) to be administered in an efficient manner. In reality, the government sought above all to break the unity of the principal stronghold of nationalism, by exploiting the differences between the politicians of the west and of the east of the province. The Bengalis would not approve of this division between the west and the east of the province – eastern Bengal, a Muslim majority area, being attached to Assam to form a new province – and suspected the British of wanting to exacerbate the nascent conflict between Hindus and Muslims.

Contrary to the expectations of the administration, the population reacted with hostility. This was because, despite religious differences, Bengal formed a definite cultural entity, with all the Bengalis turning towards Calcutta as a metropolis whose prestige was growing incessantly thanks to the radiating influence of its writers, particularly Rabindranath Tagore. At a time when the discontent accumulated by an increasingly oppressive British presence continued to intensify, the decision taken by Curzon without any consultation, even among the representatives of the elite, seemed a provocation.

The Bengalis protested first by organizing press campaigns, petitions, meetings and conferences. Thereafter, in July 1905, as the British authorities did not show the slightest sign of giving in, the activists, some of whom belonged to the Congress movement, developed new forms of action: the boycott of British goods in favour of the exclusive use of goods manufactured in the country (*swadeshi* in Hindi and Bengali), the boycott of official educational institutions and the creation of 'national' schools, street demonstrations, which were often violently suppressed. For the first time, a mass agitation developed in India. The *Swadeshi* movement heralded the great anti-British movements that were to rock India after the First World War.

Nevertheless, the boycott movement against British goods, after a few successes, clashed with the interests of the powerful Marwari community, which controlled the trade of imported English cloth, and lost its effectiveness. Efforts to revive the local craft industry were unsuccessful and only a few enterprises created by members of the elite, like the Bengal Chemical and Pharmaceutical Works, survived. In the field of education, the legacy of the movement also seems negligible. Its most important result was the creation of *samitis*, or volunteer organizations that were engaged in diverse activities (assistance to victims of famines and floods, organization of physical activities, aid to artisans) and formed pockets of nationalism scattered all over Bengal.

The movement finally stumbled over the Muslim question. While the population of Bengal was in majority of the Islamic religion, the movement remained largely dominated by the Hindu elite, which provoked a growing hostility from the Muslim masses, a hostility that the British made haste to exploit. After a brief period of euphoria, marked by spectacular manifestations of fraternization between Hindus and Muslims, the relations between the two religious communities became the principal obstacle to expansion of the movement, which disappeared as a mass movement in 1907. The most active elements then resorted to terrorism, which developed on a large scale as early as 1908, sponsored by the secret societies (Anushilan, Jugantar).

The Bengal events infused new life into the extremist movement all across the country. Demonstrations of solidarity took place particularly in the Punjab, in Maharashtra and in the Madras Presidency. Consequently reinforced, the extremists were in a position to challenge the moderate leadership of the Congress. In December 1906, at the Calcutta session, following their insistence, the term 'self-government' or *swaraj* was for the first time included in the programme, but the two groups separated the following year during the Surat session. The government took advantage of this to launch a great campaign of repression against the extremists: Tilak was once again tried and sentenced, and extremism was reduced to its terrorist component. It was once again the hour of the moderates, more than ever confident in English liberalism, the most eminent representative of which, John Morley, became the secretary of state for India in 1906.

The methods of the moderates seemed to bear fruit when Gokhale, succeeded in persuading Morley to launch political reforms, despite the little enthusiasm shown by the viceroy, Lord Minto. In 1909, the *Indian Council's Act* (known as Morley-Minto reforms) introduced the principle of election in the appointment of the members of legislative councils, even while maintaining an official majority in the central council; the elected members were not in majority, even in the provincial councils. Above all, the new law established the principle of separate electorates for the Muslims, thus opening the way to a dangerous trend.

A growing political divergence between Hindus and Muslims had emerged. First considered the most dangerous enemies of British rule, the Muslims assumed a different image in the colonial view from the 1880s. Their slowness in getting involved in institutions of western education placed them at a disadvantage in the face of political changes. After some hesitation, the Muslim elite had in effect remained aloof from the Congress. The colonial administration, increasingly hostile to the Congress, was therefore inclined to look for potential allies among the Muslims. This explains the favourable response that Lord Minto gave in October 1906 to a delegation of Muslims notables that had come to request him to reserve a proportion of seats in the legislative councils for their coreligionists. The formation, in December 1906, of a Muslim League that projected itself as a counterweight to a Congress that they believed was dominated by Hindus, was perceived by the British as an opportunity to apply their favourite tactic, 'divide and rule'.

They were cautious nevertheless not to place all their hopes on the Muslim elite. In 1911, by replacing the division of Bengal into two provinces with a tripartite division between Bengal, Assam and Bihar-and-Orissa (which thus maintained the unity of the Bengali linguistic region), they made an overture to the moderate leadership of the Congress and disappointed their Muslim allies. The latter drew some satisfaction from the transfer of the capital from Calcutta to Delhi, which was announced in 1911: for them, this was a direct appeal to the sentiments evoked by the memory of the glory of the Mogul Empire.

On the eve of the First World War, the situation seemed to have stabilized: the Congress, controlled by moderate elements, played the role of Her Majesty's opposition, while the Muslim League represented a pro-British political force and terrorist agitation had been more or less stifled. The spectacular manifestations of loyalty at the announcement of the outbreak of the war made the British believe that that had the situation firmly under their control. Nevertheless, the quiet was deceptive. Discontent against the British spread to increasingly larger sections of the population. In 1915, an event occurred which remained largely unnoticed: the return to India, after almost twenty-five years of stay in South Africa, of a Gujarati advocate, who had gone there to defend the cause of his immigrant compatriots. His name was Mohandas Karamchand Gandhi.

XX

THE DECLINE OF THE EMPIRE
AND THE RISE OF NATIONALISM

(1914–42)

In 1914, when the First World War broke out, India appeared as one the most solid pillars of the British Empire. In 1942, the English had to face an uprising of the masses. In three decades, the nationalist movement, initially confined to a small section of the westernized elite, had gained ground and popular support. At the beginning of the 1930s, this led to a widespread confrontation with the British, which forced the latter to grant substantial political concessions. Both the parties seemed ready to embark on a very gradual process of transfer of power when the Second World War broke out, preparing the ground for a new confrontation.

The broadening of the nationalist movement

The Indian National Congress, which until 1917 had been more of a current of opinion than a true political force, transformed itself within a few years into a movement capable of organizing extensive anti-British movements. If this development, was already found in its embryonic form in the 1904–7 agitations that erupted in the wake of the partition of Bengal, nationalism crossed both a qualitative and a quantitative threshold in the course of the years 1917–19. This increase of momentum was the result of the combined impact of the First World War and the advent of Gandhi on the political scene.

It is impossible to overestimate the consequences of the war and of the Russian Revolution for the entire colonized world. The participation of millions of colonials in the great carnage changed both their perception of European civilization and of their place in the colonial system. The colonial powers came out of the interminable conflict weakened, and everywhere anti-colonial nationalisms experienced a strong upsurge, further invigorated by the revolutionary ideas radiating from Russia.

India was rocked by the full force of these upheavals. Its contribution to the British war effort, both in men and in money, was considerable. The Indian army, the strength of which reached 1.2 million men, fought on numerous fronts and suffered heavy losses. It was this army that conquered Mesopotamia for England at the end of a long and difficult campaign and it took part in the fighting on the Somme as well as in the battle for Palestine. The increase in the strength of the army was obtained, especially in the Punjab (this province supplied nearly one third of the total force), through methods that bordered on impressment, even though conscription had not been officially established. India also participated in the war effort financially, in the form of a voluntary contribution that looked more like a supplementary tax. Furthermore, the export of certain agricultural commodities, like food grains, (by way of fodder for the cavalry) was encouraged even when the country was experiencing difficulties in supplies. Lastly, the war awakened the habitual evil of opportunism and speculation among both English and Indian capitalists, which led to a soaring of prices.

The role of Gandhi

From 1917 onwards, a wave of unprecedented popular discontent swept across India. Nationalist politicians like Tilak took advantage of it to demand autonomy and created Home Rule Leagues based on the Irish model, thus supplanting a Congress that had drifted into abeyance in 1914.

Gandhi was to be the catalyst of this new situation. This Gujarati barrister situated himself within the inherited tradition of the moderates of the Congress, with Gokhale as his mentor. The struggle that he had waged in South Africa for the respect of the fundamental rights of the Indian population, a struggle that had served as a model for the Blacks, spurred him to conceive methods very different from the habitual arsenal advocated by the moderates (petitions, meetings). He thus organized in 1907–8, 1908–11 and 1913–14 three campaigns of passive resistance (called *satyagraha*, that is 'the force of truth'), so far-reaching that they constrained the authorities to make concessions. In his South-African 'laboratory,' Gandhi had developed a form of struggle using a combination of principles: the formation of a small group of disciplined cadres through whom he could control the movement; non-violent means of agitation, the deliberate but pacific violation of certain unjust laws, voluntary arrests on a large scale, spectacular marches; lastly, the alternation between pressure and negotiation. This blend of fierce determination and strict observance of non-violence generally succeeded in disarming the adversary.

When he returned to India in 1915 basking in the glow of the successes scored in South Africa, Gandhi first maintained a low profile: after a tour across the country during which he familiarized himself with the conditions of farmers, he created an *ashram* in 1915 at Ahmadabad, which served simultaneously as a place of meditation and as a training school for the cadres of the future movements. From 1917 onwards, he intervened in the public arenas in order to support or help organize certain movements like that of the peasants of the district of Chanparan, in North Bihar, victims of the exploitation of English indigo planters, or that of the farmers of the district of Kheda, in Gujarat, who were fighting against tax pressures. He also played the role of a mediator during a labour conflict in the textile factories of Ahmadabad. These actions began to confer on him the image of a popular leader.

The struggle that he organized against the emergency regulations promulgated by the British, the Rowlatt Acts, paved the way for him to make a spectacular entry into the pan-Indian political arena.

The ambiguity of his message was one of the reasons for the extraordinary influence that Gandhi would exert in the years 1917–22: if, in the eyes of the peasant masses, he embodied at the time the end of exploitation by the *zamindars*, he also personified for many *zamindars* the hope of a conciliation between landowners and peasants. In his speeches, Gandhi underscored his opposition to class struggle and his preference for solutions of compromise in agrarian conflicts. This position as arbitrator enabled him to play a major role in nationalist politics even when he had taken semi-retirement. But the tension between the rigid framework that he imposed on the movements that he led and the outburst of initiatives from the grassroots, that unceasingly threatened to overwhelm him, explains in part the fluctuating nature of anti-British mobilizations between 1919 and 1934.

The turmoil of 1919

From 1917 to 1919, the British government took a certain number of initiatives that marked a turning point in the constitutional history of India. The point of departure was the declaration made before the House of the Commons on 20 August 1917 by the secretary of state for India, Montagu, which announced that the objective of British policy would henceforth be 'the development of self-governing institutions, in view of a gradual transition to a responsible government within the framework of the British Empire'. Following the Montagu–Chelmsford Report of 1918 (Lord Chelmsford was the Viceroy of India), the change was concretized by the passing of the *Government of India Act* of 1919, which modified the functioning of the provincial governments. The autonomy of the provinces was reinforced in keeping with the theory of 'dyarchy': certain prerogatives of the provincial governments (education, health, agriculture, local bodies) were transferred to ministers accountable to the provincial legislative assembly, while others (finance, in particular) remained within the purview of ministers appointed by the British and not accountable before the assemblies.

The limited character of these reforms, which did not alter the functioning of the central government, is clear. It has, however, been interpreted by some as the beginning of the process of decolonization of India, set in motion by the colonial authorities, who had apparently already perceived that a transfer of power to Indians was inevitable in the long run. There is no proof, however, that in 1917 or 1919 the British had envisaged such a process. The reforms were aimed at consolidating their domination in India by expanding the circle of collaborators of the colonial government. In the face of the development of nationalist agitation, it seemed necessary to offer the Indian elites certain gratifications, partly symbolic (as the powers of the new ministers were limited), but partly material (as the opportunities for gain through the constitution of interest groups were not negligible) with a view to divert them away from the nationalist movement.

Concurrently, the authorities adopted measures that aggravated the prevalent tension. In February–March 1919, the Imperial Legislative Council, basing itself on the conclusions drawn by a committee presided by Judge Rowlatt, passed a series of laws, the *Rowlatt Acts*, which aimed at prolonging certain restrictions on fundamental liberties introduced during the war, as they instituted special courts of justice and authorised detention without trial for two years on grounds of 'subversive' (which had a wide meaning) activities. These unleashed a storm of protests in Indian political circles. Gandhi, who had created a *Satyagraha Sabha*[1] in Bombay in February, retaliated by calling a *hartal* (strike) on 6 April all across the country. He succeeded in enrolling numerous members of the Home Rule Leagues (which at the time were rapidly disintegrating) as well as several Muslim politicians and religious leaders. The Congress as such did not participate in the movement.

The agitation soon took a very different turn from the one anticipated by Gandhi, particularly in the Punjab, where the people had borne the brunt of mass recruitment to the war. Here, after a spate of relatively pacific *hartals*, on 10 April, a violent confrontation flared up in Amristar, in the wake of which martial law was proclaimed. All in all, the agitation engulfed five districts of the Punjab, traditionally the most loyalist province: Muslims, Hindus and Sikhs joined processions in huge numbers, not hesitating to attack emblems of European domination. Though the agitation was confined to the cities, the authorities took fright, and on 13 April, 'to set an example', General Dyer opened fire on a crowd that had peacefully assembled in Jallianwala Bagh in Amritsar. Not less than 379 people were killed, including a number of women and children. In the days that followed, the repression intensified in the Punjab and soon prevailed over this uprising that had taken everyone, particularly Gandhi, by surprise. Other important protests, at times violent, also broke out in Delhi, Ahmadabad, Bombay and Calcutta, but peace was soon restored to the entire country. Gandhi, admitting that he had committed a 'Himalayan blunder' by underestimating the explosive nature of the situation, put an end to this campaign of protest.

The repercussions of this event, which came to be called the 'Amritsar massacre', was enormous and durable. In a symbolic gesture as a mark of his protest, the great poet Rabindranath Tagore, Nobel prize winner for literature, relinquished his title of knight. While General Dyer became a sort of hero for the British colonists who thanked him for having prevented a new mutiny thanks to his prompt action, Indian opinion demanded that he be sanctioned. Never had the gulf between the British and Indians been so wide. The enforcement of the *Government of India Act* in December 1919 hardly seemed destined to restore normalcy.

The Khilafat movement and the campaign of Non-Cooperation (1920–2)

The discontent of the Muslims, who represented nearly a quarter of the Indian population, with regard to British policy in the Middle East gave Gandhi an opportunity to resume the struggle. The Indian Muslim community started to organize a movement for the defence of the caliphate (the sultan of Turkey was also the 'commander of the faithful'), a movement that became radical in nature in May 1920, after the signing of the Treaty of Sevres dismembering the Ottoman Empire. Under the impetus given by two radical Muslim leaders, the Ali brothers, the Central Khilafat Committee decided in Allahabad, in June 1920, on a programme of non-cooperation.

Gandhi exerted himself to convince the Congress to adopt this programme, but he came up against the strong opposition both of the moderates like Motilal Nehru and of former extremists and of the Bengali leader CR Das. However, during an extraordinary session held in Calcutta in September, Motilal Nehru rallied himself to a vast programme aimed at paralysing British administration and trade in India. Its salient points were, other than the re-establishment of the caliphate, the relinquishment by Indians of their British honorary titles, the boycott of official schools, the rejection of courts and abstention in the elections to the legislative councils. The Congress also advocated the boycott of foreign goods, encouraged 'national' schools, the creation of courts of arbitration and the exclusive purchase of hand-made cloth (*khadi*). At the December session of the Congress, CR Das rallied to the call for Non-Cooperation, which helped Gandhi win the day. Whatever the ulterior motives of these last minute conversions, the Congress found itself involved for the first time in the organization of a mass movement the declared objective of which was the establishment of *swaraj*: this term, deliberately ambiguous, could mean either dominion status within the framework of the British Empire, or total independence.

The adoption by the Congress of a programme of struggle was not solely the outcome of Gandhi's influence. It was also due to the wave of popular agitation that shook the country in 1919 and 1920, forcing the leaders to act if they wanted to avoid being overwhelmed. In effect, strikes multiplied in the major industrial centres: in Cawnpore, 17,000 textile workers ceased work in November and December 1919; in Calcutta, 35,000 jute workers followed suit in January 1920; in Bombay, a general strike in January and February 1920 was observed by 200,000 workers. The agitation was particularly widespread among the farmers of Oudh, who attacked the *taluqdars*. The presence of a charismatic leader, Baba Ramchandra, a *sanyasi* (ascetic), made it truly popular, even though on the whole it was non-violent.

The Non-Cooperation and Khilafat movement (December 1920–February 1922) met with great success. In an early phase, the Congress leaders laid emphasis on the boycott of official schools and of courts of law. Several tens of thousands of students left their educational institutions and hundreds of 'national schools' were founded, some of which were to enjoy a long life. Nearly two hundred advocates relinquished their practice; but on the other hand, few Indian notables sent back honorary titles. Thereafter, the Congress leaders devoted the best part of their effort to collect a national public subscription (the Tilak Swaraj Fund) and to recruit new members. During the summer, they preached the boycott of imported fabrics (which were burnt in public). The movement culminated in an immense *hartal*, organized on 17 November 1921 to protest against the visit of the Prince of Wales to India, which gave rise to violent incidents in Bombay. The country seemed to be on the verge of a generalized revolt. The Viceroy Lord Reading seemed resigned to implement political reforms, when, on 11 February 1922, Gandhi abruptly decided to suspend the movement, after hearing that a peasant mob in fury had set fire to a police station in Chauri-Chaura (in the United Provinces), leading to the death of twenty-two policemen.

The campaign ended in apparent failure since *swaraj* had not been granted. The British took advantage of the return to normalcy to arrest Gandhi and to initiate legal action against him (he was sentenced to six years' imprisonment), which they had not dared to do during the events, for fear of adding fuel to the flames of discontent. The partisans of Congress could, however, find solace in a certain number of positive gains: the remarkable unity shown between Hindus and Muslims (no communal riot took place during this period), the consolidation of the finances and of the organization of Congress, which gradually transformed into a structured political movement even as it acquired representative managing bodies (All-India Congress Committee and Working Committee), the success of the boycott of imported fabrics (the import of foreign cloths plummeted by nearly 50 per cent in value in one year) and the increasing popularity of *khadi*. For the first time, British power had had to face a protest movement which was co-ordinated at the national level (while the Swadeshi movement had been largely confined to Bengal).

Significantly the movement had an impact in the South (except in Mysore), a region that had hitherto remained politically calm, and the agitation spread especially to the deltas of Andhra. In Malabar, the Mappillai Moplah, a Muslim population that had for a long time been hostile to British rule and to landowners (generally Hindu), revolted. A police raid on a mosque, on 20 August 1921, sparked off a guerrilla war lasting for several months, with thousands of armed men confronting policemen and soldiers. Though the uprising had taken on anti-Hindu overtones (several hundreds of Hindus, especially landowners, were killed by the rebels and there were numerous cases of forced conversions to Islam), the primary target of the rebels was the colonial power. The repression that ensued was severe: more than 2,000 rebels were killed, 45,000 made prisoners.

The Moplah uprising was not recognized by Congress as a part of the Non-Cooperation movement due to the acts of violence perpetrated by the rebels. But it revealed the volatility of the Indian situation. The Gandhian credo of non-violence only involved a small group of disciples of the Mahatma. For many Indians, violent struggle seemed the only recourse against British oppression.

Some 'radical' historians have blamed Gandhi for having curbed the movement by his insistence on non-violence. This interpretation does not stand scrutiny. First we must bear in mind the importance of non-violence (*ahimsa*) in the thought of the Mahatma. Gandhi was the first to extend this idea, an idea borrowed from Jainism, signifying the absolute respect of life in all its forms, to the political sphere. Besides these philosophical arguments, Gandhi justified his rejection of violence on very pragmatic grounds: with the masses being disarmed and the army, on the whole, still loyal to the British, any attempt at a violent uprising would have been easily suppressed and would have resulted in the dismantling of the existing nationalist network. In the situation prevalent in India, non-violence was probably the only realistic option, with all due respect to the romantics of armed revolution.

Gandhi's action seems more debatable with regard to the objectives of the fight for emancipation. His refusal to support peasant revolts against the landowners no doubt dampened the dynamism of the nationalist movement, but the moderation of his social programme enabled him to gain the support, particularly the financial support, of a part of the affluent strata of society. The contributions of countless Indian merchants and capitalists to the finances of the Congress were very useful, even if their amount remains a controversial subject.

Towards a new showdown (1922–9)

The restoration of normality in February 1922 was as sudden and unexpected as the outbreak of the movement had been. With Gandhi out of the political picture, Congress was divided into two groups: the 'no-changers', who remained loyal to the Gandhian programme and opposed the participation in the new political institutions set up by the British, and the 'swarajists', who were in favour of the continuation of the struggle from within the assemblies.

The swarajists, led by Das and Motilal Nehru, created the Swaraj Party in March 1923, which presented candidates to the elections slated for November of the same year. The party won the majority in the Assembly of the Central Provinces as well as the majority of the elective seats in the Bengal Assembly, where Das concluded a pact with Muslim leaders. The swarajists, thanks to their majority in the two assemblies, could give the Indian ministers who did not belong to Congress a hard time. The latter were forced to resign: the governors had to have recourse to their extraordinary powers, which demonstrated clearly that the dyarchy was nothing but a farce. When Gandhi came out of prison after being awarded an early release, he tried in vain to convince Congress to condemn the swarajists. A few months later, in November, he had to accept a compromise that authorized the swarajists to take part in the assemblies even while remaining members of Congress. In 1925, he gave them total leeway within Congress and created a separate organization, the All-India Spinners Association, in order to pursue his campaign to promote *khadi*.

While Congress was splitting up, the tension between the religious communities worsened. Large-scale rioting broke out in Kohat, in the Northwest Frontier Province, in 1924, in Calcutta and, in 1926, in numerous localities of the United Provinces. On the political front, the reforms of 1919 had encouraged Muslim separatism by maintaining constituencies reserved for Muslims: having to get only the votes of their coreligionists, Hindu and Muslim politicians tended to emphasise what divided rather than what united the two communities. The Muslim League, which had vegetated since 1916, became infused with new life, and in 1924, during its Lahore session, it demanded more autonomy for the provinces with Muslim majorities. Blatantly pro-British political groups formed governments in several provinces, especially in Madras, where the Justice Party projected itself as the inheritor of the 'non-Brahmin' movement, which had been powerful in the province since the end of the nineteenth century.

On the surface, India seemed calm and the British position firmly consolidated once again. However, various signs betrayed the serious tensions that persisted within Indian society and that were likely to set off a new explosion at any time. The continuation of peasant agitations in certain regions like Andhra, where tribal populations revolted in 1922–4, a brief resumption of terrorism in Bengal, the large-scale strikes in the textile industry in Bombay in 1924–5, all this reflected the persistence of a strong current of opposition, despite an economic situation that was on the whole quite favourable. The birth of the communist movement in 1924, though it was dispersed, caused apprehension to the colonial authorities. In spite of their weakness, the communists began to exert a certain influence over young leaders of the Congress, especially Jawaharlal Nehru.

India erupted into turbulence once again at the close of the 1920s. The trigger this time was an inopportune British initiative: the arrival in India in November 1927 of a commission composed exclusively of Britons, charged with the task of studying new constitutional reforms. The Indian reaction to the announcement of the arrival of the Simon Commission (named after its President, the liberal politician Sir John Simon) was unanimously hostile: all the political parties and groups decided to boycott it and to organize an All-Parties Conference. This conference met four times during the year 1928 and formulated the famous Nehru Report (Motilal Nehru was its main inspirator), the first draft of a Constitution for an autonomous India within the framework of the British Empire. Eventually, it rejected the demand for total independence, despite the insistence of the more radical politicians like Jawaharlal Nehru. Furthermore, the participants could not arrive at a compromise on the question of the relation between the central power and the provinces in the future federation. The nationalists desired a centralized structure, while the Muslims demanded greater autonomy for the provinces in which they were in a majority.

The workings of the conference were largely eclipsed by the reactions on the street. Widespread protests, often violently suppressed, greeted the passage of the Simon Commission across the entire country and added fuel to the tension. Terrorist acts resumed, one of the most spectacular being the bomb attack against the Central Legislative Assembly in April 1929, the author of which, the young revolutionary Bhagat Singh, was sentenced to death. After his execution, he became a true national hero, in much the same way as the Bengali terrorist Jatin Das, who died in prison in September 1929 while on a hunger strike. The country was also swept by an unprecedented wave of strikes. It culminated in the textile factories in Bombay from April to October 1928, in which the communist-led Girni Kamgar Union, played a decisive role. In the face of the increasing workers agitation, the colonial government responded by arresting thirty-one union leaders in March 1929, accusing them of 'conspiracy'. Their trial took place in Meerut and ended only in January 1933 with the pronouncement of heavy prison sentences. The communist-led union movement with was thus deprived of most of its leaders.

Simultaneously, non-violent agitation extended into the interior of the country. The most significant movement took place in a district of Gujarat, where farmers, responding to the appeal of Gandhi's principal lieutenant, Vallabhabhai Patel, rejected a rise in land tax. The government was eventually forced to concede and the success of this campaign marked the return of Gandhi into the political arena.

In December 1928, during the session of the Congress at Calcutta, the Mahatma could impose a compromise over the issue of independence on the most radical elements: it was decided that the objective of the movement remained the obtainment of Dominion Status as it had been envisaged in the Nehru Report, but that in case the British had not granted it by the end of the following year, Congress would then claim total independence (*purna swaraj*). In the course of the year 1929, Gandhi laid emphasis on the economic aspects of the Congress's programme: 'constructive'[2] work in the villages, the prohibition of alcohol, and the boycott of imported cloth. But he also imposed the election of Jawaharlal Nehru to the presidency of Congress, which indicated that he was preparing for a new confrontation with the British.

The offer made by the Viceroy Lord Irwin in October 1929, with the support of the Labour government in London, of a preparatory constitutional conference for the granting of dominion status seemed for a moment sufficient to avert a clash. But the British refused the conditions laid down by Congress for its participation and a meeting between Gandhi and Irwin in December 1929 ended in failure. A few days later, Congress, in its Lahore session, proclaimed itself in favour of total independence and the organization of a civil disobedience movement, leaving the practical modalities to the discretion of Gandhi.

Confrontations and compromises

The civil disobedience movement (1930–34)

On 31 January 1930, after a few weeks of reflection, Gandhi submitted an ultimatum in eleven points to Irwin: while avoiding the least reference to a constitutional change, he echoed a number of popular demands, particularly a reduction in military expenditure, a decrease in the land tax by 50 per cent and the abolition of the salt tax as well as of the government's monopoly of its sale. The last point was essential, as the salt tax was the only one that all Indians, including the poorest, paid. Gandhi therefore made it the cornerstone of his Civil Disobedience campaign. The 'Salt March' that he undertook from 12 March to 6 April across Gujarat from Ahmadabad as far as the salt works of Dandi, accompanied by seventy-one members of his *asram*, caused an immense popular response. Everywhere, crowds decided to harvest salt and to sell it directly, while the farmers stopped playing their land taxes (in regions under the *raiyatwari* system).

The civil disobedience movement which was at its most active, in its first phase (1930–1), had a more visible impact than the non-cooperation movement ten years earlier; in several regions, the colonial administration was almost paralysed by the resignations of small functionaries in the villages. There were constant protests that were often large-scale: the total number of arrests rose to more than ninety thousand, and prisons were literally overflowing. The ensuing repression, rather moderate until the month of May, became perceptibly harsher thereafter. The international press echoed the brutality of the police against unarmed protesters. The movement remained on the whole non-violent, which testified to the increased influence of Gandhi both on the Congress and on the masses.

There was however a spectacular recrudescence of terrorism in Bengal, where, on 18 April 1930, a revolutionary group seized the arsenal of Chittagong and waged a pitched battle against the police. Five days later, in the Northwest Frontier Province, a predominantly Muslim region which had remained aloof from nationalist agitation up until then, the arrest of the popular Abdul Ghaffar Khan, the local Congress leader, known as the 'Frontier Gandhi', triggered a popular uprising in the provincial capital of Peshawar. Martial law was proclaimed and the repression claimed numerous victims. In the face of the refusal of a platoon of Hindu soldiers to open fire on a crowd of insurgent Muslims, the authorities despatched reinforcements. They also sent troops to repress violent protests by workers in the industrial city of Sholapur, in Maharashtra. Excesses were nevertheless exceptional. At no moment did Gandhi lose his control over the movement, even if, at the end of the year, the dramatic degradation in the economic situation in the villages fuelled peasant agitations. The tenants who refused to pay the rent to owners enjoyed the support of Congress.

This civil disobedience movement is different in many respects from the non-cooperation movement. The participation of students, of the urban intelligentsia and of the working class was much more limited. It did not coincide with a wave of strikes as in 1920–2, as unionism had been weakened by arrests and because the communists, following the policy of the Komintern, viewed civil disobedience as a bourgeois masquerade. On the contrary, the participation of merchants and capitalists was markedly more significant. Its effect was particularly patent on the boycott of foreign cloth: the imports of British fabrics dropped from 1,248 million yards in 1929–30 to 523 million in 1930–1. Though a part of the decline was attributable to the decrease in the purchasing power of the Indian population, as a consequence of the worldwide depression, the boycott considerably amplified its effects, and a wave of panic swept across Lancashire. The support given to the movement by the majority of the Marwari community, to which belonged the major importers and distributors of British fabrics, was instrumental to the success of the boycott. The fact that these men, known for their solid sense of reality, accepted these losses, that were perhaps inevitable given the stagnant economic situation, demonstrates in itself Gandhi's influence on important sections of Indian society. As for the magnates of the textile industry of Bombay, their position was ambiguous. They took advantage of the decrease in the sale of foreign fabrics to regain part of the ground that they had lost during the preceding decade, not hesitating to sell the products of their factories under the label *khadi*. After a few months, a number of those belonging to the Parsi community, traditionally pro-British, began to be concerned about the continuation of the agitation and discreetly sought a *rapprochement* with the government.

The big cities, like Bombay or Ahmadabad, appeared as the strongholds of the civil disobedience movement. The success of the movement in the countryside was, however, remarkable. In effect, even as the agitation began to betray signs of weakening in the cities, it developed in the rural regions, and especially in Gujarat and in the United Provinces. Gujarat was the land of Gandhism, supported by the Patidars, a peasant caste with close links to merchant circles in the cities. Numerous Patidars protested by emigrating to the neighbouring princely state of Baroda. In Gujarat, excesses of violence were rare. This was not true in the United Provinces, where the cadres close to Gandhi were not always in a position to control the peasants.

The 1930–1 movement was also characterized by a very marked change in the attitude of the Muslims. Whereas their participation had largely contributed to the success of the non-cooperation campaign, they kept themselves on the whole prudently aloof from the civil disobedience movement (with the exception of the Pathans of the North-West Frontier Province). The year 1930 even witnessed several communal riots, including a very serious one at Cawnpore. The Muslims did not have a specific cause to fight for as they did in 1920, neither did they have a reason to be favourable to British rule. The absence of an uncontested political leader perhaps explains the difference in the political behaviour of the two communities. The Muslim League had in effect lapsed into inaction and no figure appeared on the political scene. Gandhi's discourse, which had a marked Hindu connotation, (he evoked the perspective of a *Ramraj*, the ideal kingdom according to Rama), compounded with the intransigence shown by the Congress leaders at the All-Parties Conference on the question of the autonomy of the provinces, hardly contributed to rallying the Muslim elites of the big cities. As for the attitude of the Muslim peasantry of the Punjab and Bengal (the two regions where Muslims formed the majority of the rural population), it was no doubt shaped by more local issues. In Bengal, Congress continued to be dominated by the members of the upper castes, conservative and favourable to the maintenance of the *zamindari* system: but in eastern Bengal, a Muslim peasantry was opposed to the *zamindars*, who were Hindu in majority. In the Punjab, the Congress was also above all a party of urban Hindus, and the entire political structure of the province rested on a carefully maintained antagonism between urban and rural populations. Hence the limited impact of the movement outside the few zones with a high concentration of Sikh farmers. In spite of these limits, civil disobedience was nonetheless the most intense political movement that India had hitherto known and its impact on international opinion was considerable.

However, even as these events unfolded in India, in London, a Round Table Conference assembled representatives of the colonial government, Indian politicians known for their moderate views (including the principal Muslim leaders, among whom figured Jinnah) and a delegation of princely states, with a view to examining constitutional reforms. This conference was boycotted by the Congress, but, at the time of its closing, on 19 January 1931, the British Labour Prime Minister, Ramsay MacDonald, made an overture towards the nationalists by evoking the principle of the responsibility of the executive power before the legislative assembly.

Gandhi, who had just emerged from a few months in prison, was first opposed to it. But by mid-February, during a series of meetings that he had with the very liberal Viceroy Lord Irwin, the Mahatma seemed to have been won over to the idea of a compromise: in exchange for the acceptance of the principle of the responsibility of the executive by the British, he was ready to explore the possibility of a federal regime (demanded by the Muslim leaders and the princes) and to discuss the maintenance of a certain number of guarantees for British interests. The Delhi Pact,

concluded on 5 March 1931 between Gandhi and Irwin, provided for the participation of the Congress in the Second Round Table Conference, which was to
examine these questions in detail, and for the suspension of the civil disobedience
movement. In exchange, Gandhi gained certain concessions on the issue of salt, and
more particularly, the liberation of all political prisoners. However, in England,
Churchill was outraged that the representative of the Crown had accepted to negotiate on equal terms with a 'naked fakir'.

Gandhi's backtracking on the objectives of the civil disobedience movement was
interpreted by many in India as nothing short of a capitulation and some 'radical' historians still reproach him for it. The reasons that could have led to this sudden
change in Gandhi's attitude are still an object of study. Some have seen in it the result
of strong pressures from business circles, a hypothesis that is plausible, but necessarily
partial. Others summarize his strategy by the formula 'pressure-compromise-
pressure'. By attaching extremely ambitious objectives to the movement, Gandhi
apparently had the aim of obtaining limited concessions from the British, in order to
pave the way for the nationalist movement to conquer a position from which it could
re-launch an attack on the citadel of colonialism. The most plausible hypothesis is
that, in the face of the growing reticence of certain groups (including the capitalists),
Gandhi preferred to maintain the unity of the movement and to put the seriousness
of British intentions to the test through negotiations, even while keeping his options
open for the future. The fear of a radicalization of civil disobedience in the villages
certainly influenced his decision, but India was not yet in a 'revolutionary' situation.
The worldwide Depression brought in its train great sufferings for the peasantry
everywhere but it did not lead to a peasant revolution anywhere in the world: one
wonders why it could have been otherwise in India.

The rest of the year 1931 was a rather strange period. In India, a precarious calm
reigned and Congress took advantage of the truce and of the liberation of political
prisoners to consolidate its organization in the country. At the same time, in London,
where Gandhi had gone to participate in the Second Round Table Conference, the
government was preparing emergency plans to brave a possible resumption of the
civil disobedience movement. British business circles, worried about the perspective
of negotiations, insisted on the necessity to obtain financial and commercial guarantees before envisaging any transition towards a more representative regime. The
negotiations in London reached a stalemate over the question of guarantees to
minorities. Gandhi in effect found himself confronting a united front of the British,
the Muslims and the princes who were determined to cede nothing. As the representatives of the Hindu Mahasabha, the organization that projected itself as the
mouthpiece of the Hindu community, showed an equal intransigence and refused all
concession to Muslims, Gandhi had to accept his failure.

The Mahatma returned empty-handed to India. Congress had no other choice but
to resume civil disobedience. This time, the authorities did not allow themselves to be
taken by surprise. On 4 January, even before the movement could be organized, a
series of draconian ordinances were promulgated in order to institute a state of
emergency: massive arrests began, while all organizations coming, closely or remotely,
under the sphere of influence of the nationalist movement were struck by bans.

The second phase of the civil disobedience movement (1932–3) witnessed a markedly less important mobilization of the masses. Estimates of the total number of arrests are very high, but many people were arrested several times, so the figure is not very significant. The movement affected Bombay in particular, where the cotton market was disturbed for several months by the boycott of British firms, and Bengal, where it coincided with a new wave of terrorism. Elsewhere, the movement for the non-payment of land tax was not very successful on the whole. The boycott of foreign fabrics also flagged. By mid-1932, the failure of the movement had become obvious.

From then on, Gandhi was driven to seek an honourable escape route. From his prison he launched a campaign to protest against the creation of constituencies reserved for untouchables, one of the most controversial clauses of the *Communal Award*[3] passed by the British in August 1932 to cut short the interminable negotiations in London on the question of minorities. Gandhi undertook a fast 'unto death' in his prison and the leader of the untouchables, Ambedkar, had to agree to negotiate with him. The two leaders concluded the Poona Pact, which demanded the revocation of these separate electorates and which was accepted by the British. Busy with his effort to launch a vast campaign against the various discriminations that oppressed the untouchables and against the very principle of untouchability, Gandhi 'temporarily' suspended the civil disobedience movement in May 1933 (except for himself), then definitively in April 1934. Thus, one of the greatest political campaigns of the century ended in the middle of almost complete indifference.

Apparently, the civil disobedience movement ended, as had the Non-Cooperation movement earlier, in a failure for Gandhi and Congress. The task of elaborating constitutional reforms, after the end of the deliberations of the three Round Table Conferences (the last of which took place in November-December 1932) and following the publication in March 1933 by the British government of a preliminary report (*White Paper*), fell on a committee of the two Houses of the British Parliament, a committee of which not one Indian was a member.

The political reforms

The new *Government of India Act*, passed in August 1935 by the Parliament in London, made but a slight advance in comparison with that of 1919 and fell far short of the minimal demands of Indian public opinion. It stipulated the setting up, in due course and subject to the approval of not less than half of the princes, of a federation comprising the British provinces and the princely states. In this future and hypothetical federation, part of the powers would be transferred to responsible Indian ministers, but finances and defence would remain within the purview of the viceroy (these articles were never to be applied). The most significant step forward concerned the provincial governments: the system of dyarchy was abolished and the increased prerogatives of the provinces were transferred to ministers answerable before the assemblies. The electorate of the provincial assemblies was considerably enlarged by the extension of the franchise – to be an elector, it was however necessary to give proof of a minimum of resources – but the governors of the provinces retained certain reserve powers that enabled them to intervene in the political game.

From the point of view of the British, the increase in the powers of the provincial governments represented a fresh attempt to enlarge the circle of collaborators by offering increased possibilities of patronage and influence to Indians willing to play the game. This was a retreat, but a calculated retreat carried out in an orderly fashion, with a view to saving, at the cost of minor concessions, what was essential, that is the maintenance of Britain's financial and strategic control over India. There was, however, a risk that Congress might take advantage of the extension of the franchise to consolidate its electoral positions in the provinces, and even that it might eventually be in a position to form governments there. The British apparently did not consider this risk very great in 1935.

At the end of the years of civil disobedience, Congress appeared weakened and increasingly divided. The influence of Gandhi and other moderate leaders (Patel, Rajagopalachari, Rajendra Prasad) seemed to be threatened by the rise of more radical tendencies that found in the Congress Socialist Party, created in 1934, a rallying point and in Jawaharlal Nehru a prestigious and popular leader. The British believed that this radical menace, compounded with a marked recrudescence in labour unrest – strikes multiplied from 1933 onwards – and in peasant agitation, with the development of new organizations, the *kisan sabhas* (farmers' unions), would cause the affluent classes, landowners and capitalists, to come closer to them. It is true that a certain number of large industrialists in Bombay had concluded a pact with their Lancashire competitors in 1933 and had in exchange gained from the British measures limiting the access of Japanese textiles to the Indian markets. But the attempts to create in India a capitalist party had but a feeble response among the traders and industrialists; the latter, on the whole, preferred to maintain ties with the Congress, even while exerting pressure on the nationalists to move towards a socially conservative policy.

These pressures helped Gandhi and the moderates to impose their views within the Congress: the Lucknow session held in April 1936, presided over by Nehru, seemed at the time about to embody the triumph of the 'radicals', but it was a decisive failure for the Congress left wing. The majority of the delegates rejected the idea of transforming the nationalist movement into a sort of federation of worker and peasant organisations, and Gandhi succeeded in obtaining the election of a Working Committee composed in majority of moderates. Nehru, re-elected President of the Congress, had to compromise with the followers of Gandhi and could not gain acceptance for his views – in particular the refusal to participate in the provincial elections.

The years 1936 and 1937 were a turning point in the history of the Congress. It began to transform itself into a full-fledged party and recruited hundreds of thousands of members, particularly in the countryside among a peasantry of small and medium owners. Numerous local notables, until then pro-British, rallied to it, reassured by the moderation of its agrarian programme, and played a vital role in its electoral successes in 1937. Gandhi's prestige, the admiration elicited by the devotion of Congress cadres were considerable assets for the nationalist party in the electoral competition that concerned larger categories of the population (the electorate had grown from 6.5 to 30 million), even while excluding the poorest and most women.

The provincial elections of 1937 resulted in the undisputable victory of the Congress. Despite the efforts of the British to support non-Congress candidates, the latter, not backed by full-fledged organizations, by and large cut a sorry figure. The nationalist organization won 711 of the 1,585 seats at stake in eleven provinces, obtaining an absolute majority in five of them (Madras, Bihar, Orissa, Central Provinces, United Provinces) and a simple majority in Bombay. The success of the Congress was spectacular in Madras where the Justice Party, the inheritor of the non-Brahmin movement, was literally crushed. Congress obtained its poorest results in the three provinces with a Muslim majority, Sind, the Punjab and Bengal, where the Muslim League too suffered a severe defeat. The bulk of the seats reserved for Muslims went to regional parties (the Unionist Party in the Punjab, the Krishak Praja Party in Bengal). The Hindu electorate, to the great surprise of the British, had on the whole voted overwhelmingly in favour of Congress. The nationalists reaped the fruits of fifteen years of struggle against colonial rule. This victory however was the fruit as much of the financial support received from the local notables as of the popular enthusiasm for nationalist ideas.

Having won the elections, Congress had no reason not to form governments in the provinces in which it had the majority. In March 1937, the All-India Congress Committee, which comprised delegates of all the provinces, decided to form governments if the British gave them the assurance that the governors would not use their extraordinary powers. Though no official assurance of this nature was given, Gandhi agreed in July 1937 to play the game. Congress governments were thus immediately formed in the six provinces where the nationalist party had the majority, and a few months later, in the Northwest Frontier Province and in Assam thanks to coalitions. Three years after the rather inglorious end of the civil disobedience movement, the nationalists came to power in provinces that represented half of the Indian population.

Congress governments in the provinces (1937–9)

The Constitution of 1935 had significantly enlarged the powers of the provincial governments and these thus had the means to take measures for the wellbeing of the people. The main limit to their action was financial: the resources of the provinces were meagre, with land tax representing a large part of it. In order to overcome this shortage of funds, it had been decided that a part of the revenues of the central government would be allocated to the provinces according to a system of progressive transfer. But the financial situation in most of the provinces remained difficult.

Despite these problems, the accession to power by the Congress in six provinces in July 1937 was welcomed with joy by the population. However, each social group had its demands, and to conciliate such diverse aspirations was to prove an arduous task for the leaders. Business circles expected from the new governments a policy that was resolutely favourable to national enterprise, while the workers' unions hope‹ advances in the field of social legislations and wage increases that the industrialists were not ready to grant. In the villages, the *zamindars* were anxious about nationalist intentions to institute reforms, while the peasant unions (*kisan sabhas*) exerted pressure to pass laws favourable to the tenants. Account had also to be taken of Gandhi's ideas: the Mahatma was favourable to the prohibition of alcohol, which was likely to deprive the provincial governments of their second largest source of income, and wished that an aid be granted to the village craft industry.

Congress provincial governments soon found themselves faced with a wave of strikes, particularly in Madras and in the United Provinces. In an effort to defuse conflict, they set up enquiry commissions that recommended wage increases. The industrialists, initially reticent about granting these wage increases, eventually conceded them in exchange for guarantees that there would be no other in the future. These measures were not sufficient to bring the strikes to an end. The reinforcement of unions moreover caused anxiety in business circles. With a view to checking the wave of agitations, in 1938 the Congress government in Bombay passed the *Bombay Trade Disputes Act*, which made strikes more difficult and impeded the growth of labour organizations. It also endeavoured to establish unions hostile to the doctrine of class struggle, on the model of the Gandhian union of Ahmadabad, the Mazdoor Mahajan.[4] On the whole, the social and industrial policies of the Congress governments disappointed both the business circles and the trade unions. But the solidity of the bonds forged at the pan-Indian level between the moderate Congress leaders and a certain number of big industrialists (particularly, GD Birla, the Marwari jute and sugar magnate) limited the consequences of the opposition of the businessmen. The latter were reassured by the spirit of responsibility shown by the nationalist ministers. The divorce with one section of the labour movement was more durable, but, because its influence was still limited, it did not pose a serious threat to the Congress.

The Congress governments were more successful in the countryside. They succeeded in gratifying the small and medium landowners, who formed their principal electoral base, without excessively alienating the *zamindars* and other big landowners. The *Tenancy Bill* adopted in 1939 in the United Provinces represents the most audacious legislative measure taken by Congress: though ill-received by the *zamindars*, it preserved their essential interests while significantly improving the lot of the tenants.

In two years, these governments evidently did not have the time to usher in notable changes in the life of the people and their principal action was symbolic in nature. The fact that Indian ministers commanded the obedience and respect of a bureaucracy the members of which were still in the majority British was a sweet revenge after decades of humiliation suffered at the hands of the arrogant members of the Indian Civil Service. The liberation of political prisoners who were still crammed in the penitentiary of the Andaman Islands and the restoration of lands confiscated by the government during the civil disobedience movement announced the dawn of a new era.

Could the spirit of *entente* manifested in the provinces by the Indian nationalists and the representatives of the colonial power pave the way for a negotiated political transition? If a number of Congress leaders, including Gandhi, seemed favourable to such an evolution, the radical wing of the Congress was strongly opposed to it. As for the intentions of the British, they were far from clear. With their customary sense of fair play and realism, they had accepted the fait accompli of the electoral successes of Congress, but nothing proved that their position had fundamentally changed. They still seemed to count on the princes and the Muslims to delay indefinitely the political reforms that would allow the Congress to take over the central government. The absence of any *entente* with the princes on the question of the federation seemed to give them ample room for manoeuvre. The heightening of international tension from 1938 onwards brought to the forefront the issue of defence, on which British and Indian interests clashed. For London, it was more than ever crucial to have the Indian army at their disposal to serve as an imperial reserve force in the face of the new dangers that loomed over the empire in Asia owing to the Japanese advance and the Soviet threat that was constantly in the minds of the rulers of India. But Congress had always pronounced itself in favour of a rapid Indianization of the corps of officers of the Indian army, whereas for the British this could only be a gradual process. Thus, in August 1939, when the British decided to despatch Indian troops to reinforce the British garrisons in the Middle East and in Singapore, the Congress used this pretext to boycott the deliberations of the Central Legislative Assembly. This marked the beginning of a new break with the British.

The decision, taken unilaterally on 3 September 1939 by the Viceroy Lord Linlithgow, to declare war against Germany without consulting the legislative assembly further intensified the tension. It is true that defence was part of the domain reserved for the viceroy and that the Constitution did not oblige him to seek his decision to be approved by the Assembly. But the cavalier fashion in which the proconsul treated Indian public opinion and parliament shocked a population that was already highly critical of the policy of appeasement pursued by Great Britain towards dictatorships. The attitude of the viceroy placed the leaders of Congress in a delicate situation. In effect, all the resolutions adopted by the nationalist party before the outbreak of the conflict, at the instigation of Nehru, were favourable to extending support to Great Britain in exchange for political concessions. These resolutions were however not endorsed by Gandhi, who underscored the contradiction between the ideology of non-violence to which the Congress claimed to subscribe and support for a war effort. Nevertheless, after the outbreak of the conflict, Gandhi declared to Linlithgow that he favoured unconditional support for England. But during the meeting of the Working Committee on 16 September he was in the minority; the majority voted a resolution declaring that Congress was ready to support Great Britain in the war against fascism, on the condition that London clarified its aims and its position with regard to democracy in the empire; in the absence of a positive response, Congress would be obliged to denounce the use of India's resources for a conflict that was not of its concern.

The response of the British came in the form of a declaration of the viceroy on 'India and the war' made public on 17 October. In this declaration, the government clearly rejected the independence demanded by the Congress and contented itself with promising dominion status after the war, without fixing a precise schedule.

The only immediate measure that it proposed was the formation of a consultative group in which the political parties and the princely states would be represented. This declaration was a flat refusal and was condemned by the working committee, which decided that under these circumstances, Congress could not support the war effort and enjoined the Congress provincial governments to tender their resignation at once.

The war and its consequences

The intransigence of the British is understandable because London hoped to take advantage of the opportunity offered by the war to regain some of the ground lost since 1935. The objective of the Crown continued to be the retention of India in the empire; the British leaders believed that the situation was favourable to them, particularly owing to the growing political importance of the Muslim League led by Jinnah. Though this party was far from representing the majority of Indian Muslims, they sought to place it on equal terms with the Congress and to use it more and more as a counterweight to the nationalist party.

Despite Congress's rejection of the propositions of the Viceroy, both sides strived not to break off their relations completely. In May 1940, the defeat of France led the Congress and the government to make a new attempt to come to an agreement. In fact, the new offer that Linlithgow was now authorized to make in August hardly differed from the one made in October 1939: the intransigence shown by Churchill, hostile from the beginning to Indian nationalism, constituted a formidable obstacle to a possible rapprochement. At the same time, the Muslim League, during its Lahore session, adopted a resolution on Pakistan, but it was formulated in sufficiently vague terms to lend itself to several interpretations. The shadow of a partition would henceforth loom over India.

Gandhi returned to the front stage of politics and persuaded the Congress to adopt a programme of limited civil disobedience. This time, there was no question of a mass movement: only volunteers designated by Gandhi himself would participate in the *satyagraha* in order to preclude the excess that the previous movements had given rise to. By launching a movement that he would be able to control closely, Gandhi intended to express the resolute opposition of the Congress to the manner in which the government envisaged the participation of India in the war, without however sparking off a trial of strength and without impeding the war effort. The government reacted moderately and everything settled down in a sort of routine, despite the regular arrests of volunteers who were promptly released. In July 1940, the government granted a concession that was largely symbolic to Indian opinion by admitting a certain number of Indian notables into an expanded executive council, but the political impasse was still complete.

The principal preoccupation of the authorities was in effect the augmentation of India's defence effort. Thanks to a large-scale recruitment campaign, the strength of the Indian army increased from 205,000 men in October 1939 to 430,000 in January 1941 doubling to 856,000 in January 1942. From the end of 1940, Indian forces stationed abroad were engaged in fighting on several fronts: in Egypt, in eastern Africa, in Iraq and in Iran. Though Great Britain had taken charge of nearly half of the military expenditures of India, the burden for the Indian finances was substantial and the government had to resort to massive increases in taxes, needless to say unpopular, all the more so as the war was still a remote affair for the Indian people.

In December 1941, when Japan entered the war, the conflict came dangerously close to the frontiers of India. With the fall of Singapore in February 1942 and the conquest of Burma by Japan in April 1942, the entire eastern flank became vulnerable. The capture of a large number of Indian soldiers by the Japanese in Malaysia and the evacuation of several hundred thousand civilians from Burma under difficult conditions suddenly impressed the reality of the war on India. It is now known that the conquest of India was not one of Japan's aims in the war, but the existence of a Japanese threat could be evoked legitimately between March and June 1942, when the defeat of the Japanese fleet at Midway definitively fended off all dangers of invasion by sea.

For all this, during the great crisis in July-August 1942, all the political players acted as if the Japanese were on the verge of invading India. From the British perspective, this attitude can be easily explained: they stood to gain from exaggerating the risk run by India in order to justify their political intransigence. From the point of view of the Congress leadership, it is more difficult to understand; in effect, it is plausible that the Congress leaders had fallen victim to their own propaganda and had underestimated the capacity of the British to maintain their presence in India. The severity of the British defeats in Southeast Asia at the beginning of 1942 did not permit a lucid assessment of the situation and seemed to portend a complete collapse. The fall of Singapore, the symbol of imperial power to the east of Suez, had made a particularly striking impression on the minds of India; the rumours that spread – and it is needless to point out the importance of rumours in an illiterate society – tended to lend credence to the idea that British rule was heading towards its end. In a population, which was in its majority Hindu or influenced by Hindu modes of thought, the defeats suffered by the British in Asia assumed the proportions of a cosmic disaster that augured the end of an era. This state of mind among the masses weighed on the politicians, and more particularly on Gandhi.

In December 1941, Gandhi was at loggerheads with the majority of Congress over what attitude to adopt in the event of an invasion of India and once again withdrew from active politics: the civil disobedience movement was thus de facto suspended. The Congress leadership was divided between a minority led by Rajagopalachari, favourable to a political accord with the Muslim League in order to open negotiations with the British, and the majority led by Nehru, Patel and the *maulana* Azad, which was inclined to a wait-and-see policy.

The political initiative emanated this time from the British in the form of the Cripps Mission. Sir Stafford Cripps, the Labour leader of the House of Commons, arrived in India on 11 March 1942, heading a delegation charged with the task of exploring the possibilities of a political accord between the British, the League and Congress. The plan that Cripps carried with him provided for the immediate transformation of India, as soon as the war ended, into a self-governing dominion, with a clause allowing the secession of the provinces, which was expected to satisfy the Muslim League. Though Nehru was ready to concede this point, so great was his desire to arrive at an accord, the negotiation reached a stalemate over the definition of the powers of the new Executive Council of the viceroy, in which the Congress was to have a majority; the Congress leaders wanted to make it a ministry invested with responsibilities equal to those of the viceroy, a point that the British government, on the insistence of Linlithgow, refused to concede.

The blame for the failure of the Cripps Mission seems above all to rest with the British. Churchill had agreed to send the mission only after pressure had been applied on him by the Labour Party and the Americans, desirous of gaining the support of the Indian people in the war. But he was not keen on its success and did nothing to facilitate it: the intransigence shown by Linlithgow proved convenient for him. It seems that it also suited Gandhi, who, convinced that the British found themselves in a very difficult position, was now all set for a fight.

Gandhi demanded the immediate withdrawal of British and American troops from India, but did not succeed in rallying the majority of the Working Committee to his point of view during the Allahabad session held from 27 April to 1 May 1942. The resolution adopted did nothing but observe that 'it was contrary to the interest of India and dangerous for the cause of liberty to introduce foreign armies into the country' but condemned Nazism and Fascism in unequivocal terms. Another month would pass before Gandhi and Nehru arrived at a common position. The resolution adopted by the Working Committee at Wardha on 14 July 1942, and which was ratified on 8 August by the All-India Congress Committee under the name of the 'Quit India Resolution', demanded that the British immediately hand over the government of the country to Indians, but pronounced itself for the continued presence of the Allied troops 'in order to ward off all aggression from Japan or any other power, and to protect and help China'.

XXI

PRINCELY INDIA

(1858–1950)

Lord Dalhousie, Governor-General of India during the years that preceded the Mutiny of 1857–8, professed that it was opportune to put an end to the existence of the princely states in the subcontinent every time there were good reasons to annex them. Influenced by liberal ideas, he believed that these protected kingdoms, politically hardly reliable and often poorly administered, formed enclaves of anachronistic despotism that stood to gain from integration with British India. Furthermore in his opinion, they represented a danger for the security and the future of the British Empire in India. With respect to his last point, the reaction of the princes during the Mutiny clearly showed him wrong. With a few exceptions, the princes abstained from following the movement, thereby impeding the rebellion from sweeping throughout the entire subcontinent, and making its repression infinitely less difficult. About forty of them even extended valuable help to Great Britain at critical moments.

Lord Canning, who succeeded Dalhousie in 1856, therefore adopted a policy of conciliation vis-à-vis the princes, once peace had been restored. By the Queen's Proclamation, made public in 1858, the Crown undertook to apply scrupulously the treaties concluded with the princes at the time of the conquest and to respect their territories and their prerogatives. Rewards in terms of territories and cash, as well as titles and decorations were conferred liberally on the most meritorious: henceforth, all the princes enjoyed a security unprecedented in history. With a view to ensuring the permanence of these kingdoms, the colonial government even recognized successions by adoption in 1860. In this sense, a golden age dawned for the Indian princes.

Colonial policies would nevertheless become less favourable during the first half of the twentieth century, with Great Britain progressively abandoning the princes to their fate as the time for the emancipation of India drew closer.

The princely states in 1858

In legal terms, a princely state was defined as follows: 'Any territory, whether described as a state, an estate, a jagir or otherwise, belonging to or under the suzerainty of a ruler who is under the suzerainty of His Majesty and not being part of British India [under direct colonial administration]' (Section 311 of the *Government of India Act* of 1935). It was therefore a territory with delineated frontiers, situated within the Empire of India and subjected to the authority of a political ruler whose more or less extended privileges of internal sovereignty were recognized by the sovereign colonial power. This ruler could be as much the representative of an ancient royal Hindu dynasty as the descendant of a more recent Muslim house, or even just a lord or a local war chief recognized by Great Britain in the troubled context of the conquest.

This elastic definition applied to entities of diverse size and status, the number of which varied according to different interpretations. Most of the official documents mention five hundred and sixty-two princely states, but other governmental sources numbered six hundred or more. The variations nonetheless concerned only minuscule territories, whose privileges of autonomy were more symbolic than real.

The princely states covered two-fifths of the area of the Empire of India and embraced about a fifth of its population. The largest, the state of Jammu and Kashmir, encompassed 218,780 square kilometres, followed by the State of Hyderabad, covering 213,191 square kilometres. At the end of the colonial era, twenty-eight states had a population of more than 500,000, the largest eight of them representing half of the population, area and incomes of this group. At the other extreme, some two hundred states covered less than 25 square kilometres. The incomes of the smallest were no greater than the average salary of an artisan.

The geographic distribution of the states in the subcontinent was extremely irregular. It was the result both of the territorial policy of Great Britain at the various stages of the conquest and of the political state, sometimes unified, sometimes fragmented, in which the regions concerned were at the moment of confrontation with the British. Princely enclaves were rare in the richest and the most populated agricultural regions, namely the Gangetic basin, the Indus valley and the coastal plains of the Deccan (excepting the coastal states of Travancore and Cochin, which were situated in the far southwest of the Deccan). Most of the states were situated in the dry expanses or in the hilly and mountainous regions of India: the former kingdoms of Rajasthan (Jaipur, Jodhpur, Udaipur, Bikaner), clusters of states in Central India that emerged in the wake of the dismemberment of the Maratha empire, Sikh states on the Himalayan border and the confines of the Punjab, principalities of the hills of Orissa and the peninsula of Saurashtra, powerful kingdoms of the Central Deccan (Hyderabad, Mysore), Himalayan kingdom of Kashmir.

Owing to their geographic situation and to the relative scantiness of their natural resources, the princely states were for the most part economically disadvantaged zones. Some of them nevertheless enjoyed certain advantages: for instance, Travancore, a fertile agricultural region receiving plentiful rainfall and a former hub of maritime commerce; Hyderabad and Mysore, which possessed considerable mineral resources.

The cultural diversity of these states reflected that of the Indian subcontinent across which they were scattered. The states of mountainous and forest regions, which could cover great territories, like Bastar in Central India or Manipur on the Indo-Burmese frontier, were often populated by primitive groups, limited in number and still untouched by the Hinduism of the plains. Animistic practices were still widespread among them. The ancient states of the Rajput Kings of Rajasthan, as well as the surviving kingdoms of the Maratha Confederacy (Gwalior, Indore, Baroda, Kolhapur), were on the other hand Hindu states administered at times by brilliant and enlightened rulers. Hyderabad, the greatest of the Muslim states, formed one of the major centres of Indo-Muslim culture in the subcontinent. Its sovereign, the *nizam*, a descendant of the Mogul viceroys of the Deccan, had the reputation of being the richest man in the world and governed with the support of an opulent nobility.

As the result of the vicissitudes of political history, the subjects of several states lived under princes of foreign origin or of a different religion. In Kashmir, the prince was Hindu and the people overwhelmingly Muslim. Hyderabad presented the inverse configuration. The princes of Gwalior and Indore, Marathas by race, language and culture, governed Hindi-speaking populations of a different ethnic origin.

Political structures

The princely states were monarchies subordinated to the colonial power. Their rulers were kings. They were called princes because the only king in the political architecture of colonial India was the holder of the British crown. The political order in these states therefore rested fundamentally on the exercise of absolute power by a sovereign recognized by Great Britain. This sovereign, within the limits of the right of intervention that the paramount power reserved for itself, and of the traditional rights and privileges, if any, of its nobility (to which he was frequently related by caste or kinship), was the incarnation of the State in his domain. He was, in theory as in practice, the source of all authority. It was of his own volition that he sometimes decided to govern with the help of ministers or counsellors, and he remained free to dismiss them at any moment and to take the reins of the administration into his own hands.

The legislation in force was everywhere a heterogeneous combination of customary rules, of laws drawn from British models and of the decrees of the princes, each component being more or less modifiable at his discretion. There was nowhere a judiciary system independent of the executive, and those under his jurisdiction did not have any possibility of appealing to a higher court than the prince himself. The administrative staffs were entirely in the hands of the prince and all those who held an office of the State, from the highest to the lowest echelons of responsibilities, depended on his good pleasure.

In fact, there was no distinction between the public domain and the private domain of the sovereign: this is the characteristic of a 'patrimonial' system as defined by Max Weber. The employees of the state were not civil servants but holders of offices and came under the absolute dependence of the prince. The budget of the state was not distinct from the private budget of its ruler. There was however a certain relation of reciprocity between the monarch and his people. A subject had to obey his king and serve him by exercising his professional specialization, by paying taxes and other dues, by performing the services demanded. The prince, on his side, offered every one the possibility of earning his living and of fulfilling the vocation of his caste in peace: he extended his protection to the entire population, executed the royal rites that guaranteed the welfare and the prosperity of the kingdom.

Anthropologists have described the Hindu kingdom as a closed hierarchic system of ritual services and counter-services, organized around a sovereign who wielded material power over men, under the religious authority of Brahmins specialized in traditions and rites. If kingdoms coincided only imperfectly with this abstract view of things, the model nevertheless expressed in its coherence a representation of a kingdom that was present in Hindu ideology. This representation continued to have currency in the princely states, even if in reality the warrior dimension of the function of the prince had disappeared.

Not all the princes enjoyed the same degree of internal sovereignty. There was an abyss between princes like the *nizams* of Hyderabad, who struck money, could legislate freely and possessed the right of life and death over their subjects and the smallest princes who had almost no rights. Thus, there existed an entire gradation of executive, legislative and judicial powers that the princes enjoyed according to their origin, importance and status. The powers that the prince did not have in his territory were exercised by the representative of the British government.

This sharing of power was imposed by Great Britain in the name of its privilege of paramountcy, the legal foundations of which were highly controversial and the application of which varied in accordance with the general imperatives of colonial policy in the subcontinent.

Colonial tutelage

Forty princely states were bound to Great Britain by treaties in good and due form. The other princes had signed less elaborate engagements or had simply received written concessions (*sanads*) by which the victorious power recognized their local authority and other privileges. More than two-thirds of the population of the princely states resided in those whose relation to the Crown was governed by a treaty.

Treaties, engagements and concessions generally guaranteed the territorial integrity of the states, protection and (in a variable measure) internal sovereignty, in exchange for a pledge of friendship and alliance with Great Britain. The states lost the right to maintain independent relations with one another and naturally to engage in armed conflicts. In certain cases, the payment of a tribute was stipulated. Diverse subordinate clauses could be included: cessions or exchanges of territories, transit duties, stationing of troops, conventions on ports, post, or telegraph, conventions relative to the circulation and the right to strike money, to the production and the commercialization of salt or opium, to the construction of canals or railways, etc.

Great Britain, nonetheless, did not consider the field of application of its suzerainty ('paramountcy') as strictly defined and delimited by these accords.[1] These agreements had been drafted in a determined historical situation, that of the conquest. The East India Company had never planned to bring the whole of India under its direct governance. Except for the regions of evident economic or strategic importance, the Company had preferred to consolidate its influence through alliances or treaties concluded with native rulers who were allowed to remain in place with the status of subordinate protected princes, in exchange for a commitment of obedience: this was a special case of the imperialism of free trade. The subsidiary system thus conceived was initially nothing but an economic means of bringing regions into submission without assuming the burden of administering them.

Nevertheless, as the political climate of the conquest became more distant, as the *pax Britannica*, after the Sepoy Revolt, became administrative routine, as communication networks developed across the Indian Empire, as the imperatives of economic management came to the forefront, the content of the relations between the colonial power and these subordinate states progressively ceased to coincide with the letter and the spirit of the initial conventions. Thus, the British government affirmed repeatedly that paramountcy was an open concept, indefinite by nature, and adaptable to the context of each period. The stipulations of treaties, engagements and *sanads*, were in other words only particular and dated expressions of a general suzerainty of principle. This suzerainty, moreover, had not been granted to a recognized by Great Britain by a superior authority that could have defined it in a limited manner. It had simply fallen to it as a result of the political and military supremacy that the East India Company had acquired over the whole of India, thus becoming the heir to the Mogul emperor. The East India Company exercised this suzerainty *de facto* until 1858, because the Mogul emperor, though deprived of all powers, was always present. The Crown assumed it *de jure* in 1858.

Great Britain, in this legal framework that it had itself defined, evidently enjoyed the greatest latitude for action with regard to the princely states. It could interpret as it pleased the status of more or less great autonomy initially granted to the princes by the East India Company. The princes, in any case, had no control over their international relations. They could neither negotiate with another state nor send a representative to it, and even less declare war or make peace with it. Only the paramount power could enter into international commitments. What is more, the princes could be requisitioned for the application of these commitments in case they were concerned by them. The paramount power was also solely responsible for the defence of British India and the princely states. In consequence, it had all the powers of decision concerning the location of cantonments, the posting of army corps, the strength of armed forces of the states, the movements of troops across the subcontinent, military supply (notably arms and munitions), etc.

In practice, these prerogatives in foreign relations and in defence inevitably implied interventions of the paramount power in the internal affairs of the states. Great Britain in effect considered that its status of paramountcy invested it with such a right of intervention every time the interest of India or that of the prince himself demanded it. For example, it could interfere in order to prevent the disintegration of the state, or to restore order when a rebellion threatened a legitimate sovereign, or in serious cases of maladministration, or to put an end to crimes against humanity, against the natural law or public morality, or even simply in the interests of the economic development of the empire. It was even specifically endowed with the right to intervene in the resolution of conflicts of succession. It alone could validate successions by granting its recognition to the new ruler. It took charge of the state's princes, when they were minor, and provided for their education. Lastly, a prerogative of great importance in the princely universe, it governed precedence, conferred honours, and could regulate ceremonies. All princes were required to respect the duty of loyalty towards the Crown.

Great Britain's policy towards the princes until 1905

The policy of conciliation adopted towards the princes in the wake of the Mutiny did not mean that Great Britain would henceforth treat them as partners on an equal footing. Lord Canning believed on the contrary that the guarantee of stability that was afforded to them, as well as the recognition of their right of succession by adoption placed the paramount power before the moral obligation of being more vigilant than in the past in the detection of abuses or inadequacies of government. The sanction in the most serious cases would not be the annexation of the guilty states, but the deposition of their princes. A state temporarily deprived of its ruler, or governed by a minor prince, could be placed under the authority of a Council of regency, or administrated directly by a representative of the colonial government.

This policy, nevertheless, did not weigh heavily on the princes, apart from a few cases of spectacular sanctions (for example the trial and deposition of the prince of Baroda in 1875, the deposition of the rajah of Manipur in 1890). In matters of internal administration, or of taxation, the government had only relatively summary information on most of the states. Moreover, within the colonial executive, the Viceroy himself held *ex officio* the portfolio of political affairs, in other words the responsibility for relations with the princely states. But it was well known that he never had the time to take care of it and that he largely left the responsibility of this department to the secretary of the department of political affairs, a colonial administrator.

Only two viceroys showed a sustained interest in the question of princes, Lord Lytton (1876–80) and Lord Curzon (1899–1905). The former sought to mobilize the active support of the princes for the imperial system by playing on their appetite for symbolic distinctions. He organized in particular the great Delhi *durbar* of 1877, a sumptuous deployment of ceremonies in which Queen Victoria was proclaimed Empress of India before the gathered elite of the princes, a number of whom were gratified on this occasion with titles, banners or promotions in the hierarchy of salutes (the important princes having right to a number of cannon shots that varied according to their rank).

As for Lord Curzon, who was authoritarian by temperament and imbued with a lofty idea of the imperial mission of Great Britain, he attempted to regain control over the princes. Officially, he handled princes carefully and he too organized a spectacular *durbar* in Delhi in 1903, to announce the coronation of Edward VII, in which he bestowed honours on them, even while reminding them clearly of their status of subordination in the imperial construction. Curzon in fact had little respect for the princes whom he believed were devoid of intelligence and sense of duty, and obsessed by their concern for appearance. Intolerant of the fact that some of them were spending more time leading a life of pleasure in Europe than in administering the affairs of their states, he personally took charge of the authorization of their travels outside India. Above all, he took Great Britain's duty of intervention seriously when it came to the question of maintaining peace or of protecting the people of the states from the abuses or incompetence of their monarchs. 'The throne of princes, he said, is not a divan of indulgence, but the stern seat of duty.'[2] Fifteen princes were forced to abdicate or deprived temporarily of their office during his viceroyalty.

During the period as a whole, the dominant trend in colonial policy towards the princes was nonetheless one of pragmatic conservatism, which made a break from the reformist dogmatism (of utilitarian inspiration) that had preceded the Sepoy Revolt. Travellers, civil servants of the Political Department, viceroys on tours in the princely states could all testify that the princes were venerated by their subjects and enjoyed a legitimacy among them that Great Britain could never claim. No doubt the political risks that the maintenance of the princely states was supposed to avert in 1858 no longer existed at the close of the nineteenth century. However, the continuation of this regime relieved the colonial government from the responsibility of administrating two-fifths of the expanse of the empire of India and more than seventy million of its inhabitants.

Everyday tutelage

If the existence of princely states was no longer in question, the princes were reduced to a situation where they could receive injunctions from the colonial government at any moment or might have to justify their actions to it. Their relations with this government, to quote the terms of Lord Mayo, who became viceroy ten years after the Mutiny, consisted of 'a mixture of laissez faire and niggling interference'.[3] The government agents they had to deal with belonged to a specialized administration department, the Foreign Department (renamed Foreign and Political Department in 1914), which managed the relations with the princely states of India and with the states of the Persian Gulf and which, in collaboration with the army, ensured the control and defence of the frontiers of the Empire.

Two-thirds of these agents were officers of the Indian Army, recruited in principle on the criteria of their university education and their linguistic skills but also largely thanks to the connections they had in the higher echelons of the colonial administration. The remaining third came from the corps of colonial administrators, the Indian Civil Service. Only the four largest princely states (Hyderabad, Mysore, Baroda and Kashmir) had a full-fledged British resident. The others had to deal with a political agent, who often represented the government concurrently in several states and who himself came under the authority of an agent of the governor-general in charge of the princely states at the regional level. At the beginning of the twentieth century, the states were divided into two groups. Only 176 among them, the most important, fell under the direct purview of the governor-general.

The others passed under the responsibility of the governments of the provinces in which they were geographically situated. They came henceforth under the authority of either political agents answerable before the local government, or of the administrators of divisions and districts of British India within which they were located.

In the second half of the nineteenth century the Political Department (this was the name commonly used to refer to the cadre of colonial agents serving in the princely states) constituted the last bastion of the ideology of the 'civilizing mission' of Great Britain in India, which for the most part had lost its currency in the governmental spheres. The agents of this department had the particularity of enjoying on the field a liberty of action that the colonial administrators of British India, whose office was becoming increasingly bureaucratized, had lost for a long time. They were at the same time physically isolated in their place of posting, invested with a mission of representation and control in princely courts, which were skilful and on home ground, forced to rely on subordinates whose fidelity was uncertain, and incessantly faced with situations and government practises that often violently clashed with their modern western conceptions of efficiency and equity.

The extent of a particular agent's influence on the conduct of the politics of a kingdom depended considerably on the prince's character. When dealing with a weak ruler, the political agent could impose his law on everyday affairs. When transacting with an energetic and bold prince, skilful in averting any visible scandal, he was almost powerless. In general, a political agent was in charge of the local application of the decisions of the colonial government, of supervizing the collection and the payment of the tribute and other duties demanded by the government and of controlling the administration of the state. He also sent regular confidential reports to the government on the conduct of the prince. He had certain judicial duties: arbitration of border or territorial disputes between states, jurisdiction over Europeans residing in the states, procedures of extradition, etc.

Evidently it was in the small states that the weight of the political agent was most considerable, because he himself exercised executive, legislative and judicial powers of which the local ruler had not obtained recognition at the time of the conquest. In the smallest states, the political agent often exercised purely administrative and judicial functions of the same type that fell to a local colonial administrator in British India. If this Political Department harboured a somewhat outmoded zeal for reform, it was because it operated every day in the context of archaic and degenerating monarchies, which were for the most part a result of the colonial situation itself.

The internal evolution of the states

The irresponsibility of the protected princes

Under British protection, the political and military history of the Indian kingdoms had been suspended. The princely states were isolated from each other, confined within the fixed frontiers guaranteed by the paramount power and for the most part demilitarized. Not only had the logic of war that presided over the rise and fall of kingdoms disappeared, but the rulers no longer even needed to defend themselves to conserve their position. So powerful was the British guarantee that it protected them from all external dangers and also from the possible consequences of internal disorder.

Before the colonial period, Indian royalty was engulfed in a permanent dynamics of conflict: the kings had to protect themselves constantly not only from the ambitions of their neighbours or the rapacity of superior powers, but from the rivals who appeared in their own entourage or from among their dependents. Besides, their subjects, according to tradition, had the legitimate right to revolt against an oppressive or incapable prince who did not fulfil the duties of his office.

All these risks, during the colonial era, had more or less dissipated, as Great Britain was always likely to interfere in a state in order to put an end to serious disorders and to defend the legitimate sovereign if he was threatened.

In practice, British control was mostly inadequate to impose a correct management on a daily basis, and the princes felt sufficiently protected to be no longer concerned about ensuring the happiness of their subjects or about scrupulously executing the duties of their charge. Thomas Munro had foreseen this evolution as early as the conquest. In 1817, he wrote to the Governor-General Lord Hastings: "It is the natural tendency [of the subsidiary system] to render the Government of every country in which it exists, weak and too opressive; to extinguish all honourable spirit among higher classes of society, to degrade and impoverish the whole people. The usual remedy of a bad Government in India is a quiet revolution in the palace, or a violent one by rebellion. But the presence of the British force cuts off every chance of remedy by supporting the Prince on the throne against any foreign and domestic enemy. It renders him indolent by teaching him to trust to strangers for his security; cruel and avaricious by showing him that he has nothing to fear from the hatred of his subjects. Wherever the subsidiary system is introduced, the country will soon bear the mark of it in the decaying villages, a decreasing population".[4]

The princes, by their behaviour, often laid themselves open to criticism. The time that they devoted to the government of their state was often less than sufficient. They were seen far from their capitals, staying in the big cities of India, in hill stations and in Europe, where a number of them spent several months every year under the pretext, for instance, of taking care of their health: 'There are many princes who are never seen in their palaces,' fulminated the moderate political leader VS Srinivasa Sastri in 1926. "They are to be seen anywhere where enjoyment can be bought with people's money. You go to London, you go to Paris, you go to all fashionable cities and you meet some Indian Rajah or other, dazzling the people of Europe and corrupting those who go near him".[5]

Even the deposition of a prince by the paramount power was not an absolutely dissuasive punishment, because the ousted prince was entitled to a pension that enabled him to live abroad comfortably, while being relieved of all responsibilities. The government was thus led to depose one after another three princes of the state of Indore (the twelfth largest in India in terms of population). In fact, the princely states suffered from numerous evils: the multiplicity and the arbitrary nature of taxes; negligence in the maintenance and development of education, health and public works; subordination of the government to palace intrigues; generalized administrative misconduct; corruption of the judiciary and the police, incoherence of the systems of law and regulations that poorly dissimulated the rule of the good pleasure of the prince; misuse by the ruler of public money to defray expenses for the prestige and luxury of his private life; extensiveness of social abuse; absence of public liberties; general poverty, etc.

The protected condition of the princes nurtured or aggravated these evils. In the various echelons of power, in each state, the officials held their position as long as the favour of the ruler lasted, and performed their function with the help of their kin and dependants, without any real control. As a rule, the supervision of internal politics by the colonial political agents was partial and often superficial. It could not prevent an astute prince from doing what pleased him in his domain, provided he could avert excessively patent scandals.

Great Britain and the economic development of the states

The colonial government, always short of money for development expenses in British India, did not compensate in any way the lack of initiative of the princes in this respect. But, in the states of western Deccan for instance, the rate of taxation of the population was sometimes greater by 40 per cent than the rate that prevailed in British territory, while the per capita public expenditure could be less by over a third than in the neighbouring districts of the Bombay Presidency. It is true that the network of public services established across the empire of India – roads, railways, telegraph, perennial irrigation systems – occasionally benefited the princely states that were situated in their path, as the princes were required to sign the conventions permitting routes, lines or canals to traverse their territories. But the states did not possess any industry worthy of the name, with a few exceptions (Mysore, Travancore, Cochin, Baroda, Gwalior). The rare industries that existed came for the most under the textile sector (ginning of cotton, spinning and weaving, printing). Many of these enterprises were the properties of the princes, who established for their own profit monopolies of production.

An active policy of industrial development in a state would have presupposed access to external sources of capital. The savings rate in the princely states was low, as elsewhere in India, and the inadequacy of the organized banking system made the mobilization of the existing savings difficult. It was therefore necessary to borrow, either in British India, or in London or from foreign governments. But, the attitude of the colonial authorities in this matter was quite restrictive, as the government reserved a right of review on all borrowings contracted from abroad, or those liable to weigh heavily on the reimbursement capacity of the state if it was already indebted to the government of India. Nevertheless, it does not seem that borrowing was officially prohibited. However, in practice, the rulers of princely states believed that it was almost impossible to borrow from abroad. The government of India, constantly short of money, granted them loans only to meet exceptional needs (in case of famine, for example). Moreover, it authorized the borrowing of a state from one another only when the amounts in question were insignificant and easy to reimburse (on the other hand, it never objected to investments made in British India by rich states, like Gwalior).

The credit of the states in the capital markets was poor. Most of them, in effect, could only claim modest budgetary receipts that depended on an agrarian taxation the return of which was subject to the vagaries of the climate. Very often, the small area and population of state, compounded with the princes' frequent reputation for financial irresponsibility, sufficed to dissuade potential creditors. Only the financial guarantee of the government of India could have compensated for this handicap. However, the colonial government, which did not grumble about granting this guarantee when its local or provincial governments negotiated loans, refused to do so in the case of princely states. On the contrary, if a state contracted a loan, the government promptly proclaimed that did not stand guarantee for it. The only source of credit really open to the princes continued to be, as in the past, the informal capital market. But private financiers exacted exorbitant rates that were prohibitive in the case of development projects.

In any case, many princes, no doubt, showed only a limited interest in the economic development of their states. Even those who were actively involved were, barring exceptions, unable to finance development. The British government was prompt to demand, when its interest was at stake, that the princes should abolish customs protection in their territories or otherwise that they should construct roadways. But it systematically refrained from interfering in order to help the princes mobilize the resources necessary for the progress of their territories. This neutrality was tantamount to a policy of dissuasion. It was but the economic counterpart of the political principle of indirect rule that froze the princely states in their status of subordination for the exclusive benefit of the imperial structure.

The colonial policy of non-interference after 1905

Colonial policy towards the princes began to change in tone after the departure of Lord Curzon in 1905. The partition of Bengal, carried out by the viceroy despite Indian opposition, unleashed a wave of nationalist agitation. This agitation convinced Curzon's successor, Lord Minto, that the princes were the only political allies in India on which Great Britain could truly rely. For a long time, they had not been likely to revolt or to cause serious apprehension in the government. Henceforth, the risk of subversion loomed from the side of nationalist agitators and terrorists. The princely states represented a way of maintaining vast zones of order in the empire at a lower cost. Their chiefs embodied for the entire world the loyalty of the people of India towards Great Britain. In a speech pronounced at Udaipur in November 1909, Minto exposed the principles of the policy of non-interference that his government would henceforth pursue. The Political Department was advised not to interfere in the internal affairs of the princes, except if the abuses or shortcomings of their administration resulted in the flagrant violation of the 'fundamental laws of civilization'.

Minto knew well that this change in policy that radically transformed the ideas and habits of the agents of the Political Department could only be effected gradually with the replacement of existing staff with a new generation of administrators. But his initiative met with the immediate acceptance of the princes. The most enlightened of them promptly demanded from the government tangible proof of these new provisions. In particular, they made clear to the government that they would become efficient allies only if they were allowed to meet to discuss important political questions and subjects of common interest.

The political situation at the time of the First World War, the support given by the princes to the British war effort, the rise of nationalist agitation at the end and in the wake of the conflict, and lastly the sympathy of the secretary of state for India (Edwin Montagu) brought success to their cause. A Chamber of Princes was inaugurated in February 1921. The chamber was a consultative assembly presided over by the viceroy, and its function was to provide the princes with a framework of institutional consultation and to give the government of India an account of their sentiments and their wishes. Its creation marked the end of a hundred-year old policy of maintaining the princes in political isolation and their formal accession to the status of allies of the imperial regime.

Nevertheless, this political activity in which the princes could henceforth be involved very soon became, for the most part, a contentious debate with Great Britain around the definition of paramountcy. In their intention to possess complete control over their internal affairs, the princes were not satisfied with a hazy and elastic definition of this suzerainty, which invested the colonial government with a de facto discretionary right of interference. This issue was all the more serious, as the princes began to envisage the possibility, however distant, but without doubt appearing, of the relinquishing of India by Great Britain and of the transfer of its powers to an Indian government. They did not obtain satisfaction because Great Britain did not intend to be dispossessed of all powers of interference in the states. This disagreement was to dominate, from 1930 onwards, the debate relative to the constitution of an All India Federation; it also to a large extent led the princes to reject this project definitively in 1939.

Meanwhile, the British continued to apply their policy of non-interference. Numerous states that were liberated from the tutelage of the political agents of the provincial governments were authorized to establish direct relations with the government of India. The smaller states, in the various regions, were brought together under the responsibility of one political agent, who henceforth exercised only a distant control on them. This relaxation of colonial tutelage resulted in the rapid deterioration of administration in numerous states where despotic or irresponsible monarchs reigned.

At the time of the rapid growth of democratic and nationalist ideas, this evolution led the subjects of the states to call into question, and thereafter to defy openly, the autocratic regimes under which they lived. The Political Department, dispossessed of the sentiment of its mission, lapsed into inertia. From the end of the 1930s onwards, with the development of the Congress agitation in the states, it became evident to the British government that the princes were no longer reliable allies and that they were even becoming a political liability.

Political modernization

Some princely states had nevertheless made some progress on the path of political modernization in the course of the half-century that preceded the accession of India to independence. Mysore had an annual representative assembly from 1881 onwards, Travancore a legislative council in 1887 and a representative assembly in 1904, the state of Baroda a legislative council in 1907. These creations were accomplished by competent rulers open to new ideas, like Vishakam Tirunal of Travancore, who reigned from 1880 to 1885, or Sayaji Rao of Baroda (1875–1939).

These princes incarnated the ideal of a responsible and enlightened ruler that the British nurtured among the princes of India. This was the ideal inculcated in the sons of the princely aristocracy in the colleges that the colonial government had established for them, like the Rajkumar college of Rajkot or the Mayo College of Ajmer. Only a minority of princes truly 'fell' for this education. But paradoxically, British tutelage made the task difficult for reforming princes when they acceded to power. The bureaucratic and conservative counter-power that the Political Department represented in each state often impeded the initiatives of princes who were eager to rule effectively. It constituted for most of them a de facto incentive to hold on to the traditional mode of government that relied on networks of power over which they had perfect control.

The councils and assemblies created in a few pioneer states at the close of the nineteenth century were but embryonic representative institutions. They were convened only at spaced-out intervals and for brief sessions. Their role was purely advisory. The overwhelming majority of their members were appointed. The attribution of a seat constituted an honour with which notables influential in the court and recipients of a modern education, were gratified. At the end of the 1930s, the princely states that had made the most advances along the path towards a constitutional government were, from the point of view of public liberties, still at the stage inaugurated in British India by the Morley-Minto reforms of 1909.

Certainly, the rising pressure of democratic ideas circulated by the nationalist movement, the development of currents of protest within the states, and lastly the perspective of the departure of Great Britain opened the eyes of numerous princes to the necessity of rallying their subjects through reforms. In 1946, according to the information diffused at the time by the Chamber of Princes, more than sixty states had set up a legislative body of some sort. But these were generally only democratic façades behind which monarchic absolutism persisted and which were not sufficient to convince the leaders of the nationalist movement that the princely states deserved to survive once independence had been won.

The major princely states

The state of Hyderabad

The *Nizams* of Hyderabad, leaders of the foremost of the princely states of India, descended from the viceroy appointed in 1713 (with the title of *nizam-ul-mulk*) by the

Mogul emperor to govern his territories in the Deccan, who had acquired a de facto independence less than ten years later. After various vicissitudes, the state of the *nizam* definitively fell under the protectorate of Great Britain in 1768. A British resident was posted in Hyderabad from 1778 onwards, while, concurrently, a 'subsidiary' force was stationed there. The *nizams* thereafter resolutely made common cause with the English in the wars against the Marathas, their old enemies. Nevertheless, the chronic disorder of their finances prevented them from suitably maintaining the 'subsidiary' contingent. The English therefore conferred on themselves, within the framework of a treaty imposed in 1853, the control of Berar, the richest province of the *nizam's* state, in order to meet this expense.

That same year, Salar Jang, one of the best administrators modern India had ever known, was installed as prime minister for thirty years. When the Sepoy Revolt broke out, the state of Hyderabad, under perfect control, remained firmly in the bosom of its alliance with Great Britain. Had it become involved with the rebellion, dragged into it by the Muslims of the South, the destiny of the British Empire in India would probably have been different. As a token of its gratitude, Great Britain significantly attenuated the clauses of the treaty of 1853.

State finances, unfortunately, deteriorated once again after the death of Sir Salar Jang, in 1883. A new arrangement was concluded in 1902 at the initiative of the Viceroy Lord Curzon by virtue of which the *nizam* ceded Berar, his sovereignty over which was officially recognized, through a lease in perpetuity to the government of India in return for a fixed annual rent. The military contingent was delocalized and integrated with the Indian Army in exchange for which the government promised to ensure the protection of the state of the *nizam*. This nagging question was thus definitively resolved, despite the very strong reservations of the *nizam* whose chances of regaining control over the most beautiful of his provinces ebbed away. When he attempted in 1925 to reopen the issue by evoking his right to manage his internal affairs in complete independence, he received a letter from the viceroy Lord Reading reiterating the absolute supremacy of the British Crown over the entire territory of India, including the princely states, and refusing to recognize the slightest privilege of internal autonomy to the state of Hyderabad.

Situated in the heart of the Indian Empire, embracing a territory of more than 200,000 square kilometres, a population that exceeded 14 million in 1931, a budget of 260 million rupees and substantial natural resources, Hyderabad was in all respects the most important of the princely states of India. It enjoyed the privilege of minting money, of issuing its own bank notes and stamps and of floating public loans. On the eve of independence, it possessed an extensive, profitable railway network and a great Urdu language university. Rumour had it that its ruler was the richest man in the world. After the First World War, under pressure from the British government, the *nizam* agreed to consider the question of the modernization of its institutions, which were reputed to be retrograde, authoritarian and controlled by intrigue. He first created an executive council of six members. On the eve of independence, a legislative assembly was constituted, which met for the first time in 1946. In this assembly of 132 members, the Muslims had a majority of 10 seats over the Hindus, while the population of the state was 85 per cent Hindu.

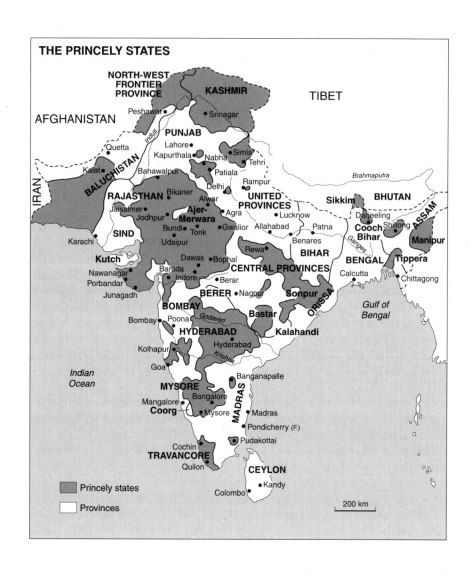

THE PRINCELY STATES

NORTH-WEST
FRONTIER
PROVINCE   KASHMIR   TIBET

AFGHANISTAN   Peshawar   • Srinagar

                    PUNJAB
        • Quetta   Lahore•
                    Kapurthala• Simla•
        Kalat   Nabha• Tehri   Brahmaputra
BALUCHISTAN Bahawalpur   Patiala•
                            • Delhi
                    Bikaner   Rampur•   UNITED   Sikkim   BHUTAN
RAJASTHAN   Alwar   PROVINCES
        Jaisalmer• Ajer- •Agra   • Lucknow   Darjeeling   ASSAM
        Jodhpur•   Merwara •Gwalior Allahabad Patna Cooch Shillong
SIND   Bundi• Tonk   Benares   Bihar   Manipur
Karachi   Udaipur   Rewa•   BIHAR   Tippera
Kutch   Dawas •   •Bophal   BENGAL
Nawanagar•   Baroda   CENTRAL PROVINCES   •Chittagong
Porbandar•   • Indore   •Berar   Calcutta
Junagadh   Nagpur   Sonpur   Gulf of
            BERER   •   •   ORISSA   Bengal
        BOMBAY   Bastar
Bombay• Poona• Godaveri   Kalahandi
        HYDERABAD
Kolhapur•   Hyderabad
            •Krishna
    Goa•
            Banganapalle•   Indian
    MYSORE   Ocean
        •Bangalore
Mangalore•   MADRAS
Mysore• •Madras
Coorg
            Pondicherry (F.)
        Pudakottai•
    Cochin•
TRAVANCORE
    Quilon•   CEYLON

                    • Kandy

        Princely states   Colombo•   200 km

        Provinces

The preponderance of the Muslim minority, which was itself composite, clearly reflected the historical origin of the state, which had been born out of the Mogul conquest of the Deccan. This minority retained a very great social and cultural autonomy in the Hindu environment. The landed aristocracy that enjoyed the ownership of land in the kingdom was entirely Muslim and lived for a large part in Hyderabad. Its sons received western education in the public schools and the universities of Great Britain. This class occupied the dominant positions in the state and the economy. Muslims belonging to the lower strata of society, were employed in the army, the police, the administration and in the service of the nobility. There were also Muslims among shopkeepers and artisans. On the other hand, the entire peasant class, in other words the bulk of the population of the state, was Hindu.

This situation could not fail to constitute an important factor of political fragility the day when the status quo would no longer be guaranteed by the colonial power. This guarantee nevertheless enabled the *nizams*, within the limits imposed by colonial tutelage, to govern their territory as more-or-less absolute monarchs until independence.

Mysore

The state of Mysore, founded in the fourteenth century, had been governed without interruption by the Hindu dynasty of the Wodeyars until the victorious usurpation of the Muslim Haidar Ali (1765). When the son and successor of Haidar, Tipu Sultan had been definitively defeated and overthrown by the English in 1799, Mysore was restored to the Wodeyars. But a great popular rebellion led by the local aristocracy broke out between 1830 and 1831, which propelled the state into a spiral of violence. The British government then decided to take over its management directly. This situation dragged on for half a century.

Under the authority of the Chief Commissioner Mark Cubbon (1834–61), a colonial administrator of the conservative school, Mysore was administrated with a firm hand but with a minimum of interference in the local power structures. The Mutiny of 1857 went almost unnoticed there. A prudent policy of modernization was initiated including expansion of the administration, the renovation of irrigation and roads, the development of market agriculture and plantations of coffee and cardamom, and the launch of an educational policy. The European population of the state grew rapidly. Access to English education paved the way for the development of a modern elite (essentially Brahmin). The commercialization of agriculture had negative effects from the point of view of subsistence production and terribly aggravated the impact of the famine of 1876–77, which claimed one million lives in the state and substantially interrupted the momentum of progress.

When the government decided in 1881 that it could reinstate a Wodeyar on the throne without risk, Mysore had already acquired the reputation of being one of the best administrated states in the Indian empire. It maintained this reputation until the end of the colonial era, surpassing all the other states from the point of view of the modernization of institutions and of economic development.

Three maharajahs succeeded each other as head of state. Under Chamarajah Wodeyar (1881–94), a young and unexceptional prince educated in the English fashion who died prematurely, the state was administered by an authoritarian and efficient *diwan*, K Seshadri Iyer. The maharajah Krishnarajah Wodeyar (1902–40), son of the former, a powerful and talented personality, also enjoyed the assistance of two highly competent administrators, M Visveswaraya (1912–18) and Mirza Ismail (1926–41). Under the leadership of these administrators, Mysore in the first half of the twentieth century became the example of a model state. This princely state as big as Scotland, with a population of 6.6 million in 1931, was one of the rare states to witness a certain industrial development (Kolar gold mines, metallurgy, chemical, engineering and textile industry, transformation of agricultural products). It also played a pioneering role in the field of hydroelectricity and perennial irrigation (Krishnaraja Sagar dam).

Mysore also set the example in the field of political modernization. In 1881, it became the first princely state to create a Legislative Council, to which an Upper House was adjoined in 1907. The proportion of elected members in the council became a majority in 1931. This council of fifty members had the vocation not only of legislating but also of voting the budget and of submitting to the government all questions of public interest by passing resolutions. The Indian National Congress, in this context, formed an organized force in Mysore as early as the 1930s, earlier than in the other states. On the eve of independence, the state was under the control of a government responsible before the Assembly, which nevertheless had no preroga-tive in certain reserved domains relating to finances, the princely family and to the relations of the state with the paramount power, which continued to come exclu-sively under the remit of the maharajah and his *diwan*.

We should not however exaggerate the scope of this institutional liberalization. Until the end, Mysore had a personal regime. The bureaucratic edifice of the British type that administered the state was accountable in the final analysis only to the maharajah. The religious and cultural homogeneity of the state, the popularity of a dynasty several hundred years old and the quality of the administration nevertheless made this state an exceptionally successful case of monarchy under protection. The chronic internecine conflicts of the ruling elite (between Madrasis and Mysoreans, between Brahmins and non-Brahmins) did not pose a serious threat to its stability in the course of the last century of colonial rule.

Kashmir

The state of Jammu and Kashmir, the largest in India after Hyderabad (218,000 square kilometres), came third in terms of the size of its population (3.6 million inhabitants in 1931). It had fallen under British protection by virtue of the Treaty of Amritsar (1846), after the defeat of the Sikh kingdom of the Punjab, which ceded this dependent territory to its victors by way of indemnity. The British placed on the throne of the state the maharaja Gulab Singh, a descendant of the ancient Rajput dynasty that ruled over Jammu before the entire region was annexed by the Sikhs in 1820.

The state was mostly an immense mountainous and almost barren expanse, dominated by the great Himalayas and the Karakorum, and encompassing Ladakh in the east and Gilgit in the west. Human presence and activity were concentrated in the two lower regions, a segment of the Himalayan piedmont situated in the south, which was a continuation of the Punjab (the districts of Jammu and Poonch), and above all the Kashmir Valley, a depression 140 kilometres long where the capital, Srinagar, was situated.

This princely state owed its existence partly to the reticence of the British, after the victory over the Sikhs, to occupy and militarily defend so vast and so unproductive a frontier zone. A buffer state, situated at the crossroads of important international frontiers, Jammu and Kashmir retained a comparatively high degree of autonomy within the Indian Empire. No subsidiary force was imposed on it. A permanent Resident, assisted by a political agent posted in Gilgit, was appointed only from the year 1880 onwards, at a time when the Russian advances and the instability in Afghanistan made the region particularly sensitive. Nevertheless, misadministration, notably an abusive taxation imposed by the Brahmins, rapidly became rife. It contributed greatly to the disaster of the famine of 1871, which devastated nearly three-fifths of the population. The inefficiency of the maharaja Partap Singh, who came to power in 1885, obliged the British to impose on him a government council supervised by a Resident.

The colonial government took direct control over certain sectors of the administration: land surveying in the Kashmir Valley, administration of the border districts of Gilgit, reorganization of the army. The maharaja could take back the personal management of the state in 1905. His successor Hari Singh, who ascended the throne in 1925, was a dominant figure in the Chamber of Princes, and was not hostile to reforms. However, he had to face a growing exacerbation of inter-communal tensions that the religious composition of his state encouraged.

Like most of the princely states, Kashmir had its share of internal dissensions between religious and cultural communities, vying with each other for access to the attributes and the advantages of power. The zone of tension here primarily was between the Muslim majority of the population (80 per cent of the total population) and the Brahmin and Rajput Hindu minority that monopolized the posts of responsibility in the administration and in the army. The oligarchy of Brahmin pundits, accused of monopolizing the favour of the maharajahs by means of intrigue, and in a dominant position at all levels of an often oppressive administration, was particularly unpopular among the Muslim population. Even though Kashmir was an ancient land of Buddhism, the Buddhist minority, concentrated in Ladakh, did not represent a significant political force. A leader of the Muslim community, Sheikh Abdullah, launched a protest organization, the All-Jammu and Kashmir Muslim Conference, in 1932. It repudiated its religious overtones officially in 1939 to transform itself into the National Conference exclusively focused on the struggle against the princely regime, and shortly later became affiliated to the All India States People's Conference which waged the same fight all across India. Owing to his action and his successive arrests, Sheikh Abdullah had by then already become the most popular leader of the state. He was to play a vital role in the independence process.

Gwalior and Baroda

In terms of area (70,000 square kilometres) and population (3.5 million inhabitants in 1931), Gwalior was fourth among the princely states of India. It was the largest of the states that emerged out of the disintegration of the Maratha confederacy in the wake of the ultimate defeat inflicted on it by the British in 1818.

Its ruler belonged to the most prestigious lineage of Maratha chiefs, the Sindhias, whose power had reached its apogee in the year 1790 under Mahaji Sindhia, who had gained supremacy over a large part of the north and central India. His successor, Sindhia Daulat Rao, after a spate of military disasters, had to sign a treaty of subsidiary alliance with the British government in 1817. The territory over which his sovereignty was recognized, within the framework of a comprehensive political settlement effected the following year by Sir John Malcolm, was essentially shaped by the accidental configuration of military forces at the end of the war. The region of Malwa, which was as a result divided by Malcolm on the basis of purely diplomatic and military imperatives, resembled in 1818 'a sea suddenly petrified in a raging storm'.[6] This explains why the state of Gwalior, a residue of Maratha expansion fossilized by colonization, still numbered only 14,000 Marathas among its 3 million inhabitants in 1920. Of the other three great Maratha princely states (Baroda, Indore and Kolhapur), the first two presented the same peculiarities.

Given the composite nature of their state, wherein Maratha *sirdars* coexisted with Rajput *thakurs* and with a Muslim minority (the peasantry being overwhelmingly Hindu), the Gwalior rulers had to construct a solid and centralized power structure in order to maintain its unity. Mutinies broke out frequently in the army, and a military insurrection flared up in 1857, which forced the maharajah to flee. Gwalior fort was recaptured after a hard-fought struggle in 1858 by the British army, which did not restore it to the maharajah until 1886. From 1860 onwards, the army of Gwalior, under firm control, became one of the best of the princely states. The administration of the state, strict and rigorous, exceptionally competent and dynamic on the economic front, was from then on cited as an example, as was that of Mysore.

The same was largely true for the state of Baroda (21,000 square kilometres, 2.4 million inhabitants in 1931). This territory was ceded by Great Britain in 1817 to one of the principal Maratha chiefs, the *gaikwad*, as the territory of Gwalior had been to Sindhia. The total Maratha population in this state formed only a minority: it was close to 12,000 in 1920. The *gaikwads* governed with the support of the local notables to whom they leased the collection of land taxes, the primary source of income for the state. These notables, with their village forts and their private militia, were minor potentates. Their deeds, often oppressive towards peasants, formed a permanent source of conflict. The rivalries between these notables for obtaining leases of taxes represented another factor of instability. This system could only function under strong and respected princes. It progressively plunged into chaos from the 1860s onwards under two incompetent *gaikwads*; the second of whom was forced to abdicate by the colonial government in 1875.

The British then chose to place on the throne a twelve-year old child, Sayaji Rao

III, to whom they gave an English tutor charged with educating him according to western principles. His reign was to endure until 1939. As the prince was a minor, they assigned him a talented administrator, T Madhavo Rao, the former *diwan* of the state of Travancore, who became the de facto regent. This *diwan* was entrusted with the mission of reforming the government of the state: he began to exert himself to fulfil it, but he had to withdraw prematurely in 1881 owing to the rivalry that had arisen between him and the tutor of the young prince. It was this tutor, FAH Elliot, who de facto governed the state until 1895, even though he had espoused the cause of Baroda to the point of frequently alienating the colonial government. Sayaji Rao ruled alone thereafter for twenty years, then withdrew from politics and took on a new *diwan*, Manubhai Mehta (1916–1926) and then another, VT Krishnamachariar (1926–44), both of whom were capable and imbued with the spirit of modernization.

Sayaji Rao, despite his irritable temperament that involved him in many troubles with the British government, was a very popular ruler, efficient, open to the advice of competent councillors, and convinced of the superiority of the western model of government. His reign was characterized by the restoration of ordered relations between the throne and the peasantry, by the development of a modern type of administration and by a relatively sharp growth of trade and industry in the state. The systematic registration of land rights and the rigorous establishment of the tax base (revenue settlement) for each farmer regularized land and tax administration while enhancing the budgetary receipts of the state. A Legislative Council was instituted in 1907. If it initially had but an advisory role and consisted of only eighteen members most of whom were appointed, it represented, at the time it was created, a pioneering innovation. Local administration was reorganized according to the model of districts and subdivisions (*taluqs*) of British India. The budget of the state, two-thirds of which were still reserved in the 1870s for the maintenance of the *gaikwad*, of his troops and his bureaucracy, gave an increasingly important share to education, public works and developmental expenses. The literacy rate of the state in 1931 was nearly two times higher than that of the neighbouring British Gujarat (21 per cent against 13 per cent). Baroda was the first princely state to construct railway lines. A significant textile industry (43,000 workers in 1944), as well as diverse chemical firms developed from the inter-war period onwards with the financial support of the important Bank of Baroda. The springhead of these successes, modest but real, was the agricultural wealth of the villages of the state, but also the solid alliance between the princely government and the prosperous stratum of the rich and medium landowning peasants (mainly of the Patidar caste), which represented nearly half of the rural population and which did not have to suffer the adverse effects of landlordism.

Baroda did not witness any significant popular agitation before the end of the 1930s, whereas the Gandhian nationalist movement had become entrenched among the peasants of Gujarat as early as the 1920s. The climate started to change only from 1938 onwards when Vallabhbhai Patel, the main nationalist leader of Gujarat, began to criticize the land tax system in force in the State. VT Krishnamachariar successfully defused the agitation by reducing the land tax and by enlarging the representation of the Legislative Assembly. There were no serious troubles after this in the state until independence.

The Rajputana states (Rajasthan)

The twenty-two princely states that were amalgamated in 1949 to form a political entity called Rajasthan constituted the heart of the political space occupied by the military and royal caste of the Rajputs. There were certainly princely states ruled by the Rajput dynasty all across the north and centre of India, but Rajputana was Rajput land par excellence.

This region of 330,000 square kilometres, populated by 13 million inhabitants at the time of independence comprised some of the most ancient and the most prestigious states of India (Udaipur, Jaipur, Jodhpur, Bikaner, Alwar). The Rajput oligarchy here represented less than one million people. With its clannish social organization and its belligerent traditions, it embodied the mode of Hindu political organization that dominated the subcontinent until the colonial conquest, grounded on a logic of incessant martial competition. Its glorious military past, in particular the fierce resistance that it offered against the successive Muslim invasions had taken on the aura of a legend. It reigned over a peasantry of which the most enterprising, the most prosperous and the most structured component was the caste of the Jats. The region, however, situated in the most arid part of the subcontinent, was largely a vast desert or sub-desert zone plagued by economic backwardness.

The Rajputana states fell under British protection at the end of the last Anglo-Maratha War, in 1818. Colonial peace immobilized the Rajput political system everywhere in its decentralized configuration, between a king who was the chief of a clan and a nobility that descended from this clan, each lineage of which constituted a rival for all others and for the king himself. The dynamics of the system were henceforth frozen, as the colonial power threatened to intervene militarily against all belligerent enterprises. It could henceforth express itself only in a symbolic way through the game of matrimonial alliances, honours and precedence.

Taking advantage of this protected situation, various princes exerted themselves to further the process of administrative centralization for their own benefit by instituting, in their territories the limits of which were henceforth fixed and guaranteed, the system of districts and subdivisions in force in British India, and by developing the bureaucracy. However, the recruitment of administrative staff was nowhere carried out on the impersonal basis of educational qualifications before the inter-war period. A de facto indistinctness continued to reign everywhere between the private budget of the princes and the budget of their states. Rajputana also lagged far behind from the point of view of representative institutions. Public education, communications and the economy in general stagnated during the entire colonial period. Progress in urbanization was insignificant.

Likewise, the impact of modern political ideas in these states remained almost nil until the middle of the 1930s, as information was strictly controlled everywhere and the rare attempts at popular mobilization were invariably crushed by vigorous repression. However, associations came into existence towards the end of the 1930s in various states with the external support of the Congress, generally at the initiative of Brahmin or Kayasth school masters, at times backed by members of the trading castes. The bulk of these movements in the villages was often constituted by the wealthy peasants of the Jat caste, who demanded the recognition of their land rights and the eradication of the abuses of which they were victims.

The awakening of popular protest across Rajputana, the growing power of the pan-Indian nationalist movement to which it was affiliated and the circumspect attitude of the colonial government in this uncertain context, made the pursuit of intransigent repressive policies more difficult. Nevertheless, with the exception of the state of Bikaner, which had set up a legislative assembly (which incidentally was purely decorative) as early as 1913, the Rajput princes decided to institute a semblance of democracy among them only in the middle of the 1940s. In comparison with relatively atypical states like Mysore or Baroda, Rajputana, as independence drew nearer, appeared as the symbol of the anachronistic conservatism of princely India, which doomed it to disappear at the same time as the colonial situation.

The end of princely India

The princely states of India hardly had any chance to survive after the withdrawal of Great Britain. The dominant democractic, unitary ideology of Indian nationalism was not compatible with the survival of hundreds of antiquated monarchies across Indian territory. Even the princes who tolerated the exercise, at least partially, of public liberties and who had reformed their administration in a spirit of modernization, as was the case for instance of Mysore, had to face from the 1930s onwards movements of contestation inspired by the Indian National Congress.

For the most part poor in resources and with limited sizes, the states could not in any case hope to persist as autonomous entities against the will and without the protection of the supreme political power of the Indian subcontinent. The only guarantees on which they could have relied as independence drew nearer was the expression of a massive popular demand in favour of their survival, or the negotiation by Great Britain, on the eve of its departure, of legal safeguards ensuring their recognition by free India. However, there was no popular upsurge in favour of the princes, but on the contrary, a growing mobilization against their absolutism. And Great Britain, no longer having any imperative political reasons at the time of decolonization to strive for their survival, left them to fend for their own survival, without any great chance of success.

The federal organization of India, as stipulated by the *Government of India Act* of 1935, had a place for the princely states in their own right. However, while the provinces of British India were to enter automatically into the new constitutional structure, the entry of the princes had to be voluntary. For the Federation to really come into existence, the representatives of the states would have had to occupy not less than fifty-two seats in the State Council and these member states to represent at least half of the total population of princely India. The scope of authority that each member prince would grant to the government and to the parliament of the Federation was open to negotiation and was to make the object of specific clauses in each particular treaty of accession. The reticence of the princes in the face of the real or supposed threat that this project of federation posed to their internal sovereignty caused protracted difficulties. Their falling back on reactionary positions consummated their alienation from progressive nationalist opinion. This proved, along with the growing hostility of the Muslim League towards a constitutional schema that maintained a single centre for the whole India, to be a major reason for the ultimate failure of the formula, which was officially abandoned in 1939.

The Cripps Plan of 1942, and then the Simla Conference of 1945, new fruitless efforts to come out of the political impasse, made it clear that the destiny of the princely states was henceforth relegated to second place in the priorities of the British government. The victory of the Labour Party in the British elections of July 1945, and their determination to extricate themselves rapidly from the Indian tight corner, only accelerated this trend. Great Britain only reiterated several times that there was no question of imposing a solution on the princes without their negotiated consent.

The Cabinet Mission of 1946, however, established clearly in the plan that it made public in May that Britain would not become the determined advocate of princely India in the political settlement that would follow its departure. Paramountcy would not be transmitted to the power that would succeed the colonial power, but would die out by itself with the end of the British regime. The states would be represented at the stipulated constituent assembly, according to modalities that were yet to be discussed with the Chamber of Princes. It was their responsibility to negotiate for themselves the shape that their political relation with the future Indian Union would take. The attitude adopted by Great Britain in 1946 would not fluctuate until its effective departure from the subcontinent the following year.

The internal political situation of the princes had in the meanwhile considerably deteriorated. The All India States' People's Conference, created in 1927 under the influence of the Congress to federate and to develop progressive popular associations (*praja mandals*) in the states, was in the beginning an organization of moderate inspiration, with leaders such as CY Chintamani or Ram Chandra Rao (a former *diwan* of Mysore). The Congress did not intend at the time to be involved as such in the states, because the political climate there was very different from the one in British India (poor popular mobilization, the violently repressive attitude of the established regimes), and because it wanted to avoid turning the princes straightaway against the independence movement. The passing of the *Government of India Act* in 1935 modified this position, because the text laid down that the representatives of the states should occupy one-third of the seats of the federal assembly and that these representatives would not be elected but appointed by the princes. The Congress interpreted this as a manoeuvre. This third of the assembly, in effect, would constitute a retrograde and anti-nationalist force, capable of making the Congress into a minority by forging alliances with the other conservative sections of the future assembly. It therefore became urgent to demand the democratization of the princely regimes.

In 1937, the accession of the Congress to power in the new provincial governments of British India infused a new determination in the militants of the cause of liberties in the states. *Praja mandals* multiplied, and serious conflicts with the princely regimes flared up in numerous states (Jaipur, Kashmir, Rajkot, Patiala, Hyderabad, Mysore, Travancore, the states of Orissa). It was then in 1938 that, being won over to the already ancient wish of its radical wing, the Congress, with the approval of Gandhi, decided to give up its policy of non-interference and to create openly Congress committees in the states. Nehru himself became the President of the All-India States' People's Conference in 1939. Against the backdrop of the Second World War, and after the resignation of Congress provincial governments, the agitation in the states lost its momentum. But it was infused with new strength with the Quit India Movement of 1942, launched by the Congress all across India, including the princely states.

In the negotiations that preceded the accession of India to independence, the problem of the princely states occupied a central place. The British Crown, as the paramount power, represented by the viceroy, constituted the link between the states on the one hand and the central and provincial governments on the other. The passing of the Indian Independence Act, in 1947, radically modified the situation by relieving the states from all obligations towards the Crown. The extinction of the paramountcy made them legally independent. With a view to disentangling a particularly complex situation, the government of India decided on the creation of a Ministry of States, which was entrusted in July 1947 to Sardar Patel, with VP Menon as secretary. From the outset, it was demanded that the states abandon to the government of India the responsibility for their defence, their foreign relations and their communications. Negotiations were conducted promptly. Patel and Menon succeeded in persuading the princes to integrate with the new India by combining guarantees, appeals to their patriotism and threats, supported by the pressure of the local popular movements, and by the obvious fact, generally conceded by the interested parties themselves, that independence did not constitute a realistic alternative except in a very few cases. Some states like Hyderabad, Kashmir, Travancore and the small Muslim state of Junagadh, in Gujarat, resisted until the last minute. But on 15 August 1947, all had finally accepted their unification with the new dominion, except Hyderabad, which ceded only the following year in the face of a military operation. The administrative modalities of their integration with independent India were then negotiated state by state, and were completed, with the exception of Kashmir, at the end of 1949.

XXII

THE WORLD OF THE COUNTRYSIDE

(1860–1950)

During the century that followed the Sepoy Revolt, the countryside went through two somewhat differing periods. The first, which came to a close with the First World War, marked a phase of economic growth, characterized by the continuation of the expansion of cultivated land, a slow but steady rise in agricultural prices and the creation of vast infrastructures (railway networks, networks of perennial irrigation). There were, however, several severe famines that revealed the persistent fragility of the agrarian economy and the inequitable distribution of its profits. After the First World War, the general trends in the countryside became markedly unfavourable with the rapid acceleration of demographic growth, the fall in per capita income, the widening of social inequalities and an economic situation punctuated by deep crises. The enhancement of the famine prevention system nevertheless precluded the return of the scourge after 1900, except for the famine that devastated Bengal in 1943, in the exceptional context of the Second World War.

This century as a whole was also marked by the slow progress in the Indian countryside of what is conventionally called modernization: the incorporation of agriculture into the market universe, the propagation of a contractual idea of agrarian relations, embodied in a corpus of new laws, the awakening of the peasant world to new forms of political protest in connection with the rise of the nationalist movement. Despite the visible economic success of a few privileged agricultural regions and of certain strata of peasant society, the Indian configuration of agricultural under-development assumed its current form, characterized by bottlenecks and growth disparities.

The agricultural conjuncture

Agriculture and population

Between 1871, the year in which the first general census of the British Empire in India was started, and 1941, the Indian population grew (in adjusted figures) from 255 to 389 million. These figures correspond to a rise of 52 per cent in seventy years and to an annual growth of 0.61 per cent. This rate of growth was close to that of the world population during the same period, but it was less rapid than that of the countries of Western Europe, the United States or Japan. It was furthermore attended by very marked irregularities in time, as shown by the percentages of growth per decade:

1871–1881	0.9 per cent	1911–1921	0.9 per cent
1881–1891	9.4 per cent	1921–1931	10.6 per cent
1891–1901	1.0 per cent	1931–1941	15.0 per cent
1901–1911	6.1 per cent		

These fluctuations were perhaps nothing but a prolongation of previous oscillations, with the difference that periods of depression before 1872 often corresponded to actual population decreases with the overall consequence in the long run being a more or less stationary growth. This abatement of demographic fluctuations was primarily due to the disappearance of war and insecurity as major causes of mortality. Famines and epidemics, on the contrary, continued to be widespread and represented until 1921 the principal factors of demographic crises: the famine of 1876–8, the famines of the closing years of the nineteenth century, the Spanish influenza of 1918. During the intermediate periods, there was a rapid increase in population. From 1921 onwards, these oscillations ceased through the disappearance of famines and thanks to the advances made in public health. India then entered into the period of the highest demographic growth in its history, which continues even today.

India's population remained essentially rural: only 9 per cent of Indians lived in agglomerations of 5000 inhabitants or more in 1881, and 16 per cent in 1951. This population lived on agriculture and cattle rearing: 72 per cent of the Indian working population in 1881 belonged to the agricultural primary sector, and 76 per cent in 1951. The quasi stability of this distribution is a significant indicator of stagnation, if we consider that economic growth goes in tandem with a relative growth of the secondary and tertiary sectors to the detriment of the primary sector. From the agricultural point of view, this stability resulted in a considerable rise in absolute figures of the demographic pressure weighing down on the land. The expansion of cultivated land, which continued during the second half of the nineteenth century, gradually lost its momentum. The average progress was about 0.4 per cent per year during the period 1891–1947. In effect, within this half-century, it slowed down, as the frontiers, except in certain regions of relatively recent colonization such as Assam or the Central Provinces, advanced henceforth into less and less fertile zones. Moreover, a part of this increase in areas was obtained, when technical conditions allowed, by the simple acceleration of the agricultural cycle in cultivated lands, with the farmer introducing an additional annual crop in lands that already yielded one or even two harvests.

The gradual exhaustion of the capacity for expansion of cultivated land was not offset by a rise in yields. The average growth of yield per acre between 1891 and 1947 was in effect close to nil (+ 0.01 per cent per year). However, this zero growth did not characterize all crops uniformly. But the persistent decline (- 0.18 per cent per year) in the yield of foodgrains (cereals and pulses), which formed the bulk of agricultural production, statistically annulled the rapid increase in the yields of other crops, particularly commercial crops (tea, cotton, sugarcane and groundnut in particular), which rose by 50 per cent in half a century. In terms of per capita output, the general decline commenced only in the second decade of the twentieth century, owing to the fluctuating nature of the previous demographic growth. Thereafter, this decline stabilized at an average of − 0.72 per cent per year until 1947.[1] It was more severe in the case of foodgrains alone, the per capita production of which seems to have dropped by 1 per cent every year between 1891 and 1947. It is not however impossible that the real trend was slightly less disastrous, as the official agricultural statistics were perhaps artificially inflected downwards from the 1920s due to taxation policies resulting from the development of nationalist agitations in the country.

These overall figures relative to the period after 1891 mask significant variations from region to region, from decade to decade and from crop to crop. The favoured destiny of non-food crops was partly due to the growing tendency of farmers to reserve the best lands for them with a view to using market opportunities to the full (which, incidentally, proves that they were sensitive to the market). The spectacular decline in the foodgrain yields cannot be reduced to any single explanation, but it was clearly attributable to the state of agriculture in eastern India (Bengal, Bihar, Orissa). This region alone produced half the cereals of British India. But it underwent a regression in its cultivated area, and the average yield of foodgrains declined by 0.4 per cent per year since the beginning of the period in question, thus by itself annulling the increase in the yield of these crops in the other regions. The crop that was the most directly responsible for this decline was rice, particularly in the Bihar-and-Orissa region.

From the point of view of the range of crops, the only notable changes in the course of the century occurred in non-foodgrain crops. The Indian agricultural production remained overwhelmingly a production of grains. The countryside of British India (excluding the princely states) contained in 1904 about 25 million hectares of rice (half of which was in the eastern regions of Bengal, Bihar and Orissa), 10 million of wheat (in the Punjab and the western half of the United Provinces in particular), 32 million of millet and pulses. The total area of these crops increased by 0.31 per cent per year between 1891 and 1947 (a little slower than the total cultivated land: + 0.40 per cent), closely followed by cotton (cultivated especially in Central India and the Bombay Presidency), and far behind by jute (1 million hectares, exclusively in Bengal), sugarcane (1 million hectares, essentially in the Ganges Valley), tobacco (400,000 hectares), indigo and opium (300,000 hectares each) and tea (200,000 hectares). The area of these non-foodgrain crops recorded an overall growth of 0.42 per cent per year, but their production, as we have just seen, increased much more rapidly owing to the spectacular advances in yields. Within this category, considerable changes occurred. Indigo (challenged by synthetic indigo) and opium (the controlled production of which was abandoned by the government) totally disappeared in the 1930s. Sugarcane, on the contrary, benefiting from strong customs protection, experienced a veritable boom during the inter-war period (+ 70 per cent between 1929 and 1937). As for the area devoted to cotton, it exceeded 7 million hectares in 1925.

Forms of intensification

The widening gulf between the growth of population and that of agricultural production, once the possibilities for the expansion of the cultivated land had been exhausted, posed the problem of the intensification of production in the existing areas. Intensification by the expansion of double-cropping was possible only in lands that were adequately fertile and irrigated. But progress in this direction had already been made in the major agricultural regions as early as the end of the nineteenth century. The furthering of this intensification would have required technological advances, and above all the development of irrigation.

Agricultural techniques during the last century of colonial rule did not make any significant progress. In 1951, there were still thirty times more indigenous country ploughs than modern ploughs in the Indian countryside. The use of fertilizers by farmers presupposed capital resources that most of them lacked. Agronomic research and the dissemination of its findings were inadequate, notwithstanding the creation of a Department of Agriculture in every province from 1906 onwards, as budgetary resources allocated for these bodies were very limited. Even the distribution of improved seeds that they had undertaken fell far short of meeting the needs.

The intervention of the state was considerable, however, in the area of perennial irrigation, which contributed to the opening of dry lands for agriculture, the intensification of rain-fed farming and the regularization of annual yields by escaping to a large extent from the vagaries of the monsoon. The policy of public works pursued in this field between 1820 and 1850 was resumed towards the end of the century following the recommendations of the Famine Commission of 1880. New canals were constructed, especially in Oudh (the Sarda Canal), in Orissa, in Sind (inundation canals connected to the Indus) and above all in the Punjab, a rich but arid region, whose agriculture was revolutionized by a series of canals built from the Himalayan tributaries of the Indus. Perennial irrigation networks covered about a quarter of the cultivated land in India at the time of independence.

This form of irrigation, however, produced adverse secondary effects: the sterilization of the soil by saline deposits or waterlogging and the propagation of malaria. But its beneficial effects cannot be denied. It enabled the management of cultivation to be rationalized, freed from climatic constraints, to multiply the double-cropped area, to produce more for the market without sacrificing subsistence crops, to have more access to credit on the guarantee of more valuable lands, to provide better fodder for cattle. The impact of these beneficial effects was not, however, as great as anticipated, owing to the rigidities arising from small-scale cultivation, corruption, social inequalities in access to water, inadequacy or poor maintenance of village distributaries and lastly the cost of water.

From acute famines to latent crises

In the course of the second half of the nineteenth century, famine continued to be a major risk all over India. It is believed that the famine of 1860–61 left two million dead in its wake in North India. The famine of 1866–7 claimed nearly one million lives in Bihar-and-Orissa, and that of 1876–7 about four million in the Deccan. Lastly, the great famine of 1896–7 that struck the major part of the subcontinent claimed more than five million lives; it was compounded in 1899–1900 by a new crisis that killed yet another million in central and western India. This sinister hit parade, one of the most tragic in the history of the planet at the time, is an eloquent testimony to the state of poverty in which the rural masses of the country lived, of the uncertain nature of an agriculture still heavily dependent on the monsoon, and of the inadequacy of inland communications and public relief.

It is all the more striking to note that subsistence crises, from the beginning of the twentieth century, ceased to pose a major demographic threat. It was mortality by epidemic that became predominant from then on. From one crisis to another in the course of the preceding half-century, diverse advances had contributed to limiting deaths. These advances include: the rapid growth of domestic trade consequent upon the development of rail and road networks; the elaboration of a Famine Code in every province laying down the rules to be observed in the grain market, preventive measures to be taken depending on the economic situation, modalities for the organization of relief during times of crisis. After 1900, famine mortality became comparatively negligible, while agricultural crises continued to occur. In the 1860s, it became evident that this mortality was due not so much to the absence of supplies but because the poorest could not afford to buy them at a time of massive price inflation. It was work that poor farmers needed above all during the crisis, and for this reason the organization of relief work formed one of the essential chapters of the Famine Codes.

If mortality due to famine dropped in a spectacular way after 1900, it reappeared during the famine that desolated Bengal in 1943, which demographers believe claimed between 3.5 and 4 million lives, compounded as it was by the excess mortality caused by epidemics. This was undoubtedly a calamity of exceptional magnitude, due not to a crisis of major agricultural under-production caused by climatic inclemency, but due to deadlock in the circuits of import and distribution of grains, to the paralysis of the administration, to inflation and to hoarding reflexes engendered by the war against the Japanese advance on the Indo-Burmese border. This tragedy however once again brought to light, at the end of colonial rule, the precariousness of the food resources of the rural population and its vulnerability to the scourge of hunger.

Trends in agricultural prices

Indian agriculture benefited from an exceptionally favourable economic situation for more than half a century after the Sepoy Revolt. The rise in prices, triggered as early as the 1850s by the inflow of British capital for the construction of the railway network, thereafter sustained by growing foreign demand for Indian agricultural goods, had been further consolidated by the strong devaluation of the rupee in 1876. During a phase of rampant depression in world agricultural prices, this depreciation of the silver currency resulted in maintaining the rise of Indian prices, while world prices for Indian goods remained stable. India exported 1 million tonnes of rice per year around 1870 and more than 1.5 million tonnes of rice and wheat in the 1890s. The decrease in the cost of maritime freight, consequent upon the opening of the Suez Canal, encouraged this trend for wheat. The international prices of Indian cotton, jute and tea likewise pursued an upward trend. In India itself, the rise was caused by foreign demand, but also by the increase in domestic demand engendered by demographic pressure.

The rise in agricultural prices continued almost without abating until the First World War and was further accelerated by the inflation that attended it. Subsequently the economic conjuncture remained stationary during the greater part of the 1920s, until the Great Depression, which intervened abruptly. The prices of wheat and millet plummeted by half between the spring of 1929 and the summer of 1931. Rice, however, reached its lowest ebb only in 1933. The crisis took a heavy toll on farmers, including those who had but few contacts with the market, because the revenue assessment and credit rates that they had to bear had been fixed on the basis of high selling prices. It was all the more severe as it was attended by a spectacular contraction of credit. The collapse in the prices of agricultural goods on the international market also produced calamitous results. Recovery was slow and became total only in the context created by the Second World War, with the return of a moderate but regular rise in agricultural prices during the early years of the war, before inflation soared from 1942 onwards.

The expansion of the market

The development of communications

Against the backdrop of the contrasted agrarian conjuncture of the second century of colonial rule, rural India pursued its slow transition towards commercialization and the modern universe of the market. On the one hand, communication networks as well as commercial and banking circuits extended and diversified, thereby contributing to the increasing integration of agriculture within the system of monetary exchanges at the level of the region, but also of the entire country, if not at the international level. On the other hand, the colonial government had during the course of the years undertaken the development of agrarian legislation in most of the regions, codifying the relations between man and the land and the transactions related to agriculture in accordance with market notions that had currency in the West, and which were foreign to the mental universe of the majority of farmers.

The construction of the Indian railway network started in 1853. This network, which comprised 25,000 kilometres of tracks in 1890, reached 57,000 kilometres in 1920, thus claiming the fourth place in the world. To descend the Ganges Valley from Meerut to Calcutta, not less than twenty-seven days were required in 1819, and only forty hours in 1880. The development of the telegraph accelerated the transmission of economic information. The opening of the Suez Canal in 1869 radically reduced the length and cost of maritime trade with the West. These advances propelled the rural economy of India onto the path of fundamental transformation. This economy was traditionally compartmentalized into small-scale regional markets, where prices fluctuated independently depending especially on local climatic variations. The new transport facilities, associated with the upward trend in demand and prices of agricultural goods, spurred on the commercialization of these goods, and the tendency towards the homogenization of prices and the integration of the domestic market. They also opened Indian agriculture to the influence of the international market. In most of the provinces of India, there was a perceptible attenuation of seasonal fluctuations of agricultural prices from the 1880s onwards, and a growing influence in the twentieth century of the trends of the world economic situation on the movements of agricultural prices in the country.

Peasant commercialization

The cultivator generally commercialized his produce through the intermediary of specialized middlemen, except for the small share that he himself went to sell on the neighbouring market. Among these middlemen, the rural trader-moneylender occupied a predominant place. Often, the indebted cultivator, in order to pay his debt, would pledge his entire crop, or a part of it, and sell it to him at the time of harvest at low prices. He commonly accepted an advance from him for undertaking the production of a market crop, which he delivered when the time came at the stipulated price. The village trader-moneylender was connected within a network with his counterparts in urban centres. The latter themselves acted in collusion with big commerce and the modern banking system, where Europeans had the most important roles, especially in transactions with Great Britain and the rest of the world. The cultivators, situated at the base of the system, generally earned only a partial profit from the market, except for the largest of them. The peasant sold the middleman a fraction of his harvest under the coercion of indebtedness, or in order to settle taxes or the land rent in cash, and in the worst conditions, at the time of the seasonal depression of agricultural prices. The middleman, in his turn, performed a series of necessary functions that the average producer would have been unable to perform, unfamiliar as he was with the world of commerce, and not having sufficient means of transport nor means of stocking, and most often needing immediate liquidities. The same middleman represented the indispensable agent regulating tax revenues from the point of view of the government.

Contact with the market however functioned a little differently for a number of non-food commercial crops. These had experienced rapid expansion in the course of the nineteenth century and India, which primarily exported agricultural goods, had become a large exporter not only of rice and wheat, but also of raw cotton, opium, tea and indigo, and had a world monopoly on jute production. Crops like oilseed or tobacco also occupied an important place, and sugarcane was to develop considerably after the First World War. Non-food crops in British India (excluding the princely states) covered 11.6 million hectares in 1891 and 15.4 million in 1941. Oilseed and tobacco were commercialized relatively freely through the same middlemen as rice, wheat and the other food grains produced for the market. The trade in opium, on the other hand, until its interruption in 1907, was a state monopoly, and farmers could cultivate the poppy only under the close supervision of the Opium Department, in exchange for a remuneration fixed by it. Indigo plant (the cultivation of which disappeared after the First World War, owing to the competition of synthetic indigo) was grown by farmers for factories of which they were tenants, under contractual regimes from which coercion was not absent, and for a price that was also fixed without any relation with the price of the finished product on the market. The system of sugarcane cultivation was similar to that of indigo in many respects. The farmer worked for and was dependent on the sugar factories in his vicinity. He could not commercialize his produce at free market prices. As for tea production, it did not come under the peasant agricultural sector, but under plantation agriculture.

The amount of agricultural produce marketed every year is therefore not an accurate indicator of the prevalence of speculative farming in peasant agriculture. Commercialization by peasants was often through forced sales or distress sales, carried out under the pressure of urgent needs for cash, and under hardly lucrative conditions, which left a disproportionate share of the profit from the harvest in the hands of the middlemen. The farmer in general sold only a negligible fraction of his harvest, constrained as he was to retain the bulk of his produce to ensure the subsistence of his family, and secondly for payments in kind. Lastly, the crops that he produced for industrial purposes or for exports were often bought from him by client firms under a more or less arbitrary system of fixed remuneration, which divorced him from direct contacts with the price system of the free market.

Peasant commercialization was therefore highly imperfect. It coexisted on the one hand with a vast non-trading agricultural sector where self-subsistence and redistribution in kind remained the rule, and on the other hand with a diversified and sometimes sophisticated professional trading sector, well connected with the national market and export channels. We must nevertheless be careful not to consider the peasantry as a homogeneous entity, as not all farmers were equal before the market. Access to the free market was fraught with difficulties that varied according to the wealth and social status of the peasant. The minority of farmers who produced a surplus, employed a labour force permanently, lent money and grains, possessed a means of transport and had the monopoly of influence and power in the villages, met the conditions required for practising truly speculative agriculture and for commercializing their produce under more profitable conditions. Therefore, only these powerful farmers and merchant-moneylenders accumulated the profits created by the sharp growth of commercial agriculture in the colonial context and the attendant potentialities for agricultural improvement.

The market for the factors of production

The advances in the commercialization of agricultural goods occurred in tandem with the development, uneven from sector to sector but real, of the market for the factors of production (land, capital, labour). They were also accompanied by an evolution in agrarian relations which, under the influence of colonial legislation, began to emerge out of the age of relations of dependency and patronage to enter the era of contractual relations, with a primarily economic content and subject to the laws of the market. In the middle of the nineteenth century, these developments, however, were only in their initial stages, as the legislation that prepared the ground for them defined the rights and duties of the agents in the peasant society in exclusively economic terms, far removed from traditional concepts. A century later, they still had not been completed, as the provisions of these enactments had often met with failure or produced perverse effects.

Even though there is evidence of the sale of land rights throughout the history of India, in the middle of the nineteenth century there existed no land market in the modern sense of the term, wherein land itself and not just the rights over a part of its produce, was subjected to a generalised demand and supply, and changed hands freely, without the interference of considerations of power. This was the case despite the fact that landownership had been instituted in practice within the framework of land systems set up in the various provinces after the conquest. Things changed in the second half of the nineteenth century, especially under the influence of the growing demand for land consequent upon demographic growth and the rise of agricultural prices. A veritable land market functioned in all the major agricultural regions at the beginning of the twentieth century.

Simultaneously, the land rental market underwent a sharp growth. The tenants had had to suffer from the establishment of colonial land systems, which conferred the rights of full and undivided ownership on the masters of the land recognized by the government, without giving the dependents who cultivated the lands of these masters any guarantee against their arbitrary power. Until then, the relation between masters and tenants functioned as a hierarchical relation of interdependence within the framework of a caste society and in a village community, grounded on a mutual recognition of reciprocal duties, in particular of a codified sharing of the produce of the land, of which none was the exclusive owner. The absolute authority with which the colonial law invested the owner constituted an exorbitant privilege in this environment that warranted in return a definition of the rights and guarantees of the tenants. The initial legislative efforts in this direction in Bengal in the first three decades of the nineteenth century proved to be inconclusive, due to the difficulties in controlling the actions of omnipotent local magnates in thousands of villages, always capable of ignoring or circumventing the regulations in force. The situation of a tenant, at least, was not desperate as long as land remained abundant and he could flee to escape an oppressive master with the hope of finding a better situation elsewhere. But the condition of the tenants worsened inexorably as the expansion of cultivated land reached its limits, as the pressure on the land intensified and as agricultural labour became overabundant.

The first important law aimed at the protection of tenants was passed in 1859 in Bengal. It proved to be ineffective and was replaced in 1885 by another, the *Bengal Tenancy Act*, which thereafter served as a model for the agrarian laws introduced in other provinces. These laws were the fruit of difficult compromises. They defined rigorously and in modern economic terms the various categories of tenants, their rights and their duties, as well as the condition under which the owners could fix and increase their rents, and obtain reparation in case of default. They aimed at preserving peace and equity in the rural world, but did so at a time when, having learnt a lesson from the revolt of 1857–8, the British were resolved to preserve the established hierarchies and to secure the faithful support of the elites of rural society. Within the colonial staff itself, controversies raged between the advocates of the rights of tenants and those who believed all interference of the state in the affairs of owners as a potential obstacle for the progress of agriculture. This was an echo of the great debates that rose in the home country when the British Parliament was preparing an agrarian legislation for Ireland, the *Irish Land Acts* of 1870 and 1881.

These laws, though constantly amended between their initial promulgation and the agrarian reforms of the middle of the twentieth century, could never succeed in effectively reducing the abuses that were rife in the countryside. The distance, not only physical but also social and cultural, that separated the ordinary illiterate peasant from the colonial court of law was too great, and a village magnate, even when declared guilty by justice, remained all-powerful in his locality and had the last word against an adversary of lesser calibre. Nevertheless, the law resulted in the introduction of a new conception of agrarian relations wherein the relationship between an owner and a tenant, in theory, was no longer a relation of interdependence the modalities of which varied according to the social status of the partners (and notably their caste status), but a contractual business relation between economic agents with defined rights, and subject to objective rules laid down by the legislator.

From the last third of the nineteenth century onwards, in effect, a land tenure market emerged, though slowly and not without imperfections, even as the demand for land intensified. The owners did not fail to take advantage of this to the fullest. But their feudal-like behaviour, the exactions that they made on the cultivators over and above the regular rents henceforth, were clearly stamped as illegal. Vast operations of survey and settlement of land rights and dues were carried out systematically by the colonial administration in the various provinces, thus equipping the farmers with unquestionable documents admissible in a court of law; they were completed, for the most part, at the time of the First World War. From then on, the legal conditions of the functioning of agrarian relations in compliance with the objective laws of demand and supply were established. But the government still had to be capable of enforcing the law in the villages. This was far from being the case at the end of colonial rule.

With the increase in the market value of land, the capital market developed. Each farmer could borrow more on the guarantee of land rights that he possessed (ownership rights and tenancy rights). The extent of rural indebtedness in the second half of the nineteenth century is unknown, but it is estimated that about three-quarters of the agricultural population was indebted. The creditors were professional merchant-moneylenders, but also farmers to a large extent, as whoever had liquidities maximized them through lending. Rural indebtedness consisted on the one hand of small short-term loans pledged on the forthcoming harvest at the ordinary rate of 24 or 25 per cent; this small-scale indebtedness, an indispensable recourse for the poor peasant, was normally paid back during the same year. On the other hand, there were mortgage loans for longer terms; the sharp growth in the land market and the growing value of properties and tenures rapidly multiplied the number and volume of such loans. Thus in the region of Bihar, in 1930, nearly half of the rural debt was composed of loans guaranteed on land.

Colonial legislation contributed to this development. In effect, in the second half of the nineteenth century, it rigorously codified relations between creditors and debtors and the practice of land alienations, by placing all the cards in the hands of the lender in the name of a modern notion of the inviolability of contracts. This evidently incited the lenders to expand the horizon of their operations, to an extent that, for a moment, the authorities feared a massive expropriation of peasants by the moneylenders. Restrictions, which were of little effect, were imposed on the professional moneylenders through legislation towards the end of the century in the Punjab, in western India and in a part of central India, but the credit market remained free elsewhere. The check that the colonial government inclined towards, rather than restrictions on the freedom of transaction, was the development of cooperative credit, which, however, demanded time-consuming work of organization and education in the villages. The cooperative movement was officially launched in 1904. But, for cooperation to have a chance to succeed presupposed autonomous and united peasantries, while those in India were largely disinherited and characterized by violent inequalities. Cooperatives covered only about 3 per cent of the credit needs of the Indian agricultural population in 1950.

As for the labour market, it was only at its initial stages of development at the second half of the nineteenth century. It was only during this period that domestic slavery disappeared little by little and even then only incompletely. The condition of agricultural labourers was most often that of an unfree labour force. A family of agricultural labourers was normally a household of a very low caste, bound to one or more families of cultivators by relations of patronage that at times dated back to several generations. In return for the work performed by the employee and his family (agricultural work, domestic service, performance of ritual tasks), the employer provided subsistence, protection, credit and other forms of assistance. Conditions of bondage for debts were widespread everywhere. Forced labour imposed by the local magnates on their tenants, sometimes remunerated, sometimes paid at very low rates, was still widespread in the middle in the twentieth century. Unfree labourers were necessarily not very mobile. There was nonetheless a certain mobility among agricultural labourers, to short and long-distance. But this, whether it was temporary seasonal migration guided by rumour or chance, or long-term migrations organized by recruitment networks towards plantations in the mountains or overseas, was not synonymous with an integrated and competitive labour market. Remunerations were composite in nature, money was involved only to a negligible extent, and were fixed by local custom. The levels of remuneration could vary considerably from one village to another.

There are indications that at least from the beginning of the twentieth century, agricultural wages began to vary in accordance with the price trends. The employers sought to adopt remunerations in cash when the price of grains soared in the market, and there is evidence of cases of collective resistance of agricultural labourers against these conversions. But the underprivileged labour force gradually found itself more at a disadvantage in defending itself after the First World War, because its number began to increase rapidly, and the labour supply chronically exceeded the demand. In this area where the colonial power hardly interfered (except in matters relating to the labour force employed in plantations and to overseas emigration), the impact of the market in times of demographic inflation was clearly a factor of increase in difficulties.

Social differentiation

The combination of the factors we have examined in the preceding paragraphs – trends in the agricultural conjuncture, demographic growth, the development of communications and perennial irrigation, the multifarious advances of the market economy – led to a social polarization within the rural world.

An entire historiography in the course of the 1950s and 1960s, for the most part of nationalist inspiration, has presented this widening of social disparities as a tragic phenomenon, sometimes reiterating the idea of the dispossession of peasants by moneylenders, an idea that had emerged much before the independence in the writings of certain colonial administrators. According to this view, owing to the aggravation of indebtedness in the villages, and within the framework of the provisions made by the new agrarian laws, the poorest of cultivators were massively expropriated of their lands by speculators and driven to swell the ranks of the rural proletariat; nonetheless, agriculture did not become more dynamic for it, as the buyers, not traditionally being cultivators, contented themselves with living as parasites of the land instead of investing in it. This thesis is not entirely baseless. The inquiry commission on the Deccan riots of 1875 officially concluded that the major cause for the troubles had been the antagonism between peasants and moneylenders. The decennial censuses of the working population seem to indicate furthermore a sharp increase in the number of landless peasants during the last century of colonial rule. Lastly, the paradox of the recurrence of great famines during a long period of agricultural growth can be explained by this phenomenon.

Recent historiography has considerably qualified this interpretation. The transfer of lands, if it assumed new legal forms in the nineteenth century, had been less important then than in the turbulent course of the preceding century. Social inequality in the villages between dominant farmers and tenants on the one hand, and between landless peasants and the rest of the villagers on the other, was very pronounced even before the conquest. The percentage of lands acquired by non-farming 'speculators' seems to have been modest on the whole, except perhaps during acute economic crises (especially during famine), as the most frequent purchasers were rich farmers. Lastly, the analysis of statistics on the working population does not allow us to conclude that, at least for India as a whole, there was a sharp increase in the percentage of the category of landless peasants in the agricultural population. The number of agricultural labourers between 1901 and 1951, in adjusted figures, represents a constant of about 30 per cent (this corresponds nonetheless to a significant increase in absolute figures).

The relative stability of rural social stratification in its broad outlines, which is today generally conceded, does not eliminate the possibility that economic relations between the groups concerned underwent changes, and that social disparities widened. The grip of the moneylenders did not lead to a massive proletarianization of poor peasants, but it is unquestionable that the moneylenders normally wanted less to buy the lands of their debtors than to maintain them in a situation of inextricable mortgage indebtedness, and to transform them into tenants at will subject to crushing conditions (share-cropping on a half-and-half basis being the most advantageous status). Furthermore, it is now clear that the buyers of land were not overwhelmingly professional moneylenders but rich farmers, who were commonly engaged in usury, and whose dominant situation in the village environment was no doubt reinforced in the second half of the nineteenth century.

It has been maintained that the period 1860 to 1900, which saw the rapid growth of the market in the villages, was a 'golden age' for the rich farmer in India.[2] This affirmation, subsequently contested, needs to be adjusted according to region. It is clear that the economic situation, the institutional evolution (above all that of agrarian legislation) and the specificities of rural social structure in India created especially favourable conditions for the rapid development of this social category. The village magnates were not necessarily proprietors. In the regions where aristocratic types of land systems had been instituted, dominated by an elite of big landowners (*zamindars* of eastern India, *taluqdars* of Oudh, etc.), the dominant farmers were the rich tenants, who cultivated directly with agricultural labourers or who sublet their holdings in fragments to sharecroppers, generally under a regime of informal lease with payment of rent in kind. The large domains were customarily managed by their masters (who were most often absentee landlords) not as agricultural enterprises but for the sole prospect of collecting the rent, which was carried out through the intermediary of *patwaris* (village accountants) and village headmen. It was the minority of principal tenants, among whom figured these local agents, who truly exercised power in the village, a privilege that belonged everywhere else to the dominant peasant proprietors. Owners or tenants, the dominant farmers were cultivators belonging to the upper, or at least respected, castes; they held a central place in the economic and social life of the village, as they provided land, work, credit, means of transport, aid and other relief at times of crisis and played the role of arbitrators in local disputes, and of protectors if necessary, for the rest of the village population.

More educated than the mass of peasants, more open to the external world, enjoying an economic size sufficient to produce veritable surpluses in a normal year, the dominant peasants were naturally best armed to use the new economic and institutional conditions in the agrarian life to the full. They were, as we have mentioned earlier, the principal beneficiaries of the expansion of commercial agriculture because, having more land than they needed for their subsistence, they could store their surpluses to sell them at the best prices, select crops in function of market opportunities, and lend grain at interest to commercialize the surplus obtained thereafter. The rise in agricultural prices could not be profitable to the same degree to a cultivator who sold smaller quantities or to the one who only sold under coercion and in the most disadvantageous conditions. It was even harmful to those who did not produce sufficiently for their subsistence, if for the complement of their needs they were driven to resort not to work remunerated in kind but to the market.

Colonial agrarian legislation also conferred other advantages on the richest. If they were landowners, they continued to benefit from the ordinary impunity that the local magnates enjoyed. If they were tenants, they now had new arms in the face of big landowners, as, contrary to the majority of peasants, they had the skills, the means and the relations necessary to take the best advantage of the colonial law and courts. As moneylenders, they stood to gain in a legal context that, with a few regional variations, hinged on the inflexible principle of the inviolability of the contract.

The cooperative movement itself, in the twentieth century, proved to be conducive to their pre-eminence. A credit cooperative in effect was a group of solvent individuals who came together to obtain loans of money at the most favourable rates. It functioned all the better if its members were richer and it had to exclude from its structure cultivators without credit in order to survive. When these disadvantaged peasants formed not a mere disinherited minority but a significant percentage of the peasantry, the cooperative served only to consolidate the privileges of the affluent minority, who had access through it to cheap credit, while the mass of the poorest remained under the onerous dependence of the traditional moneylender. The same logic was at work even in perennial irrigation, the beneficial effects of which were distributed unequally. The new networks were managed at the top by the colonial administration, but at the base, they functioned within the framework of the structures of village society. Access to water was conditional on caste status and local power, compounded by an omnipresent corruption. It was therefore the elite of medium and large cultivators that strengthened yet again its dominant position.

Regional trends

North India

Once the effects of the famine of 1860–1 had dissipated, the salient traits of the economic development of the countryside in North India were on the one hand the agricultural dynamism of the Punjab-Haryana region, and on the other, the widening gulf in the development between the east (Oudh) and the west (Doab, Rohilkhand) of the United Provinces.

From the point of view of agricultural performance, the Punjab-Haryana zone was way ahead among the Indian regions from 1891 onwards. This fertile but dry region had an average density of population half that of eastern India, and certain zones were still uninhabited in the middle of the nineteenth century. Agricultural colonization developed rapidly at the end of the century, when the large-scale networks of perennial irrigation the construction of which had been launched in the 1850s were put into service. In this vast region that produced wheat (which accounted for half of the total production of grains) and cotton (which represented two-thirds of non-food production), the cultivated area progressed at an average of 0.93 per cent per year between 1891 and 1947, and the average yield by 0.62 per cent. Per capita output increased by 45 per cent between 1891 and 1921, then its growth slowed down as everywhere else in India, but less than elsewhere, and never became negative.

In the United Provinces, the regional 'dimorphism' between the East and the West, owing to the difference in geographical features and in socio-economic structures, as well as to the influence of history, intensified greatly during the second half of the nineteenth century. In the west, the development of railways and roads and of large-scale irrigation projects implemented in the Doab between the Ganges and the Jamuna produced the anticipated spread-effects. The region became a large exporter of wheat and sugar. Urbanization developed in a comparatively dynamic way. The rapid growth of a class of rich farmers was apparent. In the East, on the contrary, it was the old rural elite with feudal-like practices that continued to reign over the countryside. All across the United Provinces, however, the limits of the expansion of cultivated land were reached in the 1880s. Medium and large-scale properties were kept afloat, but small properties entered a process of continuous fragmentation due to demographic growth and the pauperization of the masses. Agrarian difficulties worsened seriously in the twentieth century, taxes and land rents increased in tandem with the prices, while per capita income, from the 1920s onwards, began to decline. In 1950, 9 per cent of the cultivators of the United Provinces (that is one million people) occupied 43 per cent of the cultivated land, while two-thirds of the farmers shared a fifth of it.

Eastern India

From the point of view of agricultural performance, eastern India (that is principally Bengal, Bihar and Orissa) found itself at the other extreme of the Punjab-Haryana region at the close of the period. In this predominantly rice-producing region (rice accounted for 90 per cent of the production of grains), characterized by very high densities of population, the possibilities of expansion of the cultivated land were already almost nil in the second half of the nineteenth century. Cereal production witnessed an unprecedented decline: 0.73 per cent per year from 1891 to 1947. This region was the only one in British India where the growth rate of the production of grains was less than that of the population as early as 1891. Per capita food production declined by about 1 per cent per year during the first half of the twentieth century. The cultivated area declined slightly in absolute figures, while it continued to increase everywhere else, though often negligibly. Lastly, the average yield also decreased in this region (by 0.38 per cent per year on an average), while its growth was general in the rest of British India.

The exhaustion of marginal lands, rural outmigration and the sterilization of land due to the migration of the principal course of the Ganges in the delta – a variety of factors were at work, the exact nature and influence of which can only be ascertained if we pursue our analysis to the local level of the district. It then appears that this regional decline was imputable largely to the particularly poor performance of Bihar. It goes without saying that the agrarian structure also played a role. The landed aristocracy of the zamindars hardly seemed inclined to productive investments, if not, as has too often been told, due to a lack of a spirit of enterprise that was supposedly entrenched in their mentalities, at least due to objective economic circumstances. The first among these was the limited market for agricultural goods, due to the weakness of industrial and urban development which made land speculation, loans on interest and trading more attractive than the enhancement of the productive capacity of the land. The rich farmers, a social stratum the existence of which was well attested in the region, acted in accordance with the same principles, and for the same reasons.

Western India

In western India (West of the Deccan and Gujarat), the predominant crops were millet (accounting for three-quarters of the production of grains) and cotton (which alone accounted for four-fifths of non-food production). After decades of stagnation, the region witnessed a period of rapid agricultural expansion in the 1860s. The decisive fact from this perspective was the cotton boom provoked by the American Civil War (1861–5), which abruptly increased foreign demand for Indian cotton. The price of cotton soared by 132 per cent and the cotton-producing area expanded by 97 per cent between 1860–1 and 1869–70. Cultivated area and food-grain production also increased. This windfall benefited above all trader-moneylenders and wealthy farmers, but it produced beneficial effects all round, at least by enabling innumerable peasants to pay off their debts.

Economic circumstances, however, once again became gloomy at the end of the decade with crises caused by climatic conditions and the drop in prices that occurred in the course of the 1870s. The rural distress of this period found expression in the Deccan riots of 1875, which were largely directed against the moneylenders, even though more rich farmers than moneylenders had been snatching the patches of land that the indebted peasants were forced to sell. From the 1880s onwards, the development of railways gave a new impetus to commercial crops (cotton, sugarcane, groundnut, tobacco), the production of which underwent sharp growth. Concurrently, the value of the land increased and the land market developed, favouring the richer farmers.

The history of rural western India then fell in line with the general trends in the other regions: great famines at the close of the nineteenth century, upward trends in agricultural prices rapidly gaining momentum during the period of inflation at the end of the First World War, the vicissitudes of the economic situation in the 1920s, the collapse of prices during the Great Depression, slow recovery at the end of the 1930s and a new inflationist tendency during the Second World War. In keeping with the rest of India this region saw neither massive growth in the rural proletariat nor clear tendencies towards the concentration of landownership.

South India

In the regions of southern India were the *zamindari* system prevailed, the rise in agricultural prices enhanced the condition of the *zamindars* in the second half of the nineteenth century. But the progress made in the commercialization of agriculture benefited, above all, wealthy farmers, who prospered thanks to cotton and tobacco. Serious tensions erupted between the *zamindars* and their tenants during the depression of the 1930s, further aggravating the difficulties of the former. In the regions subject to the *raiyatwari* system of rural ownership (that is the bulk of South India), the excessive levels of land taxation enforced in the first half-century of colonial rule led to a reform of the system of revenue assessment whose principles were framed in 1864. The level of tax imposition was then fixed at half the net produce of the land, with revision of the tax base every thirty years. The upward trend in prices, thanks to the length of this interval, considerably attenuated the tax pressure. Only the crisis of the 1930s, in these *raiyatwari* zones, was to bring about serious difficulties in this respect.

For the South Indian countryside, the third quarter of the nineteenth century was a period of opulence during which cultivated land increased much faster than the population, even as the colonial government pursued large-scale construction of infrastructure in the areas of irrigation and railway and road communication, and as the cultivation of cotton, groundnut and oilseed experienced sharp growth. The famine of 1865–6, then that of 1876–8, which killed between 10 and 20 per cent of the population, essentially among the poor classes, dealt a severe blow to this expansion. Recovery was nonetheless rapid from the 1880s onwards, and South India experienced relative agricultural prosperity once again up until the First World War. A few regions practising commercial agriculture developed brilliantly during this period, especially the rich common delta of the Krishna and the Godavari. After the First World War, as the growth of the population gained momentum while that of agricultural production ran out of steam, the per capita production of grain plummeted by 30 per cent in three decades (1916–45). Nevertheless, no clear trend towards the proletarianization of the peasantry emerged, despite the rapid aggravation of the average indebtedness of cultivators in the course of the 1930s.

Agrarian movements and the Peasant question

Rural agitation before Gandhi

After the revolt of 1856–7, as before it, the disinherited of the rural world, poor or tribal peasants, continued to express their sufferings in difficult economic circumstances through age-old forms of resistance such as violations of communal or forest regulations, the withdrawal of work, services or dues, protest migrations, individual or collective acts of violence directed against the agents of the government or of the employees of the big landowners, theft of food and pillages of shops during times of shortage, etc. These classical forms of agrarian crime or violence were generally disapproved of by the peasant elite. Their repression by the police or the judiciary was hardly difficult, as they almost always resulted from localized, unorganized initiatives stemming from ephemeral economic conditions, deprived of elaborate political perspectives. The only peasant agitation that really mattered, in the eyes of the government, by its magnitude and by the efficiency of its methods, was the one that flared up occasionally at the initiative of wealthy farmers, who were the major beneficiaries of the rapid growth of commercial agriculture initiated in the 1860s.

This peasant elite, prosperous and well informed, was capable of mobilizing with a view to defending its interests against the European indigo planters who exploited it (in Bengal in 1859–60, in Bihar in 1868 and 1877), against oppressive *zamindars* (as in the district of Pabna and other regions in eastern Bengal in the 1870s), against the moneylenders making abusive demands (the Deccan riots, 1875) and lastly against the revenue authorities (in the north of Assam in 1893, in Maharashtra in 1896–1897, in the Punjab in 1907). Under the leadership of its notables, it implemented mostly non-violent customary modes of protest (though untoward incidents inevitably occurred): petitions addressed to the authorities, refusal to pay taxes, dues and land rents, collective emigration. It often seemed to be animated by the conviction (classical in peasant movements) that the sovereign power was on its side in the fight that it waged against its oppressors. The farmers of Pabna thus appealed to Queen Victoria in their struggle against their *zamindars*.

These movements animated by the wealthy peasantry, which did not seek the subversion of the established order and which expressed themselves on the whole pacifically, often mobilized significant fractions of the rural population in the zones concerned, through the traditional solidarities of caste, clan, religious or cultural community that cut across the social classes. This type of agitation, when it was directed against the European planters or the revenue officials, often enjoyed the prudent approval and the support, at least verbally, of the moderate nationalist intelligentsia that had begun to emerge in the big cities. This was especially the case in Calcutta during the indigo riots in Bengal and Bihar, and during the Pabna movement.

The Gandhian movements (1917–47)

Gandhi returned from South Africa in 1915 at the age of forty-six, already well known as an apostle and tactician of non-violence. First, he organized peasant movements limited in scope but pregnant with symbolic value (in Champaran district in Bihar, 1917, in Kheda district in Gujarat, 1918), thereafter a workers' strike (Ahmedabad, 1918) and a national day of action against governmental repression (Rowlatt *satyagraha*, 6 April 1919). The great mobilization that he could achieve made him unquestionably the leading figure of the nationalist movement by 1919.

The extent of peasant participation in these campaigns seemed to indicate that a meeting point had been reached between agrarian agitation and the political demands of the liberal intelligentsia, thanks to the mediation of Gandhi. There are two common explanations, often linked together, for this conjunction of interests. The first, elitist in view, interprets these great surges towards unity as the fruition of the efficient work of organization and propaganda carried out by the intelligentsia to reach the inert and naïve peasant masses: this is the gospel that the national leaders propagated in their writing, especially in their memoirs. The second explanation, of mechanistic inspiration, establishes a direct relation of cause and effect between the recurrent scourge of bad harvests, the inflation of the First World War, the world depression, the resumption of inflation around 1940 and the upsurges in rural agitation. The analysis of these movements, nevertheless, does not reveal any decisive correlation, either chronological or geographical, between the maximal impact of economic difficulties and the eruptions in peasant effervescence, and at times there are even blatant contradictions. These restrictive interpretations that attribute the predominant role to ancillary factors share the common defect of underestimating the capacity of the peasantry for autonomous initiative.

The popular impact of Gandhi

One fact stands uncontested: the announcement of the intervention of Gandhi, during the course of these large-scale protest campaigns, unleashed the effervescence of the masses. Waves of collective turbulence then surged autonomously, largely overwhelming the tactically calculated calls of the nationalist Congress and overcoming the control of local committees. Thus in 1920–2, the call for 'Non-Cooperation' launched by Gandhi and the Congress leaders firstly consisted in instructions for boycott, which met with undeniable success. But at the same time, there was a sudden rise in criminality, and mobs were seen pillaging markets and destroying excise 'liquor' shops (symbols of the indirect taxation of the government), workers going on strikes, prisoners mutinying, tribal communities violating forest regulations, farmers refusing to pay their land rents and taxes, violating fishery rights, throwing the land settlement operations out of gear, etc. Where these excesses occurred, the name of Gandhi was constantly invoked. Events unfolded as if the advent of the Mahatma on the scene had suddenly created in the minds of the people the feeling that all the structures of authority were collapsing, that all prohibitions had vanished, that the world was turning upside down.

The effective message communicated by Gandhi did not reside in his explicit discourse (which in any case was only perceived in bits and pieces, and which was reinterpreted thoroughly), but in the image of Gandhi that circulated among the masses: that of an 'ascetic', of a pilgrim of truth in the garb of a poor peasant, of a man of God possessed of miraculous powers. This popular image was a projection of the archetype of the divine hero of folk culture, a saint and a worker of miracles. The effectiveness of Gandhi's style was such that it soon spawned a number of emulators: agitators and propagandists modelled on the familiar character of an ascetic and an itinerant preacher multiplied in the course of the 1920s.

Rumour also played an essential role in an overwhelmingly illiterate society wherein information was primarily disseminated by word of mouth. It was rumour that propagated all across the villages the messianic image of Gandhi and the news of an imminent salvation that he had come to spread among the oppressed multitudes. In the heart of these innumerable tales, which often echoed the fabulous aspects of oral tradition, was the conviction that the entire existing edifice of the structures of power and coercion that weighed down on the peasant condition was collapsing. This picture of the breakdown of the perverse order of the world had overtones of the universal revolutions that attended, in the medieval literature of India, the birth of certain divinities. Gandhi, on whom the farmers often conferred devout titles (*baba, bhagwan*), seemed to be perceived as an avatar, as an incarnation of God come down to earth to bring back the respect of eternal laws and to restore justice. The refusal of the established disorder, naturally, expressed itself in the language of religion, and under the cover of a legitimizing intervention coming from above.

This mobilization through messianic rumour contained an essential weakness. It gave rise only to intermittent, sporadic explosions, separated by long interludes of passivity. And it hardly contributed to the creation of awareness that leads to the maturity, continuity, and in the long run to the effectiveness of popular movements. On the other hand, it gave a spectacular impact to protest campaigns launched by the nationalist elite recruited from the middle class, which thus drew considerable political mileage from it.

The social failure of the peasant mobilization

The massive mobilization of the peasantry in the wake of the return of Gandhi played a crucial role in the success of the struggle for freedom. But the gaining of independence was not attended by any social revolution. In other words, the poor masses had been mobilized to serve a fight entirely conceived and directed by the middle class, which has become, in independent India, the hegemonic class.

The ranks of the nationalist movement, before and during the Gandhian era, came overwhelmingly from the educated middle class of cities and market towns, which was to a great extent a class of rentiers. They stood to gain from the non-capitalistic organization of agrarian relations that prevailed in the villages. This largely explains the hesitant and tardy nature (1936) of the agrarian programme of the Congress. They furthermore belonged in majority to liberal and intellectual professions, the traditional monopoly of the upper castes. The social distance that separated them from the poor masses continued to be vast, despite the populist connotations that Gandhi had given to the nationalist commitment. This middle class did not desire to change the world, but only to establish its political dominion.

In the countryside, it was the dominant peasantry, the stratum of village society that was the closest to the world of modern politics, that formed the bulk of the rural base of the Gandhian Congress. The peasant movements that it animated and organized were unitary movements, in which Gandhian orders to abide by non-violence served to avert radicalization and to control excesses. There was thus a convergence of interest between the urban middle class and the rural elite, and a de facto consensus over the Gandhian programme of limited mass agitation.

Nevertheless, there existed, during and before the Gandhian era, a more or less endemic autonomous agitation of the poorest. These were subsistence riots and other forms of popular protestation against the rising cost of living, as well as tribal movements motivated by the amputation of the customary rights over forests, by the abuses of moneylenders, by the requisitions of labour, etc. But these movements were often repudiated by the nationalist elite as social disorders and, in the absence of organized political backing, were easily struck down by repression.

On the other hand, the Gandhian era witnessed the emergence, on the fringes of the nationalist movement, of peasant protest movements directed against the big landowners: for instance, the movements launched by Swami Bidyanand in Bihar in 1919–20 and by Baba Ramchandra in Oudh in 1920–1, the movements of tenants in Bengal in the 1920s, the *kisan sabhas* (peasant associations) in the United Provinces in the 1930s, the movements organized by NG Ranga in Andhra, etc. These movements that claimed to be unitary were often led by the affluent peasantry or by intellectuals. Some of them assumed socialistic undertones. Autonomous initially, they generally ended up being absorbed by the nationalist movement. Only some of them were taken up by the political left wing, which, however, remained weak. This largely explains the social failure of peasant mobilization.

Furthermore, peasant agitation did not bring into play any clear class struggle, but involved multiple solidarities that interpenetrated: solidarities of caste, tribe, race, religious community, regional identities, through which the peasants perceived their collective interests. The peasants of a same region could mobilize themselves alternatively against the *zamindars*, against the Muslims who slaughtered cows, against the colonial revenue authorities or the administration. Internal economic oppositions that separated the different strata of the peasantry did not constitute a decisive driving force. The wide support that the rural elite extended to the nationalist Congress from the 1920s did not lead to any massive disaffection towards the latter among the disinherited sections of the village world.

In short, if political liberation was dissociated from social revolution despite the magnitude of mass mobilization among the peasants, it was largely because this mobilization had been effected around Gandhi, not around a radical Left, and in the religious language of popular culture. The radical Left was in any case much too weak to unify the movement around itself. The nationalist movement, on its side, constituted a rallying force that transcended all particular social identities, and only its cadres were capable of organizing peasant action at the national level. Peasant unanimity was certainly fissured here and there when the mobilized peasants had proved to be more radical than their leaders, but their enthusiasm had not found a political translation, and the moderating ascendancy of Gandhi had always contributed to curbing this ebullience effectively. It was only as the very end of colonial rule that more radical and violent peasant movements, spurred on by the Communist Party, began to develop (the Tebhaga movement in Bengal in 1946, the insurrection of Telangana between 1946 and 1951), prefiguring the politically more modern nature that peasant struggles would assume in independent India.

The agrarian problem at the end of the colonial era

At the end of the colonial era, rural India presented the classical picture of agrarian under-development, characterized by excessive demographic pressure on the land and an unlimited supply of labour in a context marked by an accelerated growth of population, stagnation or excessively slow progress in agricultural techniques, the low average yields, mass poverty, the predominant role of subsistence agriculture, the persistence of coercion in agrarian relations, the wide range of social disparities, chronic agrarian delinquency and recurrent upsurges of peasant agitations. The dominant factor in this agricultural stagnation was not, as was often suggested during the colonial era, the conservative mentality of the peasant, or his incapacity for change. It has now been proved that the cultivator, in India as elsewhere, was capable of rational decision, and that he was responsive to price changes when determining the share (most often limited) of his produce that he commercialized, at least when he enjoyed a sufficiently easy and direct access to the free market, which was not the rule. But it was no longer possible for him, in the middle of the twentieth century, to expand his cultivated land, and he had already reached a high degree of efficiency in the available state of technology. Furthermore, the low per capita income in the agricultural sector impeded the formation of capital, as shown by the negligibly growing or even declining figures of the quantity of land, of cattle and ploughs available for each cultivator. Under these conditions, the increase in the labour force in the twentieth century could only lead to an increase in unemployment. Credit did not constitute any recourse, as under its traditional form it was much too onerous, and cooperative credit instituted by the government was too selective to offer a serious competition.

Owing to the inequality in the access to land, credit and the market, capital accumulated only in the hands of the dominant minority of big landowners, wealthy farmers and rural merchant-moneylenders. This primitive accumulation was essentially parasitic in nature. It was made up of the profits earned on the small production that the ordinary peasants commercialized under archaic and restrictive conditions to these middlemen (creditors or landowners) to whom they were bound. It flourished in the colonial economic setting, wherein capitalist firms and in certain economic sectors the state itself resorted to, thereby reinforcing them, the traditional forms of influence and coercion existing in the countryside for their own commercial ends, and in which the moneylender consolidated his supremacy over the peasantry as never before in history. A significant part of the capital thus accumulated was dissipated in non-productive consumption, in particular among the big landowners, or was hoarded. The rest was invested in the commercial speculation on agricultural goods, or in loans on interest, which aimed less at the acquisition of lands for purposes of dynamic management than at the parasitic exploitation of insolvent debtors reduced to a state of quasi-bondage. The formation of capital in agriculture thus did not lead to productive investment.

Analysts have very often sought to adduce cultural factors to explain the mediocrity of productive investment. Such factors played a role in particular regions or social milieus: for instance, the conservatism of certain elites, or their feudal rather than capitalist notions of land ownership. But the more universally decisive factor seems to have been the comparative profitability of the various possible forms of investment. It was primarily the unattractive quality of productive investment that was at issue, especially where the State had not intervened to remove the technical impediments affecting yields or the commercialization of goods (irrigation, agronomic research, distribution of improved seeds, transports, etc.), in a country where the level and structure of income restricted the market for agricultural products to the extreme, despite the large size of the population.

XXIII

TRADE, INDUSTRIES, CITIES
(1860–1950)

The slow progress in rural India did not preclude a significant growth in the export of agricultural products, which stimulated trade as a whole. At the same time, the birth of modern industries contributed to the decline of handicraft production. But industrial development remained limited, which partly explains the low level of urban growth that colonial India witnessed.

The beginnings of the railways

The 1850s were characterized by several innovations that, if they did not represent a marked break, augured the transition towards a new phase of colonial economic domination. Thus in 1851 the first *Companies Act* was passed, conferring a legal recognition on joint stock companies: it was followed in 1857 by a law that entrenched the principle of limited liability. These legal measures favoured the development of capitalist enterprises and the number of joint stock companies grew rapidly.

The most important innovation, however, was indisputably the beginning of the construction of a railway network. The first lines were laid in 1853 and 1854, connecting the ports of Bombay and Calcutta to their immediate hinterlands. The first master plan for the railway network had been formulated by Lord Dalhousie and aimed at meeting both economic and politico-strategic objectives. The colonial government hoped that railways would spur on the development of the country, promote the export of raw materials and the import of British manufactured goods; besides, it would enable the transport of troops more rapidly in case of unrest. The mutinies of 1857 confirmed the strategic importance of railways as, where they existed, they greatly facilitated the transport of British reinforcements.

The major problem was to attract capital from England, as the cost of construction of railway lines in India, owing to natural obstacles and climatic conditions, was relatively high and beyond the reach of local resources. With a view to attracting capital, the authorities did not hesitate to infringe the sacrosanct principles of laissez-faire: the government gave the shareholders of the railway companies the guarantee of an annual dividend of 5 per cent. As the shares of these companies represented an investment that was both safe and lucrative, it was ideal for small British rentiers and capital flowed in from Great Britain between 1855 and 1875.

It was in the 1860s that the railway network was launched, its total length increasing from 1,349 to 7,678 km in the course of the decade. Once the work had got going, it proceeded rapidly: in 1890, the network reached a total length of 25,495 km, and in 1920, with the completion of the intensive phase of construction, 56,980 km. As early as 1867, all the principal cities were connected and towards 1920, most of the districts were also, except in certain regions of the northern and central India.

The first companies were private enterprises. For the construction and the management of a certain number of lines of strategic interest that were commercially unprofitable, the state however had to intervene directly. Thus, a mixed system in which several types of companies coexisted gradually emerged: companies belonging to the government and managed by it; companies with government ownership but private management (big companies like the East Indian Railway, the Bombay, Baroda and Central India, the Great Indian Peninsular); companies belonging to princely states, and lastly private companies. Despite this diversity, the different railway companies competed little with each other and agreed on the prices.

The advent of the railways enabled roads and waterways to be substituted by a means of transport that was both safer and less costly. The average cost was considerably scaled down, thanks especially to the fall in insurance rates that had been a heavy burden on it until then. India however did not draw all possible advantages from this revolution, as the price policy practised by the companies promoted port-inland travels to the detriment of inland-inland itineraries and long journeys to the detriment of short ones. This orientation reflected the influence of British commercial interests, primarily concerned with transporting export agricultural goods towards the ports and redistributing manufactured goods from the ports to the interior. Domestic trade was therefore stimulated to a lesser degree than it could have been if a different price policy had been adopted.

The most negative aspect of the railway policy pursued by the British authorities is reflected in the absence of consequences on the local iron industry, as the companies procured their supplies from Great Britain for all the necessary equipment (engines, wagons, rails, track equipment) and did not encourage the development of local suppliers. With the end of the 'railway boom' in England, the British railway industry thus found in India a surrogate market for its products, a market that it was determined to safeguard. The bulk of the qualified staff necessary for the smooth functioning of the network (engineers, engine drivers, workshop technicians, etc.) also came from England, so that the railways did not play the role of an industrial school as it had done in a number of European countries.

Nonetheless, the extension of the rail network did have an impact on one sector: the development of coal mining. Railways facilitated the transport of coal from the coal-producing regions (the Raniganj basin, situated on the Bihar-Bengal border) towards the ports and industrial centres. Moreover, it offered an important market for the production of coal (on an average, 30 per cent of the total consumption). The latter increased from less than 500,000 tonnes in 1869 to more than 15 million tonnes in 1914, which enabled a reduction in imports from Britain and South Africa.

The rapid growth of foreign trade

Despite its limitations, the railway represented the fundamental factor in the economic transformation caused by colonization. It played a critical role in the sharp growth of foreign trade, which was by far the most dynamic aspect of the Indian economy during the period 1860–1914. This was further stimulated by the port works implemented by the British in Bombay (the construction of three docks in 1880, 1888 and 1914) and in Calcutta (the construction of jetties in 1869, of docks in 1892), the two large ports that carried out the bulk of India's foreign trade, the former being the largest importer while the latter was above all engaged in exports (jute, tea).

The trends in Indian exports which multiplied almost eight-fold (in current prices), between 1860 and 1914, reflect above all the advances made in commercial agriculture.

Principal Indian exports (1860–1911)
(in millions of rupees)

Year	Indigo	Opium	Cotton	Jute	Tea	Total
1860–1861	20	90	56	3	1.3	330
1870–1871	32	117	191	20	11	553
1880–1881	30	143	112	44	31	746
1890–1891	31	93	165	76	55	1,002
1900–1901	21	95	101	109	97	1,077
1910–1911	3	128	361	155	125	2,099

In half a century, the growth rate underwent considerable variations, sustained as it was during the period 1860–90, very low between 1890 and 1900 and very high in 1900–14. The share of the five major primary export goods swung between a maximum of 65 per cent of total exports (in 1870–1) and a minimum of 35 per cent (in 1910–11). An increasing share of jute production was exported in the form of manufactured products (for a value of 170 million rupees in 1910–11) while in the first decade of the twentieth century indigo fell victim to the growing competition of chemical colorants. If we add to these goods, cereals, oilseed and leather and hides (respectively 18.4, 12 and 6.2 per cent of India's export sales in 1910–11), we observe that non-processed agricultural products throughout accounted for not less than 70 per cent of total exports.

The sales curve of the various products reflects highly contrasted trends. Indigo shows a slow progression until 1870, followed by a long period of stagnation and a sharp decline after 1900; opium witnessed a steady growth until 1880, thereafter a market regression followed by a recovery (the collapse would occur in the next decade); cotton also underwent significant fluctuations, especially after 1870 (the high growth from 1860 to 1870 being attributable to the boom caused by the

American Civil War); only jute and tea progressed at a regular rate. These fluctuations were largely due to price trends, particularly in cotton prices. The reversal in the overall price trend from the end of the 1890s onwards, with the end of the Great Depression, contributed to the sharp rise in Indian exports during the period 1900–14.

Until 1880, India primarily exported to two countries: the United Kingdom (which absorbed 41.6 per cent of Indian exports in 1880–1) and China (29 per cent during the same period). The share of China was mostly accounted for by opium. After this date, there was certain diversification, with the rise of purchases by France (7..6 per cent of Indian exports in 1910–11), Germany (9.4 per cent), Japan (6.4 per cent) and the USA (6.4 per cent), concurrent with a decline in the relative position of the United Kingdom (24.9 per cent) and China (9.2 per cent). The fall of exports to China was largely the result of the decrease in the sales of opium. As for the decline in the share of the United Kingdom, it was due partly to the fact that a number of goods, previously shipped to English ports to be re-exported towards the Continent, reached the European ports directly after the opening of the Suez Canal in 1869. There was also a downward trend in British purchases of Indian cotton in favour of cotton from the south of the US better adapted to the demand of the Lancashire factories. Great Britain however continued to be by far the largest buyer of tea (a part of which was re-exported from London) and raw jute (for the textile mills in Dundee). But the growing exports of manufactured jute were above all bound for the rising cereal-producing countries of the 'New World' (the USA, Canada, Argentina, Australia). Germany and France were important customers for oilseeds, leather and hides, while Japan became in the beginning of the twentieth century a large purchaser of raw cotton for its rapidly growing textile industry.

The changes in the destinations of Indian exports nevertheless served British interests. From 1890 onwards, the dominant position of Great Britain in the world economy began to be called into question by the rise of Germany and the USA, two countries with which British trade showed a deficit. The increase in the sales of Indian products to these two countries enabled Britain, within a system of multilateral payments, to partly compensate for its deficit. The role of India in the British imperial system was therefore not so much to supply raw materials to the United Kingdom for its industries as to contribute, by its exports to third countries, to the imperial balance of trade.

It was therefore not so much British demand (except for tea and to a lesser extent jute) as the demand of New World countries and industrialized European countries (besides France and Germany, Belgium and Italy) that stimulated an export-oriented agriculture. However, British firms played an essential role in this development (though there were European and Japanese firms active in the cotton trade, especially in Bombay), in connection with an important class of Indian middlemen, who financed and commercialized the crops. These middlemen bore the bulk of the cost of cyclic fluctuations, which they in their turn passed on to the cultivators. The British firms established in the ports contented themselves with transporting the crop, with carrying out the primary processing (the ginning of cotton, the pressing of jute) and exporting the end product.

The development of an export-oriented agriculture thus firstly served the interests of the big British commercial firms of Calcutta, Bombay or Madras, which reaped considerable profits from minimal investment. But it also favoured the rise of a class of Indian middlemen, generally usurers and merchants, who gradually extended the scope of their operations (for instance, creating cotton-ginning factories and jute presses). Among them figured numerous Marwaris: the already ancient migration of this enterprising community of *banias* of Rajasthan received a new impetus and the migrants of this region occupied an increasingly important place in the commercial economy of the Deccan and central India, the great cotton and opium producing zones, as well as in the delta of Bengal, which produced jute; they started to flock in great numbers to the ports, particularly to Calcutta and to a lesser extent to Bombay. In Calcutta, they gradually supplanted the Bengali natives in the role of brokers to large British managing agencies – sort of trusts. Some of them acquired an important place in the commercial sector of the big metropolis of Eastern India and thus embarked on a process of capitalist accumulation. The development of an export-oriented agriculture thus proved conducive to the growth of an Indian commercial and financial capitalism closely intertwined with British interests.

The birth of large-scale modern industries

The textile industry

Large-scale industry came into existence even as manufactured goods from Great Britain increasingly penetrated the Indian market. Between 1860 and 1914, Indian imports in effect multiplied nearly eight-fold, even while the share of the United Kingdom remained preponderant (though it regressed from 84.8 per cent in 1860 to 62.2 per cent in 1910). Manufactured goods accounted for the quasi-totality of British sales to India and cotton cloths represented by far the principal product. The sales of the latter soared from 300 million yards in 1857 to more than 3 billion yards in 1914. In this year, Indian absorbed 45 per cent of British exports of cotton goods.

Nevertheless, it was cotton textiles that emerged as the major modern industry in India. The first profitable factories were created in 1854, two in Bombay by Indian capitalists, and one by an American in Broach, a city in Gujarat. The sudden success of these enterprises, after a number of failures, is not easy to explain: the railway line in the heart of the cotton-producing region, connecting Bombay to Nagpur and traversing the mountain range of the Ghats by a series of tunnels, was not completed until 1867. Despite difficulties in the access to the raw material and the very high cost of installation (machines and technical staff were imported from England at huge cost), the first factories in Bombay prospered. They benefited from an increase in customs duties on imported spun yarns and cotton goods, an increase to which the government had to resort for financial reasons. This measure triggered the protests of the cotton lobby of Lancashire, which, in 1862, forced the government to bring down the duties to a lower level.

At the beginning of the 1860s, the Indian cotton industry numbered only about ten factories equipped with 340,000 spindles and a few mechanical weaving looms. In the course of the following decade, a trend towards geographical diversification crystallized with the creation of the first factories in Ahmadabad in Gujarat and in Cawnpore, in the Gangetic plain. In 1869, out of sixteen factories, seven were situated outside Bombay. In 1873–4, construction fever broke out and eighteen companies were incorporated. The same year witnessed the first movement of cotton yarns towards China; this country was to become the principal market for the textile mills of Bombay, absorbing up to 80 per cent of their production. The growth of the industry was steady from then on until the First World War.

Growth of the cotton industry (1876–1910)

Year	Number of factories	Number of spindles	Number of looms
1876	47	1,100,000	9,100
1880	56	1,460,000	13,500
1890	137	3,270,000	23,400
1900	193	4,950,000	40,100
1910	263	6,200,000	82,700

This industry tended, at least until the early years of the twentieth century, to specialize in spinning rather than weaving. Its principal market was represented by Chinese and Indian artisan weavers who had adopted the use of industrial yarn. Bombay sold its yarn especially to China, while the other centres, Ahmadabad in particular, catered primarily to Indian artisans. By concentrating on the production of yarn, the Indian industry could thrive even as English cloth began to command the Indian market owing to the remarkable distribution network established by the Lancashire cotton mills– they employed the services of a number of Indian merchants, particularly Marwaris – and thanks to the benevolence of the colonial government. The latter, after having re-instituted customs duties in 1894 for financial reasons, gave in to the pressure from Manchester and imposed on Indian industrialists the payment of a duty on fabrics manufactured locally.

This period thus witnessed a certain symbiosis between large-scale industry and cotton handicraft industry. The latter had faced a very serious crisis in the course of the first half of the nineteenth century, but it survived, at the price of a sharp decline in wages, on the basis of very localized markets. The development of the railway network in the second half of the century dealt it another blow by facilitating the penetration of imported fabrics to regions far removed from the ports. However, in 1900, according to official estimates, handlooms supplied nearly a quarter of total cotton cloth consumed in India (23 per cent against 66 per cent for imports and 11 per cent for Indian factories).

Nevertheless, from 1904 onwards, Indian factories embarked on a process of reconversion, towards the production of fabrics for the domestic market. The reasons for this trend were on the one hand, the growing competition of Japanese textiles in the Chinese market, and on the other hand the influence of the *swadeshi* movement on the behaviour of Indian consumers, particularly among the upper classes of society. The wearing of clothes made of English fabric had become a status symbol over the course of the preceding decades. But a reversal in values occurred: *swadeshi* cloth, more expensive than imported fabrics, became in its turn a status symbol. The industrialists of Bombay and Ahmadabad took advantage of this new trend to increase the sales of their cloth with the latter practically doubling in the course of the decade 1904–14, so that the market share of Indian factories stood at around 20–25 per cent in 1914. This growth had been realized at the expense of both imports (whose share fell from 66 to 60 per cent) and handlooms (whose share fell below the 20 per cent mark). In 1914, with its 6 million spindles, the Indian industry ranked sixth in the world and employed 260,000 workers.

Remarkably, this industry was dominated from its very beginnings by Indian capital. Admittedly, British nationals also invested in it but they never controlled this sector. Investments in the first factories came from the substantial profits earned by Indian merchants in the China trade, especially in the opium trade. This explains why the first entrepreneurs in Bombay were generally Parsis, as this community had held a predominant place in the trade between India and China. Once the impetus was given, the industry developed through the ploughing back of profits, which were in general high. The role of Parsis gradually tended to weaken, and a class of Hindu entrepreneurs of the merchant castes, the *banias*, emerged: they enjoyed an important place in Ahmadabad, the second largest centre of the industry.

The situation in the cotton industry contrasts with the one that prevailed in the other modern industry that developed in India during the course of the second half of the nineteenth century, the jute industry. Here, the initiatives were purely British and this sector continued to be dominated by British firms until 1947. The growth of this industry, exclusively concentrated in Calcutta and its environs, the beginnings of which dated from 1855, gained momentum from the 1870s. Almost entirely oriented towards foreign markets (jute bags were in high demand in wheat-exporting countries like the United States, Australia and Argentina), it thrived at the expense of on the one hand the British industry concentrated in the Scottish city of Dundee, and on the other of an Indian rural cottage industry.

The decline of the traditional jute industry was more brutal and more radical than that of the traditional cotton industry. Thus, at the beginning of the 1870s, handicraft production of jute fabrics and bags offered employment to several hundreds of thousands of people, the majority of whom were women, in the villages of Bengal and contributed to a non-negligible export trade. Thirty years later, it had fallen victim to competition from factories and practically disappeared. These factories employed a large labour force around Calcutta (two hundred thousand workers), the majority of whom were migrants recruited from North India. The firms that owned the factories were themselves controlled by the powerful managing houses of Calcutta. Indian capital was therefore absent from this industry until 1918, even though the profit rates were very high on the whole.

A very embryonic modern industry

Up to 1905, modern Indian industry was more or less limited to the textile sector, both cotton and jute. From then onwards, partly under the influence of the *swadeshi* movement, industrial diversification began to crystallize, essentially through Indian initiatives. Cement factories, chemical factories, paper mills, all oriented towards the domestic market, emerged, but, in the absence of tariff protection, they often faced considerable difficulties.

The most remarkable initiative was the creation of an iron and steel industry by an exceptional entrepreneur, JN Tata. A Parsi of Bombay, Tata started in the textile industry: he bought out or created several factories that he transformed into very profitable enterprises. When he discovered the existence of rich deposits of iron in eastern India close to coalmines, he conceived the project of endowing his country with an integrated iron and steel industry. He came up against innumerable obstacles: bureaucratic regulations, governmental indifference, the hostility of certain British interest groups keen on protecting their position in the Indian market. But he overcame them one by one, and on his death, in 1904, he had set up a coherent plan that his four sons implemented. In 1907, they created the Tata Iron and Steel Co., whose capital in its totality was subscribed for in three weeks by eight thousand Indian shareholders in a wave of enthusiasm that owed much to the *swadeshi* movement. As early as the following year, the construction work on the factory and the new city of Jamshedpur began. In 1913, the first steel was cast; India could thus pride itself on its own steel industry much before more advanced countries, thanks to the vision of JN Tata. However, this steel factory was situated in the heart of an industrial desert; in the absence of an Indian metallurgical and engineering industry, its primary outlet was the railways, but the construction of the network being completed, it did not represent a big market.

On the eve of the First World War, India thus possessed a very embryonic modern industry. This sector employed only a few hundreds of thousands of workers scattered in large factories located for the most part in Bombay and Calcutta, but also in Ahmadabad, Cawnpore, Coimbatore, Madras and Nagpur, and highly dominated by the textile industry. A highly diversified handicraft production coexisted with this modern sector, which employed several million artisans in cities and villages, and supplied agricultural tools and domestic utensils for the Indian population. Some branches of handicrafts had begun a process of modernization: for example the dyeing industry in Madura, in South India, had successfully adopted the use of synthetic dyes. But on the whole, this sector offered very low wages and did not allow entrepreneurs to earn sufficient margins to be able to reinvest.

The lack of demand for industrial goods in an overwhelmingly rural and agricultural society formed a considerable obstacle to industrial growth. All the more as this narrow market was, in the absence of tariff protection, wide open to goods manufactured in Britain and other industrial countries. Investment in this sector was therefore not very attractive, while trade and finance offered high rates of return on capital. Furthermore, the official financial system, dominated by the three Presidency Banks,[1] was hardly geared towards supporting industrial enterprises.

The native banking system, however, played a more active role in the development of enterprises, as industrial firms were often controlled by families of merchant-bankers. In spite of this, the modern industrial sector, on the whole, found it difficult to raise the necessary capital.

The apparent prosperity of the Indian economy before the First World War, largely the upshot of the favourable international economic situation, involved especially the export sectors. It is true that there were no famines, the tragic cycle of the period 1875–96 seemed to have come to close for good. India even exported cereals for a few years, but this reflected the low purchasing power of Indians rather than a boom in production. The bulk of the Indian people, as proved by the inquiries and as proclaimed by the pamphlets, lived in great poverty. To remedy this situation, the nationalists at the beginning of the century believed industrialization to be the only panacea. The control of British capital over the major financial and commercial channels of the Indian economy appeared more and more as an obstacle on the path towards an industrial development centred on the domestic market.

British interests were indeed largely concentrated in the export sector of the Indian economy: tea plantations, jute factories, exchange banks that financed foreign trade, import-export companies, all branches wherein an 'oligopolistic' structure existed that enabled to earn high profits. The large British managing agencies of Calcutta (Andrew Yule, Jardine Skinner, Bird Heilgers), Bombay (Killick Nixon) or Madras (Parrys, Binnys), most often connected with the City, exported the bulk of the profits made in India to reinvest them in other more promising regions of the empire (Malaya, Australia, South Africa). Apart from coalmines and a few cotton mills, they were little involved in activities oriented towards the domestic market. Through associations that played the role of powerful lobbies, like the Bengal Chamber of Commerce, these companies maintained close links with the colonial government, which consequently showed little interest in the industrial development of India, all the more so as pressure groups in the home country (Lancashire, the railway industry) fiercely defended their position in an Indian market that was for them essential. Therefore, the government soon came under the growing criticism of Indian business circles, which demanded a more active support to domestic industry.

Industrial development (1914–47)

The First World War marked the beginning of a complex period of transition in the economic history of India. The salient features of this change were the decline in the role of the subcontinent in the British imperial system, the adoption of a tariff policy that favoured the development of industries, and lastly, the rise to supremacy of Indian capital in comparison with British capital.

The First World War, which led to power shifts all over the world, in particular a further weakening of Great Britain in favour of the USA, as well as the emergence of Japan as an important industrial and military power, could not fail to cause repercussions. The commercial position of Great Britain weakened in the Indian market, as the share of the United Kingdom in the total imports of India decreased from 62 per cent in 1914 to 43 per cent in 1930 and 30 per cent in 1939.

This decline affected all the products but was spectacular in cotton goods: the sale of English fabrics plummeted from 3 billion yards in 1914 to 1.25 billion in 1930 and 200 million in 1939. After 1930, India ceased to be a large market for the cotton mills of Lancashire. The erosion of the British position benefited the USA in particular, whose sales represented an average of 7 to 10 per cent of Indian imports in the course of the 1930s, and Japan, whose share reached 10 to 15 per cent especially thanks to the sale of cotton goods that, from 1936 onwards, exceeded that of Great Britain in volume. The diminution of the surplus in the trade between India and industrial countries – other than Britain – a consequence of the sharp increase in imports from these countries while Indian sales stagnated – reduced India's contribution to the imperial balance of payments. The surplus earned by Great Britain in its trade with India also tended to drop, owing to the rise in Indian sales in that country (they reached 34 per cent of total exports on the eve of the Second World War).

The reorientation of India's foreign trade can be partly explained by the new tariff policy adopted by the authorities from 1919 onwards. In this year, within the framework of the so-called Montagu-Chelmsford political reforms, the government of India acquired limited but real financial autonomy. Partially liberated from the niggling control of the India Office, the colonial government was in a better position to meet the demands of Indian business circles in favour of a more protectionist tariff policy. In 1921, the government accepted the conclusions of the report submitted by a fiscal commission that recommended the adoption of a policy of limited protection, designed to promote the growth of newly created Indian industries that were not yet able to face international competition. The first concrete measure, the *Steel Protection Bill* of 1924, granted tariff protection to the Indian steel industry, at the time threatened by the dumping of cheap goods from Belgium and Luxembourg. Other measures in the same vein followed suit, including the establishment of duties on imported cotton goods from 1930 onwards. However, protectionist measures were generally accompanied by provisions granting preference to British products, on which were imposed lower import duties than on non-British products.

This so-called policy of 'imperial preference' was entrenched in 1932 when India signed the Ottawa agreement which, after England had repudiated free trade, created an imperial economic zone within which preferential tariffs were established. This system, which came under strong criticism from Indian business circles, favoured Indian exports bound for the British Empire, in particular Great Britain, and enabled it to compensate in part for the loss of market consequent upon the wave of protectionism that then swept across the world. The adoption of a moderately protectionist customs system contributed to the growth of a certain number of Indian industries (sugar, paper), but its impact remained limited on the growth of the cotton industry.

The First World War especially favoured the growth of Indian industries catering to the domestic market that took advantage of the fall of imports. The first and the major beneficiary of this situation was the cotton industry, which could increase its share of the Indian market, thanks to the significant drop in the import of English fabrics owing to difficulties in maritime commerce during times of war. But once the war was over, Lancashire could not recover its dominant position. Indian factories had almost doubled their production of fabrics between 1914 and 1916, then, after a period of stagnation, production leapt once again between 1925 and 1930, followed by steady progress in the course of the 1930s. All in all, between 1914 and 1939, the production of cotton fabrics by these factories soared from a little over 1 billion to almost 4 billion yards, the number of looms doubling during the same period to reach 200,000 while the number of spindles also multiplied two-fold to stabilize around 10 million. Most factories were engaged both in spinning and weaving, except in South India where traditional weaving witnessed a renaissance and where artisans continued to form the principal outlets for textile mills. In the entire country, handicraft production also developed and reached 1.7 million yards in 1939. In that year, factories met 62 per cent of the consumption of cloth and handlooms 28 per cent, while the share of imports was reduced to 10 per cent (of which Japanese fabrics made up the majority).

The reconquest of the domestic market for cotton fabrics by the Indian textile industry was only partly due to the introduction of tariff protection. It was in terms of cost that the Indian industry had a decisive edge over its competitors from Lancashire, thanks to a more intensive use of machines and men. The efficiency of the Japanese industry made it a more dangerous rival and only the imposition of a system of quotas succeeded in curbing the wave that came from there. In a market that did not record any notable expansion, notwithstanding the reversal in the demographic trend after 1921, the growth in the sales of Indian factories was possible only by seizing from Lancashire the market for ordinary cloths and of certain semi-luxury fabrics. The English industrialists succeeded in partly maintaining their position only in the field of luxury fabrics.

The growth of the cotton industry was attended by geographical diversification: the place held by Bombay declined markedly in favour of Ahmadabad, Cawnpore, Coimbatore, Sholapur, etc. In 1938, out of 10 million spindles, Bombay had 2.9 million, and 67,000 looms out of a total of 200,000. Ahmadabad had in the same year nearly 2 million spindles and 47,000 looms. Cawnpore, which came third, had 550,000 spindles and 10,000 looms. Then came Coimbatore (467,000 spindles), Madurai (300,000 spindles and 5,800 looms) and Indore (212,000 spindles and 6,200 looms). Bombay ceased to expand after 1922 and it bore the brunt of Japanese competition, as it was specialized in ordinary fabrics. On the contrary, Ahmadabad, more oriented towards semi-luxury fabrics, was the main beneficiary of the decline of Lancashire.

Among the industries oriented towards the domestic market that benefited from the change in the tariff policy, the most important was the steel industry. The facilities in Jamshedpur were expanded on two occasions, at the end of the 1920s and during the 1930s, and in 1939, their capacity reached the one million tonne mark (six times the initial capacity). The Tatas had succeeded in cornering the lion's share in the Indian market, their progress being primarily at the expense of non-British competitors. Their monopoly in India was nevertheless threatened by the creation of a second steel factory in 1939 by a group of British and Indian businessmen. The outbreak of the Second World War, which increased the demand for steel products, averted an overproduction crisis.

Among the other industries, the sugar industry benefited from the protectionist measures implemented in 1932 enabling it to oust Javanese sugar from the Indian market, while the paper and cement industries developed in the course of the 1930s. The jute industry also recorded progress in the course of the 1920s (the number of factories increased from 76 to 100 and that of looms from 40,000 to more than 60,000), but suffered in the 1930s from the drop in world demand consequent upon the economic depression. A new fact was the appearance of factories controlled by Indian capitalists (Birla, Hukumchand), bringing a sixty-year-old British monopoly to an end.

Concurrently with the growth of industries, the production of coal underwent a spectacular rise reaching 28 million tonnes in 1938. A growing percentage of the production was supplied by the large mines, a sector that continued to be dominated by British managing agencies but in which Indian firms consolidated their positions. The inter-war period also witnessed the beginning of the production of hydroelectricity. On the initiative of the Tatas, three power stations were constructed in the region of the Ghats, near Bombay: they enabled the cotton industry of Bombay to break free from its dependence on coal from the northeast. Other power stations constructed in South India promoted the industrialization of the region (the Mettur station supplying electricity to the factories at Coimbatore).

Overall, the production of the manufacturing industry increased by half during the decade of the 1920s and doubled between 1930 and 1947 – a growth, which, without being spectacular, was nonetheless not negligible. The depression of the 1930s, of which the Indian countryside bore the brunt, did not bring industrial growth to a halt. This was because it coincided with the reinforcement of tariff protection measures and with the sudden decline in the sales of British fabrics, in part due to the Civil Disobedience movement. The Second World War, by limiting the possibilities of imports and by stimulating the setting up of new branches of industry responding to war needs (chemicals, aluminium), also had positive effects on industrial development. During the period 1920 to 1947, the labour force employed is estimated to have increased from 1 to 3 million workers (including more than 1 million in the textile industry). The textile industry and other light industries (food, leather) continued to predominate. Despite progress in metallurgy, spurred on by the Second World War, India lacked the essential link of an engineering industry. On the eve of independence, the industrial growth of India was almost entirely dependent on imported machinery.

The outcome of nearly a century of development of modern industries under colonial rule is quite meagre in the final analysis. The major achievement was the creation of a powerful cotton industry capable of meeting the bulk of the country's need for fabrics. But this development was attained partly at the expense of artisans, and the net result was less positive in terms of employment, as the number of jobs created in the factories was markedly less than the number of artisans who were driven to abandon their craft. The creation of a steel industry represented a significant success but it started when the railway network, for the main part, had already been constructed, which deprived it of a market. Railways did not form the basis for the development of an engineering industry as the lobby of the English railway industry succeeded in frustrating all the projects for the fabrication of locomotives in India itself. From 1865 to 1941, India produced 700 engines while it imported 12,000 of them from Great Britain. Likewise, the development of the textile industry was not attended by the establishment of a textile machinery industry. There were therefore a certain number of missed opportunities that would not present themselves again.

The limited development of large-scale industry without any doubt contributed to the survival of the craft industry. After 1914, the renaissance of village crafts became, under the influence of Gandhi, one of the objectives of the nationalist movement. His efforts to revive the *charkha*, the traditional spinning wheel, hardly met with any success, but the consumption of *khadi*, hand-made fabrics, benefited from its identification with nationalism. Even though industrialists did not hesitate to sell as *khadi*, cloth produced by their factories, traditional weaving gained from the change in fashion. This sector showed relative dynamism, particularly in South India, whence handcrafted *lungis* and saris were exported to Southeast Asian countries with large Tamil communities (Burma, Malaysia). From 1937 onwards, the Congress provincial governments adopted measures to promote the textile craft industry, which benefited from the introduction of technical improvements (the use of fly shuttles). Nonetheless, handicraft production tended to become more concentrated in the cities, and village craft industries declined all through the century.

Parallel to the development of industries catering to the domestic market, there was a marked ascendancy of Indian capital, which, towards 1947, was on an equal footing with British capital. Cotton industrialists formed the most powerful sector, and along with the traditional groups of Bombay (Wadia, Thackersey, Tata), there was a spectacular growth of groups from Ahmadabad (Kasturbhai, Sarabhai, Mafatlal) and North India (Shri Ram who controlled the Delhi Cloth Mills, J K Singhania at Cawnpore). However, industrial diversification propelled to the fore groups with interests in several branches (Birla in jute, paper, sugar, Dalmia in sugar and paper, Thapar in coal, paper and sugar, Walchand in construction, sugar and automobiles). The majority of these new groups were controlled by members of the Marwari community, which played an increasingly active role in Calcutta and all across East and North India. The Marwaris in particular made a spectacular entry into the jute trade and the jute industry, until then preserves of the British. The latter continued to dominate in the export sectors, but the stagnation of exports after 1930 hardly encouraged investment of capitals A few large Western industrial firms (ICI, Dunlop, British American Tobacco) nevertheless created subsidiaries to circumvent tariff protection by producing in India itself goods previously imported from England.

The class of industrial entrepreneurs that emerged in India during colonial rule did not participate very actively in the development of the country. Hailing from the merchant world, it paid more attention to the commercial and financial aspects of industrial production than to technological developments. It therefore tended to seek agreements with foreign companies to procure technologies rather than engineer a native technological effort. These shortcomings in the Indian industrial circles were to have far-reaching consequences on the development of independent India. They partly explain why the State played so great a role in Indian industry after independence and adopted a 'planning' policy.

The industrial proletariat, this 'modern' and urban class par excellence, presented, since its inception towards the middle of the nineteenth century, particular characteristics in comparison with the standard 'working class' (though it is doubtful that such an ideal-typical working class had ever really existed, even in Victorian England). The cotton workers of Bombay or Cawnpore like the jute workers of Calcutta, all these men (this labour force being primarily male), even those born in cities, retained a rural mentality, in as much as their outlook was dominated by family strategies centred on the village and the land. The money saved from a meagre wage, and sent to the village, not only served to guarantee the subsistence of the worker's wife and children, but was also used to acquire a few acres of land with a view to enlarging the family plot. At the factory, the worker, recruited through the intermediary of a *sardar*, or 'jobber,' often from the same village, of the same caste, even of the same lineage as him, continued to be a member of the same 'gang' throughout his career and to recognize the authority of the *sardar* before that of the white foreman.

The persistence of such pre-industrial loyalties did not preclude the adaptation of the worker to the universe of the factory, even though it led to a high rate of absenteeism. The employers, both English and Indian, accepted this mode of organization of labour which was so different from the one prevalent in England. It was only in the course of the 1930s that the advent of unions changed this scheme of things, inaugurating a new era in the history of Indian industrial practice. Previous to 1930, however, the world of Indian factories had not been characterized by the passivity of the labour force: on the contrary, fits of fury, often fuelled by the *sardars* themselves when they were at odds with the employers, were frequent, but generally short-lived and labour organizations were temporary in nature. If the consolidation of unions in the course of the 1930s and 1940s resulted in spectacular waves of strikes, it never sparked off any revolutionary agitation. The major labour confederations (AITUC with communist connections, the more moderate NFL) primarily put forward economic demands and obtained, particularly thanks to the relative shortage of labour that the Second World War brought about, a few successes (institution of a 'dearness allowance', which corresponded to a rudimentary system of wage indexing, still in practice today).

Towards 1947, the industrial proletariat – including railway workers, dockers and miners – formed a mass of 4 to 5 million men whose living and working conditions remained highly precarious. Notwithstanding the gradual development of a labour legislation from 1881 onwards (the first *Factory Act* limited the daily working period to nine hours for children under 12 years of age), the workers enjoyed meagre social protection and the rate of industrial accidents was high. Housing was another black spot in the condition of the Indian worker: the great majority of workers lived either crammed into slums with their families, or in dormitories for men alone (the *chawls* of Bombay); suffering deplorable standards of hygiene in both types of accommodation. Only a few enlightened employers, like the Tatas, made an effort to provide decent housing for their staff. The others left the matter to the government, which did nothing.

The evolution of cities

The censuses carried out from 1872, and especially from 1881 onwards, enable us to follow the development of the urban network. They point to a slow growth of the population living in cities between 1881 and 1931 (from 9.3 to 11.1 per cent), followed by a very marked acceleration during the period 1931 to 1951 (from 11.1 to 16.1 per cent). From 1931 onwards, the number of agglomerations considered urban increased markedly, which leads us to believe that the growth in the rate of urbanization was in part a statistical illusion stemming from changes in the definition of urban agglomerations.

Whatever the case, the overall growth was far from impressive. However, the figures taken as a whole indicate diversified trends. The first three decades of the century were marked by the slow growth of all the agglomerations. Calcutta and Bombay, the two large ports and industrial cities, recorded moderate growth (+ 50 per cent in thirty years, that is an average annual growth of a little over 1 per cent). On the other hand, Delhi, Bangalore and Ahmadabad developed rapidly. The growth of Delhi was in part due to the transfer of the capital from Calcutta in 1911, while that of Ahmadabad occurred in the wake of the rapid expansion of the cotton industry. In the other cities, the growth rates were low. This urban anaemia was the consequence of economic factors, in particular slow industrial development and in the former princely capitals (such as Lucknow and Hyderabad) of the decline in their political functions that had its impact on the level of economic activity (extinction of craft industries attached to the princely court).

Population of the major Indian agglomerations (in thousands of inhabitants)

	1901	1911	1921	1931	1941	1951
Calcutta	1510	1750	1890	2140	3620	4670
Bombay	810	1020	1250	1270	1690	2970
Madras	590	600	630	780	930	1540
Delhi	210	230	300	450	700	1430
Hyderabad	450	500	400	470	740	1130
Karachi		150	220	250	360	1100
Ahmadabad	200	220	270	310	590	880
Lahore		230	280	430	670	850
Bangalore	160	190	240	310	410	780
Cawnpore	200	180	220	240	490	710
Poona	160	170	200	250	320	610
Lucknow	260	260	240	280	390	500

Low demographic growth does not mean that the cities did not attract migrants from the countryside: in fact, as the birth rates in the cities were lower than those in the countryside (partly because of the lower proportion of women in the population), while death rates were generally higher (due to particularly precarious standards of hygiene), the demographic growth of the cities during the period 1901–31 was mostly due to migrations from the countryside. The big Indian cities were like machines that absorbed migrants from the countryside a number of whom died in the process. Calcutta well illustrated this type of urban growth: since the 1880s, the city had attracted a large number of villagers from Bihar, Orissa, the east of the United Provinces as well as from the countryside of Bengal proper, who all came to seek an often precarious employment in the jute factories and the harbour facilities; others were employed as servants and porters. They lived crammed in slums that grew like mushrooms around the factories of an industrial belt that sprawled over forty kilometres along the Hoogly River. During the period 1881–1931, the proportion of migrants in the agglomeration varied between a minimum of 53 per cent and a maximum of 62 per cent. Bombay recruited its migrants from a more circumscribed radius, the most important contribution being that of Ratnagiri district, on the Konkan coast: in the course of the same period, the proportion of population born in the city itself swung between 16 and 28 per cent. In the other cities, the great majority of migrants came from adjoining rural districts.

The rate of these migrations suddenly gained momentum in the period 1930–50. One of the causes for this development was the reversal in the demographic situation from 1921 onwards. The growing pressure on the land at the time led a large number of villagers to try their fortune in cities. These trends were further reinforced by the upheavals caused by the Second World War and the disarray caused by partition in 1947–51. Hence the veritable urban explosion of the years 1941–51, during which considerable masses came to swell the few big agglomerations.

This spotlight must not make us forget that urban India was – and continues to be – made up of a multitude of small and medium-scale cities. Their development varied from region to region, considerable contrasts being perceptible even between agglomerations situated a few kilometres from each other. Tamil Nadu, with a fairly solid urban fabric, underwent steady urban growth that was primarily evident in small and medium-scale cities. Thus the small city of Tiruvanamalai,[2] in the North Arcot district, expanded from 10,000 inhabitants in 1881 to 40,000 in 1951. The growth curves do not correspond with those of the large agglomerations as the highest rates were recorded in 1881–1931 while the period 1931–51 was characterized by relative stagnation. In this small town, urban growth was linked to fluctuations in the rural economy: the years of rapid growth coincided with the extension of lucrative crops, in particular groundnut, the years of relative stagnation coincided with the shrinking of the rural economy in the wake of the Great Depression of the 1930s. In other regions, rural prosperity and urban growth were not connected: thus in eastern Bengal, which achieved relative prosperity between 1890 and 1930 thanks to the extension of jute cultivation, the rate of urbanization remained extremely low, less than 5 per cent, and the pauperization of the countryside after 1930 did not lead to a massive exodus towards the cities.

It was from 1860 onwards that an imperial theory and practice of the city was elaborated. The Raj then had the ambition to build monuments capable of vying with those of the Moguls and to symbolize the advent to India of a new age of imperial splendour. The British encountered difficulties in their effort to define an architecture adapted to the country and at the same time capable of projecting an image of the empire. The neo-gothic style characteristic of Victorian England inspired a certain number of architects, in Bombay especially: the Victoria Terminal, constructed from 1878–87, is the most remarkable example of this style. But it was too European to satisfy the desire of the authorities to arrive at a sort of synthesis between imported and 'native' elements. Thus, the officials increasingly showed a predilection for the 'Indo-Saracenic' style.

This style, developed in the last quarter of the century by the architects Mant and Chisholm, borrowing certain elements both from Hindu and Saracenic architectures, or at least from the conception that the British had of these styles, was an original contribution of Victorian India to architectural vocabulary.[3] Reflecting the naïve cultural arrogance of the British, it presented itself as a synthesis of what was best in the native traditions. The most famous examples of this style are the main post office in Madras and Mayo College in Ajmer. It had a notable success in the Indian princely states and in Madras, but established itself in Bombay only latterly with the Gateway of India and especially the Prince of Wales Museum. From the beginning of the twentieth century onwards, it was gradually supplanted by the classical style, the renaissance of which marked in England the phase of imperial apogee. In India, Lord Curzon appeared as a determined upholder of classicism and directly intervened in the creation of the Victoria Memorial, the grand project of his reign. Designed by Curzon in an effort to counter the wave of nationalism and to prove the loyalty of the Indian population (it was entirely financed by a public subscription in India), this grandiose building, completed in 1921, appears today as a sort of a mausoleum of the Raj.

The predilection of the British for the classical style was to manifest itself even more spectacularly in the construction of a new city, New Delhi. Undertaken in 1913 and completed in the course of the 1930s, New Delhi was designed by Lutyens and Baker with a view to eclipsing Shahjahanabad, the Mogul capital. The symmetrical plan, the vast avenues with grandiose perspectives, the gigantism of the buildings (the viceroy's palace covers an area larger than that of the Castle of Versailles), the systematic use of the most noble materials sought to elicit from Indian subjects a mixture of pride and admiration aimed at inducing loyalty. This grandiose décor was also to house a few thousand civil servants. But the contrast between the facade of grandeur and the reality of a declining imperial power soon became obvious. Far from being the affirmation of a revival and of a permanence, New Delhi was the swan song for the Raj. It formed an awkward legacy for independent India, which would have to organize its central power in an oversized and overformal setting.

Apart from a few spectacular productions in the main cities, the architectural legacy of the British period in the rest of the subcontinent consists of a few thousand railway stations, constructed according to a single model, of public buildings stamped with the 'PWD' style (Public Works Department), characterized by a more utilitarian than aesthetic concern, and the bungalows of cantonments in the great majority of administrative centres and garrison towns where the British population of India was concentrated.

British influence was incontestably evident in Indian domestic architecture: Calcutta illustrates all the styles that were highly popular in Europe at one time or another in the houses of rich *zamindars* and traders. However, most Indians, even the rich, remained faithful to traditional styles and indigenous models continued to dominate the cities. Thus, in Benares,[4] (Varanasi) the localities (*mohallas*) retained their role and a sort of urban local patriotism, founded on the espousal of values shared by a large majority of inhabitants of the city (*banarsipan*), in particular merchants and artisans, emerged. Even in the large industrial city of Ahmadabad, the organization of space remained in tune with Indian notions and the introduction of the discipline of time, arising from the organization of mechanized industrial work, did not transform lifestyles or patterns of thought. A whole urban India situated at a distance from the great currents of colonial trade thus made its own way towards a modernity that owed little to British influence.

The Indian urban milieu was little affected by industry. Except for Jamshedpur, Cawnpore and the jute cities of the industrial belt around Calcutta, agglomerations in which modern industry represented the principal source of employment were rare. Artisans were more numerous than factory workers, but their condition remained very diverse. Indian industrialists formed only the upper, in any case the most visible, stratum of a commercial world with multiple ramifications, from which they hardly differentiated themselves in values or lifestyles. Urban India continued to be dominated by the triad rentier-merchant-artisan, which testified to the strength of the links maintained with the countryside. It was this urban India, the India of the bazaar, much more than the India of the capitalists and the proletarians, that served as the breeding ground for the nationalist movement in the first half of the twentieth century.

XXIV

SOCIO-RELIGIOUS REFORMS
AND NATIONALISM

(1870–1948)

The dominant trend in Indian nationalism could be defined as 'secularist' in approach. It advocated not the separation of the state and of religion, but the recognition of all religions as equal. For secularist nationalists – from the moderates of the pre-1914 Congress to Nehru, and including Gandhi – the nation was defined above all as a territory: whoever inhabited this territory, irrespective of their race or their religion, belonged to the nation. Secularists were not antireligious. Gandhi considered religion as the only source of values, but he did not conceive it in sectarian terms: Hindus and Muslims, he said, worshipped the same god under different forms. On many occasions, he declared that he was a Hindu but also a Muslim, a position that earned him little sympathy from either of the two communities. As for Nehru, an atheist (a position not incompatible with Hinduism), he construed the nation as a grouping of individuals and did not give any particular place to religious communities.

Other trends, which remained in a minority, defined the nation in ethnico-religious terms. For the extremists of the pre-1914 Congress, as well as for latter-day Hindu nationalists, the Indian nation could only be a Hindu nation. It was in reaction to this idea that Jinnah, initially a secularist, put forward his theory of two nations. This theory acknowledged the existence of a Hindu nation, but claimed in return the recognition of a Indian Muslim nation, which he defined more in territorial than in ethno-religious terms.

Most of these movements were favourable to social reform without however calling into question the caste system per se. Some of their leaders, including Nehru, demanded more radical reform, because for them egalitarian democratic ideas were incompatible with the idea of a social hierarchy.

Even though the secularist current remained politically dominant, as testified by the secular constitution of India, the dynamics of nationalism continued to be interlinked with the socio-religious reform movement that had a bearing on the entire society, whereas secular nationalism emanated primarily out of a small elite. It was his dual role as a social reformer and a political leader that made Gandhi the key figure of Indian nationalism. However, other reform movements had laid the groundwork for him.

Hindu reform movements

In the second half of the twentieth century, Hindu socio-religious reform movements diversified even as they became institutionalized.

The multiplication of the Brahmo Samajs

The Brahmo Samaj is the first to illustrate this trend. Its leader, Debendranath Tagore, tended more and more to return to mainstream Hinduism from which he had always refused to break away: in 1864, he authorized 'the twice born' (members of the three upper castes) to retain their sacred threads when they participated in the Brahmo Samajist cult. This manifestation of conservatism, added to many others, incited the protest of young radicals and led to a schism. From that time onwards, Debendranath became the head of only a small sect, the Adi Brahmo Samaj, which would not survive his death in 1905.

The conflict that provoked the schism had been latent since the rise into prominence of Keshab Chandra Sen (1838–84) within the Brahmo Samaj. Hailing from a Baidya Vaishnavite family and well-versed in English – he had worked for some time in the Bank of Bengal – K C Sen entered the organization in 1857 and in 1860 founded a circle (the Sangat Sabha, or Association of Believers) whose social reformism attracted young members. His rejection of caste distinctions and his concern for promoting the condition of women resulted, in 1862, in the clandestine organization of an inter-caste marriage, a ceremony that would be repeated in 1864 with a widow, a more flagrant act of defiance in the eyes of the orthodox, attached as they were to the interdiction on the remarriage of widows, branded as impure. This social reformism intensified after the schism, when K C Sen formed his Brahmo Samaj of India with the help of his young supporters and particularly after his stay in England, from where he returned in 1870. He then created an Association for Indian reform, which addressed the condition of peasants and militated for the legalisation of inter-caste marriages, a demand finally granted in 1872 by virtue of the *Brahmo Marriage Act* that instituted a more pared down ritualism.

However, from 1875–6 onwards, K C Sen turned away from social action to devote himself to a syncretic spirituality that was no doubt influenced by his encounter with the Bengali saint Ramakrishna Paramahansa. In 1881, he founded the New Doctrine that was supposed to realize the synthesis of Hinduism, Christianity and Islam, but whose form was particularly reminiscent of the devotional *bhakti* of Chaitanya. He projected himself as the inheritor of this famous Bengali saint of the sixteenth century, who developed the cult of Krishna by elevating himself to the status of a guru. Once again, after the return of Debendranath Tagore to orthodox Hinduism, it seemed impossible to remain on the fringes of Hindu models. A number of Brahmo Samajists interpreted this as a drift reducing the organization to the level of a mere sect and founded in reaction, as early as 1878, the Sadharan Samaj, which inherited the bulk of the regional, and even all-Indian, network of the Brahmo Samaj of India.

The spread of Brahmo Samaj branches was in fact the first contribution of K C Sen: in 1868, eastern Bengal had 65 branches and in 1872 there were 101 units in India, concentrated in Bengal but also present in Bihar, in the United Provinces and in the Punjab. The impact of the tours of K C Sen was particularly clear in the Bombay Presidency, where the Brahmo Samaj was developed out of the already existing foundation of an ancient tradition of socio-religious protest. As early as 1844 members of the anglicized intelligentsia of Surat had founded a Manav Dharma Sabha whose vocation was to fight against conversions. One of its instigators, Dadoba Panderung (1814–82), hailing from a merchant family and the head of the teacher training college of Bombay in 1846, founded the Paramahansa Mandali in this city on an even more affirmed reformist program. Of this movement, confined to a fraction of the intelligentsia, there remained only a sensibility to reformist themes in certain sections of the society of Bombay, when K C Sen went there in 1864, and in 1867. The receptivity of these circles to his discourse led to the institution of a Prarthana Samaj (Association of Prayer), that simultaneously embraced the theism of Rammohan Roy, the founder of the Brahmo Samaj, the devotional syncretism of K C Sen and a defence of Hinduism motivated by a concern not to break away from the Hindu society. The risk was all the more real as the Prarthana Samaj recruited its members almost exclusively from Brahmin circles, as for example Mahadev Govind Ranade (1842–1901), its principal leader. The bridgehead of the Bengali Brahmo Samaj – in 1872–3, a Brahmo Samajist of Calcutta, P C Majumdar, was despatched to assist it in developing the evening classes for lower castes – the Prarthna Samaj in its turn spread out its roots across the Bombay Presidency and the princely states of the region (in Poona, Surat, Ahmadabad, Karachi but also Kirkee, Kolhapur and Satara), even in the Dravidian South, with eighteen branches opened in the Presidency of Madras.

The second achievement attributed to the action of K C Sen concerns his influence on attitude. This of course involves his social reform action, but also the impact of his discourse in terms of the reconquest by the Hindus of their self-esteem. Compared to Roy's impact, K C Sen crossed a new frontier in the rehabilitation of Hindu culture, in the face of European denigrations. He was in a position to describe England after his voyage in 1870, but he did so by drawing a parallel with a Vedic golden age to conclude: 'I did not see much devotion in England. I have seen it in India in my noble ancestors.'[1] Socio-religious reformism appeared increasingly as a breeding ground for nationalism. Besides, the Sadharan Samaj would give the national movement one of its leaders in the person of Bipin Chandra Pal (1858–1932); above all, revivalist groups emerged as the continuation, even as the offshoot, of Brahmo Samajist reformism.

Ramakrishna, Vivekananda and the Ramakrishna Mission

In Bengal, this movement was embodied in the work of Vivekananda (1863–1902). Son of an advocate of Calcutta and himself educated in law, he became the disciple of Ramakrishna Paramahansa (1836–86) in 1882.

Originally a priest at the temple of Dakshineswar, near Calcutta, Ramakrishna had acquired, thanks to his devotion for the goddess Kali, the status of a guru. Even though he had not had the benefit of a modern education and he expressed himself in a rustic language, Ramakrishna gained numerous disciples among the Bengali intelligentsia, notably among the educated upper castes exercising modern professions, but frustrated in their ambitions for want of opportunities. This guru fell in line less with the logic of reformism than with the tradition of the *bhakti* that aimed at attaining *moksha* (spiritual liberation) through the worshipping of the deity. However, he distinguished himself from the masters of traditional sects by demanding from his followers only a very flexible level of discipline that suited the westernized intelligentsia very well. From this point of view, he appeared as a pioneer. He also taught the unity of the Muslim, Christian and Hindu religions of which he had explored the mystical aspects.

Before his death, this master asked his disciple, Narendranath Datta, who subsequently became Swami Vivekananda, to take care of his peers, a duty that he barely fulfilled, notably because he challenged two pillars in the teachings of Ramakrishna. On the one hand, he diluted the emphasis laid on *bhakti* to give prominence to *karma* (disinterested action, social action in this instance) as the way to reach the divine; on the other hand, he substituted the religious universalism of the master with an occasionally militant Hinduism.[2] In 1893, he attended the World Congress of Religions in Chicago where he underlined the superiority of the spiritual East over the materialistic West. His discourse so captured a part of Anglo-Saxon opinion that Vivekananda postponed his return to India until 1897. But the news of his oratorical successes reached home before him. Welcomed as a hero, he assembled the disciples of Ramakrishna and other supporters in a monastery, Belur Math, situated in front of the temple of Dakshineswar, and founded a Ramakrishna Mission devoted to the tasks of social service that he had seen fulfilled by western charitable associations. He therefore invested the best of his energy in social action wherein he discerned a variant of *karma yoga* (the yoga of action). Vivekananda thus inaugurated a new type of asceticism, that of a man devoted to the service of his contemporaries, who were perceived as a upholders of a threatened culture.

The Arya Samaj

The Arya Samaj represents an even more characteristic case of cultural nationalism. Its founder, Swami Dayananda Saraswati (1824–83), a Gujarati Brahmin who had opted at a very young age for the path of renunciation, was convinced by the teaching of his guru of the necessity to work for the reform of Hinduism in the 1860s. The campaign of this itinerant *sadhu* against idolatry and the misdeeds of Brahmins – in his opinion self-interested interpreters and religious intermediaries – brought him to Calcutta in 1872 where he met the Brahmo Samajists.

The first exposition of this doctrine, penned in 1875 in a book called *Satyarth Prakash* (The Light of Truth), however, marked a cultural closure in comparison with the Brahmo-Samajist theses: Dayananda in effect elevated the Vedas to the position of an infallible authority invested with a universal vocation and reduced all the other religions to a subordinate level. This radicalization, however, should not mask certain continuities: Dayananda also preached the discarding of the worship of images, denounced the role of Brahmin priests as religious intermediaries and also the alienating system of *jatis* in general; he campaigned in favour of inter-caste marriages and against child marriages which he saw as a major cause for the decline of Hindu society that had allowed colonization. However, his entire doctrine rested on the image of a Vedic golden age, an age where, in the origin of time, the Aryan people, virile, egalitarian and monotheistic, presumably dominated the world.

This reconstruction drew its inspiration from Orientalist works on Indo-Europeans – as proved by the usage given to the term 'Aryan' and the presentation of Sanskrit as 'the mother of all languages'.[3] But it fell in line with the effort initiated by Roy to resist western influence: it always aimed at countering the influence of Europeans by claiming a prestigious mythical past, the emphasis being laid in this instance more on social issues. Thus, Dayananda implicitly endorsed western criticisms of the caste system, but he argued that in the Vedic era the system in force relied on the four *varnas* (*brahmans, kshatriyas, vaishyas* and *shudras*) that conformed to the principle of individualism, as children were categorized by their masters under one of these categories depending on their qualities and their merits. This invention of a tradition sought to accredit the idea that Vedic India surpassed the West with respect to the latter's own conceptions of justice. Dayananda showed a much greater aggressiveness than manifested until then by the Brahmo Samaj, as the activities of the Arya Samaj would confirm.

This organization was created in 1875 in Bombay with the support of certain members of the Prarthna Samaj and of merchants. The movement nevertheless thrived in reality only in the Punjab where Dayananda went in 1877 on the invitation of Brahmo Samajists. The latter came above all from among the Bengali employees of the administration who had been 'imported' to this region to offset the scarcity of trained personnel at the time of the annexation of Punjab in 1849. The Government College of Lahore, opened in 1870, thereafter produced an intelligentsia that had broken with the orthodoxy, but was offended by the too Christian syncretism of KC Sen, who had visited the city in 1867 and 1873. Dayananda presented an attractive middle way in two respects: on the one hand, he retained only a rationalized form of the Hindu ritual: the weekly participation in the ceremonies of Vedic inspiration (the *havan*, performed without the mediation of a Brahmin priest) constituted the principal obligation demanded from the followers whose numbers increased rapidly in Lahore, and thereafter in other cities of the Punjab. On the other hand, the message of Dayananda allowed the educated youth to conciliate its loyalty to Hindu culture and the western modernity with which it was in touch. This effort towards a cultural synthesis was epitomised by the Dayananda Anglo-Vedic College, founded in Lahore in 1886, which, as the name suggests, combined teachings of the European sciences and other sciences that were strictly speaking 'revivalist' in nature.

This institution was administered by a council to which each local branch of the Arya Samaj designated a member. This system served as a model for the organization of the Arya Samaj of the Punjab itself, which formed in 1886 an Arya

Pratinidhi Sabha (Assembly of Arya representatives). Such a system is revelatory of the associative nature of the Arya Samaj: beyond the religious dimension symbolized by the weekly office, appurtenance to the movement was the sign of an ideological commitment, formalized by the payment of a contribution and the registration on the list of members. These 'workers' increased rapidly in number, growing from 14,000 in 1891 to 22,979 in 1901 and 100,846 in 1911. Members were above all, apart from intellectuals, urban traders who no doubt sought in Arya Samjist reformism a way to escape their ritualistic status of the third *varna*, all the more frustrating as the growing prosperity of Punjabi commerce elevated them to the rank of the dominant elite of the Hindu community.

However, a fraction of the Arya Samaj conceived the movement as a sect of which Dayananda was the founder guru. They militated, under the leadership of one of his disciples, Guru Datta, for adherence to his message, which, they claimed, exhorted a return to the strictest vegetarianism and the exclusive use of Sanskrit in the Dayananda Anglo-Vedic College. As the teachers at this college, Lajpat Rai (1865–1928), Lal Chand (? -1912) and Hans Raj protested, a schism occurred in 1893 between the so-called 'College' wing and the 'Vegetarian' wing. The latter, dominated by Munshi Ram (1857–1926), thereafter created its own educational institutions, with a girls' school at Jullundur in the beginning of the 1890s, then in Hardwar, with a *gurukul* imitating the Vedic system of education where the disciple of the guru was bound to complete asceticism during the period of his studies. Above all, Munshi Ram, as early as 1893, gave priority to reconversions that imitated the missionary methods in order to resist them better. The invention of tradition took another step forward insofar as a purification ritual of the upper castes, the *shuddhi*, was reinterpreted and turned into a procedure of reconversion or of the elevation of status of the lower castes. The preachers (*updeshaks*) of the Arya Samaj naturally met with the hostility of the Christian community, but also that of Muslims and Sikhs.

In 1873, the Sikh community had established a Singh Sabha in reaction to the conversion of two Sikh students to Christianity. This organization was similar to that of the Arya Samaj, with which it collaborated until the time when the *shuddhi* movement (literally, purification) sparked off a divorce that led to the emergence of a more affirmed sentiment of Sikh identity, as suggested the new slogan: 'We are not Hindus!'[4] The proselytizing mission of the Arya Samaj also poisoned Hindu relations with the Muslims, and in particular with the Ahmadiyya movement. Lekh Ram, a very close associate of Munshi Ram, held a long and violent debate with Mirza Ghulam Ahmad, before being assassinated by a Muslim in 1897.

In short, the revivalist variant of Hindu socio-religious reform proved to harbour not only a deep-rooted pride in a reinvented Vedic golden age, but also a sectarian aggressiveness towards the other religious communities. The Arya Samaj however cannot be construed as representative of the entire Hindu community in the light of this conflict; not only because it failed to establish itself beyond the Punjab (even though regional branches were formed in all the Hindi-speaking regions between 1886 and 1889), but also because it was rejected in orthodox circles.

Muslim reform movements

In the wake of 1857, which marked the end of medieval Muslim India with the Sepoy Revolt, and the repression and deposition of the last Mogul emperor, the Muslims had to take a stance with vis-à-vis Western values and institutionalize their reforms. A new division occurred then between the modernists, who attempted to make religion a private affair, and the fundamentalists, for whom religion had to impregnate all aspects of life, rivals within the same camp, both of them springing from Wahhabite reformism.

The fundamentalists: The Ahl-i Hadiths, Deoband

The reorganization of the fundamentalists widened a division that had appeared after the death of Sayyid Ahmad Barelwi. The radical wing of the School of Patna gave rise in 1864 to the Ahl-i Hadiths, who represented the most radical trend.

The Ahl-i Hadiths acclimatized the thought of Al-Shaukani to India: like him, they refused to submit to the medieval law and rejected the consensus (*ijma*) of the doctors to look for fundamental solutions in the traditions of the Prophet (*hadith*), hence, the name of the school which signifies 'people of traditions'. Their great master was Nadhir Hussain of Delhi; their great patron was Siddiq Hasan Khan, prince consort of the State of Bhopal in central India, who maintained close ties with Arabia and Yemen. The Ahl-i Hadiths mobilized an important minority of ulemas and established a network of schools all across North India.

But they were outplayed in this game by what was soon to become the most important fundamentalist organization in the subcontinent, Deoband, in North India, founded in 1867 by Muhammad Qasim Nanotawi and Rashid Ahmad Gangohi, who also claimed the heritage of Shah Waliullah and of Sayyid Ahmad Barelwi. It mobilized the moderate disciples of the latter who remained loyal to the solutions offered by the medieval law of the Hanafite school: this moderation, which permitted them to gather a large section of ulemas, was one of the reasons for its success. The second reason was the remarkable organizational ability of the Deobandis: they withdrew into small cities, like Deoband, while borrowing from the West, (with a view to resisting it better), its institutional arms (colleges with exams and boarding schools, lithography, a post to launch subscriptions and answer legal consultations that rivalled the British courts). Their seminary at Deoband, where the language of instruction was Urdu, trained generations of reformed ulemas. They created the largest network of Muslim schools at the time across North India. They printed in great quantities and at reasonable prices a vast religious literature, from catechism in Urdu to legal and theological works in Urdu and even in Arabic: missionary activity among the disadvantaged masses began to develop. A Muslim society – or rather the polite society of the Ashrafs – redoubled itself in this manner by employing the arms of the West; temporarily closed in on itself, it was ready to launch itself into politics when the occasion arose during the First World War.

The modernists: Aligarh and its emulators

Often hailing from the same circles of polite Muslim society as the fundamentalists, often imbued, as were the latter, with Wahhabism, the modernists refused the path of withdrawal after 1857. They looked for a compromise with the West on the four fronts of politics, educational institutions, science and theology.

The spearhead of the modernists, Sayyid Ahmad Khan (1817–98), had initially been a Wahhabite. Faithful to the British during the revolt of 1857, he advocated loyalty to the Raj until his death. It was for him the only way of preserving the interests of the Muslim community in the face of a rising Hindu elite. To form a Muslim elite class imbued with English culture and capable of vying with its Hindu counterpart, he founded a college at Aligarh near Delhi, in 1875 (which became the Muslim University) on the model of Oxford, where the language of instruction was English, and where the professors themselves were often British: here generations of westernized cadres were educated who were as active in the struggle for independence on the Indian side as on the Pakistani side. Sayyid Ahmad Khan was also the author of books on history and archaeology; a sincere believer, he wanted to fight against the lure of Christian missionaries and western culture and to offer religious justification for his political and educational activities. He elaborated to this end a Biblical and a Koranic exegesis and a theology that was modernist in approach, one of the most radical that the Muslim world had ever known, that he called 'naturalist' theism *(nachari)*. Acknowledging the Koran as the sole source of revelation, he refused medieval law, making religion a private affair: beliefs had for him a rational foundation in harmony with the laws of nature discovered by science.

If Aligarh was the only current that was organized into a school, it did not have the monopoly of modernism. On its fringes or outside its orbit, numerous bold attempts have been made to this day. We may mention the Shiite jurist, apologist and politician Amir Ali, who was influential in Calcutta and in London, and above all the poet philosopher Muhammad Iqbal (1877–1938) who took up the task of reconstructing Islamic thought and who was the spiritual father of Pakistan.

Reformed Islam in India therefore had two components: the one a fundamentalist approach that crystallized around the ulemas, notably those of the Deoband school; and the other modernist and westernized, which rejected the tutelage of the ulemas.

Reactions to reform

At the end of the nineteenth century, reform movements had been established that elicited varied reactions. Among the Hindus as among the Muslims, the traditionalists who rejected them mobilized themselves to resist them. However, there were also, particularly among the Muslims, attempts to reconcile these diverse ideas.

The reorganization of Hindu traditionalists

Traditionalist movements developed most often as a response to the initiatives of reformers. The principal architect of this variety of reaction was Pandit Din Dayal

Sharma (1863–?), a teacher at Hardwar, one of Hinduism's holy cities, situated in a frontier zone of the Punjab, where the Arya Samaj was active. In 1886, a collection of funds organized in this city by the Arya Samaj triggered the formation of a first movement for the defence of orthodoxy, led by Din Dayal Sharma. Thereafter, he went on a tour as far as Calcutta with a view to forming Sanatan Dharma Sabhas (Associations of Eternal Dharma), which he federated in 1887 into the Bharat Dharma Mahamandala (The Great Circle of the Dharma of India), founded at Hardwar. This organization institutionalized itself from 1900 onwards in the course of annual conferences, held in part thanks to the help of maharajas, such as the maharajah of Darbhanga (Bihar). It then spread its wings to encompass the entire subcontinent. Its principal intermediaries came from the milieu of landowners (from small *zamindars* to princes who had retained possession of their domains) and conservative Brahmins, whether they were *mahants* (priests in the temples) or pandits well-versed in the prestigious knowledge of Sanskrit scriptures.

Despite its reactive traditionalism, this movement can be considered as one of the poles in the typology of reform movements. Its mobilization certainly appears conservative in as much as it was firstly motivated by the infringements made on the socio-religious order by the reformers or by the laws that the British edicted. This calling into question of the religious neutrality of the colonial power sparked off an unusual agitation in 1891 with the passing of the *Age of Consent Bill*, which forbade child marriages. Nevertheless, like the reformers, the traditionalists conceded that India was in a position of decadence that warranted measures being taken. They recommended as a remedy the return to the institutions prescribed by the *dharmashastras* through the abolition of *jatis*. On the social front, this signified the rehabilitation of the *varnashramadharma*, the reestablishment of the hierarchic system of *varnas* and the observance of the stages of life (*ashrama*) prescribed by the normative texts. Not only does this reveal an aspiration towards social reform, but the implementation of this project brought the traditionalists close to the Arya Samaj who advocated a return, though in more egalitarian terms, to the *varnas*. The structure of the orthodox organizations (remunerating full-time preachers) was comparable to that of modern associations, while education resurfaced as a priority.

As early as 1899, Din Dayal Sharma was instrumental in the opening of a Hindu College in Delhi. An institution with the same name had been founded in 1898 by the theosophist Annie Besant in Benares where it served as the base for the laborious edification of a Benares Hindu University (1916).[5] This imposing establishment was firstly the work of Pandit Madan Mohan Malaviya (1861–1946), an orthodox Brahmin who epitomized the traditionalist movement in the United Provinces and who received in this capacity the support of the pandits of Benares and the financial support of a very large number of maharajahs and traders. For them, the university deserved the same gifts as the religious works that they patronized in order to act in keeping with their rank and acquire merits. Nevertheless, the Benares Hindu University did not content itself with dispensing a traditional knowledge in Sanskrit: English and the works of Europeans authors eventually found acceptance.

The reorganization of Muslim traditionalism: the Barelwis

The traditionalists, who had raised their voices against the Wahhabites as early as 1825, had to wait until the end of the nineteenth century for the advent of a theoretician and leader who would justify their viewpoint and organize them into a school. They found him in a scholar of high calibre, Ahmad Riza Khan (1855–1921) who founded the so-called Barelwi School at Bareilly in the north of India that maintained the exact opposite of the doctrines of Sayyid Ahmad Barelwi (1786–1831), the initiator of Indian Wahhabism who himself came from the city of Rae Bareilly.

The image of this traditionalism has been distorted by its fundamentalist adversaries who accused it of condoning superstitions of Hindu origin. This is a misunderstanding: the Barelwis observed a scrupulous orthodoxy, but the norms that they restored were those that had currency before the intrusion of Wahhabism; they reaffirmed, in all its medieval dimensions, Sufi mysticism, the miraculous powers of saints who could lawfully be worshipped, and the greatness of the Prophet who was not only the legislator, but also an object of veneration. There is no doubt that they reflected the profound spirituality of the silent mass of Muslims: at the time, reformers still formed a minority.

To fight these reformers, both fundamentalist and modernist, the Barelwis employed their own arms. They organized a 'movement' in the course of the 1890s, with its annual congresses, its newspapers and its network of schools. The Barelwis were, and remain, influential in the territory of present-day Pakistan: they also have their partisans in Bihar and Hyderabad. Unlike the reformed ulemas, as those of Deoband who made a fray into the politics as soon as an occasion arose, the Barelwis maintained a quietistic position until towards 1940: they then started to support the creation of Pakistan.

A new Muslim prophecy: the Ahmadiyya

An original reaction to the Muslim reforms and to the challenges posed by the proselytizing activities of the Hindus of the Arya Samaj and Christian missionaries, was that of Mirza Ghulam Ahmad (c. 1838–1908), founder of the sect of the Ahmadiyyas, outcast today. His doctrine was also seriously warped by his detractors: he projected himself to the Hindus as an avatar of the god Vishnu, to the Christians as a reincarnation of Jesus, and to the Muslims as a new Prophet: this could very easily look like a frenzied syncretism. In fact, nothing could be further from the truth: a recent study of his works has shown that he elaborated a theological response for the challenge of his time, a response that built on the Sufi speculations on continuous revelation. He posed as a prophet bringing a new revelation for modern times, abolishing in particular the obligation of the holy war and encouraging Muslims to devote themselves to pacific proselytizing.

The Ahmadiyyas created, during the inter-war period, the first great worldwide Muslim missionary network. Rejected by all other currents of thought, traditionalist, fundamentalist and modernist, on the grounds of a restrictive and modern interpretation of the dogma of the finality of the prophecy of Mahommad, driven to live in closed communities, the Ahamadiyyas opted in 1947 for Pakistan. . . and therefore for misfortune, as they would be excluded in 1974 from the Muslim community and legally persecuted from 1984 onwards.

An attempt at conciliation: the Nadwatululama

The Ahmadiyyas had, in one sense, attempted a reconciliation by moving towards medieval mysticism. Another attempt was made in the other direction by the Nadwatululama, the 'House of Ulemas', established in Lucknow, in North India, towards 1894, in the wake of the double impetus given by an ascending bourgeoisie and by ulemas and mystics resolved to adapt themselves to the needs of the time without sacrificing the tradition in any way: it strove to create a middle ground between fundamentalists and modernists. At its beginning, it was innovative both in theology and in pedagogy (Arabic as a living language, Western sciences) with Shibli Numani (1857–1914), marked by the modernism of Aligarh and his two students, Abul Kalam Azad (1888–1958) and Sayyid Sulaiman Nadwi (1884–1953), who created ties with Egyptian modernists such as Rashid Rida (1855–1935) who came to Lucknow. But, like the Egyptian modernists, Nadwatululama returned to fundamentalism: its administration was practically always administered by a single conservative family, that of the great scholar Sayyid Abdulhayy (1869–1923), and thereafter, from 1930 onwards, by his two sons.

Hindu reformism and political action

The Indian National Congress, as early as its formation in 1885, had decided to exclude the problems of socio-religious reform from its field of action. This decision reflected its desire to embody the Indian nation in its totality – which was hardly compatible with its taking into consideration debates internal to such and such a community – and its concern for avoiding issues on which its members were often divided. The party therefore created, in 1886, an Indian Social Conference entrusted to the leadership of MG Ranade, a former member of the Prarthana Samaj of Poona (Maharashtra) whose annual session took place concurrently with that of the Congress, in the same city but under a different canopy. This Conference drew its inspiration from the programme of early movements of socio-religious reform and thus advocated the remarriage of widows and the elevation of the minimum age of marriage, even for inter-caste marriages. In this respect, it reflected the dominant sensibility within the milieu of the founders of the Congress, who for the most part belonged to a westernized intelligentsia that, we must emphasize, did not easily gird itself for action when it came to openly breaking away from Hindu customs.

From the 1890s onwards, another branch of the Congress, called 'extremist' owing to its anti-British activism, would call into question the reformist discourse of the founders of the party – henceforth described as 'moderates'. Thus, its main leader, Bal Gangadhar Tilak, who also came from Poona, protested against a British measure, the *Age of Consent Bill*, which aimed at prohibiting child marriage, explaining that this was an element of the traditional Indian heritage. The 'extremists', if they subscribed to certain social reforms, tended to subordinate them to political action, which they believed was the priority: from their point of view, these problems would be automatically resolved once India was liberated from foreign rule; whereas, for certain 'moderates', social reform had to precede independence.

To this so-called 'extremist' political and social sensibility was added the pressure group of the Hindu Sabhas (Hindu forums) in the 1900s. This movement was in its beginning circumscribed to the provinces of the North. In the Punjab, it developed from 1906 onwards, for the most part in reaction to the Muslim demand for a separate electorate (granted by the British in 1909). Its architects, like Lajpat Rai, were none other than Arya Samajists of merchant castes who were afraid of losing their socio-political supremacy to the Muslim majority, a supremacy hitherto guaranteed by privileged access to education. In the United Provinces, the Hindu Sabhas emerged after the right to a separate electorate had been granted to the Muslims, in 1915, for the elections of corporations that designated the Legislative Council of the region. Their advocates, like their leader Madan Mohan Malaviya, came above all from the Sanatan Dharma Sabhas, the militant Hinduism of which assumed a political dimension. The various Hindu Sabhas of the North of India were federated to form an All India Hindu Sabha, thereafter a Hindu Mahasabha in the second half of the 1910s, notwithstanding the past divergences of their leaders – Lajpat Rai had been an 'extremist' whereas Malaviya had figured among the early 'moderates'. The Hindu Mahasabha was constituted as a movement for the defence of Hindu interests within the Congress. If its influence remained limited, it institutionalized the division that had appeared in the 1890s between the Congress leaders who campaigned for adequate social reforms – represented then by Motilal Nehru – and others who expressed reservations and even hostility.

Gandhi favoured, in this domain as in others, a sort of compromise: on the one hand, by his reformism, he followed the line of the moderates, whose last great leader Gokhale, had initiated him into politics; on the other hand, he remained loyal to the Sanatan Dharma, as he himself affirmed. This ambivalence, which was propitious to compromise, clearly stems from his conception of the problem of untouchability, around which the debate on social reforms in the Congress, during the period 1920 to 1930, increasingly tended to focus.

As early as the beginning of the 1920s, Gandhi advocated the abolition of untouchability in his newspaper *Young India*. A resolution was voted to that effect at the session of 1920, which saw the advent of Gandhi to the leadership of the party. Social reform was for the first time recognized as falling within the fully legitimate field of action of the Congress. The key issues in the fight against untouchability were the access of all to schools, wells, hospitals, temples etc. that certain untouchables had been demanding officially since 1917. A memorandum had then been addressed by a delegation of the 'depressed classes' of Bombay to the Secretary of State for India, Montagu, within the framework of his preparatory consultations for the constitutional reform of 1919. Gandhi focused his attention primarily on the opening of temples to the untouchables. He participated, in 1924, in the *satyagraha* of Vaikom (Travancore, in present Kerala) which had been launched on this theme.

This was because he believed that untouchability was essentially a religious problem: a category of human beings cannot be excluded from access to the divine, nor to its representation in the form of an image. The social dimension of this question appeared to him less acute because, as a partisan of the Sanatan Dharma, he did not envisage calling into question the economy of the caste system.

Concurrent to his denunciation of untouchability, Gandhi declared himself in favour of a reinterpreted system of *varnas*: his social ideal consisted of statutory categories, acquired by dint of merit, collaborating with each other in a harmonious way. This was a vision that had no room for conflict. Gandhi avoided participating in other protest movements of untouchables after the *satyagraha* of Vaikom in an effort to avoid exacerbating social tensions. This was denounced as 'paternalistic' by certain untouchable leaders, among whom B R Ambedkar (1891–1956) was the foremost. Convinced that the emancipation of untouchables presupposed the conquest of specific political rights, Ambedkar demanded a separate electorate during the Round Table Conferences of 1930 and 1931. When this demand was acceded to by the British in 1932, Gandhi undertook a fast unto death because he saw it as calling into question Hindu social unity. The compromise at which he arrived with Ambedker under the name of the Poona Pact (the city where Gandhi was at the time incarcerated) substituted separate electorates with a significant quota of seats reserved for untouchables in the elected assemblies. Immediately afterwards, Gandhi launched, with the financial support of Marwaris like G D Birla, a Harijan Sevak Sangh (association for the service of *harijans*, that is, 'the children of god') whose proposal for the reform of the Hindu social system from the inside could necessarily come to fruition only in the long term. Ambedkar, disillusioned, then concluded that conversion was the only way to circumvent the hierarchy of castes, but he only acted out his decision in 1956, the year in which thousands of untouchable families became Buddhist.

If Gandhi elevated social reform to the status of a legitimate field of action of the Congress, he did so, in the final analysis, from a conservative point of view. This ambivalence stemmed to a great extent from his constant concern for conciliation, from his effort to preserve the unity of his party, and beyond it, of society at large. Indeed, the tensions between traditionalists and reformists within the Congress did not degenerate into a schism during Gandhi's lifetime. If Lajpat Rai and Malaviya had formed parties aimed at promoting their sensibilities, they did so within the framework of the Congress in 1926 and 1934 respectively. The only rift that occurred, and only partly on the question of social reforms, was caused by other minor chiefs of the Hindu Mahasabha. This schism attracted only a small number of followers, but it marked the emergence of Hindu nationalism as an autonomous political force.

Hindu nationalism

Hindu nationalism was embodied from the 1920s by two different organizations, the Hindu Mahasabha and the Rashtriya Swayamsevak Sangh (RSS – Association of National Volunteers), which in certain respects were the offshoots of socio-religious reform movements.

The former bartered, in the course of the 1930s, its status as a pressure group within the Congress for that of an independent political party. Whereas its long-standing leaders, like Malaviya, rallied under Gandhi's banner, even while asserting their difference, its radical current – particularly well represented in Maharashtra – came out of the Congress and transformed the Hindu Mahasabha into a political party in 1937. V D Savarkar (1883–1966), who was its president from 1937 to 1942, imbued it with a Hindu nationalist ideology.

This doctrine – codified by Savarkar in 1923 in *Hindutva – Who is a Hindu* – in many respects fell in line with the doctrine of the Arya Samaj. It described the Hindus as a race descended from 'Vedic fathers' who, as the inheritors of this glorious past, epitomized the Indian national identity. Religious minorities – *a fortiori* because they were essentially composed of converts – were therefore commanded to keep their cultural practices in the private sphere and to pay allegiance to Hindu symbols that were presented as the summation of Indian identity. Hindi – even Sanskrit – had to be adopted by all as the national language. Muslim separatism was denounced all the more virulently as the Indian territory – so clearly outlined in the eyes of Savarkar by the Himalayas and the seas – constituted a pillar of Hindu nationalism. This ideology in short represented an ethnic nationalism where religious communities were organized into a hierarchy in accordance with their value, with Hindu culture invested with the vocation of dominating Indian identity. This conception ran counter to the one maintained by Gandhi and Nehru for whom the Indian nation was defined as a collection of communities and individuals, on an equal footing.

The Hindu Mahasabha enjoyed for some time the prestige of Savarkar who, in 1937, completed serving a twenty-seven year term of imprisonment for his anti-British activities in terrorist societies. But during the Second World War, the party opted for a strategy of cooperation with the British in an effort to influence the colonial power into favouring Hindus and, above all, to allow their recruitment in the army so as to acquire the martial virtues necessary for 'resisting' the Muslims. This 'collaboration' was ill perceived by Indian public opinion, aware as it was of the sacrifices incurred at the same moment by the Congress for the sake of independence.

Besides, the Hindu Mahasabha, apart from a team of leaders who came from the intelligentsia, relied on a poorly structured network of conservative notables. Not only were the latter ill-suited for militant work, but they also lived divorced from the masses. Some leaders of the party themselves considered the traditional system of the *varnas* as a model of the Hindu nation owing to the emphasis laid on unity. Notwithstanding the efforts of S P Mookerjee, who succeeded Savarkar as the head of the party, and whom Nehru would appoint as minister in his first government, the Hindu Mahasabha was reduced to the insignificance of a minuscule group during the general elections of 1945–6 in which it did not win even a single seat.

At the same time, the RSS witnessed a rapid growth that reflected its very specific character. This movement had been established in 1925 in reaction to the Muslim mobilization in the context of the Caliphate Movement. Its founder in Nagpur (Maharashtra), K B Hedgewar, like many a member of the Hindu Mahasabha, had interpreted this pan-Islamic mobilization, and the riots between Hindus and

Muslims that had punctuated it, as a threat to the Hindu community. This inferiority complex of the majority took root in the conviction that the Hindus were too divided – into castes, sects, and regional appurtenances – to be able to confront the Muslims. Upon this idea was built Hedgewar's plan to forge a Hindu nation by influencing society. This long-drawn-out enterprise rested on the ideology that he had read in *Hindutva*, but was developed independently of any involvement in the political game, despite the pressing solicitations of the Hindu Mahasabha.

The basic unit of the RSS was – and continues to be – the *shakha* (branch) the young members of which, in each locality, met every day, in their uniforms, to perform physical exercises and hear nationalistic Hindu sermons that most often dealt with history (in particular with Shivaji's empire). This discipline aimed at strengthening the 'muscle' of, and at indoctrinating, the Hindu youth, but also at eroding the caste divisions by assembling members from all sections of society in a common place. This objective – which confers a reformist dimension to the RSS – only began to crystallize with great difficulty, so much was the ethos of the RSS inseparable from that of the Brahmins of Maharashtra, marked as they were by the history of the Maratha Empire and the subsequent Confederacy. But this movement eventually succeeded in integrating members of the lower castes, especially when it was extended towards the north, where the opposition between Brahmins and non-Brahmins was less problematic.

This proclaimed and premeditated indifference to caste status is reminiscent of Hedgewar's Hindu nationalist project, but above all testifies to the affinity of the RSS to certain values of another Hindu institution, the sect. The sect, in theory, was in effect open to all castes: ascetic disciples of the founder guru formed the core of a sect after renouncing the world and with it their social status. Besides, the steel-frame of the RSS was composed of *pracharaks* (remunerated full-time preachers) who had often abandoned their studies, renounced family life, or exercised a profession in order to devote themselves fully to the Hindu nationalist cause. This body of 'activist ascetics' was founded by Hedgewar in his image; he was indeed venerated as a guru. The paramilitary dimension of the RSS also, in part, evokes religious traits insofar as it stipulated certain practices of traditional *akharas* (gymnasiums) like the emphasis on moral and physical discipline, the worship of an idol and the authority of the guru. The importance of the ritual is evident in the complex liturgy performed every day in the *shakhas* (prayer, salutation of the saffron flag, etc.) and in the cycle of the six annual festivals that the movement observed (some of which belonging also to the Hindu calendar).

If in the 1930s the expansion of the RSS outside Maharashtra was above all the fruit of the devotion of the corps of *pracharaks*, and of the attraction for its ritualistic sectarian dimension, in the 1940s, its rapid growth stemmed from its paramilitary character, that seemed a means of reinforcing Hindus in zones where the Muslims were in a majority. From 1940 to 1948, the followers of the movement grew from one hundred thousand to six hundred thousand, with the most spectacular growth being registered in the northwest, where the RSS was party to the violence sparked off by partition, notably in Delhi.

In January 1948, Gandhi was assassinated by a former member of the RSS, subsequently a disciple of Savarkar, who held the Mahatma responsible for partition. The Nehru government forthwith banned the RSS and arrested twenty thousand members of the organization.

Muslim nationalism and separatism

At the dawn of the twentieth century, the various trends among Muslim reformists and their traditionalist adversaries had assumed a certain form, and their doctrine would no longer be subject to any modifications. They would only fine-tune their thought with respect to two points: the attitude towards the colonial power and the strategy of proselytizing. Their development would continue concomitant to that of the Hindu reformers.

Composite nationalism and the ulemas

Until the beginning of the twentieth century, any true debate on the relation of Indian Muslims with power was impossible. Only loyalty towards the British could be expressed freely; it could find religious justification only in the theologies, marginal as they were, of Sayyid Ahmad Khan and Mirza Ghulam Ahmad. The adversaries of the British presence were cowed into silence. With the coming of elections into India, the rise of the pan-Islamic wave in the world and the beginnings of the national movement, the debate on power was opened. It engendered in effect the most tragic rift in the history of the subcontinent between the Muslim leaders who were keen to collaborate with the Hindus and those who refused such collaboration.

The majority of ulemas, and a part of the westernized elite, opted for the fight against the British by allying with nationalist Hindus. Abdul Kalam Azad was, in 1910, the first architect and theoretician of this alliance, which was sealed by the Pact of Lucknow in 1916. This branch enjoyed the support of the Deobandis, who founded in 1919 – with the avowed intention of entering the political arena and of using religion to mobilize the masses – the powerful Association of the Ulemas of India (Jamiyyatululama-yi Hind); from 1920–24 they participated with Gandhi, against the backdrop of the Caliphate movement that strived to make the Ottoman Sultan a sort of Pope of Islam, in the first campaign of non-cooperation. According to the doctrine of this school, composite nationalism, Muslims and Hindus formed a single nation. The champions of this current were, on the side of the ulemas, the rector of Deoband, Husain Ahmad Madani, and the historian Muhammad Mujeeb, rector of the Nationalist University (Jamia Millia) of Delhi.

Separatism: Iqbal, Jinnah and Pakistan

Feeling threatened by the possibility of being absorbed by the Hindus who dominated the Congress party, other Muslims, particularly the modernists, opted for the course of separatism charted out by Sayyid Ahmad Khan and organized themselves to defend their interests. They created the Muslim League in 1906 and obtained a quota of seats in the assemblies. This process was to eventually lead to the partition of the subcontinent. It was toned down from 1916 to 1924, under the leadership of a graduate of Aligarh, Muhammad Ali, associated with an authentic mystic and theologian of Lucknow, Abdulbari (1878–1926), with a view to fighting shoulder to shoulder with the Hindus against the British. It was infused with new life under the leadership of Iqbal, who demanded as early as 1930 a separate state for Muslims, and in 1936 by Muhammad Ali Jinnah (1876–1948), elected to the presidency of the Muslim League. Taking the opposing view to the theory of composite nationalism, he declared that the Muslims formed a nation distinct from that of the Hindus. He rallied to his banner – with the backing of a minority of the Deoband ulemas, like Muhammad Shafi and Shabbir Ahmad Usmani, and the support of the Barelwis – the majority of the westernized elite. He obtained a massive vote for Pakistan, which was created in 1947. This country has its 'ideologists,' such as the historian Ishtiaq Husain Qureshi.

The neo-fundamentalists

In the growing chasm between Hindus and Muslims that followed the failure of the Caliphate movement, there appeared new forms of fundamentalism more radical than those of the nineteenth century, and which, in their highly centralized organization, often drew heavily on western models, in particular those of totalitarian political parties and on another plane, those of the missionaries.

The dream of an Islamic state: Maududi and the Jamaat-i Islami

Two movements, which have left behind an important tradition, distinguished themselves by the place that they afforded to politics.

The first, the Jamaat-i Islami movement, was one of the precursors of the Islamic radicalism today so prevalent in the Muslim world. Muslim separatism, the work of a modernist elite that often considered religion as a private affair, lacked a theological justification. It was outlined by Iqbal (1877–1938), who, relinquishing as early as 1930 the chimera of pan-Islamism, wanted to construct the new Muslim man in only one country, Pakistan, of which he was considered the spiritual father. Before his death, he established an obscure self-taught man of religion, Abdul-Ala Maududi (1903–79) as the director of an Islamic institute at Gurdaspur, in the Punjab. Like his Egyptian contemporary Hasal al-Banna, the founder of Muslim Brothers, the latter believed that the integral application of the Muslim Law rested on the seizure of power by a dynamic and devoted minority that had to be trained secretly. This audacious doctrine was sketched out as early as 1928 in the Urdu work titled *Of the Holy War in Islam*. He pursued his project in another book published in 1939, *The Political Theory of Islam*, and by the foundation in 1941 of an educational and religious movement that became a political party, the Jamaat-i Islami. He surged to fame by launching, in 1948, the fight to make Pakistan a model Islamic State which he theorized in his book *Islamic Law and the Constitution*; he dragged along with him religious parties: the traditionalist ulemas forming two associations (and subsequently political parties): the Association of the Ulemas of Islam (Jamiyyatululama-yi Islam, the Deobandis) and the Association of the Ulemas of Pakistan (Jamiyyatululama-yi Pakistan, the Barelwis). He dominated the debate that led to the first constitution in 1956, declaring Pakistan an Islamic Republic; he also put forward the first theory of a state founded on the revealed Law, the *Shariah*.

The Tablighi Jamaat and 'apolitical' proselytizing

Around the 1930s, one of the greatest issues in the struggle between Hindus and Muslims was the conquest or the reconquest of converts. In response to the Hindu movements that wanted to reconvert Muslims of Hindu origin to Hinduism, there was a proliferation of missionary organizations, created by politicians like Hasrat Mohani (1878–1951), Saifuddin Kitchlew (1878–1951), or by religious leaders like Hasan Nizami (1878–1955): they aimed above all at confirming the Muslims in their faith and, more rarely, as in the case of Hasan Nizami, at converting Hindus. Among these missionary organizations, often short-lived, was one destined for a great fortune, the *Tablighi Jamaat*, or 'The Group of Predication,' created in Delhi in 1927 by Muhammad Ilyas (1885–1944), a fundamentalist religious leader within the Deobandi sphere of influence. This movement ostensibly declared itself apolitical; however, the analysis of its strategies lay bare the ultimate political aims that it harboured. Its missionary network, which soon became international, is today the largest in the Muslim world.

XXV

THE END OF THE BRITISH EMPIRE IN INDIA

The birth of the Indian Union and of Pakistan (1942–50)

The Quit India movement, launched in 1942 by the Congress to force the British to depart, inaugurated a decisive phase in the history of the subcontinent. In the space of a few years, the British imperial edifice would fall to pieces, giving rise to two independent dominions, India and Pakistan – a painful birth, accompanied by blood and tears. Between 1942 and 1948, one of the greatest tragedies of the century was to be played out in what was British India.

The truth about these terrible years is only now beginning to come to light, even as the myths meticulously fabricated are being shattered one after another. The myth of successful decolonization epitomized by the flamboyant personality of the last Viceroy of India, Lord Mountbatten. The myth of the birth of Pakistan, the doing of a single man, Muhammad Ali Jinnah, execrated by some, adulated by others. What is becoming more and more obvious, apart from the extraordinary acceleration of history during the few years that witnessed the collapse of one of the greatest imperial edifices of all times, is the accumulation of errors, wrong calculations and cowardly acts that led to the tragedy of the partition: hundreds of thousands of dead, fourteen million uprooted. This open wound is still far from being healed.

The publication of the most confidential British archives has largely torn away the veil, but there still remain a number of obscure areas; in particular, we are far from a consensus on the interpretation of events. Two schools maintain a sharp opposition: the first sees in Jinnah the primary instigator of partition and blames the British, particularly the last but one viceroy, Lord Wavell, for having abetted him to a great extent in his task; the other tends to exonerate Jinnah of one part of the responsibility and judges the Congress and Mountbatten with greater severity.

From the Quit India movement to
independence and partition

The British government interpreted the Quit India movement as a declaration of war from the Congress and took advantage of the occasion to deal a decisive blow to the nationalist organization. In the morning of 9 August 1942, it launched a vast crackdown all over India and almost all the leaders and cadres of the Congress were arrested as they got out of bed and were placed under lock and key. The ease with which these arrests were carried out shows that the Congress leaders were completely taken by surprise, and casts doubt on the genuineness of the accusations of 'premeditated subversive conspiracy' that the authorities subsequently hurled on the Congress. In reality, it seems that neither Gandhi nor the others leaders had yet taken any concrete measures for the organization of a campaign of agitation. The situation would have been kept under control, were it not for the reaction, largely spontaneous, of the popular masses that confounded the calculation of British. On hearing the announcement of the arrest of Gandhi and his companions, large crowds, often led by militant Congress leaders who had escaped the arrests, took to the streets. In several regions, protests degenerated into riots, sounding the alarm of an anti-British popular uprising. In Bihar and in the east of the United Provinces, British authority indeed dissipated and several weeks were needed to re-establish a semblance of normality. The viceroy Linlithgow conceded that this was the most serious challenge to the Raj since 1857.

The police having been overwhelmed, the British called upon the army, and during the following few months fifty-seven battalions were assigned for the maintenance of order. The presence on Indian soil, owing to the war, of a large number of British military (around twice the number in peacetime) facilitated the repression of the movement, because the government avoided engaging Indian units as much as possible. An official statement published at the end of 1943, but surely underestimated, records a total of 91,836 arrests, 1,060 protesters and 63 policemen killed. Material losses were considerable: 208 police stations, 332 railway stations and 945 post offices were destroyed or seriously damaged and 664 explosive attacks were reported. The violence of the masses was far from blind – it was directed against the most accessible symbols of British rule.

With the exception of Muslims who, in general, observed the orders of abstention given by the Muslim league, all sections of the population participated in the movement. In the urban milieu, schoolchildren and students were particularly active, but traders and workers did not allow themselves to be outdone. The big cities became the scene of widespread turmoil in August 1942: in Bombay, strikes and protests paralysed all activities for five days. The most spectacular event was the total stoppage of the textile mills of Ahmadabad, employing more than 100,000 workers, which, following a secret agreement between the employers and the unions, remained closed for three and a half months. There was also a strike of fifteen days at Jamshedpur, in the Tata steel factories, which hampered the war effort.

In the rural regions, the uprising was marked by a massive participation in Bihar and in the east of the United Provinces, but was quite rapidly repressed. In other regions, situated at a distance from the important strategic arteries, the mayhem persisted at times for longer. In Bengal, in the Tamluk subdivision of Midnapur district, Congress leaders formed a parallel government (the Tamralipta Jatya Sarkar), which succeeded in maintaining itself until September 1944. In Orissa, in the princely state of Talcher, a popular insurrection broke out and the British air force had to bombard the capital to prevent it from falling into the hands of the insurgents. In Maharashtra, in the region of Satara, where a tradition of political activism existed among the lower castes, a parallel government was formed in 1943 and survived as late as 1945. Lastly, near the Nepalese border, a leader of the Congress Socialist Party (the socialist Left of the Congress), Jayaprakash Narayan, waged a guerrilla war for several months against the British before being captured.

The 'Quit India' movement apparently ended in total failure, since the British not only did not quit India, but used it further as a rear base for the war in Asia. However, if they succeeded one more time in mobilizing the resources of the country to meet their own war objectives, they could not win hearts to their cause. In a long-term perspective, 1942 therefore marked an essential turning point in the history of the nationalist struggle. The unexpected magnitude of the uprising opened the eyes of the British to the fragility of their position: they did not realize this at that time but, after the war, the memory of 1942 influenced their decision not to remain in India by dint of force.

Conversely, the Congress leadership came out of this apparent defeat with renewed strength. The years spent in prison conferred an aura of martyrdom to the politicians who had opted for the way of compromise in 1937. The Congress also made mileage from the discredit incurred by the communists for having collaborated with the British authorities. In 1945, it seemed to be in a position to succeed the British as the rulers of the country. Above all, the spontaneous popular reaction of 1942 was a warning for all Indian politicians. Henceforth, seeking a compromise with the British appeared dangerous: it was clear that the Indian masses would not accept a drawn-out political transition towards an independence negotiated within the framework of the empire: they wanted total independence as quickly as possible.

India and the war

From 1942 onwards, India became an important rear base in the fight of the Allies against Japan while its armed forces, whose strength had been raised to one million and a half men, participated in military operations in Africa and in the Middle East (they suffered considerably less loss than during the First World War). The country, especially the eastern regions, became covered with military bases and aerodromes that accommodated, in addition to Indian and British troops, a large American contingent and elements of the Chinese army of the Kuomintang. At the same time, the British reoriented Indian heavy industry towards the production of arms and munitions, while the textile industry worked for the needs of the armies. The establishment of a real war economy produced disastrous effects. The presence of American soldiers with high purchasing power, the emergence of a shortage of labour in the industrial and construction sectors contributed, coupled with the enormous increase in governmental expenses, to spur on unbridled inflation. The salaried employees of the cities managed to escape the brunt of the situation thanks in part to the action of unions, but this was not the case with the peasants. To guarantee every one a minimum subsistence, the government had to regulate the economy and adopt measures of rationing. It could not, however, prevent the development of speculation and black market.

The most serious manifestation of the imbalances caused by the war was the great famine of Bengal of 1943, the only one to strike India in the twentieth century. It resulted not from a deficit in the rice harvest, but from the destruction of several thousands of boats that transported rice in the delta of eastern Bengal; this destruction had been decided on by the British authorities as part of their scorched earth policy, with a view to preventing a Japanese invasion. The impossibility of transporting part of the harvest disrupted the market and further increased speculation. The poorest of villagers, in particular agricultural workers, who had to buy all or a part of their daily ration, could not face the rise in prices. Hundreds of thousands of them flocked towards Calcutta, begging a bowl of rice or even a little stock in which the rice had been cooked. Weakened by malnutrition, they fell easy prey to cholera, malaria and other diseases. The incapacity of the Bengal government, led by the Muslim League, to act, heightened political tension. The central government had to take charge of the provision of supplies but had difficulty in feeding the population. The number of victims of the calamity exceeded the three million mark. No doubt the Indian population saw in this return of the scourge of famine yet another sign of the end of the British era.

Another severe blow to the prestige of the British was the formation of an Indian National Army (or INA, in Hindi: Azad Hind Fauj) among the Indian prisoners of war captured by the Japanese in Malaya and in Singapore in 1942. It was created in October 1943 at the initiative of the dissident nationalist politician Subhas Chandra Bose. Bose, former president of the Congress, had broken away from Gandhi and Nehru in 1939 and had formed his own party, the Forward Block, which adopted violently anti-British positions when the war broke out. Placed under house arrest by the British, he escaped to Afghanistan and via the Soviet Union, at the time an ally of Hitler, reached Berlin, where he attempted to obtain the support of the Nazis for the cause of Indian independence. As Hitler saw in the British Empire an important factor of stability, and as he harboured no sympathy for the Indians, in his opinion degenerated specimens of the Aryan race, Bose went to try his luck in Tokyo. There he was well received and met another Indian nationalist, Rash Behari Bose, who had created a government of free India under the aegis of Japan. Subhas Chandra Bose rapidly ousted his colleague and placed himself in the service of the Japanese, in exchange for the promise of their support for the independence of India.

By a combination of threats and appeals to patriotism, Bose succeeded in rallying to his cause a section of the soldiers and officers of the Indian Army captured by the Japanese, about 20,000 men, and launched a call for a march on Delhi. The INA fought in March 1944 on the side of the Japanese in the invasion of Assam from Burma. This diversionary operation ended in a complete fiasco after a few weeks of combat, but symbolically, the entrance of the INA into India had a considerable impact. For the first time since 1858, Indian soldiers in uniform had faced the British (in fact the Indian Army, that is other Indian soldiers) on Indian soil. At a time when the Congress leaders were in prison and when nationalist sentiments could not be expressed openly, a section of the Indian public experienced a surge of enthusiasm for the lost soldiers of Bose. The latter, who died in 1945 in a mysterious plane accident, remains a national hero in India, and particularly in Bengal.

The formation of the INA was a severe blow to the British, because they considered the loyalty of the soldiers and officers of the Indian Army as the ultimate guarantee of the Raj. The betrayal of one-third of those who had been captured showed that the Indian Army was no longer a force on which they could count in the event of an anti-British revolt.

Between 1942 and 1944, the political situation remained deadlocked: the leaders of the Congress were still in prison and all the contacts between them and the government seemed to have been broken off. The primary difficulty concerned the provinces, which, as provided by the constitution of 1935, enjoyed important prerogatives. After the dismissal of the Congress governments, the centre directly administrated most of the provinces. But the Muslim League could form governments in some of them: in Assam, though a province with a Hindu majority, in August 1942, in Sind in October 1942, in Bengal in March 1943 and lastly in the North-West Frontier Province in May 1943. Of the provinces with a majority of Muslims, only the Punjab escaped the control of the League and continued to be governed by the Unionist Party, a coalition of the powerful Muslim, Hindu and Sikh landowners; this party was, however, weakened in December 1942 by the death of its leader, Sikandar Hayat Khan.

Jinnah took advantage of the years of war to endow the Muslim League with an embryonic organization and a popular base that it had largely lacked until then. This lawyer from Bombay, who had started his political career in the Congress, was a confirmed constitutionalist and wary of the methods of agitation advocated by Gandhi. Increasingly marginalized from 1921 onwards, he had abandoned politics and had settled down as a lawyer in England. He returned to India in 1934 and embarked on a second political career as the representative of the Muslim community. Even though he was highly anglicized and did not manifest very evident religious sentiments – it has often been alleged that he used religion to gratify an unbridled political ambition – he reorganized the moribund Muslim League to turn it into the principal political organization of Indian Muslims. However, on the eve of the war, the League continued to be weak in Bengal and in the Punjab, the two provinces where the majority of Muslims were concentrated. It was influential especially in the United Provinces, where Muslims represented a minority (around 16 per cent of the total population), but where the principal spiritual centres of Indian Islam were to be found and the bulk of the cultured Muslim elite. Jinnah was careful at the time not to air openly separatist views, but accused the Congress of being the representative of Hindu interests. Even when he swayed the League in 1940 into adopting the resolution over Pakistan, it appears that he did not envisage the creation of a separate Muslim state, but wished to convince the British and the Congress to grant the Muslims a place equal to that of the Hindus in an autonomous India.

As for the communists, in exchange for their support for the war effort, they could act in broad daylight for the first time. Thus, they gained a certain influence among workers and intellectuals, in particular in Bengal and in Madras.

In 1944, despite its popularity, the Congress was, therefore, not the only political force in India. It now had to reckon with the Muslim League, and to a lesser extent, with the Communists. But, the Congress leaders, isolated in their jails, did not gauge the significance of the changes underway and especially the magnitude of the gulf that had developed between them and the Muslim population. Only bold initiatives could have broken the deadlock, but nobody seemed resolved to take them.

The first attempts at ending the deadlock (1944–5)

In October 1943, Viceroy Lord Wavell, former commander-in-chief in the Middle East, then in India, succeeded the intransigent Linlithgow. This soldier, little in touch with politics, proved a capable administrator and a man of good will. From the beginning of his mandate, he attempted to make political overtures but came up against the obstinacy of Churchill, who desired to maintain the *status quo* by making the fullest possible use of the divisions among Indians. Six months after his arrival, in a speech pronounced before the Legislative Assembly in February 1944, Wavell seemed to extend a hand to the Congress, but could not announce the liberation of the imprisoned leaders, a precondition indispensable for any serious effort towards discussions. It was only in May that Gandhi was liberated, officially on grounds of ill health.

No sooner did he come out of prison than Gandhi invited Jinnah for negotiations over a plan formulated in March 1943 by the Congress leader from Madras, Rajagopalachari. The latter, convinced that the creation of a Muslim state was inevitable, wanted to negotiate with Jinnah to obtain from him certain concessions, so as to preclude the districts with a majority of non-Muslims in the Punjab and Bengal from being included in this state. The Mahatma therefore made Jinnah an offer: as soon as the war ended, referendums would be organized in these districts, in which the people could choose to be incorporated into either one of the states. This was tantamount to recognizing Pakistan without naming it, which caused apprehension among a number of Congress leaders. Jinnah, on his side, during his address to the council of the League on 30 July 1944, rejected this formula contemptuously: he described it as a 'ridiculous proposal' declaring that it offered only 'a shadow, an empty shell, a Pakistan disfigured, mutilated and moth-eaten'. He agreed to discuss the matter with Gandhi in September, but eighteen days of talks ended in failure. Gandhi was ready to envisage serious concessions to the League, but only *after* the British had granted independence to India, while Jinnah demanded solid guarantees *before* talking of independence. It was clear that the latter counted more on the British, than on the Congress, to grant him these guarantees.

What did Jinnah really want? On this point, opinions diverge even today. According to the most widespread view, he wanted an independent Muslim state, but according to a recent theory,[1] Jinnah in reality had as his objective the union of two sovereign states bound to each other by a defence pact, but he could not openly reveal his true intentions because he believed himself to be in a position of weakness vis-à-vis the Congress, as he did not control the situation in the provinces with a Muslim majority, in particular the Punjab. He therefore pushed up the bidding in the hope of reaching a favourable compromise. Even if we were to suppose such were indeed his intentions, none, neither the British nor the Congress leaders, perceived them clearly. In fact, Jinnah acquired the reputation of a devious negotiator, whom no one trusted, which did not facilitate compromises.

After the failure of the talks between Gandhi and Jinnah, Wavell, conscious that the British could not remain indefinitely in India solely by force, pressed London to seek an agreement in view of the formation of an interim government associating the Congress and the League, but he came up once again against the disapproval of Churchill. In view of the paralysis on the British side, the Congress and the League attempted fresh negotiations. In January 1945, Bhulabhai Desai, head of the Congress group at the Central Legislative Assembly, signed an agreement with his counterpart of the League, Liaqat Ali Khan, providing for the formation of an interim Central government in which the Congress and the League would have equal representation (40 per cent each, the remaining 20 per cent reserved for minorities, Sikhs, Christians, etc.). This government was to function within the framework of the existing constitution, passed in 1935, but the viceroy was to relinquish the use of his discretionary powers. Even though the two negotiators had certainly received the green light from their respective leaders, Gandhi as well as Jinnah became evasive after the signature of the agreement and refused to endorse it in public.

In an effort to accelerate the process, Wavell decided to intervene directly. He attempted to obtains the agreement from London to a plan for the formation of an interim government composed only of Indian members (only defence was to remain a British prerogative) and for the organization of a Constitutional Round Table. But he could not convince London before the allied victory in Europe. Churchill, who was then unable to oppose his initiative, gave the green light to Wavell to form an interim government following the guidelines that he had suggested. As a sign of good will, the imprisoned Congress leaders were released.

On 15 June 1945, at the same time as he announced these liberations, Wavell also invited the Indian leaders to discussions in Simla, the summer capital of India, with regard to the formation of the interim government, an offer that was immediately accepted by the Congress and the League. The conference opened on 25 June and an agreement was easily concluded on the principle of parity between Hindus and Muslims. However, no agreement could be reached on the names of the Muslim members. Jinnah intended to decide on the matter alone, a demand that Wavell, supported by the Congress, rejected. The conference was then adjourned to give time to each party to prepare its list of nominations to the government. But Jinnah, who wanted to be known as the sole spokesperson for the Muslims, became evasive and Wavell had to dissolve the conference. The viceroy has generally been accused of allowing Jinnah to sabotage his efforts by giving him a sort of right of veto in all attempts towards a settlement. But could he have acted otherwise? Had he tried to form a government without the League, he would have run the risk of further fuelling the hostilities between Hindus and Muslims.

The failure of the Simla conference took place after the victory of the Labour Party in the British elections. The change of government in Great Britain was welcomed in India, as a Labour government was thought to be more open than the Conservatives on the Indian problem. However, the Attlee government, which took office on 26 July 1945, showed very great circumspection. In the face of serious internal problems, it opted for a prudent approach, which also suited the Congress, certain that time was playing against Jinnah.

In India, the end of the war with Japan inaugurated an era of tumult. Strikes and protests multiplied. In their effort to restore order, the British announced as early as 21 August that elections were to take place shortly to the Central Legislative Assembly and the Provincial Legislative Assemblies, and on 11 September, in a speech delivered in Parliament, Prime Minister Attlee reiterated the intention of his government to promote the evolution of the Constitution in the direction of the Cripps offer of 1942, in other words, a greater autonomy for India.

However, these promises were not sufficient to satisfy Indian opinion and popular agitations increased at the end of 1945. These protests stemmed from economic difficulties during the immediate post-war period, in particular owing to the vertiginous increase in prices and to the emergence of serious food shortages. However, very quickly, they took on political overtones because of the tactlessness of the English. In the autumn of 1945, the latter decided to bring several hundreds of officers and soldiers of the Indian National Army to justice on charges of treason. The first trial, which took place in the Red Fort in Delhi, docked three officers, a Hindu, a Muslim and a Sikh, which was a manner of causing a rapprochement between these three communities. Nehru and Jinnah, both lawyers, undertook the defence of the accused. All the political parties, including the Muslim League, joined in a wave of mass protests. The movement culminated between 21 and 23 November, during riots in Calcutta in the course of which Muslims and Hindus, students and striking workers, communists and Congress leaders confronted the police and the army.

A fresh confrontation seemed inevitable but, unlike in 1942, neither the British nor the Congress stood to gain by it. The former were too weakened by the war to launch a massive repression and the latter greatly feared possible excesses that the communists might exploit. As early as 1 December, the government announced that it had abandoned some of the legal proceedings against the members of the Indian National Army. The Working Committee of the Congress returned the compliment by condemning the violent protests during its session in December. The moderation of the riposte of the Congress was also because it was at the time in the swing of its electoral campaign.

The 1945–6 elections were above all an occasion for the Muslim League and for Jinnah to prove that they enjoyed the massive support of the Muslim population. The League in effect won the thirty reserved Muslim electoral constituencies in the Central Assembly with 86.6 per cent of votes and obtained in the provinces 442 of the 509 reserved seats. It missed by a small margin majority in the Punjab (it won only 79 seats of the total 175) where the Unionists, led by Khizar Hyat Khan, formed a coalition government with the Congress and the Akalis (the Sikh party). It was nevertheless in the Punjab that it obtained the success that was most significant and important for its future. In the beginning, its chances seemed bleak: its organization was still embryonic and torn by serious factional conflicts, while its Unionist adversaries, closely associated with big landowners, enjoyed the support of the administration and of a smoothly functioning vote-catching system. Nevertheless, they could not counter the propaganda of the League, centred on the theme of 'Islam in danger'. The defection of a certain number of Unionist notables, the espousal of the League by a large number of Muslim students of Lahore inspired by the writings of the poet Iqbal, the inventor of Pakistan, lastly the support of numerous leaders of Sufi brotherhoods (*pir*), whose spiritual influence was great in rural Punjab, were so many factors that led to the very clear victory won by the League in the Muslim constituencies of the province. Its success in these constituencies did not, however, give it an absolute majority of the seats. But, for the first time, the creation of Pakistan, inconceivable without the Punjab, became possible.

As regards the Congress, if it confirmed its overwhelming pre-eminence among the non-Muslim electorate by obtaining 91.3 per cent of the votes and 57 seats to the Central Assembly, its failure in the provinces with a Muslim majority (except in the North-West Frontier Province, where it obtained a slight majority) was fraught with consequences.

The Cabinet Mission Plan and its failure

In the face of mounting danger, the British government was obliged to rise out of its torpor and find a solution. On 22 January 1946, Attlee announced the arrival in India of a Cabinet Mission composed of Secretary of State for India, Pethick-Lawrence, Cripps and Alexander. This was the ultimate attempt at arriving at a settlement.

This initiative marked a watershed in British policy. At that time, the British government still envisaged, in case the Mission should fail, the maintenance of its rule by the use of force for a certain period. But, one month later, under the pressure of the events, it was forced to amend its position. On 4 February, the General Staff intimated that it could not send reinforcements of troops to India. On the 18th, serious mutinies flared up in the Indian Air Force and the Navy. The mutiny of the airmen was easily repressed but in Bombay, the insurgent sailors took control of over twenty vessels and only the threat of air bombardment, coupled with the entreaties of the leaders of the Congress and the League, for once united in the fear of chaos, forced them to surrender. In Karachi, they opened fire with canons on the vessels of the Royal Navy before being brought into submission. It was clear that the British, in the absence of reinforcements, did not have any other choice but to negotiate.

It was in this context that, on 14 March 1946, the Cabinet Mission arrived in India. The following day, Attlee delivered a speech to the House of Commons, in which he promised to grant independence to India as early as possible and underlined that the Muslim minority would not be entitled to right of veto and block any settlement. The British wished to transfer power to a single central government, which would maintain the unity of the army. They feared that the break-up of the Indian army might create a strategic void in the region which would be profitable to Moscow. But their talks with the representatives of the Indian parties led the British delegates to formulate two different proposals. The first, which had been their preference, provided for the maintenance of a united India in the form of a federation where the prerogatives of the central government would be restricted to defence and to foreign relations. The second envisaged the creation of a sovereign Pakistan but which would not embrace the regions with a non-Muslim-majority district of eastern Punjab and western Bengal (even while including the district with a Muslim majority of Sylhet, in Assam). Subsequently, they thought, Pakistan would be led to conclude a defense pact with Hindustan. These two options were submitted to the British government, which, during a historic meeting held on 11 April, expressed its preference for the former, even while envisaging a partition, if it was the only way to avert chaos and massacres.

Having received the green light from London, the Mission made more detailed proposals. Plan A provided for a three-tier federal system: a union at the highest level, limited to defence and to foreign affairs, 'sections', sort of sub-federations, forming an intermediate level between the centre and the provinces, and lastly the provinces and the princely states or groups of states that would have the possibility of joining with either one of the sub-entities. This complicated scheme, which combined the maintenance of the unity of India with the constitution of provinces enjoying a very large autonomy, offered the advantage of appeasing Muslim anxieties. Plan B put forward the principle of a division into two sovereign states, Hindustan and Pakistan (set apart from the regions with a non-Muslim majority), with the princely states opting for either one or the other. The Mission did everything possible for the Congress and the League to accept Plan A. But both refused. Even though the plan seemed largely to meet the aspirations of Jinnah, the latter did not accept it. This left the ball in the Congress's court, who found that the plan made too many concessions to the provinces.

In an effort to arrive at a final consensus, a tripartite conference between the delegates and the representatives of the Congress and the League met in Simla on 5 May 1946. The discussions floundered over the question of grouping into sections: was it mandatory or not? The Congress declared its opposition to it, whereas the League considered it indispensable: Jinnah did not sufficiently control the Muslim provinces to be sure that they would voluntarily join the sub-federations. There was also disagreement on the nature and the power of the Constituent Assembly. The Mission then announced that it would communicate its own plan in the form of a statement on 16 May.

The British pursued the talks until this date. It seems that their different interlocutors were not presented with the same proposals. To the representatives of the League, Pethick-Lawrence and Cripps promised that the grouping of provinces in the sub-federations would be obligatory, whereas Wavell, at the behest of Pethick-Lawrence, adopted a more evasive stance on this point with Gandhi, even while confirming the principle of the sovereignty of the Constituent Assembly.

Thus arose a serious misunderstanding: the League and the Congress accepted the plan, but each one interpreted it in its own way. The League was the first to make known its acceptance on 16 June, but the two parties could not come to an agreement on the composition of the interim government that would be in force during the transition period. Jinnah, believing that he had received assurances from the British, demanded absolute parity between the Congress and the League with a ratio of 5–5–2 (five members of the League, five member of the Congress, two representatives of other communities), which the Congress refused. On 13 June, Nehru, on behalf of the Congress, made proposals based on the ratio of 7–4–4 (seven members of the Congress, four members of the League, four representatives of other communities) and on 16 June the Mission proposed a ratio of 6–5–3 (six members of the Congress, five members of the League, three members of other communities). The Working Committee of the Congress then announced its refusal to take part in the interim government, but accepted the Mission's plan while maintaining reservations on certain points, in particular on the question of sub-federations. The British government then decided in favour of 6–5–3, which Jinnah regarded as a capitulation to the Congress.

Jinnah was up against the wall: his strategy, founded on the idea that the British would act as arbitrators in his favour and to the detriment of the Congress, had proved to be erroneous. In sheer desperation, he decided to take a gamble: on 29 July, he made the League adopt a resolution rejecting the statement of 16 May and called the Muslims of the entire country to a day of protest (Direct Action Day) on 16 August. His resort to non-constitutional methods appeared as a surprising volte-face. In fact, Jinnah wanted to show to the Congress that he could also mobilize the masses. But he did have any experience in launching this kind of movement and it would not be long before his gamble turned into tragedy.

The ultimate attempt of the British to reach an agreement between the League and the Congress within the framework of a confederal system had failed. It was time for the daggers to be drawn.

The Great Calcutta Killing and its consequences (August 1946–March 1947)

On 6 August, Viceroy Wavell invited Nehru to submit to him his proposals in view of the formation of an interim government, and the Working Committee of the Congress therefore authorized Nehru to seek an agreement with the League. During this time, preparations for the day of protest were in full swing all over India.

When the dreaded day arrived, India remained calm on the whole. The Congress had given instructions not to retaliate and there were protests, but very few serious incidents, except in Calcutta where a massive massacre was unleashed.

Muslim groups launched attacks against Hindus, who soon retaliated: *goondas* (louts) of both the communities waged a war, which claimed ten thousand lives (of which the majority were Muslims). In these tragic events, the chief minister of Bengal, Suhrawardy, member of the League but also often opposed to Jinnah, played an essential role by paralysing the action of the police and by openly inciting

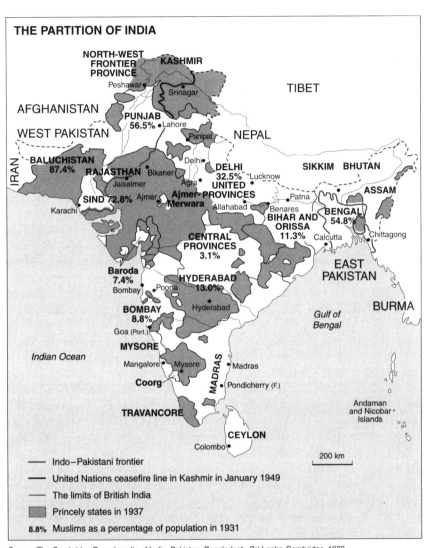

THE PARTITION OF INDIA

NORTH-WEST FRONTIER PROVINCE
KASHMIR
Peshawar
Srinagar
TIBET
AFGHANISTAN
PUNJAB
56.5%
Lahore
WEST PAKISTAN
Panipat
NEPAL
IRAN
BALUCHISTAN
87.4%
RAJASTHAN
Bikaner
Delhi
DELHI
32.5%
Lucknow
SIKKIM
BHUTAN
Jaisalmer
Agra
UNITED
ASSAM
SIND 72.8%
Ajmer
Ajmer-
Merwara
PROVINCES
Patna
Karachi
Allahabad
Benares
BENGAL
54.8%
BIHAR AND
ORISSA
11.3%
Calcutta
Chittagong
CENTRAL
PROVINCES
3.1%
EAST
PAKISTAN
Baroda
7.4%
Bombay
Poona
HYDERABAD
13.0%
BURMA
BOMBAY
8.8%
Hyderabad
Gulf of
Bengal
Goa (Port.)
MYSORE
Indian Ocean
Mangalore
Mysore
Madras
MADRAS
Coorg
Pondicherry (F.)
Andaman
and Nicobar
Islands
TRAVANCORE
CEYLON
Colombo
200 km

— Indo–Pakistani frontier

— United Nations ceasefire line in Kashmir in January 1949

— The limits of British India

Princely states in 1937

8.8% Muslims as a percentage of population in 1931

Source: *The Cambridge Encyclopedia of India, Pakistan, Bangladesh, Sri Lanka.* Cambridge. 1989.

Muslims towards violence during a public meeting. Governor Burrows also played a discreditable role, waiting for more than twenty-four hours before ordering the intervention of the army when the police were overwhelmed. It is certain that Jinnah was surprised by the magnitude of the turmoil in Calcutta. By opening a Pandora's box, he had inadvertently revealed the limits of his control over his party, since Suhrawardy had played his own game. Jinnah was reduced to a strategy of attrition.

This explains the apparently surprising decision of the League to join the interim government that Nehru formed on 2 September. On 13 October, the League designated its representatives, among whom featured an untouchable Hindu, supposed to compensate for the presence of a Muslim among the Congress ministers. The League, by entering the government, wanted above all to prevent the Congress from taking control of the administration. However, the result was an almost complete paralysis of the executive.

This paralysis came to light on 10 October, when clashes between religious communities broke out in several regions. In eastern Bengal, in the districts of Noakhali and Tippera, Muslim groups attacked the Hindu population and there were instances of rape and forced conversions to Islam. As soon as the news spread to neighbouring Bihar, Muslims were in turn attacked; in a space of a few months, it is estimated that twenty thousand of them were massacred. Nehru had to threaten to call the air force against the rioters before a precarious normality returned to Bihar.

India then entered a decisive phase. On 6 December, the British government clarified the plan of the Cabinet Mission on an essential point: the groupings within the sub-federations would be decided by simple majority, which would make them obligatory for all intents and purposes. It left the door open for Pakistan. Meanwhile the tension did not stop increasing. Confrontations between the communities multiplied, and the state machinery was collapsing. The administration, in particular the British members of the Indian Civil Service, was demoralized. The police, more and more eaten away by communalism, were incapable of maintaining even a semblance of order. In the face of these dangers, Wavell asked the government in London to formulate a plan for the gradual withdrawal of the British from India, but the government turned a deaf ear. On 8 January, London decided to fix a deadline for the transfer of power to an Indian authority.

At this time, the Congress still believed it possible to avoid the partition. Two days earlier, it had accepted the British statement of 6 December, in the hope of obtaining the participation of the League in the Constituent Assembly, which had met on 9 December without the participation of the representatives of the Muslim organization. However, on 31 January the Working Committee of the League reiterated its refusal to sit in the Constituent Assembly. The League was now striving to consolidate its control on the provinces with Muslim majorities. It was already in power in Sind and in Bengal, but in the Punjab, the fragile government headed by Khizar still impeded its ambitions. On 20 February 1947, the British government, convinced that only the announcement of a precise date for the British withdrawal would bring the various parties to an agreement, proclaimed that Great Britain would transfer power to an Indian authority at the latest by 30 June 1948. Attlee added that in case a constitution was not adopted before this date, the government would make arrangements, remaining deliberately vague on this point. At the same time, he announced the replacement of Wavell by Mountbatten.

But the announcement did not produce the anticipated effect. The Muslim League was not more conciliatory and intensified its protest movement in the Punjab where the Khizar government resigned on 2 March. Mountbatten arrived in an India on the verge of chaos. He had been charged with the mission of carrying out the liquidation of the Raj as early as possible and at the least cost for the British.

'Divide and Quit': *the last days of the British Raj (March–August 1947)*

Lord Mountbatten, the last viceroy of India, was a legendary character. He had commanded the allied forces in Southeast Asia before being entrusted with the delicate task of putting an end to two centuries of British presence in India. He had been chosen because he had the reputation of being a 'political' soldier and because his membership of the royal family – he was a cousin of the King – was expected to enable him convince the Indian princes to renounce their privileged relationship with the Crown. London invested him with extraordinary powers so that he could take decisions very rapidly. Mountbatten can be reproached for having reacted hastily and for not having done everything he could have to avert a bloody partition. He was not capable of maintaining the impartiality necessary for the accomplishment of his mission either. If he established excellent relations with the leaders of the Congress, in particular with Nehru (his wife, Lady Edwina, being very close to the Congress leader), he could not forge relations of confidence with Jinnah, a man who, it might be added, had a difficult character.

Mountbatten was convinced by mid-April that partition was inevitable. Unrest was spreading to the Punjab. Even as negotiations were underway at Lahore between the different political parties for the formation of a new provincial government, Muslims attacked the Hindu and Sikh populations of several districts of western Punjab, who had to be partly evacuated, as the authorities were incapable of ensuring their security. In May, Hindus and Sikhs in their turn attacked Muslims in eastern Punjab. The Punjab, the richest province of India, was plunged into a bloody chaos.

Mountbatten proposed a first plan of partition, which offered the provinces and the princely states the choice between India, Pakistan and independence. Nehru rejected it without any hesitation because he believed that this was an open door to the balkanization of the region. Mountbatten then proposed the plan formulated by an Indian high official VP Menon, which provided for the transfer of power to two independent dominions, India and Pakistan. There was still the question of the future of the non-Muslims regions of the Punjab (where Hindus accounted for 33 per cent and Sikhs 11 per cent of the total population, with a clear majority in the districts of the eastern part) and of Bengal (where the Hindus formed a distinct majority in Calcutta and in the districts of the West and a minority representing 25 per cent of the population in the districts of the East), as well as that of the North-

West Frontier Province. By 7 March, the Working Committee of the Congress had demanded the partition of the Punjab and Bengal. Mountbatten had to acquiesce in exchange for the acceptance by the Congress of the partition of India. It was decided to hold a referendum in the North-West Frontier Province which had a majority Muslim population (90 per cent) but also a Congress government hostile to the League.

This plan was accepted on 2 June 1947 by the leaders of the Congress, of the League and the Sikhs, and was announced publicly the next day while Mountbatten fixed 15 August as the date for the effective transfer of power to the two new dominions. It served as the basis for the India Independence Act voted by the British Parliament on 18 July. In Bengal and in the Punjab, while the Muslim members of the Legislative Assembly voted in favour of accession to Pakistan, the representatives of the regions with a non-Muslim majority voted for a separation from the rest of the Province and the two new provinces of eastern Punjab and of western Bengal joined the Indian Union (the official name for India). A commission presided by the British Judge Radcliffe undertook the task of accurately delineating the frontier between the two new states, which posed a problem in the Punjab, owing to the mesh of the communities, but its final decision (the Radcliffe Award) was announced publicly only on 17 August, when the situation had reached a point of no return. A Muslim majority district in Assam, Sylhet, joined Pakistan, along with eastern Bengal. In Sind, the Provincial Legislative Assembly voted for joining Pakistan, despite the protestation of the representatives of the Hindu minority (25 per cent of the population). In the North-West Frontier Province, the referendum resulted in a very narrow majority in favour of unification with Pakistan.

There remained the problem of the 562 princely states, of which 140 enjoyed real powers. Most of them, despite the reticence of the princes, joined India. They signed a treaty, an instrument of accession, by which they surrendered all powers to the Union with respect to defence, foreign affairs and communications. In the other domains, the princes retained their prerogatives. On 15 August only three states adjoining India, Junagadh (whose ruler chose Pakistan despite geographic realities), Hyderabad and Kashmir had not signed any treaty. They would subsequently be integrated into the Indian Union under difficult conditions. A few states, the most important among which was Bahawalpur in the confines of the Punjab and of Sind, joined Pakistan.

On 14 and 15 August, Pakistan and India became independent dominions, members of the British Commonwealth. For India, dominion status was temporary; it was to cease as soon as the Constituent Assembly had adopted a constitution, which happened on 26 January 1950. India then became a republic. For the time being, the last viceroy, Lord Mountbatten, remained in India as governor-general, henceforth a decorative post. In Pakistan, Jinnah became governor-general.

The British Indian Empire had seen its last day: ninety years after the proclamation of Queen Victoria as the Empress of India, the Union Jack was lowered for the last time. On either side of the new frontier (the exact contours of which would be only known two days later), people celebrated liberty regained. In Delhi, Nehru hailed independence in a lyrical speech that remains one of the most eloquent pieces composed in the language of Shakespeare. In Karachi, Jinnah, again in

English, was more sober. Did these speeches delivered in the language of the colonizer imply a sort of homage to Britain? They rather revealed that the anglicized elite occupied an important place in the new states and that British political culture had become acclimatized to this part of the world, at least superficially. There were even scenes of fraternization between Hindus and Muslims. But the heart was not in it. In each of the new dominions, the religious minorities knew that their destiny depended on the good will of the majority. Only the civil servants, soldiers and policemen could opt for either of the two states; the others could only hope that they would be left in peace. These hopes were to be cruelly shattered.

Why partition?

The Indian nationalist movement, born between 1870 and 1890, had set total independence as its objective in 1929, even though there was no unanimity on this point (certain moderate nationalists were willing to be content with dominion status); none at the time envisaged the division of India into two states. The first to speak of a separate homeland for the Muslims was the poet Iqbal in 1930. Ten years later, the Muslim League had rallied to the idea of a Pakistan that had hitherto been a mere slogan. At this time, the League represented only a fraction of the Indian Muslim elite, and its influence on the Muslim masses was very limited. But, in 1945, by voting massively for the League, Muslim voters (that is only a part of the Muslim population, as universal franchise had not yet come into existence) overwhelmingly voted in favour of Pakistan. How did this unitary conception of nationalism transform into a theory of 'two nations' and lead to a territorial partition? And before that, was the British policy of 'divide and rule' responsible for partition?

This viewpoint is often aired in India even to this day. In support of this theory, its advocates cite the institution of separate electorates for Muslims in the wake of the Morley-Minto reforms of 1909, and the de facto alliance between the League and the government against the Congress during the Second World War. It is unquestionable that, in the face of the rise of Indian nationalism from the beginning of the twentieth century, the British relied primarily on a fraction of the Muslim elite and on the princes, but for all this, they did not seek a division into two states, as they feared that it might favour Soviet enterprises in the region.

Did religious division necessarily have to lead to territorial partition? It is certain that the Indian Muslim elite had never come to terms with the loss of the political supremacy that it had exercised over a large part of the subcontinent from the close of the twelfth century to the beginning of the eighteenth century. For many Muslims, subjection to the hegemony of Hindu politicians was hard to accept on the grounds of mere electoral arithmetic But certain geographic and demographic realities, often forgotten, also offer an explanation for the territorial division of India. The Muslim separatist movement developed above all in regions where Muslims formed a minority, in particular in the United Provinces, the former heart of the Mogul Empire, home to a highly urbanized Muslim elite. On the other hand, in regions where Muslims were a majority, particularly in the Punjab, separatist ideas were much slower to take hold.

We must emphasize here the regional dimension of separatist dynamics. Sind, western Punjab and eastern Bengal, the three regions that formed the core of the Pakistani State from 1947 to 1971, were not distinct from the rest of India solely by the fact that their population was of Muslim majority. Sind, conquered by the Arabs in the eighth century and very open to Islamic influences and march of the Mogul Empire, had passed under the Afghan sphere of influence in the eighteenth century, and had had, before its annexation by the British in 1843, only minimal relations with the rest of India (except with neighbouring Punjab). Incorporated into the Bombay Presidency, the Sindhis strove to escape the domination of the metropolis of West India and hailed the transformation of Sind into a separate province in 1936 as a liberation, even though the significant Hindu minority of the province showed more reserve. The personality of the Punjab was even more affirmed: already discernable during the medieval age, it was reinforced under Sikh rule. The last important native state to be annexed by the British, the Punjab was subject to a particular form of colonial regime, which was reflected in the close alliance of the colonial state with landowners and the dominant farmers of the very dynamic Jat caste. This specificity was manifested on the political front in the existence of a strong regional party, the Unionist Party, which prevented the Congress from establishing itself in the villages. In 1945, rural Punjab passed directly from Unionist rule to that of the League. The strength of the Punjabi regional sentiment was also manifest among the Sikhs, some of whom, in 1947, accepted the incorporation of the Punjab into India as a lesser evil, but deplored the division of the province, which cut them off from some of their holy places.

The question of eastern Bengal is complex: this area of India, a delta region that came to be inhabited by man relatively recently, and whose Islamization presents specific traits, had a Muslim majority, but a fraction of landowners and the majority of traders were Hindus. In 1947, the Muslims of this region vacillated between the formation of a united and independent Bengal and an incorporation into a Pakistan that was hardly to offer any advantages. As early as the beginning of the 1950s, they began striving to break free from the yoke of Pakistan, which they accomplished in 1971 with the creation of Bangladesh. For all this, they would not at the time seek a reunification with their compatriots of western Bengal, so great was their mistrust of Hindus and their fear of the preponderance of Calcutta over the entire Bengali zone.

Rather than a contention between Hindus and Muslims all across India, it was therefore the relations between the two communities in the regions that formed Pakistan that explain the partition. In these regions, there was an economic and social conflict between the Hindu elites who associated wealth from both real estate and personal properties and the Muslim elites who drew from the soil almost all their resources. The former monopolized credit, which enabled them to block the progress of their Muslim rivals. The Hindu-Muslim conflict was, therefore, not fundamentally a class struggle between a Muslim peasantry and Hindu landowners and moneylenders (even if such conflicts existed locally), but rather a conflict between elites. It was, however, true that the Muslim elite could mobilize the masses considerably better than the Hindu elite. The conflict was therefore resolved once and for all in favour of the former, by the physical expulsion of the Hindu elite.

The movement in favour of Pakistan fundamentally represented a circumstantial coalition between regionalisms, which, in the political context, assumed anti-Hindu undertones and a pan-Indian Muslim political class without any solid social base, as it came from regions where Muslims were a minority. Jinnah, for example, belonged to a small Shiite community in Bombay, most of whose members were traders. The rapid disintegration of the Muslim League in Pakistan after the death of Jinnah shows the fragility of this coalition. But had its moment in 1947.

Lastly, this coalition owes its success to the weaknesses and shortcomings of the Indian nationalist movement. Though the Congress had proclaimed its attachment to a secular conception of politics, the Muslims increasingly viewed it as a Hindu party. Nehru's attempt to play the Muslim masses against the elites in 1936 and 1937 was fruitless. Neither the masses not the elites could identify themselves with the Congress. From the time when the British determined to leave India and the Congress ready to assume the mantle of seccession, pride and fear incited the Muslims to seek the security of a separate state. This security proved to be largely illusory as a third of Muslims, despite massive population movements, stayed back in India where they still form a very vulnerable minority. Partition did not resolve in any way the problem of the relations between the religious communities in the subcontinent.

For all this, was there an alternative? Given the weakness of the Congress in the three regions with a Muslim majority, the partition could have been averted only if the nationalist party had accepted sharing its power with the Muslim League in the central government and affording very great autonomy to the provinces with Muslim majority within the framework of a very flexible federation.

Why did the Congress give in to a partition that ran counter to all its principles rather than envisaging such concessions, which were also largely incompatible with its conception of the future of India? Some have interpreted its attitude as a manifestation of its political realism, but should this be the case, it would have rallied as early as 1944 to Rajagopalachari's plan, which conceded that the creation of Pakistan was inevitable and strived merely to limit the cost thereof.

For almost another three years, the Congress continued to deny representation to the League, even when the results of the election of 1945 to 1946 proved the contrary. It ignored the warnings of its own leader, Maulana Abul Kalam Azad, who, in 1945, reiterated that the Muslims harboured fears concerning their future in an India governed by the Congress, and that the only way to appease these fears was to accept the principle of parity between Hindus and Muslims in the central government. The Congress rejected the theory of two nations that the League advocated, all the more as this theory fuelled the arguments of Hindu extremists, eager as they were to identify a 'Hindu nation' with the 'Indian nation'. However, its position proved to be disastrous on the political front. The Muslim masses that the nationalists had never mobilized in the struggle against the British found themselves propelled into action, but against the Congress, for Pakistan.

The intransigence of the Congress towards the League had its roots also in a certain conception of the state. In this respect, the divorce between Gandhi and his two main lieutenants, Nehru and Patel, was becoming increasingly obvious. Abandoning the vision of Gandhi, who envisaged independent India as a federation of village communities, the Congress leaders declared themselves in favour of the construction of a strong centralized state. They sought a compromise with the Indian high officials of the Indian Civil Service (which, since 1939, had begun a rapid process of Indianization) and favoured the continuity of the state. In this perspective, they could not agree to relinquish important powers (with regard to finances or communications) to provinces or groups of provinces, as demanded by the Muslim League. Nehru and Patel preferred an amputated India, but with a strong central power, to a confederacy with a weak central government.

Under these circumstances, it is clear that there was no viable alternative to partition. On the other hand, the human cost of the operation could have been markedly less if each of the three players, the British government, the Congress and the League, had gauged the gravity of the impending perils. But this was not the case: while London sought above all to extricate itself from the Indian quagmire, Jinnah proved to be incapable of controlling the passions that he had unleashed, and Nehru could not overcome the profound repulsion that the League and its leaders inspired in him. Only Gandhi proved equal to the situation, but he was, despite his immense prestige, only one man. What is more, he was to pay with his life for his refusal to passively accept the tragedy that unfolded in 1947 and 1948.

The legacy of Partition: the establishment of the new States

The solution hastily elaborated by Mountbatten in 1947 soon revealed its limitations. The announcement on 17 August of the definitve boundaries of the frontier (Radcliffe Award) only aggravated matters in a Punjab already given to fire and the sword, while Kashmir became the scene of an armed conflict between the two new dominions.

Massacres in the Punjab

In mid-August, the situation in a number of districts in the Punjab was extremely tense. At Lahore in particular, there were pitched battles between communities, and Hindus and Sikhs were driven out of the capital of the Punjab, with heavy human losses. On either side of the frontier, anarchy reigned. The Radcliffe Award sparked off the indignation of the Sikhs, as Pakistan had been allotted territories where a number of holy places were located and where a prosperous Sikh peasantry lived (the Canal Colonies in particular, the richest agricultural region of the provinces, were home to an important Sikh minority). The turmoil spread like wildfire, particularly stirring up the rivalry between Muslims and Sikhs. Both these communities had a solid military organization, formed especially of a number of retired members of the army, and increasingly of deserters. In western Punjab, the Sikhs were the primary target of the attacks launched by Muslim bands, often acting in collusion with the authorities and the police, against villages and against the convoys of refugees who were trying to reach India. In all, from March to December 1947, four million Hindu and Sikh refugees of western Punjab and from the North-West Frontier Province (where the Hindu minority accounted for 10 per cent of the population) left for India, but many of them never reached their destination.

In the beginning, the convoys were organized spontaneously: caravans of refugees walked across western Punjab in the hope of arriving at the Indian frontier. Without any protection from the army, they often fell victim to bloody ambushes. In the face of the magnitude of the exodus, the governments were forced to intervene. The Indian government created a mission, which, in liaison with the Pakistani authorities, was to ensure a more orderly evacuation. Trains and trucks were placed at the disposal of the refugees, as well as military escorts. However, the local authorities in western Punjab extended little cooperation, and, in the face of the growing hostility of the people, the escorts could not always succeed in protecting the refugees: a number of them were massacred before they reached the frontier. Abductions and rapes were also perpetrated on a large scale. The same situation was observed on the other side of the frontier: Muslim refugees of eastern Punjab and Delhi who were trying to reach Pakistan were attacked by Sikh bands operating from the princely states of Patiala and Kapurthala. Massacres and rapes of the same magnitude as in western Punjab were committed. In the princely state of Patiala, whose maharajah was a Sikh, a large part of the Muslim population (one-third of the total population of the state) was massacred, the survivors forced to flee. On either side, the initiative for these massacres came often from freshly arrived refugees who were driven by the desire for vengeance against the coreligionists of those who had attacked them. Thus began an infernal cycle of retaliation and counter-retaliation.

The second half of the year 1947 saw the unleashing in the Punjab of a wave of violence and pillage that the authorities on both the sides of the frontier were largely powerless to control. The disorganization of the police, the inefficiency of the Punjab Boundary Force, a special unit hastily created and soon dissolved, obliged the new states to solicit the help of the army, which, in the process of being reorganized, did not always act with the necessary effectiveness. It was only at the end of the year 1947 that a semblance of order was restored in the Punjab and that the administration and the police of the two dominions began to function normally. The province had been the scene of an exchange of population unprecedented in human history: more than eight million people had been 'displaced'. There were practically no Hindus or Sikhs in western Punjab and in the North-West Frontier Province, and very few Muslims in eastern Punjab.

It is impossible to quantify with accuracy the massacres perpetrated. The exodus claimed at least 180,000 lives in 1947 and 1948. There was also a very large number of wounded, not to mention the terrible psychological trauma inflicted on the millions of human beings who witnessed these massacres. The tragedy poisoned relations between the two dominions for a long time, each accusing the other of not having protected the refugees. A number of women were also abducted, and few of them were restored to their families. Furthermore, the refugees had been forced to leave behind their houses, fields and movable property. The problem of compensation put a further strain on Indo-Pakistani relations for a long time. On either side of the frontier, millions of people, having lost all their possessions, crowded into refugee camps where living conditions were precarious. They sometimes had to stay in camps for several years. Their rehabilitation would cost both the young nations considerable effort and weigh on their meagre resources.

Transfers of population in the other regions

Apart from the transfer of population in the Punjab, other movements of lesser magnitude were observed. Between 1947 and 1949, the great majority of the Hindus of Sind, that is about one million people, left the province though there had been no massacres comparable to those committed in the Punjab. In Sind, pillage was systematic but attacks on persons were rare. The Hindu population of the province, which included a minority of very affluent merchants and a majority of small shopkeepers and tenants, took fright and opted for an exodus towards Gujarat, Bombay and Rajasthan.

At the same time, a million and a half Muslims left North India for Pakistan. The majority were from Bihar and the United Provinces. The Muslims of Bihar, the bulk of whom were villagers, fled in fear of fresh massacres, while those of the United Provinces belonged primarily to an urban elite and went to Pakistan above all on the grounds of ideological conviction. They were the 'Zionists' of the movement, of which the United Provinces had been the cradle. These emigrants (muhajirs), who spoke Urdu, maintained an identity distinct from that of the Muslim Punjabis and Sindhis. This was, and continues to be, a source of grave tension in Pakistan.

Hindus from eastern Bengal settled down in western Bengal, but in smaller numbers. From 1947 to 1949, about one million of them emigrated, driven less by massacres as by latent hostility. The movement gained strength in 1950, as in the course of this single year, one million refugees established themselves in western Bengal; from 1950 to 1971, the rate of emigration stabilized at around two hundred thousand per year. The concentration of refugees in Calcutta and its immediate environs aggravated the economic situation of the metropolis of Eastern India. There was also an inverse, but quite limited, movement of Muslims from western Bengal towards eastern Pakistan.

Indian and Pakistani censuses of 1951 record more than seven million departures from India to Pakistan, from 1947 to 1950, and an equal number from Pakistan to India, in other words a total of more than fourteen million 'displaced persons'.

The question of the princely states: the crises in Kashmir and Hyderabad

On 15 August 1947, only two princely states, Kashmir and Hyderabad, had refused to opt for either one of the dominions. A third state, Junagadh, whose ruler was Muslim, but the majority of whose population was Hindu, had opted for Pakistan, though the state did not have a common border with this country and was landlocked within Indian territory. In the wake of a popular uprising supported by the Indian authorities, the state was integrated into India.

On the other hand, India and Pakistan entered into open conflict over Kashmir. Partition created a thorny situation for the maharajah of Kashmir as the principal access to the Kashmir Valley passed through western Punjab, which had become Pakistani, while its population, including the majority of Muslims, were rather hostile to Pakistan. But he hesitated to choose India out of fear of economic reprisals from Pakistan.

Notwithstanding the conclusion of a standstill agreement between Kashmir and Pakistan, high tension reigned on the frontier of the two states. On 22 October 1947, a motorized column of about five thousand men penetrated Kashmir from the North-West Frontier Province and overpowered the meagre forces of the princely state. A government of free Kashmir (Azad Kashmir) was proclaimed in the 'liberated' territory. Two days later, the column arrived at the gates of Srinagar. The maharajah then appealed for help from the government of India, which agreed to intervene on the condition that the maharajah signed an instrument of accession to India. On the request of Mountbatten, the agreement stipulated that the integration of Kashmir into India would become effective only after a referendum. On the 27 October, an airborne operation brought an Indian battalion to Srinagar. It launched a first indecisive battle. For a few days, the Pakistani government, which India strongly suspected of having instigated and organized the entire operation, did not adopt any official position, but on 30 October, it condemned the Indian military operation and declared that it did not recognize the agreement between Kashmir and India.

The negotiations between Mountbatten and Jinnah did not lead to any agreement between the two states. On 8 November, thanks to the arrival of reinforcements, the Indians recaptured Baramulla, a strategic position that commanded the route to Srinagar. Then a war of attrition broke out in the course of which Indian and Pakistani forces confronted each other directly. The situation did not lack spice, as the commanders-in-chief of both the armies were British officers directly subordinate to the supreme commander, General Auchinleck, in charge, for a temporary period, of carrying out the division of the former Indian Army into an Indian army and a Pakistani army. At the close of the year 1947, the two governments brought the Kashmir affair before the United Nations and it was under the aegis of UNO that a ceasefire was concluded, which came into force on 1 January 1949.

The confrontation came to a close rather to the advantage of India, which retained the largest part of Jammu and the Kashmir Valley, as well as a part of Ladakh, but lost Gilgit. Kashmir was therefore divided in two: one part incorporated into India, an accession that was proclaimed definitively in 1957 without a referendum, as the Indian authorities maintained that the Pakistani occupation of a part of the territory prevented the organization thereof; and Azad Kashmir, officially independent, but in reality integrated into Pakistan. The ceasefire did not put an end to the contention between the two states. In the eyes of New Delhi, the whole of Kashmir has been an integral part of the Indian Union since 1957 and Azad Kashmir was a fiction masking the illegal occupation of an Indian territory by Pakistan. For Islamabad, the Kashmir issue must be resolved through a referendum organized under the aegis of the United Nations, and the accession of one part of the territory into India is by law null and void. In its view, Azad Kashmir is a provisional structure that would be dissolved as soon as the referendum is held.

Thus Kashmir, which was the scene of renewed combat during the Indo-Pakistani Wars of 1965 and 1971, remains a bone of contention between the two countries. The most burning heritage of partition, it risks provoking a new conflict at any time.

In comparison with the Kashmir crisis, the question of Hyderabad appears relatively minor. Although this state was landlocked within Indian territory, its ruler, the *nizam*, refused to rejoin India in 1947. He obtained respite in the form of a standstill agreement for a period of one year. But, instead of using this interval to undertake political reforms in favour of the establishment of a representative regime, he allowed a Muslim militia, the *razakars* (volunteers) to terrorize the Hindu population. Concerned about the development of a rural communist guerrilla army in the Telangana region, on the border between the state of Hyderabad and the Madras province, the Indian government launched a military operation on 15th September 1948. On the 17th, the army of Hyderabad capitulated and the next day the Indian army occupied the capital. This brief campaign left 800 dead, almost entirely on the Hyderabad side. The occupation of the princely state enabled the army to defeat the communist guerrilla army, which surrendered its arms in 1951. With the incorporation of Hyderabad into India the first phase in the process of political reorganization in the wake of the end of the British Empire in India came to a close.

The beginnings of India and Pakistan

The beginnings of both the states were fraught with difficulties. Hardly had a precarious normality been restored in the Punjab that occurred, one after another, the death of Gandhi, assassinated on 30 January 1948 by a Hindu extremist, and that of Jinnah, who succumbed to an illness. Despite the emotion that it aroused and the indignation that it fuelled in India against Hindu extremist movements, Gandhi's death did not produce any serious political consequences, because the Mahatma had retired from active politics. Nehru and Patel governed India competently with the support of the Indian Civil Service, renamed the Indian Administrative Service. The turmoil of the partition had affected only a small region and did not have any durable repercussions on the functioning of the country, where the economic situation gradually recovered.

The two principal leaders of independent India were different from each other in many respects, but they knew how to work together. Nehru, who hailed from a Brahmin family, originally from Kashmir but settled since the eighteenth century in Allahabad, in the United Provinces, was born to rule: his father, Motilal, had been one of the key leaders of the Congress in the 1920s. He had a very privileged childhood and pursued his studies in Cambridge. Very anglicized, much more comfortable with English than with Hindi, he was none the less radical in his political viewpoints. He flirted for a time with the communists, but moved away from them to adopt a moderate leftist position, close to that of the Fabian socialists in England. A democrat and a liberal, he was sensitive to the adulation of the masses and came to exercise a very personal power in India, especially after the death, in 1950, of his only serious political rival, Vallabhabhai Patel.

Patel, who came from the peasant caste of the Patidars in Gujarat that formed a sort of rural elite, initially practised as an advocate before making a fray into politics in Ahmadabad, the big city of Gujarat. This inveterate Gandhian rose into prominence all across the country through the campaign that he organised in Bardoli in 1928. He then remained in the shadow of the Mahatma, but succeeded in creating a political base for himself, thanks in particular to his excellent contacts with business circles. His deep-rooted conservatism made him the ideal counterbalance for a Nehru, whose views occasionally frightened some. The two men shared the ideal of a centralized state, and it was indeed Patel who ensured, with the help of a high official, VP Menon, the effective integration of the princely states into India.

Between 1947 and 1950, India, where Mountbatten was replaced as governor-general in June 1948 by Rajagopalachari, was endowed with a democratic constitution. The text, in the elaboration of which the untouchable leader BR Ambedkar played a vital role, represented an original synthesis of the British and American constitutions. The presidency and the federal system drew directly from the American model, but the preponderance of the prime minister and the Parliament, which soon became entrenched in practice, reveal the force of the tradition of Westminster. Another important feature was the proclaimed secularism of the state. On 26 January 1950, snipping the last link with the British Crown, India became a republic and entered the era of five-year plans. A plan for economic development was in effect launched that year: the objectives that it set for itself were still quite modest.

The beginnings of Pakistan were more chaotic. The disappearance of the *Qaid-i- Azam* (the 'Great leader', Jinnah's official name) considerably weakened the Muslim League, which was torn apart by internecine conflicts. The assassination of the prime minister Liaqat Ali Khan, in 1951, aggravated the crisis in the political system and paved the way for the military dictatorship which seized power in 1958. The elaboration of a constitution was long-drawn-out, because of the intervention of theologians in the political debate; it was only in 1956 that Pakistan was proclaimed an Islamic republic, which nevertheless did not satisfy the fundamentalists. On the economic front, the country had to brave numerous difficulties: given its population and gross product, the burden of refugees was much harder for it to bear than for India, as western Punjab had borne the brunt of the turbulence of the partition. The massive departure of Hindus and Sikhs, attended by the outflow of capital, deprived the new state of a part of the qualified personnel required for the functioning of the economy; the arrival of Muslim businessmen from Bombay or Calcutta only partially compensated these departures. Furthermore, the regions that formed the new state, in particular eastern Bengal, had under-developed transport infrastructures. The country therefore had to start from scratch to build a modern state. However, Pakistan had the advantage of possessing the greatest part of the Punjab, the granary of the subcontinent. But its separation into two entities by 1,700 kilometres of Indian territory cast a doubt on its long-term viability. Towards 1950, the situation seemed, despite everything, on the way towards improvement.

PART SIX

ON THE MARGINS OF
THE EMPIRE

This book closes with two chapters that retrospectively throw light on the history of modern India.

Chapter 26 traces the evolution of the French trading posts in India in the nineteenth and twentieth centuries. Scattered on the flanks of India, the French establishments, notwithstanding their Lilliputian sizes, were the thorn in the paw of the British lion. In the first half of the nineteenth century, the authorities of Madras and Calcutta greatly feared a resurgence of French influence in India spreading out from these few enclaves; they were apprehensive about the possibility of revolutionary contagion when the Third Republic introduced universal suffrage and representative institutions in these regions. They offered France compensations in Africa in exchange for relinquishing these enclaves when, at the beginning of the twentieth century, the Indian nationalists transformed them into 'bomb factories'.

More populated than the West Indies and Reunion, the trading posts, which numbered nearly 300,000 inhabitants at the dawn of the twentieth century, were not, as has often been affirmed even in France, 'a few poor and insignificant market towns'. Better located than Madras, Pondicherry, whose roadstead was the safest on the Coromandel coast, became one of the largest ports of the French colonial empire in the second half of the nineteenth century, with a turnover of around 30 to 40 million francs per year. The liberalization of British and French tariffs, the advances made in navigation, the spectacular growth of the 'coolie trade' towards Mauritius and the West Indies, the quality of the cotton goods produced by its mills, the progress of speculative crops, like groundnut imported by the oil mills and soap factories of Marseilles, contributed to the renaissance of the ancient capital of Dupleix. The economic potential of the trading posts was nevertheless not optimized by the home country, which, convinced that the English would ruin all investments likely to make Pondicherry the rival of Madras, had since long renounced exerting the least influence in this part of the world, to devote its efforts to Indochina and Africa.

The appearance of the chapter on Sri Lanka (XXVII), here is justified by the incontestable fact of the island's belonging to the Indian sphere of influence. The chapter shows significant lessons for the understanding of the general history of the subcontinent. The special case of

Sri Lanka can throw light on certain aspects of the history of India through a comparative study. From the perspective of a pan-Indian history, Ceylonese history appears intrinsically specific; but if we adopt a regional or local approach of the Indian entity, Ceylon finds its place therein: there are probably fewer differences between Ceylon and Kerala than between Kerala and the Punjab.

The modern history of Sri Lanka offers significant parallels with that of India. But the island has been marked by a more ancient colonial rule, which developed an export-oriented economy founded on plantations, and favoured the rapid growth of a westernized bourgeoisie. It witnessed a less active national movement, influenced by the Buddhist revival in the Singhalese majority, which led to a peaceful independence, but which failed to forge a shared national conscience, making room for the separatist demands of the Tamil minority.

XXVI

FRENCH INDIA

(Nineteenth – Twentieth century)

Captured by the English on 23 August 1793, at the beginning of the revolutionary wars, Pondicherry was restored to France, along with the other four trading posts and a few factories, by virtue of the Treaty of Paris of 30 May 1814. Of the achievement of Dupleix, there remained henceforth but these 'debris,' a few 'poor and insignificant market towns,'[1] whose public buildings had been destroyed by the occupying forces who 'did not leave us a brick'.[2]

In the beginning of the nineteenth century, British supremacy in India was still fragile: the Marathas would be brought under submission only in 1818. Aware of the precariousness of their position, the authorities in London and Calcutta were resolved to prevent France from recovering its former economic, political and military power. For the administrators of the East India Company, haunted by the memory of Dupleix, Bussy, Madec, Perron and de Boigne, it was imperative to reduce France to insignificance and to proscribe it from defining a policy for India.

The government of the Restoration, confronted by the determination of the British, had neither will nor policy. The colonies were no doubt the least of its preoccupations and the establishments in India were the least of its colonies. As testified by the *Mémoire du Roi pour Servir d'Instruction au Sieur Comte Dupuy*, (Count Dupuy was the civil governor in charge of taking back possession of the trading posts), the sole ambition of Paris was to pursue the administrative, fiscal, judicial and commercial practices of the end of the reign of Louis XVI.

Until the Second Empire, the centralization of the administration of the trading posts, the sacrifice that they were forced to make to the detriment of their own economic development in order to favour that of the home country and the prudence of the native policy that was followed there – all were reminiscent of the *Ancien Regime*.

The burdensome heritage of the *Ancien Regime* (1816–52)

A 'humiliating vassalage'[3]

To the severity of the Treaty of Paris, by which France promised notably 'not to undertake the construction of fortifications [. . .], to station, in these establishments, only the number of troops necessary for the maintenance of order' (article 12), the old Count Dupuy added a reprehensible ineptness prejudicial to the interests of his nation. In effect, he tolerated the presence in Pondicherry of a British resident, Colonel Fraser, who exercised the 'greatest influence' and enjoyed 'the same honours, the same prerogatives as the residents that the Company [East India Company] places with the nababs that it has subjugated.' This was a 'humiliation to which the Dutch and Danish governors of Sadras and Tranquebar had refused to submit'.[4]

The 'resident' Fraser no doubt played a role in the serious prejudices suffered by France, in 1817, at the time of the *de facto* transfer. The lands of Villenour and Bahour were indeed restored to Count Dupuy, but not the rich district of Valdavur, whose cession consented by Chanda Sahib in favour of Dupleix, in 1749, had been confirmed later by a *parvana* of the *subadar* of the Deccan, Muzaffar Jang. The Marquis de Saint-Simon, one of the successors of Dupuy, would denounce in 1836 the 'bad faith' of the English and the 'reprehensible ineptness' of the French: 'By the treaty of 30th May 1814, England promised (Article 8) to restore to France all the portions of the territory of India that it possessed as on 1st January 1792. The terms of this treaty have not yet been fulfilled [. . .]. The large district of Valdavur was included among the possessions that were to be restored to France [. . .] and by a mistake that is difficult to explain, and of the motives of which it would be justifiable to be wary, Bahour has been restored to us instead of Valdavur which remained in the hands of the English.'[5]

Amputated as a result, the territory of Pondicherry resembled a 'puzzle'.[6] It was 'a game of draughts whose white squares represented the English districts and the black squares the French districts'.[7] This 'monstrous dissection'[8] was designed to prevent the French from being masters in their territory and to enable the English 'to conserve, even if it were by strips of land, all the positions suitable for the installation of batteries. Consequently, the territory seems, at places, as it were mutilated.'[9]

In Malabar, despite the evidence of the rights of the French, the East India Company refused to restore the right bank of the Mahé river, a vital artery for its economic activities in the region. As the control of the mouth of the river would enable the French to defeat the monopoly of the trade of salt, in which it earned profits to the tune of 1,000 per cent, of spices and precious woods, it did not hesitate to 'substitute force for law'.[10]

The British, determined to prevent French India from reviving its prosperity of the preceding century, succeeded in depriving it of a large part of its resources with the consent of the government of Louis XVIII. By signing the Treaty of London, on 7 March 1815, the French authorities renounced selling the production of the salt marshes of Pondicherry and Karikal in Bengal, in exchange for a meagre indemnity, the 'annuity of India' (four lakh *sikha* rupees). A convention signed in Pondicherry on 13 May 1818, consummated the ruin of this industry: for a symbolic annual indemnity (4,000 starred pagodas, that is 33,600 francs), the French authorities undertook to prohibit the manufacture of salt in their territory.

The government of the Restoration has long been blamed for having sacrificed in this manner national fortune to a foreign monopoly. 'This diplomacy is unfortunate,'

PONDICHERRY TERRITORY: 'A GAME OF CHECKERS'

Calapett ●

Alancoupam ●

● Souttoukerny

● Sedrapett

Mouttalpett ●

■ PONDICHERRY

Vadanour ▨ ● Sorapett

● Oulgaret

Ariancoupam River

● VILLENOUR

● Tiroubouvane

● Arougour

Ariancoupam ●

● Madagadipett

Chounambar ●
Pournancoupam

● Nettapacom

Maltar

☐ French territory

▨ Mixed territory

● BAHOUR

|__ 2 km __|

Ponnear

wrote the *Journal d'Outre-mer* on 11 January 1872. 'It is anti-French, as it leases out a French industry for the exclusive advantage of a foreign monopoly, for the benefit of the Treasury of the King [. . .]. This is a deplorable act as it is not worthy of a government [. . .] to speculate on the lease of its subjects.' Besides, the Danish governor of Tranquebar, to whom the East India Company proposed an indemnity in exchange for the cessation of the manufacture of salt, 'replied with dignity that he did not wish to resort to foreigners for all that his territory could produce'.[11]

The two treaties of 1815 and 1818 were disastrous for the trade and industry of Pondicherry and Karikal, which were drawing an annual profit of 500,000 livres tournois from the export of salt to Bengal in 1789, and perhaps even more from sales in the south of the peninsula. The trading posts could not find any compensation for these losses as the 'annuity of India' that they were to receive was cornered by the home country.

As Louis XVIII had recalled in his *Mémoire* that it was 'essential from the political point of view to retain the power to strike money in Pondicherry,' one of the first decisions of the Governor Dupuy was to re-establish the mint. The rupees that it produced soon enjoyed the same 'great favour' as in the preceding century. Apart from the incomes that the right to their manufacture earned for the government, they were a 'means of observing in the eyes of the Indians the reinstatement of the pavilion of the king, as [they] spread out all over the peninsula'.[12] But the government of Madras, 'jealous of our successes and the quantity of the rupees of Pondicherry that spread out particularly in Mysore,' decided in 1817 to bring this to a halt by ordering the collectors to reject them.[13]

The prosperity of Karikal, the 'garden of the Carnatic,' was another source of stress for the British. Its alluvial lands which produced exceptional yields attracted populations from the inland. Its port, eclipsing those of Nagore and Nagapatinam, became the principal exporter of rice from Tanjore, brought here by leather boats called '*perichous*' that descended the numerous arms of the delta of the Kavery that flowed across the trading post. In the 1830s, the flow of these rivers decreased to such an extent that the rice cultivation of Karikal was jeopardized and the *perichou* boats could no longer reach the French port. The administrator of Saint-Hilaire explains that the dams built upstream by the English were the cause for the drop in the water level. It is indubitable, he says, 'that the English have sought, in the works that they have constructed, all means to harm our cultivation and in particular our trade'.[14]

No sooner had France taken back possession of the trading posts than Chandernagore became inaccessible to French vessels. 'It seems,' the word went around in Bengal, 'that the English have silted up the passage from Calcutta to Chandernagore as the vessels above a draught of thirteen feet can no longer go to Chandernagore and are forced to anchor and unload in Calcutta.'[15] The double duty of 16 per cent levied on all French merchandise, introduced into the Madras Presidency as well as on all Anglo-Indian products entering Pondicherry, 'was tantamount to a prohibition'; despite the exemption from duty proclaimed by Dupuy in reaction to this 'blockade', it diverted the traffic in favour of Madras. The resident Fraser conceded that this discriminatory customs legislation, which did not penalize

Portuguese trade (which was subject to a single duty of 8 per cent), had been designed 'to affect French commercial interests in concrete terms'.[16]

These 'disastrous measures', legal nonetheless, were aggravated by the abuses of the agents of the English customs, the *joucaniers*. Taking advantage of the mutilated appearance of the territory of Pondicherry, they exacted a duty of 16 per cent for a product every time it entered or left their territory before reaching the French port. The collectors used the vagueness of the texts to overestimate the value of goods in transit, in such a way that, in reality, the duties frequently exceeded 100 per cent. To such an extent did some *joucaniers* carry their zeal, that they demanded 16 per cent or more on the clothes that the Indians wore when they crossed the frontier.

The last nababs and the first servants of the state

The hounding of the British was not the sole reason for the deplorable situation of the trading posts. The Baron Desbassayns de Richemont, inspecting the colony in 1821, imputes the economic stagnation and the political vassalage to 'this general torpor, which, starting from the chief, had crept into the employees of all classes' more than to the bad faith of the English. The Pondicherry of Dupuy, this 'valetu-dinarian old man transplanted under the burning sun of Asia, in effect evokes in [him] the image of this palace of a marvellous memory the inhabitants of which had plunged into the deepest of drowsiness. Cursed is he who seeks to awaken them; he shall be in their eyes an importunate guest.'[17]

In reality, while the governor busied himself in a thousand futilities and most of the officials 'do not want to do anything and do not want anyone to make them do anything', a few favourites, imbued with the mentality of the eighteenth century, this 'age of great carnivores',[18] were bursting with activity. The administrator of Yanaon, Courson, used all the revenues of the locality for personal speculation, which elevated him to the rank of 'a true nabab'. Denis Dayot, charged by Dupuy with the task of commanding the establishments in Bengal, invested the first instalments of the 'annuity of India' in highly risky personal commercial operations. After his death, in August 1817, his brother Joseph, entrusted with the mission of restoring the financial situation in Chandernagore, continued to plunder the public treasury and instituted so oppressive a tax regime that 'it was difficult to believe that such a tax system exists among a civilized people.'[19]

On the death of Joseph Dayot, in March 1821, when the new administrator of the trading post, Scipion, undertook to restore order and legality and threatened to punish the profiteers of the previous regime, the 'revolution' broke out. An assembly of the partisans of the Dayot brothers, led by Leprévost, 'with a bottle of brandy and a glass in hand', decided to destroy all the compromising documents, to arrest Scipion and to nominate a new chief, Delaunay, whose first decision was to award himself a salary higher than that of the governor. Only when the government of Calcutta threatened to put an end to the sedition did Dupuy finally sent a ship to Bengal. Order was restored, but the guilty were gratified with a strange clemency: they were recalled to Pondicherry, with the interdiction of setting foot again in

Chandernagore. 'Thus,' concludes Desbassayns, 'this affair, which has all the characteristics of a revolution, which at least tends to make it feared by foreigners, is treated with great moderation. All that has happened degrades and demeans the name of the French.'[20]

The recall of Dupuy, decreed on 25 September 1825, put an end to an era 'of our history in which the ruler, sleeping on his throne, abandoned the reins of the government, leaving the affairs to be resolved according to the interests of courtesans and the caprice of women, in which all the resources of the state were employed for frivolous and useless expenses, in which all the seeds of industry and prosperity were as if crushed: a fatal era in which France, unhappy within its boundaries, had lost all consideration outside.'[21]

The colony renewed its strength and affluence thanks to a new governor, the Viscount Eugène Desbassayns. A nephew of Villèle, the minister of Charles X and son of the baron, Desbassayns may be compared to a surgeon entrusted with the task of carrying out 'painful operations' in order to 'draw the patient out of his lifelessness'. Between July 1826 and August 1828, he restored order in the administration and the finances, inaugurated the royal college and founded schools for children of both the upper classes and the pariahs. He encouraged agriculture, granting concessions to Europeans who wanted to undertake 'special cultivations', sugarcane, indigo, cotton, mulberry, etc. Lastly, he attracted French industrialists who opened a cotton weaving factory on 30 June 1828 'in the European fashion', the first of its kind in India.

When the viscount left India, in August 1828, after two years of intensive work, Pondicherry had to a large extent recovered its fortune and its pride. However, 'like all that moves away from the beaten path, all that comes to break old habits to enter a new order', his administration had 'zealous friends and violent detractors, it left behind deep-rooted memories of hatred and affection'.[22] Apart from the profiteers of the Dupuy administration, the few liberals that Pondicherry numbered had fought against Desbassayns's authoritarianism. These liberals, who placed their hope in the change in regime in 1830, would be soon disappointed.

As early as 1830, Article 73 of the *Charter of 1814*, which stipulated that the colonies should be governed by particular laws and regulations, was amended. It laid down that henceforth 'the colonies shall be governed by particular laws'; as it were, 'the regime of laws succeeded the arbitrary regime of regulations' decreed by the executive. This was however a derisory reform. What is more, the *status quo* was maintained for India, which as yet did not have the least representation, while in Reunion, the promulgation of the revised charter was forthwith attended by measures of decentralization and liberalization, such as the nomination of deputies directly by the general council and no longer by the king.

The Act of 24 April 1833, described as a 'colonial charter,' which transformed the general councils of the West Indies, Guyana and Bourbon into colonial councils elected by universal suffrage and invested with the responsibility of voting the budget and of distributing the taxes, was not extended to India, which continued to come under the purview of a special regime. Article 25 of this Act even stipulated that 'the

French establishments in India shall continue to be governed by the ordinances of the king,' which represented a step back in comparison with Article 73 of the *Charter of 1830*, which had placed them under the regimes of laws.

The 'colonial charter' of 1833 sounded the toll for the hopes of decentralization and assimilation nurtured by the Pondicherry liberals. The institution of a local representation and a parliamentary representation was postponed to a later date. French India, subjected to a regime of ordinances and having at its head an omnipotent governor, remained, more than any other colony, 'the conservatory of forms of the exercise of authority that, in Europe, were associated with the anciens regimes'.[23]

The colony experienced new vicissitudes under the government of the Marquis de Saint-Simon (1835–40). Having fallen out with the Creoles whom he accused of harbouring 'national antipathies', the Marquis on the other hand extended his support to the cause of Indians, to whom he granted, by the decree of 18 February 1838, the right to form a representative Committee of the upper and lower castes. While this 'small convention of Indians' henceforth enjoyed the right of review in the affairs of the colony, the government 'excluded the entire class of Europeans, which it punished with political incapacity' by depriving it of the same advantages. With the Creoles refusing to be 'delivered, feet and wrists bound, to the adversary', whose civilization, 'stamped with superstitions, sorceries and prejudices' was that of twelfth century Europe, the situation soon turned 'volcanic'.[24]

In an effort to bring the crisis to an end, Paris decided to recall Saint-Simon and to endow the colony with a proper constitution. Despite the acknowledged necessity of 'protecting, in the future, from the dangers of too unlimited a power', the organic ordinance of 23 July 1840 hardly undermined the powers of the governor. He was admittedly assisted by a board of administration, of which the head of the administrative department, the public prosecutor and the colonial inspector were the permanent members, but he was not at all required to comply with the opinion of the majority. On the other hand, the people had taken the first step in obtaining representation thanks to the institution of a general council, which nominated a delegate in charge of defending the interests of the colony in Paris. Nevertheless, its ten members were elected by an assembly of twenty-five to forty-five notables chosen by the governor himself, and its powers were purely consultative: the general council could only give its opinion on the budget and voice the needs and wishes of the population.

After four years in existence, the general council continued to remain paralysed by incessant internecine disputes, which is indicative of the 'difficulty in making harmony reign among the colonials'.[25] It had not yet pronounced 'a single word in favour of trade and industry which were suffering and which desperately required that the government of the home country did not abandon them entirely to the arbitrary power of the government of the English East India Company'. One of the general councillors, Frion, conceded that the proceedings of the first four sessions were entirely 'negative for the interests of the colony'.[26]

A colony sacrificed to its home country

The development of the colony and its prosperity did not preoccupy the home country any more than they had before the ordinance of 23 July 1840. In the colonial conception of the *Ancien Regime*, colonies did not enjoy any economic and financial autonomy. They were sacrificed to the home country, for which they had to be profitable. This economic subjugation would be inconceivable without a total administrative and political dependence. Between the autocracy of the *Ancien Regime* and the system of 'debarment', the correlation is evident. Mercantilist theories, which still had currency in the first half of the nineteenth century, required that the colonies be maintained under submission. Like the others, French India was placed 'at the exclusive service of national interests',[27] without even being able to express its grievances.

The misappropriation by Paris of the annuity of India was the most serious of the 'spoilations' suffered by the trading posts. While this million benefited a 'privileged colony' it was a drop in the ocean of the immense budget of the home country. Pondicherry had to grapple with unsolvable financial difficulties. The Governor, Saint-Simon, was the first to denounce what he considered 'the greatest of all injustices'.[28] His successor, Du Camper, affirmed that 'it is thus one million that these possessions pay as contribution, as it was to the detriment of a trade that they had gained that France received it.'[29]

Under Saint-Simon, Hindu notables denounced the consequences of this misappropriation and especially the magnitude of the land duties, the primary source of budgetary income, which accounted for 50 per cent of the gross product, whereas 'under the domination of Hindu princes they had to pay only a sixth of the net product [. . .]. Slavery cannot have anything more odious that this deplorable state', they concluded. 'The idea of leaving us even further in this condition cannot befit a constitutional government, nor become the dignity of a nation that has shed so much blood to re-conquer its rights and to renounce all enterprises against those of others.'[30]

The Indians, deprived by the tax authorities of a large share of the produce of their fields, had no hope of finding compensation in handicrafts, industry or trade. The products of the trading posts were practically prohibited in France and in the other colonies, burdened as they were by heavy duties designed to protect the economy of the home country. From 1826 onwards for instance, *guinées*, that is cotton goods dyed with indigo that formed the reputation of Pondicherrian artisans, were subject to a duty of 20 per cent upon entry into Bourbon. The other productions of the trading posts, especially 'furniture and shoes that were one of the most productive branches of the industry of Pondicherry,' were prohibited. 'Bourbon, by levying duties on the blue cloths of India, has dealt a severe blow to our small-scale Indian trade,' it was protested in Pondicherry. 'They have not been satisfied with depriving us of this income; they have prohibited the entry of soap, furniture, pottery, which has completely crushed our industrial trade.'[31]

A large number of distributors, encouraged by the privileges, particularly tax benefits, granted by Desbassayns, devoted themselves successfully to the cultivation of mulberry, indigo and sugarcane. They were promised that their production 'would enjoy advantages equal to those that the other colonies enjoyed and in any event would not be considered as foreign products'. But Pondicherrian sugar that arrived in Nantes in 1830 was declared 'foreign' and subjected to the 'enormous, quasi prohibitive, tax of the time'. Since then, in Pondicherry, 'everything has been falling into ruin! How, by virtue of what law,' asked an industrialist, 'could we place outside the general law this colony where the French flag has been flying since 1672? By virtue of the absurd and iniquitous.'[32]

The mechanical textile mill, the first in India, which was inaugurated in 1828, was the only enterprise to boast of a brilliant expansion, precisely because it had a market, Senegal. Despite the impossibility of trading directly between Pondicherry and Senegal and the obligation of transiting the Indian productions bound for this colony via Bordeaux or Marseilles, regardless of the various attempts by the home country to impose its own textile productions, the *guinées* of Pondicherry, 'which made the men blue in Mauritania, thanks to a deliberately indelible golden brownish blue dye,'[33] flooded the markets of the western coast of Africa. Notwithstanding the high cost owing to the transit, the 'Moors of the Sahara,' who appreciated 'the excellence of their dye [. . .] and recognized them with ease by the odour that they exhale,'[34] preferred them to European imitations.

The exploitation of which the colony was victim, and the misery of the population that resulted, sparked off only sporadic protests. In 1824, while food shortage was rife in Pondicherry, there was very little agitation in the bazaar. 'They bore the misery and all the deprivations with remarkable perseverance and resignation,' observed with surprise the appropriator of funds, Achille Bédier,[35] an official in the administration placed under the orders of the governor. The Pondicherrians were, on the other hand, inflexible whenever their religion or the honour of their caste was at stake.

The reign of the mamul

The native policy pursued by France since the beginning of the eighteenth century was therefore marked by great prudence. The regulations decreed in Pondicherry on 30 December 1769 and 27 January 1778 confirmed the right of the Indians to be judged in accordance with their practices, customs and laws (the *mamul*) and guaranteed them the respect of their personal status.

Louis XVIII, in the instructions that he addressed to Dupuy, recalls that 'if there were a region where religious tolerance is required, it is particularly in India [. . .]. The ownership of their temples, the free practice of their religion, the use of external ceremonies were entitled to absolute tolerance. Tolerance was expressly required of the magistrates whom the trust of His Majesty places at the head of our establishments in Asia.' Consequently, Dupuy announced solemnly, on 6 January 1819, that 'Indians, whether Christians, Moors or Gentiles, shall be judged as in the past in accordance with the laws, practices and customs of their caste.'[36] A consultative committee of Indian jurisprudence was created in 1827 in order to enlighten the magistrates as to the highly complex laws of the country.

From then onwards the French judges had to allow polygamy in Pondicherry and polyandry in Mahé, authorize child marriages and prohibit the marriage of widows and lastly punish the pariahs who wore slippers, a privilege of the upper caste of Vellajas. Just as the tolerance of Malabar rites and walls separating the *choutres* (Christians of caste) and the pariahs in the churches enabled the priests of foreign Missions to retain their flock, this scrupulous observance of the *mamul*, this abdication of the Civil Code in the face of the laws of Manu won the French administration, if not the attachment of the Indians, at least their indifference: it was evident, in Paris, that this price had to be paid to retain possession of the trading posts.

After the Revolution of February 1848, however, the provisional government decided to resume the policy of assimilation that Boissy d'Anglas begged for under the Thermidorian Convention: 'Let the colonies be a part of our indivisible Republic and let them be supervized and governed by the same laws and the same government; let their deputies called to this House be the indistinct from those of the entire people [. . .]. There can be only one good way of administration and if we have found it for the European countries, why should those in America be disinherited thereof?'

On 5 March 1848, for the first time, a decree called the Indian population to elect a deputy by universal franchise, without distinction of religion or caste. The pariahs, persuaded that the egalitarian republic was determined to elevate them to the rank of the Vellajas, immediately assumed the privilege of wearing slippers. It was not long before the upper castes reacted: pariahs were massacred and their villages set on fire. In the face of such an outburst of violence, Governor Pujol proclaimed the return to the *status quo ante* and announced that pariahs wearing slippers would be liable to pay heavy fines. Thus, the rights of man and the citizen, declared the press in Madras ironically, did not include, in Pondicherry, the right to wear slippers.

At the end of fictional polls, it was a trader from Nantes, Lecour, who was elected deputy on 31 January 1849. The government had come to know of a contract concluded between Lecour and the leader of the Vellajas, Sidambara Modeliar. In agreement with the notables of the upper castes and confident of his authority over the Indians of Pondicherry, Sidambara had promised to send battalions of ignorant and docile electors to vote massively for Lecour, who, in return, was to employ his influence in the Parliament for the service of the 'people of caste.' But the Act of 15 March 1849, which abolished the seat of the deputy of India, soon snatched their victory from Lecour and Sidambara. It had become clear in Paris that it was not advisable to give India 'a representative whom, if he was a native, would represent only a certain part of the French population'.

Without affording the least scrap of autonomy to the colony nor the least political rights to its inhabitants, the Second Empire succeeded in part in what the Second Republic had failed. Its administrators managed to make a few breaches into the fortress of *mamul* and caste, without seeking to alarm the Indian consciences by hasty reforms. Assisted by a favourable economic situation, they paved the way for the colony to enter the age of Industrial Revolution.

The trading posts under the Second Empire: reforms and progress

A favourable economic situation

The abolition of slavery in the French colonies in 1848 opened new horizons for the Indo-French business world. As the cultivation of the 'invasive sugarcane' continued to gain ground and as liberated slaves were reluctant to work in the place of their servitude, the sugarcane islands had to resort to free labourers, African, Chinese and Indian.

Between 1849 and 1885, nearly one hundred and forty thousand coolies were introduced into the French colonies. They have given rise to the large Indian communities that today populate the overseas departments.

Indian emigration in the trading posts

Host colony	Coolies embarked in the trading posts		Coolies embarked at Calcutta		Number of coolies received in each colony
	Period of emigration	Number of coolies	Period of emigration	Number of coolies	
Reunion	1849–1882	63,573			63,573
Martinique	1853–1872	16,915	1872–1883	7,232	24,147
Guadeloupe	1854–1872	21,749	1872–1885	20,577	42,326
Guyana	1856–1872	4,706	1872–1876	3,710	8,416
Total		106,943		31,519	138,462

Some coolies from Bengal were introduced to Reunion. But the planters of Mascareignes in general showed very little appreciation for the 'Calcuttas'. Owing to clandestine emigration, probably quite extensive, the official statistics are lower than they should be. Some Indians, very small in number, were repatriated at the end of their five-year contract.

Simultaneously, one million coolies, perhaps two, were introduced to Mauritius, to South Africa and the British colonies in America, which faced the same needs for labour as the French sugarcane islands.

The authorities of Bombay, Madras and Calcutta hardly approved of this exodus that coincided with the opening in India itself of vast sites for the construction of telegraph, irrigation canals and railway lines, mobilizing all available hands. All the more were they opposed to the French recruitment that was organized in the three Presidencies for the benefit of the colonies of a rival power. In the 1850s, the coolie trade thus sparked off diplomatic incidents, occasionally serious in nature. In 1860 and 1861, while Franco-British relations were improving in Europe, two conventions were finally signed authorizing recruitment by the French even while subjecting it to the control of the collectors.

This extensive transfer of labour, during its time, met with reprobation. In Pondicherry itself, public opinion did not hesitate to 'denigrate with the epithet of traders of men'[37] the merchants who controlled the recruitment and the ship owners and the captains who ensured the transport.[38] It is true that abuses and scandals punctuated the coolie trade. It would, however, be risky to compare it too closely to the slave trade, at least in consideration of the niggling regulation that the government decreed to protect the hired workers, and from 1860 onwards, of the double control, French and British, that was exerted on all the operations. The mortality rate on the coolie ships connecting Pondicherry and the West Indies was only 2.7 per cent for a crossing of one hundred and ten to one hundred and sixty days. It was about 15 per cent on the slave ships of the eighteenth century, whose voyage between Africa and America lasted from five to six weeks. In the nineteenth century, mortality was at times much higher on certain ships transporting European emigrants to the USA.

The utility of the immigration for the host colonies themselves has often been called into question. Victor Schoelcher, for instance, explains, with the evidence of figures, that the coolies introduced into Martinique finally 'cost more than they contributed'. Emigration on the other hand was instrumental in the revival of the trading posts. In 1856, an administrator observed that 'well-being has begun to become evident [. . .] since six to eight years. It is,' he added, 'to the money circulated by emigration that this well-being is due.'[39] The trading houses of Pondicherry and Karikal, which formed an emigration company enjoying the monopoly of recruitment, earned considerable profits by delivering their recruits to captains for the price of 39 rupees for Reunion and 42 rupees for the American colonies. In 1856, Jules Bédier-Prairie, who was the head of the company, could invest, with the gains of the coolie trade, one hundred thousand rupees in a factory in Karikal and the same amount in two fine ships that he purchased. The coolie trade attracted a number of vessels to port of Pondicherry, whose turnover doubled between 1850 and 1855. On 17 December 1853, the Governor Verninac observed that a third of the hundred and twenty ships that had been lying at anchor since the beginning of the year had come to transport hired workers. They completed their cargo by loading rice, sesame, groundnut, indigo and cotton goods, contributing to the agricultural, industrial and commercial prosperity of the trading post.

The advances in maritime navigation were, according to the economist Leroy-Beaulieu, the principal economic phenomenon of that time. Their beneficial effects became evident from 1860 onwards. Until then, it was necessary at times to wait for three or four months for a ship bound for France and the crossing through the Cape of Good Hope still lasted from one hundred to one hundred and twenty days. The opening of the French line to Indochina in October 1862 inaugurated a new era and brought the colony closer to the home country. Henceforth, thanks to the steamers of the imperial freight forwarding, Pondicherry was only twenty-seven days away from Marseilles. The opening of the Suez Canal would reduce the crossing to twenty-two days. *The Godavery*, called to serve the secondary line Pointe-de-Galle-Calcutta via Pondicherry and Madras, would be the first ferry to cross the canal after its inauguration in December 1869.

The Act of 19 May 1866 and the Decree of 9 July 1869, which put an end to the monopoly of the national flag in the relations between France and its colonies, caused a decrease in the number of French ships frequenting the trading posts, as the French ships could henceforth face competition from 'country' boats and English ships. But the dismantling of the system of debarment, marked among others, by the abrogation of the monopoly of the national flag, was largely beneficial to the colony.

Likewise, the adoption of free trade by England, under the government of Peel, between 1846 and 1852, produced the most fortunate consequences on the trading posts: the double duties that were levied on their trade were abolished in 1848. The new tariffs, very moderate, no longer established the least discrimination. In June 1860, the Governor d'Ubraye conceded that so satisfactory was the customs system of British India for French interests that no more negotiation was necessary in this regard.

The revolution of customs tariffs brought about a revival of inter-asian trade, on which so many fortunes had been built during the times of Dumas and Dupleix. Pondicherry became the warehouse where the products of the Coromandel, Madurai, the Nilgris, Salem, Bengal and the 'East coast' (Burma) converged for redistribution. Karikal, more than ever the largest exporter of rice from Tanjore, strengthened its ties with Colombo and Singapore.

Napoleon III, converted to the theories of free trade, set out to dismantle the colonial pact in the wake of the signature of the Franco-British Trade Treaty of 23 January 1860. The Decree of 6 October 1863 was received with enthusiasm in French India: except for sugar, coffee and cacao, the colonial products were admitted duty free into the home country. Immediately, industrialists, assured of a market, founded new enterprises, oil mills and soap factories, especially in Pondicherry, Karikal and even in Yanaon. Exports towards France recorded at the time a rapid growth and the commercial turnover of Karikal, which rarely reached two million francs per year before 1850, exceeded the ten million mark from then onwards, while that of Pondicherry multiplied four-fold during the same period, growing from ten to forty million francs.

Partly due to favourable economic circumstances, this prosperity also resulted from the construction works and the reforms implemented in the colony.

Investments and reforms

'We have, as the emperor, many a conquest to make,' declared Napoleon III in his speech in Bordeaux. 'We have immense uncultivated territories to clear, routes to open, ports to dig, rivers to make navigable, canals to terminate, our railway network to complete.' This programme had been to a large extent executed in India.

On 14 August 1865 the harbour at Pondicherry was inaugurated. This work, which had cost the largest sum ever invested in the colony (495,000 francs), was to facilitate the operations of loading and unloading of laid-up ships, until then carried out by flat bottomed boats, the '*chelingues*', and made dangerous by a sand bar. Karikal also benefited from port construction works: the river Arselar, where trading ships dropped anchor, was banked up. Thanks to these works, completed in 1856, Karikal soon supplanted its rivals, Nagore and Nagapatinam. At the same time, roads were raised, enlarged and macadamized. New arteries were opened and splendid engineering works henceforth made it possible to cross all the rivers. At the end of the Second Empire, the ports of Pondicherry and Karikal were well connected with their hinterland and no *aldee* was isolated from its administrative centre any more.

Agriculture also benefited from the hydraulic works that were then carried out. In Pondicherry, tanks were built to allow the irrigation of rice fields. The capacity of the largest of these tanks, the one in Oussoudou, was raised from twelve to eighteen million cubic metres. The area that it irrigated (*ayakkat*) increased from seven hundred hectares to more than thousand. In Karikal, the exceptionally fertile alluvial soils were irrigated either directly with the water of the eight arms of the Kavery delta that flowed across the region, or by the dozens of diversion canals. Large-scale works were undertaken between 1857 and 1864 with a view to perfecting this complex work of hydraulics: the system set up in Manamoutty, including dams, lock gates, weirs and two irrigation canals that were also navigable, was to improve the irrigation of a third of the lands in the south of the area. As in France, where the ploughed area grew from twenty-five to twenty-six million hectares, cultivated lands expanded significantly. In Karikal for instance they increased from 6,850 hectares in 1830 to 8,720 in 1858 and to more than 9,000 hectares after the completion of the Manamoutty complex.

In the same way as the irrigation works, tax reforms implemented from 1853, designed to alleviate the burden of the cultivators and to stimulate their spirit of initiative, contributed to the extension of cultivated lands. In *L'Extinction du Paupérisme*, Napoleon III explains that the wealth of a nation depends not only 'on the prosperity of agriculture and industry, on the development of domestic and foreign trade,' but also 'on the equitable distribution of public revenues.' In this regard, there remained a lot to be done in the trading posts, whose cultivators had to pay to the treasury a tax of 50 per cent of the gross product of their fields, while real estate property, handicrafts, industry and trade were totally exempted.

Since 1840, the most educated of the Indians had been increasingly voicing their protests against this 'extortion'. 'This is no longer a government, but a robbery,' they wrote. Never had Indians been pressurized to such an extent. Manu authorized the ruler to levy a sixth of the harvest and the legislator Vidiariannia added that the rajah who exacted more than this would be 'regarded as infamous in this world, and in the other, subjected to the flames and to hell.' The Mogul emperor Aurangzeb, it is true, had imposed 'the tribute that the victor made the vanquished to sweat out, to the beat of the drum and with the wick on fire', that is 50 per cent, but after him, 'the most despotic of Muslim dominators', Haidar Ali, had not dared to 'adopt a taxation system similar to that one that afflicted the population under the government of the French': he had contented himself with 30 per cent in Malabar. In France, the Act of 23 November 1799 fixed tax, as Manu had, at a sixth part of the net product. By establishing a due of 50 per cent, the French thus infringed the Indian law and their own legislation: 'Administer us, Your Excellency, according to either one or the other,' the cultivators demanded the Governor. 'If you do not want ours to benefit us, let yours at least decide our fate.'[40]

The Governor Verninac, who arrived in Pondicherry in August 1852, set himself the mission of curing the 'tax plague'. His decree of 19 February 1853, ratified by the imperial decree of 18 October 1855, granted the farmers a reduction of 33 per cent: it thus reduced the tax amount to a quarter of the gross product. The Decree of 27 April 1854 awarded the *mirasdars* (landowners) of Karikal an equivalent reduction. But the diminution of the income of the government consequent upon these reforms was soon compensated by the increase in the amount of indirect contributions. As foreseen, the affluence resulting from the tax relief led to a rise in consumption and, consequently, in the revenues that the Treasury earned from the taxes on tobacco, betel and the alcoholic drinks, *calou* and arrack.

The French, since the foundation of their establishments, considered the State as the sole owner of land, with Indians being but usufructuaries liable to be evicted from the lands that they cultivated, called *adamanom*, in the event of the non-payment of their dues. In the first half of the nineteenth century, the idea gained ground that 'the right of national ownership' was a 'pure fiction' and that the Indians ought to be given back the right to private ownership that they had enjoyed in the distant past before it was 'buried under the rubble of the Muslim rule'. Some Indians nevertheless affirmed that 'the Mohammedans, who violated everything, did not dare to touch ownership' and that it was the French who had called into question this right 'as old as the world'. The proof of their statements was found, they added, in Karikal where the 'right to single ownership' had remained 'intact'. This was contested in Pondicherry by the Judge Eugène Sicé:[41] the *mirasdars* of Karikal might possess the lands in their *aldees*, but they did so collectively and not singly: the proof thereof was that they regularly carried out redistributions, which paralysed individual initiatives.

In Pondicherry as in Karikal, caste was a major obstacle to individual ownership. An Indian did not belong to himself. He belonged 'body and soul' to his caste. He was 'in the impossibility of owning his own person, this first property of man [. . .]; as he was strictly prohibited from any act pre-supposing the exercise of his free will, how can one concede that ownership is accessible to the Indian especially with respect to land?' As private ownership had never existed in India, the duty of France, concluded Sicé, was to institute it.

The Decree of 16 January 1854 proclaimed that 'in Pondicherry and in the districts falling under its administration, holders of land in any capacity whatsoever, who shall settle the statutory tax, are declared inalienable owners of the lands that they cultivate.' According to Sicé, this reform aimed at leading the trading posts towards 'civilization' and drawing them closer to the home country. Ownership being 'a religion that was even more universal and more absolute than the religion of Christ,' its introduction would contribute to the progress of equality, this 'base' of Christianity, which, despite the efforts of the missionaries, Indians still failed to understand.

A few years later, Eugène Rouher, speaking of Algeria, would also see in ownership a factor of civilization and of the rapprochement between the colonies and the home country: 'Ownership is, in Algeria, collective and undivided; several ownership did not exist. But, what is the first symptom of civilization if not the duly constituted right to ownership? [. . .] The first condition, in view of preparing the work of civilization, is therefore the constitution of ownership.'

It was therefore decided to replace the dogma of opposition to change, religiously respected since the eighteenth century, with a faith in progress. Denouncing the observance of the 'hierarchy of contempt' and the reign of the *mamul*, the public prosecutor Ristelhueber affirmed that it would be disgraceful 'if we were to abdicate the principles of our nationality and cease to be French and be more Indian than the Indians themselves'.[42] This did not signify, for all that, as an effort to revolutionize the laws and mores of the country, as the Second Republic had tried to do by introducing universal suffrage. Ristelhueber in effect deplored that 'France wants to do everything in its image and does not believe itself to be consistent if the least parcel of French soil does not enjoy in some way this fine political organization of which universal suffrage is the foundation.'

Between the policy of opposition to change, humiliating for France, and political assimilation, which would lead either to the consolidation of the hegemony of the privileged castes or to a war between communities and castes, there was, according to Ristelhueber a third way, 'The expectant progressive policy.' The policy of France ought to be 'prudent, reserved,' but also 'progressive'. Far from being immobile, Indian society could in effect, 'by the sole progress of time and ideas', evolve slowly to be eventually assimilated into France: 'However slow the tortoise might be, it arrives none the less surely,' summed up the *Moniteur Officiel des Établissements Français dans l'Inde*, on 28 July 1854.

The introduction of private property fell in line with the 'expectant progressive policy'. The abolition of dualism was nevertheless the most remarkable success of the Second Empire in this regard. The castes of Pondicherry, Karikal and Yanaon were divided into 'Right Hand' and 'Left Hand'. The origins of this dualism, unknown in Kerala and in Bengal, are still controversial, as are the reasons for the adherence of a particular caste to one Hand rather than the other. On the right side, or *valangai*, came the noble castes of the Vellajas (owners, functionaries, liberal professions), of the Cavarés (sepoys, policemen) and the Comouttys (traders), but also the Vallanga pariahs. The left side, or *idangai*, was dominated by the Chettis (traders) and the Kammalars (artisans), but the Pallys and the Pallars, almost as much despised as the Vallangas, were its most ardent champions. Certain castes, including the Brahmins, were neutral.

Each Hand had privileges that it defended with tenacity. For instance, when the Pallys belonging to the Left Hand laid claim to the right of putting out, during times of festivals, the pavilion with the effigy of the tiger and the five-coloured flag, a prerogative of which the Right Hand demanded the monopoly, bloody combats broke out in Pondicherry. Verninac was particularly shocked by the practice that forbade an Indian to cross on horseback, in a carriage or on a palanquin the street of the rival Hand. The situation was all the more absurd as, following real estate transactions, Indians of the Right hand had settled down in the streets of the Left hand and vice versa. On various occasions, the police had to 'pierce the walls of eight or ten houses to enable the participant of a marriage, burial, etc. to reach the street into which he is allowed.'

The governor, determined to abolish this dualism, had no difficulty converting Indian businessmen to the freedom of circulation. The committee of Indian jurisprudence, to which he referred the matter, proclaimed that the division 'does not have a legal foundation, that it harms the prosperity of the population and that it serves only to cause troubles'. This opinion was corroborated by eight Brahmin scholars who affirmed that dualism was attested neither in the *Vedas* nor in the *Shastras* and the neutrality of their caste had never had any other cause. A first decree passed on 5 November 1856 thus granted all Indians the right to build their house or to settle down in any street whatsoever. Another, passed on 25 February 1857, entrenched the full freedom of circulation for all the castes, in all the streets.

This was admittedly not a fusion of castes, but it was the end of dualism and the turmoil that it engendered. 'We are not of those who condemn India to immobility,' declared a successor of Verninac. 'Under the progressive action of our laws, all that can remind the Indians of the abuses of their national sovereignty, confusion or despotism in the game of powers, the love of privilege, misappropriation of public funds (concussion), is fading more and more.'[43] The results were significant, but they were the work of Hindu authorities as much as that of the imperial administration. This much hailed victory of progress over tradition was in the last analysis possible because the *mamul* called into question did not have any foundation.

Failures and humiliations

A few resounding successes can not eclipse the failures, no more than the prosperity regained can conceal the humiliating position of France in India. The 'prospective progressive policy', to use the expression of the public prosecutor Ristelhueber, had its limitations: the imperial government failed both to introduce civil status and to officially abolish the infamous sentence of caning, which could be passed only against the condemned of the lower castes.

There was still a lot to be done for the development of the colony. In January 1858, the banker Hippolyte Worms proposed to connect Karikal with the British railway network, under rapid expansion at the time. This project was never to come to fruition. It came up against the opposition of the business circles of Pondicherry, who did not want Karikal to steal the priority. At the end of a 'parish-pump war' that dragged on for ten years, the Karikalese had to give in. The victory of the Pondicherrians soon left a bitter taste: the British, fearing that Pondicherry might attract all the productions of the south of the peninsula to the detriment of Madras, finally vetoed the construction of a French line on their territory. After prolonged negotiations, the railways of Pondicherry and Karikal were respectively inaugurated in 1879 and in 1898, but in both the cases, the British would impose a route that was the least prejudicial to their interests.

Resolved to settle the affair of the dependencies of Mahé once and for all, the imperial governor concluded an agreement with Palmerston in 1853. The minister of foreign affairs, Drouyn de Lhuys, was 'very pleased that this affair has finally been closed in a satisfactory manner' but Verninac was aware that 'we have not been restored to all that had belonged to us previously.' Admittedly, the British had returned to France all the three 'arid and desolate' peaks that overlooked the right bank of the Mahé River, but not the slopes that it lapped.[44]

Napoleon III also approved the idea of an exchange of territories that would bring to an end the humiliating dispersion of the trading posts and to the fragmentation of Pondicherry, imposed by the vanquishers of his uncle. Admiral Hamelin, minister of the Navy and Colonies from April 1855 to June 1858, proposed that France ceded, in exchange for a homogenization and an expansion of Pondicherry, the territories of which the government of Louis XVIII should never have taken possession, namely the secondary factories and establishments, excepting the rich trading post of Karikal. The negotiations were on the verge of producing an agreement when the Sepoy Revolt broke out. Paris believed that henceforth the exchange ought to be adjourned until the end of the mutiny 'because in the event of the triumph of the rebels, it would be more important for us to have many different small points than to possess bigger ones that would be less scattered.'[45]

Whereas in 1843 the consul of France at Bassora, Fontanier, had advocated an alliance with the rajahs of Cochin and Travancore, and even with the Afghans, in order to 'liberate India from the English yoke', the French authorities contented themselves, in 1857, with cautiously observing the events and were pleased with the loyalty of the Indian notables of the trading posts, which reiterated that their attachment to France had no other reason but its tolerance and its respect of the *mamul*. Powerless to play a political and military role in India, France had the satisfaction of seeing its trading posts prosper and order reign in them.

A laboratory of republican assimilation

The dogma of assimilation

Anxious to disseminate its ideals and to uplift the most despised of castes, the Third Republic broke away, in 1871, from the principles that had guided the previous regimes. No sooner was it instituted than it resumed the policy of political assimilation. The Decree of 1 February 1871 enabled the population of the trading posts to elect a deputy by universal franchise.

On 28 May 1871, a 'liberal' committee led by the Creole, Emile Hecquet, and the advocate of the Vellaja caste, Ponnoutamby, ensured the election of the baron Desbassayns de Richemont, son of the governor of the Restoration whose memory was still alive in all their minds. While Paris cast a veil of discretion over the manoeuvres that enabled this legitimist royalist, allied to the republicans for the need of his cause, to defeat Ristelhueber, the candidate of the 'conservative' committee led by the trader, Gallois-Montbrun, Hecquet demanded the end of the omnipotence of the governor and the institution of councils elected by universal suffrage.

Hecquet obtained only partial satisfaction, no doubt because of the warnings of the Governor Michaux, for whom 'universal suffrage would be a disastrous application in the colony'.[46] The local councils created in each establishment by the Decree of 13 June 1872 were certainly elected by universal franchise, but they were presided by the head of department and had only consultative powers. The colonial council, which represented the collective interests of the colony, was composed of representatives of the people, designated by the local councillors, but also of functionaries, ex-officio members, including the governor who presided. Despite the prudence of this decree, the criticisms against assimilation became more and more virulent. Three major arguments were put forward by the administration of Pondicherry and the monarchist opposition of the Parliament:

1. Indians are not French, as, free to retain their personal status, they are subject not to the Civil Code, but to the laws of Manu if they are Hindus or Catholics and to the Koranic law if they are Muslims. 'Can you admit for an instant,' queried the legitimist deputy Champvallier in November 1875, 'that the 48,000 electors of India, enjoying this personal status, could nominate a deputy who would come to this Chamber to vote our civil laws that are not applicable to them?' [47] Although less refractory to French values, the Algerians had not been called to elect their representatives, because they remained subject to their own laws. 'Inconsistency! Illogicality!' cried out Ristelhueber. 'How can what is true, sensible, reasonable for Algeria be not so for India?'[48]

If the Indian, born on French soil, is not *ipso facto* French, all the more should the one from British territory be excluded from the polls. But a decree passed on 5 August 1872 grants the right to vote to Indians 'who have been exercising an industry on our territory for several years or whose family resides there or who possesses personal properties,' which is tantamount, for the adversaries of assimilation, to an invitation to the infringement of national sovereignty. With very few exceptions, Indians do not speak French and know nothing about France, its institutions and its culture. 'Most of these poor people,' wrote Governor Bontemps when he heard that India was to elect a deputy, 'understand nothing about moderation and are more wary of it than they are jubilant.' By granting the right to vote to Indians before placing 'at their disposition all the riches of western science and culture'[49] France has put the cart before the horse.

2. While France is offering self-government to its establishments, the British 'are refusing [it] energetically' to their subjects 'because they find that the Indian has not yet arrived at the necessary maturity and nobility to exercise these rights with all the desirable wisdom'.[50] Unknown in England, universal suffrage is all the more so in British India.

3. Republican institutions, incompatible with the Indian social organization, can produce disastrous effects in this country. 'The myriad division of castes is an insurmountable obstacle for any institution founded on election,' explained Governor Michaux. 'It would not be long before we see the dramatic rise of the preponderance of the higher castes over the lower castes and the oppression of the latter.' The exclusion of the pariahs from certain polling stations, 'owing to their social indignity', can in effect arouse fears. The untouchables would not be the only victims of the Hindu aristocracy: 'Christians first, the Europeans next would be excluded from the

polls and the administration of the country would fall into the hands of pagans; to reach this goal, they only have to count themselves.'[51]

Assimilation was, nevertheless, not called into question. Far from voting 'the parliamentary death of the colonies,' called for by the spokesperson of the legitimist Right, Champvallier, the authorities of the home country granted them, by the constitutional statute of 24 February 1875, the right to be represented in the Senate. The progress of the republicans in France, the election in 1876 of 'liberal' candidates – Richemont to the Senate and the lawyer Jules Godin to the Chamber of Deputies – as well as the emergence, under the impetus given by the lawyer Ponnoutamby, of a movement of the renunciation of personal status and of caste gave rise to new measures towards assimilation:

1. The colonial council was replaced by a general council elected by universal franchise and invested with extended fiscal and budgetary powers (decree of 25 January 1879).
2. Ten communes were created by the decree of 12 March 1880. The establishment of Pondicherry numbered four of them (Pondicherry, Oulgaret, Villenour and Bahour); that of Karikal three (Karikal, the Grande-Aldee and Nedouncadou). The municipal councils were elected by universal franchise. However, as for the elections to the general council, the electors were registered on two lists, one for Europeans and descendants of Europeans and the other for Indians.
These reforms were, for the traditionalist Hindus, the straw that broke the camel's back. Their leader, Chanemougam, son of Sidamabara Modeliar, who had been instrumental in causing the people to vote massively for Lecour in 1848, demanded the government to put an end to its reform policies. In vain.
3. The decree of 24 June 1880 promulgated in the colony a number of provisions of the Civil Code. Though exemptions were granted to Hindus and Muslims, there was considerable unrest in Pondicherry where the wind of revolt was beginning to blow.
4. The decree of 21 September 1881 enabled the Indians who so desired to renounce their personal status and to come under the purview of the French laws, with the objective of 'facilitating the progressive assimilation of natives' and of contributing to 'the uplift of the pariah by fraternity'. Its immediate result was to spark off a drawn-out war between what the Governor Richaud (1884–6) would call 'the French idea' and 'the Hindu idea', which had coexisted harmoniously for the last two centuries.

These measures, which aimed at ethnic (or cultural), not only political, assimilation marked in Chanemougam's opinion the beginning of the process of 'absorption.' But he did not seek to organize a bloody revolt. By granting the right to vote to those who did not renounce their personal status (the *non-renonçants*), France had given him the means to achieve his ends without bloodshed. All that he needed to do, in his capacity as the leader of the upper castes (*nadou*) who wielded great authority over all the Hindus, was to send cohorts of ignorant and docile electors to fill up the ballot boxes. Far from wanting to oust the French, Chanemougam had decided to become their master: fraud and manipulation would be his arms.

An Indian republic

An unrivalled 'master fraudster', Chanemougam was distinguished, as early as 1880, in the art of 'stuffing' ballot boxes and falsifying reports. An institution of his invention, the corps of *bâtonnistes* (louts armed with sticks) enabled him to even do without the cooperation of the electors: while these redoubtable henchmen exerted themselves to keep the citizens away from the polling stations, a few zealous 'chanemougamists' drew up a report that awarded all the votes on the list, and sometimes more, to the candidate chosen by the 'Hindu Machiavelli'.

On four occasions (1881, 1885, 1889 and 1893), the journalist Pierre Alype, a republican close to Gambetta, was overwhelmingly voted the deputy of India, in the wake of entirely 'fictive' polls. In exchange for the sinecure that his *grand électeur* offered him, he had promised to execute without questioning the least of his orders and never to set foot in India. He was thus the only French deputy never to have visited his constituency. To those who accused him of betraying the republican ideals by serving the interests of a retrograde oligarchy, he replied that an elected official ought 'to represent the opinion of the country and not his personal opinion', that 'progress does not consist of making a people whose civilization is legendary embrace the European civilization of today' and that the pariahs were 'shameful people, coming from the sordid parts of the cities'.[52]

In their desire to reconquer their hegemony, the 'liberals', who had become much less liberal since they had lost their power, henceforth maintained that the *non-renonçants* were not French citizens and harassed the minister to deprive them of their right to vote. Failing this, they demanded that these Indians should no longer be drowned in the mass of 'Brahminics' and Muslims of the second list and that they should be allowed to vote on the first list, with the Europeans.

Victor Schoelcher, on his side, was conscious of the necessity of rewarding the patriotism of the friends of Ponnoutamby (who became Laporte at the time of his renunciation), even while conserving the influence of Europeans and not wronging the 'Brahminics.' On the strength of the support of Alype and Hébrard, the senator 'fabricated' by Chanemougam, he proposed to institute three lists each electing ten general councillors. The decree of 26 February effectively ordered the registration of Europeans, 'the civilizing element,' on the first list; the *renonçants*, about whose sincerity doubts still persisted, would be entered on the second list; Indians subject to their personal status would form the third list. The government had conceded that it was impossible, without spoliation, to deprive them of their right to vote: 'The Republic is like the God of Saint Paul, it does not take back its gifts'.[53]

Three lists, three categories of French citizens, 572 European electors electing as many general councillors as 69,819 Indians, the ways of assimilation are indeed tortuous. In any case, the Schoelcher decree was a lesser evil for Chanemougam, who feared the success of the manoeuvres of Laporte. He did not denounce any less astutely its discriminatory nature and even conferred on himself the titles of progressive leader and democrat by demanding a single list, which would give him all the seats in the different councils.

No doubt Chanemougam had to brave the coalition of the first two lists for five years, but in 1890, he put an end to his sojourn in the political wilderness. At the price of a cynical blackmailing, he rallied to his cause the unscrupulous Rassendren, the successor of Laporte, who died in 1886. Contrary to the forecasts of Schoelcher, he succeeded in forging the 'unnatural' alliance between the Indian *renonçants* and *non-renonçants*. He also enjoyed the support of a few Europeans, including the lawyer Gaston Pierre, whom he made the mayor of Pondicherry.

The 'French party' of the trader Gallois-Montbrun and the industrialist Gaebélé, supported in the home country by the future Nobel prize for peace winner, Constant d'Estournelles, multiplied in vain the protests against 'the scandals of the electoral system of India.' The Chamber of Deputies indeed recognized on several occasions that 'there are in our colony of India deplorable electoral mores, to which we must at all cost put an end[54],' but perhaps because, between the interests of the colonies and the interests of the colonial deputies, it had, according to Estournelles, opted for the latter, the election of Alype was duly validated.

Henri Gaebélé succeeded, however, in drawing a few castes, the rich Chetti merchants and the humble Vannias led by Sadassivanaiker, away from the Brahminic fortress. This was not however sufficient to defeat the electoral monopoly that Chanemougam exercised over the third list. At the most, these dissidences contributed in once more sparking off the caste war that flared up during the least partial election. The control of the polling stations, and consequently of the reports, gave rise to pitched battles culminating in blood baths. This was because, according to the expression of the Governor Martineau, 'the stick of happy memory' had soon given way to gun, vitriol and bomb. Long since 'the land of frauds', French India became the breeding ground for electoral terrorism in 1893, a tragic outcome of the policy of assimilation.

The rallying to the French party of the progressive *renonçants* led by Gnanadicom, who reproached Rassendren, 'this Ganelon of the motherland',[55] for having betrayed the ideal of Laporte, proved detrimental to Chanemougam who lost several seats of the second list. For the 'chief sorcerer,' a reform of the Schoelcher decree was the best remedy. With Alype compromized in several scandals, having lost all credit in the ministry, he decided to entrust this delicate operation to a new deputy: it would be Louis Henrique-Duluc, the influential director of the newspaper *La Politique Coloniale*, as unknown as his predecessor had been in the colony, but 'elected' in 1898 with the same quasi unanimity. When France was becoming radical, the Brahminic oligarchy astutely acquired a radical representative.

Henrique-Duluc, supported by Jules Godin, who in 1891 had bartered his liberal and assimilationist convictions for the seat of the senator of India, snatched from the minister of Colonies the decree of 10 September 1899 that abolished the second list, and even the first in the communes and establishments where the number of European electors was less then twenty. This was the apogee of Chanemougam, the 'king of French India,' henceforth the sole master of the budget and of 'all that concerned the political, administrative and judicial personnel'.[56] A true 'black Louis XI', he discarded as vulgar 'oafs' the magistrates, officials and governors who refused to be his 'toys'. His network in Paris was so well organized that he could assert arrogantly that if his deputy were a cat, the ministry would mew with him.

Master of the general council, Chanemougam was the sole 'custodian' of the budget: officials in need of a promotion, entrepreneurs in the quest of markets by private agreement, humble Indians seeking an employment, all had to apply to him: 'He was the bridge in the colony that it was mandatory to cross to reach the governor or to obtain the most legitimate of favours, and this was a toll bridge.'[57] 'Under the despotism of this fanatic',[58] the lot of the lower castes – 'an army of paupers, lying on the ground pell-mell under a hut, dressed in rags, people who were never satisfied [. . .], exploited, in tatters and emaciated, whom cholera and the plague periodically cut down and whom physiological misery decimated incessantly'[59] – worsened. The pariahs especially, whose rights were, according to the writer Edmond About, 'approximately the same as those of a pig in the suburbs of Paris',[60] had to be maintained in 'their prison of misery and abjection': perpetuating the supremacy of the upper castes was for Chanemougam a sacred duty.

For this 'Hindu ascetic' who 'yearns for the time – and he makes no secret of it – when the widow of a Malabar burned on the pyre of her husband',[61] economic development was the least of his priorities because it would emancipate the lower castes by spreading wealth among them and would benefit the businessmen of the French party. On the contrary, all means were good to hamper the growth of the colony: the bard of opposition to change thus successively fought against the project of building a deep-water port in Pondicherry, which the baron de Reinach had decided to finance, the construction of coal yards in the administrative centre and Mahé, the preparation of land registers and the construction of the Cuddalore-Pondicherry railway line. Only agricultural works, profitable to the rich landowners of the 'noble' castes, were provided the necessary funds.

If Pondicherry did not collapse, it was because, firstly, the productions of its textile mills continued to be marketed in other colonies – despite the discriminatory tariffs imposed by the protectionist act of 1892 inspired by Jules Méline – and secondly, because the export of groundnut from the south of India, towards Marseilles in particular, had grown considerably.

While he was in the zenith of his power, 'Chanemougam I' was brutally dethroned in 1906: to everyone's surprise, Henrique-Duluc was defeated by the 'Gaebélist' candidate, the former governor Lemaire, ousted two years earlier at the behest of the *nadou*. But the French party could achieve this result only by resorting to the same arms as its enemies, namely fraud and terror, and by playing the Muslim community against the Hindu community, thereby inflicting on the colony another scourge, communalism, the ultimate mishap of political assimilation.

The end of French India

The influence of Gandhi

The hegemony of the Gaebélé party, interrupted between 1910 and 1924 by the return to power of a violently anti-French 'neo-Chanemougamic' party, was unchallenged until 1928. The mayor of Pondicherry, master of the general council, the senator of India in 1922, Henri Gaebélé distinguished himself especially by his firmness towards the British: in 1918, for instance, he opposed the extradition of the nationalist philosopher Aurobindo, who had been in refuge in Pondicherry since 1910.

Dominated by the personality of Joseph David, who succeeded Gaebélé as the 'grand électeur' of French India, the decade that preceded the Second World War was marked by the massive entry of Indian nationalists pursued by the British police and by social agitation, which were at the centre of the preoccupations of the new political movements.

The *Jeunesses de l'Inde françaises* (Youth of French India), which emerged in 1931 under the influence of the personality of Gandhi, declared itself against European domination and for radical social reforms. They contributed to the birth, in December 1933, of the Harijana Seva Sangham. This movement, aimed at the emancipation of the pariahs, encouraged the workers of textile mills to 'fight against the exploiters' and was no doubt party to the violent strikes that broke out in June and July 1936, under the Popular Front government, and the repression of which claimed a dozen victims.

Born in 1937, another political movement, the Mahajana Sabha, drew its inspiration from the methods of the Indian nationalists: in order to achieve its objectives, which were the reduction of the powers of the governor, a single list and the sincerity of the polls, it advocated non-cooperation and civil disobedience.

The Second World War brought to an end the tension between the party of Joseph David and the new formations. The rallying to liberated France, decided in 1940, was barely contested and hundreds of young Pondicherrians expressed their attachment to France by joining de Gaulle.

The merger

In 1946, the Democratic National Front, which had been formed during the war around socialist and communist leaders, won the municipal elections and the elections to the Representative Assembly, which replaced the general council. It was instrumental in the election of professor Lambert Saravane to the National Assembly.

The Front disintegrated in July 1947: the socialists, lead by Lambert Saravane and Edouard Goubert, denouncing the radicalism of the communists, seceded and founded the Socialist Party of French India, which immediately won the sympathy of the administration. The communists, for their part, came closer to the National Congress of French India, born in the beginning of the year 1947, in order to claim the 'merger' of the trading posts with the Indian Union.

The agitation that attended the independence of India was such in the French enclaves that Governor Baron had to go to Calcutta to solicit the intervention of Gandhi. The Franco-Indian agreement, signed in June 1948 and which provided for the organization of a referendum for self-determination, calmed the passions for some time.

A referendum was held in Chandernagore on 19 June 1949, in which 99 per cent of the population declared themselves in favour of the integration of the city into the Indian Union, but this would not be the case in the other trading posts. The Congress leaders, who had doubts about the sincerity of the polls, were hostile to consulting the people. The victory of the partisans of Goubert in the municipal elections of October 1948 and particularly his election to the seat of deputy, on 17 June 1951, with 90,053 votes out of the 90,667 votes cast, could justify their fears.

As the French authorities were seeking to stall for time, the Nehru government decided to act and to implement finally the resolution adopted by the Congress at Jaipur in December 1948 in view of the incorporation of the French and Portuguese colonies into the Indian Union. A blockade was put in place, in the beginning of 1954, which soon threatened to asphyxiate Pondicherry. The sudden rallying of Goubert to the nationalists shattered the last hopes of the partisans of French India.

The government of Mendès France, resolved to settling the Indo-French question simultaneously with the Indochina problem, opened negotiations. An agreement was signed at New Delhi on 21 October 1954: the *de facto* transfer came into force on 1 November 1954.

The secession treaty, signed at New Delhi on 28 May 1956, by French ambassador, Ostrorog and Nehru, stipulated in particular that French nationals born in the territory of the establishments and who resided there at the date of its enforcement should become Indian nationals. However, they had six months to opt by a written declaration in favour of French nationality. The treaty was ratified by the French Parliament in 27 July 1962, that is a few months after the Evian accords. It came into force on 16 August. More than five thousand families, of Tamil origin, made use of the right of option.[62] While the *pieds-noirs* of Algeria left their native land in a climate of violence, 'the largest democracy of the world' permitted these French Pondicherrians, admittedly few in number, to stay in the soil of their ancestors, to enjoy their possessions and to perpetuate the French language and traditions. No doubt it was believed at the time that they could contribute to make this city 'an open window to French culture' as desired by Pandit Nehru.

XXVII

SRI LANKA
Specificities and similarities

The island of Sri Lanka occupies a marginal space in relation to India. However, it holds a position of importance at the crossroads of two trade routes: a north-south route, taken by movements of population, religious trends, forms of social organization and agricultural techniques; and an east-west route, maritime, animated by the flow of trade, but also by political, religious and cultural influences. This means that the island is within the orbit of both the Indian subcontinent and Southeast Asia.

Sri Lanka, in certain respects, forms a microcosm of the Indian world but it is very different from it in others. The natural environment and the cycle of monsoons resemble those of the south of India: the escarpments of the Kandyan up-country are the continuation of the relief of the Ghats and the Nilgiris; the coastal plains of the Southwest, receiving regular rainfall, are similar to those of Kerala; the slopes of the mid-northern region, which experience a long dry season from March to October, are comparable to the uplands of Tamil Nadu.

Its society and culture are the result of the juxtaposition, and to a large extent of the combination, of elements of the north and of the south of India. The population of the island has been formed by a succession of waves of immigration from the continent. Some of them carried with them a language and culture originating from the Indo-Gangetic regions; they became those of the majority of the population, under the combined influence of the dynasties established in the mid-northern part of the island and of the great Buddhist monasteries that they protected: this is the origin of the Singhalese (*sinhala*) cultural group – a community and not a race. The others descended from the closer southern India – from Tamil Nadu and from Kerala; many of them merged with the Singhalese cultural group during its formative phase.

In the first millennium AD, in the wake of the affirmation of new forms of Hindu religiosity and the emergence of expansionist centres of power in the Deccan, Tamil identity consolidated itself in the north and in the east of the island. Under the effect of climatic changes and the upheaval caused by the Chola conquests, the populated regions of the Mid-north, whose economy relied on sophisticated systems of irrigation, were deserted. From the twelfth century onwards, the centres of Singhalese population

drifted towards the humid zone of the southwest, while the Jaffna peninsula, to the
far north, became the home of a homogenous Tamil population: the emergence of
a no man's land widened the cultural distance between the two communities. The
ties of the island with the continent were not cut off for all this: groups continued to
migrate towards Ceylon, integrating, depending on the geographic location of their
settlement, into the Tamil or the Singhalese society, or forming distinct minorities,
like the Muslims.

The internal organization of the society of the island draws heavily on its Indian
origins: the caste of cultivators was dominant, both hierarchically and in number,
among the Singhalese (the Goyigama caste) as well as among the Tamils (the Vellalar
caste), similar to the situation that prevailed in the irrigated regions of Tamil Nadu.
The dependant castes at the service of the former were largely comparable in the
island and on the continent, as were the castes of fishermen on either side of the
Palk Strait. Kinship structures and vocabulary are identical. Lastly, notwithstanding
the persistence of Buddhism and the absence of Brahmins in Ceylon, the forms of
religiosity prevailing all over the island have been highly influenced by South-Indian
Shivaism.

Unlike in India, Buddhism survived in the Singhalese community, even as it was
disappearing form the subcontinent under the pressure of Hindu religious dynamics and the irruption of militant Islam. This survival was due to the persistence of a
monarchic system that offered protection to the community of monks (the *sangha*),
while in the Islamic states of the north of India they were being persecuted, and the
Brahminic domination in the states of the south were jeopardizing their very existence. This political system emptied the caste system of its religious substance to
make it a social structure at the service of the monarchy.

Another element of differentiation is the precocity and the depth of the colonial
impact, facilitated by the maritime nature of the country: four and a half centuries
of western domination in the coastal regions, nearly one and a half centuries in the
inland. The integration of the island into the world market was more precocious and
more general than in India: subsequent to the economy of transport established by
the Portuguese and the Dutch for obtaining supplies of cinnamon, the system of
plantations (coffee, and tea and rubber) imposed by the British in the interior, occupied a decisive place in the overall economy of Ceylon. Consequently, colonial
taxation weighed less heavily on the subsistence agriculture of the island than on that
of the continent, but the system made the country much more dependant on the
fluctuations in the world market for export-oriented agricultural products.

In addition, the colonial administration, with the exception of a few years in the
beginning of the British rule, remained distinct from that of India, which contributed to maintaining the particularities of Ceylon. It favoured the introduction of
a new group of Indian origin, the Tamil coolies, who came to work in the plantations
opened in the interior of the island from 1840 onwards, but it discouraged the integration of these immigrants into the island society.

The subsequent development among the Singhalese, and to a certain extent
among the Tamils of Jaffna, of a heightened consciousness of their uniqueness,
grounded on mythical representations of an elected people, led them to discount

their Indian origins and to minimize the parallelism between their two historical experiences. Lastly, the British colonizers, who introduced the concept of 'race,' contributed to the construction, during the colonial period, of separate Singhalese, Tamil and Muslim identities.

The beginnings of the modern era

The modern age dawned in the fourteenth century with the spectacular development of maritime commerce, under the impetus given by Arab traders. The momentum was maintained thanks to the western demand for spices and precious stones, the monopoly of which the Portuguese exerted themselves to obtain from the beginning of the sixteenth century. Afterwards, the east-west exchanges tended to dominate the north–south exchanges, without supplanting them. The desertion of the dry zone of the northeast did not reverse for several centuries, while the population concentrated in the humid zone of the southwest and the centre. The rice-growing Goyigama cultivators who retreated to this region were subsequently joined by the castes that had immigrated more recently from the South of India: Karava fishermen, Salagama weavers who became cinnamon peelers, Durava *toddy*[1] extractors and probably Batgama serfs. The extension of coconut farms and of areca nut gardens, the peeling of cinnamon, the mining of precious stones and the oyster beds for cultivation, and pearl fisheries supplied important resources for export. It was the Muslims who carried out the bulk of this commerce.

The stable and relatively centralized Singhalese kingdoms of the great hydraulic civilization were succeeded by small instable principalities. In the Tamil north, a kingdom with Jaffna as capital was formed under the influence of the kingdom of Madurai. In the south, after numerous vicissitudes marked by a progressive displacement of capitals towards the humid zone, the Singhalese and the South Indians created a state more powerful than the others around the city of Kotte – whose port would give rise to the city of Colombo – while a secondary centre of power emerged in the mountainous regions, at Gampola, then at Senkadagala, which the Europeans would call Kandy.

But the political fragmentation of the pre-colonial epoch was not a sign of a decline: in the kingdom of Kotte, where the bulk of the population was concentrated, a prosperous barter economy developed and the use of money became generalized. The literature in the Singhalese language became secular and broke free from its Pali and Sanskrit origins, without renouncing them, to flourish for the first time in its history – a growth that was contemporary to that of Indian literatures in vernacular languages: poetry, the so-called minor chronicles and topographical descriptions shed more light on the society of the time than the great monastic texts of the earlier period.

While the Europeans were striving to establish their power in the island, Ceylon was not, therefore, in a position of weakness: the image of decline put forward both by colonial historiography and by nationalist writings arises from the excessive value attached to the civilization of the dry zone, based on the testimony of the great monastic texts and the exclusive importance given to the archaeology of antique cities.

It is true that the state of Kotte disintegrated in the beginning of the sixteenth century (1512) against the backdrop of the rivalry between Arab and Portuguese traders. But with the support of the prince (*Zamorin*) of Calicut, the Singhalese king, Mayadunne, formed a new kingdom with Sitawaka as its capital, in the interior of the country, midway between Kotte and the mines of precious stones at Ratnapura; he succeeded in impeding the expansion of the Portuguese power. The Portuguese, established in the port of Colombo, supported the kings who had remained in Kotte, who became obliged to them and whose territory they annexed at the end of the sixteenth century; they seized from the Tamil princes of Jaffna the region of Mannar, which they converted to Catholicism, before taking possession of the whole of their territory in 1619. But their domination remained tenuous, without any comparison to the British colonization that was to come.

The Portuguese exerted themselves to take control of the kingdom of Kandy, but without success: the mountains of the centre became, for two centuries after the decline of Sitawaka, the breeding ground for resistance against colonial domination. The regions of the median country, between Colombo and Kandy, were the scene of an indigenous guerrilla war, which depopulated them but also exhausted the Portuguese forces, until the momentary alliance between the king of Kandy, Rajasinha II, and the Dutch put an end to their presence in the island, in 1658.

Despite its transience and its fragility, Portuguese rule left profound marks: the conversion to Catholicism of a part of coastal population (essentially from the fishing castes, Tamil speakers in the North and Singhalese in the South) was sustained by the action of Oratorian priests from Goa during the Dutch domination, perceived as a period of persecution, and thereafter by Italian and French missionaries. The use of Portuguese, the language of communication in the Asiatic maritime space, continued as late as the nineteenth century. The port sites chosen by the Portuguese would witness continuous urban development, and the commercial network founded on the export of cinnamon towards Europe, areca nut and elephants towards India and on the import of Indian rice and cloths, would persist for a long time.

The colonization of the coastal regions

From the beginning of the seventeenth century, the establishment by the Portuguese, and later by the Dutch, of a regime of direct rule in the coastal regions, brought the island close to the Javanese model and differentiated it from the forms of control that were taking shape in the continent. Ceylon was integrated at this time into a system that took advantage of the possibilities offered by maritime trade but also from the relative weakness of the political regimes situated at the southern fringe of Asia, which contrasted with the power of the continental empires of the North, notably the Mogul state. The Dutch East India Company sought to seize possession of the productive territories. It was only at the end of the eighteenth century that it experimented with the first plantations: it would be left to the British from 1840 onwards to impose a new model of economic exploitation in Ceylon.

The cost of collecting cinnamon was apparently infinitesimal in comparison with the vertiginous rise in prices after 1660. But this production was based on coercion: the Salagama caste – weavers turned cinnamon peelers – was assigned to forced deliveries and was not up to meeting the demand. The resistance of the entire population of the coastal regions against the restrictions imposed by the Dutch on subsistence agriculture threatened to overthrow the system. All the more as the independent kingdom of Kandy which supported these revolts represented a permanent challenge to the Dutch power: Holland, powerless to conquer it, strived to enclave it by depriving it of access to the sea.

The strength of the Kandyan state rested on the defence offered by a relief that made the highlands a natural fortress, on the social organization into castes that the monarchy had placed at the service of a tax and military system founded on tenures of service and lastly, on the revival of Buddhism in the eighteenth century, encouraged by a dynasty of Dravidian stock (the Nayakkars of Madurai), which found in it a source of legitimacy to counterbalance its South Indian origins. Its weakness resided in the absence of external support, in coterie fights that undermined the ruling aristocracy (the Radalas, the highest section of the Goyigama caste), in the latent discontent caused by the despotic nature of the regime and in the growing alienation between the Tamil entourage of the ruler and the powerful Kandyan families. In 1796, when the British seized the coastal regions, in the wake of the disappearance of the Dutch provoked by the French occupation of the Netherlands, the economy of Ceylon was integrated with the world trade and the monopoly of the Company was seriously eroded by the illegal trade and smuggling with India organized by the Muslims and by the Tamils of Jaffna.

Local society was more profoundly transformed in the Singhalese low land than in the rest of the island or in the coastal areas of India. The Dutch had imposed in this part of the world their version of Roman law: a regime of individual ownership of land was established to the detriment of the principle of undivided ownership and of the traditional tiering of land rights. The colonial power openly supported a landed aristocracy (the Mudaliyars of the low land) whose power it consolidated by recognizing its full and undivided ownership of vast domains in the southwest of the island. The judicial machinery gave rise to a class of lawyers, largely hailing from among the Creoles of Dutch stock (called Burghers). Along with the native chiefs accumulating wealth through the collection of agrarian taxes, they formed the beginning of an urban elite as early as the eighteenth century. The early development of education ensured the continuity of the power of this composite bourgeoisie by entrenching it in a 'colonial culture'. On the other hand, the Dutch and, to a certain extent, the British, recognized and codified the personal rights of the Tamil communities, notably in the Jaffna peninsula, and thereby contributed to maintaining their particularity and rigid caste structure.

The depth of the British impact

At the dawn of the nineteenth century, colonialism was not new to Ceylon. The British had not been confronted, as they had in the subcontinent, by the vestiges of an imperial political machinery, or the dynamism of an autonomous barter economy, nor by the complexity of a highly hierarchic rural society. The island would be governed by men who were not to make a career in India, but in Africa, Malaysia or in the Caribbean. In general, the colonial policy pursued in Ceylon reflected the one followed in India, without it resulting from deliberate coordination. But the authorities here had a much denser network of administrators (the district in Ceylon was much smaller and less populated than an average Indian district), of means of communication and information and, consequently, the best tools to impose their policy. Nevertheless, there was a good measure of improvisation, of opportunism and of contradictions in the practice of the Raj.

After 1815, the English consolidated their dominion in Ceylon, which they considered indispensable for the control of the south of India where they were in the process of expanding their territories. The ports of Trincomalee and Galle presented in this regard a strategic interest for the surveillance of the maritime routes connecting the eastern and western coasts of the subcontinent. Until 1802, the island was placed under the administration of the East India Company, which governed it from its base in Madras, even while continuing to use the services of Dutch administrators. An attempt to reorganize public finances, and more particularly the employment of South Indian tax agents by the Company, which deprived the native chiefs of the lowlands of their prerogatives, sparked off a revolt in 1796–7. Order was restored when Governor North chose to rely on the landed aristocracy. After a period of trial and error, London resolved to change the status of Ceylon, which became a direct colony of the Crown in 1802 and would be governed independently of India throughout the entire colonial period. From the British imperial perspective, the island was an essential link in a system of control and exploitation that extended from the Red Sea to the Straits of Malacca and to Australia, and from Bombay to Calcutta and to Rangoon. But until the creation of a telegraphic network and the opening of the Suez Canal (1869), the control wielded by London remained distant and the initiative of the local governors often predominant.

British domination, firstly maritime as that of its predecessors, encompassed larger and larger territories. But while it allowed vassal princely states to subsist in the subcontinent, it undertook the annexation of the kingdom of Kandy, which hindered the security of its communications and its control of the cinnamon-producing regions. An ill-prepared expedition ended in a crushing defeat in 1803. From then on, the strategy of the British was to add fuel to court intrigues with a view to destabilizing a young ruler, hitherto popular, but not experienced, and who was to attract the hatred of the aristocracy by a series of executions in response to the plots of his ministers. In 1815, believing that the time was ripe, the British sent a second expedition which, meeting no resistance, resulted in the cession of the kingdom, which was sealed by a convention signed with the principal Kandyan chiefs and Buddhist dignitaries, by which the colonial authorities undertook to respect their privileges and to grant their support to the *sangha* (the Buddhist 'Church').

But the Kandyan aristocracy was soon disillusioned by the unexpected extent of British supremacy, which excluded all prospects of a restoration of the monarchy. It joined *en masse* the popular insurrection of 1817–8, which prefigured on a smaller scale the revolt of 1857–8 in the North of India. The rebellion was provoked by the appearance, in the isolated provinces of the east, of a pretender – a former monk who claimed to be a descendant of the royal Nayakkar family and who invoked the support of the Hindu god Skanda who had been revealed to him at the sanctuary of Kataragama. The mobilization of the Kandyan population and the efficiency of the guerrillas threatened the colonial presence, but the divisions among the rebels enabled the British to reconquer the ancient kingdom, by practising a scorched earth policy, which devastated entire regions. The repression decimated most of the great Radala families, with the result that the beginnings of subsequent revolts, always motivated by trends aiming at a restoration, were easily crushed, all the more as the construction of roads (the Colombo–Kandy road was inaugurated in 1831) prevented the extension of the breeding grounds of the guerrillas.

In 1848 a new rebellion flared up, led this time by the Singhalese of the lowlands, but which found support above all from the Kandyan peasantry. The causes of the revolt were, firstly, the fears of the Kandyans, provoked by the rupture of the link between the colonial government and Buddhism, as well as by the social upheaval consequent upon the setting up of coffee plantations, and secondly, the action of the liberal press of Colombo, which denounced the establishment of new taxes and reported with sympathy the echoes of the French Revolution. It soon met with failure because it did not obtain the support of a debilitated aristocracy: the dominant families had lost their ascendancy shortly after the conquest, and it is significant that the initiative of the revolt came from the immigrants of the coastal regions.

The influence of Protestant missionaries was stronger in Ceylon than in the India of Bentinck, but Buddhist practices did not give cause for them to issue moral condemnations as they had done against Hinduism. On the other hand, the missionaries found in the terms of the convention of 1815 an occasion to denounce the lack of firmness of the colonial authorities: they demanded the dissociation of the State and Buddhism and the support of the authorities for Protestant churches and largely obtained satisfaction. But in the wake of the rebellion of 1848, their influence decreased even as an interest for Buddhist doctrines developed in the West. In the long term, the response to the action of the missionaries would take the form of a movement of Buddhist renaissance, which would follow ways significantly different from those of the religious and social reform movements characteristic of India during the same period. In the short term, the missionary activities gave a decisive impetus to education in English, in Colombo, Galle, Kandy and Jaffna, leading to the emergence of an anglicized elite that conformed to the dreams of Macaulay, and whose conversion to Christianity the authorities overtly promoted.

This anglicized class, of which the Burghers constituted the elite, was associated with the political game earlier than in India: a commission of enquiry composed of two men with liberal ideas, W Colebrooke and C Cameron, was charged by London with the task of proposing reforms aiming at creating embryonic legislative power, following the example of the evolution which was crystallizing in Australia and in Canada. As early as 1833, two councils, legislative and executive, including a few appointed members not belonging to the administration were created to assist the governor. This initiative established a precedent that would place the island, during the entire colonial period, a step ahead of the continent in the matter of constitutional reform. But it introduced the principle of representation based on communities – there was initially one Singhalese representative, one Tamil, one Burgher and three Europeans – which would contribute to a long-lasting division; when the number of seats was increased in 1889, caste-based rivalries loomed large on the political scene.

This system calmed any vague radical inclinations among the members of the elite, who did not demand an evolution towards the principle of election. The reality of power continued to be concentrated in the hands of the governor and his representatives in each district: called 'government agents' (and not 'collectors' as in India), they were more and more rarely natives of the island and depended on the collaboration of the loyalist local chiefs. The Tamil regions of the north were administrated autonomously: the government agents, who remained for a very long time in office in Jaffna, acted as proconsuls and contributed to the maintenance of a conservative social structure. The Kandyan districts were especially subject to close surveillance, owing to their growing economic importance.

The economic strategies inspired by the home country were parallel in India and in Ceylon: from the 1830s onwards, they aimed at dismantling the restrictions on the freedom of enterprise. Until 1832, the East India Company enjoyed the monopoly of the trade in cinnamon whose production it encouraged and whose prices it manipulated to the detriment of Ceylon and for the benefit of India that it was governing. In a space of a few decades, prices collapsed and the cinnamon of Ceylon lost its pre-eminent place in the European market. However, the first coffee plantations began to prosper from 1824 onwards. Furthermore, the colonial government transformed into compulsory labour service the system of *rajakariya* – inherited from the Dutch and the Kandyans – which made the recognition of land ownership conditional upon the fulfilment of services for the benefit of the king or the colonial government. The Salagamas (the group forced to deliver cinnamon) complained of the burden of their obligations, while the Kandyan peasants conscripted for the construction of roads manifested a discontent intensified by the sentiment that service had been deprived of any symbolic compensation.

The Colebrook–Cameron commission proposed to abolish the monopolies of the state, to remove the obstacles to trade, to liberate the labour market by abolishing the system of compulsory labour service and to support private ownership of land, which had been permitted to Europeans as early as 1812. The integral implementation of this programme facilitated the extension of coffee plantations, at the initiative of British planters and occasionally of the Singhalese of the low land, for whom the Kandyan regions became a hinterland open to their enterprises. The monetarization of the economy, already advanced in the lowlands, generalized in the highlands, but the Kandyans themselves did not benefit from it: traders, middlemen and speculators were either Muslims who had already established themselves there or immigrants from the coastal regions. Moreover, the reluctance of the villagers to accept the conditions close to serfdom imposed by the planters, led the latter to resort to Tamil coolies, attracted from India, initially on a temporary basis, then permanently. Thus a multi-communal society was formed in the ancient Kandyan kingdom, the different sections of which maintained economic relations, but which were not either functionally or symbolically integrated as they had been during the time of the monarchy.

At this stage, the evolution of Ceylon diverged from that of India as a whole, despite similarities with certain regions like Assam, Coorg and Travancore where plantation economies had also developed that relied on an immigrant labour force. In Sri Lanka, the colonial state came to depend on the export resources procured by plantations to such an extent that the crisis that annihilated the coffee plantations in the beginning of the 1880s represented a major collapse. It was surmounted by a rapid conversion to substitution crops, essentially tea, occasionally cinchona and cocoa and rubber. The success of tea was due to the regularity of the harvest throughout the year and the possibility of cultivating at different altitudes, but also to the growth of British consumption, encouraged by the marked preference of the traders of the home country of the end of the nineteenth century for a product that they could control within the framework of the imperial market. At the turn of the century, a crisis of overproduction led to a concentration of capital and a rationalization of structures: the age of owner-planters gave way to the age of large companies based in the home country, like Brooke Bond, Lipton, which administered their estates through 'managing agencies' established in Asia. Besides, the least profitable of the plantations of the low and median land were reconverted for the production of rubber. The economy of the island was henceforth founded, directly or indirectly, on tea, which represented more than half of the export revenue.

The emphasis laid solely on the plantation economy meant that subsistence farming became neglected. The rice cultivation of the dry zone fell victim, until the middle of the nineteenth century, to the disinterest of the administration regarding irrigation and to the abolition of the *rajakariya*, which had allowed the maintenance of hydraulic works. In the centre and the southwest, a large part of the lands available for slash-and-burn farming and the extension of gardens planted with trees were absorbed by plantations. Timid efforts towards the restoration of village reservoirs and a few large dams came up against the prevalence of malaria and yaws, a chronic infectious disease, in the dry zone; the opposition of planters, who considered it a futile expense; and competition from the massive imports of Indian and Burmese rice destined to provide food to the people in the cities and plantations. They succeeded only in limited zones of the east (Batticaloa) and of the south (Matara). The abolition of taxes on the production of subsistence corps (in sharp contrast with the situation prevailing in colonial India) did not prove to be an incentive to the growth of productivity. During the first third of the twentieth century, the government stopped financing irrigation works. In addition, the repression of slash-and-burn cultivation by the colonial authorities deprived the peasants of a complementary resource, indispensable for their balance: those who could do so replaced it by the profits earned from commercial agriculture, salaried work on the plantations and petty trade. The rest were condemned to a greater economic precariousness.

Nevertheless, there was no conflict between a traditional native sector and a colonial modern sector, but rather interdependence. The spirit of enterprise was not the monopoly of European planters: numerous Ceylonese amassed wealth thanks to the renting of taxes, their activities as middlemen and above all, the various advantages offered by subaltern positions in the administration. By the middle of the nineteenth century, they began to invest in plantations, particularly in coconut trees; for this purpose, they also obtained mortgage loans from Tamil trader-bankers, the Nattukottai Chettiars. This trend became massive at the turn of the century: non-Europeans acquired 72 per cent of the land sold by the Crown between 1868 and 1906. Coconut plantations, whose production was partly destined for the domestic market, seemed a safe investment, which did not require the use of new techniques or considerable capital: their area quadrupled in the space of half a century. The plantations supplied a series of resources to the various categories of the local population: regular employment on the plantations of coconut and rubber trees, more casual on tea plantation; the fabrication of latex, arrack and coir; handicrafts made of wood; professions linked to transport, felling, construction, urban development and port activities. They led to a rise in the standard of living of the majority of the population of the wet regions of the island, evident in the beginning of the twentieth century: early and continuous demographic expansion testifies to it. It contrasted with the situation on the continent and contributed to attracting to Ceylon Indian immigrants, who at the beginning of the century became more numerous than the native Tamils of the northeast.

The colonial state supported the planters because its budget depended largely on the taxes linked to the prosperity of this sector – essentially customs duties on imported rice and on exported agricultural products. In the absence of land registration and a settlement, as had been established in India, the administration proved incapable of fixing the base for a general land tax that could have been simultaneously imposed on planters and peasants. The only tax levied on rural agriculture was the tax on paddy (one tenth of the harvest), which brought in little income and which became a source of permanent discontent. The sporadic attempts aimed at converting it into a fixed land tax were systematized after 1878: in the course of the 1880s, the multiplication of legal actions for the non-payment of tax brought about evictions against which sectors of public opinion mobilized itself, with the support of the liberal press. In 1892, the government resolved to abolish the tax, with the result that Ceylon became the only country of the region where subsistence agriculture was not taxed.

This exceptional situation explains the quasi absence of agrarian movements in the island, which contrasted with India and Southeast Asia. A poll tax towards the maintenance of routes had been instituted in 1848; viewed by the Kandyans as a restoration of the forced labour, it was maintained until 1922, but did not represent a very substantial income. Only the taxes on alcohol continued to have a considerable weight, notwithstanding the opposition of the nationalist circles, which launched a campaign in favour of prohibition in the beginning of the century.

The 'plantocracy' founded its power on the close links that it maintained with the administration. In the beginning, there was confusion between the two activities:

the colonial administrators of the 1840s often devoted more time to their estates than to their official tasks. Subsequently, the Association of Planters, founded in 1854, became the most influential lobby in the country. It relentlessly claimed cheap lands and above all unassailable land titles, means of communication and the organization, for its benefit, of the immigration and control of Tamil coolies. The state met the expectations of the planters by devoting a substantial part of its public expenditure to the construction of roads in the Kandyan region by imposing forced labour on peasants, and by establishing a railway network serving the zone of plantations.

In 1840, an order proclaimed the Crown's ownership of the forestlands and a large part of the areas until then used for slash and burn farming. The Crown resold the spaces in which they were interested to the planters at very low prices. When the lands available consequently became rare, villagers also began to sell what remained of their uplands, at the instigation of a class of Ceylonese and European land speculators, who often made their fortune in this manner. At least until the authorities, from 1897 onwards, apprehending the long-term effects of this buying-up, instituted a department of land registration and settlement with a view to amiably determining the respective rights of owners and of the Crown. But it was too late to ward off the threat of a shortage of land, which hampered the expansion of villages in the zone of plantations. Moreover, to a much greater extent than in India, the plantations adversely affected the environment: deforestation made the flow of the rivers that irrigated the rice fields irregular, grazing grounds and resources of firewood and timber dwindled, methods of culture, founded on integral weeding, caused widespread erosion and silting up of paddy fields situated in the foothills.

The planters demanded that the state ensured them an abundant and docile labour force. As long as the villagers had enough lands for their needs, they were loath to work in large estates, all the more as the planters sought to force them to reside there. Hence the recourse to an immigrant labour force from the south of India according to modalities quite different of those that prevailed for migration under contract to long distance, towards the plantations of the islands of the Indian ocean and of the West Indies. This immigration remained seasonal and male for the best part of the coffee period (1835–80): the coolies, the majority of whom were untouchables, were recruited in the Tamil country through intermediaries called *kanganis*. Working and living conditions on the plantations were miserable, deaths on the outward and return journey were numerous, the workers were paid only at the end of their stay and through their *kangani*, who withheld the amount of the advances that he had made to them. But despite the meagreness of the income that they earned, this temporary employment enabled the migrants to brave the vagaries of the climate responsible for terrible famines in the south of India, in as much as the coffee harvest season in Ceylon did not overlap with the season of paddy cultivation in Tamil Nadu.

Things changed completely after the conversion to tea and rubber. Employment then became permanent and largely female: entire families settled down permanently on the plantations, under the strict control of the *kanganis* and to the greatest advantage of the planters; even while retaining a certain mobility, owing to the proximity of the country of origin, which enabled them to preserve their cultural identity intact. The population of Ceylon grew more rapidly because of this than all the other regions of South Asia, with the exception of Assam and Lower Burma, despite the high mortality rate. The presence of a large community of South Indian workers on the plantations and in Colombo (where a large number of Keralites were engaged in manual work, notably in the port) reinforced the multi-communal character of island society, into which immigrants had until then assimilated rapidly.

Lastly, the economic specialization of Ceylon took place in the framework of an imperial system wherein India occupied a central place. The same banks, commercial import and export firms and British managing agencies controlled the market economy in the island and on the continent. Indian businessmen were active in Ceylon. Nattukottai Chettiars controlled land and commercial credit, Bohras, the important rice trade, Sindhis textile imports. A part of the distributive trade was carried out by Muslim traders of Keralite origin.

The Indian predominance in trade gave rise, as early as the beginning of the twentieth century, to xenophobic reactions, orchestrated by the Singhalese merchants of the lowlands. In 1915, after a dozen years of commercial rivalry, the regions situated between Colombo and Kandy became the scene for riots directed against Indian Muslim traders, the repression of which marked the kick-off of the national movement. Shortly thereafter, during the depression of the 1930s, it would be the Chettiars who would be accused of being the agents of Indian expansionism and the Tamil coolies of forming its troops. As in Burma – the other Buddhist country in the region – India was, even before its independence, perceived as a great power with which it was advisable to avoid association.

Responses to the colonial system

The apogee of the Raj brought to Ceylon, as to India, the ferment of a crisis in the established order. But while the 1880s heralded the formative phase in the emergence of national sentiment in the continent, it was marked in the island by movements for the quest for its identity that did not lead to a comparable political mobilization: this difference merits an explanation.

In the course of the last third of the nineteenth century, the colonial power increasingly relied on the powerful landowners of the lowlands, of which the Bandaranaike family represents the archetype. It strove, generally without success, to invest the Kandyan elite classes with authority and dynamism: the administration legally recognized and registered the services that the tenant peasants owed to the temples and to the Kandyan chiefs. It legitimized the hierarchies of caste without giving them an official status, nor enumerating them as had been done on the subcontinent. It sought to favour a conservative Buddhism and to moralize society, by denouncing the corruption of the administrators of ecclesiastical properties and of certain monks, but also practices such as polyandry. The decadence of the Kandyan aristocracy can be put down to the adverse effects of alcoholism, widespread ever since the fiscal policy encouraged the intensification of a traffic in alcohol: certain leaders

demanded the imposition of a system of prohibition. At the same time, the authorities restricted the access of the Ceylonese to posts of responsibility in the
administration and in the judiciary, and sought to impose the image of an irre-
proachable administration, the defender of the public good against the private
interests of a handful of native exploiters hailing from the lowlands. This policy was
the offshoot of reflexes of conservatism nurtured by the emergence of a Ceylonese
bourgeoisie whose prosperity was founded on the activities based on the plantation
economy.

This bourgeoisie was diverse in its origins. The nouveaux riches of the Singhalese
lowlands, including many Karavas and Salagamas, occupied an increasingly important place, but the Goyigama notables were numerous, as were the Tamil Vellalas of
Jaffna, the Burghers and a few powerful families of Muslim traders. Its economic
interests converged, given the place that the plantations occupied in its heritage. It
was the material prosperity that came from the plantations of coconut and rubber,
graphite mines and commerce that served as the base for the formation of this
class. The education that its children received in the private English schools of
Colombo, Kandy or Jaffna contributed to a social homogeneity. The predilection for
careers as judges, lawyers and doctors, which were the most prestigious, led to the
creation of law and medical schools, but the absence of a university incited families
that had the means to send their children to Great Britain to pursue their studies,
more often than to India.

Although very anglicized, the elite was not as cut off from the mass of the population as was claimed by the administration, which made itself out to be the
protector of the 'real country' against the pretensions of the bourgeoisie. It was from
its ranks that movements of religious renaissance arose, in reaction to the missionary
influence that was exercised in education. It was, as in India, an effort to oppose the
cultural defiance of the west by drawing from a largely reinvented tradition, with the
difference that Ceylon lacked the dimension of social reform that played a significant
role in the birth of Indian nationalism.

This tendency appeared before the middle of the nineteenth century among the
Tamils of Jaffna, where American Protestant missions were particularly active: a
movement urging the return to the sources of Saivaism was launched by Arumuga
Navalar, a scholar who had collaborated with the missionaries: he edited the great
Tamil religious texts, created a network of Hindu schools and organizations of
laymen, published numerous brochures and preached the Saivaite doctrine: his
influence even radiated to the south of India. But contrary to the Brahmo Samaj
and the Arya Samaj, the movement initiated by Navalar was fundamentally
conservative in nature and his message cannot be interpreted in a nationalist sense.
On the contrary, he contributed to the reinforcing of the caste spirit of the Hindus
of Jaffna and their specificity by presenting their society as the conservatory of
Shivaite orthodoxy and of the purest form of Tamil culture, which external influences
had caused to degenerate on the continent. Concurrently and contradictorily, the
Tamils of Jaffna opened themselves to the outside world: the quality education that
they received enabled them to find employment all across the British Empire, while the
University of Madras offered the others the possibility of pursuing higher studies.

This ambivalence, characteristic of the issues surrounding emigration, persisted until the end of the twentieth century and formed one of the factors of the separatist movement.

The insularity of Navalar was the exact counterpart of the representations promoted by the defenders of Buddhism, which made Ceylon 'the island of the Doctrine' (*Dhammadipa*) – the home of Buddhist orthodoxy. The renaissance of Buddhism in the low land crystallized in the beginning of the nineteenth century, on the initiative of the Salagama, Karava and Durava laymen, who did not accept that monastic ordination was reserved for the members of the Goyigama high caste: as early as 1802, a delegation of novices travelled to Burma for obtaining a valid ordination, thus founding the order of Amarapura. While the Kandyan monks of the order of Siam became fossilized in conservative attitudes, those of the lowlands took up more effectively the challenge put forth by the Protestant missionaries during public controversies which engrossed the crowd and which culminated, in 1873, with the triumph of Migettuvatte Gunananda at Panadura. This episode drew the attention of the American theosophists, whose founder, Olcott, visited Ceylon several times after 1880, contributing to the organization of a militant Buddhism that gained renewed strength from this western support. But as early as 1883, conflict between Buddhists and Catholics flared up in the outskirts of Colombo, of which the government accused the Buddhists of being the instigators.

At the beginning of the twentieth century, the movement described by some as 'Protestant Buddhism' broke free from the influence of theosophists, even while retaining Western methods of mobilization and themes. It was spearheaded by a young admirer of Olcott, who, choosing the existence of an ascetic and a propagandist of Buddhism, had adopted the name Anagarika Dharmapala. This character, whose bearing and message evoked in certain respects Gandhi, preached moralization of society as a precondition for the reconquest of national identity. He gave a decisive impetus to a movement of temperance, which accused the government of encouraging the consumption of alcohol for the profits that it earned from it and which, as a result, targeted the distillers of arrack, Catholic in the majority. The rich laymen who supported it founded schools, seminaries (*pirivena*) and newspapers, and then formed influential pressure groups, such as the All Ceylon Buddhist Congress and the Young Men's Buddhist Association. But this agitation remained essentially of a social and religious character: unlike in India, it did not lead to a political movement. A reason for this was the absence of Dharmapala, who had settled in Bengal, where he fought for the restoration of the high places of Buddhism, but even more, the absence of a political organization comparable to the Congress, and the prosperity of large sections of the society that numbed any desire to protest. By granting in 1910, to the English-educated Ceylonese, the right to elect a representative to the Legislative Council, the power aroused coterie rivalries that diverted the elite from an authentic political action.

The First World War was marked, as in India, by political activism. Following the example of Tilak, AE Goonesinha created a Youth League and developed a union movement among the working class of Colombo. This resulted in the hardening of the colonial authorities, which portended an open conflict, but the troubles that broke out in 1915 were provoked by 'communalist' attitudes and not by a nationalist movement. Tensions between Buddhist activist traders, and South Indian Muslims who had settled recently, largely motivated by commercial rivalries but expressed in religious terms, degenerated into acts of violence and looting at the time of the celebration of the centenary of the cession of Kandy. These troubles, perceived by the colonial authorities as a plot aiming to destabilize them, were quelled with the help of Indian troops, with a violence incommensurate with the real violation of public order, as would be four years later the protest meeting at Amritsar. The executions of rioters and the imprisonment of the principal Singhalese Buddhist leaders (notably the Senanayake family) created a movement of solidarity, spearheaded by the Tamil leaders Ramanathan and Arunachalam. A national movement seemed on the point of emerging, with the foundation, in 1919, of Ceylon National Congress, which brought together the representatives of all the communities and of all leanings.

But the mobilization had disintegrated by 1921, without giving rise to a mass movement. The governor, Manning (1918–25), exploited, if not aroused, coterie fights and cleavages between castes and between communities in the wake of the expansion of the suffrage to the Legislative Council: the Tamils broke away from the Congress, with Arunachalam leaving its leadership in 1921; the Kandyans asserted their demands in the face of the preponderance of the Singhalese of the lowlands. This policy of division was successful only because the nationalist movement remained inconsistent: no dynamics came to revitalize it and the moderates who dominated the Congress were frightened of the daring of a Goonesinha, who organized a general strike in Colombo in 1923.

The phenomena observed in Ceylon were not radically different from those that encouraged the birth of Indian nationalism and the vicissitudes that attended its growth. Yet, in the Ceylonese case, the movement met with failure. The ancientness and the depth of the colonial impact in Ceylon could have contributed to the frailty of the reaction. The non-existence of groups capable of catalyzing the nationalist reaction, and notably the absence of Brahmins, needs to be taken into account: the monks, sequestered from civil society, would not be able to assume this role and the Buddhist activist circles did not have either the network nor perhaps the legitimacy to create a political mass movement. The provincialism of Colombo produced neither the intellectual effervescence of Calcutta, nor the activity of the business world of Bombay, and where all that came from, India, was regarded with distrust – the prestige of Gandhi here remained very limited – this was hardly conducive to political activism. Until independence, political activity was for the most part confined to the acts of individuals or of coteries refractory to party discipline, which exposed them to the manipulations of the colonial authorities. The break between the anglicized urban bourgeoisie, and the local notables educated in the vernacular schools, seemed more marked than in the regions of India where the national movement developed. Nonetheless, the growth of local branches of Buddhist movements of temperance where these notables militated, and their transformation into popular associations (*mahajana sabhas*), show that it was possible to create such a network. The advanced development of western education was not sufficient to incite a national political mobilization. Politics in Ceylon rarely succeeded in going beyond the level of coterie fights: a typical example in this regard is the opposition between the Senanayake and Bandaranaike clans, which persisted, and was transformed after independence by the creation of the two principal parties of the island. These local potentates did not feel the need to oppose colonial interference as in India, insofar as their power depended very largely on their collaboration with the Raj.

Furthermore, the island, at least since the abolishing of agrarian taxation, no longer experienced tensions likely to spark off protest movements in rural areas which could serve as a base for a mass mobilization like the one that made the success of the Indian Congress in the 1920s. It is true that the repression of slash and burn cultivation and the scarcity of land consequent upon the extension of the large tea, rubber or coconut estates fomented a latent discontent. The hunger for land was felt all the more as the preceding decades had been marked by very high demographic growth (more than 1.5 per cent per year), well before that in India and probably owing more to the rising standards of life than to progress in medical infrastructure. But until the great depression of the 1930s, the resources earned from the system of plantations offset negative effects. And when these resources began to dwindle, the colonial government, in agreement with the Ceylonese political leaders, was prompt in inversing its land policies and in stopping the expansion of plantations, on the recommendations of an agrarian commission, which met between 1927 and 1929. At this time, the transfer of power to the bourgeoisie had already been initiated and the political interests of the Ceylonese leaders converged with those of the Raj to impede at all costs the emergence of Gandhian type of movement. With a view to forming political supporters in the rural areas, they projected themselves as the defenders of the peasantry and started, from 1935 onwards, to distribute the lands that were still available in the humid zone and to undertake extensive irrigation works designed to restore to rice cultivation the vast spaces of the dry zone, which had been the heart of the ancient civilization. Hailing from a family that had made its fortune in coconut plantations and graphite mines, DS Senanayake was the advocate of this policy.

The depression dried up the sources of prosperity; it revealed the limits of the colonial growth and showed to what extent the majority of the peasantry was integrated into the market economy. The malaria epidemic that broke out in 1934–35 was aggravated by the effects of the crisis, which reduced peasant families of the rubber and coconut regions to a state of extreme need. It became the occasion for the setting up, in the rural areas, of the rudiments of a welfare state. The principal beneficiaries of this evolution were the Singhalese – in particular the Kandyan villagers – and the authorities sought to exclude Indian immigrants from it. A characteristic trait of the crisis was the development of xenophobic sentiments, which were directed against the Indian presence and which borrowed the European arsenal of the time: the Tamil immigrant workers were made responsible for unemployment by the unionists, like Goonesinha, who had shortly before been defending class positions. The bourgeoisie, whose revenues earned from coconut plantations collapsed and who feared a process of dispossession on a vast scale – which did not take place – accused Indian moneylenders and businessmen, especially the Chettiars, of ruining the country and of appropriating its lands. Nevertheless, these verbal outbursts did not lead to physical violence, as was the case in Burma during that time. From the perspective of a transfer of power, the bourgeoisie preferred the parliamentary way that was opened to it and obtained, among others, the creation of a system of state credit for its use.

The transfer of power

The appointed Legislative Council – established in 1833 – had been progressively opened up, from 1910 to 1923, to representatives elected by a very narrow suffrage based on a tax qualification and separate colleges. Concurrently with the Simon commission, sent to India to investigate the possibilities of expansion of the representative system, the Donoughmore commission (1927) examined the opportunities for the evolution of the regime. Despite a smokescreen boycott, the entire political class seized the opportunity given to it to express its demands, where factional interests and oligarchic preoccupations dominated: factionalism, casteism, regionalism and communalism were given free rein.

Marked by the personality of the British Labour leader, Drummond Shiels, the commission took up a position against these tendencies and chose to combat the ferments of division, hitherto nurtured by colonial power, refusing to give recognition to particular interests. It recommended the abolishing of the separate colleges and the institution of universal suffrage for both the sexes, against the opinion of the colonial machinery and of the great majority of local politicians. Among the latter, the representatives of the Tamil minority of Jaffna understood that the law of the majority might be imposed on them, while the Singhalese were worried at the thought that the Tamils of the plantations could elect one of their own in several Kandyan districts, where they formed the majority. As regards the colonial administration, it viewed the system of dyarchy proposed by the commission with the greatest scepticism. It had been stipulated that the governor would retain control of the finances, justice, maintenance of order and foreign relations, with the other domains of public intervention being devolved to the assembly, called the State Council. The Council had to elect, within its framework, specialized commissions, each appointing as its head a minister, without there being either a prime minister, nor collective ministerial responsibility, before the assembly.

This constitution was initially ill received by the political class: universal suffrage was forcing it to enter the electoral arena, without the power granted to it meeting its expectations. The goal it pursued was a parliamentary system based on the British model, within the framework of a dominion, with an administration controlled by a parliament. But the members of the State Council soon discovered the advantages that they could draw from their position. The system enabled the emergence of a strong character, DS Senanayake, who would dominate the political game during the period of decolonization. Against him, while the then unionist Goonesinha, who had believed he could create a labour party on the British model, had lost all influence, emerged a Marxist movement, created in 1936, the Lanka Sama Samaja Party. This party had two of its leaders elected to the Council, led efficient campaigns of anti-colonial mobilization, demanded total independence, but split up in the face of Stalinism; the majority of its members joined with the Trotskyist International in 1940.

The non-Singhalese on their side, were anxious about the dismantling of the separate colleges. Under the pressure of the Youth League of Jaffna, inspired by the Indian national movement, which outflanked the moderates, the Tamils of the north of the island boycotted the elections during two years. Subsequently, their representatives demanded equal representation for the Singhalese majority (about 70 per cent of the population) and all the minorities. This process of radicalization prefigured the separatism that appeared forty years later. In response, an openly communal Singhalese organization, the Sinhala Mahasabha, was created in 1937 by SWRD Bandaranaike, but it would be only in 1956 that this movement would become politically credible. The rise of political 'communalism' in the course of the 1930s was the outcome of a system where the groups, until then represented through separate colleges, henceforth perceived themselves as minorities, reduced by definition to a position of opposition: the same logic was at work in India, which would lead to the secession of Pakistan. In the meantime, the rupture between the Tamils and the Singhalese was being repaired: after 1942, Senanayake succeeded in integrating the Tamils of Jaffna into national political life for about ten years. At the same time, he excluded the Tamils of the plantations who, for the most part, became stateless at the time of independence: the Singhalese politicians of the lowlands believed that they could secure in this manner the support of the Kandyans. But they contributed to aggravating a contention with India, which arose at the end of the 1930s, with the dismissal of a part of the employees of Indian origin and the exclusion of Indians from the distribution of lands, to which the Indian authorities responded in 1939 with the cessation of migration between the two countries, a cause for tension and inter-communal conflicts on the plantations. As early as 1943, the Ceylonese ministers obtained from the Governor the power to negotiate directly with the Indian authorities, thus gaining recognition of the sovereignty of the island, in the face of the great continental power in the process of coming into existence: more than the destiny of the coolies, this was their principal objective.

The path towards the total independence of Ceylon was very different from that of British India: the new circumstances created by the war had almost opposite effects here. After 1942, the island became the headquarters of the anti-Japanese fight in Southeast Asia. The economy of Ceylon benefited largely from this opportunity by the contracts it offered, by the setting up of a machinery of planned economy guaranteeing prices at production and controlling them at consumption and by the creation of a durable infrastructure of services, one of the most decisive contributions of which was the eradication of malaria by the use of DDT. On the political front, the extensive powers granted to the military, far from doing a disservice to the evolution towards the independence, consolidated it. The unfailing support extended by DS Senanayake to the war effort, at the time when the British presence on the continent was weakened by the Quit India movement, made him appear as an interlocutor worthy of complete confidence in a perspective of the transfer of power. It was Lord Mountbatten, then commander-in-chief, who persuaded the War

Cabinet to take into consideration, as early as June 1944, a Constitution project submitted by Senanayake: the report of the Soulbury commission, sent to Ceylon at the end of 1944, served as the basis for a negotiation that dragged on for three years. The Attlee government gave the priority to the resolution of the Indian question, for which also he solicited the services of Mountbatten, with the result that the independence of Ceylon, though ripened for a long time, became effective only in February 1948, in the wake of Indian independence.

In comparison to India, Pakistan and Burma, the transfer of power was experienced in Ceylon as an operation as peaceful as the cession of Kandy had been in 1815. The transition was all the more imperceptible as the agreement of defence and cooperation safeguarded the place of Britain in the foreign relations and economy of the island. In the eyes of the most radical nationalists, this decolonization appeared inauthentic. In many respects, 1948 did not represent a major watershed in the history of the island. The peaceful nature of the transition masked a certain number of fragilities. These would be come to light a decade later, sparking off a succession of increasingly serious crises, which would make the country, considered in 1948 a model of decolonization, the sick man of South Asia.

CONCLUSION

At the end of five centuries of tumultuous history, had India changed in essence? The persistence of the caste system and the absence of a technological revolution in its rural areas, where, towards 1950, an army of small cultivators continued to till the land with the same tools as their ancestors of the fifteenth century, could make India appear an extraordinary conservatory of archaisms. Such a view is deceptive. If we were to place its history in the balance, it is towards change that the scale tilts, without any doubt and by a long way.

Demographic changes first. They are not specific to India, but the scale on which they occurred makes them spectacular. The Indian population in the middle of the fifteenth century was certainly less than 100 million. In 1951, the Indian and Pakistani censuses put forward a figure of 434 million habitants. Until around 1920, the growth of the Indian population was regular but slow, evolving in fits and starts, due to famines and epidemics. From 1920 onwards, it gathered momentum owing to a decline in mortality sharper than that of the birth rate, explicable in part by the disappearance of famine (with the exception of the famine of 1943 in Bengal), and heralding a demographic transition. A comparison of the rates of the growth of population and food production between 1920 and 1950 could suggest that India was entering a Malthusian spiral. But the vigorous recovery of the growth of food production, which in the 1950s exceeded demographic growth, proved the pessimistic prophets wrong. This tendency has persisted until today. Thus, the Malthusian vision often applied to the subcontinent is not justified, with the exception of Bangladesh, where agriculture is struggling to meet the needs of a rapidly expanding rural population. On the other hand, the population explosion from the 1920s onwards has brought about, due to the age pyramid, the exponential growth of needs in the fields of education and health. The states of the subcontinent were inadequately armed to face them. However, towards 1950, no one could gauge the real magnitude of needs in these domains.

The economic situation that India and Pakistan had inherited seemed extremely worrying. It is true that there were some positive aspects: a railway network covering most of the country, well equipped ports, a dynamic private capitalist sector and a corps of good quality administrators. But the negative aspects were numerous: a stagnant agriculture, characterized by the burden of rural indebtedness, by an inequitable distribution of the cultivated lands, by a very embryonic and expensive system of rural credit and an industry that was still little developed. The principal obstacle to economic growth continued to be the lack of creditworthiness caused by the extreme poverty of the greater part of the rural population.

In this globally negative state of affairs, are the factors of inertia specific to Indian society, or are they the result of colonial policies? The debate continues to rage. Neither the culturalist theories that make Hindu or Islamic values the primary obstacle to the economic development of India, nor the theories that see in imperialism the principal cause of its economic backwardness, can be proved. On the other hand, it is evident that the policies followed by the colonial authorities, at least up till 1920, produced negative effects: the preference given to the British suppliers of railway equipment hampered the development of the metallurgic and engineering industry of India, and the subordination of the financial interests of the subcontinent to those of the City in London limited the possibilities of capital accumulation.

The economy of India and Pakistan towards 1950 was, therefore, characterized by limited modernization, which had hardly any impact on the rural areas, where the bulk of agricultural production continued to be used for subsistence and to rely on traditional techniques. There nevertheless existed, notably in the Deccan and the delta of Ganges, an important sector of commercial agriculture represented by cash crops (cotton, jute, tea). It was thanks to the profits of this commercialization that the Indian trading communities, in particular the Marwaris and the Gujaratis, could expand their activities towards the industrial sector, above all the textile industry. At the time of independence, India was probably the only colonial country in which native capital was more powerful than the foreign capital. This was because British capital was concentrated in a few export sectors (tea plantations, jute factories) and had started to cut down its investments since 1930, an evolution that would gain momentum after independence.

British colonization modified the society more than the economy, where transformations were limited in the final analysis. If the social hierarchy was not profoundly revolutionized, the changes at work in the eighteenth century tended to become more radical. British rule favoured the Brahmins, the trading castes and certain peasant castes, while the warrior castes, except for a few princely states, lost much of their prestige and their power. The Brahmins (and the members of several other castes like the Kayasths) were the first to frequent the new institutions of western education, which enabled them to occupy the highest and the most lucrative positions open to Indians in the administration, the judiciary, the bar and liberal professions. The trading caste, in particular those of the west and the northwest of India, were the largest beneficiaries of the development of the commercialization of agriculture and played an important role in the beginnings of the modern industrial sector, characterized by high profit rates. The peasant castes like the Jats of the Punjab and Northern India and the Patidars of Gujarat benefited from the progress of agriculture due to irrigation (the Canal Colonies of the Punjab). Generally, without the very principle of hierarchy being called into question, certain castes situated at the bottom of the social ladder succeeded in elevating their status. The losers were a section of the Muslims and the warrior castes, which suffered from the abolition of numerous native states as well as from the reorganization of the army after 1858. As regards the untouchables and the members of the lowest castes, their lot hardly changed despite the efforts undertaken by the social reform movements to fight against the most serious discriminations of which they were victims (the fight to grant the untouchables the right to enter temples in the south of India). Nevertheless, thanks to the effort of leaders like Dr. Ambedkar, the untouchables were granted by the constitution of India special rights (quotas in universities, in the administration and elected assemblies, etc). This was not the case for Muslims in post-1947 India.

It is on the political front that changes were the most striking. India in the fifteenth century was fractioned into multiple sovereignties. The Mogul Empire, which consolidated itself at the close of the sixteenth century and endured for one and a half centuries, only superimposed an additional sovereignty on the existing power structures. The eighteenth century witnessed a new disintegration of the country, but British rule put an end to it by gradually creating the embryo of a modern bureaucratic state. The two new states created in 1947 pursued the way charted out, by strengthening the process of centralization and by seeking greater efficiency. These states, jealous of their frontiers, and which arrogated the monopoly of force, have nothing in common with the pre-colonial states. The idea of the nation state that was imposed in the subcontinent was not just colonial: even the parties that fought against British rule, and primarily the Congress party, made themselves the instruments of this idea.

It was at the end of the nineteenth century that modern politics emerged: it came of age in the twentieth century with the creation of true political parties and the beginnings of a parliamentary life, which grew spectacularly after independence. Thus, democratic regimes could be established in the states born out of the former British Indian empire. Fragile democracies they might be, Pakistan and Bangladesh having experienced long periods of military dictatorship and India a 'state of emergency' in 1975 to 1977. Imperfect democracies born in a social environment that was hardly comparable to that of western democracies. Democracies nonetheless, above all in India, where the vitality of political institutions stands out in sharp contrast to the neighbouring regimes of the Middle East and of Southeast Asia.

Transformations in mentality are more difficult to pin down. It could be asserted that Indian mindsets showed themselves reluctant to change. To western eyes the preponderance of religion in everyday life, the myriad interferences between the religious and political domains appear as the most striking illustration of this. But this strong religious inclination should not be interpreted as an archaism. It is perhaps there that the most significant evolutions have occurred since the beginning of the nineteenth century. The introduction of the Christian religion, the followers of which are very few in number (2 to 3 per cent of the total population, with the highest percentages in Kerala and in certain tribal regions), did not have a great impact, but the religious world underwent profound transformations. They were not always positive. In Islam, the fundamentalist or modernist schools (Deobandi, Barelwi) attempted to fight against the worship of saints and certain others forms of popular

Islam. At the same time, numerous attempts were made to create a purged Hinduism, laying claim to Vedic purity (Brahmo Samaj, Arya Samaj) and a movement is striving to make Hinduism an organized and centralized religion, which it had never been in the past. The most evident sign of a change in mentalities is perhaps the aspiration to dignity, that has manifested itself among the most oppressed and despised sections of the population. Even if it has not led to powerful revolutionary movements, even if words have not always been translated into acts, communism has been a considerable political force in India up to the end of the twentieth century and beyond. Its impact has been profound. In its own way, in harmony with its own genius, without allowing itself to be jostled, India has undoubtedly entered the modern age.

NOTES

INTRODUCTION

1. For a clear and concise presentation, which served as our reference, see Hulin, M 'L'hindouisme', in Delumeau, J (Ed), *Le fait religieux* (Paris, 1993), pp. 351–374.
2. Deleury, G, *Les Grands Mythes de l'Inde* (Paris, 1992), p. 30.
3. Cf Dumont, L, *Homo Hierarchicus. The Caste System and its Implications* (Chicago and London, 1980). Also refer Deliège, R, *Le Système des Castes* (Paris: PUF, 1993).

I A CHANGING WORLD

1. Term by which Indians referred to the Greeks and, by extension, to the Mediterranean people.
2. The exodus of Jews to India, traditionally dated from the occupation of Jerusalem by Titus (AD 70), continued during the medieval age. The Christian community in India claims to follow the preaching of the apostle Thomas. Its presence was signalled for the first time in the sixth century by the Byzantine adventurer Kosmas Indicopleustes.
3. *The Babur Nama: Memoirs of Babur, Prince and Emperor*, ed. and trans. WM Thackerton (Oxford, 1996).
4. Varthema, L, *The Itinerary of Ludovico Di Varthema of Bologna: from 1502 to 1508*, trans. JW Jones (New Delhi, 1997).
5. Pires, T, *Suma Oriental*, p. 367.

II THE INDIAN STATES

1. Koranic exegesis, theology and law, which do not require any mystical initiation are called 'exoteric', in opposition to mysticism, which is 'esoteric'.
2. In AD 680, the death of Ali, the fourth caliph and the son-in-law of the Prophet, led to the major schism in Islam. From the Sunni majority separated the Shiite sect or the 'party', which recognized only the descendants of the Prophet, called imams, as being invested with legitimate authority. Among the Shiites, another schism isolated the Ishmailis who did not agree on the identity of the seventh imam; the majority of the Shiites acknowledge a series of twelve imams, and therefore they are called Twelver Shiites.
3. Kolff, DHA *Naukar, Rajput and Sepoy. The Ethnohistory of the Military Labour Market in Hindustan, 1450–1850* (Cambridge, 1990).
4. The Hindi dialect of the Delhi region, adopted by the Muslims as the common language, used the Arabo-Persian script; it was then called Hindi or Hindawi. In the nineteenth century, when the Hindus appropriated this dialect by writing it in the Devanagari script used by Sanskrit, they monopolized the term 'Hindi.' The form written in the Arabo-Persian script was then called urdu.

5. These themes are vouched for independently in sufi poetry dating from an earlier time outside India as well as in the more ancient Hindu and Buddhist mysticism.

6. Bouchon, G and Thomaz, L-F *Voyage dans les Deltas du Gange et de l'Irrawaddy* (Paris, 1988). This recently discovered text is the most ancient chronicle of the sultanate, anterior to the Persian chronicles written during the Mughal period.

7. In general, the title 'Sayyid' is reserved for the descendants of the Prophet. In this case, it refers to an Indian dynasty, of obscure origin, whose founder only claimed to be a descendant of the Prophet.

8. Digby, S, trans., 'Dreams and Reminiscences of Dattu Sarvani, a Sixteenth century Indo-Afghan soldier', in *Indian Economic and Social History Review*, vol. II, 1965, pp. 52–80 and 178–194. This is the only contemporary testimony on the Afghans in India at the beginning of the sixteenth century, as their history has come to our knowledge only through the chronicles dating from the Mughal period. These Afghans belonged to the clans of the Lodis, the Lohanis, the Niyaziz, the Kararanis, the Farmulis and the Surs. . .

III THE INDIAN STATES

1. From the Malayalam *samuttiri*, 'lord of the sea', title of the kings of Calicut.

2. Vijayagupta, *Padma Purana* (Calcutta, 1965), p. 7.

3. Total devotion to a god.

4. Word used in India to denote any artificial pool of water, pond, lake etc.

5. The title of the ancient kings of Eli (Kerala).

6. Sassetti, F, *Lettere* (Florence: Marcucci, 1855), vol. II, book II, p. 313.

7. Pires, T, *Suma Oriental*, p. 362. 'Gentiles', that is pagans, according to the expression used in Christian Scriptures.

8. An amalgam of base metals (copper, tin, lead), made out of the debris of various utensils (Sanskrit: *kansa*).

9. Lévi, S, *Le Népal. Étude Historique d'un Royaume Hindou* (Paris, 1905), vol. I, pp. 5–8.

IV THE NEWCOMERS

1. *Seaborne empire*, an expression coined by Charles R Boxer.

2. Aldee: from the Portuguese, *aldeia*. An expression used by the European residents of India.

3. Sassetti, F, *Lettere*, Florence, vol. II, part II, p. 343.

4. *The Babur Nama*, op. cit.

5. Sarwani, Abbas Khan *Tarikh-i Shar Shaki*, trans. Ambrishthya BP (Patna: 1974).

6. Vambery, A *Travels and Adventures of a Turkish Admiral* (London: 1899; 2nd edition, Lahore: 1975).

V AKBAR AND THE CONSTRUCTION OF THE EMPIRE (1556–1605)

1. This is called the 'communalist' vision of Mogul history. It appears in the historical works written in English by Indians, like Jadunath Sarkar, the first historian of Aurangzeb, and AL Srivastava, who authored a great biography of Akbar, and even in the works of English historians, like Vincent Smith, one of the first to have given Akbar credit for breaking away from the Islamic tradition.

2. The Pakistani historian Istiaq Husain Qureshi, who also wrote a biography of Akbar, has given the most scholarly and complete expression to this interpretation.

3. In particular, those of SAA Rizvi, John F Richards and Douglas Streusand.

4. Abdul-Fazl Allami was the son of a Indian Muslim, Shaikh Mubarak Nagauri, and the brother of the poet Faizi, who, like him, exercised a powerful influence in the Mogul court from 1574, when Akbar began to model the institutions of the empire.

5. This book promulgates the official ideology of the reign and the empire by presenting the

history of Akbar as the progressive revelation of perfection directly inspired from God, like an epiphany. Contrary to the other Mogul chronicles, the third part of this work is a sort of gazette of the empire, entitled *Ain-I Akbari*, 'The Laws of Akbar'; compiled from the archives of the empire, it describes at length the institutions and provides fiscal statistics, the only figures that we have for Mogul history.

6. Hodgson, M, *The Venture of Islam, vol. 3, The Gunpowder Empires and Modern Times* (Chicago, 1974).

VI MOGUL SPLENDOUR

1. Recent works on this period have been produced in particular by specialists of economic history and of art history. Political history essentially relies on works written between the two world wars and most often, it is remarkable to note, by Hindus: Beni Prasad on Jahangir, BP Saksena on Shah Jahan and Jadunath Sarkar on Aurangzeb. Since the last war, researchers have focused their attention selectively on the two extremities of the empire: its formation under Akbar and its decline from the end of Aurangzeb's reign.

2. After the death of its founder Guru Nanak, the sect of the Sikhs was led until 1708 by a series of nine other gurus (including Arjun) who welded it into an independent religion.

3. It is only recently that historians of architecture, WE Begley and Z Desai, have started to review the history of the reign in the light of its great chronicle, the *Badshah-nama* by Abdulhamid Lahauri, and of its abridged version, compiled by Inayat Khan.

4. Since the 1920s, it has been customary to attribute this turnaround to the influence of the Naqshbandiyya brotherhood, which presumably delegated its master Muhammad Masum (1597–1670), a descendent of Ahmad Sirhindi, to Aurangzeb. The aim was to establish a hardline Islamic State and to incite the Hindus to mass conversions. It is true that the *Letters* of Ahmad Sirhindi, in keeping with the medieval norms, recommend the humiliation of the Hindus. But a recent examination of the sources of the time has demonstrated that Muhammad Masum never had any influence in the court. The Naqshbandiyya did not play a greater political role under Aurangzeb than under Jahangir.

5. This hypothesis has been recently put forward by Satish Chandra, who rightly underscores that the measures taken against the Hindus were transitory.

VII THE EMPIRE IN ITS PROSPERITY

1. On the one hand, the University of Aligarh has constructed the image of an extremely centralized and very prosperous empire; the American historian JF Richards generally concurs with this view. On the other extreme, Indianists like JC Heesterman have called into question the capacity of the empire to exercise any sort of control outside the cities and the major arteries. Indian historians, particularly Muzaffar Alam and Sanjay Subrahmanyam, have put forward criticisms that are more moderate.

2. This task of extrapolation, initiated between the two world wars by WH Moreland, has been pursued by the University of Aligarh; the latest conclusions have been published in the first volume of the *Cambridge Economic History of India* and in the more recent book by Shireen Moosvi on the economy of the empire at the end of Akbar's reign.

3. WH Moreland has estimated the population in 1600 to be 60 million for the empire and 100 million for the whole of India. Closer to us, Kingsley Davis has put forward an estimate of 125 million for the entire country. Shireen Moosvi arrives at an assessment of 96 million for the Mogul Empire and 145 million for India.

4. The calculations made for the period of Akbar by Athar Ali, of the University of Aligarh, give the following results: in 1595, the *jagirs* accounted for 82 per cent of the revenue of the empire; they were distributed only among 1,671 people; among them, the 122 high officials alone, nobles strictly speaking, cornered 62 per cent of the revenue.

5. There were only four workshops producing gold coins, four for silver rupees and forty-

two for copper coins under the reign of Akbar. Their number increased subsequently.

6. All taxation statistics were at the time expressed in *dams* or *paisa*, that is copper coins (22 mm, 21 g) worth a fortieth of the silver rupee.

7. The historians of the University of Aligarh have arbitrarily maintained that 90 per cent of the tax resources came from agriculture, in other words, 89.10 million rupees under the reign of Akbar.

8. Based on Richards, JF, *The Mughal Empire*, (Cambridge: 1993).

9. *The Babur Nama*, op. cit.

VIII MARITIME ECONOMY AND THE TRADING COMPANIES

1. Pyrard de Laval, F *Discours du Voyage des Français aux Indes Orientales*, (Paris, 1615).

2. Term used to denote Jews recently converted to Christianity.

3. In the ancient Portuguese army, superior officer in charge of the artillery.

4. *The Voyage of John Huyghen van Linschoten to the East Indies*, (London: J Burnell and P A Tiele publications, 1884).

5. An establishment of foreign trade, less important than a trading post and of varying sizes. It could sometimes be only a shop.

6. Every year, the Spanish galleon linked Acapulco (Mexico) to the Philippines.

7. Pyrard de Laval, F *op. cit.*, 'Prologue'.

8. Quoted by L Dermigny, 'East India Company and Compagnie des Indes', p. 456, in *Sociétés et Compagnies de Commerce en Orient et dans l'océan Indien*, 8th International colloquium on maritime history, Beirut, 1966, (Paris: M Mollat publication, 1970), pp. 453–466.

IX SOCIETY AND CULTURE

1. One is more astounded to find it reiterated by Louis Dumont, who opposes the hierarchical polytheism of Hinduism and the egalitarian monotheism of Islam. Dumont, L, *Homo hierarchicus*, op. cit.

2. In other words, '*veda* of longevity': the science of medicine is considered as a supplement to one of the four revealed texts, the *Atharvaveda*, which contains magical formulas.

3. Abul-Fazl echoes this idea in the beginning of *Ain-i Akbari*, though he places warriors at the highest level.

4. This exposé of castes draws on the descriptions left behind by the British administrators of the nineteenth century (earlier documents are silent on this subject). We could perhaps project into the past the salient features of contemporary social structure, as it is difficult to imagine that the colonizers could have had the idea of inventing such a complex and puzzling structure.

5. Cf. recent ethno-historical researches, particularly by Dirk Kolff.

6. Linguists distinguish supra-regional languages of communication – called common languages – from purely regional traditions.

7. The texts of these chants were collected by R Greeven, in Benares in the last century, just as similar legends were compiled in the Punjab by Richard Temple.

X THE DISINTEGRATION OF THE MOGUL EMPIRE

1. The history of this period had been neglected for a long time. Contemporary researches have above all dealt with the history of the successor states of the Mogul Empire and with the rise to supremacy of the British in the wake of their conquest of Bengal in 1765. It has been only recently that young historians, like Muzaffar Alam and André Wink, have studied the beginning of the eighteenth century, showing how the transformations that occurred at the time conditioned the following period.

2. They were Europeans, like William Irvine or Percival Spear, or Indians like Jadunath Sarkar and Irfan Habib.

3. It was put forward by the Muslim University of Aligarh: it was constructed by the specialists of the economic history of medieval India, spearheaded by Irfan Habib. Satish Chandra announced this theory in 1959 in his work on the parties and politics at the Mogul court; Irfan Habib formulated it in a radical manner in the conclusion of his book on the agrarian structures of India published in 1963. The historians of this school have reiterated this explanation, albeit in a more moderate form, and remain attached to the central idea of decline as the inevitable consequence of Mogul institutions.
4. It was proposed by Karen Leonard in 1979.
5. This thesis has been maintained particularly by Muzaffar Alam.

XI THE SUCCESSOR STATES

1. Bayly, CA, *Indian Society and the Making of the British Empire* (Cambridge: 1988), p. 15.
2. Barnett, RB, *North India between Empires. Awadh, the Mughals and the British (1720–1801)* (Berkeley, 1976), pp. 21–2 and 241–2.
3. PJ Marshall's works are as important for the understanding of Bengal as RB Barnett's are for Oudh: *East Indian Fortunes. The British in Bengal in the Eighteenth Century* (Oxford, 1976) and *Bengal, the British Bridgehead. Eastern India (1740–1828)* (Cambridge, 1989).
4. Little, JH, *The House of Jagatseth* (Calcutta: 1967), p. 121 and Marshall, op. cit., p. 63.
5. Barnett, op.cit. p. 46.
6. Marshall, op. cit. p. 69.

XII FRENCH INDIA AND FRANCO-BRITISH RIVALRY

1. Among the more recent works: Chaudhuri, KN, *Trade and Civilization in the Indian Ocean. An Economic History from the Rise of Islam to 1750* (Cambridge: 1985); Arasaratnam, J,. *Merchants, Company and Commerce on the Coromandel Coast, 1650–1750* (Delhi: 1986); Das Gupta, A and Pearson, M, eds, *India and the Indian Ocean* (Calcutta: 1987).
2. Furber, H, *Rival Empires of Trade, 1600–1800* (Minneapolis: 1976), p. 203.
3. This has been proved, with supporting figures, by Philippe Haudrère in his thesis *La Compagnie Française des Indes au XVIIIe Siècle (1719–1795)* (Paris: 1989).
4. Ibid., pp. 404–6.
5. Wolpert, S, *A New History of India* (New York: 1977), p. 175.
6. European demand is believed to have led to the creation of one hundred thousand jobs in the textile industry in Bengal. See Om. Prakash, 'Bullion for Goods. International Trade and the Economy of Early Eighteenth Century Bengal', *Indian Economic and Social History Review*, XIII, 1976, pp. 173–175.
7. Marshall, PJ, *Bengal, the British Bridgehead. Eastern India (1740–1828)* (Cambridge, 1989), p. 66.
8. Haudrère, Ph., *La Compagnie . . .*, op. cit., pp. 965–969.
9. *Deux Officiers français au XVIIIe siècle. Mémoires et correspondance du chevalier et du général de La Farelle*, published by E Lennel de la Farelle (Paris: 1846).
10. Ranga Pillai, A, *The Private Diary of Ananda Ranga Pillai, Dubash to Joseph Dupleix* (Madras: 1904–8).
11. Guyon, Abbé, *Histoire des Indes Orientales Anciennes et Modernes* (Paris: 1744), vol. III, p. 253.
12. Cited by Haudrère, Ph., *La Compagnie . . .*, op. cit., p. 316.
13. Chaudhuri, KN, *Trade and Civilisation*, op. cit., p. 127.
14. National Archives, Colonies, C2 80, fo. 15.
15. Martineau, A and Hanoteaux, G, *Histoire des Colonies Françaises et de l'Expansion Française dans le Monde* (Paris: 1932), vol. V, p. 132.
16. National Archives, Colonies, C2 79, fo 68 and Haudrère, Ph *La Compagnie . . .*, op. cit., p. 979.
17. Cited by Crépin, P, *Mahé de La Bourdonnais* (Paris: 1926), p. 146.
18. Haudrère, Ph., *La Compagnie . . .*, op. cit., pp. 987.

19. Furber, H, *Rival Empire of Trade . . .*, op. cit.
20. Cited by Jouveau-Dubreuil, G, *Dupleix ou l'Inde conquise* (Paris: 1942), pp. 37–39.
21. Haudrère, Ph., *La Compagnie . . .*, op. cit., pp. 993–994.
22. Ranga Pillai, A, *The Private Diary . . .*, op. cit., p. 308.
23. Martineau A and Hanoteaux, G, *Histoire des Colonies Françaises . . .*, op. cit., vol. V, p. 196.
24. Martineau, A, *Bussy et l'Inde Française, 1720–1785* (Paris: 1935), p. 47.
25. Ibid., p. 80.
26. Chassaigne, M, *Bussy en Inde* (Chartres: 1976), pp. 5–6.
27. Haudrère, Ph., *La Compagnie . . .*, op. cit.
28. Martineau, A, *Dupleix et l'Inde Française, 1749–1754* (Paris: 1928), vol. IV, pp. 300–301.
29. Revenues from concessions (Villenur, Bahur,
    Karikal, Masulipatnam and its dependencies):   7,066,437 livres
    Revenues from the district of Arcot: 6,090,000 livres
    Amounts paid by the 'Moor' princes':   3,492,000 livres
    Funds from the Deccan: 21,500,000 livres
    Total: 38,158,437 livres
    Cf. Martineau, A, *Dupleix et l'Inde Française . . .*, vol. III, pp. 5–27.
30. Haudrère, Ph., *La Compagnie . . .*, op. cit., pp. 1003–1004.
31. Ibid.
32. Martineau, A, *Bussy . . .*, op. cit., p. 187.
33. Haudrère, Ph., *La Compagnie . . .*, op. cit., p. 1007.
34. The historian PE Roberts, who quotes these witnesses, observes furthermore that the revenues from French territories added up to 800,000 sterling pounds per year while those of the English amounted only to 100,000 pounds. This profit is, in his opinion, all the more remarkable as it was earned even as Bussy was under the threat of an Anglo-Maratha offensive launched from Bombay, with reinforcements from the troops disembarked by Watson, and under the command of Clive. Roberts, PE, *History of British India* (London: 1952), pp. 114–115.
35. Martineau, A and Hanoteaux, G, *Histoire des Colonies Françaises . . .*, op. cit., vol. V, p. 222.
36. Perrod, PA, *L'Affaire Lally-Tollendal. Une Erreur Judiciaire au XVIIIe Siècle* (Paris: 1976), pp. 44–47.
37. Perrod, A, op. cit.
38. Voltaire, *Fragments sur l'Inde, Sur le Général Lally et le Comte de Morangies*, 1773.
39. Labernadie, MV, *Le Vieux Pondichéry, 1673–1815* (Pondicherry: 1936), pp. 305–306 and 311.
40. Haudrère, Ph., *La Compagnie . . .*, op. cit., p. 1012.
41. Roberts, PE, *History of British India*, op. cit., pp. 95–96.
42. Haudrère, Ph., *La Compagnie . . .*, op. cit., and 'Jalons pour une histoire des companies des Indes', in *Compagnies et Comptoirs. L'Inde des Français, XVIIe siècle-XX siècle*, Revue française d'histoire d'outre-mer, no. 290, I trimester 1991, pp. 21–22.
43. Annual averages calculated on the basis of statistics given by Haudrère, Ph., *La Compagnie . . .*, op. cit., p. 1199.
44. Averages calculated on the basis of statistics supplied by Chaudhuri, KN, *The Trading World of Asia and the English East India Company, 1660–1760* (Cambridge, 1978), pp. 508–510.

XIII THE BRITISH CONQUEST OF BENGAL

1. Bayly, CA, *Indian Society and the Making of the British Empire* (Cambridge: 1988), p. 48.
2. Markovits, C, 'L'État colonial vu par les historiens', in *De la Royauté à l'État dans le Monde Indien, Purusartha*, no. 13, (Paris, 1991), p. 194.
3. See Frank, AG, *World Accumulation, 1492–1789* (1978), p. 150, and the critique of this thesis in Marshall, PJ, *Bengal, the British Bridgehead. Eastern India (1740–1828)* (Cambridge, 1989), p. 90.

4. Cited by Firminger, WK, *Historical Introduction to the Bengal Portion of the 'Fifth Report'* (Calcutta: 1917), p. CLXXVI; Marshall, PJ, *Bengal . . .*, op. cit., p. 117; and Wolpert, S, *A New History of India* (New York: 1977), p. 188.

5. Letter from the governor and the Council to the directors dated 3rd November 1772, cited by Marshall, PJ, *Bengal . . .*, op. cit., pp. 118–119.

6. Letter from the governor and the Council to the directors dated 3rd November 1772, cited by Marshall, PJ, *Bengal . . .*, op. cit., pp. 118–119.

7. Marshall, PJ, *Bengal . . .*, op. cit.

8. Ibid., p. 112.

9. Marshall, PJ, *East Indian Fortunes, the British in Bengal in the Eighteenth Century* (Oxford, 1976), p. 56.

10. Ibid., p. 154.

11. Singh, SB, *European Agency Houses in Bengal* (1783–1833) (Calcutta, 1966), and Tripathi A,. *Trade and Finance in the Bengal Presidency* (1783–1833) (Calcutta, 1979).

12. Table based on Marshall, PJ, *East Indian Fortunes . . .*, op. cit., p. 97–98.

13. Ibid., pp. 104–105.

14. Ibid., pp. 20–24.

15. Ghosh, JC, *The Social Condition of the British Community in Bengal, 1757–1800* (Leyde, 1970).

16. Marshall, PJ, *East Indian Fortunes . . .*, op. cit., p. 40–49.

17. Bayly, CA, *Indian Society . . .*, op. cit., pp. 53–55.

XIV THE BIRTH OF THE BRITISH EMPIRE IN INDIA

1. Cited in Roberts, PE, *History of British India* (London, 1952), p. 169.

2. Thornton, *History of the British Empire in India*, vol. II, p. 247.

3. Letter of 11 May 1799 to the Court of Directors, in Martin, RM, ed., *The Despatches, Minutes & Correspondence of the Marquess Wellesley during his Administration in India* (London: 1836), vol. I, p. 578.

4. Sarkar, J, *The Fall of the Mughal Empire* (Calcutta: 1951), vol. IV, p. 7.

XV THE BEGINNING OF THE RAJ

1. Stokes, E, *The Peasant Armed. The Indian Revolt of 1857* (Oxford, 1986).

2. Kaye, JW, *History of the Sepoy War in India, 1857–1858* (London, 1864).

3. This thesis was first expounded by a British historian, GB Malleson.

4. *The Indian War of Independence of 1857, by an Indian Nationalist*, s.d., s.e. The author is VD Savarkar, and the date of publication is 1907. The book was published clandestinely and was banned for a long time in India.

5. Literally, 'Franc,' a word applied to Europeans.

6. A pejorative term denoting non-Hindus.

7. Kaye, JW, *History of the Sepoy War . . .*, op. cit.

8. As for the nature of the participation of peasants, detailed studies undertaken by Eric Stokes regarding a certain number of districts in the Northwest Provinces reveal strong variations from one district to another, even from one locality to another.

9. Based on Malleson, GB, *History of the Indian Mutiny, 1857–1858* (London: 1878), 2nd edition, pp. 407–408, cited in Mukherjee, R, *Awadh in Revolt, 1857–1858. A Study in Popular Resistance* (Delhi, 1984, reprinted Anthem Press, 2003), p. 81.

XVI THE AGRARIAN ECONOMY AND RURAL SOCIETY

1. Cited in Wilks, M, *Historical Sketches of the South of India* (1810, 2nd edition: Mysore, 1930), vol. I. p. 139.

2. Cited in Ballhatchet, K, *Social Policy and Social Change in Western India, 1817–1830* (London: 1957), p. 37.

3. Cited in Marshall, PJ, *The New Cambridge History of India*, vol. II, *Bengal, the British Bridgehead. Eastern India (1740–1818)* (Cambridge: Cambridge University Press, 1989), 2, p. 151.
4. Until 1856, the districts of the west of the Gangetic Plain were called the North-Western Provinces. Following the annexation of Oudh (1856), the official name became the United Provinces.

XVII MECHANTS AND CITIES

1. Bayly, CA, *Rulers Townsmen and Bazaars* (Cambridge, 1983).
2. *Ibid.*
3. Furber, H, *John's Company at Work* (Cambridge, Mass., 1948)
4. Since the publication in 1901 of the book by Dutt RC, *The Economic History of India under Early British Rule*, in London.
5. Bagchi, AK, 'De-industrialisation in Gangetic Bihar, 1809–1910' in B De (ed.), *Essays in Honour of Prof. S.C. Sarkar* (Delhi, 1976).
6. Sarada Raju, A, *Economic Conditions in the Madras Presidency, 1800–1850* (Madras, 1941), p. 179.

XVIII CULTURAL AND RELIGIOUS TRANSFORMATIONS

1. Said, E, *Orientalism* (London: 1978).
2. This definition is taken from the *Trust Deed* (charter) of the Brahmo Samaj. For the Christian dimension in Roy's monotheism, see: Mitter, P, 'Rammohum Roy and the New Language of Monotheism' in Schmidt, F, ed, *The Inconceivable Polytheism* (London: Hardwood Academic Publishers, 1987), pp. 117 *sqq.*
3. Muller, M, 'Raja Rammohun Roy (1774–1893)' in *Chips from a German Workshop. Vol. 2 Biographical Essays* (London, 1898), p. 19.
4. The majority of Indian Muslims were Hanafite Sunnites, with a few Shafites on the coasts; there is a minority of Twelver Shiites and Ismailians.

XIX THE BIRTH OF THE BRITISH EMPIRE IN INDIA

1. Cohn, B, 'Representing Authority in Victorian India', in Hobsbawm, E and Ranger, T, eds, *The Invention of Tradition* (Cambridge, 1983).
2. Bayly, CA, *Local Roots of Indian Politics. Allahabad, 1880–1920* (Oxford, 1975) and Washbrook, DA, *The Emergence of Provincial Politics: the Madras Presidency, 1870–1920* (Cambridge, 1976).

XX THE DECLINE OF THE EMPIRE AND THE RISE OF NATIONALISM

1. *Sabha*: council, assembly.
2. By this term, Gandhi meant the help that the volunteers must render to villagers with a view to bettering their existence.
3. Decision establishing the political representation of the religious communities.
4. Created in 1919, this union comprised the majority of the workers of the textile industries of this city.

XXI PRINCELY INDIA

1. The term paramountcy is to be taken in its wider meaning, as the Indian princes were not *stricto sensu* vassals. British paramountcy was neither synonymous with sovereignty nor with military protextion, even if these notions coincided partially with it. Sir William Lee-Warner, an eminent colonialist and theoretician of paramountcy, writes: 'There is a

power in the British crown that it has been wise not to define. There is a subordination in the Indian States that is understood but not explained'; cited in Sharma, H, *Princes and Paramountcy* (New Delhi, 1978), p. 22.

2. Cited in Chudgar, PL, *Indian Princes under British Protection* (London, 1929), p. 112.
3. Cited in Ashton, SR, *British Policy towards the Indian States, 1905–1939* (London, 1982), p. 26.
4. Cited in Government of India, Ministry of States, *White Paper on Indian States* (New Delhi: Government of India Press, 1950), pp. 9–10.
5. Cited in Chudgar, PL, *Indian Princes . . .*, op. cit., p. 17.
6. Lee-Warner, W, *The Native States of India* (London, 1920).

XXII TRADE, INDUSTRIES, CITIES

1. Blyn, G, *Agricultural Trends in India, 1891–1947: Output, Availability, Productivity* (Philadelphia, 1966).
2. Stokes, E, *The Peasant and the Raj: Studies in Agrarian Society and Peasant Rebellion in Colonial India* (Cambridge, 1978).

XXIII THE WORLD OF THE COUNTRYSIDE

1. Official banks created at the close of the nineteenth century in the three Presidencies of Bengal, Bombay and Madras.
2. Guilmoto, C Reiniche, ML Pichard, P, *Tiruvanamalai, un Lieu Saint Sivaïte du sud de l'Inde* (Paris, 1990).
3. Metcalf, TR, *An Imperial Vision. Indian Architecture and Britain's Raj* (Berkeley, 1989).
4. Kumar, N, *The Artisans of Benares: Popular Culture and Identity. 1880–1986* (Princeton, 1988).

XXIV SOCIO-RELIGIOUS REFORMS AND NATIONALISM

1. Sen, KC, *Lectures in India* (London, 1904), p. 210.
2. On Ramakrishna and Vivekananda, see Sarkar, S, 'Kaliyuga, Chakri and Bhakti – Ramakrishna and his time,' in *Economic and Political Weekly*, 18 July 1992, pp. 1543–1556.
3. Swami Dayananda, *Satyarth Prakash* (Paris: Maisonneuve, 1940), p. 252.
4. Jones, K, 'Ham Hindu Nahin: Arya Sikh Relations 1877–1905' in *Journal of Asian Studies*, 32(3), May 1973.
5. Founded in 1857 in the United States and directed from 1907 onwards by Annie Besant in India, the Theosophical Society showed a great interest for the religions of India, firstly in a perspective close to occultism but also of cultural defence.

XXV THE END OF THE BRITISH EMPIRE IN INDIA

1. Jalal, A, *The Sole Spokesman. Jinnah, the Muslim League and the Demand for Pakistan* (Cambridge, 1985).

XXVI FRENCH INDIA

1. Minande, P, *Le Mamoul* (Paris: 1904), p. 278
2. Overseas archives of Aix, carton India 372, file 369, report of the intendant Dayot of 14th March 1817.
3. Overseas archives of Aix, carton India 545, file 1083. Inspection mission of the baron Desbassayns.
4. Ibid.
5. Archives of the Ministry of Foreign Affairs, Memorandums and Documents, Asia 53, pp. 14–31.

6. Mouzon, C, *Pondichéry. Étude de Géographie Humaine* (Paris, 1954), p. 9.
7. De Charolais, L, *L'Inde Française. Deux Années sur la Côte de Coromandel* (Paris: 1877), p. 109.
8. Mouzon, C, *Pondichéry* . . ., op.cit.
9. Henrique-Duluc, L, *Les Colonies Françaises. Notices Illustrées* (Paris), vol. 1, *Colonies et Protectorates de l'Océan Indien* (1893), p. 364.
10. Overseas archives of Aix, carton India 372, file 369, passim.
11. Ibid., Carton India 545, file 1084.
12. Overseas archives of Aix, carton India 545, file 1084, op.cit.
13. Overseas archives of Aix, carton India 372, file 378. Report of Cordier on his administration as the interim Governor-General (14th August 1828 – 10th April 1829)
14. Ibid., Karikal, 1838, 18th March, p. 40V, no. 43.
15. Ibid., carton India 372, file 169. Extract of a letter from Bordeaux dated 1st July 1837, entitled 'Impossibility for the French ships to dock at Chandernagore owing to the silting up by the English of the passage between Calcutta and our trading post, 1817.'
16. India Office Library and Records, London, *Madras Foreign Proceedings*, 334/72, Fraser file (15th May 1820), see pp. 460–462.
17. Overseas archives of Aix, carton India 545, file 1083, passim.
18. Expression coined by Bainville, F, cited by Perrod, PA, *L'Affaire Lally-Tollendal. Une Erreur Judiciaire au VIIIe Siècle* (Paris: 1976), p. 27.
19. Overseas archives of Aix, carton India 372, file 1083, passim.
20. Overseas archives of Aix, carton India 372, file 1083, passim.
21. Ibid.
22. Sicé, E, *Un Mot sur la Représentation des Établissements Français de l'Inde à l'Assemblée Nationale* (Pondicherry, 1848)
23. Guillaume, P, *Le Monde Colonial XIXe – XXe Siècle* (Paris, 1974).
24. On the government of the Marquis de Saint-Simon and the elaboration of the organic ordinance of 23rd July 1840, see Overseas archives of Aix, carton India 380, file 427 and 432, and carton India 505, file 877.
25. Glanchant, R, *Histoire de l'Inde des Français* (Paris, 1965), p. 33.
26. Overseas archives of Aix, carton India 380, file 435.
27. Glanchant, R, *Histoire de l'Inde* . . ., op. cit.
28. Archives of the Ministry of Foreign Affairs, memorandums and documents, Asia 53, pp. 14–31.
29. Overseas archives of Aix, carton India 380, file 43o. Letter of Du Camper to Joyau senior, 10th June 1840.
30. Ibid., carton India 471, file 642. Memorandum of the Hindu notables, addressed to the President of the Republic, 7th July 1851.
31. Overseas archives of Aix, carton India 372, file 378, op. cit.
32. Overseas archives of Aix, carton India 471, file 642, op. cit.
33. Ch. Mouzon, op. cit.
34. *Bulletin du Comité de l'Asie française*, no. 53, August 1905.
35. Overseas archives of Aix, carton India 383, statistics of Pondicherry, book VIII, population.
36. Ibid., manuscript archives, 5384, '*Memorandum pour Servir d'Instruction au Sieur Comte Dupuy*', 9th May 1816, and 5607, decree of 6th January 1819.
37. Ibid., carton India 465, file 599, report to the Emperor, February 1857.
38. British historian H. Tinker entitled his book *A New System of Slavery. The Export of Indian Labour Overseas, 1830–1920* (London, 1974).
39. Overseas archives of Aix, carton India 465, file 596, memorandum of Buirette-Saint-Hilaire dated 8th July 1856.
40. Ibid., carton 471, file 641, Pondicherry, 15th May 1844. The association of landowners at Olandé, signed Moutoussamy, to the Governor De Camper.
41. Sicé, E, *Essai sur la Constitution de la Propriété du Sol, de l'Impôt Foncier et des Divers Modes de*

Perception de cet Impôt dans l'Inde (Pondicherry, 1866).

42. Overseas archives of Aix, carton India 538, file 1043, letter of Ristelhueber to d'Ubraye dated 2nd November 1857.

43. *Voyage de M. le Gouverneur à Karikal (8th – 22nd March 1864)* (Pondicherry, 1864), p. 8. The reference is to Governor Bontemps.

44. Overseas archives of Aix, carton India 386, file 463, letters of Drouyn de Lhuys of 1st March 1854 and of Verninac of 1st December 1853.

45. Ibid., carton India 364, file 340, memorandum of the handing over of the service of the Governor Bontemps, dated 31st March 1871.

46. Ibid., carton Political affairs 717, file 4, letter of Michaux to the minister dated 30th September 1871, no. 482.

47. Moracchini, *Les Indigènes de l'Inde française et le Suffrage Universel* (1883).

48. Overseas archives of Aix, carton Political affairs 717, file 4, undated note of Ristelhueber.

49. Ibid., letter of Michaux.

50. Ignace, A, *Le Progrès Social dans l'Inde* (Karikal, 1907), p. 2.

51. Overseas archives of Aix, carton Political affairs 717, file 4, passim.

52. Ibid., carton India 360, file 308, profession of faith of Pierre Alype, cited by the Governor Drouhet in his letter of 18th December 1881, no. 52.

53. Schoelcher, V, *Polémiques Coloniales (1871–1882)* (Paris: 1882–1886), vol. II, pp. 163–164.

54. *Journal Official*, session of 2nd December 1893 of the Chamber. Report of Paul Doumer.

55. Ignace, A, *Mémoire sur le Droit Électoral des Assimilés et des Renonçants de l'Inde Française* (Karikal: 1907).

56. Id., *Le Progrès social . . .*, op. cit., p. 5.

57. Overseas archives of Aix, carton Political affairs 1278, file 2, letter of the Governor Angoulvant dated 30th April 1907, no. 18C. See also the note entitled 'Chanemougam, of the native policy.'.

58. Ignace, A, *Le Progrès Social . . .*, op. cit.

59. Overseas archives of Aix, carton Political affairs 1278, file 2, passim.

60. Schoelcher, V, *Polémiques coloniales . . .*, op. cit.

61. Letter of the Governor Richaud, cited in Martineau, A, *Les Débuts du Suffrage Universel dans l'Inde*, s.d., see 'Le governement et les idées de Monsieur Richaud.'

62. French Pondicherrians living in Pondicherry would today number ten thousand. About twenty thousand of them have settled in France.

XXVII SRI LANKA

1. The sap of the coconut tree that gives sugar by crystallisation or arrack by distillation.

CHRONOLOGY

1336	Foundation of Vijayanagar.
	Foundation of the Sultanate of Bengal.
1347	Foundation of the Bahmani Empire.
1382–1395	Reorganization of Nepal under Jayastithi Malla.
Circa 1403	Foundation of the Sultanate of Malacca.
1403–1433	Ming expeditions in the Indian seas.
1435–1469	Kapilendra Deva, King of Orissa.
1459–1511	Mahmud Begarha, Sultan of Gujarat.
1473–1509	Rana Malla, Rajah of Mewar (Rajputana).
Circa 1480	Division of Nepal into three kingdoms.
1489–1517	Sikandar Lodi, Sultan of Delhi.
1494–1519	Alauddin Husain Shah, Sultan of Bengal.
	Invasion of Assam.
1490–1503	Narasa Nayaka, ruler of Vijayanagar.
1498	Portuguese Vasco de Gama lands at Calicut.
1500	Outbreak of hostilities between the Portuguese and Calicut.
1501	Establishment of the Portuguese trading post of Cochin.
1502	Establishment of the Portuguese trading post of Cannanore.
1503–1504	The Islamic powers of the Indian Ocean call for a coalition against the Portuguese.
1503–1509	Reign of Vira Narasimha of Vijayanagar.
1504	Babur conquers Kabul.
1505	Foundation of Agra.
1505–1510	D Francisco de Almeida, the first Viceroy of Portuguese India.
1506	First Portuguese mission at Kotte (Ceylon).
1507–1508	Albuquerque subjugates the ports of Oman and Ormuz forcing them to pay tribute.
1509	Victory of the Portuguese against the Egyptian naval forces at Diu.
1509–1515	Albuquerque, Governor of Portuguese India.
1509–1529	Reign of Krishna Deva Raya of Vijayanagar.
1509–1527	Rana Sanga, Rajah of Mewar (Rajputana).
1510	Conquest of Goa by the Portuguese.
1511	Conquest of Malacca by the Portuguese.

1513	Peace between Calicut and the Portuguese.
1515	Ormuz brought under the authority of the King of Portugal.
1517–1526	Reign of Ibrahim Lodi.
1519–1531	Reign of Nusrat Shah in Bengal: invasion of Assam.
1526	Victory of Babur at Panipat.
1526–1530	Babur conquers North India.
1526–1537	Bahadur Shah, Sultan of Gujarat.
1527	Victory of Babur at Kanwa.
1530–1540	First reign of Humayun.
1536	The Mogul Humayun invades Malwa and Gujarat.
1534	Sultan Bahadur cedes Bassein to the Portuguese.
1535	Cession of Diu to the Portuguese.
	Annexation of Malwa to the Mogul Empire.
1538	The Turkish fleet lays siege to Diu.
1539	Cession of Daman to the Portuguese.
1539–1545	Sher Shah Sur, the Afghan ruler of Delhi.
1539–1555	Interregnum of the Afghan Sur dynasty.
1542	The Jesuits arrive at Goa.
1546	Diu besieged again by the Turkish fleet.
1555–1556	Restoration of Humayun.
1556–1605	Reign of Akbar.
1556–1561	Regency of Bairam Khan.
1561–1577	Expansion of the Mogul Empire to Rajasthan, Gujarat and Bengal.
1565	Fall of Vijayanagar. Battle of Talikota.
1571	Foundation of Fatehpur Sikri.
1572–1573	Conquest of Gujarat by Akbar.
1572–1580	Great reforms of the empire.
1575	Beginning of religious discussions at the court of Akbar.
1580	First Jesuit mission at the Mogul court.
1580–1582	Series of rebellions.
1583–1585	The Mogul administration assumes its definitive shape.
1583–1591	Travels of Ralph Fitch in Bengal and Burma.
1584	John Newberry at Akbar's court.
1585–1598	Akbar establishes himself at Lahore; he conquers Afghanistan and Kashmir.
1592	Akbar conquers Orissa.
1594	The Company of Distant Lands is created at Amsterdam.
	The first Dutch expedition to the East Indies.
1598–1601	Akbar's campaign in the Deccan: conquest of Khandesh and of a part of Ahmadnagar.
1599	The seamen of Malabar defeated by the alliance of the Portuguese and the Zamorin of Calicut.
1600	The East India Company is created in London.
1601	Rebellion of Salim.
1602	Creation of the Vereenigde Ooste Indische Compagnie (VOC).

1605	The Dutch at Masulipatnam.
1605–1627	Reign of Jahangir.
1606	Revolt of Khusrau; repression.
1607–1608	Stay of the English Captain William Hawkins at Surat and at the court of Jahangir.
1610	The Dutch at Pulicat.
1611	The English at Masulipatnam.
	Jahangir's marriage to Nur Jahan.
1615	Sir Thomas Roe, ambassador to the Great Mogul.
1616	Creation of the Danish East India Company.
1616–1624	Plague epidemic.
1619	Imprisonment of Sheikh Ahmad Sirhindi.
	The Dutch found Batavia on the site of Jakarta.
1622	Rebellion of Khurram (future Shah Jahan).
	Capture of Ormuz by the English and the Persians.
1624	Creation of the Portuguese Company of India.
1628–1658	Reign of Shah Jahan.
1630–1632	Famine.
1631–1632	Death of Mumtaz Mahal: construction of the Taj Mahal.
	Conflict with the Portuguese in Bengal.
1635–1636	the Sultanates of Golconda and Bijapur become vassals of the Moguls.
1638–1648	Construction of the new capital of Shahjahanabad at Delhi.
1639	Foundation of Madras by the British.
1641	Capture of Malacca by the Dutch.
1646–1647	Unfruitful campaign of the Moguls in Central Asia.
1653–1657	Campaign of the Moguls in the Deccan.
1656	The Dutch capture Colombo.
1657–1658	War of Succession of the Mogul Empire.
1659–1665	Reign of Aurangzeb.
1661–1666	Extension of Mogul rule to Bengal and Assam: annexation of Chittagong.
1663	The Dutch capture Cochin.
1664	Colbert creates the French East India Company.
1665	Temporary submission of Shivaji.
1667–1681	Successive rebellions in the Mogul Empire of the Marathas, the Rajputs, the Jats, the Sikhs, the Afghans.
1669	First religious measures taken by Aurangzeb; resumption of hostilities by Shivaji against the Moguls.
1674	Portugal cedes Bombay to England.
	The French establish themselves in Pondicherry.
	The coronation of Shivaji.
1679	Aurangzeb re-imposes the *jizya*.
1680	Death of Shivaji.
1685–1706	François Martin, Governor of Pondicherry.

1686–1687	Annexation of the Sultanates of Bijapur and Golconda.
1688	Establishment of the French trading post of Chandernagore.
1689	Capture and execution of the Maratha ruler Sambhaji.
1690	Foundation of Calcutta by the English.
1691	The Mogul Empire reaches its greatest expansion.
1692–1707	Unfruitful war of attrition waged by the Moguls against the Marathas in the Deccan.
1707–1712	Reign of the Mogul Emperor Bahadur Shah I.
1707	Insurrection of the Jats.
	Shahu, liberated by Bahadur Shah, becomes king of the Marathas in the Deccan.
1708	Death of the Sikh Guru Gobind Singh. Banda Bahadur becomes the head of the community.
	Rajput insurrection.
1710	Insurrection of the Sikhs.
	Banda Bahadur captures the Mogul fort of Sirhind and founds an independent Sikh state.
1712	Insurrection of the Jats.
1712–1713	Reign of Jahandar Shah.
1713	Mubariz Khan becomes autonomous at Hyderabad (Deccan).
1713–1719	Reign of Farrukhsiyar.
1713–1720	The Sayyids of Baraha unleash a reign of terror.
1715	Defeated, the Sikh leader Banda Bahadur is executed.
1716	Murshid Quli Khan becomes *nawab* of Bengal (1716–1727). He pursues a policy of independence.
1719–1748	Reign of Muhammad Shah.
1720	The Emperor recognizes the authority of the Marathas in the Deccan: Maratha raids and conquests in the North.
	Death of the *Peshwa* Balaji Vishvanath. His son Baji Rao (1720–40) succeeds him.
1721	Death of Churaman Jat. His successor, Badan Singh, pursues his work and consolidates the Jat State.
	New status of the French India Company.
1722–1739	Saadat Khan conquers his autonomy in Oudh and becomes *nawab*.
1724	Victory of Shakar-Kheda enables Nizamulmulk (1724–48) to lay the foundation of a de facto sovereign State of Hyderabad.
1725	Establishment of the French trading post of Mahé.
1725–1735	Government of Lenoir at Pondicherry.
1728	Treaty of Mungi Sheogaon, by which Nizamulmulk undertakes to pay the *chauth* and the *sardeshmukhi* to the Marathas.
1729	The *Peshwa* Baji Rao brings Bundelkhand to submission.
1735	Dumas succeeds Lenoir as governor of Pondicherry (1735–41).
1736	The Sidis, admirals of the Moguls, are defeated by the Marathas.
1737	Baji Rao menaces Delhi. He spares the city, but acquires Malwa.
1738–1740	Sarfaraz, *nawab* of Bengal.

1739	Sack of Delhi by Nadir Shah.
	The Marathas capture Bassein from the Portuguese.
	Safdar Jang becomes *nawab* of Oudh (1739–56).
	France acquires Karikal.
	Dumas establishes the authority of Pondicherry over Chandernagore and Mauritius.
1739–1740	Victories of the Maratha Raghuji Bhonsle in the Carnatic.
1740	Alivardi Khan becomes *nawab* of Bengal.
	Death of Baji Rao. His son Balaji Rao is nominated *peshwa* by Shahu.
1740	Dost Ali Khan, *nawab* of Arcot, is defeated by the Marathas and killed at Damalcherry.
1741	Battle of Gangawana, at the end of which the rival Rajput states of Jaipur and Jodhpur are fatally weakened.
	Intervention of La Bourdonnais in Mahé.
1742	Dupleix assumes office as governor of Pondicherry.
	Assassination of Safdar Ali, *nawab* of Arcot.
	The Maratha Raghuji Bhonsle pillages Orissa and western Bengal.
1744	Anwaruddin Khan, *nawab* of Arcot.
1744–1746	Capture of about a dozen French vessels by the British.
1746	La Bourdonnais captures Madras.
	French victory of Adyar over Anwaruddin's troops.
	First *ghalughara* or Sikh holocaust.
1747	Failure of the French before Fort Saint-David in Cuddalore.
1748	Failure of the siege of Pondicherry by Boscawen in October.
	Jassa Singh founds a new Sikh State in the Punjab.
	Death of the emperor Muhammad Shah (1719–48). Accession of Ahmad Shah Bahadur (1748–54) to the throne.
	Safdar Jang, *nawab* of Oudh, is appointed *wazir* by Ahmad Shah.
	Treaty of Aix-la-Chapelle, on 17 October. The French restore Madras to the British.
1749	Death of the Maratha king Shahu. Ram Raja succeeds him.
	Sangola agreements outlining the future Maratha 'pentarchy' between Balaji Rao (Poona), Holkar (Indore), Sindhia (Gwalior), Bhonsle (Nagpur) and Gaekwar (Baroda).
	Alliance of Dupleix with Chanda Sahib and Muzaffar Jang.
	French victory of Ambur on 3 August; Anwaruddin is killed.
1750	Alliance between Muhammad Ali, the *nizam* Nazir Jang and the British.
	Capture of Gingy by Bussy (12 September).
	Defeat and death of Nazir Jang (16 December). Muzaffar Jang becomes *nizam*.
	Dupleix is appointed governor of the lands situated to the south of the Krishna River. He delegates this government to his ally Chanda Sahib, *nawab* of Arcot.
1750–1753	Civil war pitching *wazir* Safdar Jang against Intizamuddaula and Javid Khan.

1751	Alivardi Khan is defeated by the Marathas and cedes Orissa to them. Assassination of Muzaffar Jang, whom Bussy replaces with Salabat Jang.
	Bussy enters Hyderabad and Aurangabad.
	French protectorate over the Deccan.
	Failure of the French before Trichinopoly.
	Clive captures Arcot, on 11 September.
1752	Bussy imposes the Peace of Ahmadnagar on the Marathas, on 17 January.
	Capitulation of Law at Srirangam, on 11 June.
	Chanda Sahib is killed. Muhammad Ali, *nawab* of the Carnatic.
	The Punjab passes under the domination of the Durrani dynasty, which comes up against the opposition of the Sikhs.
1753	Safdar Jang leaves Delhi.
	French setbacks before Trichinopoly.
	The recall of Dupleix is decided in September.
	Death of Safdar Jang. Shujauddaula becomes *nawab* of Oudh (1753–75). He is appointed *wazir* of Alamgir II, thereafter of Shah Alam II.
1754	Failure of the Sadras negotiations between Dupleix and Saunders.
	Victories of Bussy over Raghuji Bhonsle.
	Arrival of Godeheu at Pondicherry.
	Departure of Dupleix, on 15 October.
	Death of the emperor Ahmad Shah (1748–54). Accession of Alamgir II (1754–59).
1755	Treaty of 11 January between Godeheu and Saunders.
	Departure of Godeheu in February; Duval de Leyrit replaces him.
	Bussy is still master of the Deccan.
1756	Beginning of the Seven Years' War.
	Death of the *nawab* of Bengal Alivardi Khan. Sirajuddaula succeeds him.
	Capture of Calcutta by Sirajuddaula.
	Suraj Mal succeeds Badan Singh as the head of the Jat State.
	Victory of Balaji Rao, allied with the British, over the Angrias.
1756–1757	Victories of Balaji Rao against the *nawabs* of Kurnool, Cuddapah, Savanur and against Mysore.
1757	Clive re-captures Fort William of Calcutta in January.
	British victory at Plassey (Palasi). Sirajuddaula is killed.
	Mir Jafar, ally of the English, becomes *nawab* of Bengal.
	Capture of Chandernagore by the British, on 23 March.
	Bussy captures the British trading posts of the Circars.
1758	Arrival of Lally-Tollendal at Pondicherry.
	Failure of the raid of the French against Tanjore.
	Recall of Bussy, in June. In October, Forde captures the Circars.
	Salabat Jang accepts the protectorate of the British.

The Sikhs, allied with the Moguls and the Marathas, defeat Timur Shah, son of the king of Afghanistan, and become masters of the Punjab.

1759   Death of the emperor Alamgir II (1754–59). Beginning of the reign of Shah Alam II (1759–1806).

Failure of the siege of Madras by the French.

1760   Mir Jafar is forced to abdicate. Mir Kasim succeeds him as *nawab* of Bengal and cedes to the British the three districts of Burdwan, Midnapur and Chittagong.

French fiasco at Vandavashy. Bussy is captured.

Fall of Karikal.

The Marathas defeated by the Afghans and death of Dattaji Sindhia, in January.

Victory of Balaji Rao against Salabat Jang of Hyderabad, at Udgir, in February.

Capture of Delhi by the Marathas.

1761   The Marathas crushed by the Afghans at Panipat.

Death of Balaji Rao in June.

Jassa Singh is proclaimed king of the Sikhs at Lahore.

Pondicherry capitulates. The city is razed to the ground.

1762   Mir Kasim attempts to gain independence.

Sixth Afghan invasion. The Sikhs are crushed and become victims of the second holocaust or *wadda ghalughara*.

1762–1765 The Sikhs re-capture Amritsar, Sialkot, Sirhind, Multan and Lahore. Their domination over the Punjab is henceforth firmly consolidated.

1763   The Treaty of Paris restores to France five trading posts and a few factories.

British traders are massacred in Patna; beginning of the war between Mir Kasim and the British.

Mir Kasim, defeated, takes refuge in Oudh, in July.

Mir Jafar is reinstated to the throne.

1764   Mir Kasim forges an alliance with Shujauddaula, *nawab* of Oudh, with the emperor Shah Alam and the Rohilla chiefs.

The coalition is crushed at Buxar by Hector Munro.

1765   By the Treaty of Allahabad, the Company obtains from the emperor Shah Alam II the *diwani* of Bengal, Bihar and Orissa.

1766   Demobilization of the *nawab*'s troops. The Company takes charge of the defence and the maintenance of order in Bengal.

1767   Verelst succeeds Clive.

1770   Famine in Bengal. The Company faces a serious financial crisis.

Regulation of 1772: leasing of taxes for five years.

1773   Warren Hastings is appointed Governor-General. The Regulating Act forbids civil servants and judges to engage in commercial activities.

Hastings grants the East India Company the monopoly of opium.

Maratha civil war.

1775–1782	First Maratha War.
1780–1784	First War of Mysore.
1781	Revolt of the Rajah of Benares and the *zamindars* of Bihar against the taxation system.
1782	Treaty of Salbai between the Company and the Marathas.
	Death of Haidar Ali.
	Tipu ascends the throne of Mysore.
1784	Treaty of Mangalore between Tipu and the Company.
	Pitt's India Act.
1785	Mahaji Sindhia at Delhi.
1786	Cornwallis is appointed Governor-General.
1790–1792	Second War of Mysore.
	Tipu is forced to cede a part of his territories.
1793	Permanent settlement in Bengal.
1794	Death of Mahaji Sindhia.
1796	Baji Rao II ascends the throne of the *peshwas*.
	British annexation of Dutch possessions in Ceylon.
1798–1799	Third War of Mysore.
1799	Defeat and death of Tipu.
	Ranjit Singh at Lahore.
	Jaswant Rao Holkar on the throne of Indore.
1800	Death of Nana Fadnavis.
	Creation of Fort William College.
1801	The Company annexes the Carnatic and a part of Oudh.
1802	Victory of Jaswant Rao Holkar at Poona.
1803	Second Maratha War: British victories at Assaye and Laswari.
	The Mogul emperor Shah Alam is under British protection.
1804	Recall of Wellesley.
1805	Ranjit Singh become the ruler of the Punjab.
1809	Treaty of Amritsar between Ranjit Singh and the Company.
1811	Death of Jaswant Rao Holkar.
1813	Abolition of the commercial monopoly of the East India Company.
	Authorization for Christian proselytizing.
1814–1816	Anglo-Nepalese War: annexation of Kumaon and Gahrwad.
1815	Annexation of the kingdom of Kandy (Ceylon).
1817–1818	Third Maratha War.
1818	Annexation by the Company of the territories of the *peshwa* and establishment of British supremacy in India.
	Wahhabism: beginning of the preaching of Sayyid Ahmad Barelwi and the Faraizi movement.
1819	The Sikhs conquer Kashmir.
1824–1826	First Anglo-Burmese War: annexation of Arakan and Tenasserim.
1826–1831	Holy War of Sayyid Ahmad Barelwi in the North-West frontier.
1828–1835	Lord William Bentinck is appointed Governor-General.
1829	Abolition of *sati*.

1831	The British take over the administration of Mysore.
1833	The Company loses its commercial functions.
1834	Ranjit Singh annexes Peshawar.
1835	English replaces Persian as the language of the tribunals.
1839	Death of Ranjit Singh.
1839–1842	First War of Afghanistan.
1840	Radicalization of the Faraizi movement under Dudhu Miyan.
1843	Annexation of Sind.
1845–1846	First Sikh War.
1848–1849	Second Sikh War, annexation of the Punjab.
1852	Second Burmese War; annexation of Lower Burma.
1853	Inauguration of the first railway line.
1856	Annexation of Oudh.
	Legalization of widow remarriage.
1857	Sepoy Revolt.
	Creation of the first universities.
1858	Abolition of the East India Company: India falls under the British Crown.
	Trial of Bahadur Shah.
	Queen Victoria's Proclamation.
1860	First Age of Consent Bill.
1861	Creation of the Imperial Legislative Council and Provincial Legislative Councils.
1867	Foundation of the Muslim seminary of Deoband.
1875	Foundation of the Anglo-Muslim College of Aligarh.
1876	Occupation of Quetta in Baluchistan.
	Royal Titles Act.
1877	Queen Victoria is proclaimed Empress of India.
1878–1880	Second War of Afghanistan.
1881	Reestablishment of Indian administration in Mysore.
1885	First session of the Indian National Congress.
1885–1886	Third Burmese War: annexation of Upper Burma.
1891	Second Age of Consent Bill.
1893	Protest against the slaughter of cows: Cow Protection Agitation.
1897	First terrorist attack in Poona.
	Tribal uprisings on the North-West frontier.
1899	Lord Curzon is appointed Viceroy of India.
1904	The partition of Bengal.
1904–1907	Swadeshi movement in Bengal.
1906	Foundation of the Muslim League.
1907	Scission of the Congress between moderates and extremists.
1909	Morley-Minto reforms.
1913	Rabindranath Tagore is awarded the Nobel Prize for Literature.
1914	Gandhi returns to India from South Africa.
1917	Declaration of the British government on Indian self-government.

1919	Massacre of Amritsar and *Rowlatt Acts*.
	Government of India Act.
	Third Afghan war.
	Foundation of the Association of Ulemas of India.
1920–1922	Non-Cooperation and Caliphate movement.
1921	Moplah uprising in Malabar.
1923	Foundation of the Swaraj Party.
1927	Simon Commission.
	Foundation of the Tablighi Jamaat.
1929	The Congress adopts the Lahore resolution on independence.
1930	Iqbal launches the idea of a separate Muslim state.
1930–1931	First Civil Disobedience movement.
1931	Gandhi-Irwin agreement.
	Internal autonomy of Ceylon.
1932–1933	Second Civil Disobedience movement.
1935	Government of India Act.
1937	Formation of Congress governments in the provinces.
1939	Resignation of the Congress governments.
1940	Resolution on Pakistan adopted by the Muslim League.
1941	Foundation of the Jammat-i islami.
1942	Cripps Mission and Quit India Movement.
1943	Famine in Bengal.
1945–1946	Elections and inter-communal riots.
1947	Independence of India and Pakistan.
1947–1948	Massacres in the Punjab and exodus of populations.
1948	Assassination of Gandhi and death of Jinnah.
	Annexation of Kashmir and Hyderabad to India.
	Indo-Pakistan conflict over Kashmir.
	Independence of Ceylon.
1948–1956	Constitutional debate in Pakistan: first campaign for an Islamic state.
1949	Ceasefire in Kashmir.
1950	India adopts a republican constitution.

GLOSSARY

adab: etiquette, good manners.

adamanom: land the ownership of which belonged to the State (French), but which, under the legislation prior to the decree of 16 January 1854, had been granted to individuals with the right to alienation and mortgage. The grantee or *adamanaire* who did not pay his dues was evicted. This decree recognized the Indian *adamanaire* as the sole owner of the land that he cultivated, the state thereby renouncing its rights.

adimai: servile agricultural labourer (in Malabar).

afaqi: foreigner; denoted Arab, Turkish and Iranian immigrants in the Deccan.

aldee: village, market town.

ambati: calico from Bihar.

amil: finance administrator at the level of the *pargana*.

amin: finance administrator at the level of the *pargana* subordinate to the *amil*.

amir (pl. *umara*): Muslim high official.

amir al-muminin: commander of the faithful, title traditionally reserved for the Caliph.

arang: village of weavers controlled by the East India Company.

artha: the pursuit of 'interest'; second of the aims of man according to Hinduism, the first being the *dharma*.

ashraf: 'nobles'; generic term denoting all the Muslims of foreign origin: Arabs, Turks, Iranians and Afghans.

ashrafi: gold coin from Mameluk Egypt; gold coin under the Moguls (for ceremonial use or for hoarding).

ashram: place of gathering of ascetics.

ashtapradhan: assembly of eight Maratha ministers (*pradhan*).

aurang: workshop of manufacture and sale.

ayakkat: area irrigated by a tank.

badshah: Persian title for the Mogul emperor.

bafta: calico from Gujarat.

bakshi: Mogul official in charge of recruitment and management of personnel.

banarsipan: which is characteristic of Benares.

bandar: permanent market.

bania (Sanskrit: *vania*): merchant; generic term referring to the Hindu merchant castes.

banyan: broker, interpreter, authorized representative of a European.

baraka: divine flow transmitted by the saints.

bepari: trader.

bhakti: movement of devotional piety among the Hindus.

Bhatia: merchant caste from Cutch (Gujarat).

Bohra, Bohora: Muslim group from Gujarat, Ismailian Shiite in majority.

braja: high official of the kingdom of Pegu.

budha dal: 'army of veterans', led by the Sikh chief Kapur Singh.

cadi: see *qadi*.

calou or **toddy**: juice extracted from the coconut tree; alcohol highly appreciated in the south of India.

casado: in Portuguese 'married'; in India, term denoting a Portuguese man married to an Indian woman.

chakla: intermediate administrative unit of the Mogul Empire including several **parganas**, created under Shah Jahan.

charkha: primitive wheel used by women to spin cotton.

chaudhari: administrative head of the *pargana*.

chauth: 'quarter', due equal to 25% of the Mogul tax levied by the Marathas.

chawl: type of accommodation in which workers (in Bombay) lived.

chay: red vegetable dye used especially in the Coromandel.

chelingue: flat-bottomed boat used for crossing the sand bar in the Coromandel.

chhattrapati: title of the king of the Marathas.

chitnis: Maratha official in charge of correspondence.

choutre: upper class Christian (synonyms: *Tamouger* and *Malabar*).

conjon: very fine cotton goods manufactured in the region of Yanaon.

coolie: Tamil word meaning 'wage'; by extension, an employee, worker, labourer.

coolie ship: ship transporting Indian or Chinese emigrants.

crore: hundred *lakhs* or ten million.

dacoit: brigands, pillagers operating in bands.

dak: postal service.

dal: political faction, in urban milieu (in Calcutta).

dam: unit of account in copper currency, fraction of the rupee (a fortieth of a rupee under Akbar).

danda: punishment.

darbar: general audience given to the high officials of the empire for the Mogul emperor; under the British, solemn gathering of the princely aristocracy around the sovereign.

dargah: literally, 'palace'; sanctuary edified around the tomb of a renowned saint.

darshan: vision of a divinity; vision of the Mogul emperor on his balcony.

darvesh: dervish, Muslim ascetic; see *faqir*.

dastak: laissez-passer.

Dhammadipa: 'Island of the Doctrine', term applied to Sri Lanka by Buddhist authors in order to highlight the characteristic of this island as the chosen land of Buddhism.

dharma: socio-cosmic order; religious duty; religion.

dhikr: devotional exercises of Sufis with a view to inducing ecstasy through rhythmic repetition and the control of breath.

dhimmi: 'protected'; non-Muslims (Christians, Jews, Hindus . . .) subject to discriminatory measures in a Muslim State.

din-i ilahi: religious discipline imposed by Akbar on his disciples; form of Sufism and not a new religion as erroneously believed.

diwan: official in charge of the administration of finances; see *wazir*.

diwani: department in charge of tax collection.

diwan-i am o khas: hall of general audience in the Mogul palaces.

diwan-i khas: hall of special audience in the Mogul palaces.

diwan-i kull: the highest official for financial affairs in the empire.

diwani adalat: civil courts presided by the collectors, instituted under Warren Hastings.

doab: region situated between two rivers.

dubash: interpreter often doubling as broker.

durbar: see *darbar*.

fadnis: official in charge of accounting at the Maratha court.

fanam: silver coin; eight *fanams* make one rupee.

faqir: fakir, dervish, Muslim ascetic; see *darvesh*.

fatwa (pl. *fatawa*): expression of the opinion of a qualified Muslim legal adviser on a question of the law.

farman: edict, decree of the Mogul emperor.

faujdar: military official of a fraction of a province.

Firingi: 'Franc,' denotes by extension all Europeans.

ganj: market-town.

ghalughara: 'holocausts', of which the Sikhs were victims in 1746 and 1762.

gharib: 'foreigner,' denoting Arab, Turkish and Iranian immigrants in the Deccan.

goldar: wholesale trader.

goonda: lout, hired hand.

gosain: monastic order of Hindu ascetics, warriors and merchants.

granth sahib: holy book of the Sikhs, written in Hindi and Punjabi.

guinées: cotton goods dyed in indigo in Pondicherry and sold in Senegal.

Gurkha: Nepalese soldiers of the Indian Army.

gurmatta: resolution adopted by the assembly of Sikhs.

habshi: 'Abyssinians'; term applied to all Blacks from Africa.

hadith: tradition; word or example attributed to the Prophet and completing the Koranic revelation.

hajji: a pilgrim to Mecca.

hali: servile agricultural labourer (in Gujarat).

hartal: stoppage of work.

hat: temporary market.

haveli: residential house.

hazari: officer commanding one thousand cavalrymen.

hundi: bill of exchange.

ibadat khana: 'hall of adoration'; hall in Fatehpur Sikri where Akbar convened the representatives of various religions for discussions.

idangai: 'Left Hand' dominated by the caste of the Chettis.

id-gah: sort of open-air mosque situated outside the walls of the city for the recitation of the solemn prayer of the important festivals.

ijara: leasing of taxes; lease the holder of which is required to pay a lump sum to the State; the land revenues collected over and above this sum belong to him.

ijaza: 'license' granted by a master to his disciple to teach such and such a book or doctrine.

ijma: consensus of the scholars of a given period on a point of Muslim law; one of the traditional sources of Islamic law.

ilahi: 'divine'; epithet of the new era ushered in by Akbar.

ilhad: heresy.

iqta: 'assignment'; revenue of a particular land assigned to an official by way of salary, with it being his responsibility to collect it; see *jagir*.

Irani: Iranian.

irtidad: apostasy.

jagir: 'assignment'; revenue of a particular land assigned to an official by way of salary, with it being his responsibility to collect it; see *iqta*.

jagirdar: holder of a *jagir*.

jajmani: remuneration of artisans and servant classes in kind in the form of a part of the harvest on the basis of annual contracts.

jama: total land tax collected.

jati (jat): hierarchical and endogamous smallest subdivision of the Indian society; see *varna*.

jauhar: sacrifice by fire, customary among the Rajputs.

jharoka, jharoka-i darshan: balcony from which the Mogul emperor appeared before the crowd, like a Hindu god.

jihad: holy war for the defence and propagation of Islam.

jizya: poll tax; discriminatory tax levied on non-Muslims in a Muslim state.

jotedar: wealthy farmer (in Bengal).

joucanier: customs agent.

kamaishdar: Maratha tax collector, particularly in charge of collecting the **chauth**.

kamiyan: servile agricultural labourer (in Bihar).

kangani: recruiter and team leader in the plantations in Ceylon, generally of Tamil origin.

Karkhana: factory belonging to the emperor or to the nobles.

Kayasth: Hindu upper class of scribes.

kazi: see *qadi*.

khadi: handmade cloth.

khalisa: 'reserve'; part of the lands in the empire administered directly by the imperial officials.

Khalsa: 'Rally of the Pure,' armed, egalitarian and theocratic brotherhood of the Sikhs, founded by the tenth and last Guru, Gobind Singh, in 1698.

khanqah: Sufi hospice.

kharaj: land tax in the Islamic tradition.

kharif: autumn, autumn harvest.

Khatri: Hindu caste of the Punjab.

Khoja: Muslim group from Gujarat, Shiite of Ismailian faith in majority.

khutba: sermon pronounced before the Friday noon prayer all over the Islamic world.

kotwal: chief of police of a city.

kshatriya: order of rulers and warriors in the Hindu tradition.

kurnish: manner of saluting the emperor by placing one's hand on one's forehead and by bending forward.

lakh: a hundred thousand.

Lohana: merchant caste of Cutch and Sind.

lungi: men's dress.

madad-i mash: 'benefit'; assignment of a revenue of a land granted to religious leaders or to scholars.

madrasa: Muslim institution for higher religious education.

mahajan: in Bengal, changer, banker, usurer, moneylender.

mahal: smallest administrative subdivision, sort of canton; see *pargana*.

Mahalwari: system of tax collection, wherein the undivided community of farmers pays the tax to the State.

maharajah: title given to a Hindu king.

mahdi: eschatological character among the Muslims, who is believed to restore justice on the earth at the end of the world.

mahfil khana: hall of audience of Sufi music.

mahzar: 'proclamation'; denotes more particularly the text by which Akbar proclaimed his prerogative to decide on question of Islamic law.

majnun: mad, madly in love.

malguzari: variant of the *mahalwari* system of agrarian tax collection (in the Central Provinces).

malik at-tujjar: head of merchants.

mamluk: slave; particularly those who exercised political functions.

mamul: customs and practices, tradition considered as intangible (Tamil word borrowed from Arabic).

mandala: diagram representing the universe among the Hindus.

mansab: grade in the Mogul administration.

mansabdar, **mansabdari**: 'who possesses a grade'; official of the Mogul empire; political chief posted by the British administration in the tribal zones of Andhra.

Mappillai (**Moplah**): Muslim group of Malabar.

Marwari: denotes the members of the merchant castes, Hindu and Jain, of Marwar (region in Rajasthan).

mashaikh: see *shaikh*.

maulana: specialist of Islamic sciences.

mir atish: chief of artillery.

mirasdar: landowner in Karikal and in the district of Tanjore.

mir bahr: 'admiral', chief of a Mogul fleet.

mir bakshi: the highest official in charge of personnel in the Mogul administration.

mir saman: superintendent of the imperial house.

misl: Sikh warring band, having a territorial base; the *khalsa* was divided into twelve **misls** under Jassa Singh.

mleccha: 'impure,' denotes non-Hindus.

mohalla: locality in a city.

mohr: gold coin.

mokasa: made up of three quarters of the *chauth* and the incomes of the *swarajya*, it went to the coffers of the Maratha *sardars* who administrated the subjected territories.

mudaliyar: Tamil chief; term by which Europeans referred to their brokers in South India.

mufti: expert of the law who expresses legal opinions, *fatwa*.

Mogul: Mongol, Moghul.

muhajir: emigrant (in Pakistan denotes emigrants who came from India after 1947).

muhtasib: official in charge of the inspection of markets and of the vice squad.

mujaddid: renovator sent by Allah at the dawn of every century.

mujtahid: expert of the law authorized to create new laws.

mulla: scholar, specialist of religious sciences; the term was not pejorative during the Mogul period.

muqaddam: village chieftain.

mustajir: contractor of a lease, holder of a lease, leaser of revenues.

muta: temporary marriage practised by travellers in the Islamic world.

mutasaddi: 'accountant'; Hindu administrators of the financial departments of the *nawabs* of Bengal.

muttadar: local chief in the tribal zones of Andhra.

nachari: from English *nature*; naturalist theology of Muslim modernists like Sayyid Ahmad Khan.

nadhr: gift of allegiance presented to the emperor or to a Muslim saint in view of obtaining favours.

nadou: in Pondicherry, this term denotes the chief of the upper castes.

nagarseth: notable in charge of the administration of a city.

Naga Sanyasi: ascetic-warriors fighting naked, the body covered with ash.

nayak: captain, war chief in the Vijayanagar empire.

naib: 'substitute,' deputy or representative of a Mogul high official or dignitary; see **nawab**.

Nattukottai Chettiar: merchant caste of the Tamil country.

naubat-khana: orchestra reserved for the imperial palaces and the tombs of saints.

nawab (nawwab) or *nabab*: honorary plural of *naib*, governor of a province; more particularly, governors having become independent in the wake of the disintegration of the Mogul empire.

nazim: governor of a province, in charge of defence, maintenance of order and justice; see **subadar**.

nizam: Mogul governor of a province, title of the rulers of Hyderabad; see *nawab*, *nazim* and *subadar*.

nizamat: office of the *nizam*.

padshah: see **badshah**.

pagoda: gold coin; three rupees and a half make one pagoda; see *varaha*.

starred pagoda: gold coin, worth 8.40 francs in Pondicherry in the nineteenth century.

paisa: subdivision of the rupee.

panchayat: council, village assembly.

pannaiyal: servile agricultural labourer (in the Tamil country).

panth: Sikh community.

para: locality (in Bengal).

parvana: edict, letters patent delivered by a *nawab* or a *subadar*.

pardeshi: 'foreigner'; denoted the Arab, Turkish and Iranian immigrants in the Deccan.

pargana: sort of canton; smallest administrative subdivision of the empire; see **sarkar**.

parkala: percale.

parsi: follower of the Zoroastrian religion.

patel: village chieftain.

Patidar: peasant caste of Gujarat, partially urbanized.

patwari: village accountant maintaining tax registers.

perichous: leather boats meant for the transport of rice on the arms of the delta of the Kavery river.

peshkash: gift of a subordinate to the one from whom he expects or from whom he has just received a nomination or a promotion; tribute paid to the emperor by the dignitaries of the empire.

peshwa: 'the one who goes ahead, the one who guides'; Brahmin in charge of the administration of the Maratha Confederacy; Prime minister of the Maratha kings who resided in Poona; the title became hereditary as early as 1720; under Baji Rao (1720–40) and Balaji Rao (1740–61), the *peshwa* seized all powers.

phiriwara: itinerant trader.

pirivena: Buddhist seminary.

pol: habitation of caste (in Ahmadabad).

polygar: local chief in the Tamil country.

potnis: official of the Maratha tax departments.

pradhan: Maratha minister.

praja mandal: popular association (in the princely states).

purohita: Brahman acting as the royal chaplain.

qasba: the smallest town in the empire, with a majority of Muslim population and with administrative functions.

qadi: judge in charge of implementing the Islamic law, *cadi*.

qawwal: musician of low status who performs the mystical music of Sufis.

rabi: spring, spring harvest.

raiyat: subjects, peasants (has given *riot* in English).

raiyati: village paying taxes directly to the state.

rajakariya: 'service of the king'; initially denoted the system of delivery of services in exchange for land rights in force in the kingdom of Kandy; extended to denote all compulsory labour service during the colonial period.

rajbati: made up of a quarter of the *chauth* and the incomes of the *swaraja*, it went to the coffers of the Maratha ruler.

rakhi: protection granted by the *khalsa* to *zamindars* and peasants in exchange for a fifth of their harvests or of their incomes.

ramraj: ideal kingdom.

rana: title of the rajahs of Mewar (Udaipur).

rani: queen, princess.

razakar: volunteer (in the state of Hyderabad).

real: Spanish silver coin.

riot: see *raiyat*.

rupiya: 'rupee'; unit of account in silver currency (from *rup*, silver).

sadhu: Hindu ascetic.

sadr, sadr as-sudur: the highest official for religious affairs and justice in the Mogul empire.

sadr diwani adalat: supreme civil court of British India, presided by the British Governor-General assisted by two members of his council.

sadr nizamat adalat: supreme criminal court of British India.

sahajdhari: 'holders of the facility'; though not belonging to the *khalsa*, these Sikhs were considered as members of the community or *panth*.

samiti: association with a socio-educational objective.

sangha: in the large sense, the community of Buddhists; in the narrow sense, the community of monks.

sant: Hindu mystic of the Middle Ages.

sannyasi: ascetic.

sardar: Persian title of commander, important Maratha or Sikh officer; supervisor in the factories or in the plantations.

sardeshmukhi: tax corresponding to 10% of the Mogul tax levied by the Marathas.

sarf-i khas: domain exclusively belonging to the *nizam* of Hyderabad.

sari: women's dress.

sarkar: intermediate administrative subdivision including several *parganas* in the Mogul empire.

sati: term denoting a Hindu widow immolating herself on the funeral pyre of her husband; by extension, the sacrifice itself.

satyagraha: 'force of truth', technique of non violent agitation developed by Gandhi.

saudagar: wholesale merchant practising long distance trade.

sawar: mount, index of the portion of salary devoted by a noble for the maintenance of a contingent of cavalry.

seth: merchant-banker.

settlement: in India, denotes the fixation of land tax and accruing ownership charges. In Ceylon, denotes the determination and recording of the respective land rights of the Crown and individuals.

shahid: dead for Islam, martyr.

shaikh (pl. *mashaikh*): spiritual leader, mystical guide among the Sufis.

shariah: religious Law of Islam.

sharif: 'nobles'; Muslim upper class; see *ashraf*.

sherestadar: Indian chief of personnel of the department of contributions.

suddhi: ritual of purification for the reintegration into the caste and into the Hindu community.

shudra: order of artisans and servants in classical Hinduism.

sicca: silver coin used the year it is minted. Ruppee of the *sikka* year.

sijda: prostration before the Mogul emperor.

simhala (or *sinhala*): initially denoted the dynasty of North Indian origin that founded the first Ceylonese kingdom; by extension, the entourage of these kings, the language that they spoke, then the people who identified themselves as their subjects; today the majority community of the island, transcribed here 'Singhalese' (Sinhalese is also found).

singh: 'lion', term that the members of the *khalsa* add to their names.

sirdar: landowner among the Marathas.

soubab: see *subadar*.

sowcar: usurer.

stupa: Buddhist monument, a miniature replica of the universe, made up of a dome that rests on a square platform.

suba: province, division of the Mogul empire; there were 12 *subas* under Akbar, 21 under Aurangzeb.

subadar: Mogul high official, placed at the head of a *suba*; see *nawab* and *nazim*.

sulh-i kull: 'peace to all'; abolition of religious discriminations under Akbar.

sultan: war chief and head of State in Muslim politics.

suyurghal: 'benefit'; assignment of specified land revenues to religious leaders or scholars; see *madad-i mash*.

swadeshi: 'of the country'; term denoting the movement in favour of the consumption of goods made in India.

swami: master, guru, notably, an ascetic.

swaraj: self-rule; autonomy or independence.

swarajya: one's own territory, homeland of the Marathas.

taalluqa: village assigned to a *zamindar* who levies the tax.

tabaqat: class, order (of society).

taluqdar: big landowner (in Oudh).

taqlid: submission to readymade solutions of the schools of Muslim law.

Taruna dal: among the Sikhs, 'army of the young.'

taslim: manner of saluting the Mogul emperor by touching the ground with one's hand, then by raising it to one's head while getting up.

thakur: name given to the Rajputs in certain regions.

Turani: Turanian, native of Central Asia.

ulama (sg. *alim*): Muslims doctors of the Law, ulemas.

umara: see *amir*.

ummi: illiterate, receptive to divine inspiration.

Urdu: camp; capital; by extension, the variety of Hindi written in Arabic script by Muslims.

vaishya: order of traders and peasants in the Hindu tradition.

valangai: 'Right Hand', dominated by the caste of the Vellajas.

Vani: merchant caste of Gujarat.

varaha: golden coin of Vijayanagar.

varna: orders into which society is subdivided in the Hindu tradition; see *jati*.

wakil: 'representative' (of the emperor); ultimate official of the administration by delegation of the emperor.

waqia nawis: spy who transmits news from the empire to the emperor.

watan jagir: assignment that grants a high official the income from his own ancestral lands.

wazir or **vizir**: official in charge of finances in the Mogul administration; see *diwan*.

wazir-i mamalik: the highest official in charge of finances; see *diwan-i kull*.

yoga: Indian technique of controlling the body.

yunani: acclimatised Greek medicine in Muslim countries.

zabita (pl. *zawabit*): rules of the Mogul administration not subjected to the control of the Islamic law.

zakat: alms mandatory for all the Muslims; the term acquired the meaning of customs dues among the Moguls.

zamindar: local chief acting as intermediary between the administration and the peasantry during the Mogul period; powerful landowner in the colonial period, who collects land revenues on behalf of the government.

zamindari: system of collection of land tax, in which the *zamindar* serves as the intermediary between the cultivator and the State.

zamindari: function of *zamindar*.

zat: 'substance', 'status'; wage index used to fix the personal emoluments of a Mogul dignitary.

BIBLIOGRAPHY

GENERAL

Ali, D, *Invoking the past: The uses of history in South Asia*, New Delhi, 1999.
Bayly, S, *The New Cambridge History of India IV-3: Caste, Society and Politics in India from the Eighteenth Century to the Modern Age*, Cambridge, 1999.
Bose, S and Jalal, A, *Modern South Asia: History, culture, political economy*, Delhi, 1999.
Brown, JM, *India: The Origins of an Asian Democracy*, Oxford, 1985.
Cambridge Economic History of India, The, Cambridge, 1980–1983, 2 vols.
Cambridge History of India, The, Cambridge, 1922–1937, 5 vols.
Champalakshmi, R and Gopal, S, eds, *Tradition, dissent and ideology: essays in honour of Romila Thapar*, Delhi, 1996.
Davis, K, *The Population of India and Pakistan*, Princeton, 1951.
Dumont, L, *Homo Hierarchicus. The Caste System and its Implications*, Chicago, London, 1980.
Eaton, RM, *The Rise of Islam and the Bengal Frontier, 1204–1760*, Berkeley, 1993.
Forbes, G, *The New Cambridge History of India IV-2: Women in Modern India*, Cambridge, 1996.
Gadgil, M and Guha, R, *This fissured land: an ecological history of India*, Delhi, 1993.
Gommans, JJL and Kolff, DHA, eds, *Warfare and weaponry in South Asia: 1000–1800*, Delhi, 2001.
Guha, S, *Environment and ethnicity in India, 1200–1991*, Cambridge, 1999.
Habib, I, *Essays in Indian History: Towards a Marxist Perception*, New Delhi, 1995.
Kulke, H, Sharma, RS, Mukhia, H, Stein, B, eds, *The State in India 1000–1700*, Delhi, 1995.
Kulke, H. and Rothermund, D., *a history of India*, London, 1998 (3rd ed.).
Ludden, D., *India and South Asia: a short history*, Oxford, 2002.
——, *The New Cambridge History of India IV-4: An Agrarian History of South Asia*, Cambridge, 1999.
Metcalf, B.D. and Metcalf, T.R., *A Concise History of India*, Cambridge, 2002.
Robb, P., *A History of India*, Basingstoke, 2002.
Spear, P., *A History of India, vol. 2*, Harmondsworth, 1965.
——, *The Oxford History of Modern India 1740–1947*, Oxford, 1965.
Stein, B., *A History of India*, Oxford, 1998.
——, and Subrahmanyam, S.(eds), *Institutions and Economic Change in South Asia*, Delhi, 1996.
Wolpert, S., *A New History of India*, New York, 1977.

PART ONE: INDIA AT THE TURN OF THE SIXTEENTHCENTURY

Acharya, A.N., *History of Medieval Assam*, Gauhati, 1966.
Babur Nama, The: Memoirs of Babur, Prince and Emperor (transl. and ed. W.M. Thackerston), Oxford, 1996.
Barbosa, D., *The Book of Duarte Barbosa* (transl. M. Longworth-Dames), London, 1918–1921, 2 vols.

Bouchon, G., *Albuquerque, le lion des mers d'Asie*, Paris, 1992.

———, *L'Asie du Sud à l'époque des grandes découvertes*, London, 1987.

———, *Navires et cargaison Retour de l'Inde en 1518*, Paris, 1978.

———, *'Regent of the Sea'. Cannanore's Response to Portuguese Expansion, 1507–1528*, Delhi, 1988.

———, 'Sixteenth Century Malabar and the Indian Ocean', in Das Gupta,A. and. Pearson, M.N. (eds), *India and the Indian Ocean, 1500–1800*, Calcutta, 1987.

Bouchon, G and Thomaz, L.F. (ed. and transl.), *Voyage dans les deltas du Gange et de l'Irraouaddy. Relation Portugaise Anonyme(1521)*, Paris, 1988.

Boxer, C.R., *The Portuguese Seaborne Empire (1415–1825)*, London, 1969.

Brice, W.C., *An Historical Atlas of Islam*, Leiden, 1981.

Crafts and Commerce in Orissa in the XVIth-XVIIth Centuries, s.l., 1986.

Das Gupta, A. and Pearson, M.N(eds)., *India and the Indian Ocean, 1500–1800*, Calcutta, 1987.

De Souza, T., *Medieval Goa. A Socio-Economic History*, New Delhi, 1979.

Digby, S. (transl.), 'Dreams and Reminiscences of Dattu Sarvani, a Sixteenth-Century Indo-Afghan Soldier', *Indian Economic and Social History Review*, II, 1965, pp. 52–80 and 178–194.

Eaton, R.M., *The Sufis of Bijapur, 1300–1700*, Princeton, 1978.

Encyclopaedia of Islam, The(2nd ed.), Leiden, 1954 sq.

Gaborieau, M., *Le Népal et ses populations*, Paris-Pondicherry, 1994(2nd ed.).

Godinho, V.M., *L'Economie de l'Empire portugais aux XVe et XVIe siècles*, Paris, 1969.

Habib, I. and Raychaudhuri, T., *The Cambridge EconomicHistory of India, vol. I: c.1200-c.1750*, Cambridge, 1982.

Habib, M. and Nizami, K.A., *A Comprehensive History of India, vol.5: The Delhi Sultanate, A.D. 1206–1526*, Delhi, 1970.

Hardy, P., *Historians of Medieval India*, London, 1960.

Hasan, M., *Babur, Founder of the Mughal Empire in India*, Delhi, 1985.

———, *Kashmir under the Sultans*, Calcutta, 1959.

Hunter, W. Q., *Orissa*, Delhi, 1956 (reprint of 1877 ed..).

Khan, I.A., *The Life and Times of Mirza Kamran*, Bombay, 1964.

Kolff, D.H.A., *Naukar, Rajput and Sepoy. The Ethnohistory of the Military Labour Market in Hindustan, 1450–1850*, Cambridge, 1990.

Lévi, S., *Le Népal. Etude historique d'un royaume hindou*, Paris, 1985 (2nd ed.)

Lombard, D. and Aubin, J. (eds), *Asian Merchants and Businessmen in the Indian Ocean and the China Sea*, Delhi, 2000.

Longhena, M. (ed.), *Viaggi in Persia , India e Giava di Nicolo di Conti, Girolamo Adorno e Girolamo da Santo Stefano*, Milan, 1962.

Ma Huan, *Ying-yan Sheng-Ian, The Overall Survey of the Ocean Shores, 1433* (transl. J.V. Mills), Cambridge, 1970.

Manguin, P.Y., 'Late Medieval Asian Ship-Building in the Indian Ocean. A Reappraisal', *Moyen-Orient et Océan Indien*, II, 2, 1985, pp. 1–30.

Mare Luso-Indicum (ed. by J. Aubin), Paris, 1971–1980, 4 vols.

Meilink-Roelofsz, M.A.P., *Asian Trade and European Influence in the Indonesian Archipelago, between 1500 and about 1630*, The Hague, 1962.

Mollat, M. (ed.), *Méditerranée et Océan Indien*, Paris, 1970.

———, *Sociétés et compagnies de commerce en Orient et dans l'Océan Indien*, Paris, 1970.

Nikitin of Twer, A., *Voyage to India* (transl. Wielhorski), Cambridge, Ontario, 2000 (reprint of 1857 ed.).

Pearson, M.N., *Merchants and Rulers in Gujarat. The Response to the Portuguese in the Sixteenth Century*, Berkeley, 1976.

———, *The New Cambridge History of India, I-1: The Portuguese in India*, Cambridge, 1987.

Pires, T., *Suma Oriental* (ed. J. Cortesao), London, 1944.

Pouchepadass, J. and Stern, H.(eds), *De la royauté à l'Etat dans le monde indien*, collection 'Purusartha' no 13, Paris, 1991.

Prasad, I., *The Life and Times of Humayun*, Bombay, 1955.

Rizvi, S.A.A., *The Wonder that Was India, vol. II: A Survey of the Culture of the Indian Subcontinent from the Coming of the Muslims to the British Conquest, 1200–1700*, London, 1987.
Sarwani, A.K.(B.P. Ambryshtya, transl.), *Tarikh-i-Shar Saki*, Patna, 1974.
Sassetti, F., *Lettere* (ed. Marcucci), Florence,1855.
Schimmel, A., *Islam in the Indian Subcontinent*, Leiden, 1980.
Sewell, R., *A Forgotten Empire, Vijayanagar*, New Delhi, 1980 (reprint of 1900 ed.).
Sherwani, H.K. and Joshi, P.M., *History of Medieval Deccan (1296–1724)*, Hyderabad, 1973–1974, 2 vols.
Siddiqi, I. H., *History of Sher Shah Sur*, Aligarh, 1971.
Smith, V.A., *The Oxford History of India*, Oxford, 1958 (3ʳᵈ revised ed.).
Stein, B., *The New Cambridge History of India,I- 2:Vijayanagara*, Cambridge, 1989.
Subrahmanyam, S., *Improvising Empire:Portuguese Trade and Settlement in the Bay of Bengal, 1500–1700*, Delhi, 1990.
——, *The Portuguese Empire in Asia 1500–1700: A Political and Economic History*, London, 1993.
——, *The career and legend of Vasco da Gama*, Cambridge, 1997.
Tarafdar, M.R., *Husain Shahi Bengal*, Dacca, 1965.
Thapar, R., *Early India, From the Origins to A.D. 1300*, Berkeley, 2002.
Todd, J., *Annals and Antiquities of Rajasthan* (ed. W. Crooke), London, 1920.
Vambery, A., *Travels and Adventures of a Turkish Admiral*, Lahore, 1975 (reprint of 1899 ed.).
Varthema, L., *The Itinerary of Ludovico Di Varthema of Bologna: From 1502 to 1508* (transl. J.W. Jones), New Delhi, 1997 (reprint of 1863 ed.).
Vijayagupta, *Padma Purana*, Calcutta, 1965.
Vijayanagara, City and Empire, New Currents of Research (ed. A.L. Dallapiccola), Stuttgart, 1985.
Ziegler, N.P., 'Marwari Historical Chronicles, Sources for the Social and Cultural History of Rajasthan', in *Indian Economic and Social History Review*, XIII, 1976, pp. 219–250.

PART TWO : THE MOGUL EMPIRE

Ahmad, A., *Studies in Islamic Culture in the Indian Environment*, Oxford, 1964.
Alam, M., *The Crisis of Empire in Mughal North India: Awadh and the Punjab, 1707–1748*, Delhi, 1986.
——, and Subrahmanyam S., 'L'Etat moghol et sa fiscalité (XVe-XVIIIe siècle)', *Annales ESC*, 1994, 1, pp. 189–218.
——, and Subrahmanyam, S.(eds), *The Mughal State, 1526–1750*, Delhi , 1998.
Ali, A., *The Apparatus of Empire. Awards, Ranks, Offices and Titles to the Mughal Nobility*, Delhi, 1985
——, *The Mughal Nobility under Aurangzeb*, Bombay, 1986.
Alvi , S.S.(ed. and transl.), *Mir'at al-Alam: History of Emperor Awrangzeb Alamgir*, Lahore, 1979, 2 vols.
——, (ed. and transl.), *Advice on the Art of Governance: An Indo-Islamic Mirror for Princes of Muhammad Baqir Najm-i Sani*, Albany, 1989.
Arasaratnam, S., *Merchants, Companies and Commerce on the Coromandel Coast (1650–1740)*, Delhi, 1986.
Arasaratnam, S and Habib, I., *Masulipatnam and Cambay : a history of two ports, 1500–1800* , New Delhi, 1994.
Asher, C.B., *The New Cambridge History of IndiaI- 4: Architecture of Moghul India*, Cambridge, 1992.
Baljon, J.M.S., *Religion and Thought of Shah Wali Allah Dihlawi, 1703–1762*, Leiden, 1986.
Beach, M.C., *The New Cambridge History of India I-3:Mughal and Rajput Painting*, Cambridge, 1992.
Bernier, F., *Voyage dans les Etats du Grand Mogol* (introd. F. Bhattacharya), Paris, 1981.
Blake, S.P., *Shajahanabad: The Sovereign City in Mughal India, 1639–1739*, Cambridge, 1982.
Brown, P., *Indian Architecture, Islamic Period*, Bombay, 1956 (2ⁿᵈ ed.).
Cardon, D., *Guide des teintures naturelles*, Neuchâtel-Paris, 1990.
Chandra, S., *Mughal Religious policies: the Rajputs and the Deccan*, New Delhi 1994
——, *Parties and Politics at the Mughal Court, 1707–1740*, Aligarh, 1959 (reprint Delhi, 1972)

Chaudhuri, K.N., *The English East India Company: the Study of an Early Joint-Stock Company, 1600–1640*, London, 1965.

Corbin, H., *En islam iranien: aspects spirituels et philosophiques*, Paris, 1971–1972, 4 vols.

Dale, S.F., *Indian merchants and Eurasian trade, 1600–1750* , Cambridge, 1994.

Deloche, J., *Recherches sur les routes de l'Inde au temps des Mogols*, Paris, 1968.

Dermigny, L., *East India Company et Compagnie des Indes*, Paris, 1958.

Desai, Z.(transl.) , *The* dhakhirat ul-khawanin *of Shaikh Farid Bhakkari (a biographical dictionary of Mughal noblemen)*, vol. 1 , Delhi, 1993.

Digby, S., 'Abd-Al-Quddus Gangohi (1456–1537): The Personality and Attitudes of a Medieval Indian Sufi', *Medieval India. A Miscellany*, Bombay, 1975, vol.3, pp. 1–66.

Disney, A., *Twilight of the Pepper Empire*, Harvard, 1978.

Ernst, C., *Eternal Garden. History and Politics at a South Asian Sufi Center*, New York, 1992.

Faroqi, N.R., *Mughal-Ottoman Relations: A Study of Political and Diplomatical Relations between Mughal India and the Ottoman Empire, 1556–1748*, Delhi, 1989.

Friedmann, Y., *Shaykh Ahmad Sirhindi. An Outline of this Thought and a Study of his Image in the Eyes of Posterity*, Montréal-London, 1971.

Gaborieau, M., *Ni Brahmanes, ni ancêtres : colporteurs musulmans du Népal*, Paris, 1994.

——, (ed.), *Islam et société en Asie du Sud*, collection 'Purusartha' no 9, Paris, 1986.

Gopal, S., *Commerce and Crafts in Gujarat, XVIth and XVIIth Centuries*, New Delhi, 1973.

Gordon, S., *The New Cambridge History of India,II- 4: The Marathas, 1600–1818*, Cambridge, 1993.

Greeven, R., *The Heroes Five*, Allahabad, 1893.

Habib, I., *The Agrarian System of Mughal India (1556–1707)*, Bombay, 1963.

——, *An Atlas of Mughal India*, Delhi, 1982.

——, *(ed.), Akbar and his India.* , Delhi 1997

Hasrat, B.J., *Darah Shikoh, Life and Work*, Calcutta, 1953 (reprint, Delhi, 1982).

Heesterman, J.C., 'Was There a Reaction?', in H. Wesseling (ed.), *Expansion and Reaction*, The Hague, 1978.

Hodgson, M.G.S., *The Venture of Islam, vol. 3, Gunpowder Empires and Modern Times*, Chicago, 1974.

Irvine, W., *Later Moghuls*, Calcutta, 1922, 2 vols (reprint Delhi, 1971).

Islam, R., *Indo-Persian Relations*, Tehran, Lahore, 1970.

Jackson, P. (ed.), *The Muslims of India, Beliefs and Practices*, Bangalore, 1988.

Khan, A.M., *Chieftains in the Mughal Empire*, Simla, 1977.

Kling, B.B. and Pearson, M.N., *The Age of Partnership*, Honolulu, 1979.

Koch, E., *Mughal Architecture: An Outline of its History and Development (1526–1858)*, Munich, 1991.

——, *Mughal Art and Imperial Ideology: Collected Essays*, Delhi, 2001.

Leonard, K . 'The "Great Firm" Theory of the Decline of the Mughal Empire', *Comparative Studies in Society and History*, XXI, 2, 1979, pp. 161–167.

Linschoten, J.H. van, *Voyage to the East Indies* (eds J. Burnell and P.A. Tiele), London, 1884, 2 vols.

MacLagan, E., *The Jesuits and the Great Mogul*, London, 1932.

Mallison, F. (ed.), *Littératures médiévales de l'Inde du Nord*, Paris, 1991.

Marshal, D.N., *Mughals in India : A Bibliographical Survey of Manuscripts*, Delhi, 1987.

Meilink-Roelofsz, M.A.P., *De V.O.C. in Azie*, Bossum, 1976.

Metcalf, B.D.(ed.), *Moral Conduct and Authority. The Place of* Adab *in South Asian Islam*, Berkeley, 1984.

Moosvi, S., *Episodes in the life of Akbar : contemporary records and reminiscences*, New Delhi,1994

——, *The Economy of the Moghul Empire c. 1595: A Statistical Study*, Delhi, 1987.

Moreland, W.H., *Agrarian System of Moslem India*, Cambridge, 1929.

——, *India at the Death of Akbar: An Essay in Economic History*, London, 1920.

Moyen-Orient et Océan Indien, special issue on 'State and Trade in the Indian Ocean Region, XVI-XVIII th centuries', vol. VII, 1990.

Mujeeb, M., *The Indian Muslims*, London, 1967.

Nanda, M., *European travel accounts during the reigns of Shahjahan and Aurangzeb*, Kurukshetra, 1994.

Naqvi, N.K., *Urbanisation and Urban Centres under the Moghuls*, Simla, 1970.

——, *Urban Centres and Industries in Upper India 1556–1803*, New York, 1968.

Naqvi, S. , *Muslim religious institutions and their role under the Qutb Shahs*, Hyderabad , 1993.

Narayan Rao, V., Shulman, D. Subrahmanyam, S., *Textures of time : writing history in South India 1600–1800* , Delhi 2001.

Porter, Y., *Peinture et art du livre. Essai sur la littérature technique indo-persane*, Paris-Tehran, 1992.

Prakash, O., *The New Cambridge History of India II-5 : European commercial enterprise in pre-colonial India* , Cambridge 1998.

Prasad, B., *History of Jahangir*, London, 1922.

Price, D. (transl.), *Memoirs of the Emperor Jahangueir*, New Delhi, 1995.

Ptak, R. and Rothermund, D., *Emporia, Commodities and Entrepreneurs in Asian Maritime Trade c. 1400–1750*, Stuttgart, 1991.

Pyrard de Laval, F., *Discours du voyage des François aux Indes Orientales*, Paris, 1611.

Qaisar, A.J., *The Indian Response to European Technology and Culture (A.D. 1498–1707)*, Delhi, 1982.

Qureshi, I.H., *The Muslim Community of the Indo-Pakistan Subcontinent*, The Hague, 1962.

——, *Akbar*, Karachi, 1978.

Richards, J.F., *The Imperial Monetary System of Mughal India*, Delhi, 1989.

——, (ed.), *Kingship and Authority in South Asia*, Madison, 1978.

——, *Mughal Administration in Golconda*, London, 1975.

——, *The New Cambridge History of India, I-5: the Mughal Empire*, Cambridge, 1993.

Rizvi, S.A.A., *Religious and Intellectual History of the Muslims in Akbar's Reign*, Delhi, 1975.

Saksena, B.P., *History of Shahjahan of Delhi*, Allahabad, 1959 (2nd ed.).

Sarkar, J.N., *History of Aurangzeb, Mainly Based on Persian Sources*, Calcutta, 1912–1930, 5 vols.

——, *The Life of Mir Jumla*, Delhi, 1979 (2nd revised ed.).

——, *Studies in the Economic Life of Mughal India*, Delhi, 1975.

Shayegan, D., *Les Relations de l'hindouisme et du soufisme d'après le* Majma-al-Bahrayn *de Darah Shukoh*, Paris, 1979.

Siddiqi, N.A., *Land Revenue Administration under the Mughals, 1700–1750*, Bombay, 1970.

Singh, C., *Religion and Empire: Panjab in the Seventeenth Century*, Delhi, 1991.

Skelton, R.W., *The Indian Heritage: Court Life under the Mughals*, London, 1982.

Smith, V., *Akbar the Great Moghol*, Oxford, 1917 (reprint Delhi, 1962).

Sources of Indian Tradition, vol. I: From the Beginnings to 1800 (ed. by A.T. Embree), New York, 1988.

Srivastava, A.L., *Akbar the Great*, Delhi, 1972 (2nd ed.).

Streusand, D.E., *The Formation of the Mughal Empire*, Delhi, 1989.

Subrahmanyam, S., 'The Mughal State: Structure or Process? Reflections on Recent Western Historiography', *Indian Economic and Social History Review*, XXIX, 3, 1992, pp. 291–321.

——, *Penumbral visions : making polities in early modern South India* , Delhi, 2001

——, *The Political Economy of Commerce. Southern India, 1500–1650*, Cambridge, 1990.

Temple, R.C., *Legends of the Panjab*, Bombay-London, 1884–1885, 2 vol.

Troll, Ch. W. (ed.), *Muslim Shrines in India. Their Character, History and Significance*, Delhi, 1989.

Varadarajan, L., *South Indian Traditions of Kalamkari*, Bombay, s.d.

Vaudeville, Ch., *Kabir*, London, 1974.

Vincent, R. (ed.), *Pondichéry, 1674–1761, un rêve d'empire*, Paris, 1993.

Winius, G.D. and Vink, P.M., *The Merchant-Warrior Pacified: the VOC (the Dutch East India Co) and its Changing Political Economy in India*, Delhi, 1991

PART THREE:INDIA BETWEEN TWO EMPIRES

Arasaratnam, S., 'Trade and Political Dominion in South India, 1750–1790', *Modern Asian Studies*, XIII, 1, 1979.

Barnett, R.B., *North India between Empires: Awadh, the Mughals and the British (1720–1801)*, Berkeley, 1976.

Bayly, C.A., *The New Cambridge History of India, II-1: Indian Society and the Making of the British Empire*, Cambridge, 1988.

Brittlebank, K., *Tipu Sultan's search for legitimacy : Islam and kingship in a Hindu domain*, Delhi 1995.

Chassaigne, M., *Bussy en Inde*, Chartres, 1976.

Chaudhuri, K.N., *The English East India Company and the Trading World of Asia, 1660–1760*, Cambridge, 1978.

Cohn, B., 'Political Systems in Eighteenth-Century India: the Banaras Region', in *An Anthropologist among the Historians and Other Essays*, Delhi, 1990, pp.483–499.

Cultru, P., *Dupleix, ses plans politiques, sa disgrâce. Etude d'histoire coloniale*, Paris, 1901.

Das Gupta, A., *Indian Merchants and the Decline of Surat, 1700–1752*, Wiesbaden, 1979.

Deleury, G., *Les Indes florissantes. Anthologie des voyageurs français (1750–1820)*, Paris, 1991.

Firminger, W.K., *Historical Introduction to the Bengal Portion of the 'Fifth Report'*, Calcutta, 1917.

Furber, H., *Rival Empires of Trade in the Orient, 1600–1800*, Minneapolis, 1976.

Ghosh, J.C., *Social Condition of the British Community in Bengal, 1757–1800*, Leiden, 1970.

Glachant, R., *Histoire de l'Inde des Français*, Paris, 1965.

Gommans, J.J.L., *The rise of the Indo-Afghan empire, C. 1710–1780*, Leiden, 1995.

Grewal, J.S., *From Guru Nanak to Ranjit Singh*, Amritsar, 1972.

——, *The New Cambridge History of India II- 3: The Sikhs of the Punjab*, Cambridge, 1990.

Gupta, H.R., *History of the Sikhs*, Delhi, 1980.

Habib, I.(ed.), *Confronting colonialism : Resistance and modernisation under Haidar Ali & Tipu Sultan* New Delhi, 1999.

Hasan, M., *History of Tipu Sultan*, Calcutta, 1971.

Haudrère, Ph., *La Compagnie Française des Indes au XVIIIe siècle (1719–1795)*, Paris, 1989, 4 vols.

——, 'Jalons pour une Histoire des Compagnies des Indes', *Revue Française d'histoire d'outre-mer,* LXXVII, 290, 1991, pp. 9–27.

——, *La Bourdonnais. Marin et aventurier*, Paris, 1992.

Husain, I., *The Ruhela Chieftaincies : The Rise and Fall of Ruhela Power in India in the Eighteenth Century*, Delhi, 1994.

Labernadie, M.V., *Le Vieux Pondichéry, 1673–1815*, Paris, 1936.

Leonard, K., 'The Hyderabad Political System and its participants', *Journal of Asian Studies*, XXX, 2, 1971, pp. 569–582.

Little, J.H., *The House of Jagatseth*, Calcutta, 1967.

Malleson, C.B., *Histoire des Français dans l'Inde depuis la fondation de Pondichéry jusqu'à la prise de cette ville (1674–1761)*, Paris, 1874.

Markovits, C., 'L'Etat Colonial vu par les Historiens', in Pouchepadass, J. and Stern, H. (eds), *De la Royauté à l'Etat dans le Monde Indien*, collection 'Purusartha', vol. 13, Paris, 1991, pp. 193–206.

Marshall, P.J., *The New Cambridge History of India, II-2 : Bengal, The British Bridgehead. Eastern India, 1740–1828*, Cambridge, 1989.

——, 'British Expansion in India in the Eighteenth Century: a Historical Revision', *History*, 60, 1975.

——, *East Indian Fortunes: the British in Bengal in the Eighteenth Century*, Oxford, 1976.

——, *Problems of Empire: Britain and India, 1757–1813*, London, 1968.

Martin, R.M. (ed.), *The Despatches, Minutes and Correspondence of the Marquess Wellesley during his Administration in India*, London, 1836.

Martineau, A., *Bussy et l'Inde française, 1720–1785*, Paris, 1935

——, *Dupleix et l'Inde française, 1749–1754*, Paris, 1920–1928, 4 vols.

Martineau, A and Hanoteaux, G., *Histoire des colonies françaises et de l'expansion française dans le monde*, Paris, 1932, 5 vols.

McLane, J.R., *Land and local kingship in eighteenth-century Bengal*, Cambridge, 1993.

Meyer, J., Tarrade, J., Rey-Goldzeiguer, A. and Thobie, J., *Histoire de la France coloniale des origines à 1914*, Paris, 1991.

Nightingale, P., *Trade and Empire in Western India, 1784–1806*, Cambridge, 1970.

Orme, R., *Historical Fragments of the Mogul Empire*, London, 1805.

Perrod, P.A., *L'Affaire Lally-Tolendal. Une erreur judiciaire au XVIIIe siècle*, Paris, 1976.

Philips, C.H., *The East India Company, 1784–1834*, Manchester, 1961 (2nd ed.).

Pinto, C. and De Souza, T.R. , *Trade and Finance in Portuguese India: A Study of the Portuguese Country Trade, 1770–1840*, New Delhi, 1994.

Pluchon, P., *Histoire de la colonisation française*, Paris, 1991.

Ramaswami, N.S., *Political History of the Carnatic under the Nawabs*, New Delhi, 1984.

Ranga Pillai, A.., *The Private Diary of Ananda Ranga Pillai, Dubash to Joseph Dupleix*, Madras, 1904–1908, 13 vol.

Relations historiques entre la France et l'Inde, XVIIe-XXe siècles (Les), Sainte-Clotilde, Réunion, 1987, 2 vols.

Roberts, P.E., *History of British India*, London, 1952.

Roy, A., *The Islamic Syncretistic Tradition in Bengal*, Princeton, 1983.

Sardesai, G., *A New History of the Marathas*, Bombay, 1948.

Sarkar, J.N., *Fall of the Mughal Empire*, Calcutta, 1932–1950, 4 vol.

——, *The Bengal Nawabs*, Calcutta, 1952.

Sen, A., 'A pre-British Economic Formation in India of the late Eighteenth Century: Tipu Sultan's Mysore', in B. De (ed.), *Perspectives in Social Sciences, vol. I: Historical Dimensions*, Calcutta, 1977, pp. 46–119.

Sen, S.P., *The French in India: First Establishment and Struggle*, Calcutta, 1947.

——, *The French in India, 1763–1816*, New Delhi, 1971.

Singh, S.B., *European Agency Houses in Bengal (1783–1833)*, Calcutta, 1966.

Tripathi, A., *Trade and Finance in the Bengal Presidency (1783–1833)*, Calcutta, 1979 (2nd ed.).

Vigié, M., *Dupleix*, Paris, 1993.

Vincent, R. (ed.), *The French in India. From Diamond Traders to Sanskrit Scholars*, Bombay, 1990.

Weber, J, (ed.), *Compagnies et Comptoirs. L'Inde des Français, XVIIe-XXe siècles*, Paris, 1991.

Wink, A., *Land and Sovereignty in India. Agrarian Society and Politics under the Eighteenth Century Maratha Swarajya*, Cambridge, 1986.

PART FOUR: INDIA IN TRANSITION

Ahmad, Q., *The Wahhabi Movement in India*, New Delhi, 1994(2nd ed.).

Alavi, S., *The Sepoys and the Company: Tradition and Transition in Northern India 1770–1830*, Delhi, 1995.

Albuquerque, T., *Urbs Prima in India: an Epoch in the History of Bombay, 1840–1865*, New Delhi, 1985.

Bagchi, A.K., 'De-Industrialisation in Gangetic Bihar, 1809–1910', in B.De (ed.), *Essays in honour of Prof. S.C. Sarkar*, Delhi, 1976, pp. 499–522.

——, *The Evolution of the State Bank of India, vol. I: The Early Years, 1806–1860*, Delhi, 1987.

Bayly, C. A., *Empire & information : intelligence gathering and social communication in India, 1780–1870*, Cambridge, 1996.

——, *Rulers, Townsmen and Bazaars: North Indian Society in the Age of British Expansion, 1770–1870*, Cambridge, 1983.

Beaglehole, T.H., *Thomas Munro and the Development of Administrative Policy in Madras, 1792–1818: the Origins of the "Munro System"*, Cambridge, 1966.

Chatterjee, I., *Gender, slavery and law in colonial India*, Delhi, 1999.

Chatterjee, K., *Merchants, politics and society in early modern India : Bihar 1733–1820* , Leiden, 1996.

Chatterjee, P. and Pandey, G.(eds), *Subaltern Studies VII: Writings on South Asian History and Society*, Delhi, 1992.

Chaudhuri, K.N.(ed.), *The Economic Development of India under the East India Commany, 1814–1858. A Selection of Contemporary Writings*, Cambridge, 1971.

Chaudhuri, S. (ed.), *Calcutta, The Living City, vol. 1, The Past*, Calcutta, 1990.

Chaudhuri, S.B., *Civil Rebellion in the Indian Mutinies, 1857–1859*, Calcutta, 1957.

Cohn, B.S., *Colonialism and its forms of knowledge : the British in India* , Princeton, 1996.

Commander, S., 'Colonial Rule and Economic Subordination: the North Indian Agrarian Economy in the Nineteenth Century', *Etudes rurales*, 89–91, 1983.

——, 'The *Jajmani* System in North India: An Examination of its Status and Logic Across two centuries', *Modern Asian Studies*, 17, 1983, pp. 283–311.

Dirks, N.B., *Castes of mind : colonialism and the making of modern India.*, Princeton , 2001.

Edney, M. H., *Mapping an empire : the geographical construction of British India, 1765–1843*, Chicago , 1997

Fisher, M. H.(ed.), *The Politics of the British Annexation of India, 1757- 1857*, Delhi , 1993.

Frykenberg, R.E., *Guntur District, 1788–1848*, Oxford, 1965.

——, (ed.), *Land Control and Social Structure in Indian History*, Madison, 1960.

Furber, H., *John's Company at Work. A Study of European Expansion in India in the Late XVIII th century*, Cambridge, Mass., 1948.

Gaborieau, M., 'A XIXth Century Indian Wahabi Tract Against the Cult of Muslim Saints: Al-balagh al-mubin', in Troll, Ch.W. (ed.), *Muslim Shrines in India*, Delhi, 1989, pp. 198–239.

Guha, R., *A Rule of Property for Bengal: an Essay on the idea of Permanent Settlement*, Paris, 1963.

——, *Elementary Aspects of Peasant Insurgency in Colonial India*, Delhi, 1983.

——, (ed.), *Subaltern Studies I-VI: Writings on South Asian History and Society*, Delhi, 6 vols, 1982–1989.

Guha, S., *The Agrarian Economy of the Bombay Deccan, 1818–1941*, Delhi, 1985.

Hardy, P., *The Muslims of British India*, Cambridge, 1972.

Hawes, C. J., *Poor relations : the making of a Eurasian community in British India 1773–1833*, Richmond ,1996.

Hossain, T., *The Company Weavers of Bengal. The East India Company and the Organisation of Textile Production in Bengal, 1750–1813*, Delhi, 1988.

The Indian War of Independence of 1857, by an Indian Nationalist, s.d., s.l.

Irschick, E. F., *Dialogue and History. Constructing South India, 1795- 1895* , Berkeley , 1994.

Kaye, J.W., *History of the Sepoy War in India, 1857–1858*, London, 1864, 3 vols.

Khan, M.A., *History of the Fara'idi Movement*, Dacca, 1984 (2nd ed.).

Kling, B., *Partner in Empire. Dwarkanath Tagore and the Age of Enterprise in Eastern India*, Berkeley, 1976.

Kopf, D., *British Orientalism and the Bengal Renaissance*, Calcutta, 1969.

Kumar, D., *Land and Caste in South India: Agricultural Labour in the Madras Presidency*, Cambridge, 1965.

——, (ed.), *The Cambridge Economic History of India, vol. 2, c. 1757-c. 1970*, Cambridge, 1983.

Kumar, R., *Western India in the Nineteenth Century. A Study in the Social History of Maharashtra*, London, 1968.

Ludden, D., *Peasant History in South India*, Princeton, 1985.

Markovits, C., Pouchepadass, J., Subrahmanyam, S., *Society and Circulation: Mobile People and Itinerant Cultures in South Asia 1750–1950*, Delhi, 2003.

Metcalf, T. R., *The New Cambridge History of India,III-4 : Ideologies of the Raj*, Cambridge, 1994.

Mitter, P., 'Rammohun Roy and the New Language of Monotheism', in Schmidt, F. (ed.), *The Inconceivable Polytheism*, London, pp.117ff.

Mukherjee, R., *Awadh in Revolt, 1857–1858: A Study of Popular Resistance*, Delhi, 1984.

Muller, M., 'Raja Rammohun Roy (1774–1833)', in *Chips from a German Workshop, Vol.2, Biographical Essays*, London, 1898.

Oddie, G. A. (ed.), *Religious conversion movements in South Asia : continuities and change, 1800–1900*, Richmond 1997.

Palmer, J.A.B., *The Mutiny Outbreak at Meerut in 1857*, Cambridge, 1966.

Peers, D.M., *Between Mars and Mammon: colonial armies and the Garrison State in India, 1819–1835*, London, New York, 1995.

Powell, A.A., *Muslims and missionaries in pre-mutiny India*, Richmond, 1993.

Prakash, G., *Bonded Histories: Genealogies of Labor Servitude in Colonial India*, Cambridge, 1990.

Price, P. G., *Kingship and political practice in colonial India*, Cambridge, 1996.

Ray, R., *Change in Bengal Agrarian Society (c. 1760–1850)*, New Delhi, 1979.

Robertson, B. C., *Raja Rammohan Ray : the father of modern India*, Delhi, 1995.

Sarada Raju, A., *Economic Conditions in the Madras Presidency, 1800–1850*, Madras, 1941.

Sen, S., *Distant Sovereignty: National Imperialism and the Origins of British India*, New York, 2002.

Sen, S.N., *Eighteen Fifty Seven*, Delhi, 1958.

Siddiqi, A., *Agrarian Change in a Northern Indian State: Uttar Pradesh, 1819–1833*, Oxford, 1973.

Singha, R., *A despotism of law: Crime and Justice in Early Colonial India*, Delhi, 1998.

Sinha, N.K., *The Economic History of Bengal, 1793–1848*, Calcutta, 1970.

Sinha, P., *Calcutta in Urban History*, Calcutta, 1978.

Stanley, P., *White mutiny : British military culture in India, 1825–1875*, London , 1998.

Stokes, E., *The English Utilitarians and India*, Oxford, 1959.

——, *The Peasant Armed. The Indian Revolt of 1857*, Oxford, 1986.

——, *The Peasant and the Raj: Studies in Agrarian Society and Peasant Rebellion in Colonial India*, Cambridge, 1978.

Subramanian, L., *Indigenous capital and imperial expansion : Bombay, Surat and the West Coast*, Delhi, 1996.

Vicziany, M., 'The De-Industrialisation of India in the Nineteenth Century. A Methodological Critique of Amiya Kumar Bagchi', *Indian Economic and Social History Review*, XVI, 2, 1979, pp. 105–146.

Washbrook, D.A., 'Law, State and Agrarian Society in Colonial India', in Baker, C.J., Johnson, G. and Seal, A(eds)., *Power, Profit and Politics: Essays on Imperialism, Nationalism and Change in Twentieth-Century India*, Cambridge, 1981, pp. 649–721.

Wilks, M., *Historical Sketches of the South of India*, London, 1810 (2nd ed., Mysore, 1930).

Yapp, M., *Strategies of British India. Britain, Iran and Afghanistan, 1798–1850*, Oxford, 1980.

Zastoupil, L. and Moir, M.. (eds), *The great Indian education debate : documents relating to the orientalist-anglicist controversy, 1781–1843*, Richmond, 1999.

PART FIVE: FROM THE BRITISH INDIAN EMPIRE TO INDEPENDENCE

Ali, C.M., *The Emergence of Pakistan*, New York, 1967.

Amin, S., *Event, metaphor, memory : Chauri Chaura 1922–1992*, Berkeley, 1995.

——, 'Gandhi as Mahatma: Gorakhpur District, Eastern UP 1921–1922', in Guha, R. (ed.), *Subaltern Studies III*, Delhi, 1984, pp.1–61.

Arnold, D., *The Congress in Tamilnad. Nationalist Politics in South India, 1919–1937*, Delhi, 1977.

——, 'Rebellious Hillmen: the Guden-Rampa Risings, 1839–1924', in Guha, R.(ed.), *Subaltern Studies I*, Delhi, 1982, pp.88–142.

Ashton, S.R., *British Policy Towards the Indian States, 1905–1939*, London, 1982.

Azad, A.K., *India Wins Freedom*, Delhi, 1988 (2nd revised ed.).

Baber, Z., *The Science of Empire : Scientific Knowledge, Civilization, and Colonial Rule in India* , Albany, 1996.

Bagchi, A.K., 'European and Indian Entrepreneurship in India, 1900–1939', in Leach, E. and Mukherjee, S., *Elites in South Asia*, Cambridge,1970, pp.223- 256.

——, *Private Investment in India, 1900–1939*, Cambridge, 1972.

——, *The Presidency Banks and the Indian Economy, 1876–1914*, Delhi, 1989.

Baker, C.J., *An Indian Rural Economy. The Tamilnad Coutnryside, 1880–1955*, Delhi, 1984.

——, *The Politics of South India, 1920–1937*, Cambridge, 1976.

Baker, C.J., Johnson, G. and Seal, A.(eds), *Power, Profit and Politic: Essays on Umperialism, Nationalism and Change in Twentieth-Century India*, Cambridge, 1981.

Baker, D. E. U., *Colonialism in an Indian hinterland : the Central Provinces, 1820–1920* , Delhi, 1993.

Balachandran, G., *John Bullion's empire : Britain's gold problem and India between the wars*, Richmond 1996.

Bandyopadhyay, S., *Caste, Protest and Identity in Colonial India : The Namasudras of Bengal, 1872–1947*, Richmond , 1997.

Barton, W., *The Princes of India*, New Delhi, 1983 (reprint of 1934 ed.).

Bayly, C.A., *Origins of Nationality in South Asia: Patriotism and Ethical Government in the Making of Modern India*, Delhi, 1998.

Bénichou, L., *From Autocracy to Integration: Political Developments in Hyderabad State (1938–1948)*, Chennai, 2000.

Bhattacharya, S., *Financial Foundations of the British Raj*, Simla, 1971.

Bose, S., *The New Cambridge History of India III-2:Peasant Labour and Colonial Capital. Rural Bengal since 1770*, Cambridge, 1993.

Brass, P.R. and Robinson, F.(eds), *The Indian National Congress and Indian Society, 1885–1985. Ideology, Social Structure and Political Dominance*, Delhi, 1987.

Breman, J., *Patronage and Exploitation: Changing Agrarian Relations in South Gujarat, India*, Berkeley, 1974.

Brown, J.M., *Gandhi's Rise to Power: Indian Politics, 1915–1922*, Cambridge, 1972.

——, *Gandhi and Civil Disobedience: the Mahatma in Indian Politics, 1928–1934*, Cambridge, 1977.

Buchanan, D.H., *The Development of Capitalistic Enterprise in India*, London, 1966 (2nd ed.).

Chakravartty, D., *Rethinking Working-Class History: Bengal, 1890–1940*, Princeton, 1989.

Chandavarkar, R., *The Origins of Industrial Capitalism in India: Business Strategies and the Working Classes in Bombay, 1900–1940*, Cambridge, 1993.

Chandra, S., *The Oppressive Present : Literature and Social Consciousness in Colonial India*, Delhi, 1994.

Charlesworth, N., *Peasants and Imperial Rule: Agriculture and Agrarian Society in the Bombay Presidency, 1850–1935*, Cambridge, 1985.

Chatterjee, P., *Nationalist Thought and the Colonial World: a Derivative Discourse?*, Delhi, 1986.

Chatterji, J., *Bengal divided: Hindu communalism and partition, 1932–1947*, Cambridge, 1995.

Chudgar, P.I., *Indian Princes under British Protection*, London, 1929.

Coen, T.C., *The Indian Political Service: a Study in Indirect Rule*, London, 1971.

Cohn, B., 'Representing Authority in Victorian India', in Hobsbawm, E.and Ranger, T., *The Invention of Tradition*, Cambridge, 1983, pp.165–209.

Collingham, E.M., *Imperial Bodies: The Physical Experience of the Raj, c. 1800–1947*, Cambridge, 2001.

Collins, L. and Lapierre, D., *Freedom at Midnight*, London, 1977.

Copland, I., *The British Raj and the Indian Princes: Paramountcy in Western India, 1857–1930*, London, 1982.

——, *The princes of India in the endgame of empire, 1917–1947* , Cambridge, 1997.

Dewey, C., *Anglo-Indian Attitudes. The Mind of the Indian Civil Service* , London, 1993.

Dhanagare, D.N., *Peasant Movements in India, 1920–1950*, Delhi, 1983.

Dirks, N.B., *The Hollow Crown: Ethnohistory of an Indian Kingdom*, Cambridge, 1987.

Dobbin, C., *Urban Leadership in Western India. Politics and Communities in Bombay City 1840–1885*, London, 1972.

Douglas, I.H., *Abul Kalam Azad. An Intellectual and Religious Biography*, Delhi, 1988.

Dube, S., *Untouchable Pasts: R eligion ,identity and power among a Central Indian community, 1780–1950*, Albany, 1998.

Farquhar, J.N., *Modern Religious Movements in India*, Delhi, 1967.

Freitag, S., *Collective Action and Community: Public Arenas and the Emergence of Communalism in North India*, Berkeley, 1989.

Friedman, Y., *Prophecy Continuous. Aspects of Ahmadi Religious Thought and Its Medieval Background*, Berkeley, 1989.

Gaborieau, M., 'Le néo-fondamentalisme au Pakistan: Maududi et la Jama'at-i-islami', in Carré, O. and Dumont, P. (eds), *Radicalismes islamiques*, Paris, 1986, vol. 2.

Gadgil, D.R., *Origins of the Modern Indian Business Class. An Interim Report*, New York, 1959.

——, *The Industrial Evolution of India in Recent Times, 1860–1939*, Delhi, 1971 (5th ed.).

Gallagher, J., Johnson, G., Seal, A.(eds), *Locality, Province and Nation: Essays on Indian Politics, 1870–1940*, Cambridge, 1973.

Gandhi, M.K., *An Autobiography. The Story of my Experiments with Truth*, London, 1972.

Gilmartin, D., *Empire and Islam. Punjab and the Making of Pakistan*, Berkeley, 1988.

Gopal, S., *British Policy in India, 1858–1905*, Cambridge, 1965.

——, *Jawaharlal Nehru. A Biography, vol. I*, London, 1975.

Guha, R., *The Unquiet Woods: Ecological Change and Peasant Resistance in the Himalayas*, Delhi, 1989.

Guha, S. (ed.), *Growth, Stagnation or Decline? Agricultural Productivity in British India*, Delhi, 1992.

Guilmoto, C., Reiniche, M.L., Pichard, P., *Tiruvannamalai, un lieu saint sivaite du sud de l'Inde*, Paris, 1990.

Gupta, P. S. (ed.), *Towards freedom : documents on the movement for independence in India : 1943–1944*, Delhi, 1997, 3 vol.

Handa, R.L., *History of the Freedom Struggle in the Indian States*, New Delhi, 1968.

Haq, M.A., *The Faith Movement of Mawlana Muhammad Ilyas*, London, 1972.

Hardiman, D., *The Coming of the Devi: Adivasi Assertion in Western India*, Delhi, 1987.

——, *Feeding the Baniya: Peasants and Usurers in Western India*, Delhi, 1996.

——, *Peasant Nationalists of Gujarat: Kheda District, 1917–1934*, Delhi, 1981.

——, (ed.), *Peasant Resistance in India, 1858–1914*, Delhi, 1992.

Harnetty, P., *Imperialism and Free Trade: Lancashire and India in the Mid-Nineteenth Century*, Vancouver, 1972.

Harris, F.R., *Jamsetji Nusserwanji Tata. A Chronicle of his Life*, Bombay, 1958 (2nd ed.).

Hasan, M., *India partitioned : The other face of freedom* , New Delhi 1997, 2 vol.

Heimsath, C., *Indian Nationalism and Social Reform*, Princeton, 1964.

Hettne, B., *The Political Economy of Indirect Rule: Mysore, 1881–1947*, London, 1978.

Hodson, H.V., *The Great Divide*, London, 1969.

Hurd, J., 'The Influence of British Policy on Industrial Development in the Princely States of India, 1890–1933', *Indian Economic and Social History Review*, 12, 4, 1975, pp. 490–524.

Hutchins, F.G., *Spontaneous Revolution. The Quit India Movement*, Delhi, 1971.

Inder Singh, A., *The Origins of the Partition of India, 1936–1947*, Delhi, 1987.

India (Government of), *White Paper on Indian States*, New Delhi, 1950.

Islam, M.M., *Bengal Agriculture, 1920–1946: a Quantitative Study*, Cambridge, 1978.

Israel, M. H., *Communications and Power : Propaganda and the press in the Indian nationalist struggle, 1920–1947*, Cambridge, 1994.

Jaffrelot, C., *The Hindu Nationalist Movement in Indian Politics*, London, New York, 1996.

Jalal, A., *The Sole Spokesman: Jinnah, the Muslim League and the Demand for Pakistan*, Cambridge, 1985.

Jayawardena, K. , *The White Woman's Other Burden: Western Women and South Asia During British Rule*, New York 1995.

Jeffrey, R. (ed.), *People, Princes and Paramount Power: Society and Politics in the Indian Princely States*, Delhi, 1978.

Jones, K.W., *The New Cambridge History of India, III-1 : Socio-Religious Reform Movements in British India*, Cambridge, 1989.

Kaviraj, S., *The unhappy consciousness : Bankimchandra Chattopadhyay and the formation of nationalist discourse in India*, Delhi ,1995.

Kerr, I. J., *Building the railways of the Raj : 1850–1900* , Delhi, 1997.

Kessinger, T.G., *Vilyatpur, 1848–1968: Social and Economic Change in a North Indian Village*, Berkeley, 1974.

Kosambi, M., *Bombay in Transition. The Growth and Social Ecology of a Colonial City, 1880–1980*, Stockholm, 1986.

Krishna, G., 'The Development of the Indian National Congress as a Mass Organisation', *Journal of Asian Studies*, XXV, 3, 1966, pp.413–430.

Kumar, N., *The Artisans of Benares. Popular Culture and Identity, 1880–1986*, Princeton, 1988.

Lee-Warner, W., *The Native States of India*, London, 1920.

Lelyveld, D., *Aligarh's First Generation. Muslim Solidarity in British India*, Princeton, 1978.

Lokanathan, P.S., *Industrial Organisation in India*, London, 1935.

Low, D.A., *Britain and Indian nationalism : the imprint of ambiguity 1929–1942*, Cambridge, 1997.

——, *Congress and the Raj. Facets of the Indian Struggle, 1917–1947*, Delhi, 1977.

Low, D.A. and Brasted, H.(eds) , *Freedom, Trauma, Continuities: Northern India and Independence*, New Delhi, 1998.

Manor, J., *Political Change in an Indian State: Mysore, 1917–1955*, New Delhi, 1977.

Mansergh, N., Lumby, E.W.R., Moon, P.(eds), *India, the Transfer of Power, 1942–1947*, London, 1970–1983, 12 vols.

Markovits, C., *Indian Business and Nationalist Politics, 1931–1939. The Indigenous Capitalist Class and the Rise of the Congress Party*, Cambridge, 1985.

——, 'Big Indian Capitalists', in Lombard, D. and Aubin, J., *Asian Merchants and Businessmen in the Indian Ocean and the China Sea*, Delhi, 2000.

——, *The Un-Gandhian Gandhi: the Life and Afterlife of the Mahatma*, Delhi, 2003.

Masselos, J.C., *Towards Nationalism: Group Affiliations and the Politics of Public Associations in Nineteenth Century Western India*, Bombay, 1974.

Mayaram, S., *Resisting Regimes: Myth, Memory and the Shaping of a Muslim Identity*, Delhi, 1997.

McLane, J.R., *Indian Nationalism and the Early Congress*, Princeton, 1977.

Mehta, M., *The Ahmedabad Cotton Textile Industry. Genesis and Growth*, Ahmedabad, 1982.

Mehta, S.D., *The Cotton Mills of India, 1854–1954*, Bombay, 1954.

Menon, V.P., *The Story of the Integration of the Indian States*, Bombay, 1956.

Metcalf, B.D., *Islamic Revival in British India: Deoband, 1860–1900*, Princeton, 1982.

Metcalf, T.R., *The Aftermath of Revolt: India, 1857–1870*, Princeton, 1964.

——, *An Imperial Vision. Indian Architecture and Britain's Raj*, Berkeley, 1989.

——, *Land, Landlords and the British Raj: Northern India in the Nineteenth Century*, Berkeley, 1989.

Minault, G., *The Khilafat Movement: Religious Symbolism and Political Mobilization in India*, New York, 1982.

——, *Voices of Silence. English Translation of Altaf Hussain Hali's*, Delhi, 1986.

Moore, R.J., *The Crisis of Indian Unity, 1917–1940*, Oxford, 1974.

Morris, M.D., *The Emergence of an Industrial Labour Force in India. A Study of the Bombay Cotton Mills, 1854–1947*, Berkeley, 1965.

Neale, W.C., *Economic Change in Rural India: Land Tenure and Reform in Uttar Pradesh, 1800–1955*, New Haven, Conn., 1962.

Nehru, J., *An Autobiography*, London, 1936.

——, *The Discovery of India*, Delhi, 1994.

O'Hanlon, R., *Caste, Conflict and Ideology: Mahatma Jotirao Phule and Low Caste Protest in 19ᵗʰ century Western India*, Cambridge, 1985.

Omissi, D., *The Sepoy and the Raj : the Indian army, 1860–1940*, London, 1994.

Omvedt, G., *Dalits and the democratic revolution : Dr. Ambedkar and the Dalit movement in colonial India* , New Delhi, 1994.

Page, D., *Prelude to Partition. All-India Moslem Politics, 1920–1932*, Oxford, 1981.

Pandey, G., *The Ascendency of the Congress in Uttar Pradesh, 1926–1934. A Study in Imperfect Mobilization*, Delhi, 1978.

——, *The Construction of Communalism in Colonial North India*, Delhi, 1990.

——, *Remembering Partition: Violence, Nationalism and History in India*, Cambridge, 2001.

Panikkar, K. N., *Culture, ideology, hegemony : intellectuals and social consciousness in colonial India* , New Delhi 1995.

Parekh, B., *Gandhi's political philosophy : a critical examination*, Delhi , 1995.

Patel, S. and Thorner, A. (eds), *Bombay: Metaphor for Modern India*, Bombay, 1995.

Pernau, M., *The Passing of Patrimonialism: Politics and Political Culture in Hyderabad, 1911–1948*, New Delhi, 2000.

Pouchepadass, J., *Champaran and Gandhi : Planters, Peasants and Gandhian politics*, New Delhi, 1999.

——, *Land, Power and Market: A Bihar District under Colonial Rule, 1860–1947*, New Delhi, 2000..

Prakash, G. (ed.), *The World of the Rural Labourer in Colonial India*, Delhi, 1992.

Qureishi, M. N., *Pan-Islam in British Indian politics : a study of the Khilafat movement, 1918–1924*, Leiden, 1999.

Ramusack, B.N., *The Princes of India in the Twilight of Empire: Dissolution of a Patron-Client System, 1914–1939*, Colombus, Oh., 1978.

——, *The New Cambridge History of India III-6:The Indian Princes and Their States*, Cambridge, 2004.

Ray, R.K., *Industrialization in India, 1914–1947. Growth and Conflict in the Private Corporate Sector*, Delhi, 1979.

——, *The Felt Community. Commonalty and Mentality before the Emergence of Indian Nationalism*, Delhi, 2003.

Robb, P., *Ancient rights and future comfort : Bihar, the Bengal Tenancy Act of 1885, and British Rule in India* , Richmond 1997.

Robinson, F., *Separatism among Indian Muslims: The Politics of the United Provinces Muslims, 1860–1923*, Cambridge, 1974.

Rothermund, D., *Government, Landlord and Peasant in India: Agrarian Relations under British Rule, 1865–1935*, Wiesbaden, 1978.

Roy, T., *Traditional Industry in the Economy of Colonial India*, Cambridge, 1999.

——, *The Economic History of India 1857–1947*, Delhi, 2000.

Rudner, D. W., *Caste and Capitalism in Colonial India: The Nattukottai Chettiars*, Berkeley, 1994.

Rudolph, S.H. and Rudolph, L.I., *Essays on Rajputana: Reflections on History, Culture and Administration*, New Delhi, 1984.

Rungta, R.S., *The Rise of Business Corporations in India, 1851–1900*, Cambridge, 1970.

Sarkar, S., 'The Logic of Gandhian Nationalism: Civil Disobedience and the Gandhi-Irwin Pact (1930–1931)', *Indian Historical Review*, III, 1, 1976, pp. 114–146.

——, *Modern India 1885–1947*, Delhi, 1983.

——, *Popular Movements and "Middle-Class" Leadership in Late Colonial India. Perspectives and Problems of a "History from Below"*, Calcutta, 1983.

——, *The Swadeshi Movement in Bengal, 1903–1908*, New Delhi, 1973

——, *Writing Social History*, Delhi, 1998.

Seal, A., *The Emergence of Indian Nationalism, Competition and Collaboration in the Late XIXth Century*, Cambridge, 1968.

Sen, S., *Women and Labour in Late Colonial India: the Bengal Jute Industry*, Cambridge, 1999.

Shaikh, F., *Community and Consensus in Islam. Muslim Representation in British India, 1860–1947*, Cambridge, 1989.

Simeon, D., *The politics of labour under late colonialism : workers, unions and the state in Chota Nagpur 1928–1939*, New Delhi, 1995.

Singh, H., *Colonial H egemony and popular resistance: P rinces, peasants, and paramount power.* New Delhi, 1998.

Singh, K.S., *The Dust-Storm and the Hanging Mist. A Study of Birsa Munda and his Movement in Chota Nagpur (1874–1911)*, Calcutta, 1966 (1st ed.).

Sinha, M., *Colonial masculinity : the "manly Englishman" and the "effeminate Bengali" in the nineteenth century*, Manchester, 1995.

Sisson, R. and Wolpert, S. (eds), *Congress and Indian Nationalism. The Pre-Independence Phase*, Berkeley, 1988.

Smith, W.C., *Modern Islam in India*, Lahore, 1946 (2nd ed.).

Stern, H., 'Les Rajput: guerriers, rois et paysans', in Pouchepadass, J. and Stern, H., *De la Royauté à l'Etat dans le monde indien*, collection Purusartha, no 13, Paris, 1991, pp.123–161.

Stone, I., *Canal Irrigation in British India: Perspectives on Technological Change in a Peasant Economy*, Cambridge, 1984.

Talbot, I., *Freedom's Cry: The Popular Dimension in the Pakistan Movement and Partition Experience in North-West India*, Karachi, 1996.

Tendulkar, D.G., *Mahatma: The Life of Mohandas Karamchand Gandhi*, Delhi, 1960–63, 8 vols (2 nd ed.).

Thompson, E.J., *The Making of the Indian Princes*, London, 1944.

Timberg, T.A., *The Marwaris. From Traders to Industrialists*, Delhi, 1978.

Tomlinson, B.R., *The Indian National Congress and the Raj, 1929–1942. The Penultimate Phase*, London, 1976.

——, *The Political Economy of the Raj, 1914–1947. The Economics of Decolonization in India, 1914–1947*, London, 1979.

Troll, C.W., *Sayyid Ahmad Khan. A Reinterpetation of Muslim Theology*, Delhi, 1978.

Van der Veer, P., *Religious Nationalism: Hindus and Muslims in India*, Berkeley, 1994.

Vidal, D., *Violence and Truth: A Rajasthani Kingdom Confronts Colonial Authority*, Delhi, 1997.

Waghorne, J. Punzo, *The raja's magic clothes : re-visioning kingship and divinity in England's India*, State College, Pa, 1994.

Washbrook, D.A., *The Emergence of Provincial Politics: the Madras Presidency, 1870–1920*, Cambridge, 1976.

——, 'India,1818–1860: The Two Faces of Colonialism', in Porter, A. (ed.), *The Oxford History of the British Empire, Vol. III, The Nineteenth Century*, 1999, pp. 395–421.

Whitcombe, E., *Agrarian Conditions in Northern India: the United Provinces under British rule , 1860–1900*, Berkeley, 1972.

Yang, A.A., *Bazaar India: Markets, Society and the Colonial State in Bihar*, Berkeley, 1998.

——, *The Limited Raj: Agrarian Relations in Colonial India. Saran District 1793- 1920*, Berkeley, 1989.

PART SIX: ON THE MARGINS OF THE EMPIRE

De Silva K.M., *A History of Sri Lanka*, London, 1981.

Goonetileke, H.A.I., *A Bibliography of Ceylon*, Zug, 1970–1983, 5 vols.

Manor, J., *The Expedient Utopian: Bandaranaike and Ceylon*, Cambridge, 1989.

Meyer E., *Sri Lanka, Biography of an Island*, Negombo, 2003.

Roberts, M., *Caste Conflict and Elite Formation: The Rise of a Karava Elite in Sri Lanka, 1500–1931*, Cambridge, 1982.

Spencer, J. (ed.), *Sri Lanka: History and the Roots of Conflict*, London, 1990.

de Silva K.M., (ed.), *A History of Sri Lanka*, University of Peradeniya 1995;

——, *History of Ceylon*, vol III, Peradeniya, 1973.

Weber, J, *Les Etablissements français en Inde au XIXe siècle (1816–1914)*, Paris, 1988, 5 vols.

——, *Pondichéry et les comptoirs de l'Inde après Dupleix*, Paris, 1996.

Wesumperuma, D., *Indian Immigrant Plantation Workers in Sri Lanka: a Historical Perspective, 1800–1910*, Nugegoda, 1986.

Wickramasinghe, N., *Ethnic Politics in colonial Sri Lanka*, New Delhi, 1995.

INDEX